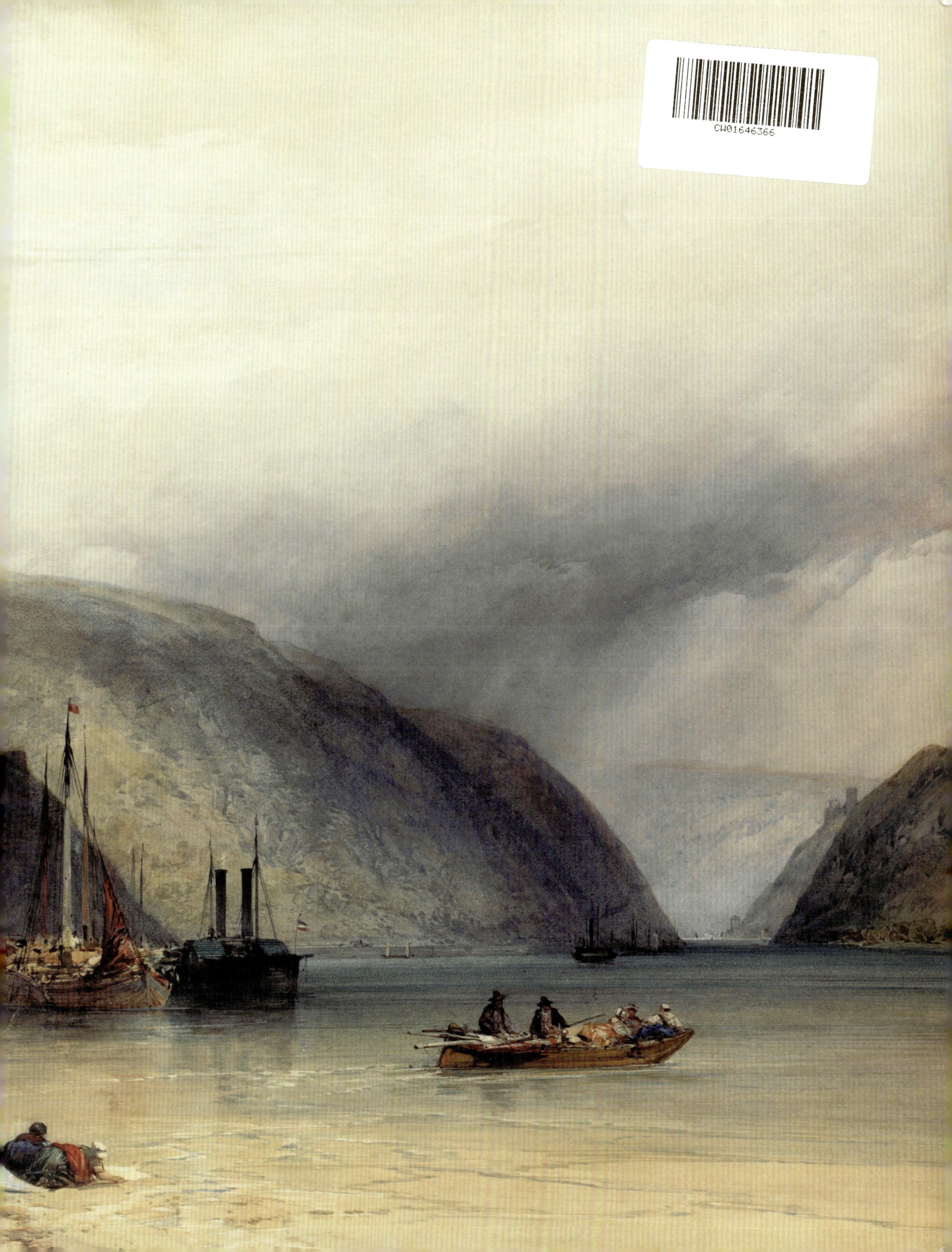

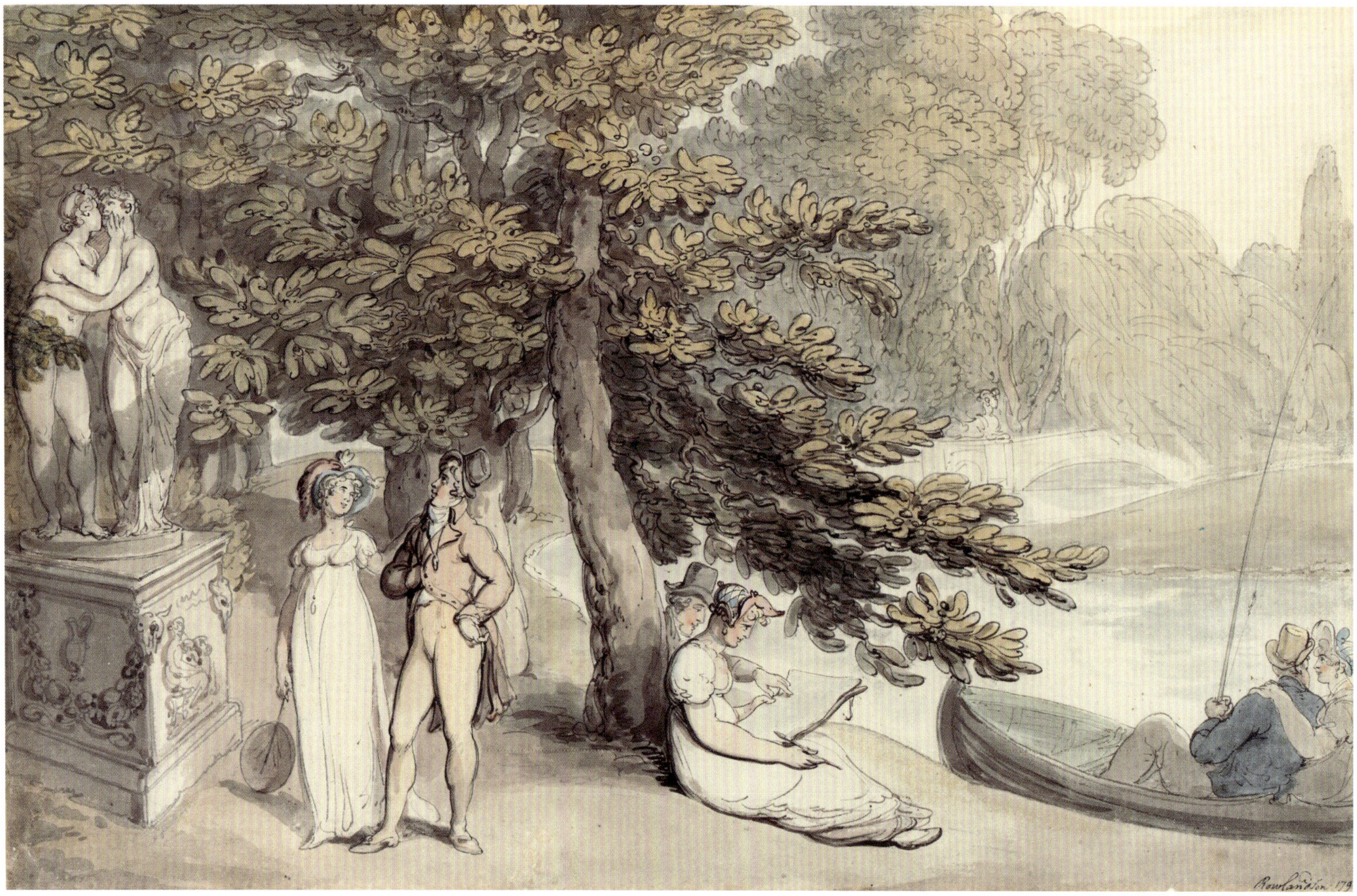
Rowlandson 179

BLISS WAS IT *IN THAT DAWN* TO BE ALIVE

BRITISH WATERCOLOURS & DRAWINGS 1750-1850

Chris Beetles Limited

8 & 10 Ryder Street
St James's
London
SW1Y 6QB

020 7839 7551
gallery@chrisbeetles.com
www.chrisbeetles.com

Catalogue in publication data is available from the British Library

IBSN: 978-1-905738-11-3

Written by David Wootton
with contributions from Max Browne and Giles Huxley-Parlour

Edited by David Wootton, Fiona Nickerson and Catherine Andrews

Design by Jeremy Brook
Photography by Red Apple
Digital Photography by Nemi Miller
Colour separation and printing by BAS Printers

Cover: John Varley, *Tintern Abbey, Wales* [**199**] (detail)
Front endpaper: William Callow, *Rheinfels and Village of St Goar* [**276**] (detail)
Frontispiece: Thomas Rowlandson, *Lovers' Recreation* [**57**]
Back endpaper: John Sell Cotman, *Leigh High Woods with the Rev James Bulwer in the foreground* [**150**] (detail)

To David Moore (1932-2008)
Friend, mentor and collector

CONTENTS

BLISS WAS IT IN THAT DAWN TO BE ALIVE: REDEFINING EARLY ENGLISH WATERCOLOURS

It is time to blow the cobwebs off one of our most characteristic artistic media, at its most vital period.

For too long, the terms '*Early English* Watercolours' and 'the *Old* Water-Colour Society' have conjured up the distant world of the antiquarian collector: with magnifying glass in hand, he examines a treasured possession by a venerable master, which he lifts expectantly from a folio, or reveals on the wall by pulling back a velvet curtain. And that antiquarianism is only reinforced by the other meaning of 'Early English', the primary stage of English Gothic church architecture, as if watercolour had been invented only to record mediaeval detail.

Admittedly, a glance at the images in this catalogue will yield a good number of churches, other ancient buildings, even ruins. But the way that those images were conceived, produced and enjoyed – and the people who conceived, produced and enjoyed them – was anything but stuffy or decrepit.

Yes, many of them had a serious interest in the past – and some even helped develop antiquarianism as a valuable study. However, they were also pioneers in their interests and skills, busy exploring, experimenting, establishing. They were *early* because they were original, and because they were so young.

Two touchstones of the period, not represented here but cited constantly, best make the point. Thomas Girtin died in 1802 at the age of twenty-seven, while Richard Parkes Bonington was born in 1802, and died at the age of twenty-five. J M W TURNER, the great figure of the age, did live to the age of seventy-six, but to his mind only at the expense of Girtin, stating that 'if Tom had lived, I should have starved', for he was as revolutionary in his approach to watercolour, and as influential. JOHN SELL COTMAN, JOHN VARLEY and SAMUEL PROUT – three highly influential nineteenth-century watercolourists – all developed in response to the example of Girtin. A generation later, Bonington had a similar effect, most immediately on the tight-knit circle of confrères that included THOMAS SHOTTER BOYS, WILLIAM CALLOW and WILLIAM WYLD, but then more widely through their lessons, exhibits, and publications.

Girtin and Bonington – two touchstones thrown into the pools of London and Paris – caused titanic ripples. In the discrepancy between their ages and their significance, they may have been alone. For the artist with the shortest lifespan to be included here – JOHN MIDDLETON at twenty-nine – was heavy with individual promise, rather than proving to be the foundation of a tradition.

However, the artists in this catalogue invariably started young, and achieved much in a short time both for themselves and their professions.

The second essay in this catalogue rehearses the origin and generation of landscape, perhaps the quintessential subject for the medium of watercolour; here is given a general flavour of the watercolourist's world at a time when the possibilities were uncertain, but seemed boundless.

Consider the boy who showed a talent for drawing in the late eighteenth or early nineteenth centuries. Whether supported by his parents, like J M W Turner, or not, like John Varley, he needed to find a way of developing. If he were an aristocrat or gentleman, he might receive drawing lessons as a matter of course. If he were a surprisingly talented servant – such as MOSES GRIFFITH – he might be lucky enough to be encouraged by his master. However, most fell somewhere in between, and an increasing number through the period started out as the sons of tradesmen.

One option for the needy was to take a job that involved some skill at drawing, as Turner did in working with architects and architectural draughtsmen. Another was to assist an established drawing master, as Varley did in joining Joseph Charles Barrow. A little money would secure a lesson from such a drawing master but, by the time that Varley was taking pupils in the early 1800s, a full apprenticeship of seven years cost £200. The term 'apprenticeship' suggests that at least some of the visual arts were still considered as trades essentially comprising a series of teachable skills – despite the foundation of the Royal Academy of Arts forty years earlier, with its aim of presenting the artist as an intellectual. However, one of the benefits of an apprenticeship at a practice such as that of Varley, was to learn from the strengths and enthusiasms of one's peers. Imagine the lively atmosphere in Varley's house when the likes of COPLEY FIELDING, WILLIAM TURNER (from Oxfordshire) and WILLIAM HENRY HUNT exchanged ideas and tips. Perhaps, luckiest of all were the artist's sons, partaking in all this without the expense of indentures.

Few of the significant watercolourists of the age would graduate to the Royal Academy Schools, most notably J M W Turner, who remained loyal to the Academy throughout his career, and never defected to any of the watercolour societies that began to be founded from 1804. Until that date, the majority had to sustain the camaraderie of their student days in more informal ways.

One popular and distinctive venue (from 1794) was the unofficial academy of Dr Thomas Monro, physician at the Royal Bethlehem Hospital. He lived at the Adelphi, between the Strand and the Thames, close to Rudolph Ackermann's Repository of the Arts, an enterprise that also offered work to promising draughtsmen. An amateur artist and collector of contemporary watercolours, Monro would invite young painters to copy works by such established artists as Alexander Cozens; and also to visit him at his cottage at Fetcham, Surrey, in order to sketch the surrounding countryside. Again, this environment, like Varley's house, can be considered a hothouse of creativity, with J M W Turner and Girtin working side by side, and even on the same drawing.

Girtin soon went on to found his own sketching society, in collaboration with LOUIS FRANCIA. Though he enjoyed the company of 'The Brothers' for just a short time before he died, its name is suggestive of the fraternal promises often made in youth, and the hope of making – in art and life – a better world. This society long survived Girtin's death in 1802, being first led by Cotman and then, reconstituted in 1808, by the CHALON brothers and Francis Stevens, as the Society for the Study of Epic and Pastoral Design. It continued into the middle of the century and spawned others.

The purpose of such a society was to meet regularly, alternately at each member's home, and for all members in attendance to produce a drawing on a given theme. They then discussed the results of the session before retiring for supper. (The Chalon Sketching Society was later known as the 'Bread and Cheese Society'.) The evening meetings might be supplemented by days spent sketching together – a practice that also encouraged more ambitious sketching tours across Britain and the Continent.

The sketching societies were, in themselves, the forerunners of a number of more formal societies, for a group similar and related to The Brothers founded the Society of Painters in Water Colours in 1804. And this pattern was replicated across the country in such regional centres as Norwich, Bristol and Newcastle. In London, certainly, this bond between artists was further strengthened by their living in close proximity; naturally, because the city had a smaller population and covered less ground, but also artificially, as, from the early nineteenth century, artists chose to move into the area around Newman Street, north of Oxford Street. In a world before telecommunication, electricity, and even the steam engine, such close proximity can only have helped created an atmosphere of mutual support, and make available the contact necessary for gaining commissions, finding pupils and selling work.

Much of this paralleled and overlapped with developments in the literary world, making pertinent the quotation that gives this catalogue its title. Taken from William Wordsworth's poem of 1805, on the French Revolution, it suggests the excitement felt by many young creative figures at the turning point from the eighteenth to the nineteenth centuries. Though few of the artists represented here were truly radical in political terms, their desire to develop their professional standing had a social as well as an artistic dimension. Initially, the words 'bliss was it that dawn to be alive' may seem an ideal match for Thomas Rowlandson's *Lover's Recreation* [**57**], so suggesting that Early English watercolours are sweet and safe. However, their origin and meaning make clear that those who made them had edge and ambition.

The first mention, in biographies and essays, of artists whose biographies are included in the catalogue, are indicated in SMALL CAPITALS.

FROM TOPOGRAPHY TO LANDSCAPE: THE ORIGINS AND DEVELOPMENT OF A GENRE

In early eighteenth-century Britain, landscape developed out of topography to become a distinct genre of painting.

Early representations of terrain had attempted to record the essential information about a place with clarity and accuracy. Rarely aesthetic in intention, these representations contributed significantly to the survey and possession of land. In this way, they aided various groups contributing to a changing society, including landowners and military leaders, explorers and tourists, architects and garden designers, and antiquarians and scientists. Such images were habitually produced on paper in media chosen for their portability – pen, pencil and watercolour – while their careful lines and flat tints made them suitable for reproduction through engraving.

Many of these elements – both semantic and technical – became intrinsic to the evolving genre of landscape. They were enhanced by two contrasting, and sometimes competing, artistic traditions: northern naturalism and Italianate idealism.

The northern tradition had a particularly direct influence on practice, as many families of Dutch and Flemish origin (such as the three generations of artists all called Bernard Lens) had settled in London by the late seventeenth century. At its best, the northern strand offered a precise and down-to-earth poetry.

On the other hand, the Italianate strand alluded to classical and biblical narratives, as well as assimilating the appearance and atmosphere of the Mediterranean. It was therefore more acceptable to those artists and theorists who were trying to establish visual art as the intellectual and moral equal of literature – of which Greco-Roman culture was the benchmark. The most notable models for this approach were Claude Lorrain and Nicolas Poussin, two seventeenth-century French artists who had worked in Rome. Their paintings were well represented in British collections by the early eighteenth century, while etchings and engravings were in circulation, so that images were accessible to the impressionable landscape painters of the period.

These two influences can be detected in the ground-breaking work of WILLIAM TAVERNER who, though an amateur, was described by the engraver and antiquary George Vertue as 'equal if not superior in some degree to any painter in England' (Vertue 1934, p 118). Some of his watercolours are distinctly Italianate in subject and composition, though inspired by Italian artists active in London, notably Marco Ricci, and by earlier prints and drawings, rather than by direct experience of Italy. Yet others take their lead from images by Antwerp-born Peter Tillemans, an artist whose work Taverner collected. They not only record precise locations around the capital (Hampstead, Richmond, Woolwich) but do so with such naturalism of colour and freedom of execution that they are likely to have been painted on the spot.

Taverner was undoubtedly significant, for such fellow artists as Paul Sandby owned examles of his work, but his reputation was limited. Equally innovatory, but of wider and more lasting influence, were Paul Sandby and his brother Thomas, and – another artistic family – Alexander Cozens and his son John Robert.

Unlike Taverner, Alexander Cozens (1717-1786) had a direct experience of Italy, being one of the first British artists to study in Rome. While there, around 1746, he worked in the studio of Claude-Joseph Vernet, who was known as 'the French Claude', and learned from Vernet's interpretation of the ideal landscape tradition. As a result of Vernet's teaching and his own experiments, he eventually developed a set of theories that he published as *A New Method of Assisting the Invention in Drawing Original Compositions in Landscape* (1785-86). Remaining true to the ideal tradition while encouraging originality, he proposed that students make almost random ink blots as a starting point for a variety of generalised compositions.

THOMAS SUNDERLAND possibly studied under Alexander Cozens and certainly under J R Cozens (1752-1798), who was heir to his father's experiences and ideas. Like his teachers, Sunderland had opportunities to travel on the Continent, and responded to his surroundings in a restrained – classicising – palette. The influence of the Cozenses is manifest in his treatment of mountains, as in *Aqueduct of Spoletta* [27] and *Terni* [25], though the introduction of quirky detail is very much his own.

By contrast with the Cozens family, Paul Sandby (1731-1809) confined his travels to Britain, initially as a Military Draughtsman and Drawing Master, and later as the guest of various patrons. Establishing a precise approach to topography to meet the demands of the army, he gradually became expert in creating a strong sense of place – by choosing an interesting viewpoint, adding atmosphere, and introducing well-observed figures. While working in a variety of media, he proved pioneering in producing a significant number of watercolours and exhibiting them at the Royal Academy of Arts, which he and his brother,

Thomas (1721-1798), helped to found in 1768. Paul's qualities as a watercolourist were upheld by his assistant, MICHAEL ANGELO ROOKER, who was one of the first students to be admitted to the Royal Academy Schools.

Despite the successes of landscape painters, landscape painting was considered of relatively low status by the Royal Academy, the most prestigious of the artistic institutions to be founded in the late eighteenth century. As the academicians attempted to raise the status of the visual arts within British culture, and British culture within the European heritage, so they privileged *historia*: large-scale canvases representing episodes from history and literature, and especially Hellenic and Hebraic history and literature. Landscape was most valued when it aspired to this genre, in providing an idealised, generalised, usually Italianate setting for figures to enact an incident from classic narrative.

The desire not only to emulate but also experience and record the European heritage spurred artists, as well as aristocrats, to undertake the Grand Tour. These included Thomas Jones and such members of his circle as WILLIAM PARS, JOHN 'WARWICK' SMITH and Francis Towne – all of whom spent time in Rome and the surrounding Campagna during the late 1770s and early 1780s. However, with the freedom to produce what they wanted, these artists made sketches – in oil and watercolour – that were personal, direct and spontaneous, and so transcended contemporary conventions. The direct study of nature may have generally been intended as an aspect of preparation at this date, but such experiments in naturalism would become the norm soon into the new century.

Even Sir Joshua Reynolds – as President of the Royal Academy and, thus, protector of artistic propriety – could be less than rigid in his private communications. In one letter of 1780, for instance, he encouraged NICHOLAS POCOCK to 'paint from nature' as well as 'imitate Joseph Vernet'.

In effect, the lively contemporary debate about aesthetic theory offered the landscape painter a wider variety of approaches than that dictated by the academy. Even before the foundation of the Royal Academy, landowners were drawing inspiration from pictorial landscapes to reshape their estates, while philosophers were making increasing connections between the natural world and moral well-being. In 1757, Edmund Burke provided the public with a basic contrast of landscape types and the emotions they had provoked, in writing *Of the Sublime and the Beautiful*; then, a decade later, William Gilpin added a third – and intermediate – category, the Picturesque, 'a term expressive of that peculiar kind of beauty, which is agreeable in a picture' (Gilpin 1768, p 2). The landscape painter could use such approaches to test his personal engagement with particular places and terrains, and frame a response appropriate to his patron, be he landowner, antiquarian or publisher.

As landscape painting developed as a distinct genre, so landscape painters increased in diversity – of class and regional identity – as well as number. A gentleman amateur such as Thomas Sunderland contrasted with both a professional draughtsman such as ANTHONY DEVIS and – admittedly an extreme case – a servant such as MOSES GRIFFITH. And, perhaps inevitably, for a genre dependent on place, regional artists – GEORGE CUIT in Yorkshire and GEORGE FROST in Suffolk – began to make local reputations, and so pave the way for regional schools. Of greater surprise, it was landscape – rather than narrative or even portraiture – that became the conduit for expressing an individual intensity of feeling, and so acted as a parallel to the Romantic poetry of William Wordsworth or Samuel Taylor Coleridge. Landscape had risen out of representation to become an art.

1: FROM TOPOGRAPHY TO LANDSCAPE

WILLIAM TAVERNER
William Taverner (1700-1772)

William Taverner has a prime position in the history of English watercolours: Tate Britain's curators have presented him as 'our first regular and systematic painter of free landscape in watercolour' (Tate display caption, 2004); while Martin Hardie has considered him a challenger to Sandby's claim 'to be father of the English school both of pure water-colour and of body-colour' (Hardie 1967, p 111). This estimate seems all the more justified when it is known that Paul Sandby himself valued Taverner sufficiently to possess two of his works.

Taverner was a grandson of Jeremiah Taverner, a minor portrait painter, and son of William Taverner, an ecclesiastical lawyer, artist and dramatist. Born in London on 25 November 1700, he was articled to his father in 1720, and in 1739 inherited the position of Procurator-General of the Court of Arches of Canterbury (the supreme ecclesiastical court of the Church of England, based in Bow Street, London).

However, Taverner devoted much time to artistic activities, becoming well-known among artists despite his amateur status and retiring manner. Indeed, the animal painter, Sawrey Gilpin, commented that 'Taverner had much quaiking about shewing his pictures, which raised their reputation' (quoted in Farington 1978, p 765).

In 1733, the engraver and antiquary, George Vertue described Taverner thus:

> this present young gentleman, about Aeta 30 (besides his practice in Law) has a wonderfull genius to drawing of Landskap in an excellent manner, adorned with figures in a stile above the common & paints in oil in a very commendable & masterly manner, a fine geneus blending the arts of his Ancestors in Painting & Poetry and his happy stile of Painting (Vertue 1934, p 68)

However, as his oils are rare, Taverner's reputation rests on a few surviving undated landscape watercolours. Many of these suggest an Italy he never visited but knew through the classical compositions of such seventeenth-century artists as Gaspar Dughet and Cornelis van Poelenburgh. Others are recognisably native in topography and commonly depict the environs of London. Some native views display such free execution and natural colour as to suggest that they may have been painted on the spot – which would be almost unparallelled for work of the time.

Technically, Taverner pioneered the use of pencil or chalk, rather than pen and ink, for underdrawing, and of bodycolour as a medium for landscape. He may have learned the latter from foreign artists working in England, such as Marco Ricci, who was based in London from 1710.

William Taverner died on 20 October 1772. After his death a writer in the *Gentleman's Magazine* called him 'one of the best landscape painters England ever produced'. A sale of his work was held at Langfords, Covent Garden, on 21 February 1774.

His work is represented in the collections of the British Museum, The Courtauld Gallery, Tate and the V&A; and the Ashmolean Museum (Oxford), the Castle Museum and Art Gallery (Nottingham), The Fitzwilliam Museum (Cambridge), Manchester Art Gallery, the Walker Art Gallery (Liverpool) and The Whitworth Art Gallery (Manchester).

Further reading:

Susan Morris, 'Taverner, William (*b* Canterbury, 1703; *d* 20 Oct 1772)', Jane Turner (ed), *The Dictionary of Art*, London: Macmillan, 1996, vol 30, pp 274-375

Andrew Wyld and Susan Sloman, 'Taverner, William (1700-1772)', H C G Matthew and Brian Harrison (eds), *Oxford Dictionary of National Biography*, Oxford University Press, 2004, vol 53, pp 843-844

Smollett on Taverner

If I am not totally devoid of taste, however, this young gentleman of Bath is the best landscape-painter now living; I was struck with his performances in such a manner as I had never seen by painting before. His trees not only have a richness of foliage, and a warmeth of colouring, which delights the view; but also a certain magnificence in the disposition and spirit in the expression, which I cannot describe. His management of the chiaro oscuro, *or light and shadow, especially gleams of sunshine, is altogether wonderful, both in the contrivance and execution; and he is so happy in his perspective, and marking his distances at sea, by a progressive series of ships, vessels, capes and promontories, that I could not help thinking I had a distant view of thirty leagues upon the back-ground of the picture. If there is any taste for ingenuity left in a degenerate age, fast sinking into barbarism, this artist, I apprehend, will make a capital figure, as soon as his works are known.*

Tobias Smollett, *Humphrey Clinker*, 1771

1 FIGURE IN A WOODED LANDSCAPE
watercolour, 7 ½ x 24 inches

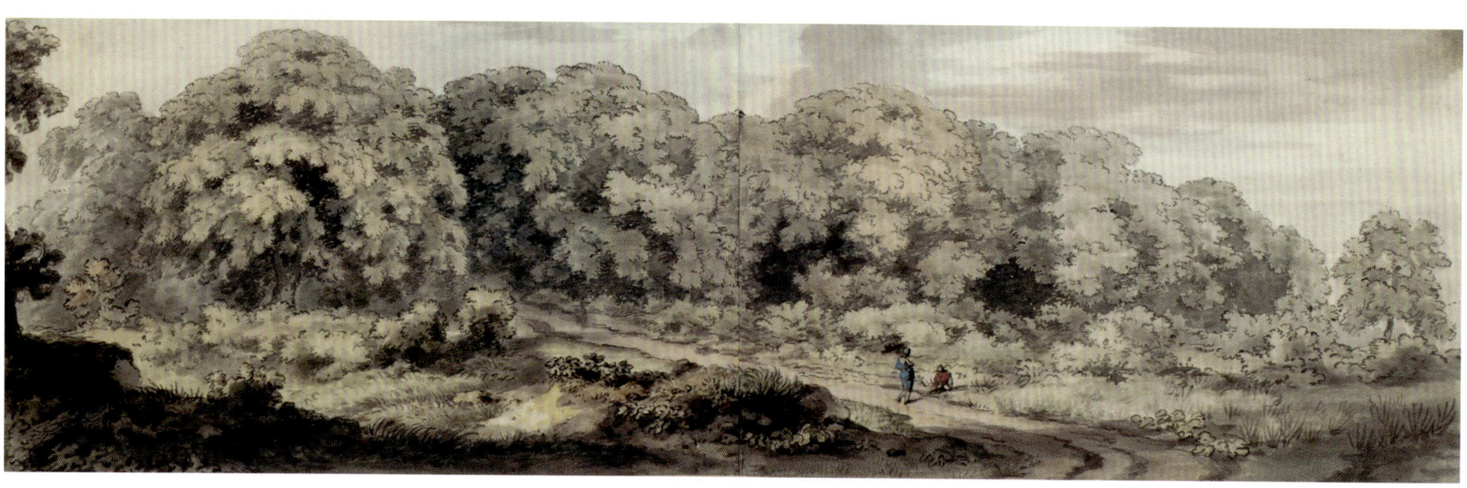

ANTHONY DEVIS
Anthony Thomas Devis (1729-1816)

Anthony Devis was a painter and draughtsman of charming landscapes inspired by Dutch and Italianate models. As a draughtsman, he produced large finished works in crayon and wash, and – as here – fresh studies in pen and ink enlivened with touches of colour.

Anthony Devis was born in Preston, Lancashire on 18 March 1729, to the councillor, Anthony Devis, and his second wife Anne. The portrait painter, Arthur Devis, was his older half-brother.

While his training remains a mystery, Devis was certainly working as a painter in London by 1742, when he was still only thirteen. Returning for a time to Preston, he was back in London by 1762, and living in Gloucester Street with his brother John, a silversmith and watchmaker; a decade later he had moved to Bedford Row. He specialised in topographical paintings, which he produced in both oil and watercolour, and exhibited – most notably – at the Free Society of Artists (1761 and 1763) and the Royal Academy of Arts (1772 and 1781). *A Cool Morning*, exhibited at the Free Society in 1763, was awarded 'The Third Premium for Landscape Painting'. He also worked as a picture restorer and a teacher.

In the early 1770s, Josiah Wedgwood commissioned Devis, among others, to produce numerous views of 'the ruins, country-houses, parks, gardens and picturesque landscapes of Great Britain'. These were intended to decorate the great creamware dinner service – known as the Frog Service – ordered by Empress Catherine the Great of Russia. This project may have instigated his extensive travels across Britain, and he subsequently undertook a number of commissions from native landowners. The completed service certainly includes views by Devis of Enville, Staffordshire and Bradgate, Leicestershire.

In 1780, Devis moved to Albury House in the village of Albury, near Guildford, in Surrey. Though there is no evidence of his exhibiting later than 1781, he did continue to work, producing among others the present watercolour, *Old Mill at Albury* **[12]**, as well as a view of his house (1792, now in the Harris Museum and Art Gallery, Preston).

There is no record that Devis travelled abroad, and his drawings of foreign views, such as *Between the Chartruse and Preppe* **[15]** are probably inspired by the work of others. Still, it is possible that Devis accompanied William Assheton of Cuerdale Hall, Lancashire, on his tour of Italy in 1783-84 – as the trees in a number of Assheton's Italian drawings are very like those by Devis. Indeed, Devis may have acted as Assheton's drawing master.

Devis died a bachelor at Albury on 26 April 1816. However, two of his nephews – Anthony Thomas Devis and Robert Marris – continued to produce work in a similar vein.

His work is represented in the Government Art Collection; and numerous public collections, including the British Museum, Tate and the V&A; Abbot Hall Art Gallery (Kendal), The Fitzwilliam Museum (Cambridge), the Harris Museum and Art Gallery (Preston), Tyne & Wear Museums and The Whitworth Art Gallery (Manchester); National Museum Wales (Cardiff); and Aberdeen Art Gallery & Museums.

Archives concerning the Devis family are held at The Courtauld Institute of Art.

Further reading:

Hugh Belsey, 'Devis', Jane Turner (ed), *The Dictionary of Art*, London: Macmillan, 1996, vol 8, pp 832-834
Ellen G D'Oech, 'Devis, Arthur (1712-1787)', H C G Matthew and Brian Harrison (eds), *Oxford Dictionary of National Biography*, Oxford University Press, 2004, vol 15, pp 978-980
Drawings by Anthony Devis, Preston: Harris Museum and Art Gallery, 1956
Sydney Herbert Paviere, 'Anthony Devis and his relatives', *The Antique Collector*, vol 6, no 3, April 1935, pp 83-85
Sydney Herbert Paviere, 'Arthur and Anthony Devis', *The Antique Collector*, vol 5, no 3, April 1934
Sydney Herbert Paviere, 'Biographical Notes on The Devis Family of Painters', *Walpole Society*, vol 25, 1936-37, pp 115-166
Sydney Herbert Paviere, *The Devis Family of Painters*, Leigh-on-Sea: F Lewis, 1950
Michael Raeburn, Ludmila Voronikhina and Andrew Nurnberg (eds), *The Green Frog Service: Wedgwood & Bentley's Imperial Russian Service*, London: The Cacklegoose Press, 2006
R Charles Walmsley, *The Sage of Albury, and the Man Mushroom*, Albury: R Charles Walmsley, undated
Stephen Whittle, *Anthony Devis (1729-1826): a 'picturesque traveller'*, Preston: Harris Museum and Art Gallery, 1993
Eric Young, 'A Watercolour by Anthony Devis', *Auckland City Art Gallery Quarterly*, no 64, May 1977, pp 8-10

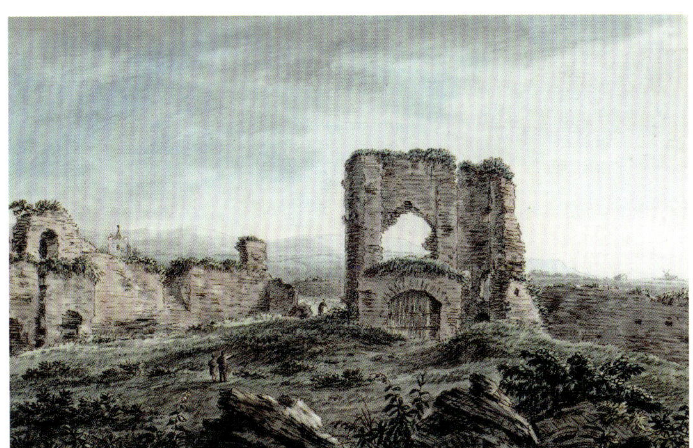

2 OLD CASTLE RUINS
watercolour, pen ink and pencil
8 ¾ x 13 inches

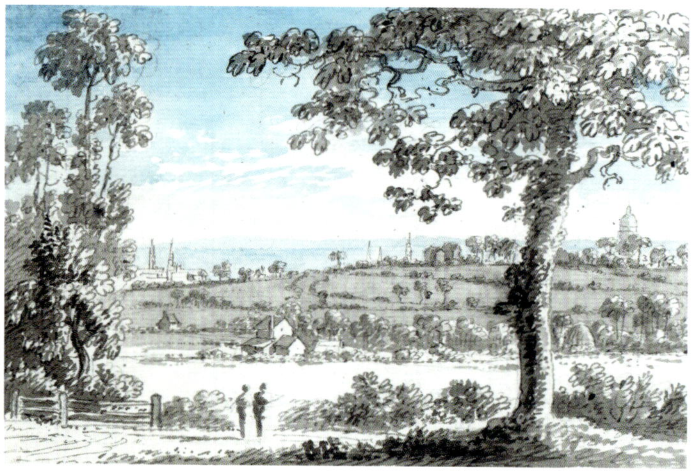

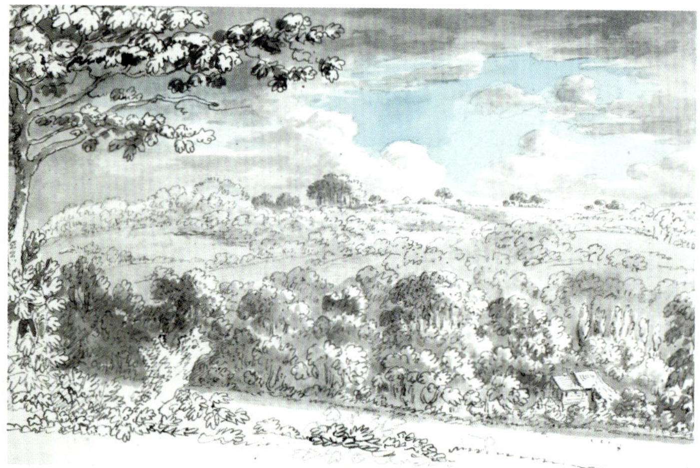

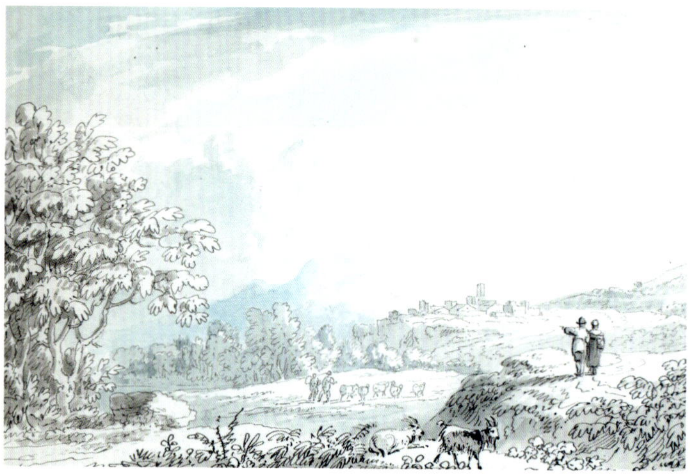

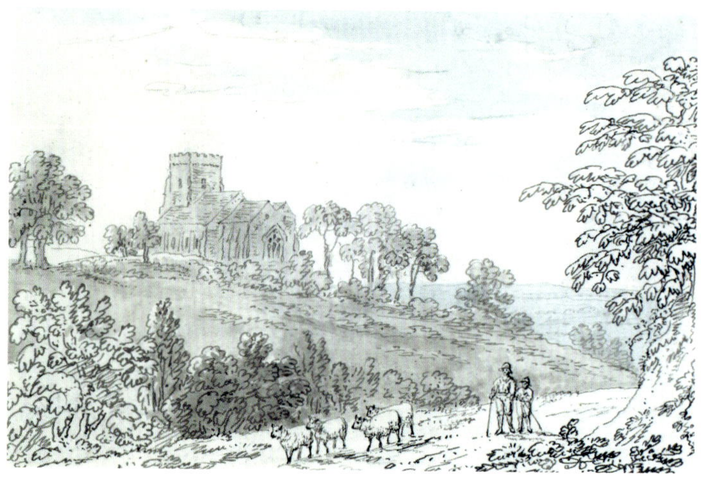

3 DISTANT VIEW OF COASTAL VILLAGE
pen ink and watercolour
5 ¼ x 7 ¾ inches

4 ABOVE MR CALLINGS HOP GROUNDS
inscribed with title below mount
pen ink and watercolour with pencil
5 ¼ x 7 ¾ inches

5 VIEW OF A HAMLET
pen ink and watercolour with pencil
5 ½ x 8 inches

6 GREEN HYTHE
inscribed with title below mount
inscribed with title on reverse
pen ink and watercolour with pencil
5 ½ x 8 inches

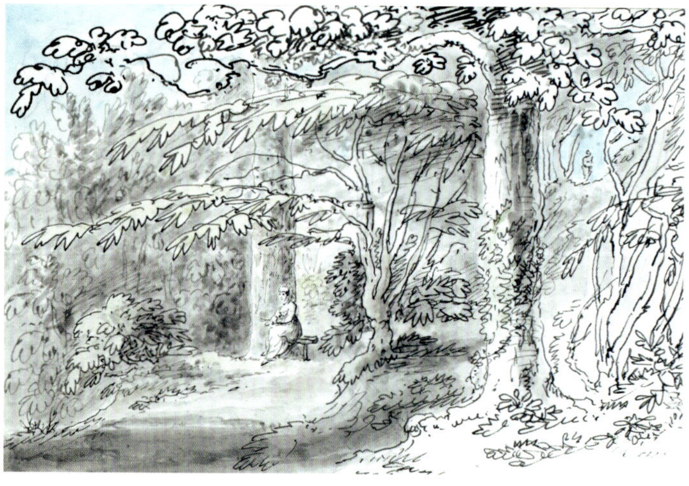

In Mr Malthus's Woods

The Malthus family lived in or near Anthony Devis's home village of Albury in Surrey. Its most famous member was Thomas Robert Malthus (1766-1834), author of *Principles of Population* (1798). Malthus was briefly curate at Albury.

7 IN MR MALTHUS'S WOODS
inscribed with title on reverse
pen ink and watercolour
6 ½ x 9 inches

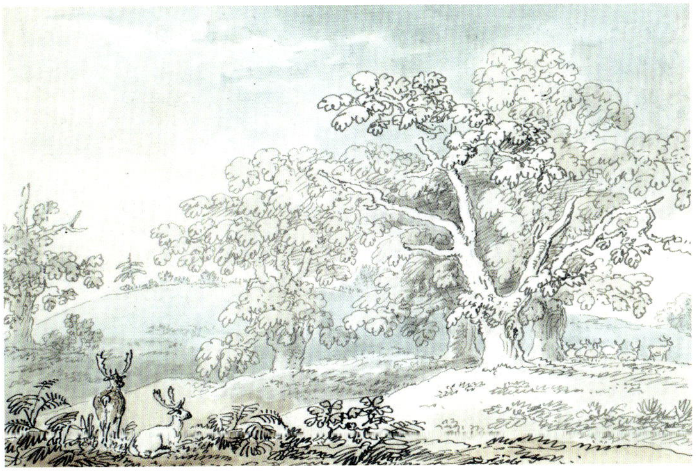

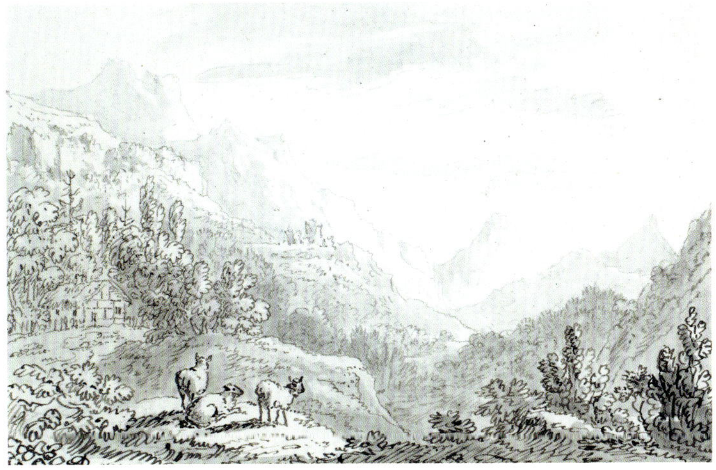

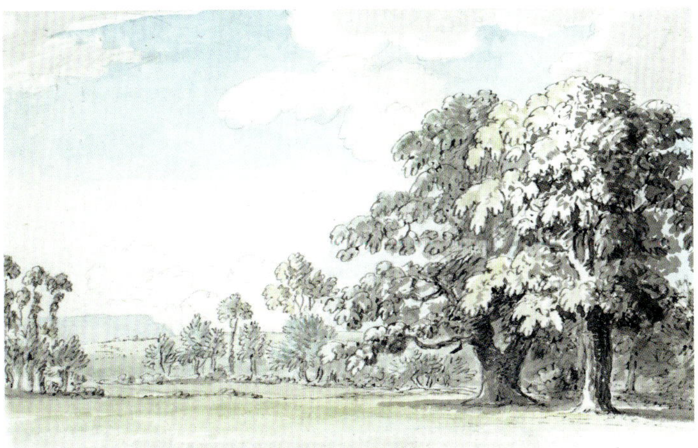

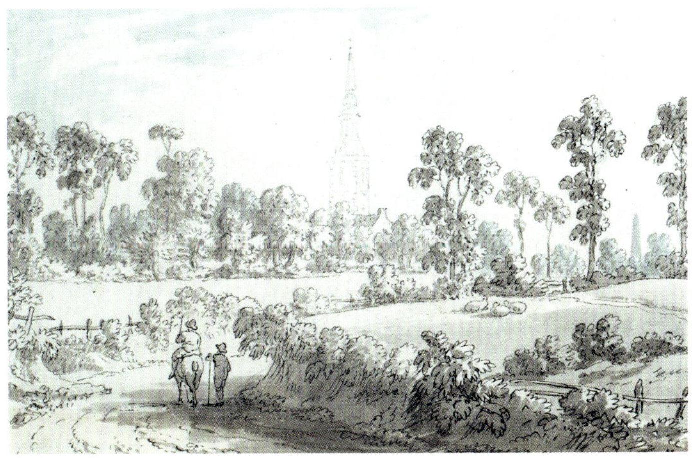

8 DEER PARK
pen ink and watercolour
5 ½ x 8 inches

10 IN THE FOOTWAY TO CLEVE
inscribed with title on reverse
pen ink and watercolour with pencil
5 ½ x 8 ¼ inches

9 SHEEP IN A ROMANTIC VALLEY LANDSCAPE
pen ink and monochrome watercolour with pencil
5 ½ x 8 inches

11 YONDER SPIRE
pen ink and watercolour with pencil
5 ½ x 8 inches

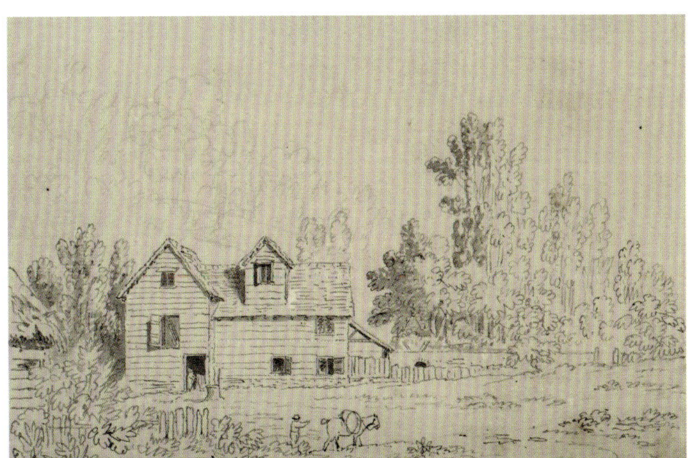

12 OLD MILL AT ALBURY
inscribed with title below mount
pen ink and monochrome watercolour with pencil
5 ¼ x 8 inches

ANTHONY DEVIS

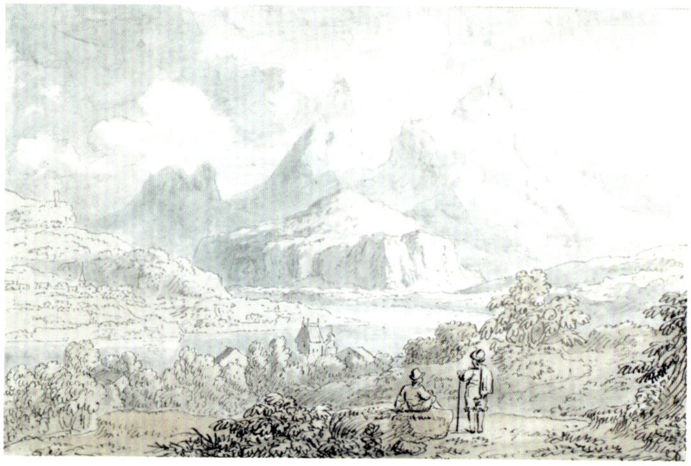

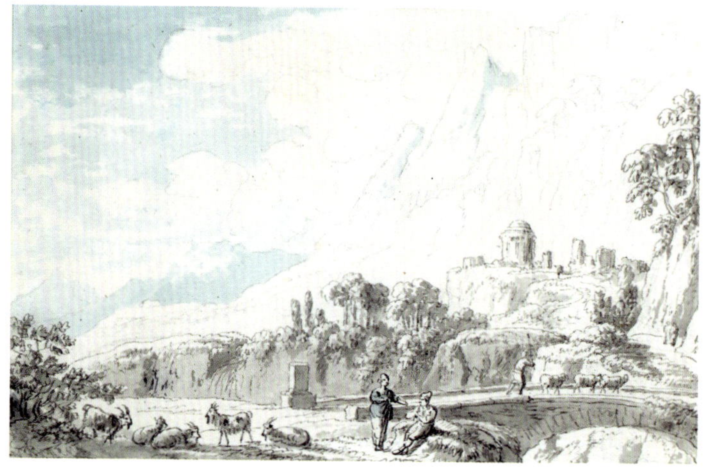

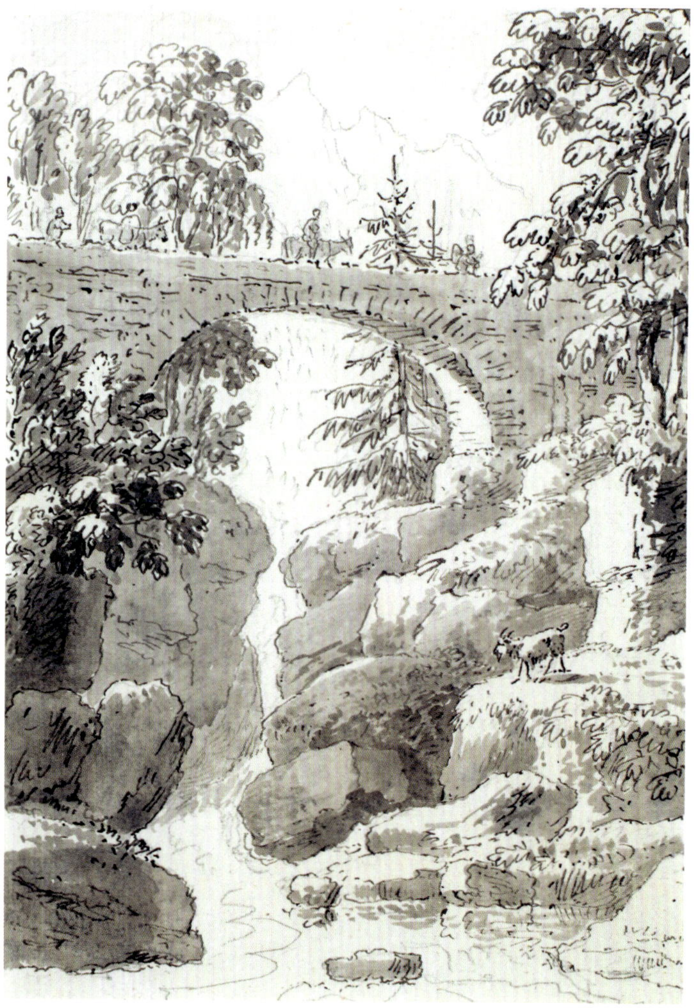

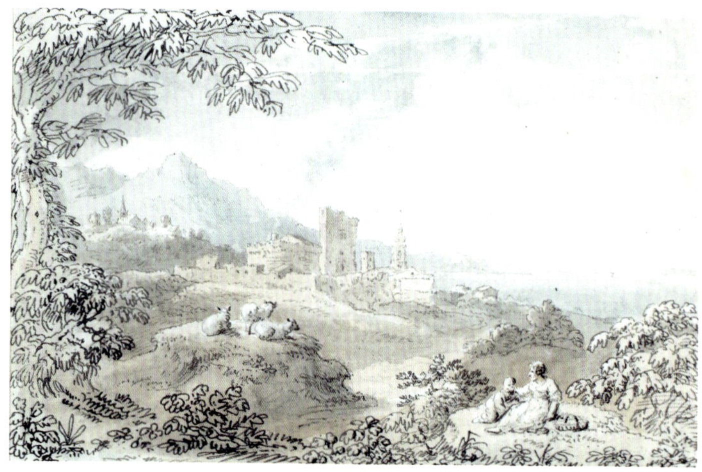

13 SALANCHE ON R ARVE SAVOY
inscribed with title below mount
pen ink and watercolour with pencil
5 ½ x 8 inches

15 BETWEEN THE CHARTRUSE AND PREPPE
inscribed with title below mount
pen ink and monochrome watercolour with pencil
9 ¼ x 6 ¼ inches

14 GOATHERDS BELOW MOUNTAIN RUINS
pen ink and watercolour with pencil
5 ¼ x 8 inches

16 PASTORAL SCENE IN AN ITALIANATE LANDSCAPE
inscribed with title below mount
pen ink and monochrome watercolour with pencil
5 ½ x 8 inches

SAMUEL HIERONYMUS GRIMM

Samuel Hieronymus Grimm (1733-1794)

A range of youthful experiences – in which he engaged with the arts and sciences, in Switzerland and France – made Samuel Hieronymus Grimm well equipped for his career in England as a draughtsman and illustrator. There he responded with a combination of precision and lyricism to the demands of his patrons: antiquaries, topographers and natural historians, who sought to record 'everything curious'.

Samuel Hieronymus Grimm was baptised at Burgdorf, in the canton of Bern, Switzerland, on 18 January 1733. He was the youngest child of a notary, Johann Jakob Grimm, and nephew of the painter, Johann Grimm. Following the death of his father in 1749, he lived with a maternal uncle and, despite his artistic leanings, was set to assist a physician, J G Zimmerman. Under the influence of the scientist and poet, Albrecht von Haller, he began to write his own poetry, publishing two volumes, in 1758 and 1762 (the second with an introduction by Haller).

During the 1750s, Grimm studied under the artist Johann Ludwig Aberli, in Bern, and then began to establish himself as a topographical painter. Though he initially worked more in oil than watercolour, it is his tinted drawings that indicated his future direction. Travelling with Alberli in the Bernese Oberland, in 1758, he produced views of glaciers that were used to illustrate G S Gruner's *Die Eisgebirge der Schweizerlandes* (1760). During the years 1764-75, he produced further illustrations, mainly for books issued by the Bern publisher Beat Ludwig Walthard.

In or soon after 1765, Grimm moved to Paris, where he entered the circle of the engraver and publisher, Johann Georg Wille. He made sketching tours in the vicinity of Paris in the company of other artists, and visited Normandy with Philipp Hackert and Nicolas Pérignon.

In February 1768, Grimm settled in Covent Garden, London. Staying initially with Mrs Susannah Sledge, the printseller, in Henrietta Street, he remained in the area for the rest of his life. Within months of his arrival, he exhibited at the Society of Artists. In the following year, he showed four works at the first exhibition of the newly formed Royal Academy of Arts, and then regularly (continuously until 1781, and then in 1784-84 and 1793). He also exhibited at the Free Society of Artists (until 1793). Elected to the Society of Arts in November 1773, he sat on its committee of polite arts until 1777.

While continuing to produce illustrations for Swiss publishers, Grimm first made a name in London with social caricatures (including some published by Carington Bowles of St Paul's Church Yard). By 1773, he was receiving commissions for antiquarian, architectural and landscape watercolours, including prefatory illustrations to the first volume of Francis Grose's *Antiquities of England and Wales*.

In 1773, Grimm recorded the Maundy Ceremony for Sir Richard Kaye, the king's sub-almoner, who would become his chief patron, providing him with work for the remainder of his life. As Kaye rose through the ecclesiastical hierarchy, eventually becoming Dean of Lincoln, he moved about the country, and Grimm would stay and travel with him. (Kaye's collection in the British Library comprises about 2500 items by Grimm.)

During the late 1770s, the number and range of commissions that Grimm received increased further. In 1776, he spent a month with Gilbert White, working on illustrations to his *Natural History and Antiquities of Selborne* (1789). In the following year, he travelled through Wales with the topographer, Henry Penruddocke Wyndham, in order to provide illustrations for his *Tour through Monmouthshire and Wales* (1781). At the time of the tour, Wyndham had recently been elected a fellow of the Society of Antiquaries, and that learned society would also employ Grimm on four occasions, between 1779 and 1791, to record a number of Tudor paintings.

Between 1780 and 1791, though excluding 1786, Grimm spent each fortnight from Whitsun working for Sir William Burrell, the Sussex antiquary. (The 900 studies from nature that he produced for him are now in the British Library.) In 1781 and 1785, he also worked for Cornelius Heathcote Rodes of Barlborough Hall, Derbyshire.

Grimm died 'of a mortification in his bowels' on 14 April 1794, at the house of William Wellings, engraver, in Tavistock Street, St Paul's, Covent Garden. Never having married, he left much of his money to a niece in Switzerland. His will also named three 'worthy friends and employers': Rodes, Burrell and Kaye.

His work is represented in numerous public collections, including the British Library, the British Museum, The Courtauld Gallery, Tate and the V&A; and The Fitzwilliam Museum (Cambridge) and Tyne & Wear Museums.

Further reading:

Rotha Mary Clay, *Samuel Hieronymus Grimm of Burgdorf in Switzerland*, London: Faber and Faber, 1941

John H Farrant, 'Grimm, Samuel Hieronymus (*bap.* 1733, *d.* 1794)', H C G Matthew and Brian Harrison (eds), *Oxford Dictionary of National Biography*, Oxford University Press, 2004, vol 24, pp 24-25

'Grimm, Samuel Hieronymous (*b* Burgdorf, Switzerland, bapt 18 Jan 1733; *d* London, 14 April 1794)', Jane Turner (ed), *The Dictionary of Art*, London: Macmillan, 1996, vol 13, pp 663-664

Georges Herzog, 'Grimm, Samuel Hieronymus', Swiss Institute for Art Research, www.sikart.ch (in German)

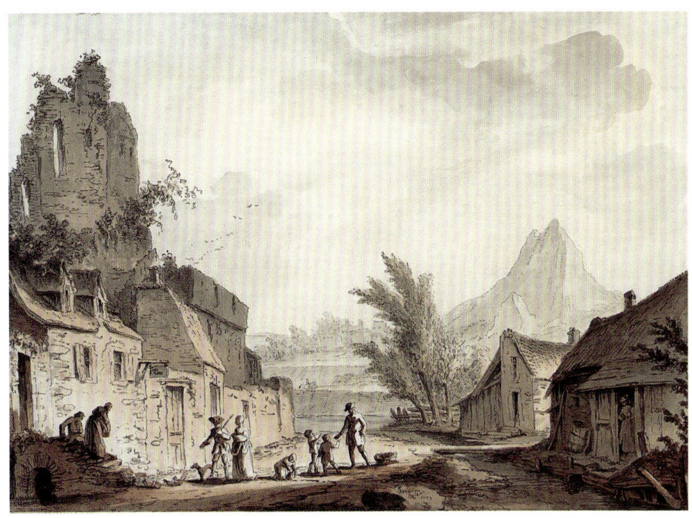

17 VILLAGE WITH A RUINED TOWER
signed and dated 1771
pen ink and watercolour
10 x 13 ¾ inches

NICHOLAS POCOCK

Captain Nicholas Pocock, OWS (1740-1821)

Nicholas Pocock was the finest and most popular marine painter in Britain during the Napoleonic period, his work being well informed by his own practical experience as a seaman. He also produced a number of distinctive landscapes.

Nicholas Pocock was born in Bristol on 2 May 1740, the son of Nicholas Pocock, a mariner. He grew up in Prince Street, close to the docks and, from 1757, was apprenticed to his father, drawing in his spare time. On the death of his father nine years later, he began to captain Bristol trading vessels (the *Lloyd*, *Betsey* and *Minerva*) for the Quaker merchant, Richard Champion, leading twelve voyages, mainly to America and the West Indies. While at sea, he developed his interest in drawing, regularly illustrating his logbooks with vignettes of the ship, its surroundings and the weather conditions.

Eventually, circumstances must have encouraged Pocock to turn from the merchant navy to professional painting; for though he lost his captaincy in 1778, when Champion became insolvent, he still married on 10 February 1780. Later in the same year, he submitted work to the exhibition at the Royal Academy of Arts and, while it arrived too late to be included, it did elicit an encouraging letter from the President, Sir Joshua Reynolds. He stated that 'it is much beyond what I expected from a first essay in oil colours', and advised that he 'paint from nature' and 'imitate [Joseph] Vernet by uniting landscape to ship painting'. As a result, Pocock exhibited four marines at the RA in 1782, and then showed without a break until 1812, with a last appearance in 1815. At the same time, he began to receive regular commissions for both oils and watercolours.

In 1789, Pocock and his family moved to Great George Street, Westminster. His combination of seafaring experience and artistic talent made him the ideal person to record the subjects required by Royal Naval and mercantile patrons and, after the death of Dominic Serres in 1793, he became the leading naval painter in Britain. A year later, he began to record the naval battles between Britain and France, witnessing at first hand the Battle of the Glorious First of June as a guest of Captain Barlow of the frigate *Pegasus*.

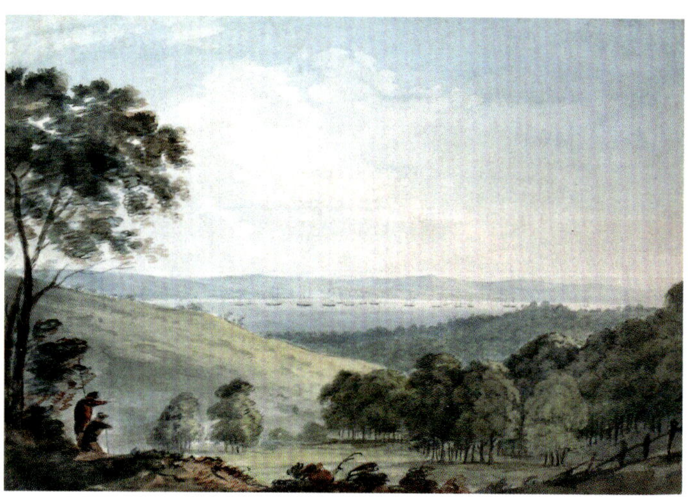

Pocock painted more peaceful marine views, exhibiting many at the Society of Painters in Water Colours, following his founder membership in 1804. His works were also engraved as prints and illustrations to books and periodicals, notably the *Naval Chronicle*.

Following a stroke in 1817, Pocock seemed to stop painting altogether and retired to Ray Lodge, Maidenhead to live with his eldest son, Isaac. He died there on 9 March 1821.

Isaac was a painter of historical subjects and portraits, including one of his father and others of naval officers; however, he had a greater reputation as a playwright. Another son, William Innes, was a skilled marine watercolourist as well as a lieutenant in the Royal Navy. Pocock's elder daughter, Mary Anne was the mother of two significant Victorian watercolourists – George Arthur Fripp and Alfred Downing Fripp.

His work is represented in the Government Art Collection, and numerous public collections including the British Museum, The Courtauld Gallery, the National Maritime Museum, Tate and the V&A; the Ashmolean Museum (Oxford), Brighton & Hove Museums, Bristol's City Museum and Art Gallery, Gallery Oldham, the Grosvenor Museum (Chester), Leeds Art Gallery, Manchester Art Gallery, Norwich Castle Museum & Art Gallery and The Whitworth Art Gallery (Manchester); and the National Library of Wales (Aberystwyth) and National Museum Wales (Cardiff).

Further reading:

David Cordingly, *Nicholas Pocock 1740–1821*, London: Conway Maritime Press/National Maritime Museum, 1986
David Cordingly, 'Nicholas Pocock's paintings of sea battles', www.nmm.ac.uk
David Cordingly, 'Nicholas Pocock's Voyages from Bristol', *in Sea Studies: essays in honour of Basil Greenhill*, London: National Maritime Museum, 1983
David Cordingly, 'Pocock, Nicholas (1740-1821)', H C G Matthew and Brian Harrison (eds), *Oxford Dictionary of National Biography*, Oxford University Press, 2004, vol 44, pp 656-657
David Cordingly, *Ships and Seascapes: an introduction to maritime prints, drawings and watercolours*, Philip Wilson Publishers, 1997
David Cordingly, 'The Watercolours of Nicholas Pocock', *The Old Water-Colour Society's Club*, vol 54, 1979, pp 24-40
Randall Davies, 'Nicholas Pocock', *The Old Water-Colour Society's Club* vol 5, 1927–28, pp 1-29
Stephen Deuchar, 'Pocock, Nicholas (*b* Bristol, 2 May 1741; *d* Maidenhead, Berks, 19 March 1821)', Jane Turner (ed), *The Dictionary of Art*, London: Macmillan, 1996, vol 25, p 61
W H Dunman, *Nicholas Pocock*, catalogue of the exhibition held at Bristol Art Gallery in 1940

18 THE STRAIT OF MENAI, CAERNARVONSHIRE
watercolour and bodycolour on laid paper, watermarked 'J Whatman 1794'
13 ½ x 19 inches

NICHOLAS POCOCK

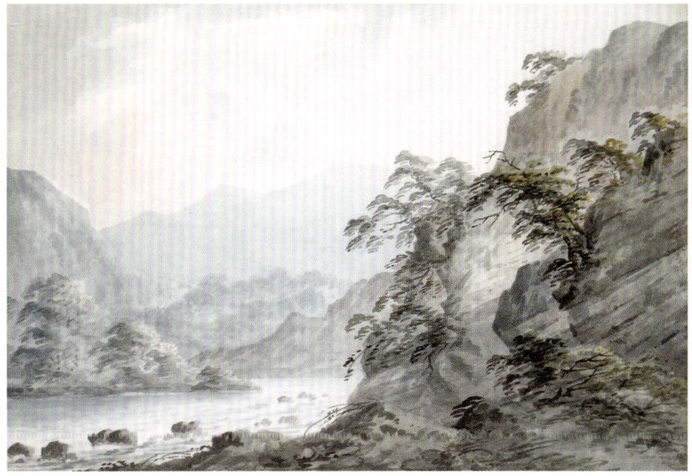

19 ENTRANCE INTO BORODALE
inscribed with title on reverse
watercolour
10 ¼ 14 ½ inches

WILLIAM PARS
William Edmund Pars, ARA (1742-1782)

William Pars is best remembered as a travelling draughtsman, responsible for some important antiquarian studies and pioneering topographical views.

William Pars was born in London on 28 February 1742, the son of a metal chaser, probably of Dutch origin. He studied at the drawing school at 101 The Strand, run by William Shipley (who had founded the Society for the Encouragement of the Arts in 1754), then in the Duke of Richmond's sculpture gallery, Whitehall, and at the St Martin's Lane Academy. He later returned to Shipley's to assist his brother, Henry, who had become its director.

Pars had trained to become a landscape and history painter, but first earned his living as a portrait painter, exhibiting at the Society of Artists (1760), the Free Society of Artists (1761) and the Incorporated Society of Artists.

In 1764, while still only 22, Pars achieved a turn in his career. Not only did he win a premium from the Society of Arts for his (untraced) painting *Caractacus before the Emperor Claudius* (one of several such prizes in his career). He was also selected by the Society of Dilettanti to accompany Richard Chandler, the antiquary, and Nicholas Revett, the architect, on an archaeological expedition to Asia Minor and Greece (1764–66).

His views of Classical monuments in Asia Minor were engraved and published in *Ionian Antiquities* (in parts from 1769). Some of those made in Greece were later included in the second and third volumes of Stuart and Revett's *The Antiquities of Athens* (1789 and 1794), while others were engraved by William Byrne for the Dilettanti. The Greek drawings included groundbreaking studies of the Parthenon. In 1769, Pars exhibited seven of the Greek subjects at the Royal Academy (now in the British Museum), which led to his election as an associate of the RA.

In 1769, Pars accompanied his patron, Henry Temple, 2nd Viscount Palmerston, on a tour through Switzerland down into Italy. In the following year, he exhibited eight of the resulting works at the Royal Academy, works which Laurence Binyon called 'the earliest revelation of the high Alps to the untravelled English' (1933, p 58), and which prefigure views by J R Cozens and Francis Towne. He travelled again with Lord Palmerston, to Ireland and the Lake District (1771), and was employed by Horace Walpole to make views of Strawberry Hill.

In 1774, the Dilettanti awarded Pars an income for three years so that he could continue his studies in Rome. In the following year, he set out with the wife of the miniaturist John Smart (though she died in 1778). On arrival, he joined Thomas Jones and his friends, and worked alongside them in Rome and its surroundings, and in Naples. Though he sent works back to London, to patrons and for exhibitions, he remained in Rome for the remainder of his life. He died in October 1782 from pneumonia having contracted pleurisy following a trip to Tivoli, during which he had drawn standing in the Grand Cascade in the Grotto of Neptune.

His work is represented in the Government Art Collection and numerous public collections, including the British Museum, The Courtauld Gallery, Tate and the V&A; the Ashmolean Museum (Oxford), Birmingham Museum & Art Gallery, Brighton Museum & Art Gallery, The Fitzwilliam Museum (Cambridge) and Leeds Art Gallery; Aberdeen Art Gallery; and the National Gallery of Ireland (Dublin).

Further reading:

Andrew Wilton, 'Pars, William (*b* London, 28 Feb 1792; *d* Rome, 1782)', Jane Turner (ed), *The Dictionary of Art*, London: Macmillan, 1996, vol 24, p 213
Andrew Wilton, 'Pars, William Edmund (1742-1782)', H C G Matthew and Brian Harrison (eds), *Oxford Dictionary of National Biography*, Oxford University Press, 2004, vol 42, pp 904-905
Andrew Wilton, 'William Pars and his Work in Asia Minor', in Edith Clay (ed), *Richard Chandler: Travels in Asia Minor, 1764-1765*, London: British Museum, 1971, pp xix-xlv
Andrew Wilton, *William Pars: Journey through the Alps*, Zurich: Dubendorf: De Clivo Press, 1979

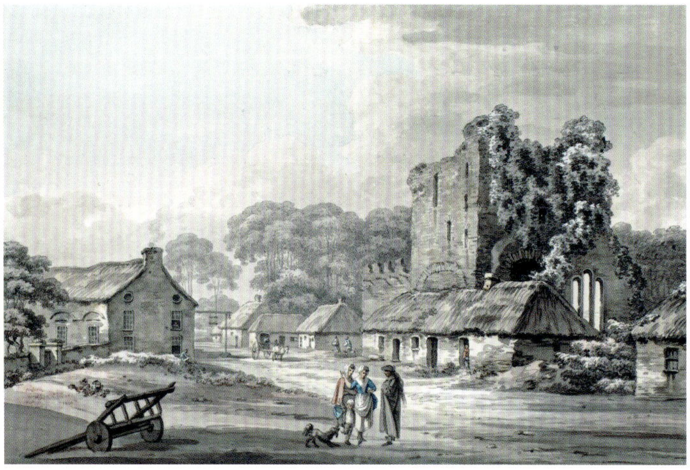

WILLIAM PARS

20 RUIN AT ADARE,
IN COUNTY LIMERICK
watercolour
10 ¼ x 15 inches

Ruin at Adare, in County Limerick
This image was likely to have been painted in or after 1771, when Pars undertook a tour of Ireland with his patron, Henry Temple, 2nd Viscount Palmerston. Lord Palmerston was an Irish peer, and his estate was in County Sligo, in north-west Ireland; County Limerick is much further to the south.

Now claimed as Ireland's prettiest village, Adare contains a number of historic buildings, including the Trinitarian Abbey, shown here in a ruined state. This thirteenth century abbey flourished until the dissolution of the monasteries by Henry VIII. Valentine Quin, 1st Earl of Dunraven restored its church to use in the early nineteenth century.

Other Irish views by Pars are held in the collections of Tate and the V&A.

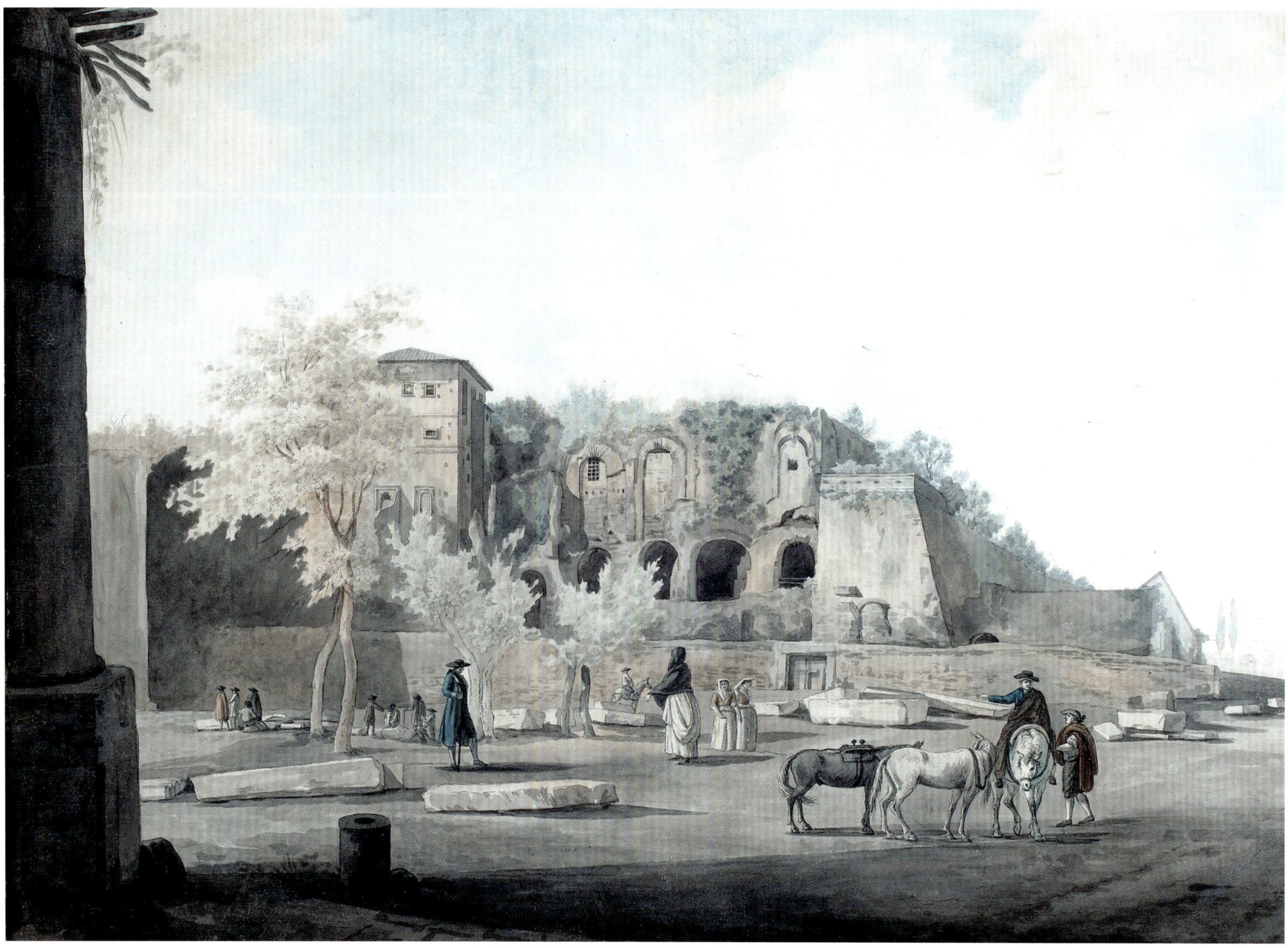

21 THE IMPERIAL PALACES, THE PALATINE, ROME
watercolour with pen and ink, 13 ½ x 18 ½ inches

GEORGE CUIT
George Cuit the elder (1743-1818)

Though George Cuit travelled as far as Italy, he made his reputation in Yorkshire, close to home; so he represents one of many regional schools of watercolour painting that developed through the later eighteenth century.

The son of a builder, George Cuit was born in Moulton near Richmond, Yorkshire on 8 September 1743. Educated at Richmond School, he showed an early talent for drawing, and was taken up by Sir Lawrence Dundas of Aske Hall. In 1769, Dundas sent him to study painting in Italy, in the company of his former schoolfriend, the architect Thomas Harrison, and he remained there for six years.

On his return to England, Cuit attempted to establish himself in London, and began to exhibit at the Royal Academy of Arts (1776-1798). However, hampered by ill health, he returned to Richmond within two years. There he enjoyed a career as a landscape and portrait painter in oil and watercolour for over two decades. He also worked as a drawing master, numbering among his pupils William Young Ottley (collector and early British historian of Italian painting). In 1788, he collaborated with Robert Coatsworth in painting the scenery for the opening productions of Richmond's Theatre Royal. In the same period, he worked for the former naval captain Constantine Phipps who, as Baron Mulgrave, commissioned a set of views of Yorkshire ports visited by Captain Cook. He died in Richmond on 7 February 1818, a month after his wife.

His son, George Cuitt, painter and etcher, may have added an extra 't' to his name to distinguish himself from his father.

22 TANFIELD YORKS
signed 'Geo Cuit Pinxt', inscribed with title and dated 1788
watercolour and bodycolour
15 ¾ x 21 ½ inches

His work is represented in the Government Art Collection, the Societies of Antiquaries of London and York Minster Library; and the following public collections: the British Museum; Leeds Art Gallery, Wakefield Art Gallery and Whitby Museum; and the Yale Center for British Art (New Haven).

Further reading:
Jane Hatcher, *George Cuit the elder, 1743-1818*, Leyburn: Tennants, 1992
L H Cust (rev Ruth Stewart), 'Cuit, George, the elder (1743-1818)', H C G Matthew and Brian Harrison (eds), *Oxford Dictionary of National Biography*, Oxford University Press, 2004, vol 14, p 571

Many thanks to Peter Boughton, Keeper of Art and Creative Development at the Grosvenor Museum, Chester, for help in compiling this entry. He is currently writing a monograph and catalogue raisonné of George Cuitt the younger.

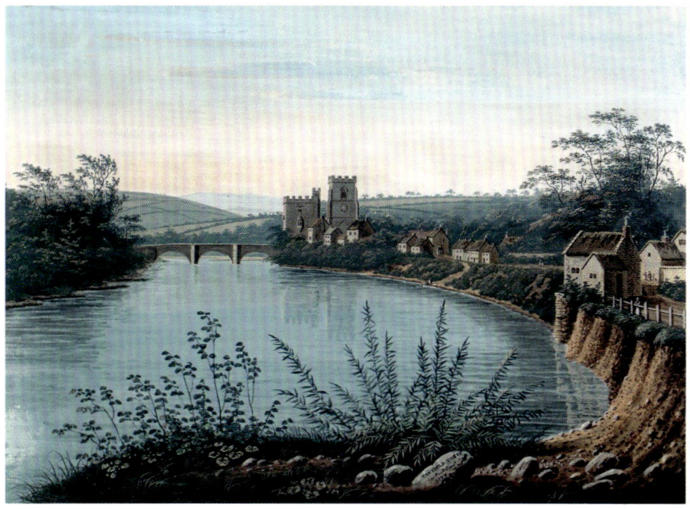

THOMAS SUNDERLAND
Thomas Sunderland (1744-1823)

Thomas Sunderland was a prolific amateur artist, best known for his landscapes and for copies after other artists, made in clear, flat watercolour washes.

Thomas Sunderland was born at Whittington Hall, near Kirkby Lonsdale, Lancashire on 3 November 1744. He became the owner of an iron ore foundry at Furness and Deputy Lieutenant for Lancashire.

In 1782, Sunderland sold the family home and built 'Littlecroft', a house at Ulverston. Two decades later, in 1803, he responded to the threat of a French invasion by forming the Ulverston Volunteer Light Infantry, and becoming its Lieutenant-Colonel.

Sunderland was a pupil of John Robert Cozens, and possibly of Alexander Cozens and Joseph Farington. The influence of all three artists is very strong in his work. He generally worked in monochrome wash with pen or pencil outlines, while also producing full watercolours. Though he made many copies after works by Old Masters, he also recorded the places that he visited on wide travels across Britain and Europe. In turn, it seems that J R Cozens stayed with him at Littlecroft. He died at home on 3 July 1823.

His work is represented in the Government Art Collection, and numerous public collections, including the British Museum, Tate and the V&A; and Abbott Hall Art Gallery (Kendal) and the Whitworth Art Gallery (Manchester).

Further reading:
Randall Davies, 'Thomas Sunderland (1744-1823). Some Family Notes', *The Old Water-Colour Society's Club*, vol 20, 1942, pp 31-39

THOMAS SUNDERLAND

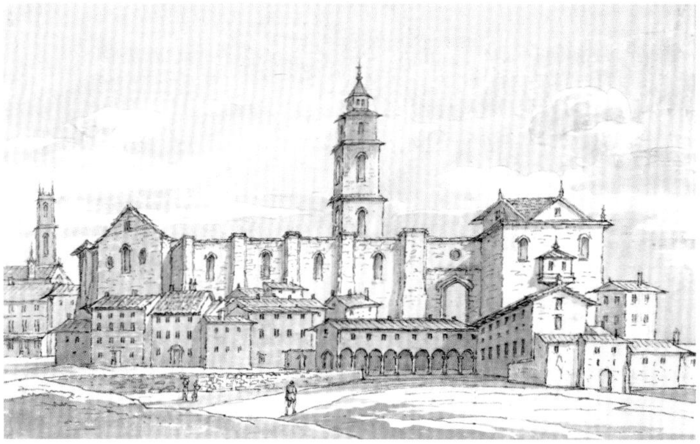

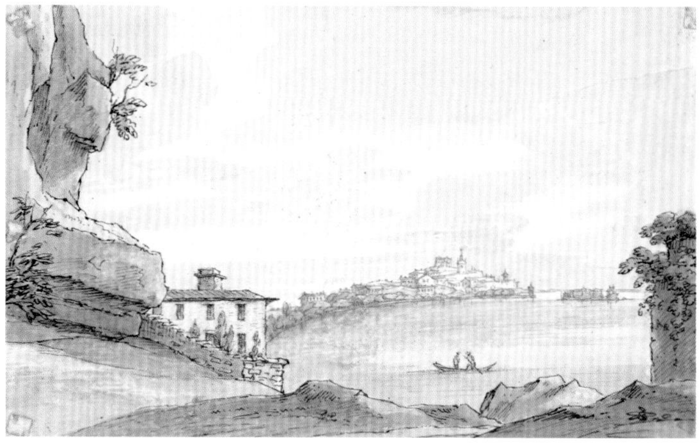

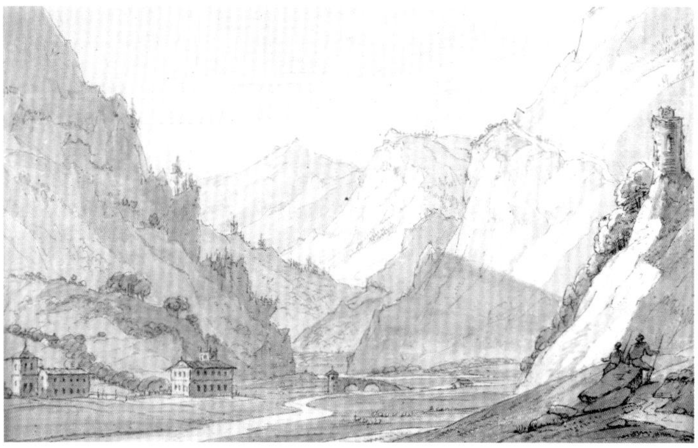

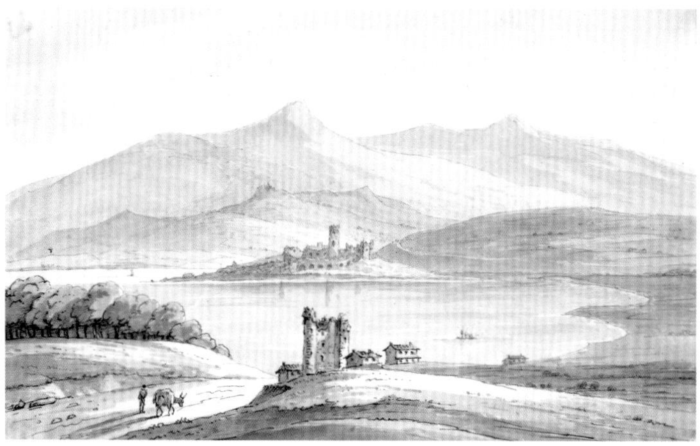

23 PERUGIA
inscribed with title below mount
pen ink and watercolour
6 ¾ x 10 ½ inches

24 THE LAKE OF PERUGIA
inscribed with title below mount
pen ink and watercolour
6 ¾ x 10 ½ inches

25 TERNI
inscribed with title and faint inscription on reverse
pen ink and watercolour
6 ¾ x 10 ½ inches

26 ITALIAN SCENE
inscribed with title on reverse
pen ink and watercolour
6 ¾ x 10 ½ inches

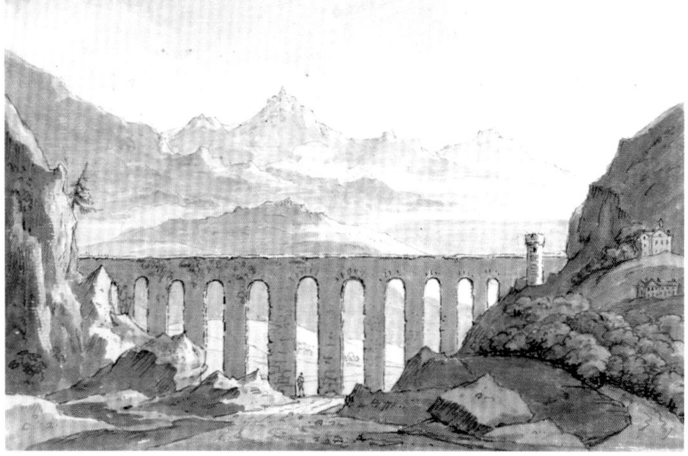

27 AQUEDUCT OF SPOLETTA
inscribed with title on reverse
pen ink and watercolour
7 x 10 inches

GEORGE FROST
George Frost (*circa* 1745-1821)

Though of amateur status, George Frost had a key role in the development of naturalism in British landscape of the Romantic period – by communicating his enthusiasm for Thomas Gainsborough to John Constable, and other pupils, through his drawings and his conversation.

George Frost was the son of a builder living in Ousden in West Suffolk. However, he was probably born in the neighbouring village of Barrow, and was certainly baptised there on 21 February 1745.

Though Frost initially worked in his father's building business, he obtained an administrative position in the offices of the Blue Coach company in Ipswich, directing the departure and arrival of the coaches. He worked there until his retirement in 1813, and lived for some years at Brook Street, near the Coach and Horses Inn.

In his spare time, Frost developed his natural skill as a draughtsman, and produced a number of watercolours and drawings of the local area (the first recorded watercolour being dated 1780). A devoted admirer of Gainsborough, he collected, copied and imitated many of his works. His interest in collecting pictures seems to have led to his dealing in them.

Beginning to give drawing lessons by 1797, Frost was able to number John Constable among his pupils within three years. Frost encouraged Constable to look at the work of Gainsborough, and took him sketching along the banks of the River Orwell. Even when Constable gained a wide reputation, the two artists remained friends.

Frost died at his home, at Common Quay, Ipswich, on 28 June 1821 after a long illness.

His considerable art collection was sold by Garrods of Ipswich on 7 June 1839, following the death of his widow, Mary, on 25 April. Many of the Gainsborough drawings in this collection were bought by William Esdaile, a friend of Frost as well as a notable collector. The present drawing was once in Esdaile's collection.

His work is represented in the collections of the British Museum; and Ipswich Museums Service.

Further reading:
L H Cust (rev Hugh Belsey), 'Frost, George (*bap.* 1745, *d.* 1821)', H C G Matthew and Brian Harrison (eds), *Oxford Dictionary of National Biography*, Oxford University Press, 2004, vol 21, p 62
John Hayes, 'The drawings of George Frost (1745-1821)', *Master Drawings*, vol 4, no 2, 1966, pp 163-168
Michael Rosenthal, *George Frost, 1745-1821*, Sudbury: Gainsborough's House, 1974
Denis Thomas, 'George Frost and the Gainsborough tradition', *The Connoisseur*, no 178, 1971, pp 108-113
Denis Thomas, *George Frost and Thomas Churchyard*, Colchester: The Minories, 1974

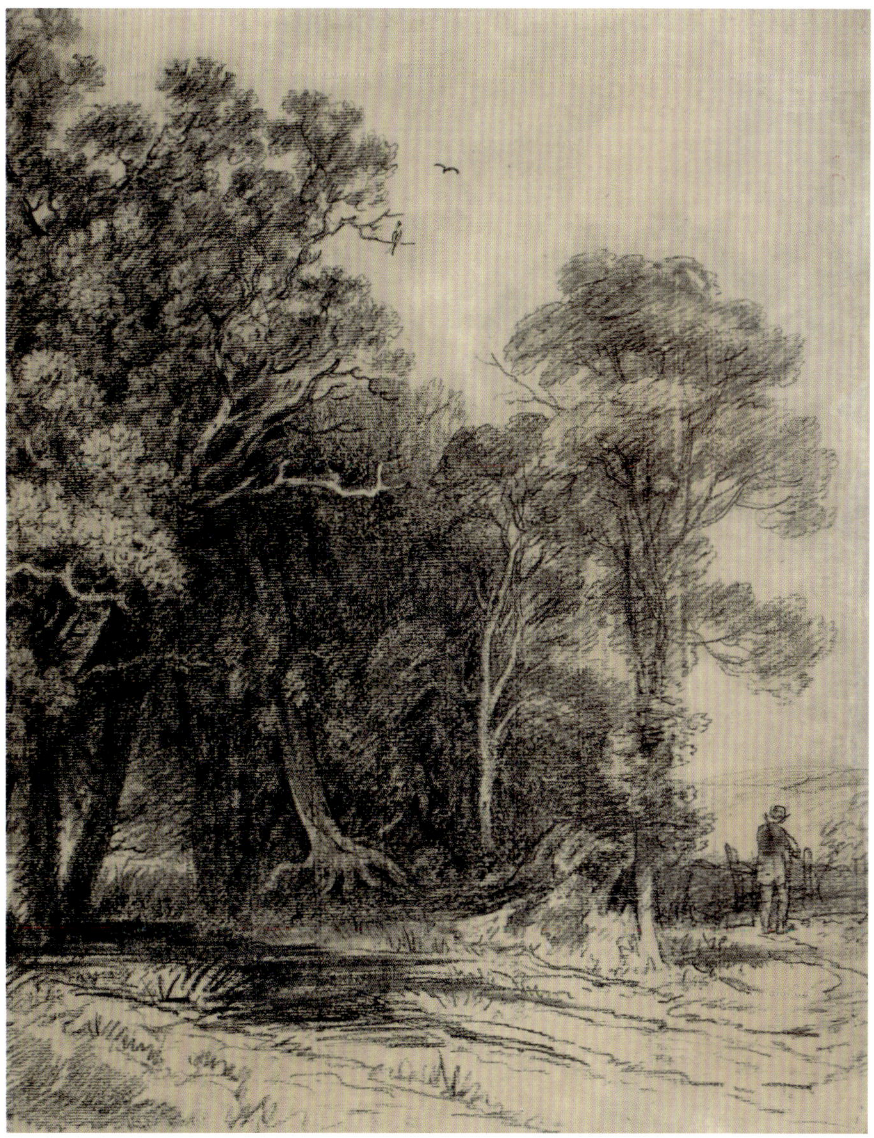

28 A WOODLAND WALK
stamped with William Esdaile's collector's mark
chalk on laid paper
18 ½ x 14 ¼ inches
Provenance: William Esdaile
Exhibited: Caroline Smythe, London, Spring 1980

MICHAEL ANGELO ROOKER
Michael 'Angelo' Rooker, ARA (1746-1801)

Michael Angelo Rooker was one of the most eminent topographical draughtsmen of the generation that followed Paul Sandby.

Michael Rooker was born in London, almost certainly on 25 March 1746. His father was Edward Rooker, who combined careers as an engraver and pantomime actor, and developed a reputation – as Ned Rooker of Drury Lane Theatre – as the most notable Harlequin of his day.

Rooker began his training in engraving and draughtsmanship under his father. Early success was suggested in 1759 when he was awarded the first share of a premium, from the Society for the Encouragement of the Arts for 'Drawings of any kind, under the age of fourteen'; while, from 1763, he exhibited watercolours at the Society of Artists.

During the 1760s, Rooker served as an assistant to Paul Sandby. He accepted the name of 'Michael Angelo' that Sandby seems to have given him, and eventually used it as his regular signature. However, he remained open to other opportunities to develop his training; in 1769, he was among the first ever students to be admitted to the Royal Academy Schools (probably for a span of six years), and in 1770 was one of the first artists to be elected an associate of the Royal Academy of Arts. From this time he regularly exhibited oil and watercolour landscapes (contributing over a hundred works to the RA).

On his father's death in 1774, Rooker maintained the family's engraving practice. In so doing, he involved himself in the developing market for topographical images, mainly through George Kearlsey's publication, *The Copper-Plate Magazine*, for which he engraved drawings by Sandby as well as himself (1774-78). However, his involvement was not extensive, and the only engraving commission he retained (until 1788) was for the frontispiece for the annual *Oxford Almanack*.

From 1779, Rooker worked as a scene-painter at George Colman's Theatre Royal, Haymarket, mostly during its regular short summer season of melodramas and comedies (some written by Colman's son). His reputation in this field led to his providing scenery for the private theatre at Blenheim Palace, near Oxford (1787-89). He also undertook occasional commissions for literary illustrations, including Colman's edition of Beaumont and Fletcher (1778) and an edition of works by Henry Fielding (1783).

The combination of a generous salary and limited commitment gave him the time to concentrate on landscape watercolours. From 1788, he undertook a series of regular walking tours in England and Wales, making sketches in pencil and wash that formed the basis of the finished works that consolidated his reputation. Consistent in his practice, he seems to have gone out of fashion by the turn of the century, so that, following his death in London on 3 March 1801, Edward Dayes could describe him as 'dejected and broken in spirit, for want of due encouragement' ('Professional Sketches on Modern Artists', in Dayes 1806, p 347).

His work is represented in the Government Art Collection, the Royal Academy of Arts and the Royal Collection; and numerous public collections, including the British Museum, The Courtauld Gallery, Tate and the V&A; the Ashmolean Museum (Oxford), Brighton & Hove Museums, The Fitzwilliam Museum (Cambridge), Manchester Art Gallery, the Walker Art Gallery (Liverpool), The Whitworth Art Gallery (Manchester) and York Art Gallery; National Museum Wales (Cardiff); the National Gallery of Scotland (Edinburgh); Ulster Museum (Belfast); and the National Gallery of Ireland (Dublin).

Further reading:

Patrick Conner, *Michael Angelo Rooker 1746-1801*, London: B T Batsford/Victoria & Albert Museum, 1984
Patrick Conner, 'Rooker, Michael (Angelo) (*b* London, 1746; *d* London, 3 March 1801)', Jane Turner (ed), *The Dictionary of Art*, London: Macmillan, 1996, vol 27, p 132
Patrick Conner, 'Rooker, Michael [known as Michael Angelo Rooker] (1746-1801)', H C G Matthew and Brian Harrison (eds), *Oxford Dictionary of National Biography*, Oxford University Press, 2004, vol 47, pp 698-699

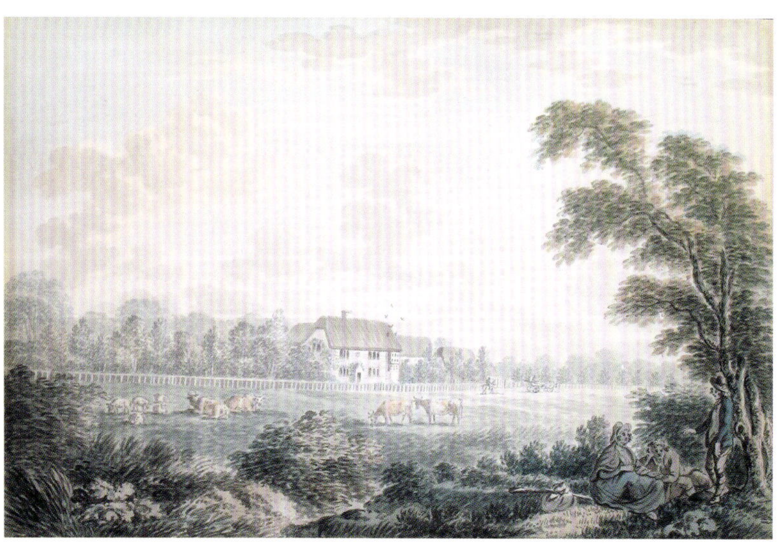

29 THE COUNTRY HALT
watercolour
9 ½ x 13 ¾ inches

MOSES GRIFFITH
Moses Griffith (1747-1819)

Moses Griffith had an unusual, if not unique, position among British topographers of the eighteenth century, in that his chief patron employed him as a servant, yet made the most of his talents as a draughtsman, watercolourist and engraver.

Moses Griffith was born at Trygarn, Bryncoes, Caernarvonshire, in Wales, on 25 March 1747. The illegitimate son of a labourer, he received a rudimentary education at the free school attached to Botwnnog Church.

In 1769, Griffith entered the service of Thomas Pennant, the squire of Downing, Flintshire, and was immediately employed as a draughtsman on a series of tours of antiquarian and scientific purpose. The most significant destinations included Scotland (1769), the Hebrides (1772), Cumberland and Yorkshire (1773), North Wales (mid 1770s), the Isle of Man (1774), the Midlands (1776), Yorkshire and Derbyshire (1777), Staffordshire (1780) and the Severn Valley (1783).

Some of the resulting drawings were engraved on copper – by Griffith or others – for use as illustrations in several of Pennant's published travelogues, including *A Tour in Scotland and Voyage to the Hebrides* (1774) and *A Journey to Snowdon* (1781); others appeared in Pennant's volumes of natural history.

Pennant also acted as Griffith's agent for work he undertook with other patrons, for example the illustrations that he contributed to Francis Grose's *The Antiquities of England* (from 1773).

After Pennant's death in 1798, Griffith was employed by his son David Pennant, and executed a group of about 200 watercolours of Welsh views between 1805 and 1813.

Marrying in 1781, Griffith lived with his family at Gwibnant, a house on Pennant's estate. He died there on 11 November 1819, and was buried at Whitford churchyard.

His work is represented in the Government Art Collection and numerous public collections, including the Grosvenor Museum (Chester) and York Art Gallery; and The National Library of Wales (Aberystwyth) and National Museum Wales (Cardiff).

Further reading:
Peter Lord, 'Griffith, Moses (1747-1819)', H C G Matthew and Brian Harrison (eds), *Oxford Dictionary of National Biography*, Oxford University Press, 2004, vol 23, p 970
Donald Moore (intro), *Moses Griffith, 1747-1819, artist and illustrator in the service of Thomas Pennant*, Cardiff: Welsh Arts Council, 1979
Iolo Aneurin Williams, 'Thomas Pennant and Moses Griffith, a Welsh Naturalist and his Welsh Artist in the Eighteenth Century', *Country Life*, July 1938, pp 8-9

30 KIRKSTALL ABBEY YORKSHIRE
signed and inscribed with title and dated 'May the 15th 1777'
watercolour with pen and ink
9 x 15 inches
This View, from the south east, is similar in composition and date to *A view of Kirkstall Abbey, from the North West*, 1777, in the collection of Leeds Art Gallery.

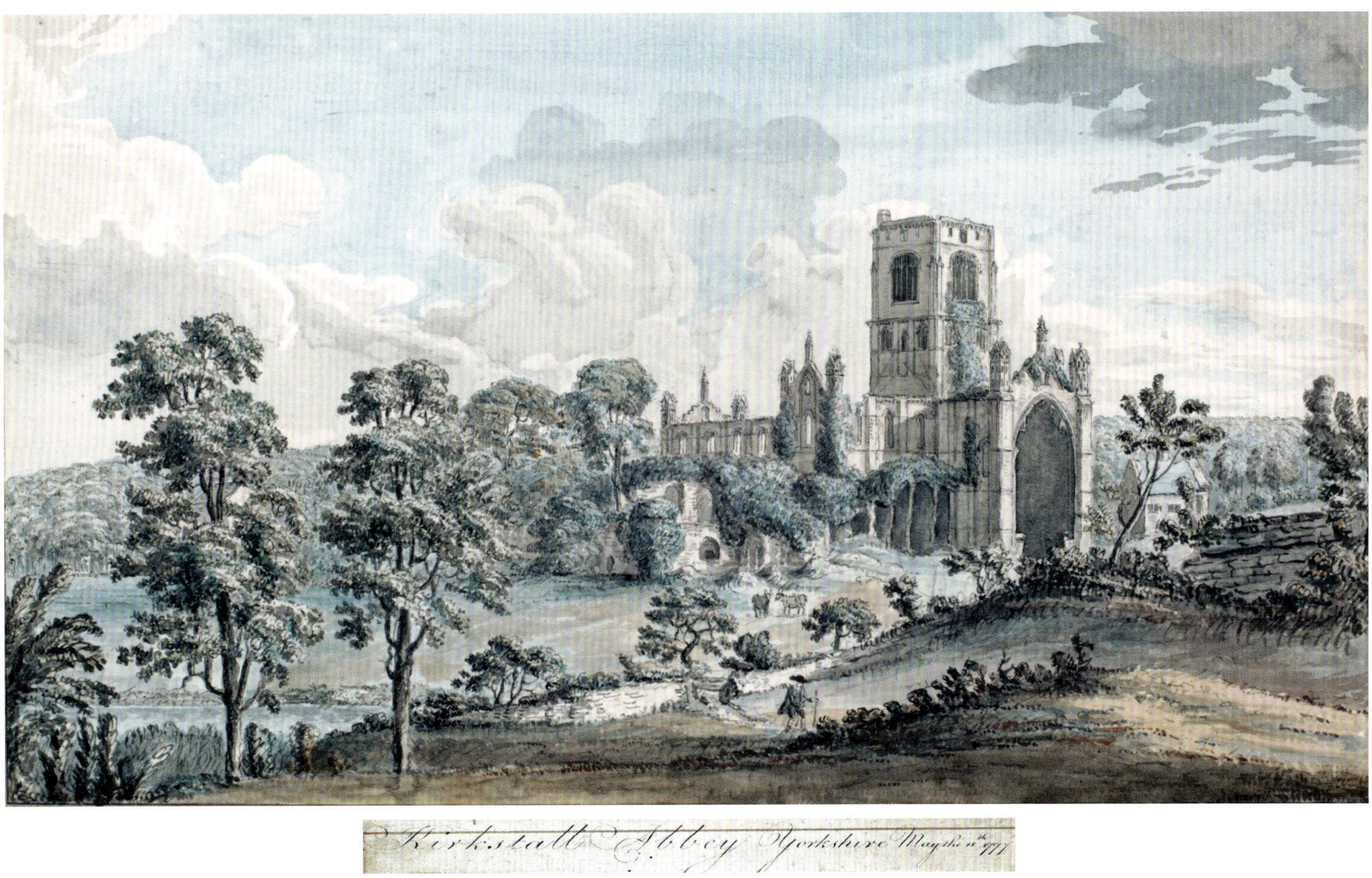

JOSEPH HALFPENNY
Joseph S Halfpenny (1748-1811)

Joseph Halfpenny made his reputation as an antiquarian and architectural draughtsman, and his work would prove invaluable in later restorations of York Minster. However, his talent for precise observation and transcription also made him an able topographical watercolourist.

Joseph Halfpenny was born on 9 October 1748 at Bishopthorpe, the official residence of the Archbishop of York, and was the son of the archbishop's gardener. Following an apprenticeship to a house painter in York, and some time in the trade, he became a drawing master at the age of twenty. As a topographical and architectural draughtsman, he made drawings of Gothic churches and monuments in Yorkshire, and was appointed Clerk of Works to the architect John Carr during his restoration of York Minster. His resulting publications include *Gothic Ornaments in the Cathedral Church of York* (1795-1800) and *Fragmenta Vetusta* (1807). He also produced etchings after portraits by other artists.

As a watercolourist, Halfpenny produced a number of views of the Yorkshire Dales and the Lake District, following sketching tours in the early 1790s.

Halfpenny died in Gillygate, York on 11 July 1811, and was buried in St Olave's church.

His work is represented in the collections of the British Museum; and York Art Gallery.

Further reading:
Bertha Porter (rev William Joseph Sheils), 'Halfpenny, Joseph (1748-1811)', H C G Matthew and Brian Harrison (eds), *Oxford Dictionary of National Biography*, Oxford University Press, 2004, vol 24, p 567

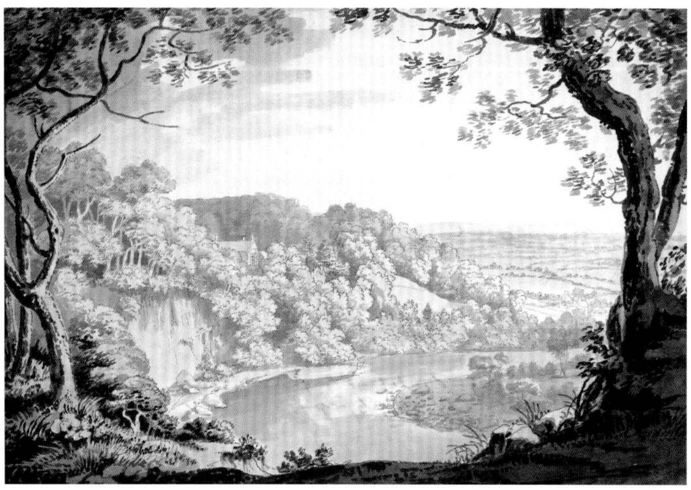

Wycliffe in Yorkshire
Wycliffe is on the River Tees, in North Yorkshire. Local Wycliffe Hall was originally built in the Elizabethan period, but remodelled in the eighteenth century by the Tunstall family. Marmaduke Tunstall (died 1790) created a notable private museum, for which a separate block was built.

31 WYCLIFFE IN YORKSHIRE
signed, inscribed 'Drew From The Tees Bank near the House of Tunstall Esq a Wycliff In Yorkshire' and dated 'Taken July 12th 1791' on reverse
watercolour with pen and ink
14 ¾ x 21 ¼ inches

JOHN 'WARWICK' SMITH
John Smith, POWS (1749-1831), known as John 'Warwick' Smith and John 'Italian' Smith

During his lifetime, John 'Warwick' Smith received much praise for his broad handling and use of local colour, qualities that anticipated 'the atmospheric watercolours of the next generation, particularly Girtin and Turner' (Stainton 1985, p 34). Furthermore, he kept alive the eighteenth-century preoccupation with the Classic ground of Italy through the watercolours he exhibited in the nineteenth century as a leading member of the Society of Painters in Water Colours.

John Smith was born in Irthington, Cumberland on 26 July 1749. His father was gardener to Susannah Maria Appleby, a sister of the amateur artist Captain John Bernard Gilpin. He received drawing lessons from both J B Gilpin and his sons William and Sawrey. Gilpin sent him to St Bees School, near Whitehaven, and subsequently set him up as a drawing master at St Bees or another local school.

Through Sawrey Gilpin, Smith met Sir Henry Harper, at whose Derbyshire seat he came to the notice of Harper's brother-in-law George Greville, 2nd Earl of Warwick, around 1775. Himself an accomplished amateur artist, Lord Warwick became Smith's leading patron: pleased with sketches that Smith made at Matlock, he sent him to Italy and supported him for five years from 1776 to 1781.

While based in Rome, Smith was in close contact with other British landscape painters – notably Thomas Jones, WILLIAM PARS and Francis Towne – and sketched alongside them. In 1781, Towne accompanied him on his return to England, which was made by way of Switzerland.

On his return, Smith lived in Warwick for a time, and was dubbed 'Warwick' either as an indication of this residence or as a result of Greville's patronage. During this period, he sketched in Devon, Worcestershire and the Lake District; and, from 1784, he made regular trips to Wales in search of the Sublime and Picturesque, some in the company of Robert Fulke Greville, the Earl of Warwick's brother.

At the same time his watercolours were reproduced as engravings or aquatints and gathered in volumes for publication: *Select Views in Great Britain* (1784-85), *Select Views in Italy* (1792-99), *Twenty Views of the Lake District* (1791-95) William Sotheby's *Tour Through Parts of Wales* (1794) and *Views in Switzerland* (1794).

By 1797, Smith had moved to London, where he continued to receive commissions and teach (JOHN GLOVER being among his pupils). Within a decade he also began to exhibit, becoming an associate of the Society of Painters in Water Colours in 1805, and a full member a year later. A stalwart of the society, he promoted its reformation as the Society of Painters in Oil and Water-Colours in 1812, and acted as Secretary (1816), Treasurer (1819) and President (1814, 1817 and 1818). He resigned in 1823.

The majority of Smith's 159 exhibits comprised views of Italy, and from the first they signalled his immediate experience of the landscape in and around Rome. This was at the time when Rome was considered the world's most important artistic centre, and Smith considered the last active survivor of the generation of British landscape artists who had worked there in the 1770s and 80s. Because of this, he was also known as 'Italian' Smith.

Smith died at Middlesex Place, Marylebone Road, London on 22 March 1831.

His work is represented in numerous public collections, including the British Museum, Tate and the V&A; the Ashmolean Museum (Oxford), The Fitzwilliam Museum (Cambridge) and Manchester Art Gallery; The National Library of Wales; and Manx Museum.

Further reading:

Simon Fenwick, 'Smith, John (1749-1831)', H C G Matthew and Brian Harrison (eds), *Oxford Dictionary of National Biography*, Oxford University Press, 2004, vol 51, pp 207-209
Basil Somerset Long, 'John (Warwick) Smith, (1749-1831)', *Walker's Quarterly*, no 24, 1927, pp 3-37
Susan Morris, 'Smith, John "Warwick"' (*b* Irthington, Cumbria, 26 July 1749; *d* London, 22 March 1831), Jane Turner (ed), *The Dictionary of Art*, London: Macmillan, 1996, vol 28, p 883
Iolo Aneurin Williams, 'John "Warwick" Smith', in Adrian Bury (ed), *The Old Water-Colour Society's Club*, vol 24, 1946, pp 9-18

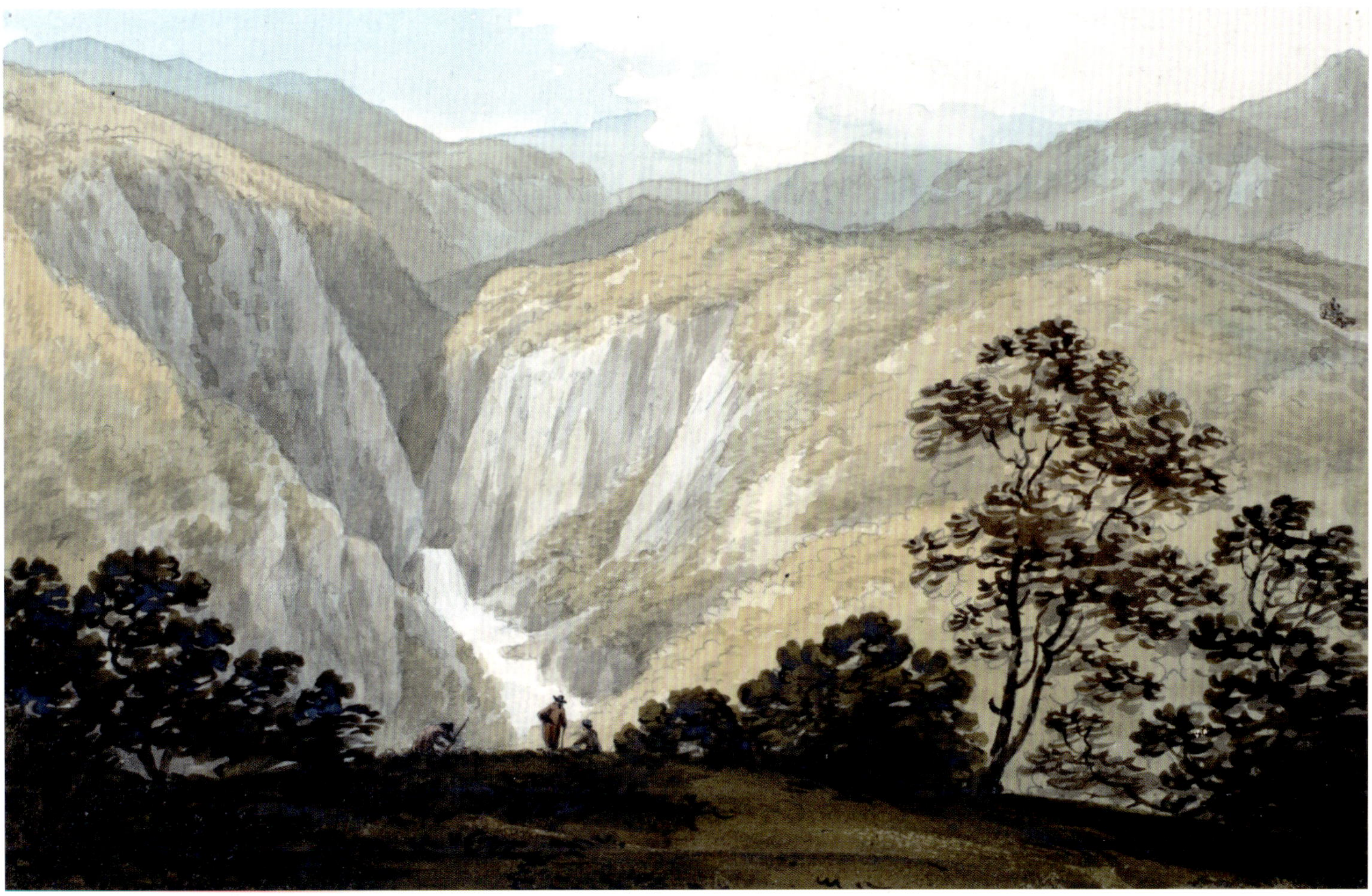

32 LOOK INTO THE GLEN OF THE RHEIDOL
NEAR ITS JUNCTION WITH THE TYNACH OPPOSITE THE DEVILS BRIDGE CARDIGANSHIRE
inscribed with title and dated 'June 14th 1795' on the original mount
watercolour with bodycolour
5 ¾ x 8 ½ inches

Similar to Sir James Edward Smith, *A Tour to Hafod, in Cardiganshire: The Seat of Thomas Johnes, Esq. (with illustrations by John Smith)*, London: White & Co, 1810, plate 13, 'Great Falls of Fynach'

2: ROWLANDSON AND HIS MILIEU

SAMUEL HOWITT
Samuel Howitt (1756/57-1822)

Samuel Howitt was self-taught as an artist. However, his enthusiastic approach to his interests in natural history and field sports translated itself into drawings that were at once vigorous and accurate.

Samuel Howitt was born into a wealthy Quaker family of Nottinghamshire origin, who were squires at Chigwell, Essex. He spent his youth enjoying sporting activities, and turned to art professionally only when he experienced financial difficulties. Moving closer to London, he took a job as a drawing master at the Rev Samuel Goodenough's Private Academy in Ealing.

Becoming a member of the artistic circle that included GEORGE MORLAND, John Raphael Smith, Henry Wigstead and THOMAS ROWLANDSON, Howitt married Rowlandson's sister, Elizabeth, in 1779. Together they had at least one child to survive into adulthood, though they separated long before Samuel died.

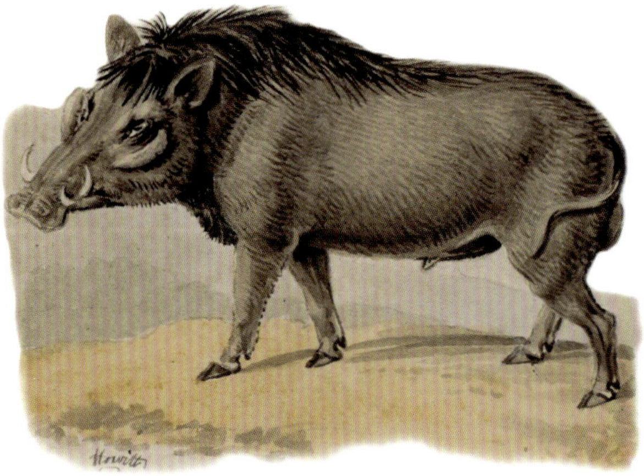

By 1783, Howitt had moved into London's West End, and was establishing himself as a painter and engraver. He began to exhibit at the Incorporated Society of Artists (in 1783) and the Royal Academy of Arts (from 1784).

Howitt accompanied Rowlandson and Wigstead on a trip to the Isle of Wight in 1791, and may have spent some time in Richmond, Yorkshire. However, he was certainly in London by 1793, building a reputation for animal and sporting subjects, and beginning to work as an illustrator. He made many studies from life, at the menagerie of the Tower of London and elsewhere, and also worked up sketches that amateur artists had made abroad.

His illustrative work first came to the public's notice through the pages of *The Sporting Magazine* (founded in 1792). Then, through the following two decades, it featured in a number of books; these included Peter Beckford's *Thoughts on Hunting* (1798) and Thomas Williamson's *Oriental Field Sports* (1807), and several issued by Edward Orme, notably *Orme's Collection of British Field Sports* (1807), *The British Sportsman* (1812) and *Fables of Aesop, Gay and Phaedras* (1811). His achievement has been compared to that of George Stubbs, and he has been considered a precursor to HENRY ALKEN.

Howitt died at home, at 103 Chalton Street, Somers Town, London in February 1823.

His work is represented in numerous public collections, including the British Museum and the V&A; and The Fitzwilliam Museum (Cambridge), the Natural History Museum (Tring) and the Museum of Island History (Newport, Isle of Wight).

Further reading:

Ruth Cohen, 'Howitt, Samuel (1756/7-1823)', H C G Matthew and Brian Harrison (eds), *Oxford Dictionary of National Biography*, Oxford University Press, 2004, vol 28, p 530

J Gilbey, 'Samuel Howitt: sporting artist', *Apollo*, vol 63, 1956, pp 25-26

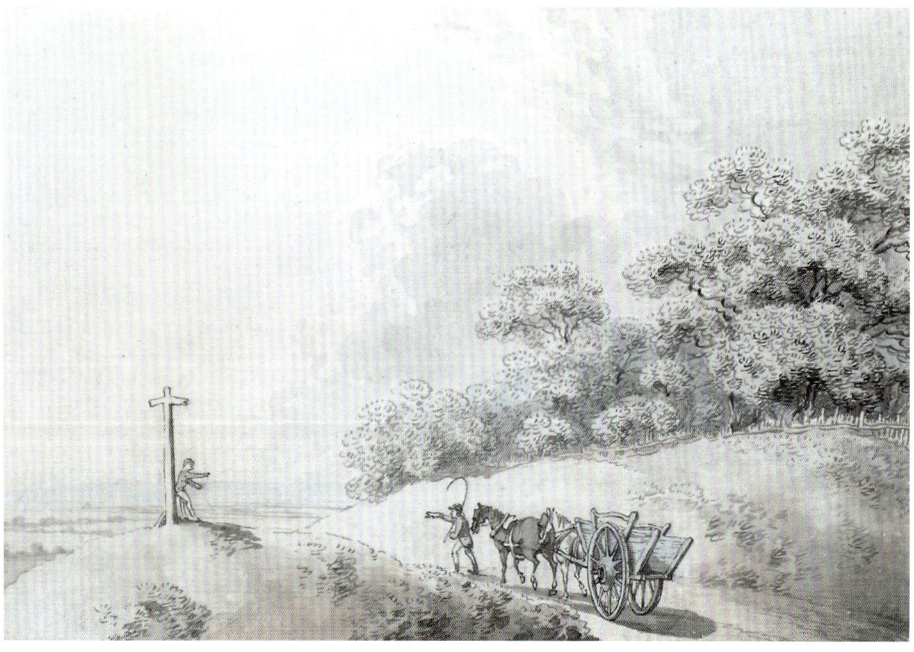

33 S ETHIOPICUS (detail)
signed and inscribed with title
watercolour
8 ½ x 5 inches

34 A BRIEF SALUTATION ON THE ROAD BACK FROM THE MARKET
pen ink and watercolour
6 x 8 inches

THOMAS ROWLANDSON
Thomas Rowlandson (1756/57-1827)

Thomas Rowlandson raised comic art to a new level by representing the panorama of contemporary life with almost unparalleled fluency – adopting lyricism or incisiveness as best fitted the subject. And, in capturing an abundance of picturesque detail, his work provided a parallel to the novels of Henry Fielding or Laurence Sterne.

Thomas Rowlandson was born in Old Jewry, in the City of London, on 14 July, either in 1756 or 1757, to a merchant in wool and silk. In consequence of the bankruptcy of his father, he and his younger sister, Elizabeth, went to live with their uncle, James, and aunt, Jane, a prosperous Spitalfields silk weaver and his French wife. Following the death of his uncle in 1764, he moved to 4 Church Street (now Romilly Street), Soho, with his widowed aunt, and attended the Soho Academy.

From the age of sixteen, Rowlandson studied art at the Royal Academy Schools, Somerset House, and received permission to draw at the Duke of Richmond's sculpture gallery in Whitehall. Between 1775 and 1787, he exhibited both subject pictures and caricatures, in pen and wash, at the Royal Academy of Arts, winning a silver medal in 1777, and making his name seven years later with the ambitious *Vauxhall Gardens* (V&A). During this period, he began to make trips to the Continent (particularly Paris) and in Britain (often accompanied by Henry Wigstead).

Rowlandson continued to live in apartments in Soho with his aunt, until her death in 1789: at 103 Wardour Street (by 1777) and then 50 Poland Street (by 1787). On her death, he received a substantial legacy, though it seems likely that he lost it through gambling. Certainly, through the 1790s, he lived in modest, even shabby, addresses in and around the Strand, finally settling in attic rooms at 1 James Street, Adelphi, in 1800, where he lived for the rest of his life.

Throughout the 1780s, Rowlandson had been engaged in political and social caricature, but his versatility enabled him to work extensively as a book illustrator, initially on the novels of Tobias Smollett and Henry Fielding (1791-1805) [see **42**], and later on volumes dependent on their visual content. Employed by the publisher Rudolph Ackermann from 1798, he depicted the *Miseries of Human Life* (1808) and added figures to Augustus Charles Pugin's architectural settings in *The Microcosm of London* (1808-11). He received the ideal commission in 1812 when asked to collaborate with William Combe, a writer, on *Tours of Dr Syntax* (1812-21). A seasoned traveller, with an extensive knowledge of Britain and the Continent, Rowlandson was well qualified to parody the vagaries of the Picturesque landscape artist. He frequently produced drawings after the Old Masters, and his own landscape style was an adaptation of that of Thomas Gainsborough.

35 THE VIRTUOUS CHAMBERMAID
inscribed with monogram 'HB' and stamped with monogram 'JG'
pen ink and watercolour
11 x 9 inches
Provenance: The Reitlinger Collection
Literature: John Hayes, *The Art of Thomas Rowlandson*, Alexandria, VA: Art Services International, 1990, p 46
Exhibited: Leger Galleries, London, February 1981, no 50

During the 1820s, the work of the Italian Renaissance artist, Giovanni della Porta, inspired him to return to caricature, the art that had made his name, and produced a number of comparative anatomy studies.

Rowlandson became seriously ill in 1825 and died at home on 21 April 1827. The executor and sole legatee of his will was Betsey Winter, his longstanding companion.

His work is represented in numerous public collections, including the British Museum, the National Maritime Museum, Tate and the V&A; the Ashmolean Museum (Oxford), The Fitzwilliam Museum (Cambridge), Hertford Museum, Manchester Art Gallery, the Museum of Island History (Newport, Isle of Wight), Tyne & Wear Museums, Wakefield Art Gallery and York Art Gallery; and the Yale Center For British Art (New Haven).

Further reading:

Adrian Bury, *Rowlandson Drawings*, London: Avalon Press, 1973
Bernard Falk, *Thomas Rowlandson: His Art and Life*, London: Hutchinson & Co, 1949
Joseph Grego, *Rowlandson the Caricaturist*, London: Chatto and Windus, 1880 (2 vols)
John Hayes, *The Art of Thomas Rowlandson*, Alexandria, VA: Art Services International, 1990
John Hayes, 'Rowlandson, Thomas (1757-1827)', H C G Matthew and Brian Harrison (eds), *Oxford Dictionary of National Biography*, Oxford University Press, 2004, vol 48, pp 13-16
John Hayes, *Rowlandson: Watercolours and Drawings*, London: Phaidon Press, 1972
Lowell Libson (ed), *Beauty and the Beast. A Loan Exhibition of Rowandson's Works from British Private Collections*, London: Lowell Libson, 2007
Ronald Paulson, *Rowlandson. A new interpretation*, London: Studio Vista, 1972
David Rodgers, 'Rowlandson, Thomas (*b* London, 14 July 1756 or 1757; *d* London, 21 April 1827)', Jane Turner (ed), *The Dictionary of Art*, London: Macmillan, 1996, vol 27, pp 277-279
Robert Wark, *Drawings by Thomas Rowlandson*, San Marino, CA: Huntington Library, 1975

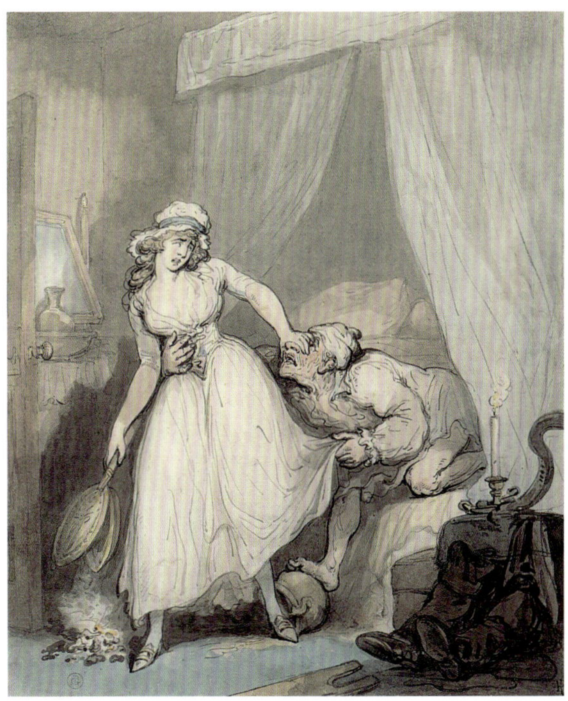

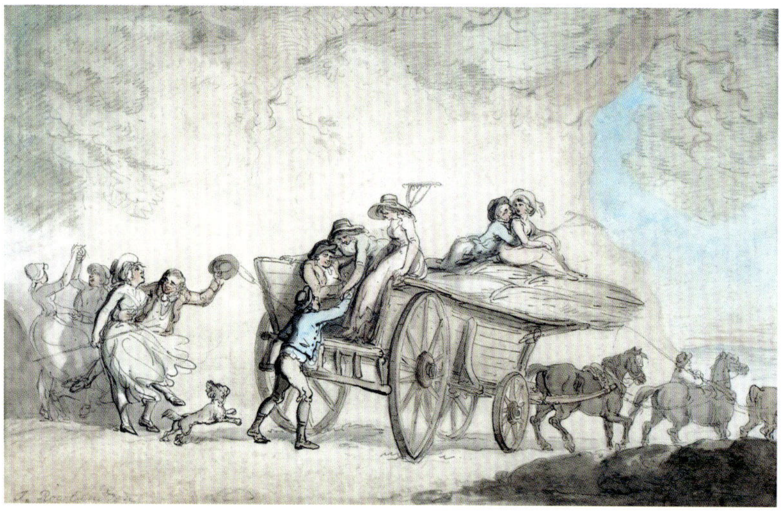

36 HARVESTERS MERRYMAKING
signed
watercolour
9 ¾ x 15 inches

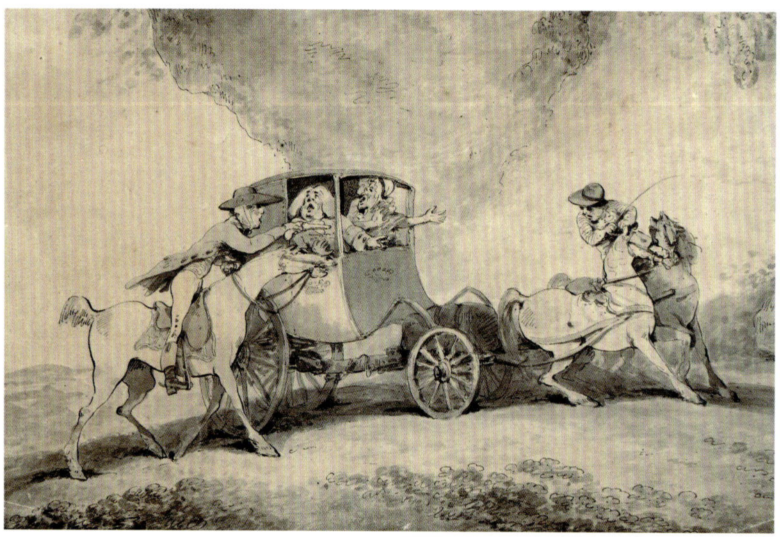

37 THE HIGHWAYMAN
pen ink and monochrome watercolour on laid paper, with GR fleur de lys and GR crown watermark
8 x 11 ¾ inches

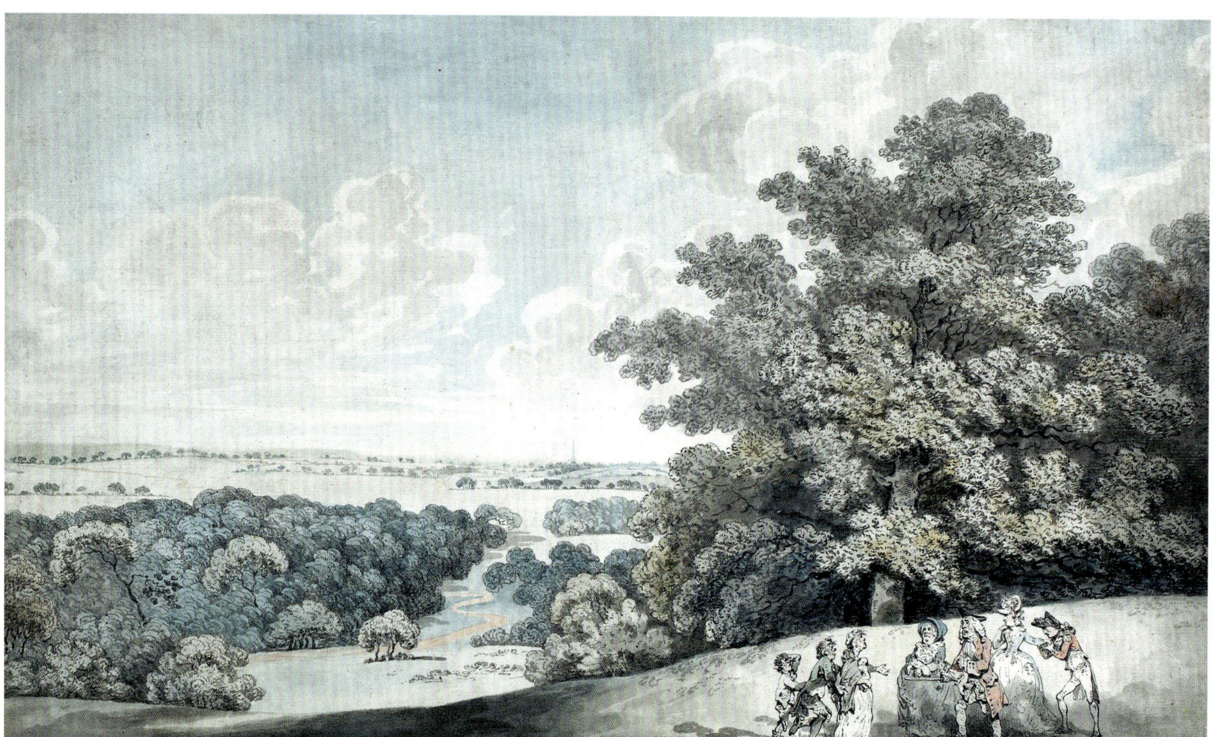

38 A MEETING OF CLASS
pen ink and watercolour
12 ½ x 20 ½ inches

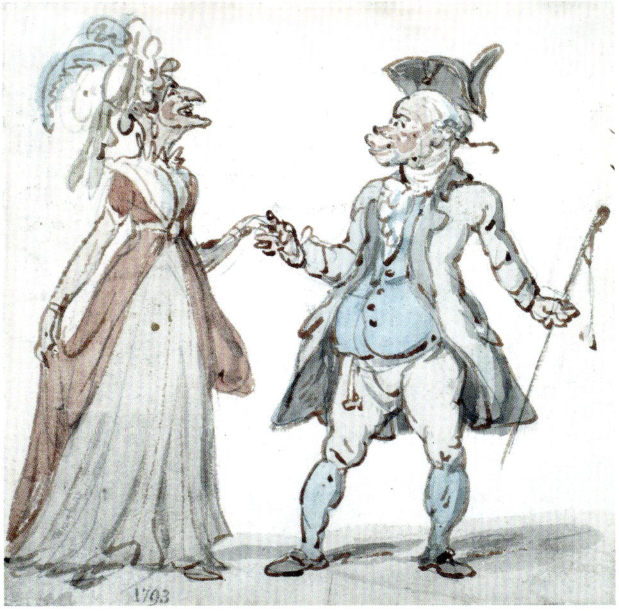

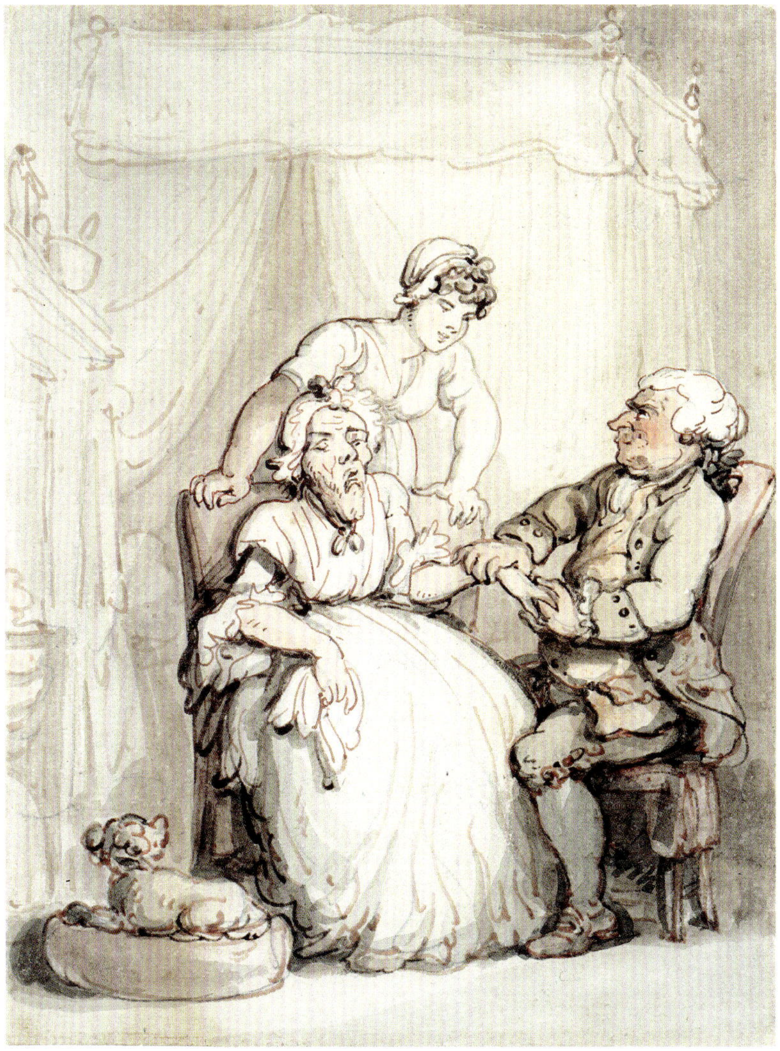

39 INVITATION TO DANCE
dated 1793
watercolour
5 ½ x 5 ½ inches

40 TAKING HER PULSE
inscribed 'Dear friend – agreeable to your request, have sent you a sett of the dwarf borders – the amount of which to the trade (which if they wont allow you to be one of you may as often as you please be accommodated through me) is £2.14- [the following is crossed out] the bath sett is incompleat but hopes have rummaged up a few others which may assist in filling up your [ ] and these being next to waste paper about th to I have added' on reverse
pen ink and watercolour
6 ¾ x 4 ¾ inches
Provenance: Gilbert Davis

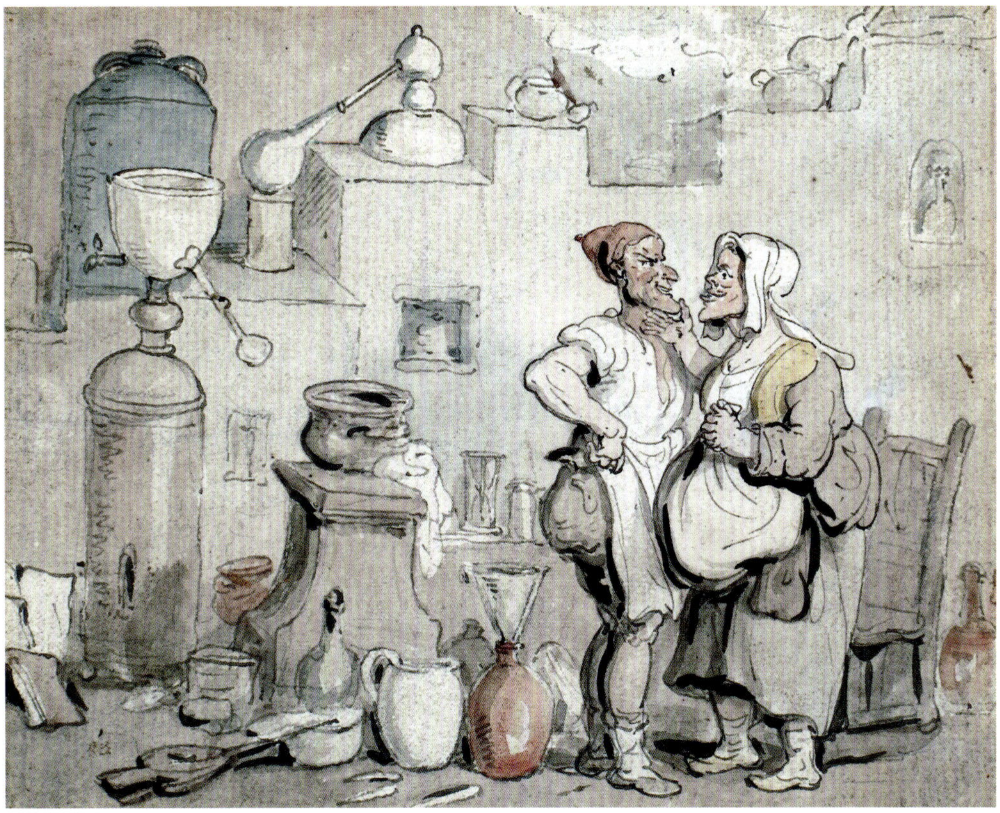

41 THE ALCHEMY OF LOVE
pen ink and watercolour
4 ¾ x 5 ¾ inches

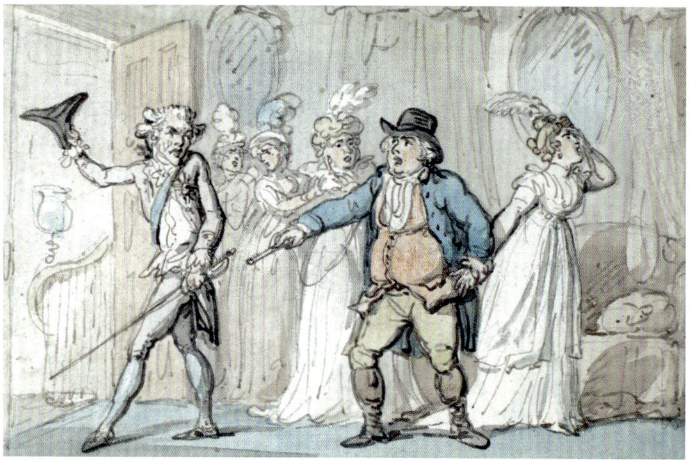

42 LORD FELLAMAR RUDELY DISMISSED BY SQUIRE WESTERN
pen ink and watercolour
4 x 6 inches
Illustrated: Henry Fielding, *The History of Tom Jones, A Foundling*, London: Longman, Rees, Hurst & Orme, 1805, vol 3
Literature: Joseph Grego, *Rowlandson The Caricaturist*, London: Chatto & Windus, 1880, vol 1, p 304

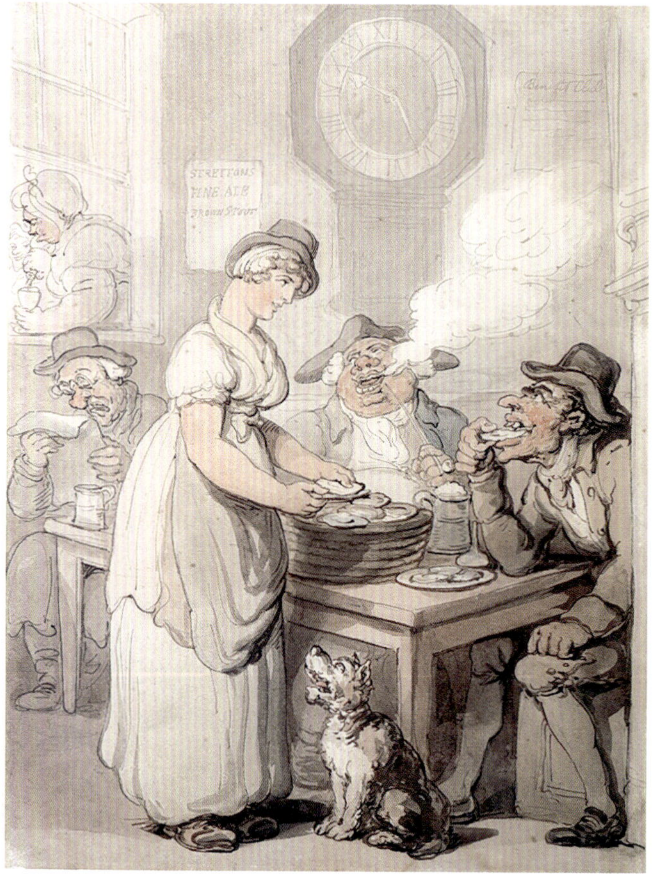

43 A PLATE OF OYSTERS
pen ink and watercolour
12 ¾ x 9 ¼ inches

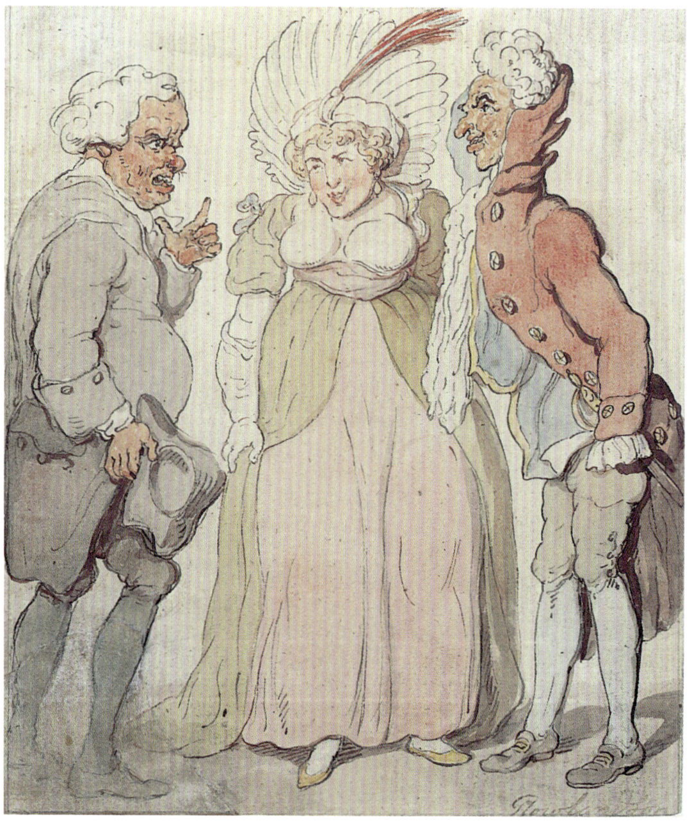

44 THE TRADESMAN
signed
pen ink and watercolour, 7 x 5 ¾ inches

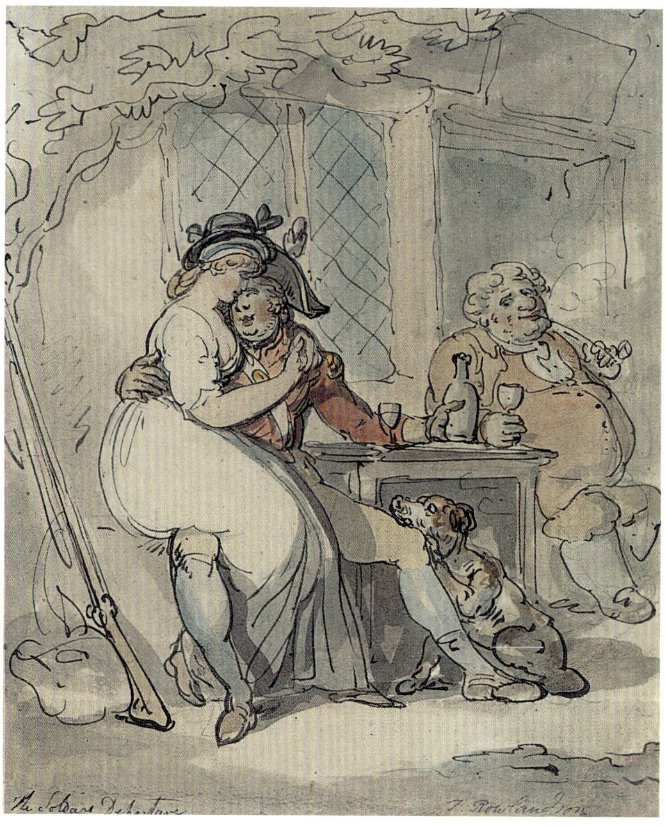

45 THE SOLDIER'S DEPARTURE
signed and inscribed with title
pen ink and watercolour, 8 ¼ x 6 ¾ inches

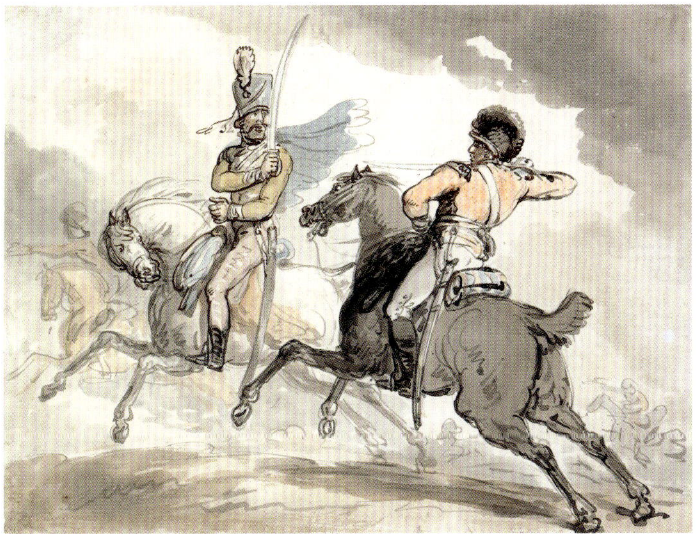

46 GIVE POINT, AND LEFT PARRY
pen ink and watercolour
8 ½ x 10 ¾ inches
Provenance: H M Lutber; Spink, London
Illustrated: Thomas Rowlandson, *Hungarian & Highland Broad Sword*, London: Henry Angelo and Son, 1799 [unpaginated]

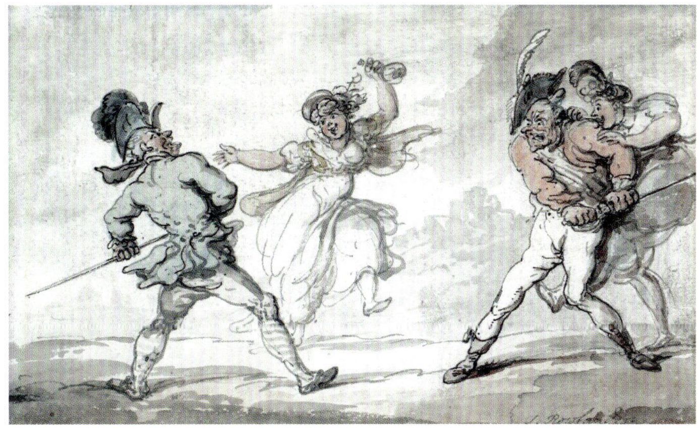

47 THE DUEL
signed
pen ink and watercolour
5 ¾ x 9 ½ inches

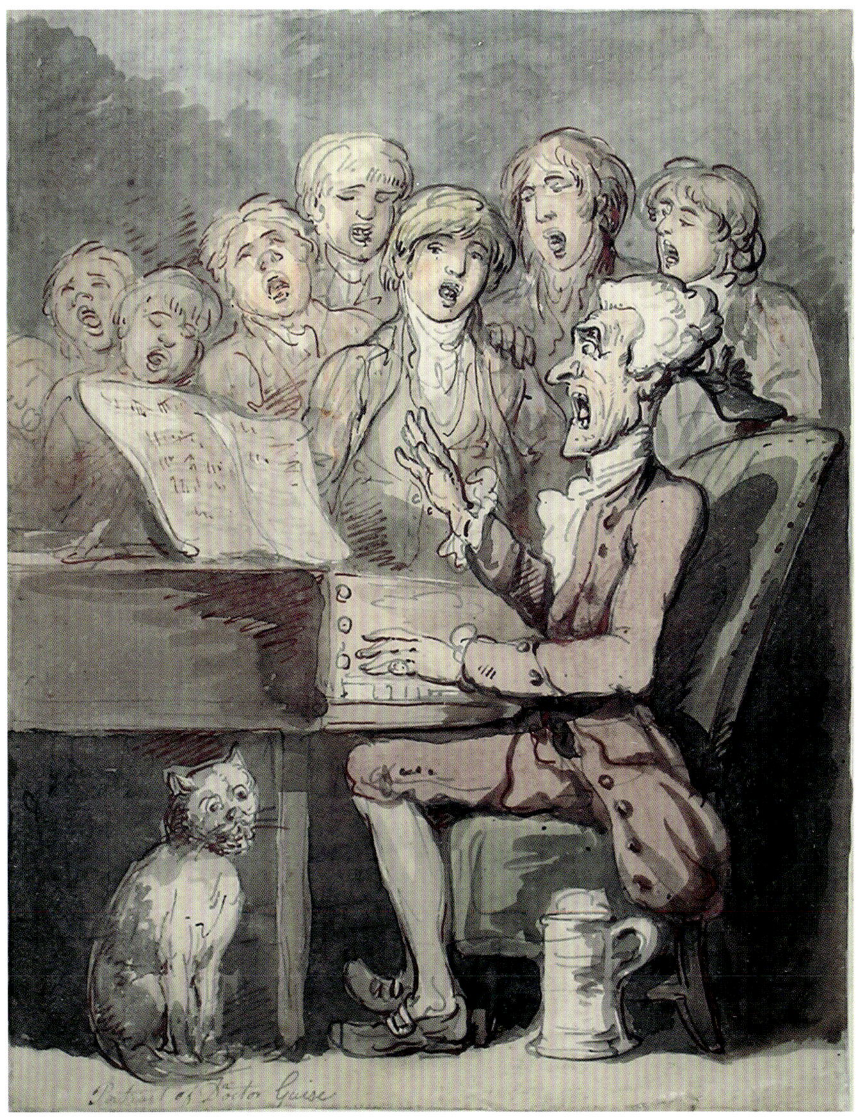

48 PORTRAIT OF DOCTOR GUISE
inscribed with title
pen ink and watercolour
11 ¾ x 9 inches

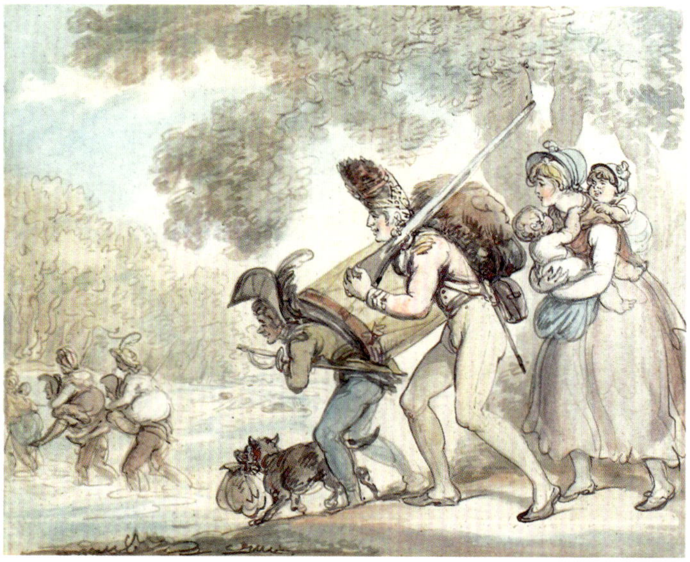

49 CROSSING THE FORD
pen ink and watercolour
9 x 11 ¼ inches

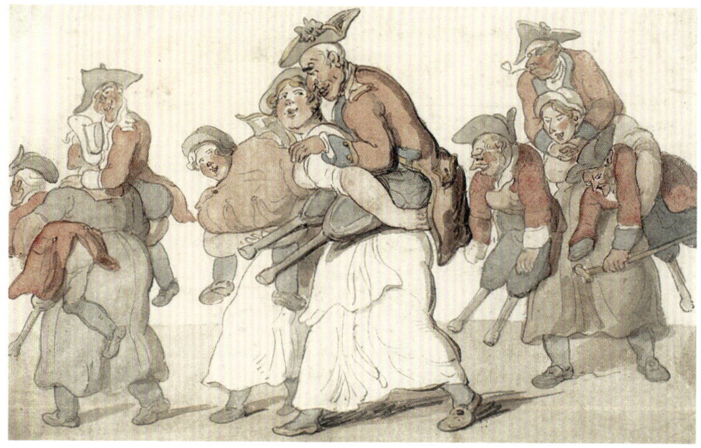

50 CHELSEA PENSIONERS
pen ink and watercolour
4 ¼ x 6 ¾ inches

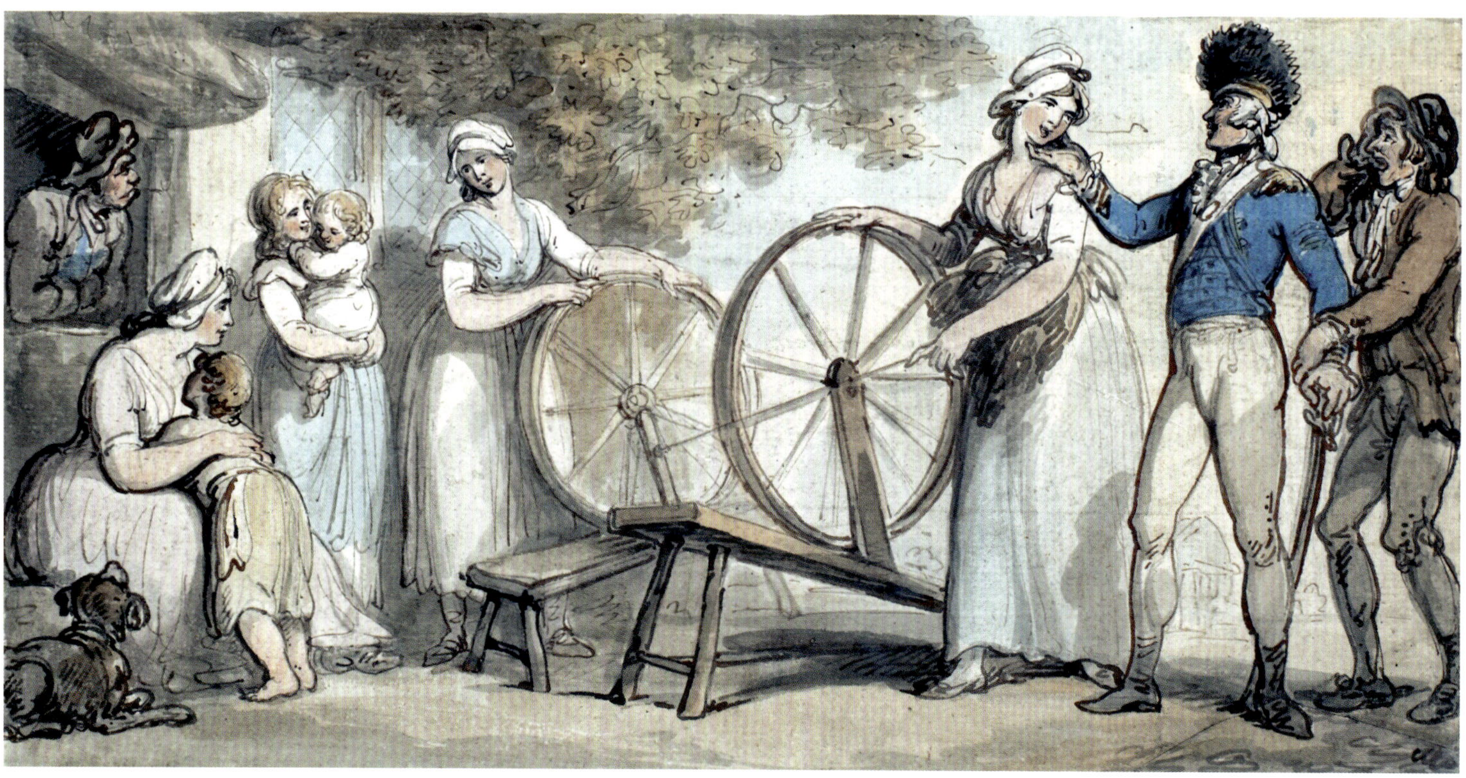

51 IDLE SPINNING
pen ink and watercolour
5 ¾ x 11 inches

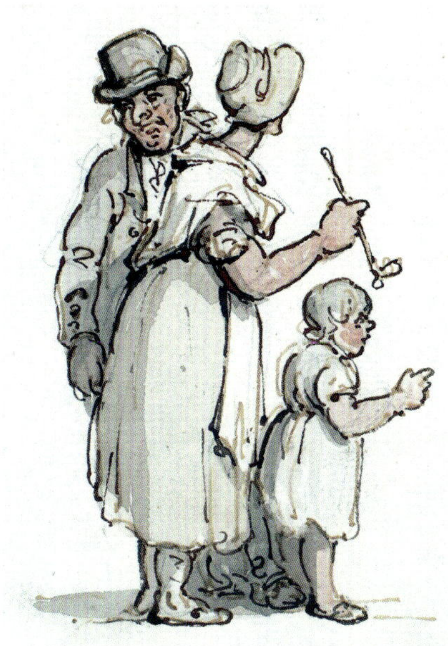

52 A PEASANT FAMILY
pen ink and watercolour
4 ¼ x 4 ¼ inches

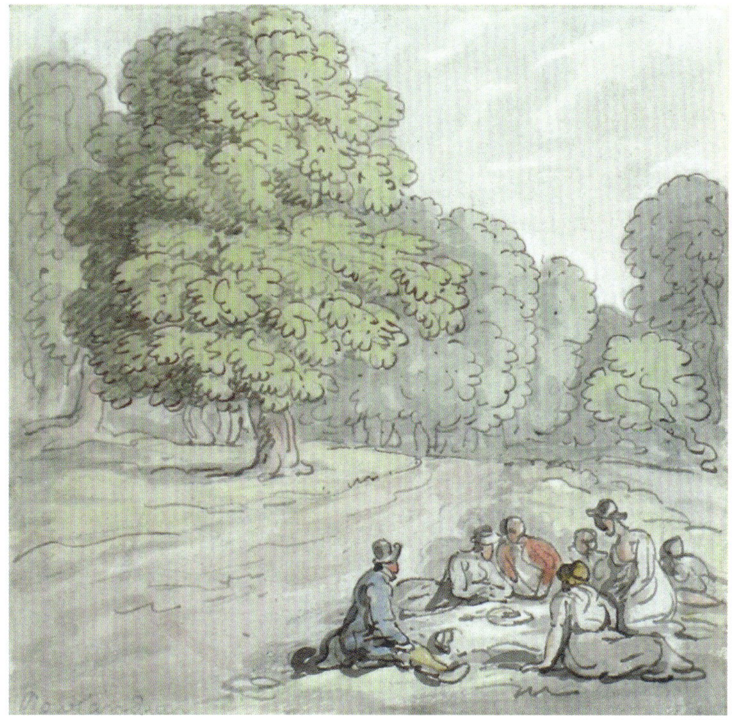

53 PICNIC AT THE ROADSIDE
signed
pen ink and watercolour
5 x 5 ¼ inches

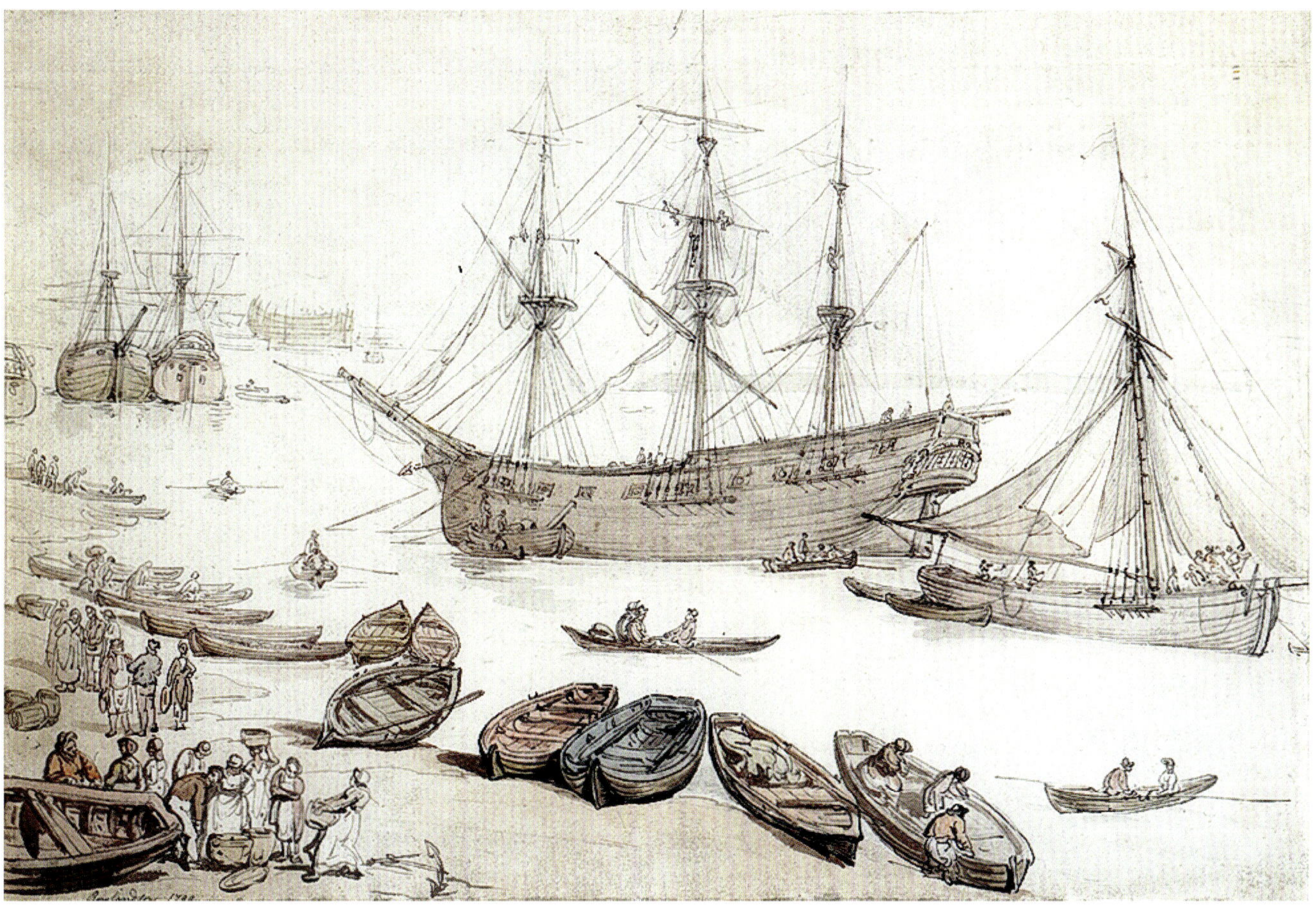

54 UNLOADING THE SHIPPING
signed and dated 1799
pen ink and watercolour
12 x 17 inches
Provenance: Albany Gallery, London

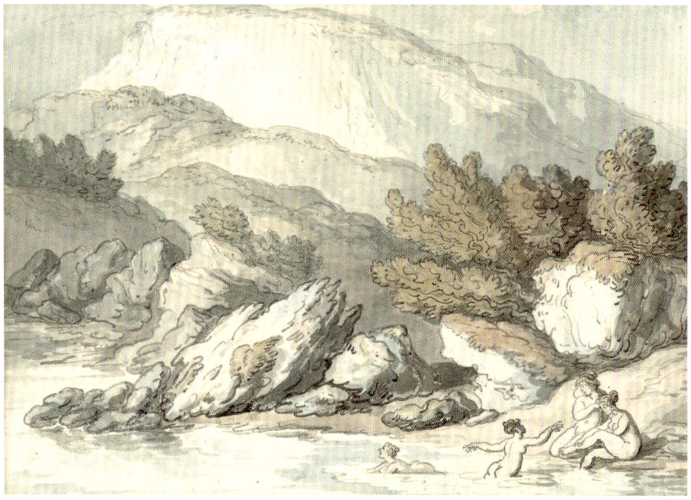

55 NYMPHS BATHING
pen ink and watercolour
7 x 9 ¾ inches

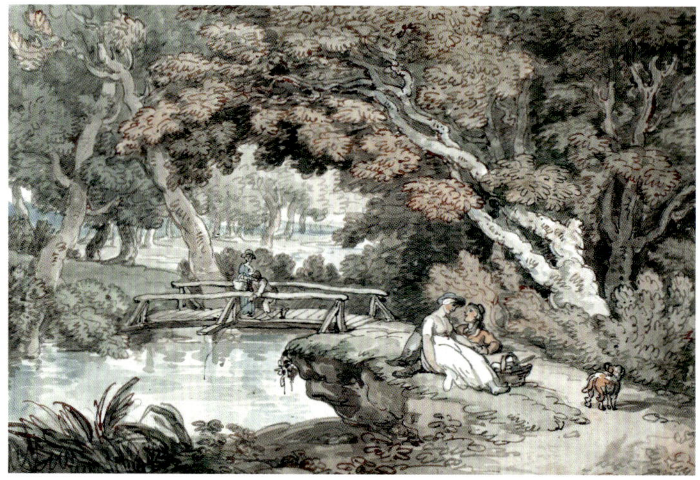

56 A SYLVAN IDYLL
watercolour and ink
7 x 10 ¼ inches

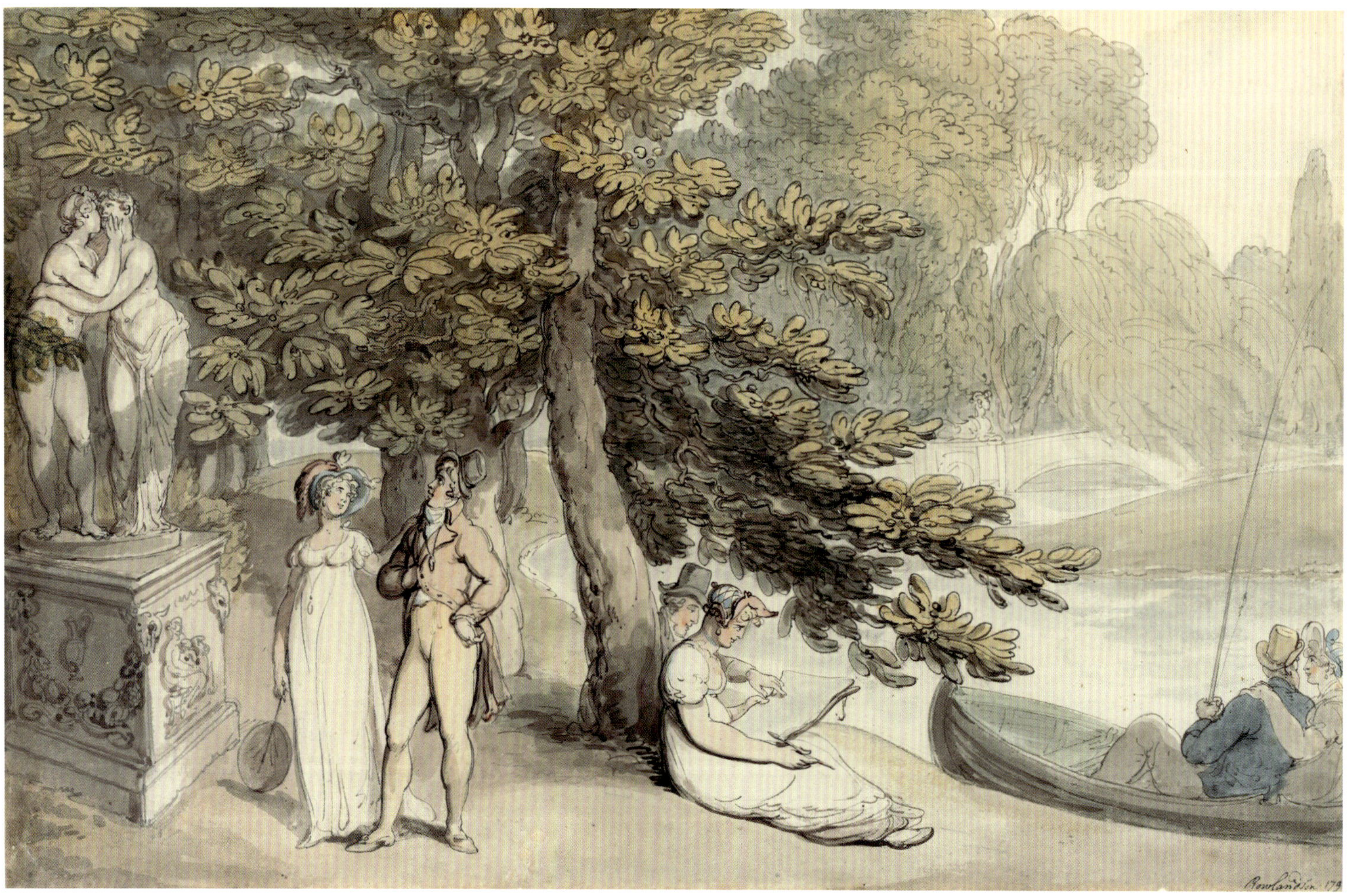

57 LOVERS' RECREATION
signed and dated 1799
pen ink and watercolour
10 ½ x 16 ¼ inches
(also illustrated frontispiece)

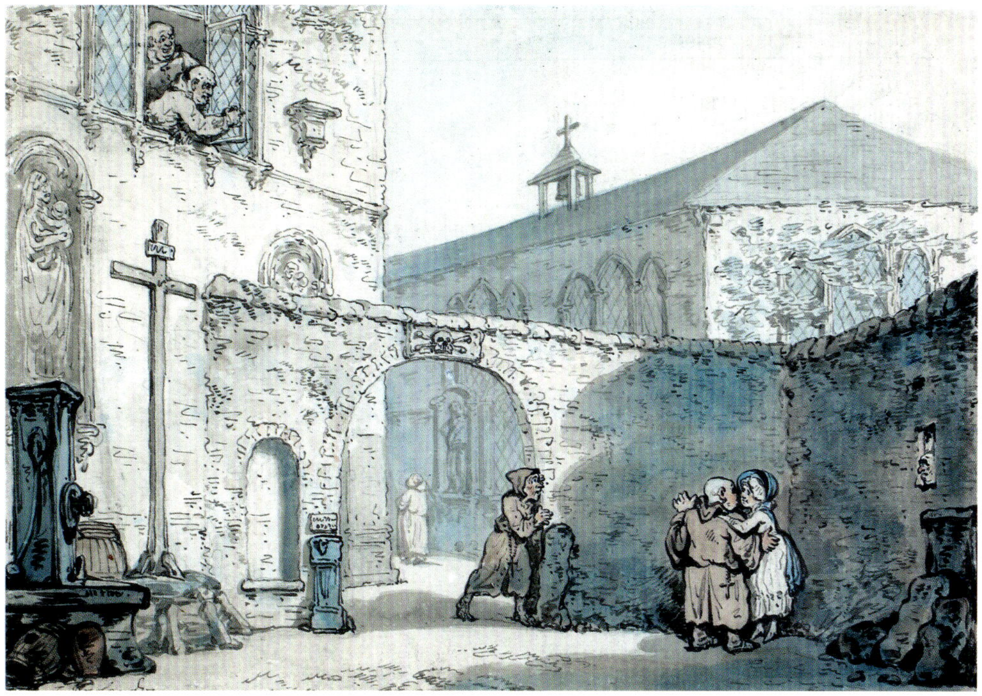

58 THE COURTYARD OF A MONASTERY
signed
pen ink and watercolour
6 ¾ x 9 ¼ inches
Exhibited: Leger Galleries, London, February 1981

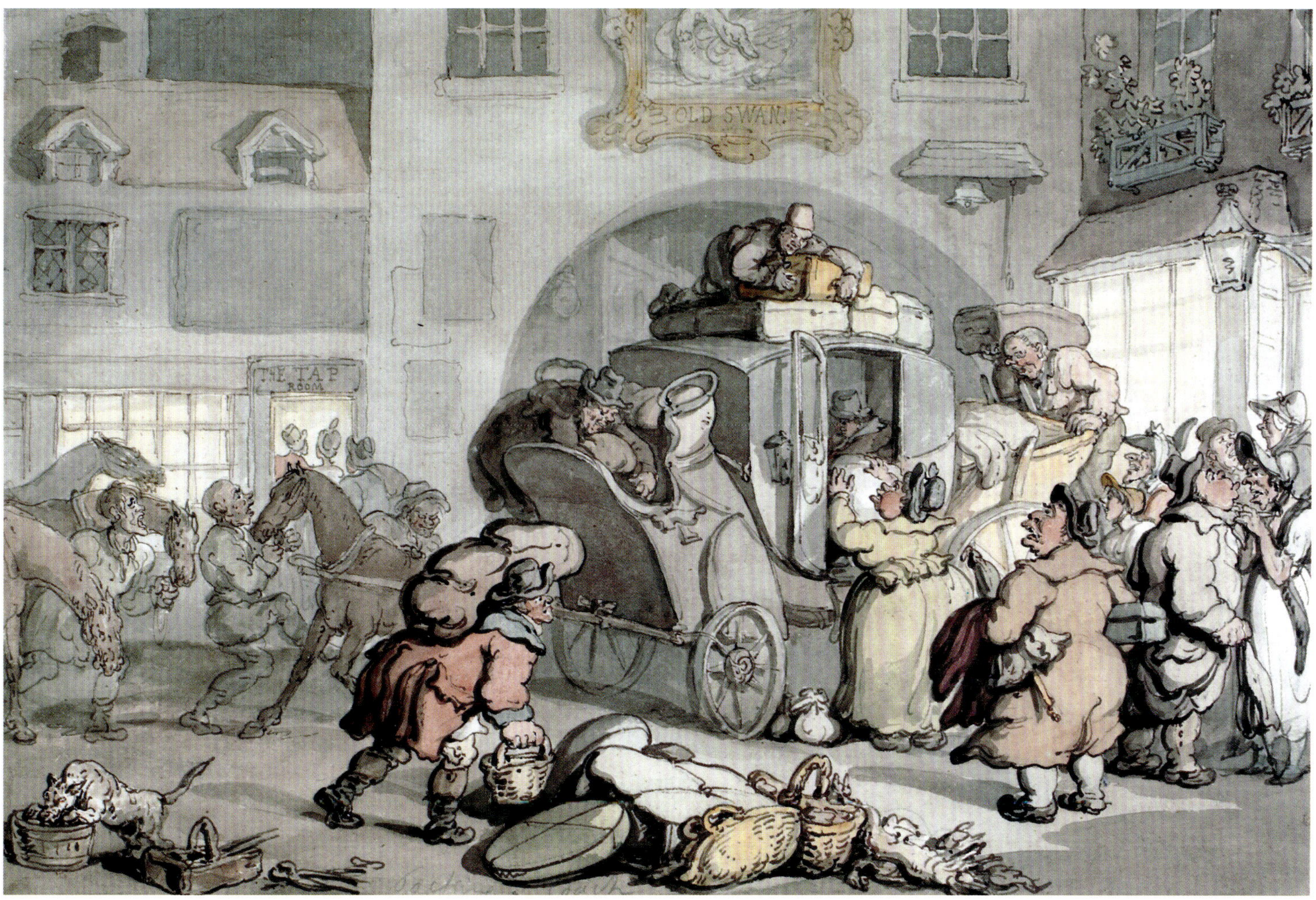

59 PACKING A COACH OUTSIDE THE OLD SWAN INN
pen ink and watercolour
9 ¼ x 13 ½ inches
Exhibited: Spink, London

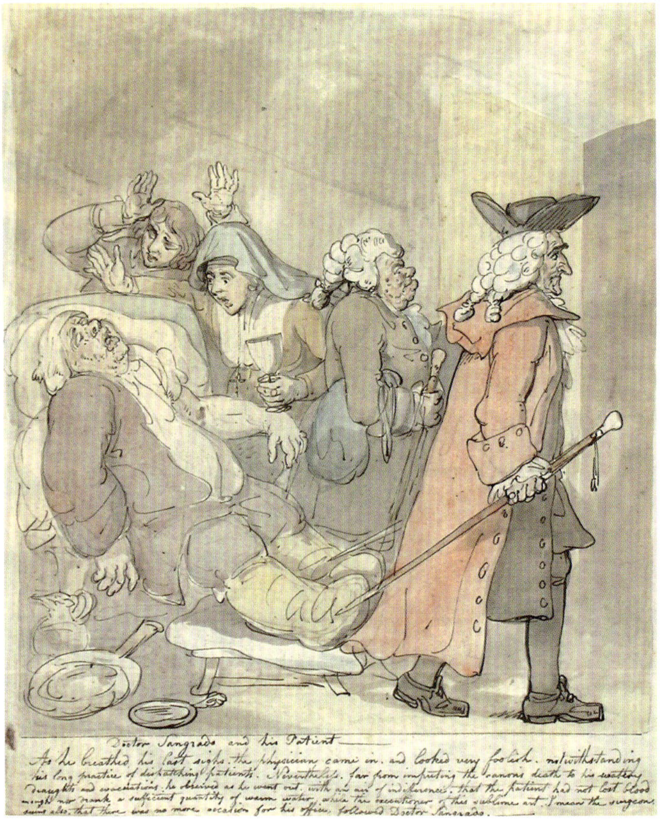

Dr Sangrado and his Patient

The quack doctor, Dr Sangrado, is a character in Alain-René Lesage's highly popular picaresque novel, *Histoire de Gil Blas de Santillane* (1715-35), first translated from French into English by Tobias Smollett for an edition printed in 1749. In 1803, Hannah Humphrey published James Gillray's caricature of Henry Addington, the Prime Minister as Dr Sangrado bleeding dry John Bull, representative of the British people. Rowlandson's drawing seems related in subject, though his composition is very different and the mood more affecting than satirical.

60 DR SANGRADO AND HIS PATIENT

AS HE BREATHED HIS LAST SIGHS THE PHYSICIAN CAME IN AND HE LOOKED VERY FOOLISH. NOTWITHSTANDING HIS LONG PRACTICE OF DISPATCHING PATIENTS. NEVERTHELESS FAR FROM IMPUTTING THE CANONS DEATH TO HIS WATERY DRAUGHTS AND EVACUATIONS HE OBSERVED AS HE WENT OUT WITH AN AIR OF INDIFFERENCE THAT THE PATIENT HAD NOT LOST BLOOD ENOUGH NOR DRANK A SUFFICIENT QUANTITY OF WATER WHILE THE EXECUTIONER OF THIS SUBLIME ART. I MEAN THE SURGEON SEEING ALSO THAT THERE WAS NO MORE OCCASION FOR HIS OFFICE, FOLLOWED DOCTOR SANGRADO

watercolour with pen and ink

11 ½ x 9 ¼ inches

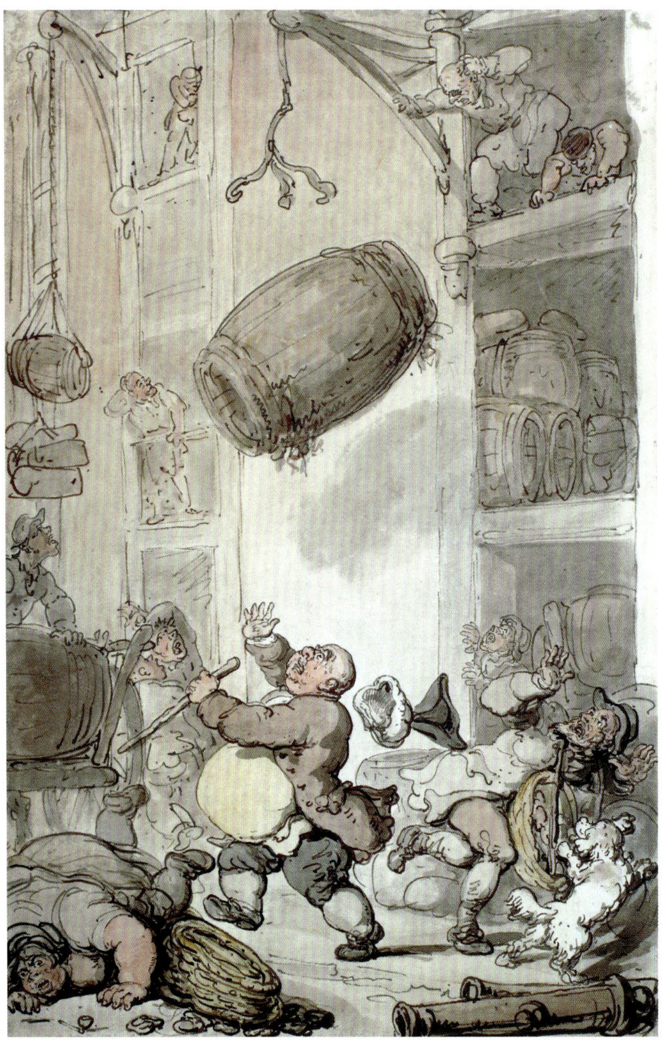

61 A FALL IN BEER

pen ink and watercolour

14 ¾ x 9 ½ inches

Provenance: Sir John Crampdon; Christie's, 1923; Desmond Coke

Exhibited: 'Humor Exhibition', Arthur Ackermann & Son, Chicago, 1925

62 THE LONG ROOM, CUSTOM HOUSE
signed and inscribed 'The Old India House'
pen ink and watercolour
8 ¼ x 10 ¾ inches
Engraved by J C Sadler, The Long Room, Custom House, and published by Rudolph Ackermann's Repository of Arts, 101 The Strand, London, 1 July 1808

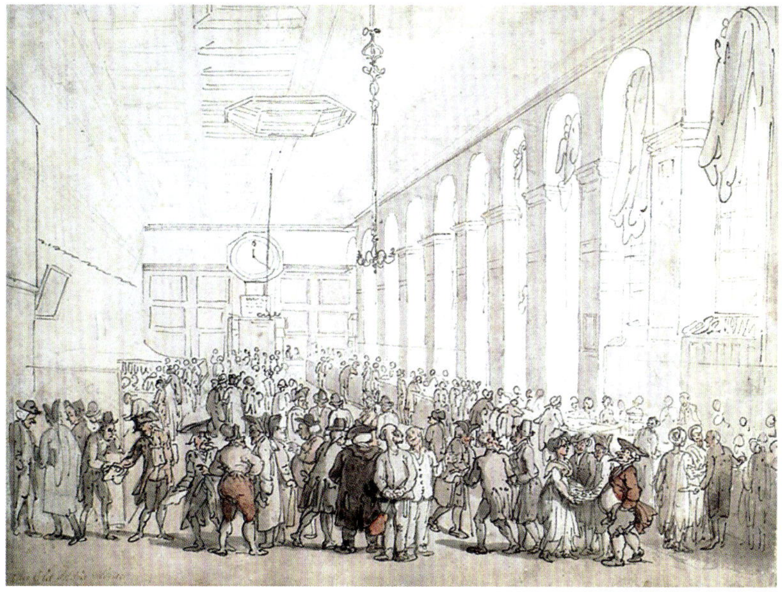

Quarterly Duns, or Clamorous Tax Gatherers
Taxation in 1805 raised a great deal of bad feeling; the satirists treated the increased imposts, and the methods of collecting them, from their point of view, and made the public smile at ills to which perforce they were compelled to submit. The house of a quack practitioner in 'Rotten Row', one Dr Humbug, at the sign of the Golden Pestle of Hippocrates, who advertises 'advice gratis' on his front door, is the scene of a general muster of the inquisitors and collectors of taxes. Window Tax, Income, Property, House, Servants, Horses, Dogs, &c, *are among the requisitions to be levied.* The Budget opened, or how to raise the wind for the year *1805 explains these visitations. The quack and his wife are declining to admit their duns; they are surveying the besieging party from an upper window, and the goodwill of their house is according to a placard,* to be disposed of. *The prospect of 'Houses to Let' and of windows 'Blocked up' shows that taxation was pressing with over-severity, and had, in reality, had been carried beyond a joke.* Joseph Grego, *Rowlandson the Caricaturist*, London: Chatto & Windus, 1880, vol 2, p 49

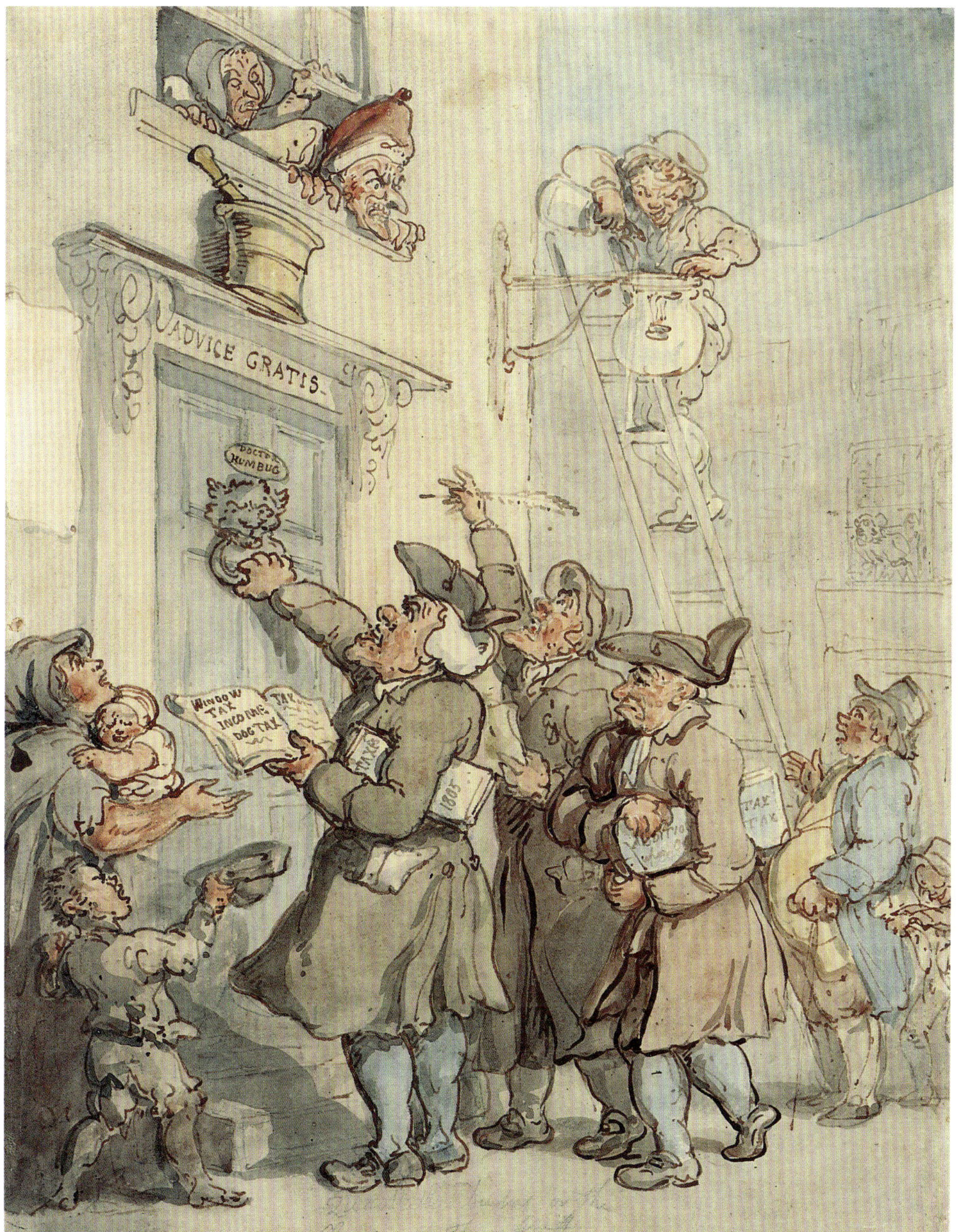

63 QUARTERLY DUNS, OR CLAMOROUS TAX GATHERERS
inscribed with title
pen ink and watercolour
12 ½ x 9 ½ inches
Published by Howitt, 73 Wardour Street, Soho, 1805
Literature: Joseph Grego, *Rowlandson The Caricaturist*, London: Chatto and Windus, 1880, vol 2, p 49

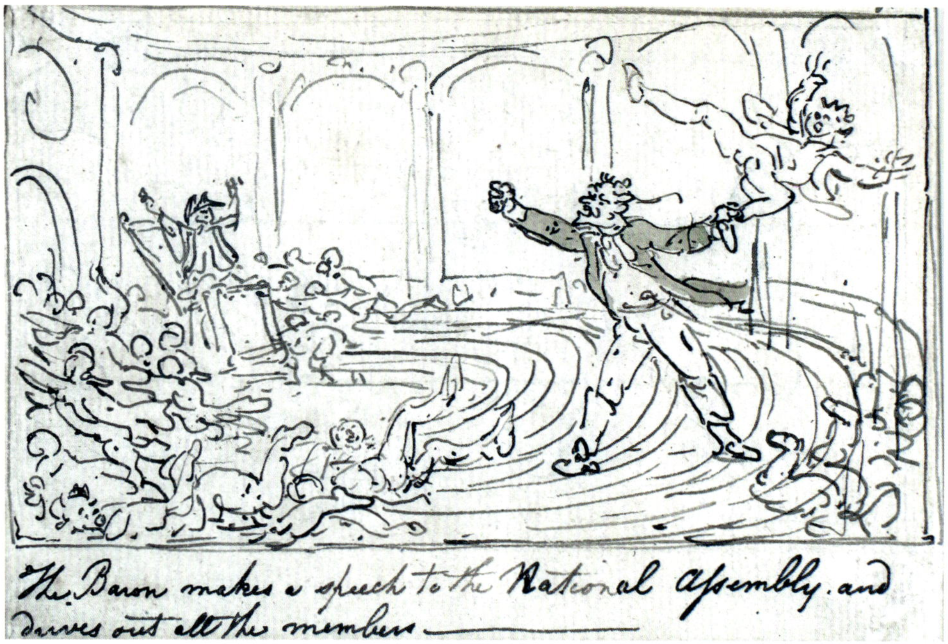

64 THE BARON MAKES A SPEECH TO THE NATIONAL ASSEMBLY AND DRIVES OUT ALL THE MEMBERS
inscribed with title
pen and ink with watercolour
3 ¾ x 5 ¼ inches
Drawn for but not illustrated in *Surprising Adventures of The Renowned Baron Munchausen containing Singular Travels, Campaigns, Voyages and Adventures*, London: Thomas Tegg, 1809

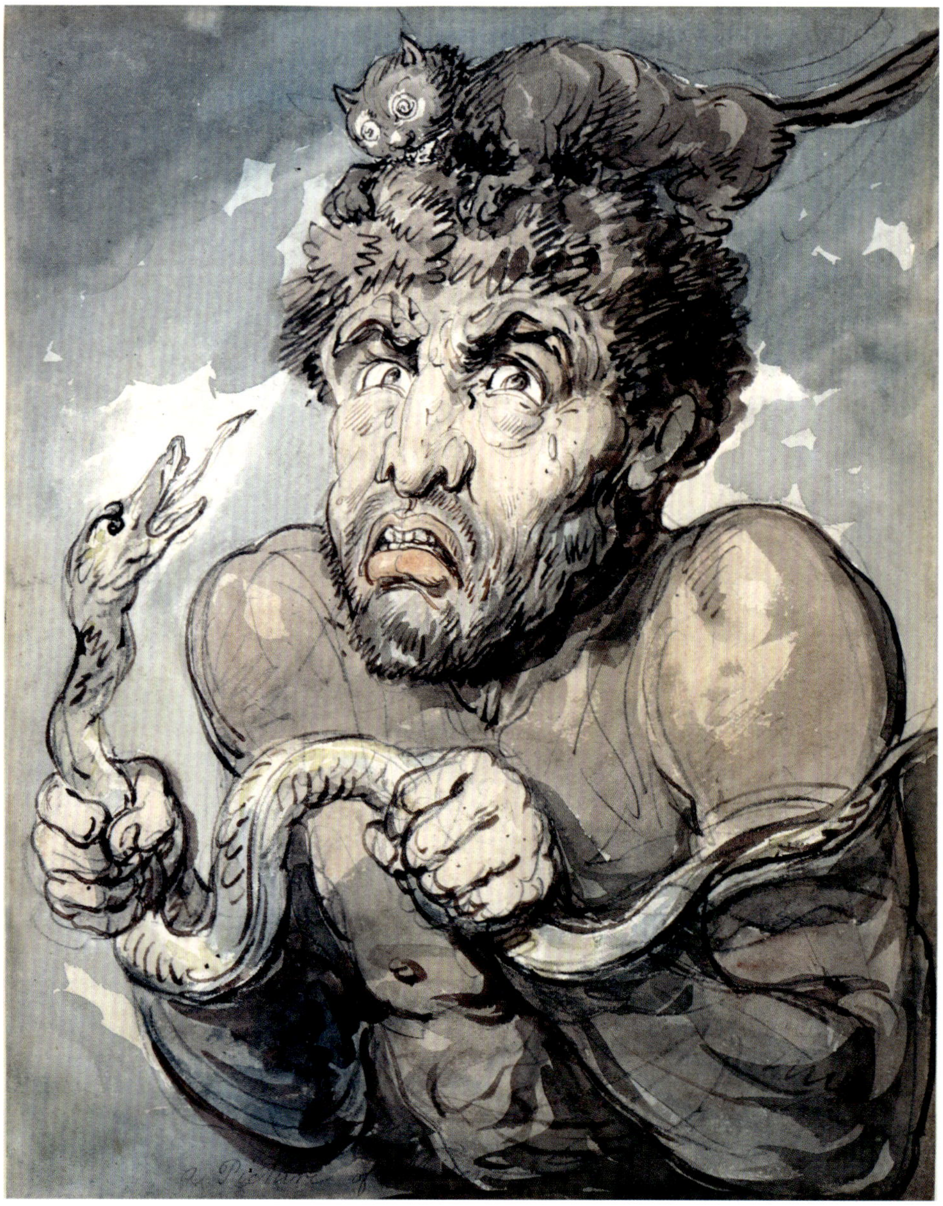

65 A PICTURE OF MISERY
inscribed with title
pen and ink with watercolour and pencil
11 x 8 ¼ inches

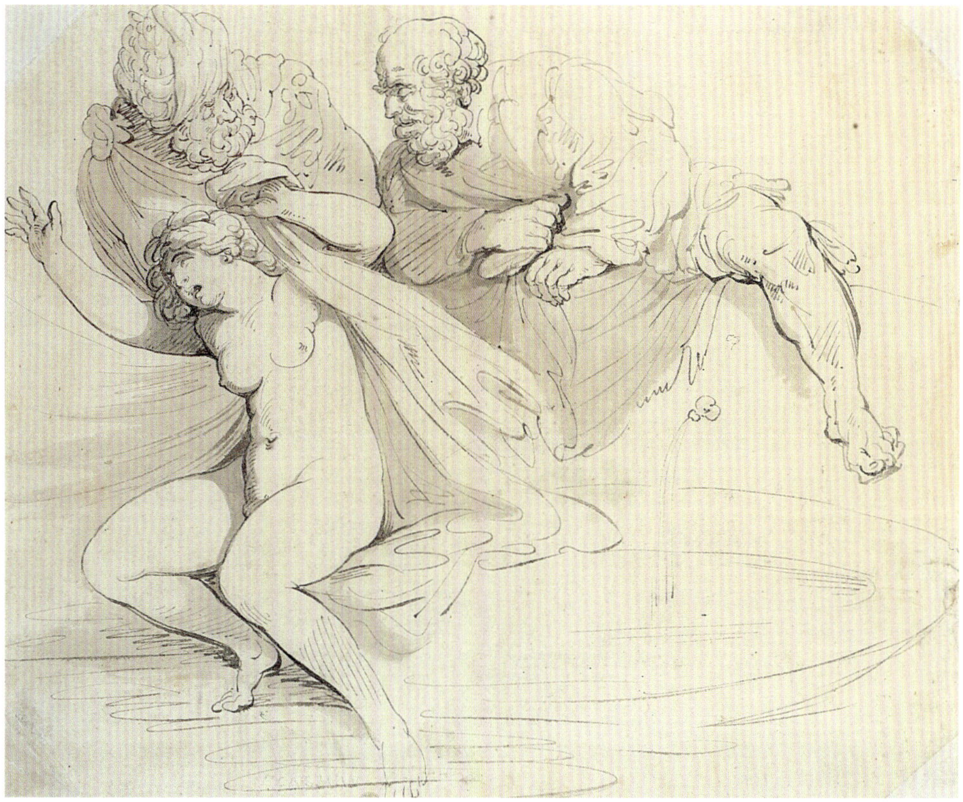

66 SUSANNAH AND THE ELDERS
pen ink and monochrome watercolour
9 ¼ x 11 inches
Provenance: W Coleman Collection; Sabin Galleries, London, May 1964

Ugolino and His Family in Prison

The subject of *Ugolino and His Family in Prison* is taken from Canto 33 of Dante's *Inferno*. Ugolino della Gherhardesca, a thirteenth-century Count of Donoratico, and his sons were imprisoned for political treachery by Archbishop Ruggieri degli Ubaldini and starved to death.

This drawing is a study for the watercolour illustrated in Adrian Bury's *Rowlandson Drawings* as plate 73. It is itself based on Joshua Reynolds' oil, *Count Hugolino and his Children in the Dungeon*. Exhibited at the Royal Academy in 1773 and purchased by John Frederick Sackville, Duke of Dorset, the painting now hangs at Knole in Sevenoaks, in Kent. A mezzotint of Reynolds' painting was published by John Boydell on 4 February 1774.

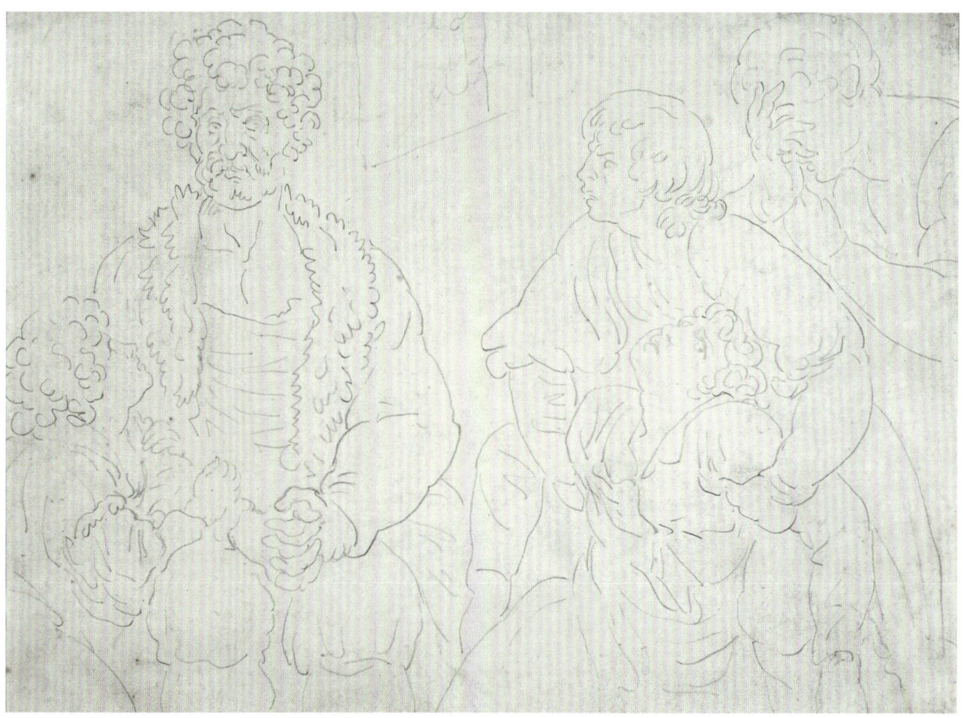

67 UGOLINO AND HIS FAMILY IN PRISON
pencil
9 ¾ x 13 ¼ inches

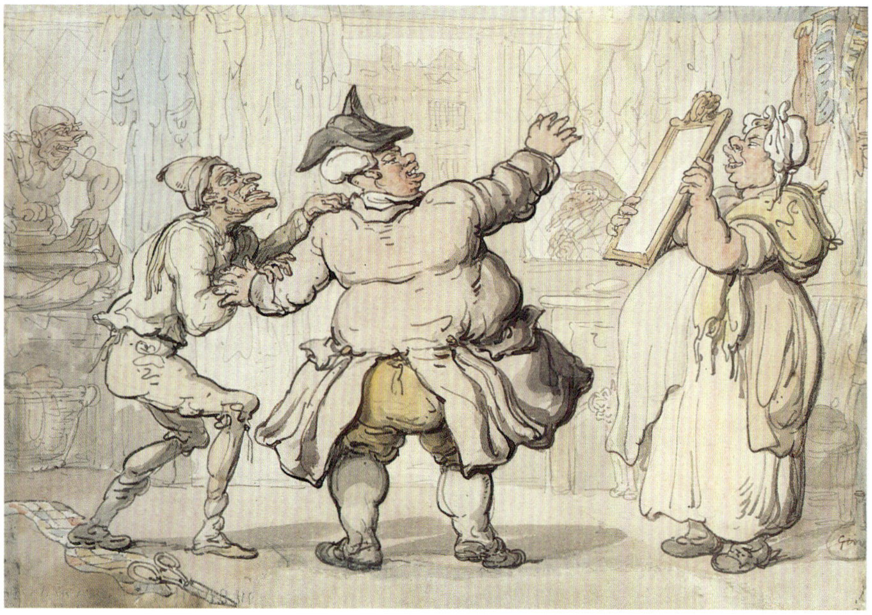

68 AT THE TAILOR'S
pen ink and watercolour
7 ¼ x 10 ½ inches

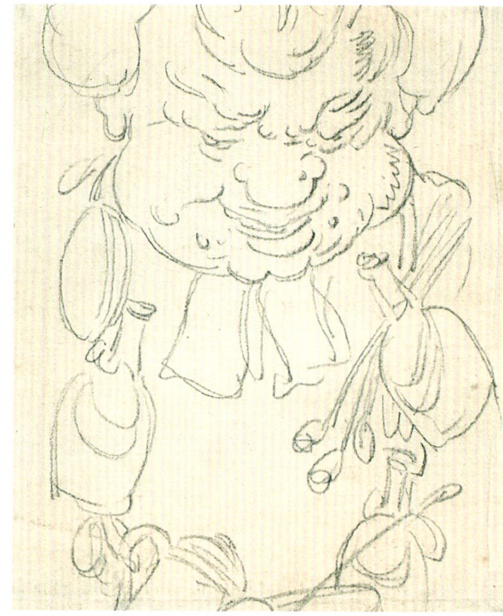

69 PARSON'S PLEASURE
pencil
5 x 4 inches

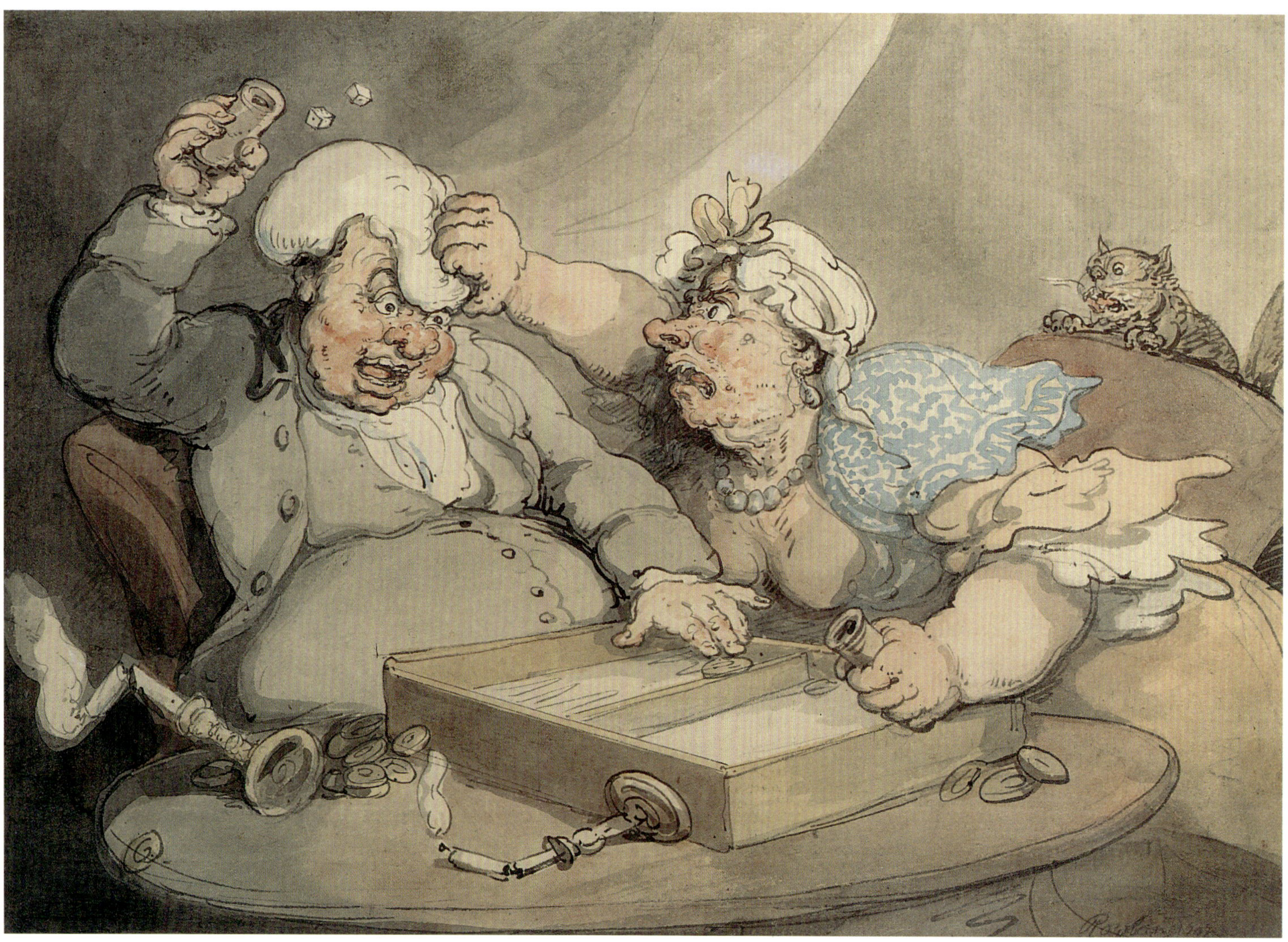

70 A HIT AT BACKGAMMON
signed
pen ink and watercolour
9 ¾ x 13 ¼ inches

Etching published on 19 November 1810 by Thomas Tegg, no 46
Provenance: Leger Galleries, London, February 1981
Literature: Joseph Grego, *Rowlandson The Caricaturist*, London: Chatto and Windus, 1880, vol 2, pp 193-194

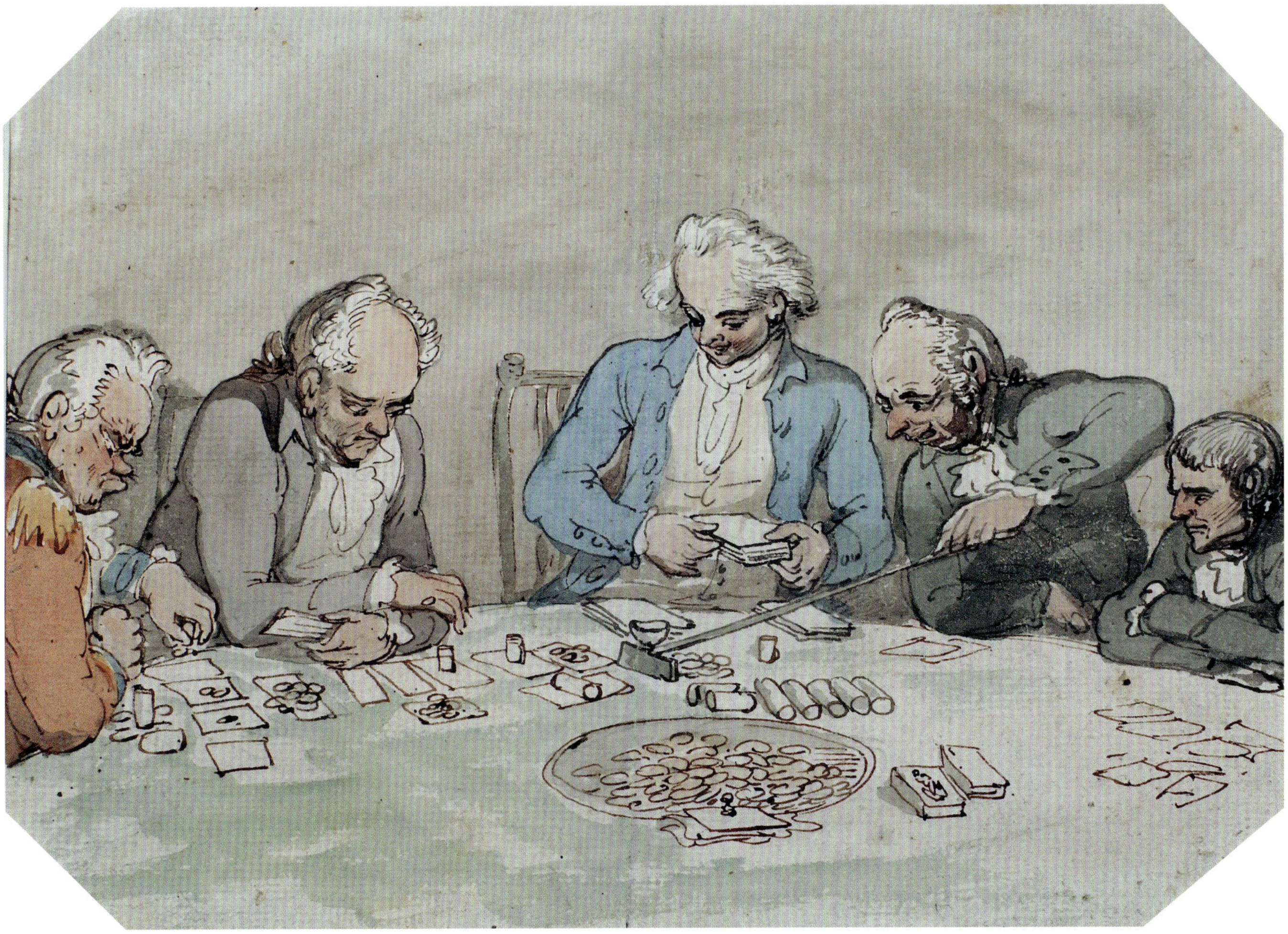

71 THE GAMESTERS
pen ink and watercolour
on paper with a whatman watermark
5 ½ x 7 ½ inches

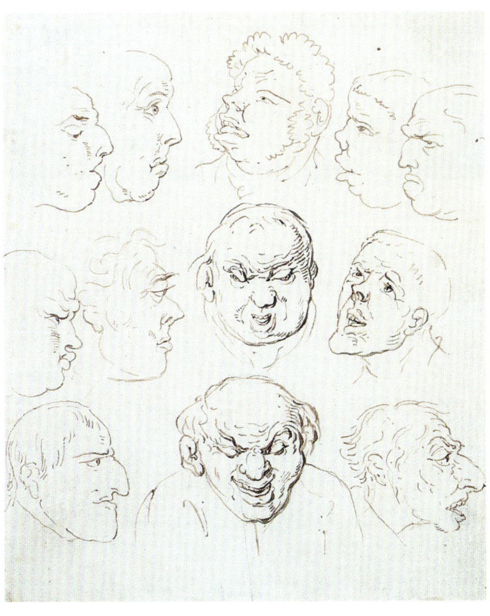

72 MALE FACE STUDIES
pen and ink
8 ¼ x 6 ¾ inches
Provenance: Gilbert Davis; Augustus Loring

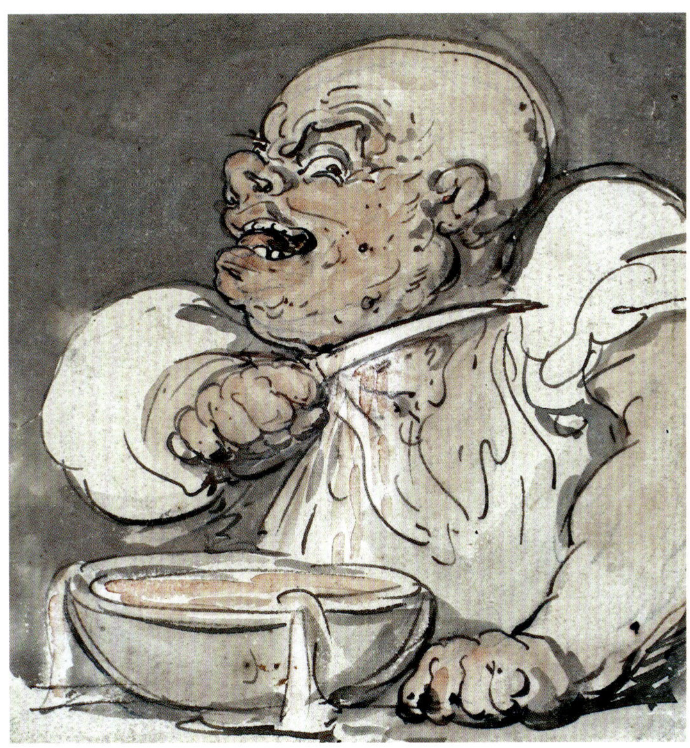

73 A CLOSE SHAVE
pen ink and watercolour
5 ½ x 5 ¼ inches

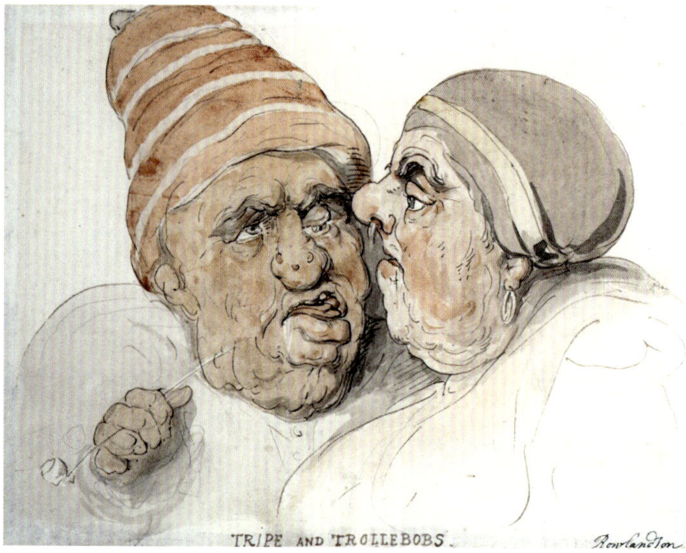

74 TRIPE AND TROLLEBOBS
signed and inscribed with title
watercolour
6 ¾ x 8 ¾ inches

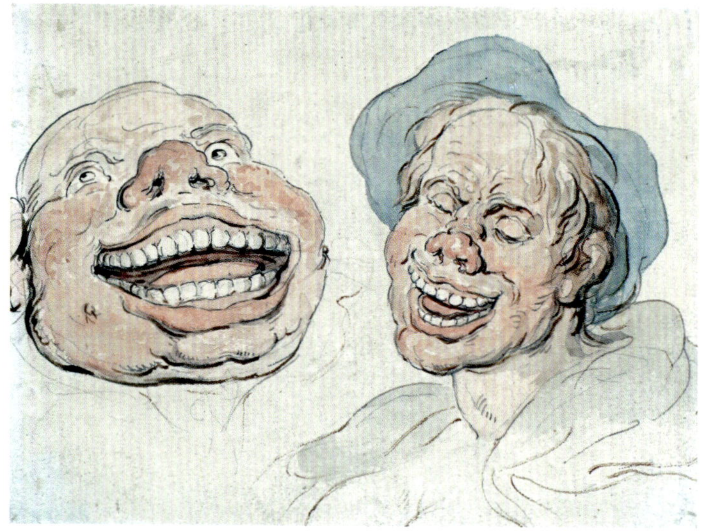

75 LAUGHING GROTESQUES
pen ink and watercolour
5 x 6 ¾ inches

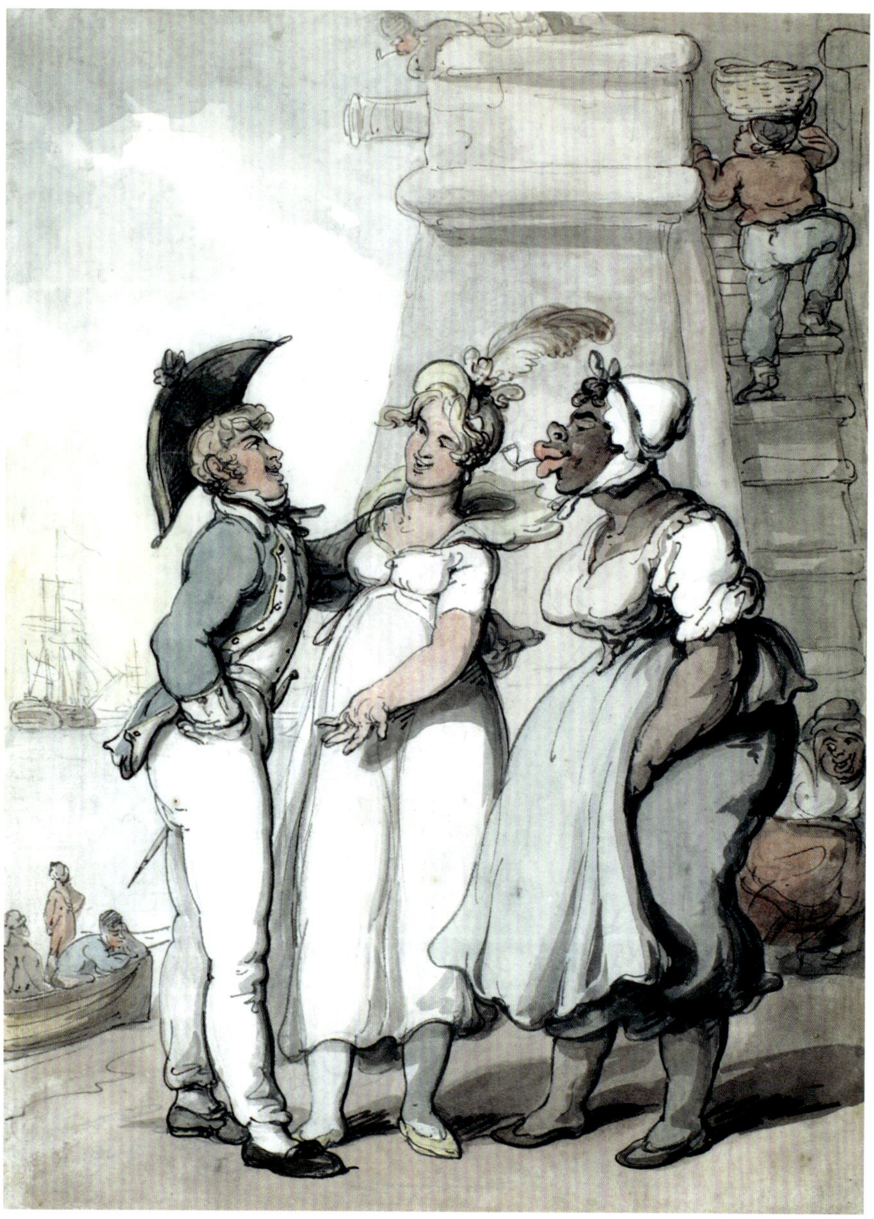

76 SEA STORES
pen ink and watercolour
13 ¼ x 9 ½ inches
Etching published on 25 March 1812 by Thomas Tegg, no 111, as a pair with 'Land Stores'
Literature: Joseph Grego, *Rowlandson The Caricaturist*, London: Chatto and Windus, 1880, vol 2, p 226; Mary Dorothy George, *Catalogue of Political and Personal Satires*, no 11960

77 THE COQUETTE
'I'LL LEAD TO YOU TO THE SPLENDID CROWD BUT YOUR NEXT DRESS WILL BE A SHROUD'
signed
pen ink and watercolour
4 ½ x 8 inches
Similar to 'The Coquette', etched and published by Rudolph Ackermann for 'The English Dance of Death', 1 October 1814, plate 21
Literature: Joseph Grego, *Rowlandson The Caricaturist*, London: Chatto and Windus, 1880, vol 2, p 331

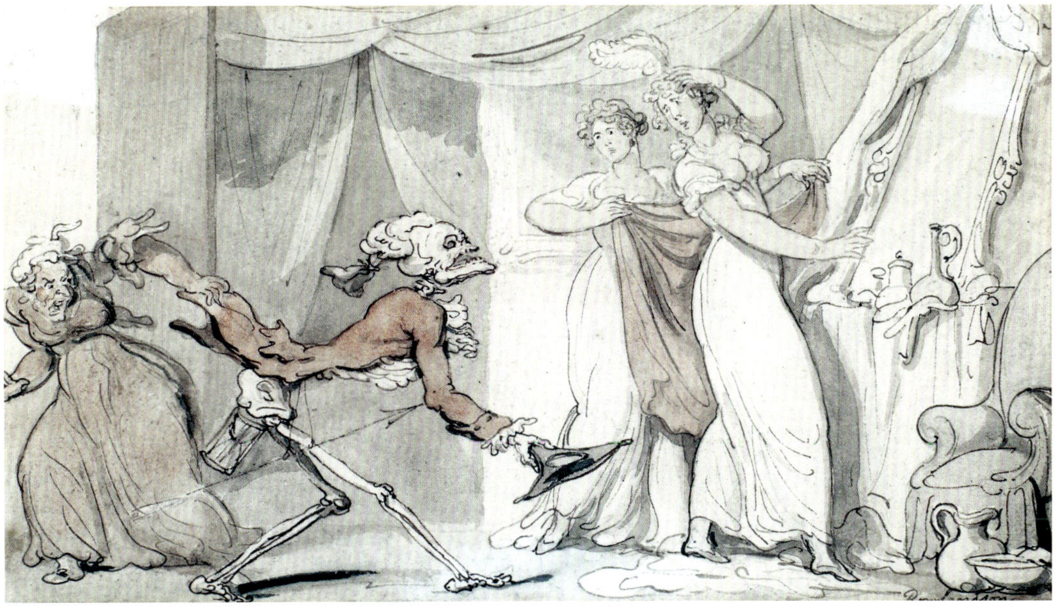

78 THE PARSON AND MILKMAIDS
watercolour
7 x 8 ½ inches
Provenance: Spink Leger, London

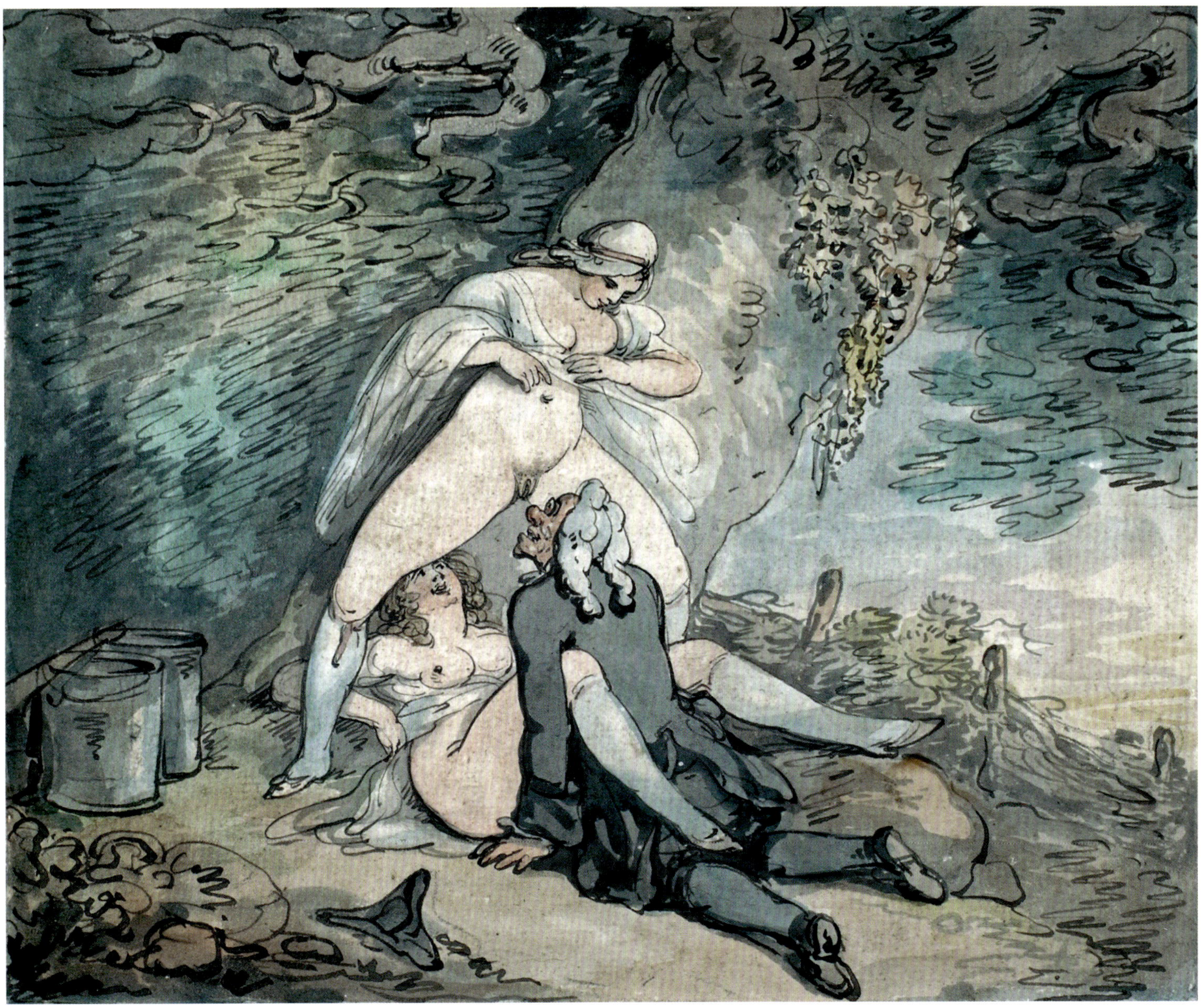

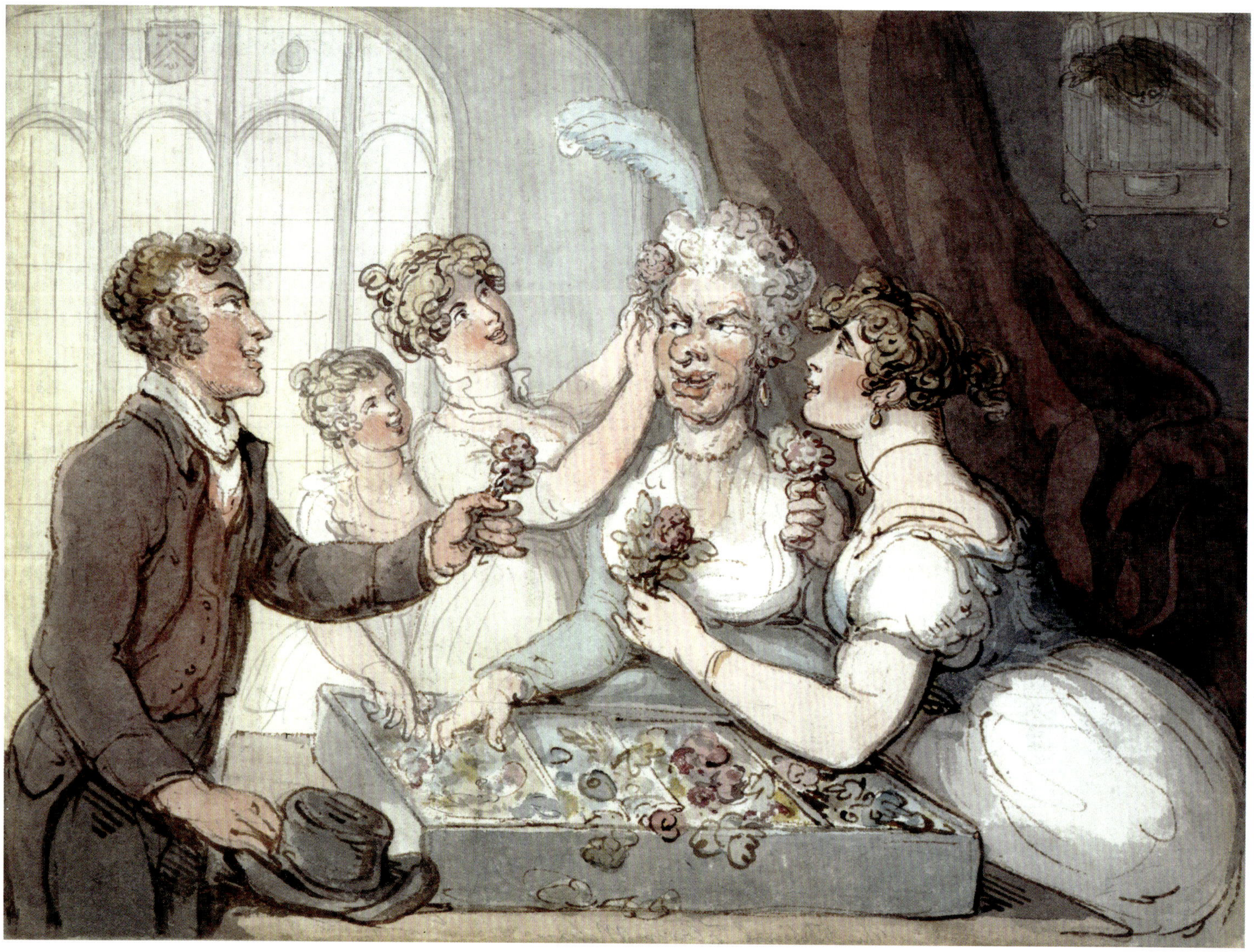

79 THE ARTIFICIAL FLOWER MAKERS
inscribed with title
watercolour
8 ½ x 11 inches

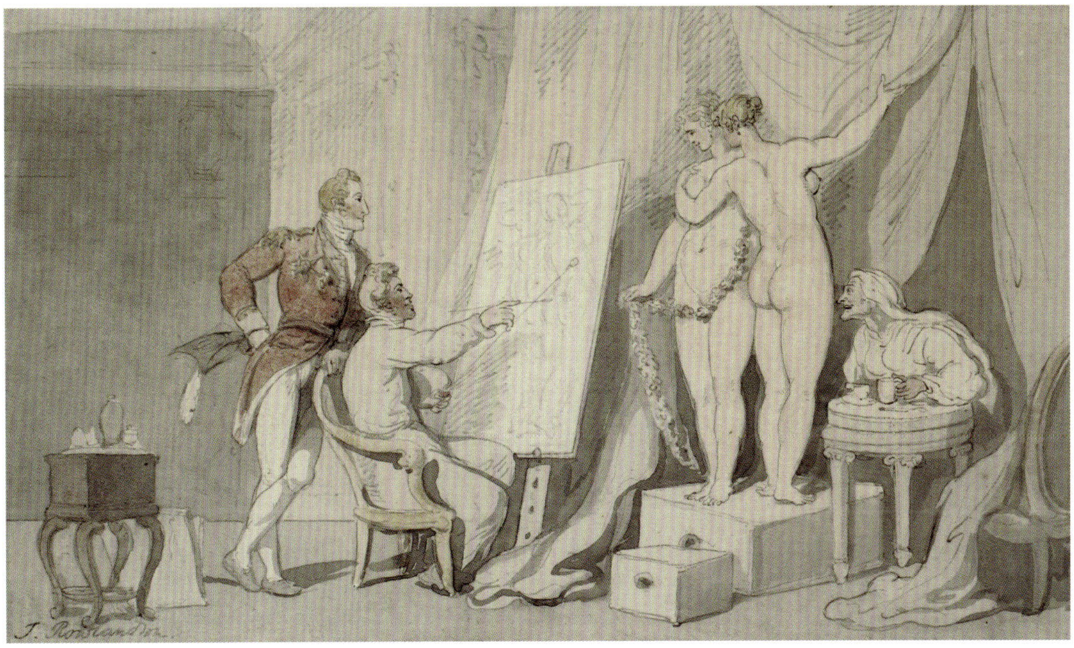

80 DRAWING FROM LIFE
signed
pen ink and watercolour with pencil
5 ¾ x 9 ½ inches
Possibly drawn for but not illustrated in Bernard Blackmantle [Charles Molloy Westmacott], *The English Spy*, London: Sherwood, Jones & Co, 1825-26 (2 vols)

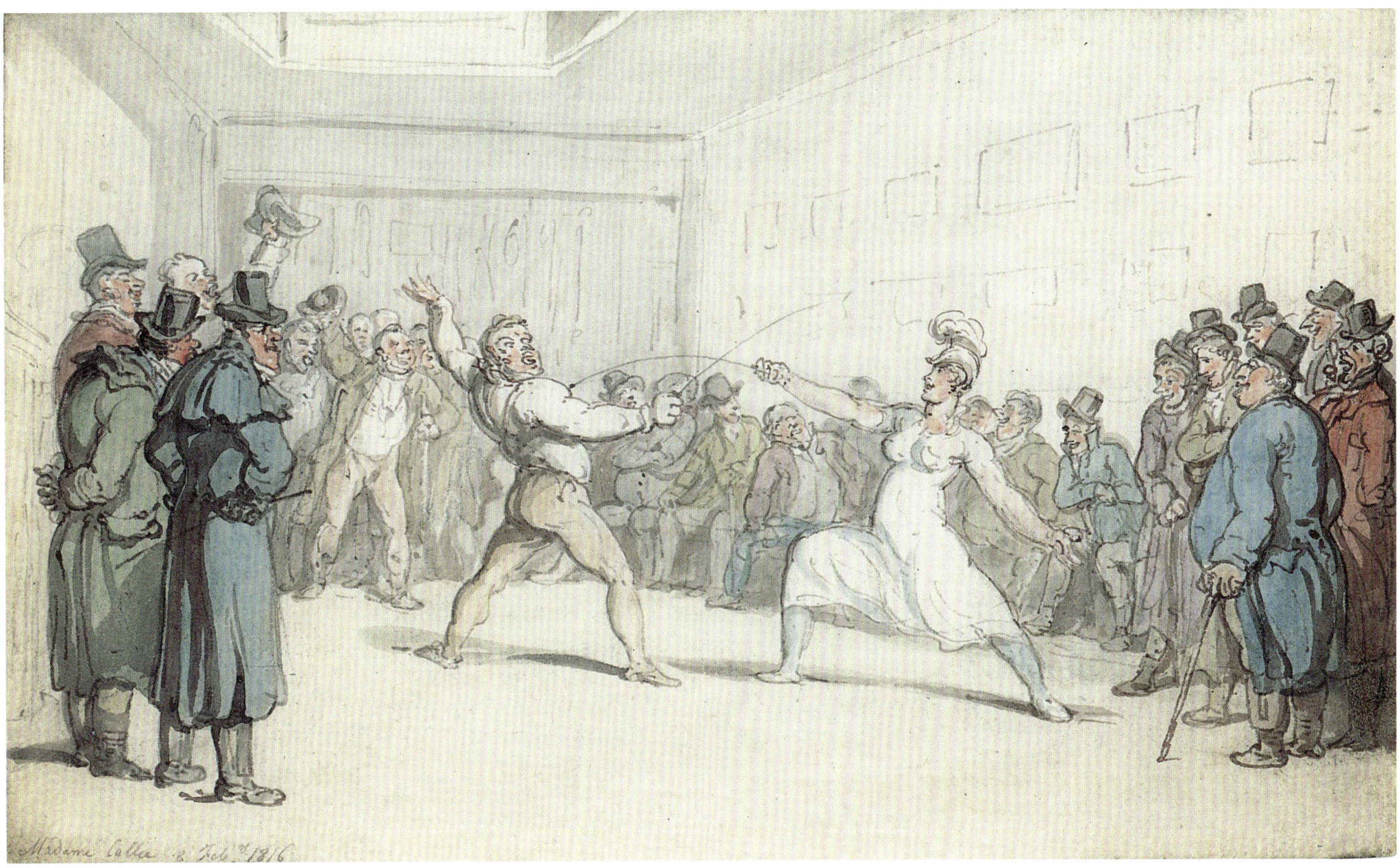

81 MADAME CALLEE (CULLONI) AND M RENAULT IN A FENCING CONTEST
inscribed 'Madame Callee' and dated '8th Feb 1816'
pen ink and watercolour
6 x 9 ½ inches

Madame Callee (Culloni) and M Renault in a Fencing Contest
There are several versions of this subject, one of which is illustrated in Robert Wark's *Drawings by Thomas Rowlandson in the Huntington Collection* as no 480. The example here appears to be the only one dated.

JOHN NIXON
John Colley Nixon (before 1759-1818)

One of the most notable amateur artists working in London in the late eighteenth century, John Nixon became best known for his caricatures of urban society.

John Nixon was the son of Robert Nixon, a successful Irish merchant. With his brother Richard, he too developed a mercantile career, living and working at Basinghall Street, near Guildhall Yard in the City. He was a special juryman at the Guildhall and a Captain of the Guildhall Volunteers. Yet at the same time, he moved in leading artistic and fashionable circles, acting as honorary secretary of the Beefsteak Club and producing a number of landscape paintings, caricatures and illustrations.

Nixon exhibited at the Royal Academy of Arts between 1781 and 1813, while another of his brothers, the Rev Robert Nixon (1759-1837), was an honorary exhibitor between 1790 and 1808. As curate at Foots Cray, Kent, Robert played host to J M W TURNER, who painted his first oil while staying with him in 1793, and gave him his first lessons in landscape painting. He also received lessons in figure painting from Stephen Rigaud. In 1798, Robert accompanied Turner and Rigaud on a sketching tour of Kent. Yet another brother, James, was a miniature painter.

John Nixon combined business and pleasure by both trading and sketching on the frequent tours that he made to Ireland in the 1780s and 1790s; he was accompanied on one such Irish trip by topographer and caricaturist, Captain Francis Grose (1791), and in turn went with THOMAS ROWLANDSON to Bath (1792).

As a result of extensive travels, across Britain and on the Continent (1783-84, 1802 and 1804), Nixon became a topographical illustrator; his drawings were included in *Seats of the Nobility and Gentry* (1779-86) and he illustrated Thomas Pennant's *Journey from London to the Isle of Wight* (1801) and a *Guide to Watering Places* (1803). He also exhibited a set of illustrations to Laurence Sterne's *Tristram Shandy* at the Royal Academy (1786). Throughout the period, he drew popular caricature prints, often published by William Holland and usually satirising social preoccupations, such as *A Country Dance*.

Nixon was a member of the set of Elizabeth Craven (Lady Craven), Margravine of Ansbach at Brandenburg House, Hammersmith, and proved a notable amateur actor in its theatrical productions.

Visiting the Isle of Wight regularly from 1789, Nixon died there, in Ryde, in 1818. Before he died he was bequeathed the estate of Upland, Ilford, Essex, by his great uncle Richard Eastland.

His work is represented in numerous public collections, including the British Museum and the V&A.

Further reading:

Frank S Brown, *A Georgian Comedy of Manners: Humorous Watercolours of Life in Bath, the West Country and London by John Nixon*, Bath: Holburne Museum, 1994

L H Cust (rev Douglas Fordham), 'Nixon, John Colley (*b* before 1759; *d* 1818)', *H C G Matthew and Brian Harrison* (eds), *Oxford Dictionary of National Biography*, Oxford University Press, 2004, vol 40, p 936

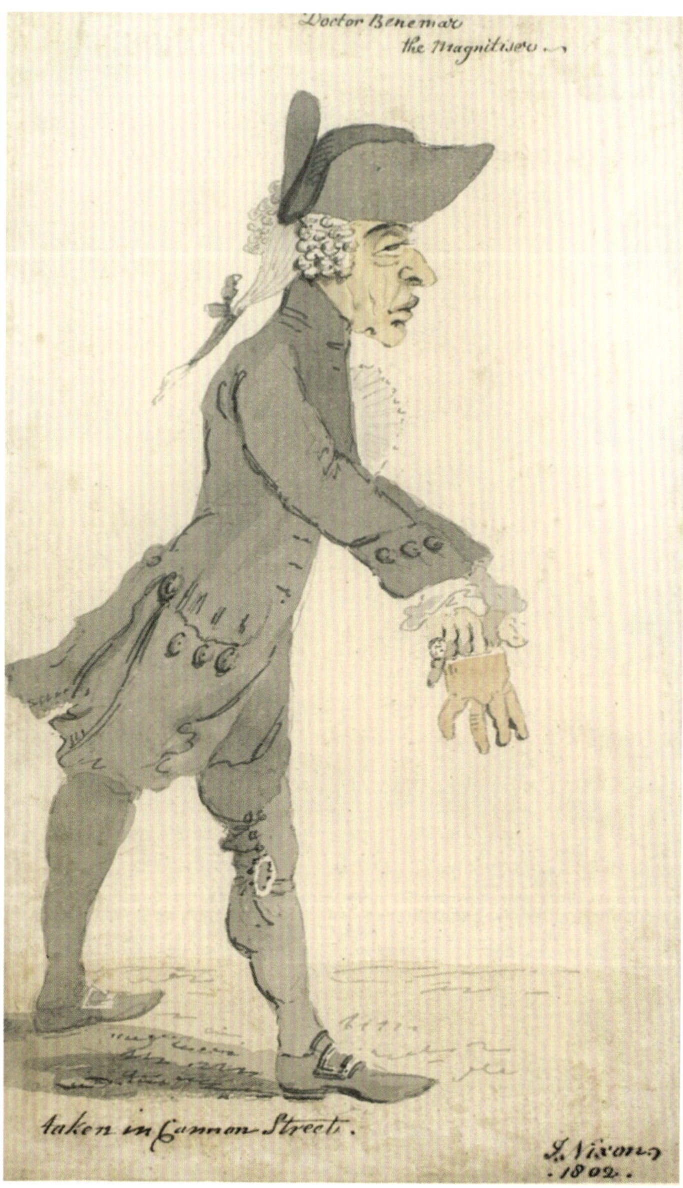

Doctor Benemar the Magnitiser

Animal Magnetism was a popular, quack medicine at the turn of the nineteenth century that developed out of the theories of the famous Swiss physician Franz Mesmer (1734-1815). Central to the concept was a mysterious, universal fluid said to run through all animal bodies, which intrinsically linked the movements of the stars and planets to health and well being. Animal Magnetism was a rare gift, held by such practitioners of the science as Dr Benemar, that could be used to restore the balance of this fluid when celestial movements provoked illness. Magnets were sometimes used, but more often than not the hands of a 'conductor' of animal magnetism were deemed sufficient.

Note by Giles Huxley-Parlour

82 DOCTOR BENEMAR THE MAGNITISER
TAKEN IN CANNON STREET
signed, inscribed with title and dated 1802
pen ink and watercolour
8 x 4 ½ inches
Provenance: Walker Galleries, London

The Naumacia to Commemorate a Peace

On the evening of 1 August 1814, grand festivities took place in London's Hyde Park, Green Park and St James's Park, to celebrate both the defeat of Napoleon and the centenary of the House of Hanover as reigning dynasty. Central to these celebrations was a *naumachia* – that is, a re-enactment of a naval battle – on the Serpentine in Hyde Park. Barges brought from the Royal Navy's dockyard at Woolwich were used to represent the Battle of the Nile of 1798, in which the British fleet under Horatio Nelson had defeated Napoleon's forces. In the present caricature, published it would seem over a week before the event, Napoleon is shown being blasted into the sky on a rocket. The actual event was recorded and disseminated through a series of engravings issued by Edward Orme in the souvenir publication, *A Historical Memento*. However, the press was less than enthusiastic in its response.

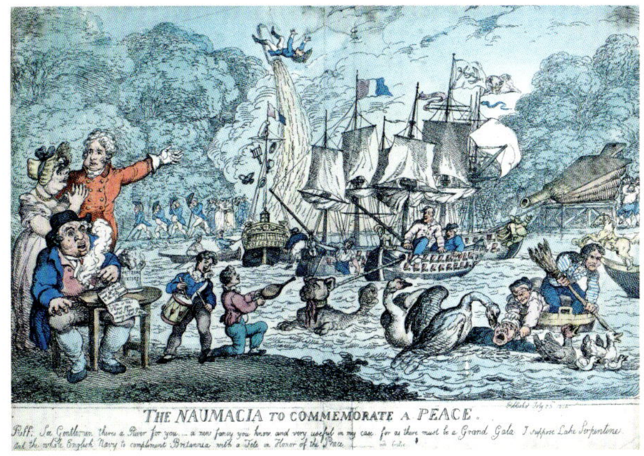

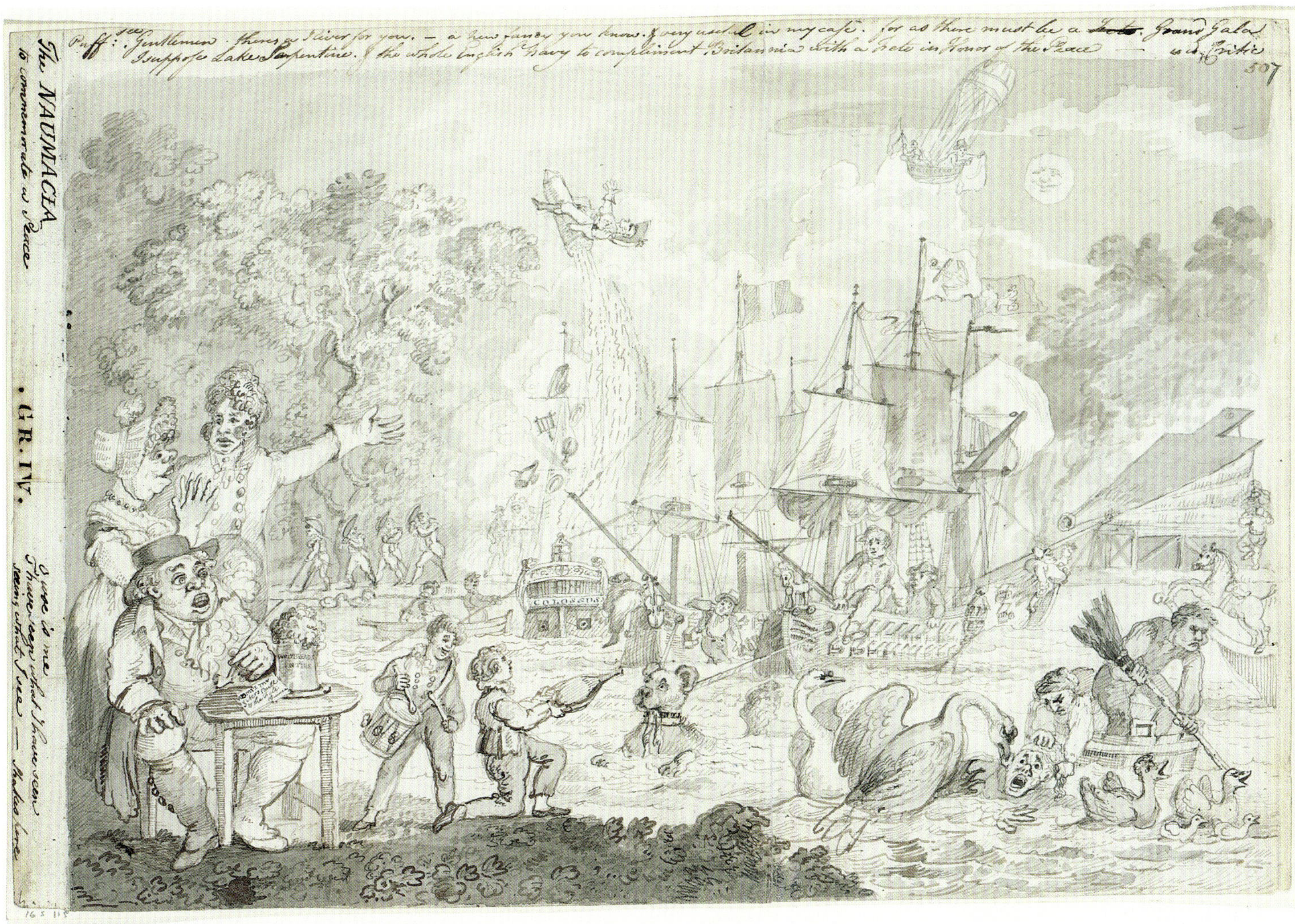

83 THE NAUMACIA TO COMMEMORATE A PEACE

PUFF: SEE GENTLEMEN, THERES A RIVER FOR YOU - A NEW FANCY YOU KNOW AND VERY USEFUL IN MY CASE. FOR AS THERE MUST BE A GRAND GALA I SUPPOSE LAKE SERPENTINE AND THE WHOLE ENGLISH NAVY TO COMPLEMENT BRITANNIA WITH A FETE IN HONOR OF THE PEACE - VIDE CRITIC

inscribed with title and 'GRR IV' and 'O woe is me I have seen what I have seen seeing what I see - Shakespere'

pen and ink with monochrome watercolour with pencil

11 ¾ x 16 ¾ inches

Published on 23 July 1814

GEORGE MURGATROYD WOODWARD

George Murgatroyd Woodward, sometimes known as 'Mustard George' (1760-1809)

The vigorous, ribald nature of G M Woodward's caricatures led one historian of caricature – Dorothy George – to call him 'a very considerable figure in caricature… original, varied, humorous and good-humoured'.

G M Woodward was the son of William Woodward, who lived at Stanton Hall, Derbyshire, and was probably steward to Mr Thornhill, the owner. During his youth, he made such a name for himself caricaturing local personalities that he decided to go to London to make his fortune.

The publication of two caricature prints in 1785 suggests that Woodward settled in London in or about that year. However, he did not make an impact until 1790, when he published a set of six caricatures under the title 'Symptoms of Drunkenness'. Once established, he proved prolific.

From the start, his caricatures owed much of their appeal to their ideas, which were conveyed in part by the inscriptions, often in doggerel verse. A number were political in subject, but most were social, and concerned the middle and working classes, including many sailors.

Sometimes claimed as Britain's first 'gag cartoonist', he was a pioneer of the strip cartoon, and his work was as popular in its day as that of THOMAS ROWLANDSON, his friend and drinking companion. However, as he was not trained as an artist, his drawings were etched by professionals, most frequently and notably by Rowlandson.

A versatile artist, Woodward designed borders, decorated screens and illustrated books, the first and most famous of which was *Eccentric Excursions*, published in 1796 (with a hundred designs engraved by ISAAC CRUIKSHANK).

He died, with a glass of brandy in his hand, at the Brown Bear public house, Bow Street, London, in November 1809, of a dropsy. He was buried at the expense of the landlord. Many caricatures were published after his death from drawings that he left behind.

His work is represented in the collections of the British Museum, The Cartoon Museum and the V&A; and Derby Local Studies Library, The Fitzwilliam Museum (Cambridge) and Leeds Art Gallery.

Further reading:
Simon Heneage, 'Woodward, George Murgatroyd (1760?-1809)', in H C G Matthew and Brian Harrison (eds), *Oxford Dictionary of National Biography*, Oxford University Press, 2004, vol 60, pp 235-236

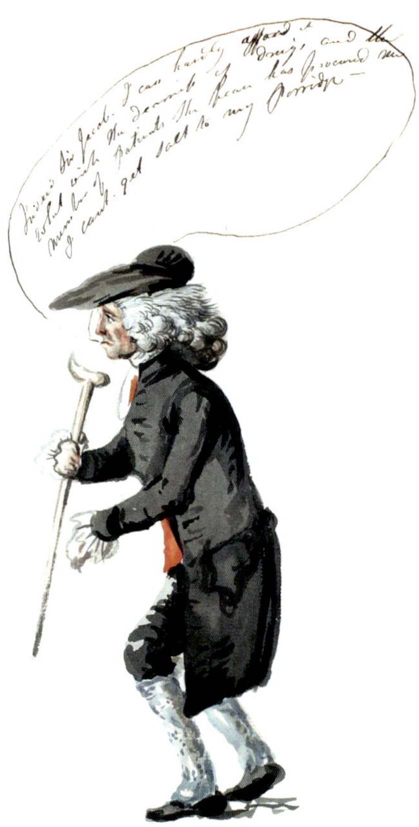

84 INDEED SIR JACOB. I CAN HARDLY AFFORD IT… I CAN'T GET SALT TO MY PORRIDGE
watercolour
11 x 7 ¾ inches

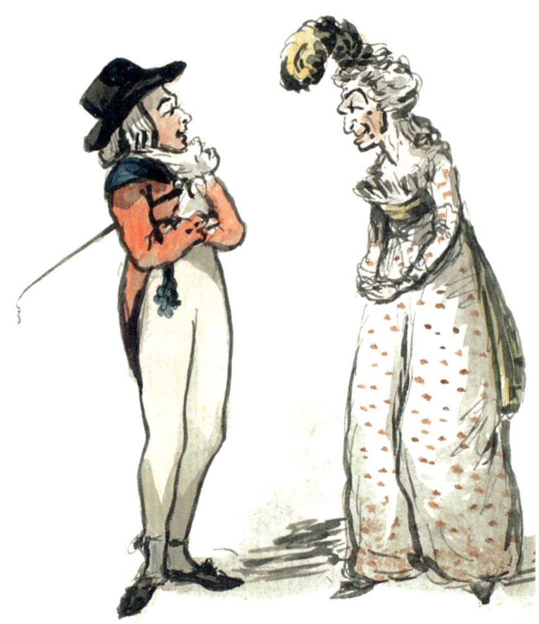

85 'KEEPING!!! YES I SHALL MAKE A PROPER SETTLEMENT AS SOON AS WE ARRIVE AT MY ESTATE IN NORTHUMBERLAND.'
'I TRUST SIR, ENTIRELY TO YOUR HONOR AND TO YOUR KEEPING A COMMANDING FORTUNE TO MY CHARMS'
inscribed with title
pen ink and watercolour
5 ¾ x 4 ¼ inches
Provenance: Iolo Aneurin Williams

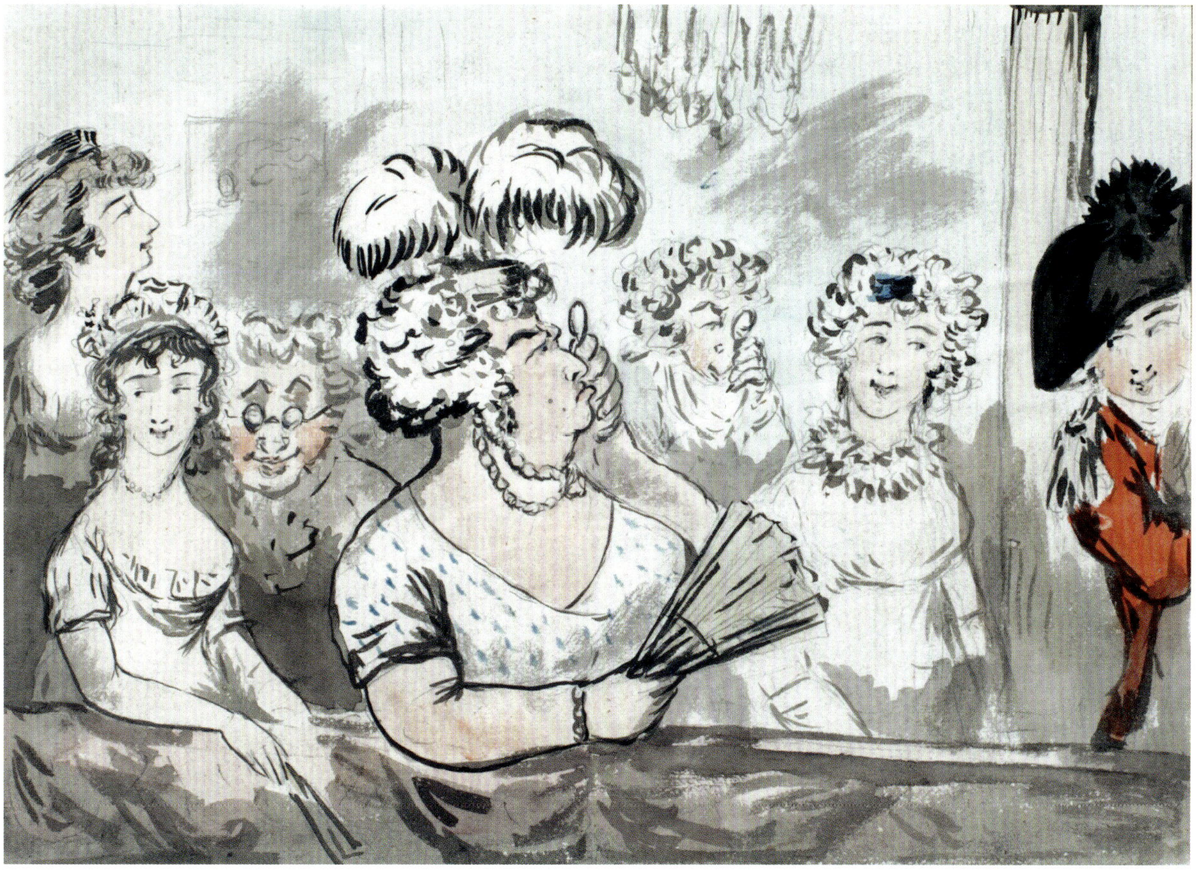

86 AT THE THEATRE
signed 'Woodward Delict'
pen ink and watercolour
9 ¼ x 11 ¼ inches

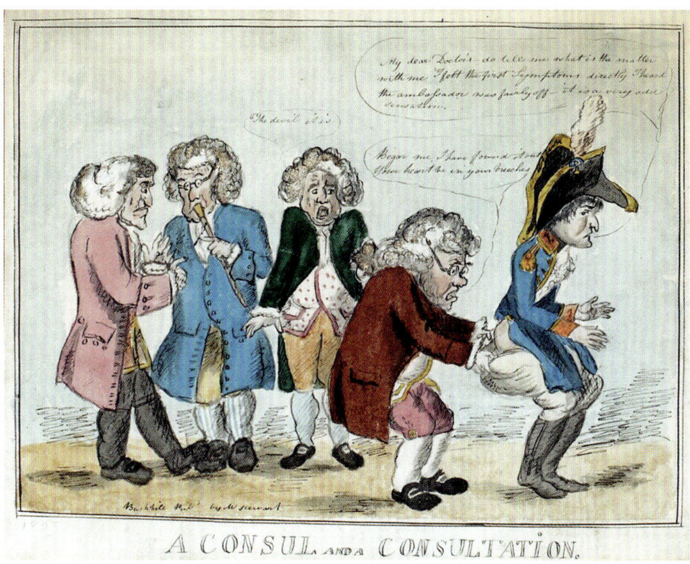

87 A CONSUL AND A CONSULTATION
inscribed with title and 'Bush Hill Pub? by M Stewart'
pen ink and watercolour
10 ½ x 12 ½ inches

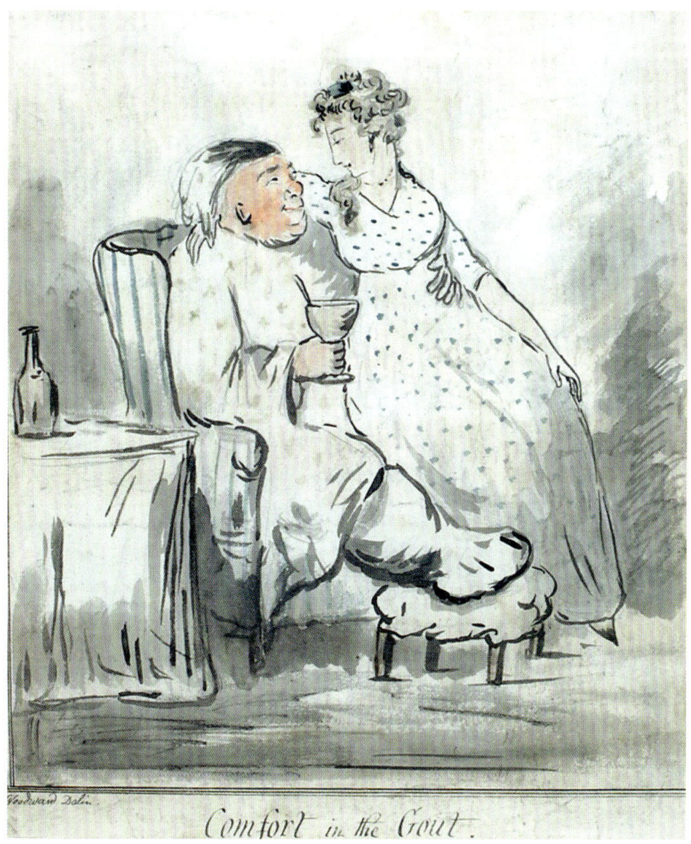

88 COMFORT IN THE GOUT
signed 'Woodward Delict' and inscribed with title
watercolour with pencil
10 ¾ x 9 inches

ISAAC CRUIKSHANK
Isaac Cruikshank (1764-1811)

Forceful as a caricaturist and imaginative as a painter, Isaac Cruikshank acted as a model for his sons and, through both them and more generally, proved an influence on the imagery of a generation.

Isaac Cruikshank was born in the Canongate, Edinburgh on 5 October 1764. His father, Andrew Crookshanks, who had once worked as a painter and, subsequently, as a customs officer, was a seller of prints and books.

Cruikshank soon decided to pursue his father's first career, and become an artist. Following his father's death in 1783, he studied under a local artist, possibly John Kay, and late in the same year master and pupil moved south to London (Cruikshank lodging at 53 Stanhope Street, Clare Market). There he worked, in the words of his son GEORGE CRUIKSHANK as 'a clever designer, etcher and engraver, and a first-rate watercolour draughtsman'. His first known publications – in January 1784 – were etchings of Edinburgh caricatures.

In 1788, Cruikshank married Mary MacNaughton. On the birth of their first child, (Isaac) Robert Cruikshank, in the following year, they moved to St Martin's Court, off St Martin's Lane. Then on the arrival of his brother, George, in 1792, they moved to 27 Duke Street (now Coptic Street), Bloomsbury. By 1808, the family would have settled at 117 Dorset Street (now Dorset Rise), Salisbury Square, close to St Bride's, Fleet Street. Three further children all died by the age of eighteen.

Cruikshank exhibited genre paintings at the Royal Academy of Arts between 1789 and 1792, exploiting a taste for Gothic humour and sentiment. However, he became better known as a caricaturist and illustrator, ranking in quality below only James Gillray and THOMAS ROWLANDSON. While he began by defending Pitt against the attacks of Gillray, he soon developed an impartial attitude, and employed the graphic skills to criticise a range of opinion. He scored a number of particular successes with his images of Napoleon. In contrast to his political subjects, his social caricatures tended towards lively and accurate observation rather than grotesque exaggeration. His book illustrations included contributions to George Shaw's *General Zoology* (1800-26).

Cruikshank nurtured the talents of his sons and, through his etched portraits of actors, introduced both Robert and George to the theatrical milieu that they so greatly valued. His early death, induced by alcohol, in April 1811 also fired George in his championship of temperance.

His work is represented in the collections of the British Museum; and the Huntington Library (San Marino, CA).

Further reading:

E B Krumbhaar, *Isaac Cruikshank: a Catalogue Raisonné with a sketch of his life and work*, Philadelphia University of Pennsylvania Press, 1966
Ruari McLean, 'Cruikshank (1) Isaac Cruikshank (*bapt* Edinburgh, 14 Oct 1764; *bur* London, 16 April 1811), Jane Turner (ed), *The Dictionary of Art*, London: Macmillan, 1996, vol 8, p 217
Edward J Nygren (ed), *Isaac Cruikshank and the Politics of Parody: Watercolours from the Huntington Collection*, Huntington Library Press, 1994
Robert L Patten, 'Cruikshank [Crookshanks], Isaac (1764-1811)', in H C G Matthew and Brian Harrison (eds), *Oxford Dictionary of National Biography*, Oxford University Press, 2004, vol 14, pp 528-529

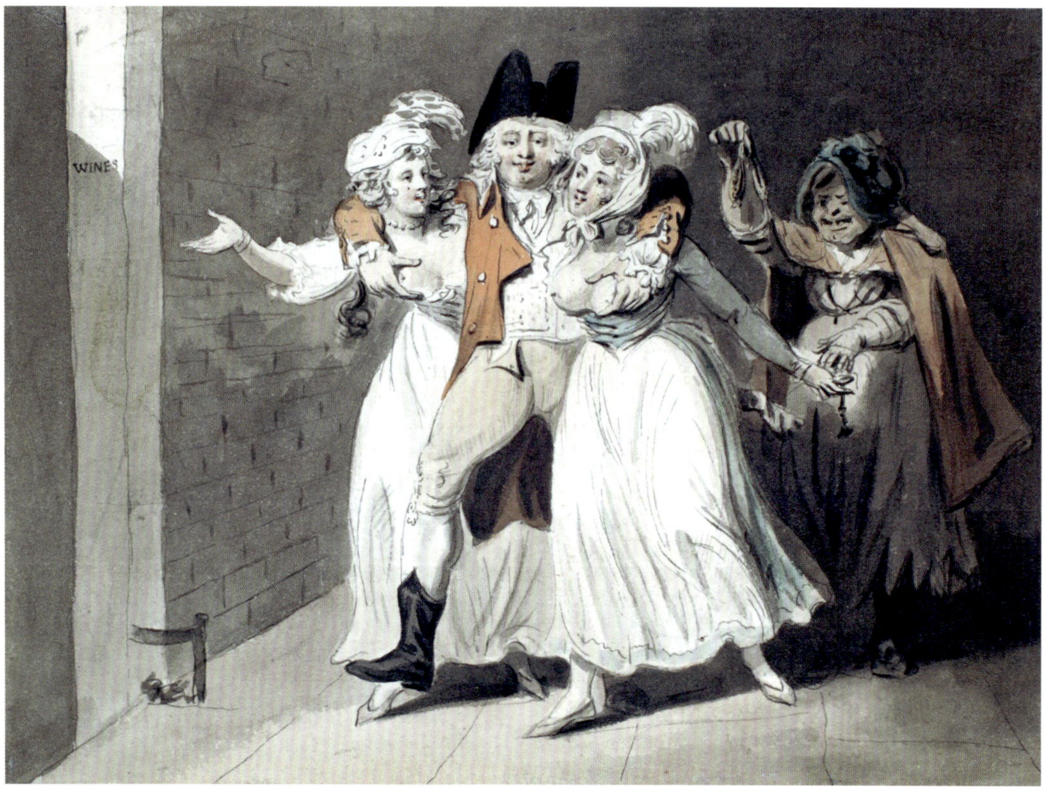

89 THE ROAD TO RUIN
watercolour
6 ¾ x 9 inches

HENRY ALKEN
Henry Thomas Alken (1785-1851)

The most distinguished member of an artistic dynasty, Henry Alken was the dominant sporting artist of the early nineteenth century.

Henry Alken was born in Golden Square, Soho, London on 12 October 1785, the third son of Samuel Alken, an architect and engraver of Danish origin. Growing up in Bedford Square, he studied under his father, and was apprenticed to the miniaturist John Thomas Barber. During this apprenticeship, he exhibited two portrait miniatures at the Royal Academy of Arts (1801-2), but seems not to have capitalised on his initial exposure. Indeed, little certain is known about the artist during the 1800s.

Alken married in Ipswich, Suffolk in 1809, and may have lived there for some years. However, he seems to have mixed with the notorious Meltonian hunting set, of Melton Mowbray, Leicestershire – and it has been suggested that he lived there, and worked as a horse breeder. His earliest sporting prints were signed 'Ben Tally Ho' from 1813, and under his own name from 1816. At this time, he had returned to London, and was living in the Haymarket, over the shop of Thomas McLean, the print publisher. By the end of the decade, he had settled in Kentish Town.

During the 1820s, Alken was at his most skilful and successful, producing many prints and illustrating numerous books, the subjects ranging across comic and serious. Volumes included *The National Sports of Great Britain* (1821), *Real Life in London* (1821-22), *A Touch at the Fine Arts* (1824) and *Sporting Scrap Book* (1824). And, while his work declined in quality and popularity from the 1830s, he continued to work, and proved a strong influence on such younger artists, as is suggested by his illustrations to R S Surtees' *Jorrocks' Jaunts and Jollities* (1843), which paved the way for JOHN LEECH.

Alken died in poverty on 7 April 1851 in Kentish Town. His funeral was paid for by one of his sons-in-law.

Of his own children, Henry Thomas and Sefferein John became artists, though Henry's output includes many copies of works by his father.

His work is represented in numerous public collections, including the British Museum and the V&A; and the New York Public Library.

Further reading:

Timothy Clayton and Anita McConnell, 'Alken family (*per* 1745-1852)', H C G Matthew and Brian Harrison (eds), *Oxford Dictionary of National Biography*, Oxford University Press, 2004, vol 1, pp 747-748

Stephen Deuchar, 'Alken (2) Henry (Thomas) Alken (*b* London, 12 Oct 1785; *d* London, 7 April 1851)', Jane Turner (ed), *The Dictionary of Art*, London: Macmillan, 1996, vol 1, p 647

George Kendall, *Henry Alken*, London: The Studio, 1929

Aubrey Noakes, *The World of Henry Alken*, London: Witherby 1952

Walter Shaw Sparrow, *Henry Alken*, London: Williams and Norgate, 1927

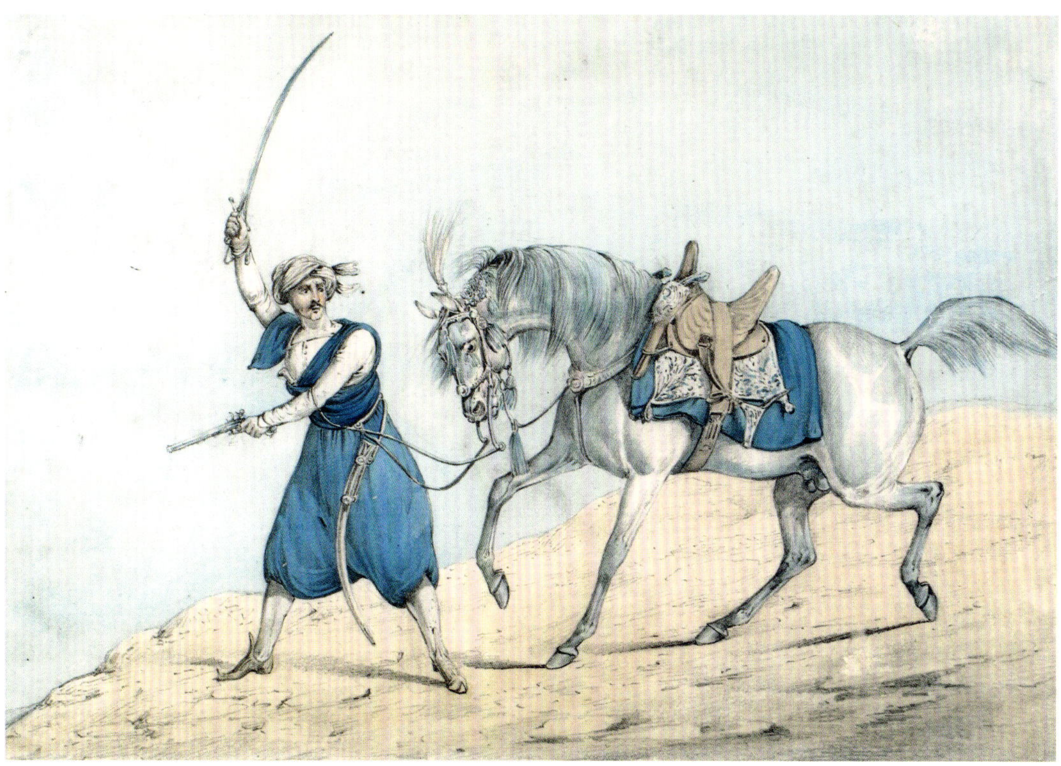

90 PERSIAN WITH HORSE
watercolour and pencil
9 ½ x 13 inches

HENRY ALKEN

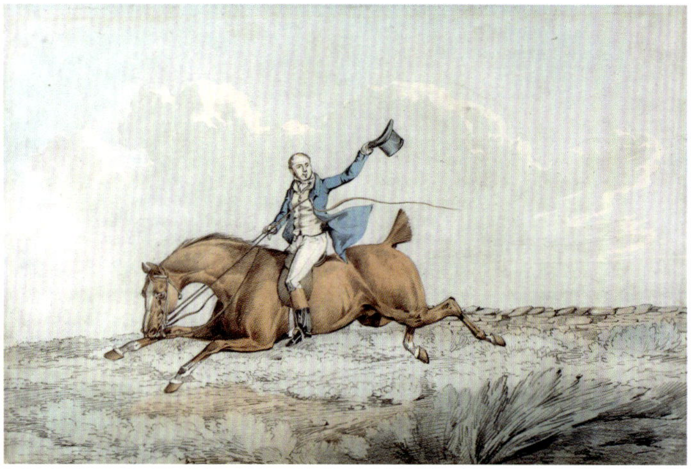

91 WHIPPING IT (left)
watercolour and pencil
8 x 10 inches

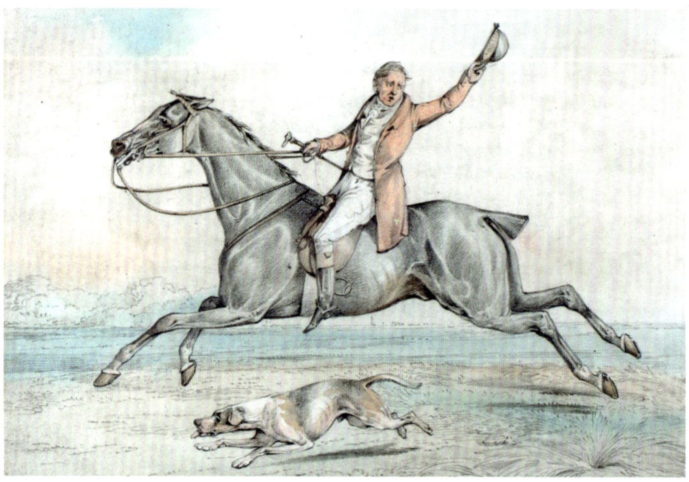

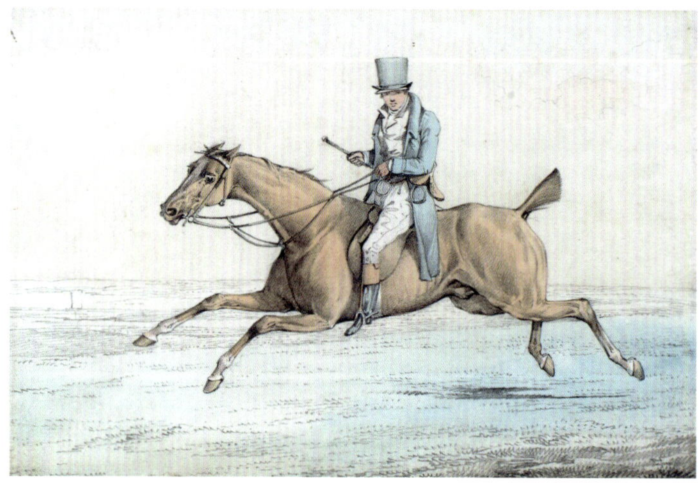

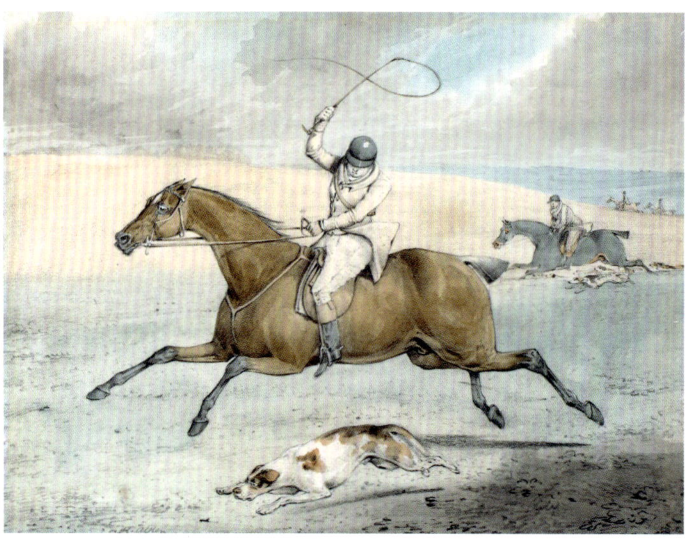

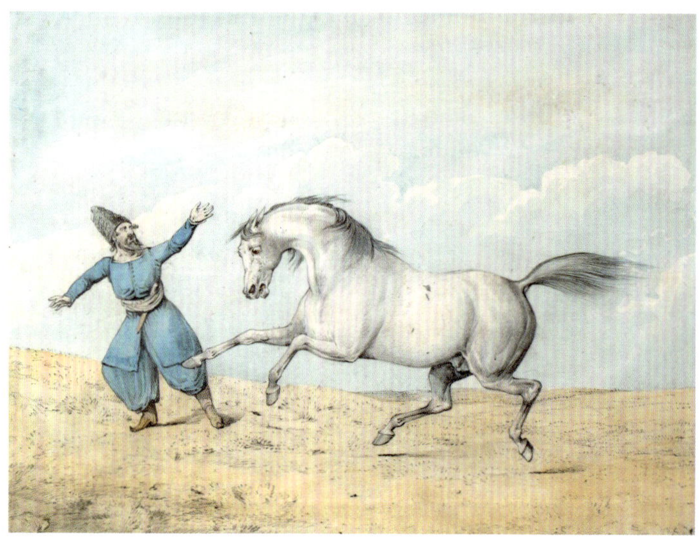

92 TALLY HO
watercolour and pencil
7 x 10 ¼ inches

93 TROTTING ON
watercolour and pencil
7 x 10 inches

94 VIEW HALLO
watercolour and pencil
8 ¼ x 12 ½ inches

95 ARAB WITH STALLION
watercolour and pencil
10 ¾ x 14 inches

GEORGE CRUIKSHANK

George Cruikshank (1792-1878)

George Cruikshank was the leading caricaturist and illustrator of his generation who, in a long and prolific career, managed to temper his style from Regency rumbustiousness to Victorian gentility.

The second son of the caricaturist ISAAC CRUIKSHANK, George Cruikshank was born in Bloomsbury, London on 27 September 1792, probably at the family home at 27 Duke Street (now Coptic Street). By 1808, the family had moved to 117 Dorset Street (now Dorset Rise), Salisbury Square, close to St Bride's, Fleet Street. Like his elder brother, Robert, he received a basic education at a school in Edgware.

Working with his father from an early age, Cruikshank began to publish in 1806. Then, following his father's death from alcohol abuse in 1811, he supported the family through his work as a graphic artist, gradually becoming the leading political caricaturist of his day. He completed James Gillray's last work for the publisher Hannah Humphrey, and collaborated with the radical publisher William Hone, as well as producing many caricatures of his own. Turning to book illustration in 1820, he worked with his brother, Robert, and the writer, Pierce Egan, on *Life in London* (1820-21), which surveyed the capital's highs and lows through the lives of two friends, Tom and Jerry.

From 1823, the Cruikshank family lived at 11 Myddleton Terrace, overlooking Claremont Square, Pentonville. In the following year, George rented 25 Myddleton Terrace, and continued to live there following his marriage in 1827. (His first wife, Mary Ann, suffered from ill health and would die childless in 1849.)

Throughout the 1820s, as he established himself as an illustrator, Cruikshank became increasingly conservative, moulding his grotesque style to the sense of humour of a respectable middle-class public. William Makepeace Thackeray wrote that it was Cruikshank who 'brought English pictorial humour and children acquainted', and this was achieved in great part by his edition of the Grimm brothers' *German Popular Stories* (1823). Almanacs were issued from 1835 to 1853 under the artist's name and these were succeeded by *George Cruikshank's Magazine* (1853-54). But he did not exclude the seamier side of life from his visual world, and showed great sensitivity towards misery, vice and crime in Charles Dickens' *Oliver Twist* (1838) and the romances of Harrison Ainsworth.

Cruikshank's conversion to the teetotal cause in the late 1840s gave a focus to his moral outrage and invigorated a flagging reputation. He worked intensively in the last thirty years of his life, primarily for the Temperance League, producing such striking images as the two series of prints, *The Bottle* (1847) and *The Drunkard's Children* (1848), and the vast masterpiece, *The Worship of Bacchus* (1863, Tate). The critic, John Ruskin did not appreciate this turn in Cruikshank's career and tried to assist him, artistically and financially, by encouraging him to illustrate a new edition of Grimm. However, his work on this project seemed coarse to Ruskin and it was never completed.

In 1850, Cruikshank had married for a second time, to Eliza Widdowson, a niece of the publisher Charles Baldwyn, who had commissioned the first volumes of *German Popular Stories*. They moved with family members and servants into 48 Mornington Place, Mornington Crescent (which would be renamed 263 Hampstead Road in 1864). However, the apparent respectability of the household proved deceptive. In 1854, the housemaid, Adelaide Attree, admitted she was pregnant, and Eliza dismissed her without realising that George was the father. George set up Adelaide in a nearby flat that he used as a studio, and is believed to have fathered a further ten children with her during the next twenty years. Maintaining two households inevitably put a strain on his finances, and at a time that his work was markedly less successful. On his death, Eliza discovered that he had left his entire estate to Adelaide while actually being insolvent.

Cruikshank died at home of an acute respiratory infection on 1 February 1878. First buried at Kensal Green, his body was later removed to St Paul's Cathedral as an acknowledgement of his work for the temperance movement.

His work is represented in numerous public collections, including the British Museum, The Courtauld Gallery and the V&A; and the New York Public Library, Princeton University Library and the University of Delaware Library.

Further reading:

John Buchanan-Brown, *The Book Illustrations of George Cruikshank*, Newton Abbot: David and Charles, 1980
A M Cohn, *George Cruikshank: A Catalogue Raisonné*, London: The Bookman's Journal, 1924
William Feaver, *George Cruikshank*, London: Arts Council of Great Britain, 1974
Ruari McLean, 'Cruikshank (3) George Cruikshank (*b* London, 27 Sept 1792; *d* London, 1 Feb 1878)', Jane Turner (ed), *The Dictionary of Art*, London: Macmillan, 1996, vol 8, pp 217-218
Robert L Patten, 'Cruikshank, George (1792-1878)', H C G Matthew and Brian Harrison (eds), *Oxford Dictionary of National Biography*, Oxford University Press, 2004, vol 14, pp 520-528
Robert L Patten, *George Cruikshank's Life, Art and Times*, Cambridge: Lutterworth, 1992 & 1996 (2 vols)
John Wardroper, *The Caricatures of George Cruikshank*, London: Gordon Fraser, 1977

GEORGE CRUIKSHANK

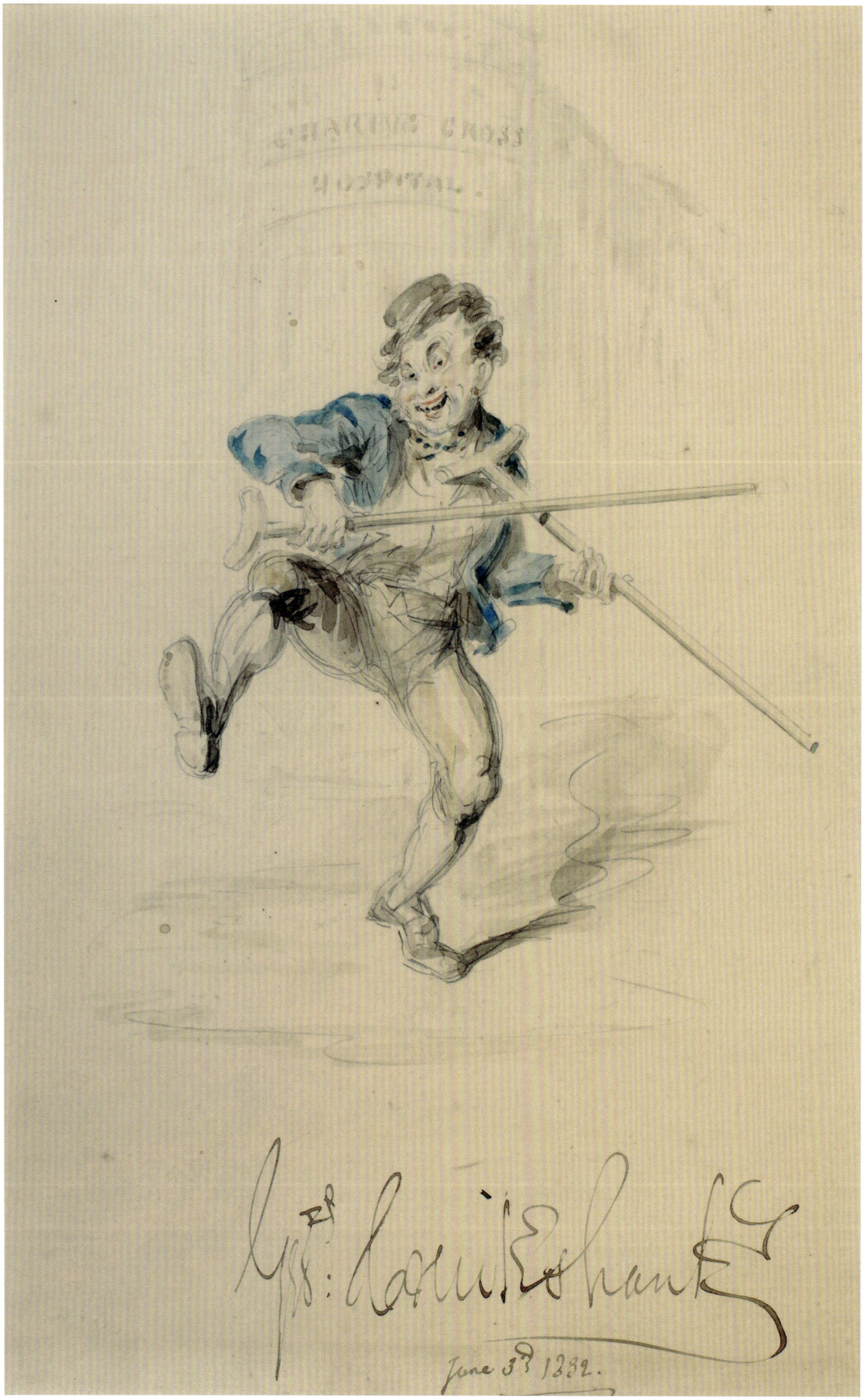

96 DANCING WITH CRUTCHES
signed and dated 'June 3rd 1832'
watercolour and pencil
12 ½ x 9 inches

HABLOT KNIGHT BROWNE

Hablot Knight Browne (1815-1882), known as 'Phiz'

Under the name of Phiz, Hablot Knight Browne became known as Charles Dickens' essential illustrator, responsible for imaging the immortal characters to ten of the major novels, from *The Pickwick Papers* to *A Tale of Two Cities*. He was also associated with the popular fiction of Charles Lever, his illustrations for which communicated his love of life, especially its equestrian aspects. A versatile artist, in technique as well as subject, he could etch his own designs, and also painted in oil and watercolour.

Descended from Huguenot refugees, H K Browne was born in Lower Kennington Lane, London in June or July 1815, and baptised on 21 December 1815 at St Mary's, Lambeth. He was brought up as the fourteenth child of the merchant, William Lowder Browne. However, it is now known (as the result of the researches of Valerie Browne Lester) that he was the illegitimate son of W L Browne's daughter, Kate, and Captain Nicolas Hablot, a cavalry officer in Napoleon's imperial guard.

In 1822, W L Browne fell in to debt and absconded to the United States, leaving his wife to bring up the children in a house in Euston Square, which she did with the help of relatives and friends.

H K Browne was educated at a boarding school in Botesdale, Suffolk, where the headmaster, the Rev William Haddock, encouraged his artistic talents. He was removed from the school by his brother-in-law (that is, his uncle) Elhanan Bicknell, who then financed his apprenticeship with the engravers William and Edward Finden, of Southampton Place, Euston Square, London. (Bicknell was a whaling magnate and one of J M W TURNER's leading patrons.) Browne's studies included visits to the British Museum and classes at William Taylor's Living Model Academy, in Upper St Martin's Lane (alongside William Etty and William Makepeace Thackeray). Though his attitude to these studies has been described as 'desultory' (Patten and Lester, in Matthew and Harrison 2004, p 165), he did win the silver Isis medal from the Society of Arts for a large etching of John Gilpin's ride in 1833.

In 1834, Browne quit his apprenticeship and set up a studio with his fellow student, Robert Young, at 3 Furnival's Inn, Holborn (across the court from Charles Dickens' lodgings). From this time until his marriage in 1840, he lived at Bedford Place, and then in the artists' quarter north of Oxford Street: at Newman Street, Warren Street, and Fitzroy Street. Browne and Young complemented each other's talents perfectly, with Browne excelling at drawing and Young at printing, and they remained friends until Browne's death.

In spring 1836, the publishers Chapman and Hall asked Browne to illustrate *Sunday under Three Heads* (1836), an anti-Sabbatarian pamphlet written by Charles Dickens, under the name 'Timothy Sparks', and to contribute illustrations to a new monthly periodical, *The Library of Fiction*.

As a result of his work on these publications, Dickens employed Browne to illustrate his first full-length novel, *The Posthumous Papers of the Pickwick Club* (1839), as a replacement for Robert Seymour (who had commited suicide) and Robert Buss (who proved incompetent). At an early stage in this project, Browne began to sign his work 'Phiz', which harmonised with Dickens' pseudonym, 'Boz'. The success of their collaboration helped establish Browne as Dickens' leading illustrator. Over the following three decades, he would provide images for ten of the major novels (up to and including *A Tale of Two Cities* in 1859), for reprints and for shorter publications.

During the late 1830s, Browne and Dickens were sufficiently close to travel together: to France and Belgium (July 1837), Yorkshire (February 1838, as preparation for *Nicholas Nickleby*), and Wales and the Midlands (autumn 1838).

At the close of the decade, Browne illustrated *Harry Lorrequer* by the Irish writer and physician, Charles Lever; so he began the second of his two close collaborations, comprising seventeen novels and a collected edition published over four decades. The subjects of these novels gave him many opportunities to draw on his love of horses and hunting, and when he visited Lever in Ireland they would go out riding together.

In the same period, Browne also began to contribute to numerous periodicals, including the *New Sporting Magazine* (1839-43), *Punch* (1842-44, 1850-51, 1861-69), the *Illustrated London News* (1844-61), the *Illuminated Magazine* (1843-45) and *Sharpe's London Magazine* (1845-47).

In 1840, Browne married Susannah Reynolds, the daughter of a Norfolk Baptist minister, at Holy Trinity Church, Marylebone, and together they rented a house on Howland Street. They would have nine children to survive into adulthood.

Always ambitious to be more than an illustrator, Browne exhibited paintings at the British Institution (1843-69), and entered two preparatory 'cartoons', apparently 'tongue in cheek' (Patten and Lester, op cit, p 167), to the competition for decorations of the Houses of Parliament. However, with the development of his reputation as an illustrator, he would be increasingly preoccupied in providing images for literary texts both contemporary and classic.

In 1844, Browne superseded GEORGE CRUIKSHANK as illustrator to Harrison Ainsworth, and illustrated six of his novels, including etchings for *Mervyn Clitheroe* (completed in 1858). Other projects during the 1840s and 1850s included illustrations to new editions of novels by Walter Scott (from 1842), Henry Fielding and Tobias Smollett (1855), and frontispieces to novels by Bulwer Lytton (from 1849).

In the late 1840s, the Brownes moved out to Surrey for the sake of Susannah's health. They lived first at Thornton House, Thornton Heath; then at a new villa on Duppas Hill, Waddon; and, finally, in rural Banstead. However, in 1859, they returned to London, and settled in Notting Hill. Living first at 2 Horbury Crescent, they moved to 19 Blenheim Crescent in 1868, and then to 99 (now 239) Ladbroke Grove in 1874.

Browne's return to London, in 1859, marked the beginning of a new

HABLOT KNIGHT BROWNE, known as 'Phiz'

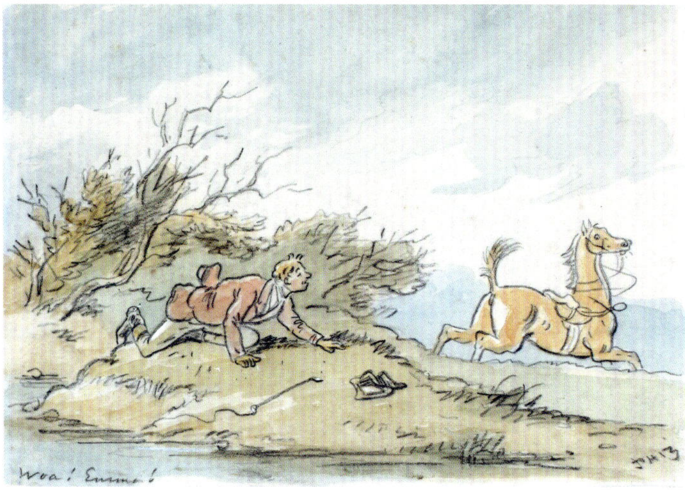

97 WOA! EMMA!
signed and inscribed with title
watercolour and pencil
5 ¼ x 7 ¼ inches

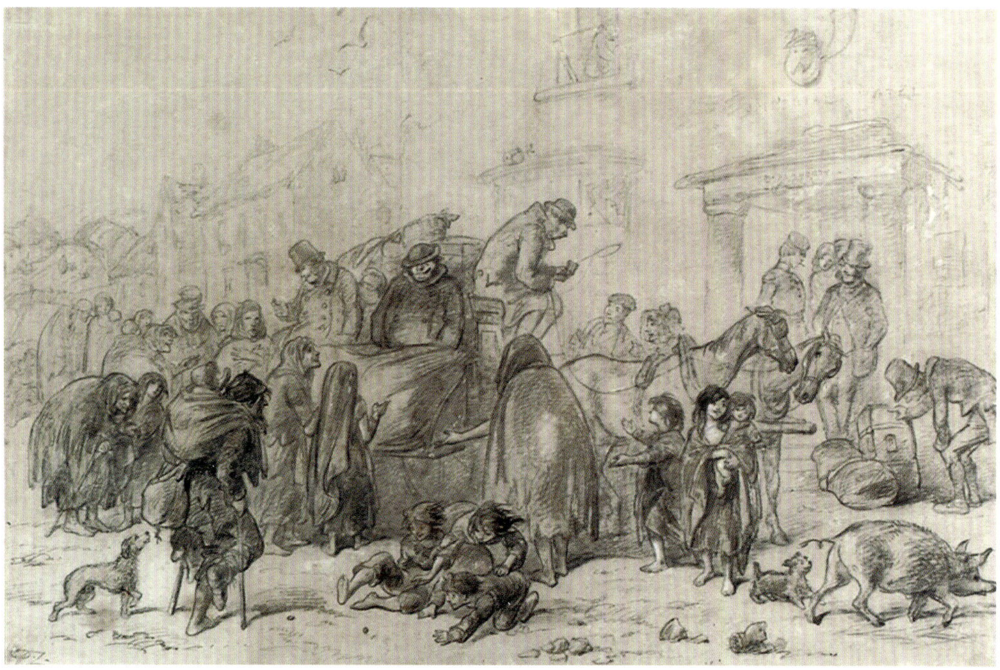

98 BEGGARS OUTSIDE THE IMPERIAL HOTEL
signed
pencil and pastel
14 ½ x 22 inches

phase in his career. Responding to changes in both the technology of the book and the tastes of readers, he diversified his talents and so re-established himself, if without recapturing the glittering success of his collaborations with Dickens and Lever. He also persevered as a painter in oil and watercolour, overcoming an episode of paralysis to his right side in 1867 to exhibit at both the Society of British Artists and the British Institution until 1869. Furthermore, he contributed illustrations to the periodical *Judy* from then until his death thirteen years later.

Never a great businessman, Browne began to suffer from poverty late in his career and, in 1880, the Royal Academy was prompted by the painters, Luke Fildes and William Powell Frith, to give him a small pension, one that had been previously assigned to George Cruikshank.

In the same year, the Brownes moved to Hove, Sussex, and lived at 8 Clarendon Villas. He died at home on 8 July 1882 of progressive paralysis and a stroke. A memorial exhibition was held at the Liverpool Art Club and the Fine Art Society, London, in 1883.

Most of Browne's children displayed and developed artistic talents, with two of his sons, Walter Robert Geoffrey and Gordon Frederick, becoming professional illustrators.

His work is represented in numerous public collections, including the V&A; and the Free Library of Philadelphia and The University of Texas at Austin.

Further reading:

John Buchanan-Brown, *Phiz! The Book Illustrations of Hablot Knight Browne*, Newton Abbot: David & Charles, 1978
Lewis Johnson, 'Browne, Hablot Knight [Phiz] (*b* London, 12 July 1815; *d* Hove, W. Sussex, 8 July 1882)', Jane Turner (ed), *The Dictionary of Art*, London: Macmillan, 1996, vol 4, pp 885-886
Valerie Browne Lester, *Phiz – The Man Who Drew Dickens*, London: Chatto & Windus, 2004
Robert L Patten and Valerie Browne Lester, 'Browne, Hablot Knight [*pseud.* Phiz] (1815–1882)', H C G Matthew and Brian Harrison (eds), *Oxford Dictionary of National Biography*, Oxford University Press, 2004, vol 8, pp 165-168

JOHN FREDERICK HERRING
John Frederick Herring junior (1815/1821-1907)

John Frederick Herring junior rivalled his father as a sporting artist, and sustained the popular family style into the late Victorian period.

John Frederick Herring junior was born in the Parish of St George's, Doncaster, South Yorkshire. He was the son of John Frederick Herring senior, a coachman who became one of England's great sporting artists.

Records show that Ann Herring gave birth to two sons named John Frederick Herring junior: one born on 21 June 1815, and the second baptised – with a sister named Sarah – on 22 May 1821. It may be that the first child had died, and the second is the artist described here, though the census of 1861 records the surviving John junior as having been born in 1815.

In 1830, the Herring family moved to Six Mile Bottom, between Cambridge and Newmarket, the headquarters of racing. During the following three years, John junior developed as his father's assistant, while two of his brothers, Charles and Benjamin, also trained as painters. Yet, when the family moved on to London, John junior remained in East Anglia and established himself as an animal painter.

By 1836, John junior began to rival his father. In subsequent years, their relationship deteriorated to such an extent that he became the only surviving child not to be mentioned in his father's will, following his death in 1865.

On the evidence of the national censuses taken in 1851 and 1861, John junior married Emma Jane of Great Wilbraham, Cambridgeshire. They settled in the village and together had at least two children. During this period, it seems that he worked as a brewer as well as an animal painter, though he was well enough known to have work reproduced in the *Sporting Magazine*.

As an exhibiting artist, John junior came to the fore in the 1860s, and began to show work at leading London societies: the Royal Academy, the British Institution and especially the Society of British Artists. The paintings were often of wider views in looser handling than those from earlier in his career.

The exhibition catalogues for the early 1860s give John junior's address as '4 Haymarket' and then '212 Piccadilly', these being the studios of Alexander Frederick Rolfe. Rolfe was a painter of angling and sporting subjects, who also showed at the Society of British Artists, and had collaborated with J F Herring senior, but was turning increasingly to photography at the time. During this decade, John junior married for a second time. His second wife was Rolfe's sister, Catherine, known as Kate, so that he and Rolfe became brothers-in-law. Kate was a member of the Society of Women Artists, who also exhibited sporting pictures. (In addition, it has been suggested that Rolfe married a woman named Harriet Ann Herring, who had been born in Nottingham in 1823; if so, she may have been related to John junior.)

In 1865, John junior built himself a tall, slightly Gothic house in Wilbraham Road, Fulbourn, Cambridgeshire. It was known as 'The Poplars', though called 'The Willows' in the census for 1881. He lived in this house until the end of his life, and died in Cambridge on 6 March 1907. He was survived by his second wife, Kate, who died in 1928.

His work is represented in the collections of the British Sporting Art Trust Gallery, Newmarket.

Further reading:
Oliver Beckett, *J F Herring and Sons*, London: J A Allen, 1981
Robert Fountain, 'Herring, John Frederick, senior (1795–1865)', H C G Matthew and Brian Harrison (eds), *Oxford Dictionary of National Biography*, Oxford University Press, 2004, vol 26, pp 813-815

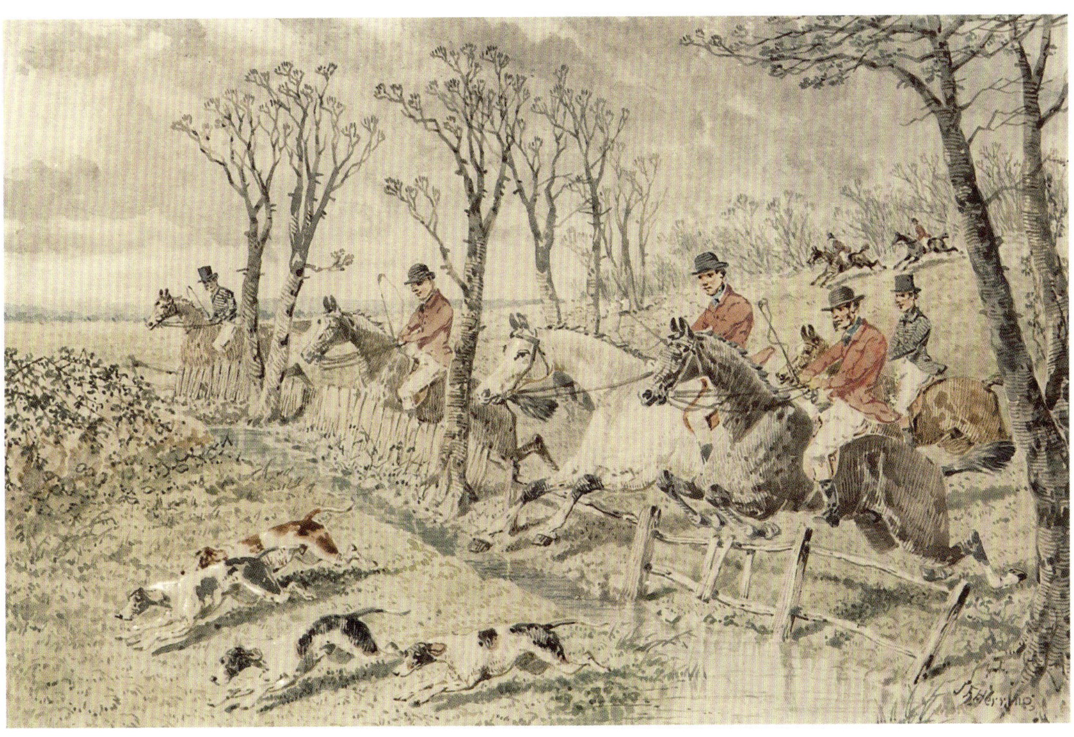

99 THE JUMP
signed
watercolour
8 ¼ x 12 ¼ inches

JOHN FREDERICK HERRING

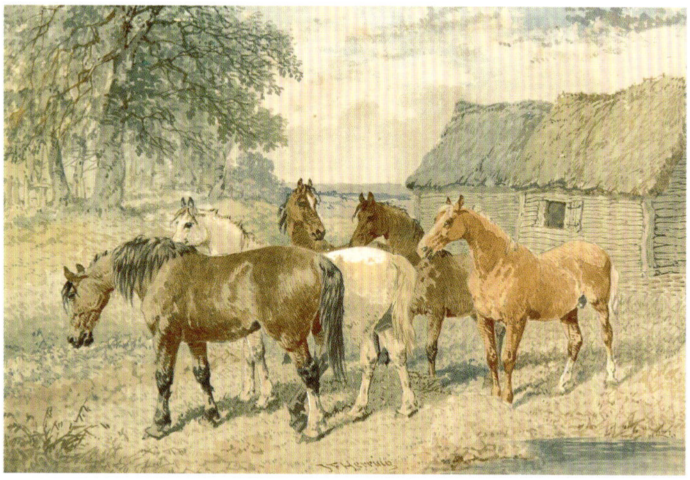

100 THE STABLE (left)
signed
watercolour with bodycolour
8 x 11 ¾ inches

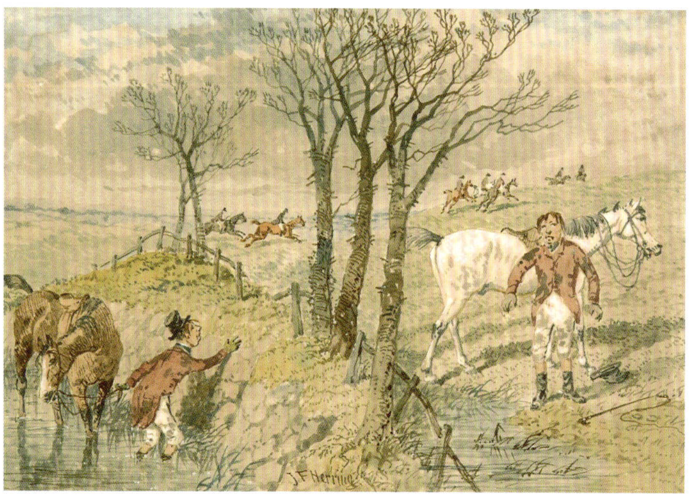

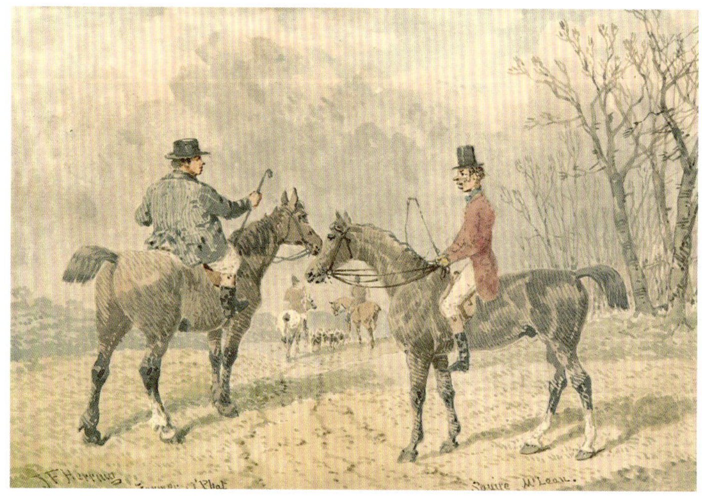

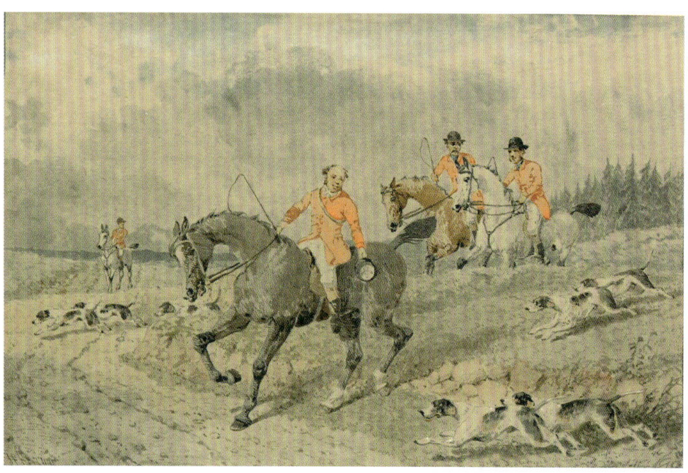

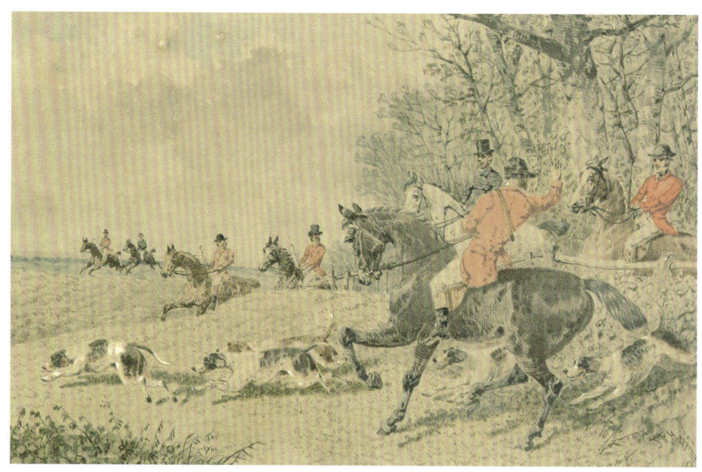

101 A REQUEST FOR HELP
signed
watercolour with bodycolour
7 ¾ x 11 inches

103 HATS OFF!
signed
watercolour with bodycolour
8 ½ x 12 ¼ inches

102 FARMER O'PHAT AND SQUIRE M'LEAN
signed and inscribed 'Farmer O'Phat' and Squire 'M'Lean'
watercolour
7 ¾ x 10 ½ inches

104 TALLY HO!
signed
watercolour with bodycolour
8 ½ x 12 ½ inches

JOHN LEECH
John Leech (1817-1864)

John Leech was a fluent and incisive draughtsman, who had great success as a cartoonist for *Punch* and as a literary illustrator, especially of John Surtees' sporting subjects.

John Leech was born at 28 Bennett Street, off Stamford Street, Southwark, London on 29 August 1817. His father, a native of Ireland, was the assistant proprietor of the London Coffee House on Ludgate Hill. Educated at Charterhouse School, he began to study medicine at St Bartholomew's Hospital at the age of fifteen, and worked for a while as an apprentice doctor. However, he was forced to abandon this medical career following his father's bankruptcy.

Soon turning to his talent for drawing to develop a career, Leech produced a pamphlet – *Etchings and Sketchings* (1835) – in his preferred medium of lithography. In 1836, he gained further, direct experience of the handling of lithography when he visited Paris and fell under the influence of such French artists as Honoré Daumier and Paul Gavarni. Later he would meet the caricaturist Comte Amedée de Noë (known as 'Cham') and the painter Edouard Manet. From 1838, he also took lessons from J Orrin Smith in wood engraving, the medium more widely used in British periodicals.

Leech established himself with contributions to *Bentley's Miscellany* in 1840, and in 1841 submitted a drawing to *Punch*. Two years later, he began to produce cuts regularly for the periodical, sharing work with John Tenniel, and excelling in images of fashionable life. During this period, he also developed close friendships with the novelists Charles Dickens and William Makepeace Thackeray. He and Dickens collaborated on a number of books, beginning with *A Christmas Carol* (1843), and throughout the 1840s they holidayed together and shared the stage in some memorable amateur productions. A former Charterhouse contemporary, Thackeray wrote in his obituary of Leech that 'he always looked at society from the gentleman's point of view'. Leech was instrumental in the 'gentrification' of *Punch*, and became well known for his many illustrations of sporting and hunting subjects, most notably for J R Surtees's *Handley Cross* (1854). As late as 1860, Leech received lessons in oils from another friend, John Everett Millais, in order to prepare for a – highly successful – exhibition at the Egyptian Hall (1862).

Leech died at his home at 6 The Terrace, Kensington, London on 29 October 1864, and was buried at Kensal Green cemetery on 4 November, with Tenniel among his pall-bearers. He had been married to Annie Eaton from 1842, and had a daughter and a son.

In the following years, John Ruskin tried to help provide for the sisters of Leech, by organising the sale of his outline drawings. In 1872, they were exhibited at the Gallery, 9 Conduit Street with an accompanying catalogue written by Ruskin. Yet, even with his support, the scheme failed, and he himself was the largest purchaser. He placed the drawings in such collections at the Museum of St George, Walkley, Sheffield (now the Ruskin Collection of Museum Sheffield).

His work is also represented in the collections of the British Museum.

Further reading:

Simon Houfe, *John Leech and the Victorian Scene*, Woodbridge: Antique Collectors' Club, 1984

Simon Houfe, 'Leech, John (1817-1864)', H C G Matthew and Brian Harrison (eds), *Oxford Dictionary of National Biography*, Oxford University Press, 2004, vol 33, pp 133-135

Simon Houfe, 'Leech, John (*b* Southwark, London, 29 Aug 1817; *d* London, 30 Oct 1864)', Jane Turner (ed), *The Dictionary of Art*, London: Macmillan, 1996, vol 19, pp 61-62

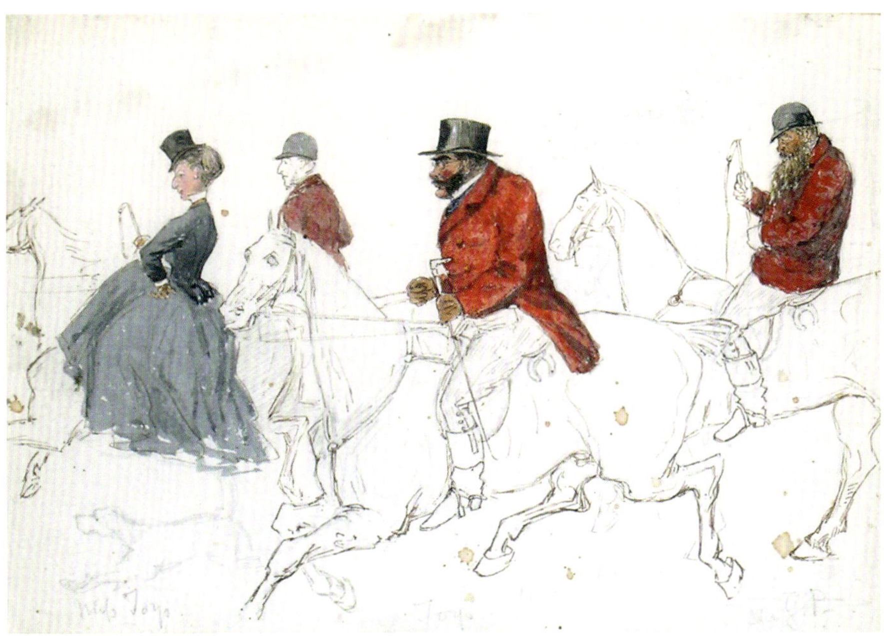

105 MR AND MRS JOYS OUT HUNTING
signed and inscribed 'Mrs Joys, joys'
pen ink and watercolour
6 ¾ x 9 ½ inches

3: THE EXPERIMENTAL DRIVE IN WATERCOLOUR

JOHN SWETE
The Reverend John Swete (1752-1821), born John Tripe

John Swete is best remembered for his illustrated journals, and other writings and drawings, which vividly describe and delineate Devon as he knew it.

John Swete was born John Tripe on 1 July 1752 at Ashburton in Devon, the son of Nicholas Tripe, a surgeon. He was educated at Ashburton Free School and then at Eton College (1767-70, through the assistance of Sir Robert Palk). He then went up to University College, Oxford (BA 1774, MA 1777).

Having taken holy orders, he became curate at Highweek, Newton Abbot, in 1775. A year later, he moved to the parish of Kenn, Exeter, at Sir Robert Palk's request, and settled at Oxton House, Kenton, the former home of the Martyns, his paternal grandmother's family. In 1780, he changed his name by act of parliament (from Tripe to Swete) to become eligible for an inheritance from the mother of his godfather, Adrian John Swete. As a result he came into the possession of Traine Manor, Modbury.

Though he was made a prebendary of Exeter Cathedral in 1781, Swete seems to have become more interested in managing his estate and in developing antiquarian and topographical interests. For instance, he excavated a number of barrows on the Haldon Ridge, west of the Exe Estuary in 1780; while, a year later, he rebuilt Oxton House.

Then, in April 1783, Swete resigned his curacy at Kenn and set out on a tour of Wales, the Lake District and Scotland. While in Matlock, Derbyshire, he met his future wife; they married on 1 January 1784, and would have fourteen children.

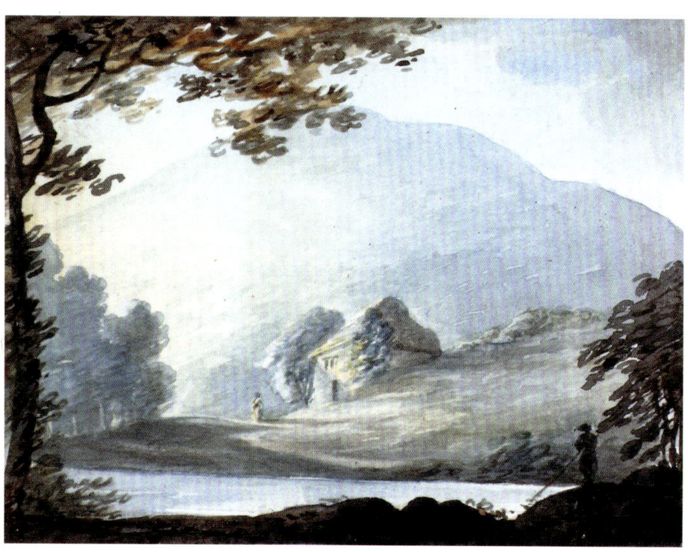

106 A DEVON COTTAGE
signed and dated 1792 on reverse
watercolour
4 ½ x 5 ¼ inches

Between 1789 and 1800, Swete undertook the project that has made his name, recording his extensive travels in Devon in a series of illustrated journals (which were published in four volumes, 1998-2001). His other antiquarian contributions include images for the *Antiquarian and Topographical Cabinet* (1808) and *Britton's Beauties of England and Wales* (1813). His watercolours show the influence of WILLIAM PAYNE.

Swete also composed at least six volumes of poetry, and contributed several poems to Richard Polwhele's *Poems chiefly by Gentlemen of Devonshire and Cornwall* (1792). However, from that year he entered a protracted dispute over plagiarism with Richard Polwhele. Eventually, Swete cut off all communication, and it was left to Polwhele to make amends, writing a tribute to Swete following his death on 25 October 1821 at Oxton House.

His work is represented in the collections of Devon County Record Office (Exeter).

Further reading:
J A Marchand, 'Swete [*formerly* Tripe], John (1752–1821)', H C G Matthew and Brian Harrison (eds) *Oxford Dictionary of National Biography*, Oxford University Press, 2004, vol 53, pp 459-460

Old Gateway, Tor Abbey
Having now made my retour to Torquay, and having scrutinised it with a picturesque eye, I shall now turn to Tor Abbey. From Torquay the proper road to the house and grounds passes by Tor Church, but there is a footpath, which by a steep and rugged ascent rises from the building of the western part of the cove, and is carried on the elevated ridge of an immense cliff of marble, protected only from the precipice by a stunted fence of brushwood.

Between the trunks of a row of noble oaks whose side and upper branches formed a sylvan arch, I had a most pleasing view of the front of Tor Abbey House with its wing and the old gateway.

(taken from Peter Hunt (ed), *Devon's Age of Elegance, described by the diaries of the Reverend John Swete, Lady Paterson and Miss Mary Cornish*, Exeter: Devon Books, 1984, p 136)

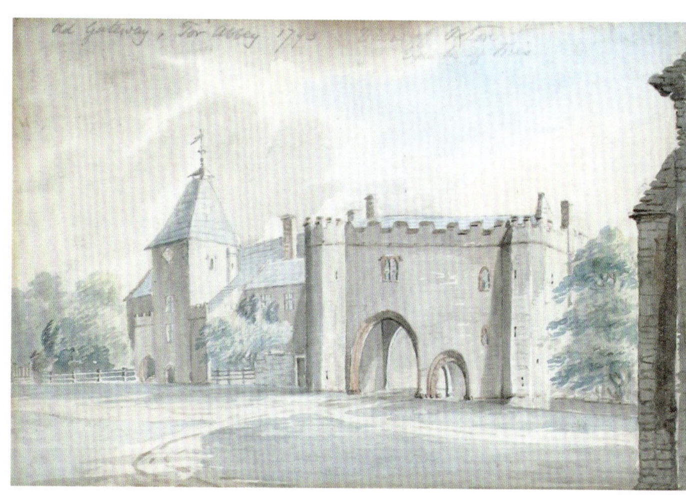

107 OLD GATEWAY, TOR ABBEY
inscribed with title and 'View of Oxton', and dated 1793
watercolour
6 ½ x 9 ½ inches
watercolour drawing of Oxton 1793 on reverse

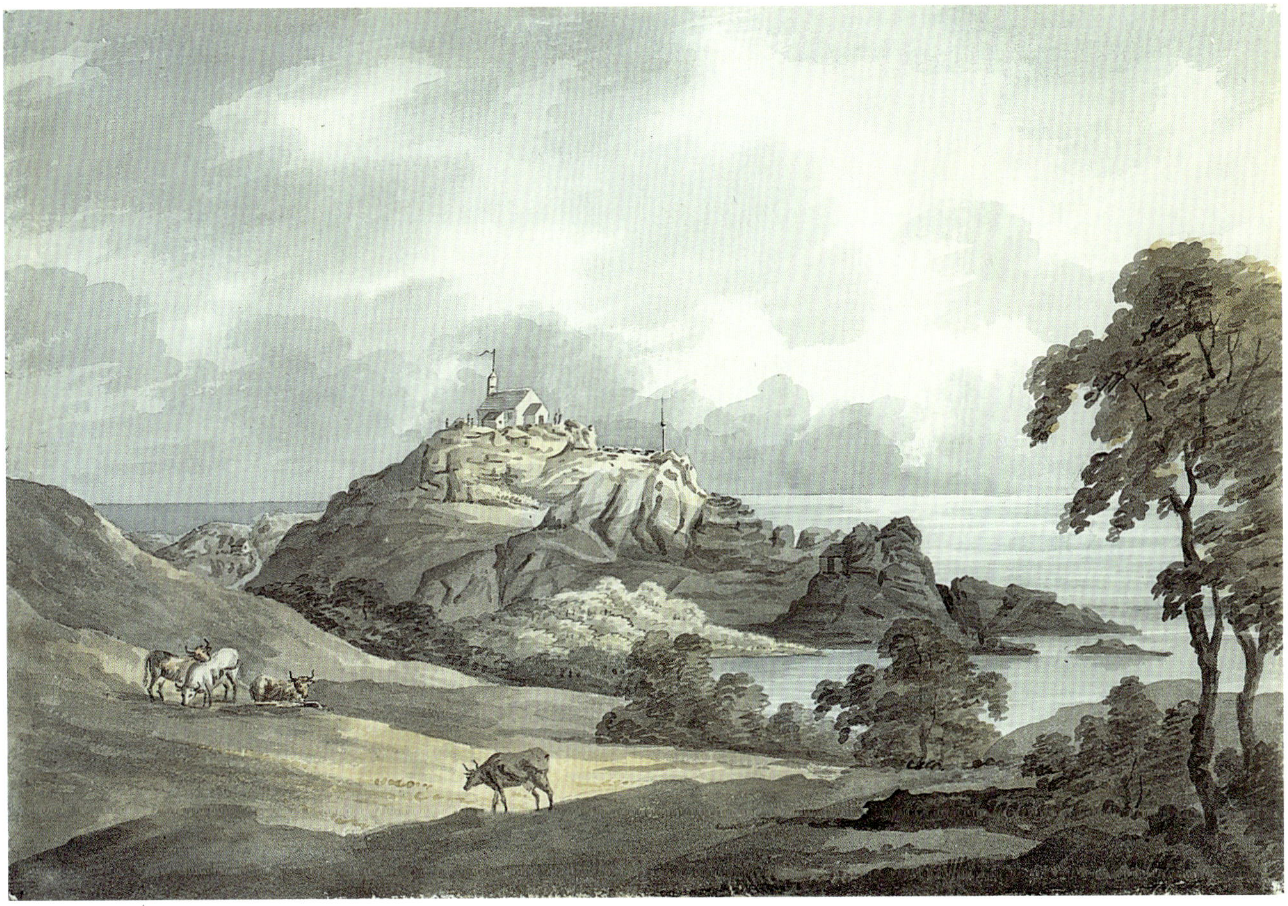

108 THE LIGHT HOUSE, AT ILFRACOMB, TAKEN NEAR THE QUAY FIELDS
inscribed with title on mount
watercolour
8 x 10 ½ inches
Literature: H L Mallalieu, *The Dictionary of British Watercolour Artists*, Woodbridge: Antique Collectors' Club, 1979, vol 2, p 522 (where it is described as 'a particularly good example')

The Light House, at Ilfracomb, Taken Near the Quay Fields

A mile or two ere I came to Ilfordcoombe, a scene extremely romantic, of wild mishapen rocks, towering to the skies presented itself. Soon after the Church appeared, seated on an eminence above the town, of which riding through a long descending street for near a mile, I at length reached the Quay, where the Inn was situated. There having breakfasted, under the guidance of a rope-walk I was insensibly led to a hill on the South West of the town; from whence I had a delightful view of the Sea – a long line of buildings stretching themselves from the South to the northern point, where they are seen terminating in a high point of land, thrusting itself far into the harbour, and on which is erected a Light House – the tops of the Vessels at Anchor in the Quay were visible over the houses and closing the scene. Cliffs at one time broken into various rude and mishapen masses, at others, towering up perpendicularly to an immense height.

The trade of this town consists for the most part in coasting voyages from Wales, transporting coals from Pembrokeshire and Glamorgan to Cornwall and bringing back Copper and tin, which are render'd a marketable commodity at the Smelting houses of Neath, Swansea and other places where Coal abounds.

Within a few years indeed, another article of Commerce hath been revived, which for the space of forty years had been unaccountably disused. I allude to the capture and seasoning of Herrings, which at periodical times are here taken in vast quantities, and (being cured) are afterwards exported to the Continent…

In addition to these articles of commerce I must not omit a manufactory for rope and cordage, which is carried on to a considerable extent, and which finds a ready sale amongst the numerous Vessels which frequent this port – than which a more commodious one is not to be met with, on the Northern coast of Somerset, Devon or Cornwall, the harbour having the advantage of a Lighthouse, and, of being secured by a strong and handsome pier build by the Ancestors of Sir Bouchier Wrey to whom the Manor belongs…

Returning through a part of the long street and ascending a steep hill towards the East, I had a charming farewell view of the town, the lighthouse, the harbour, and the wild mountainous rocks, which environ it, forming an uncommonly eccentric and romantic scenery.

The Reverend John Swete, *Tour to the North of Devon, undertaken in 1789* (taken from Todd Gray and Margery Rowe (eds), *Travels in Georgian Devon. The Illustrated Journals of the Reverend John Swete*, vol 1, Exeter: Devon Books, 1997, pp 36-37)

FRANCIS NICHOLSON
Francis Nicholson, OWS (1753-1844)

Francis Nicholson made his name as a landscape watercolourist in a Romantic vein. By combining a traditional approach to composition with an interest in technical experiments, he became a popular teacher.

Francis Nicholson was born in Pickering, Yorkshire on 14 November 1753, the son of a weaver. His father discouraged his interest in art, but did allow him to go to Scarborough to study with a copyist of Old Masters. Back in Pickering, he found work as a draughtsman of animals for members of the local gentry. After two years, he went to London, where he received lessons from Conrad Martin Metz; however, he had to return home due to a lack of money. After he painted the ceiling of a large summerhouse for a local magistrate, he began to gain commissions for portraits and sporting subjects.

In 1783, Nicholson settled in Whitby, where he married. He attempted to become a portraitist but, unable to flatter his clients, he turned to painting their houses, and this led him to produce landscapes in watercolour. His pictures were sent for sale in London and Scarborough, and exhibited infrequently at the Royal Academy of Arts (between 1789 and 1803). During the same period he also contributed drawings for John Walker's *The Copper-Plate Magazine.*

Nicholson moved to Knaresborough in 1792, and then to Ripon in 1794. There he gave lessons to John Pearson (who passed off his drawings as those of Nicholson), and was patronised by Walter Fawkes of Farnley Hall and the Marquess of Bute. The sketches that he made while touring with the Marquess, to Bute and other parts of Scotland, provided him with subjects for years to come, while his interest in the country was revived by a visit to its lowlands in 1812.

In the late 1790s, Nicholson moved south, living near friends at Weybridge, Surrey, and then in London: in Somers Town (by 1803) and at 52 Charlotte Street (from 1810). Almost immediately, he helped to raise the profile of watercolour, developing his own practice as a drawing master and, in 1804, becoming a founder of the Society of Painters in Water Colours. When the society was reformed as the Society of Painters in Oil and Water-Colours in 1812, he became its President, but resigned a year later to focus on his flourishing teaching career and, increasingly, experiments with techniques and pigments. The results of these interests were published as *The Practice of Drawing and Painting Landscapes from Nature, in Watercolours* (1820). This was soon followed by selections of 800 lithographs, issued as *Sketches of British Scenery* (1821) and *Six Views of Scarborough* (1822). He continued to accept occasional commissions, notably from Richard Colt Hoare, for a series of watercolours of Stourhead, his celebrated landscape garden (1813-16).

He died at home in Charlotte Street on 6 March 1844.

His nephew George Nicholson, his son Alfred Nicholson and his daughters Sophia (Ayrton) and Marianne (Crofton) were all watercolourists who worked in his manner.

His work is represented in the Government Art Collection, and numerous public collections, including the British Museum.

Further reading:

Randall Davies, 'Francis Nicholson, 1753-1844: Some Family Letters and Papers', *The Old Water Colour Society's Club,* vol 8, pp 1-39
Simon Fenwick, 'Nicholson, Francis (1753-1844)', H C G Matthew and Brian Harrison (eds), *Oxford Dictionary of National Biography*, Oxford University Press, 2004, vol 40, pp 813-814
Basil Somerset Long, 'Francis Nicholson: Painter and Lithographer', *Walker's Quarterly*, no 14, January 1924, pp 1-43
Huon Mallalieu, 'Francis Nicholson: a doughty biter of feeding hands', *Water-Colours and Drawings*, vol 4, no 3, 1989, pp 15-18
Scott Wilcox, 'Nicholson, Francis (*b* Pickering, N Yorks, 14 Nov 1753; *d* London, 6 March 1844)', Jane Turner (ed), *The Dictionary of Art*, London: Macmillan, 1996, vol 23, pp 104-105

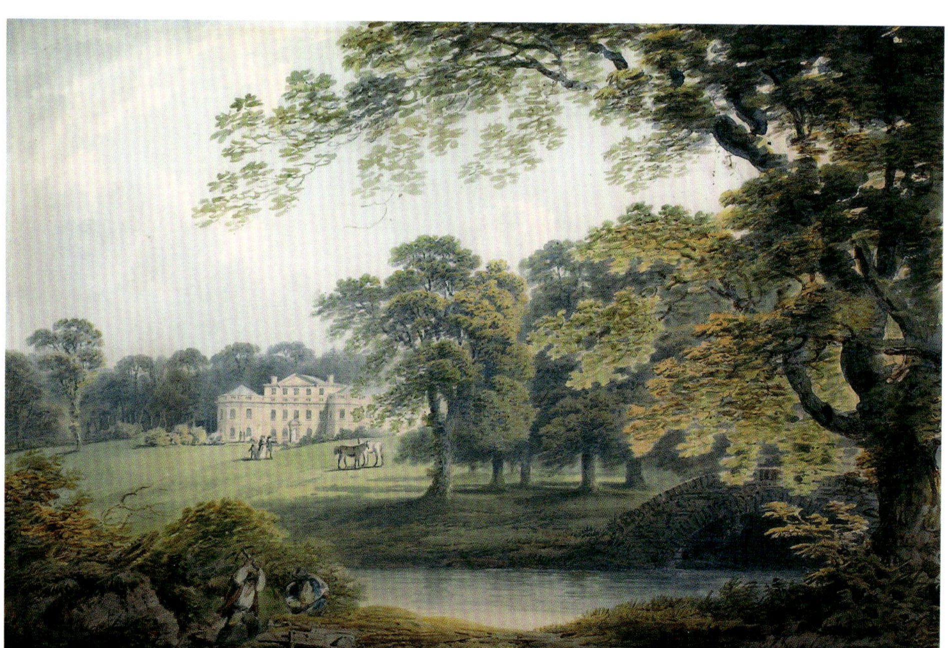

109 RUDDING HOUSE, YORKSHIRE
THE SEAT OF THE RT HON LORD LOUGHBOROUGH
watercolour
11 ½ x 16 inches

FRANCIS NICHOLSON

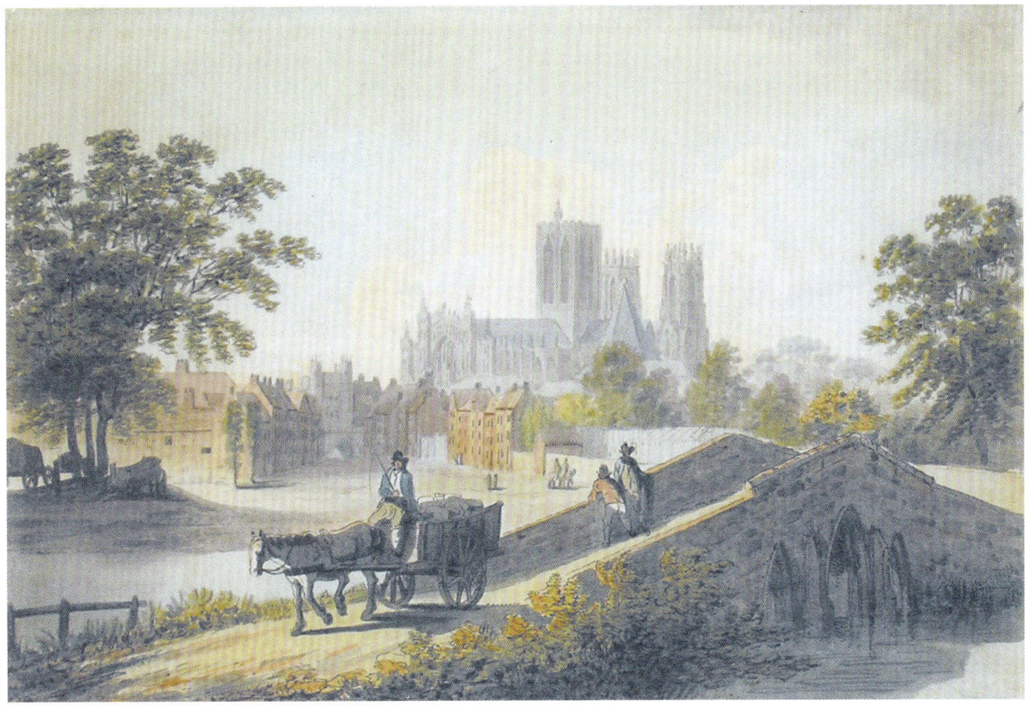

110 RIPON MINSTER
pen ink and watercolour
7 x 10 inches

WILLIAM THOMAS BREE
The Reverend William Thomas Bree (1754-1822)

William Thomas Bree was an accomplished amateur watercolourist, whose images record a small corner of Warwickshire with enthusiasm, and even obsession.

William Thomas Bree was born on 10 January 1754, grandson and son of rectors and landowners of Allesley, in north-west Warwickshire. Following in the footsteps of his forebears, he graduated from Balliol College Oxford, in 1775, and in turn became the rector of Allesley.

As an artist, Bree was most notably influenced by fellow amateur Heneage Finch, 4th Earl of Aylesford, who lived at nearby Packington Park. Bree's skilful, subtle watercolours record elements of the local area – encompassing Allesley, Packington and Maxstoke. Two of his drawings inspired poems by Anna Seward.

Also a writer, Bree contributed words and images to Thomas Purton's *Midland Flora* (1817) and published *The Plain Reader's Help in the Study of the Holy Scriptures* (1821). He died on 22 November 1822.

His son, also William Thomas Bree, succeeded him as rector of Allesley, and became well known as a botanist.

His work is represented in The Herbert Art Gallery, Coventry (which has a sketchbook containing 80 watercolours of Maxstoke Priory).

Archives concerning the Bree family are held at the Warwickshire County Record Office, Warwick.

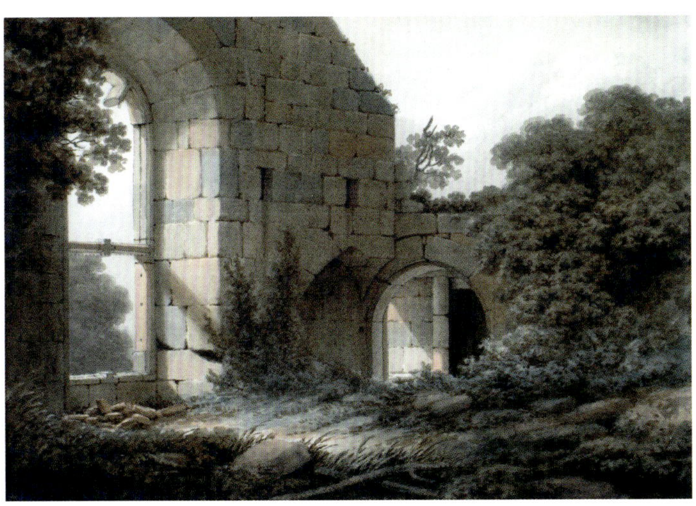

Maxstoke Priory
The picturesque ruin of Maxstoke Priory proved a favourite subject for William Thomas Bree. The foundation originated in a small College of Priests, which was established in 1331 by Sir William de Clinton, 1st Earl of Huntingdon. Twelve years later, it had developed into a full priory for Augustinian canons. However, it inevitably fell victim to the dissolution of the monasteries, being granted to Charles Brandon, 1st Duke of Suffolk, in 1538, and then sold to Robert Trappes, a London goldsmith. Over the years, its ruins provided materials for the farm buildings that were constructed on the site, so that now only the inner gatehouse remains in tact.

111 MAXSTOKE PRIORY
watercolour
9 ¼ x 12 ½ inches

JULIUS CAESAR IBBETSON

Julius Caesar Ibbetson (1759-1817)

Benjamin West described Julius Caesar Ibbetson as the 'Berchem of England'. So he acknowledged Ibbetson's emulation of the seventeenth-century Dutch naturalist tradition. Equally accomplished in oil and watercolour, and as able as a portraitist as a landscapist, he specialised in rural scenes enlivened by the reality of their animal and human figures. The watercolours are particularly valued for their delicate and atmospheric tones.

Julius Caesar Ibbetson was born on 29 December 1759 in Farnley, near Leeds, Yorkshire, apparently by caesarean section. He was probably educated by a local Moravian community and then by Quakers in Leeds. Encouraged by the talents of his father, a clothier, he was apprenticed to John Fletcher, a painter in Hull, between 1772 and 1777. From 1775, he also painted scenery for the actor-manager, Tate Wilkinson, for his Yorkshire circuit of theatres, and was invited to act in the productions.

On Fletcher's retirement in 1777, Ibbetson moved to London, where he continued to paint scenery, and worked as a picture restorer for Clarke, a picture dealer in Leicester Fields, who had also been apprenticed to Fletcher. These experiences enabled him to study techniques and obtain a thorough knowledge of the Dutch artists whose influence is apparent in his work. Gradually making a name for himself, notably as a painter of small-scale country scenes, he became one of the leading group of ruralists that included GEORGE MORLAND and James Ward. He exhibited at the Royal Academy of Arts from 1785, and illustrated John Trusler's moralising tract, *Modern Times* in the same year.

Having married in about 1780, Ibbetson moved out to Kilburn with his family in 1787. However, he soon left England with Colonel Charles Cathcart in order to act as draughtsman on the first British mission to Beijing. En route, they visited Madeira, the Cape of Good Hope and Java, where Cathcart died, in 1788, an event that forced Ibbetson's return to Britain (though with many watercolours of animals and plants). From that time, he embarked on a series of native sketching tours, particularly in Wales; instigated by a stay with Viscount Mountstuart at Cardiff Castle (1789), the tours culminated in a visit to North Wales in the company of Robert Fulke Greville and JOHN 'WARWICK' SMITH (1792). In 1790, he also visited the Isle of Wight. In 1793, the Ibbetsons moved to Paddington.

The death of his wife in 1794 and the threat of destitution to his children provoked in Ibbetson a minor nervous breakdown. However, he relieved his condition by accepting a commission from the 2nd Earl of Mansfield to decorate the music room at Kenwood House. He also undertook work as a printmaker and illustrator, contributing to *A Picturesque Guide to Bath* (1793) and John Church's *A Cabinet of Quadrupeds* (1796). Before 1802, he had also contributed images of *The Taming of the Shrew* to John Boydell's Shakespeare Gallery.

In 1798, Ibbetson spent time in Liverpool, working for Vernon, the art dealer, and patronised by William Roscoe, the radical writer. From Liverpool, he made his first visits to the Lake District, where he was patronised by Roscoe's brother-in-law, Daniel Daulby of Rydal Mount; and to Scotland, winning the friendship and patronage of the Countess of Balcarres.

His son, Julius Caesar Ibbetson the younger, followed him to Liverpool and the Lake District, and became a drawing master (and later an innkeeper in Richmond, North Yorkshire).

In 1801, Ibbetson settled in Ambleside and married the daughter of a weaver whom he had instructed in drawing. Moving to nearby Troutbeck in 1803, he published two manuals *An Accidence, or Gamut, of Painting in Oil and Watercolours* (1803) and *Process of Tinted Drawing* (1805). However, he left the Lake District for the less damp atmosphere of Masham, Yorkshire, in 1806, in order to alleviate his crippling rheumatism. He died in Masham on 13 October 1817.

His work is represented in the Government Art Collection and numerous public collections, including the British Museum, Kenwood, Tate and the V&A; Ferens Art Gallery (Hull), Temple Newsam House (Leeds), Manchester Art Gallery and the Walker Art Gallery (Liverpool); The National Library of Wales (Aberystwyth) and National Museum Wales (Cardiff); and the Yale Center for British Art (New Haven).

Further reading:

Rotha Mary Clay, *Julius Caesar Ibbetson*, London: Country Life, 1948
Bernard Lionel Kinghorn Henderson, *Morland and Ibbetson*, London: Philip Allan, 1923
Julius Caesar Ibbetson, 1759–1817, London: Kenwood House, 1957
James Mitchell, 'Ibbetson, Julius Caesar (1759-1817)', H C G Matthew and Brian Harrison (eds), *Oxford Dictionary of National Biography*, Oxford University Press, 2004, vol 29, pp 184-185
James Mitchell, *Julius Caesar Ibbetson (1759-1817). 'The Berchem of England'*, London: John Mitchell & Son, 1999
Susan Morris, 'Ibbetson, Julius Caesar, the elder (*b* Leeds, 29 Dec 1759; *d* Masham, N Yorks, 13 Oct 1817)', Jane Turner (ed), *The Dictionary of Art*, London: Macmillan, 1996, vol 15, pp 57-58

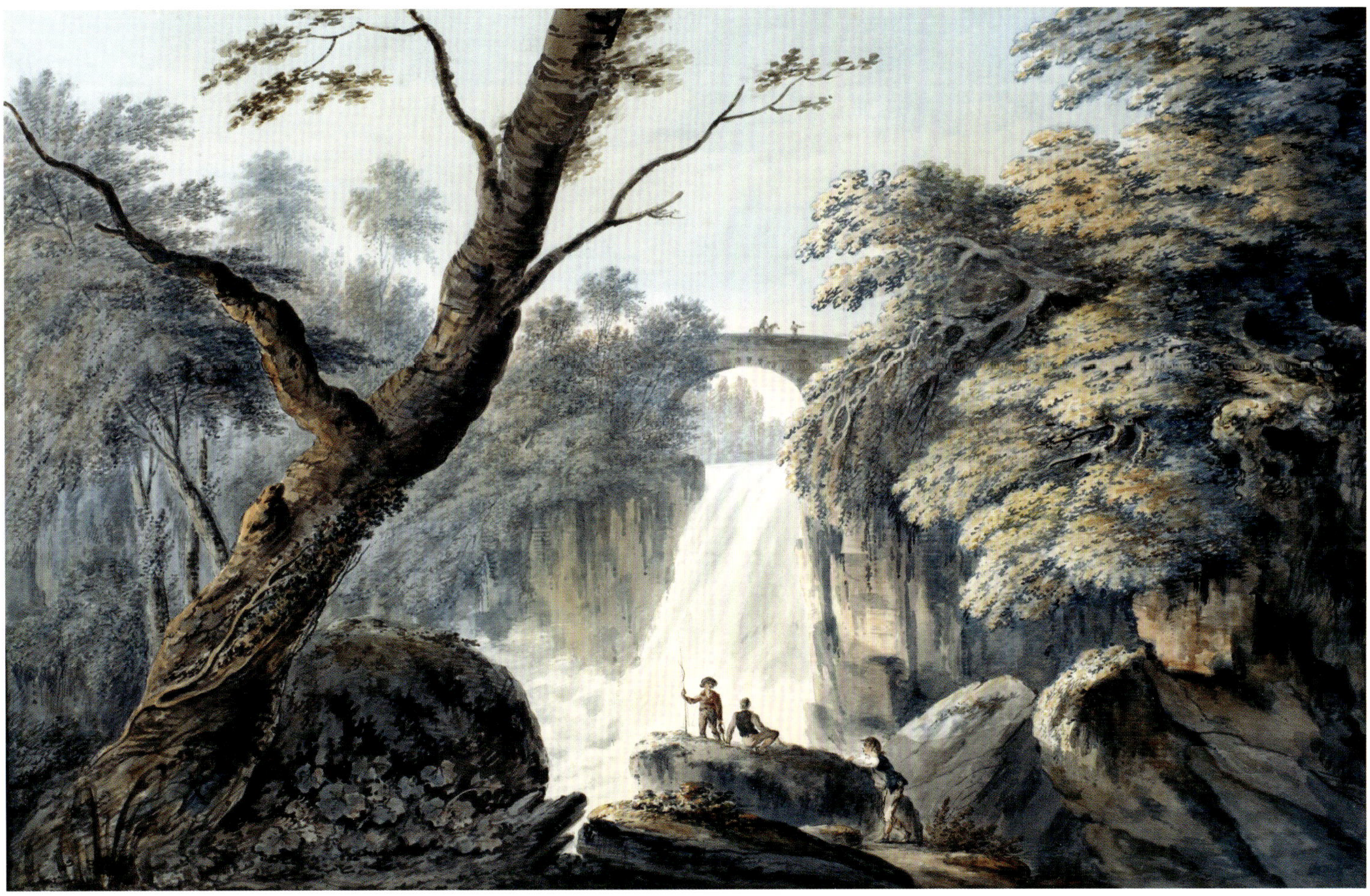

112 THE WATERFALL
inscribed '71' on reverse
watercolour with ink
18 ¼ x 27 ¼ inches

JOHN THOMAS SERRES
John Thomas Serres (1759-1825)

John Thomas Serres was a marine and landscape painter, who was drawn to portraying dramatic weather conditions, and also represented Thames-side life in sensitive detail.

John Thomas Serres was born in London in December 1759. He studied under his father, Dominic Serres, a successful marine painter of French origin. Specialising in marine subjects and landscapes, he worked as a drawing-master – both at the maritime school at Ormonde House in Chelsea and independently – and exhibited from 1780 at the Royal Academy of Arts. (However, unlike his father, he was never elected an academician.)

Staying in Paris during the fall of the Bastille in 1789, Serres went on to Rome and Naples, an experience that encouraged him to sign himself 'Giovanni T Serres' for some time after. In 1791, soon after his return from the Continent, he married his former pupil, Olivia Wilmot, the daughter of a house painter employed by the Earl of Warwick. She bore him four children between 1792 and 1802.

On the death of his father in 1793, Serres succeeded him as Marine Painter to George III. Moving to Liverpool three years later with his family, his paintings and aquatints of the city demonstrated his industry. Yet, by 1799, they had returned to London (and were sharing the same address as J M W TURNER).

In 1800, Serres was appointed Marine Draughtsman to the Admiralty, so undertaking to spy as well as record the coastlines of France and Spain. As a result of these activities, he translated and illustrated René Bougard's *The Little Sea-torch, or True Guide for Coasting Pilots* in 1801. Then, four years later, he produced *Liber Nauticum, and Instructor in the Art of Marine Drawing*, under joint authorship with his late father. During the same period, he was one of three artists involved in founding the British School, a short-lived exhibiting society (1802-4). Subsequently, he would show work at the British Institution and Suffolk Street.

Serres and his wife agreed to separate in 1802, as the result of her infidelities and his inability (or unwillingness) to support her to the degree that she desired. Yet by the time that they divorced in 1804, their animosity had increased. When Serres abducted one of his daughters, he was charged with breaching the trust by the daughters' trustee - Olivia's current lover, the artist George Fields – and consigned to prison for six years. In the intervening period, Olivia established herself as both a writer and artist, and was even appointed Landscape Painter to the Prince of Wales in 1806.

On his release in 1808, Serres began to disperse his father's collection of drawings – by Old Masters and contemporaries – in order to obtain some ready money. He then fled to Edinburgh, but was pursued by his wife's creditors, and again imprisoned for up to a decade, during which time he gave drawing lessons (the Duchess of Montrose being notable among his pupils).

Following his eventual release, Serres attempted to improve his fortune by becoming a partner of the Royal Coburg Theatre (now the Old Vic), which was built in London from 1816 and opened in 1818. He decorated its marine saloon, and designed sets for some of its early productions. Yet, he seems to have gained little from the venture, and again headed for Scotland.

In 1822, Serres attempted to secure the position of official draughtsman to George III on his royal visit to Scotland. However, the pretensions of his former wife impeded his success; for, from 1817, Olivia had begun to create a scandal by claiming to be the natural daughter of the Duke of Cumberland, the king's brother, and styling herself 'Princess Olive of Cumberland'. Undeterred, Serres still 'produced a set of large and well-crafted watercolours recording the event' (Stephen Deuchar, in Jane Turner 1996, vol 8, p 482).

Imprisoned for a third time for debt, Serres was released on health grounds in December 1825, but was required to live within the rules of the King's bench. He died in London on 28 December 1825. His memoirs were published a year after his death.

He frequently appeared in the diaries of Joseph Farington, who referred to him as Jack Serres.

His work is represented in the collections of the National Maritime Museum, Tate and the V&A.

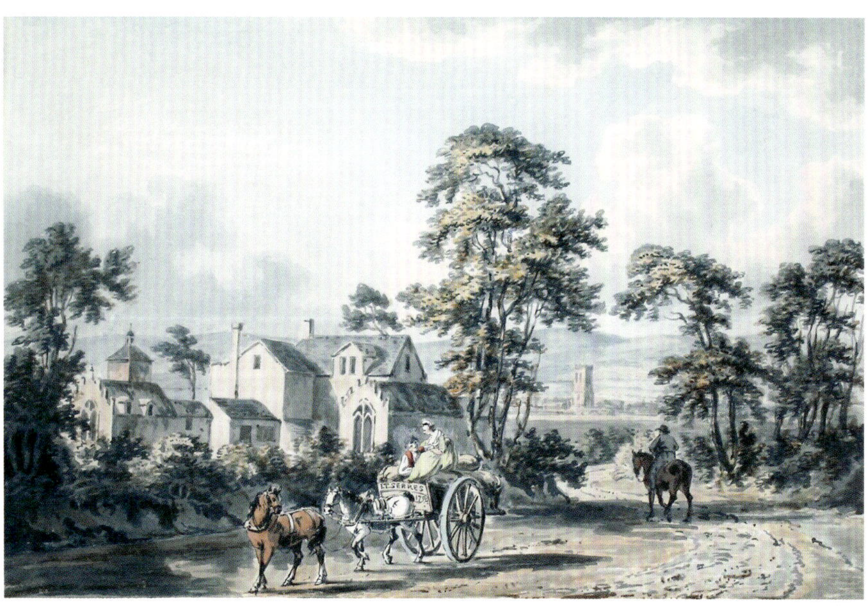

Further reading:

D D Aldridge, 'Serres, John Thomas (1759-1825)', H C G Matthew and Brian Harrison (eds), *Oxford Dictionary of National Biography*, Oxford University Press, 2004, vol 49, pp 785-786

Stephen Deuchar, 'Serres', Jane Turner (ed), *The Dictionary of Art*, London: Macmillan, 1996, vol 28, pp 481-482

113 THE VILLAGE CARRIER
signed and dated 1798
watercolour with pen and ink
8 ¾ x 12 ½ inches

WILLIAM PAYNE
William Payne, AOWS (1760-1830)

William Payne was probably the most fashionable drawing master of the day, popular for both his loose, yet clear, application of pigment and his willingness to extend the bounds of the medium of watercolour.

William Payne was born in Westminster, London, on 4 March 1760, the son of a highly successful hop and coal merchant who was originally from Burwash, Sussex. He received some drawing lessons, possibly from Paul Sandby, and in 1776 sent a drawing to the Society of Artists, though he did not exhibit again for a decade. In 1778, he was appointed a 'fifth class' draughtsman by the Board of Ordnance, and worked in its Drawing Room at the Tower of London. He received training in drawing, mathematics and perspective, the last taught by Henry Gilder, a protege and servant of Thomas Sandby. He then tested that training in an apprenticeship of surveying and mapping, and also of gun drill. By 1783, he had been promoted to the second class.

The Board of Ordnance then sent Payne to Plymouth Dock, as one of a team concerned with its defence against the French. His tour of duty ran from March 1783 to September 1788. During his time in Plymouth, Payne married and began to develop a distinct artistic career. From 1786 to 1790, he exhibited West Country views at the Royal Academy of Arts. From 1788, his work was engraved and published by Samuel Middiman. By the end of 1789, he had obtained a permanent London address (at 2 Thornhaugh Street, Bedford Square). And from 1790 to 1794, when he left the service of the Board, he made extensive tours of Wales and the West Country.

Payne's manner of work developed the watercolour from a tinted drawing to a painting which relied less on prominent pen outline and more on the build up of washes. However, he retained the use of a monochrome palette, and invented his own characteristic tint which is still known as 'Payne's Grey'. His manner was not only distinctive but easy to explain, so that he became an extremely fashionable and successful drawing master. JOHN GLOVER was among the most notable of his pupils.

In 1809, Payne relaunched himself as an exhibiting artist, working in both oil and watercolour: he showed work at the British Institution, and was elected as an associate of the Society of Painters in Water Colours (a membership which would lapse four years later). Then in the following year, at the height of his career, he moved into a new house (at 49 Upper Baker Street, Marylebone). Though he widened his subject matter (by touring the Lake District in 1811 and 1819), his popularity slowly began to decline. He died in London at home in August 1830.

His work is represented in the Government Art Collection, and numerous public collections, including the British Museum and the V&A; and The Fitzwilliam Museum (Cambridge) and Plymouth City Museum and Art Gallery.

Further reading:

Peter Hunt, *Payne's Devon*, Exeter: Devon Books, 1986
David Japes, 'Payne, William (1760-1830)', H C G Matthew and Brian Harrison (eds), *Oxford Dictionary of National Biography*, Oxford University Press, 2004, vol 43, pp 221-222
David Japes, *William Payne: A Plymouth Experience*, Exeter: Royal Albert Memorial Museum, 1992
Scott Wilcox, 'Payne, William (*b* Plymouth, *c* 1760; *d* London, after 1830)', Jane Turner (ed), *The Dictionary of Art*, London: Macmillan, 1996, vol 24, pp 296-297

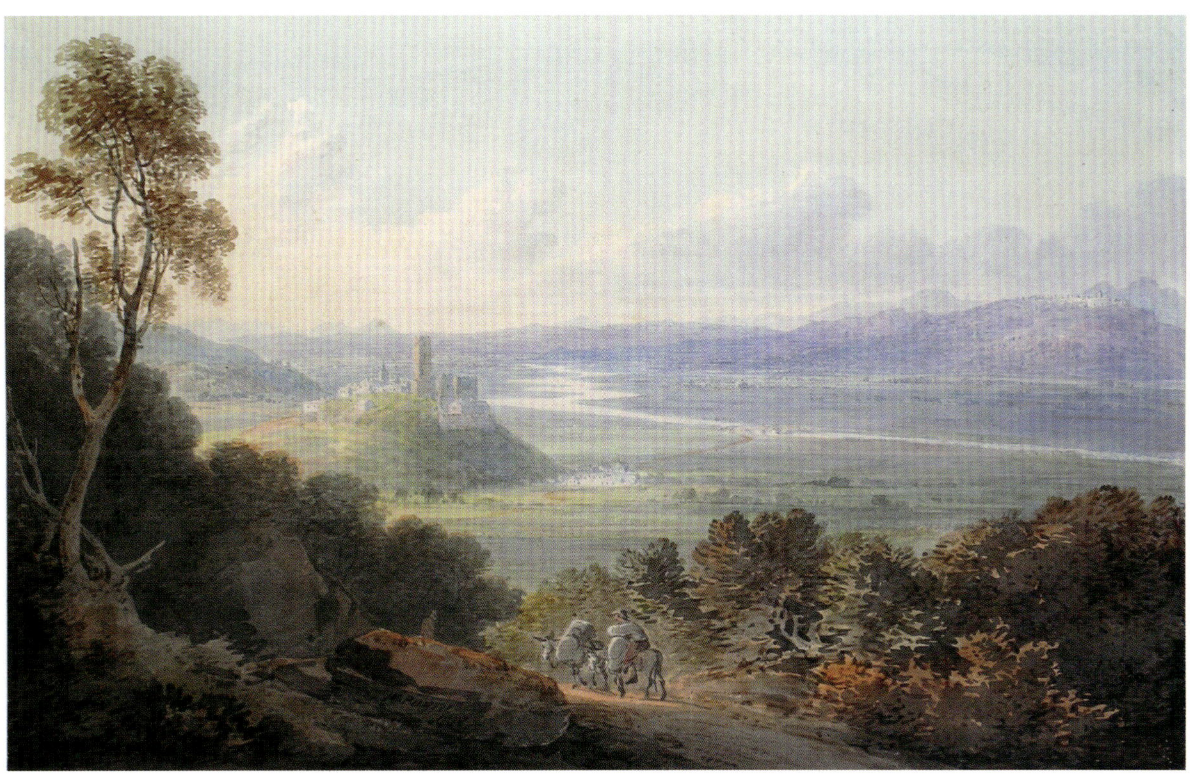

114 ACROSS THE TIBER PLAIN
signed and dated 1818
watercolour
10 ¼ x 15 ½ inches

WILLIAM PAYNE

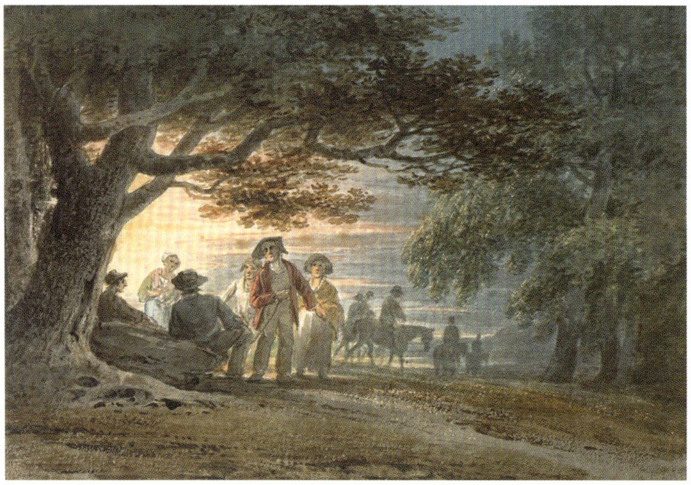

115 A REST AT SUNSET
signed on reverse
watercolour with varnish
5 ¾ x 8 ¼ inches

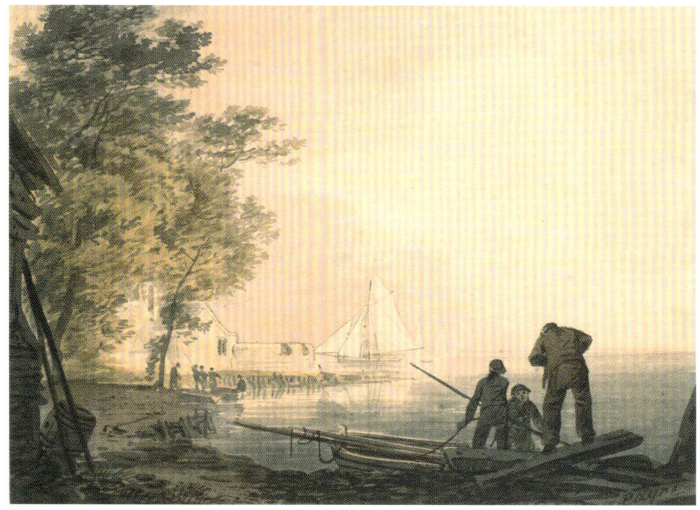

116 COWES CASTLE WITH BOATMEN ON THE SHORE
signed and inscribed 'Cowes Castle' on original mount
watercolour, 5 x 6 ½ inches
Provenance: Sir Bruce Ingham

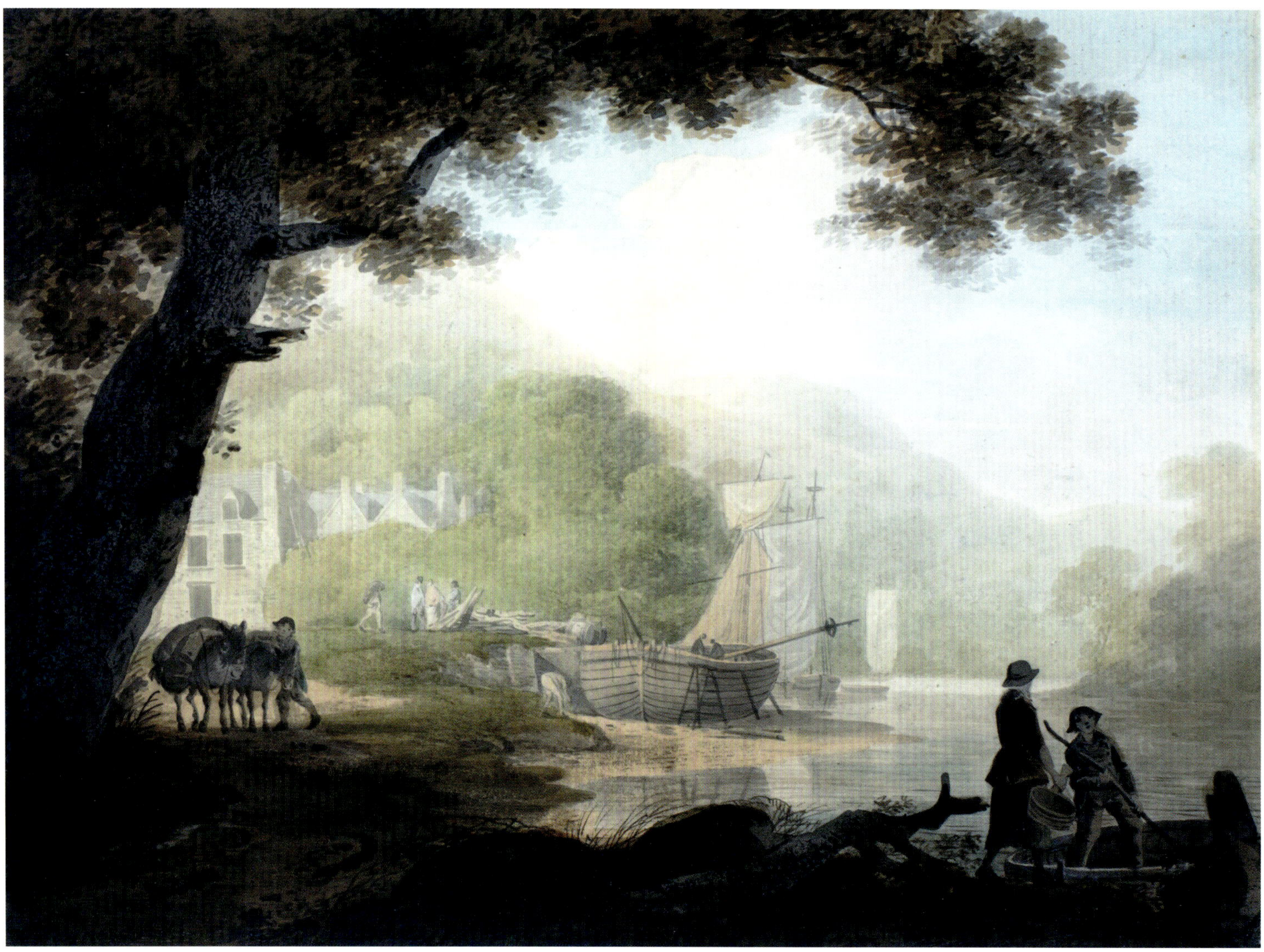

117 BROCKWEAR QUAY – ON THE WYE
watercolour
11 ¾ x 15 ½ inches

JOHN LAPORTE
John Peter Laporte (*circa* 1761-1839)

Best known as a watercolourist, John Laporte disseminated his expertise by giving lessons and writing a series of manuals.

The first known London address of John Laporte – from 1779 – was at no 3 Orange Street, Leicester Fields. This was the home of his teacher, John Melcher Barrelet, a French Huguenot born in Dublin. For this reason, it is believed that Laporte may also have been born into a French Huguenot family in Dublin. However, he may be identified equally with the child baptised at St Anne's Soho on 29 March 1761.

Exhibiting landscape watercolours at the Royal Academy of Arts (from 1779) and the British Institution (from 1785), Laporte accumulated his subjects through sketching tours, including those made to the Isle of Wight (1789), Wales (from 1792) and Ireland (from 1795). While on the Isle of Wight, he met John Hassell, the topographical artist, and they would lodge together in London at 4 Gresse Street, north of Oxford Street, in 1792-93.

Laporte worked as a drawing master, numbering Dr Thomas Monro among his pupils. In turn, Monro acquired examples of work by Laporte, as contributions to the collection he used to encourage such promising young artists as J M W TURNER and Thomas Girtin. Laporte reached a wider circle of practitioners through a series of manuals: *Characters of Trees* (1798-1801), *A Drawing Book* (1800), *Progressive Lessons Sketched from Nature* (1804), *A New Drawing Book* (1809) and *The Progress of a Water-Coloured Drawing* (1812).

By 1802, Laporte was living at 21 Rochester Row, off the Edgware Road. At this time, he began to produce a series of soft-ground etchings after landscapes by Thomas Gainsborough in collaboration with William Frederick Wells, who had also been a student of one of the Barralet brothers. While Wells became a founder of the Society of Painters in Water Colours in 1804, Laporte was a founder of the short-lived Associated Artists in Water Colours in 1808. Then in 1809, Wells was appointed first Professor of Drawing at the East India Company's Military Academy at Addiscombe, Surrey. Laporte may also have become a drawing master there, perhaps at the suggestion of Wells.

In his later phase, Laporte exhibited in Liverpool (from 1810), at the Society of British Artists (from 1825) and at the New Society of Painters in Water Colours (after 1831).

Laporte's children, Mary Anne and George Henry, both became artists, George probably studying under his father's friend, the sporting painter, Henry Bernard Chalon.

From about 1832, the family moved to 99 Albany Street, near Regent's Park. However, Laporte died at 2 Upper Coleshill Street, Pimlico (now Eaton Terrace, Belgravia) on 8 July 1839.

His work is represented in numerous public collections, including the British Museum, Tate and the V&A.

Further reading:

Basil Somerset Long, 'John Laporte and P La Cave', *Walker's Quarterly*, no 8, July 1922, pp 1-58

Huon Mallalieu, 'Laporte, John Peter (1761-1839)', H C G Matthew and Brian Harrison (ed), *Oxford Dictionary of National Biography*, Oxford University Press, 2004, vol 32, pp 552-553

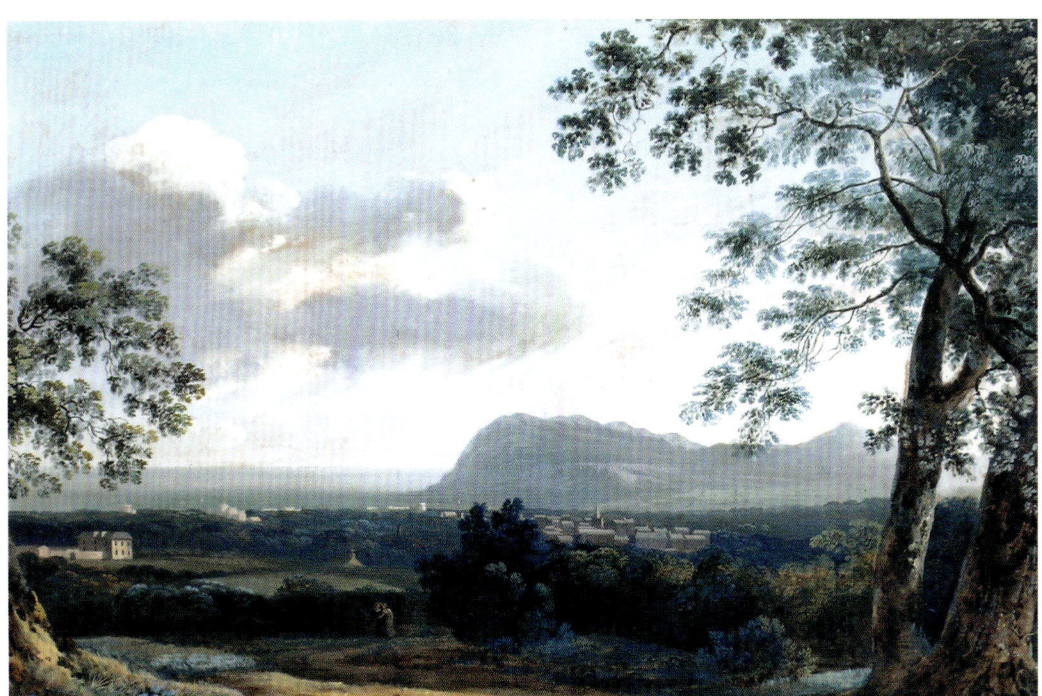

118 VIEW OF EASTBOURNE, SUSSEX
watercolour and bodycolour
14 ¾ x 22 inches

EDWARD DAYES
Edward Dayes (1763-1804)

Edward Dayes added an often dramatic sense of scale to the elegance and simplicity that he learned from the Sandbys. His topographical mastery became well known through the many engravings that were made from his watercolours.

Edward Dayes was born in London on 6 August 1763. He studied printmaking under the mezzotinter and miniaturist, William Pether and, from 1780, at the Royal Academy Schools. He exhibited sixty-four works at the Royal Academy of Arts (from 1786), and others at the Society of Artists (1790-91), in a style developed from that of Paul and Thomas Sandby. In turn, he had a great influence on the younger generation, particularly as a teacher of watercolour. For instance, the young J M W TURNER made meticulous copies of his works at Dr Monro's unofficial academy while, from 1789, Thomas Girtin was a direct pupil. Dayes could be a less than generous mentor, being so envious of Girtin's success that it was long believed that he had him imprisoned for unruliness. Nevertheless, he rose to the position of draughtsman to the Duke of York (in about 1791).

In the late 1780s, Dayes recorded the expansion of the capital in four watercolours of new squares, including Hanover Square, which were engraved by Francis Jukes and Robert Pollard. Not only did they preempt the similar achievement of Thomas Malton, but also demonstrated Dayes' skill as a draughtsman of figures.

From the early 1790s, Dayes travelled widely in Britain, notably in northern England and Wales. Responding to the landscape with bold, atmospheric watercolours of picturesque motifs, he also found employment as a topographical illustrator and in working up sketches made by amateurs. One project indicates the way in which he even interpreted terrains that were distant and unknown to him: David Collins' *Account of the Colony in New South Wales* (1798) contains engravings by Dayes after watercolours that Thomas Watling had made in Australia.

In the late 1790s, Dayes changed direction by embarking on a series of large biblical and classical subjects, some in oil, but this venture met with little success, a solo show in 1801 going unnoticed. This failure led him to commit suicide in London in May 1804. His wife had exhibited miniatures at the Royal Academy between 1797 and 1800.

Volumes of his writings were published posthumously in 1805, including the textbook *Drawing and Colouring Landscape* and the malicious commentary *Professional Sketches of Modern Artists*.

His work is represented in numerous public collections, including the British Museum, The Courtauld Gallery, Tate and the V&A; The Fitzwilliam Museum (Cambridge), Leeds City Art Gallery and The Whitworth Art Gallery (Manchester); The National Library of Wales (Aberystwyth); and the National Library of Australia (Canberra).

Further reading:

David Blayney Brown, 'Edward Dayes: Historical Draughtsman', *Old Water-Colour Society's Club*, vol 62, 1991, pp 9-21

Patrick Conner, 'Dayes, Edward (*b* London, 6 Aug 1763; *d* London, May 1804)', Jane Turner (ed), *The Dictionary of Art*, London: Macmillan, 1996, vol 8, p 584

J Dayes, 'Edward Dayes', *Old Water-Colour Society's Club*, vol 39, 1964, pp 45-55

Greg Smith, 'Dayes, Edward (1763-1704)', H C G Matthew and Brian Harrison (eds), *Oxford Dictionary of National Biography*, Oxford University Press, 2004, vol 15, pp 609-610

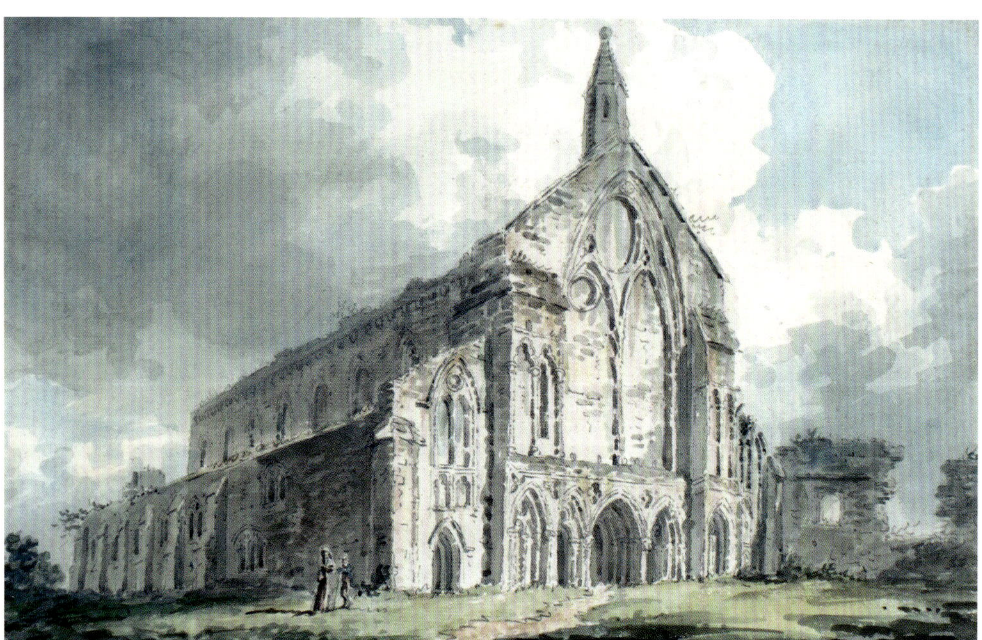

119 BINHAM PRIORY, NORFOLK
watercolour
5 ¼ x 8 inches

GEORGE MORLAND
George Charles Morland (1763-1804)

George Morland was an immensely prolific painter of landscape and rustic genre who gained widespread popularity through the dissemination of engravings of his work.

George Morland was born in the Haymarket, London on 26 June 1763, the eldest of six children of Henry Robert Morland (painter, engraver and art dealer) and Jenny Lacam (an amateur artist who was daughter to a French jeweller). His father had become bankrupt in 1762, and so latched onto the artistic promise that Morland showed from an early age as a way of restoring the family fortunes. Only ten years old when he exhibited (chalk drawings) at the Royal Academy of Arts for the first time in 1773, he also exhibited at the Free Society of Artists (from 1775) and the Society of Artists (from 1777).

In 1777, Morland began a seven-year apprenticeship under his father, during which he produced copies of old masters, passed off by his father as originals, and original works that were increasingly exhibited – and engraved (the first two by John Raphael Smith in 1780). Near the end of this period, he received an offer from George Romney to take him into his studio, but he rejected this in favour of a place at the Royal Academy. However, his attendance there was sporadic and short-lived as he chose to spend increasing amounts of time in alehouses. Thus he showed wayward characteristics for the first time, possibly in reaction to his strict upbringing.

In 1784, Morland began to work independently of his father, living close to Drury Lane, and painting portraits and genre scenes for an Irish dealer, who paid him as little as he could get away with.

By 1786, Morland was lodging in Kensal Green with the young engraver, William Ward, who, with his brother James, had studied under John Raphael Smith. During the year, Morland married Ward's sister, Anne, and Ward married George's sister, Maria, who, like George, was an exhibiting painter. Following their marriages, the two couples shared a house in Marylebone High Street, the Morlands later moving to Kentish Town (then Leicester Square and Covent Garden). In this year, Morland began to establish himself as a painter by producing *Laetitia or, A Harlot's Progress*, a series of six images modelled on a similar work by William Hogarth. However, success encouraged him into such an extravagant lifestyle that, by 1789, he had to set himself to clear his debts. He did this within fifteen months, some of which were spent on the Isle of Wight, where he went to evade his creditors. These financial problems did not stop him becoming fiercely independent so that, repelled by polite society, he is said to have refused a commission from the Prince of Wales.

The early 1790s proved relatively stable for Morland, allowing him to produce some of his best work, including the genre scenes of peasants, gypsies and smugglers that gained him a high reputation. Selling most of his paintings through his brother, Henry, who had a shop in Dean Street, Soho, he also held solo shows at Daniel Orme & Co (1792, 1793) and John Raphael Smith's temporary Morland Gallery (1793 – with 36 pictures to be engraved). At this time of industry, he took on at least five pupils.

Nevertheless, difficulties with creditors continued, pressing Morland to move continually: from Paddington to Leicestershire and possibly the Lake District, then back to London; there he had successive addresses in Charlotte Street, Lambeth, East Sheen, the Minories, Kentish Town, Soho, Newington, Kennington Green and Hackney.

Escaping with his wife to the Isle of Wight in April 1799 (Cowes, then Yarmouth), Morland returned to London by the November, and was soon arrested at his lodgings in Vauxhall. He was committed to the King's Bench Prison, living within its rules in a small, furnished house in St George's Fields. A year after his release in 1802, he placed himself in the custody of the Marshalsea, (a debtors prison), in order to avoid further harassment from creditors.

Nevertheless, on moving to live with his brother, Henry, Morland revived his mode of riotous living, so inducing a series of apoplectic fits and periods of paralysis. On 19 October 1804, he was arrested by a publican and conveyed to a bailiff's lodging house in Eyre Street, Coldbath Fields, where, in attempting to make a drawing that could be sold in discharge of the debt, he was seized with a fit that proved the beginning of brain fever. He died on 29 October 1804. His wife survived him only three days, the news of his death bringing on convulsive fits from which she died on 2 November. Their remains were interred together in the burying-place of St James's Chapel, Hampstead Road.

His continuing popularity and influence – on John Constable and David Wilkie among others – was due to the many engravings made after his work.

His work is represented in numerous public collections including the British Museum, Tate and the V&A.

Further reading:

Diane Perkins, 'Morland, George (1763-1804)', H C G Matthew and Brian Harrison (eds), *Oxford Dictionary of National Biography*, Oxford University Press, 2004, vol 39, pp 199-205
Michael Rosenthal, 'Morland', Jane Turner (ed), *The Dictionary of Art*, London: Macmillan, 1996, vol 22, pp 122-124
David Thomas, *George Morland*, London: Arts Council of Great Britain, 1954

GEORGE MORLAND

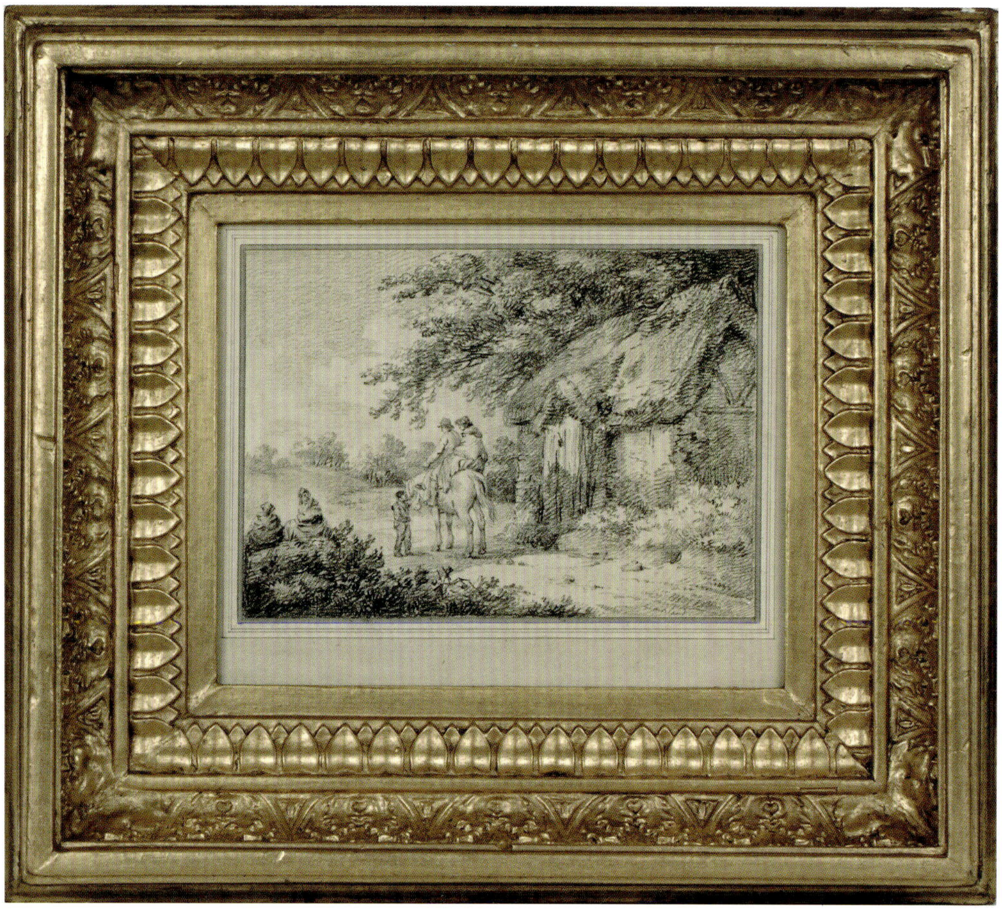

120 FIGURES ON A HORSE OUTSIDE A COTTAGE
signed
pencil
5 x 7 inches

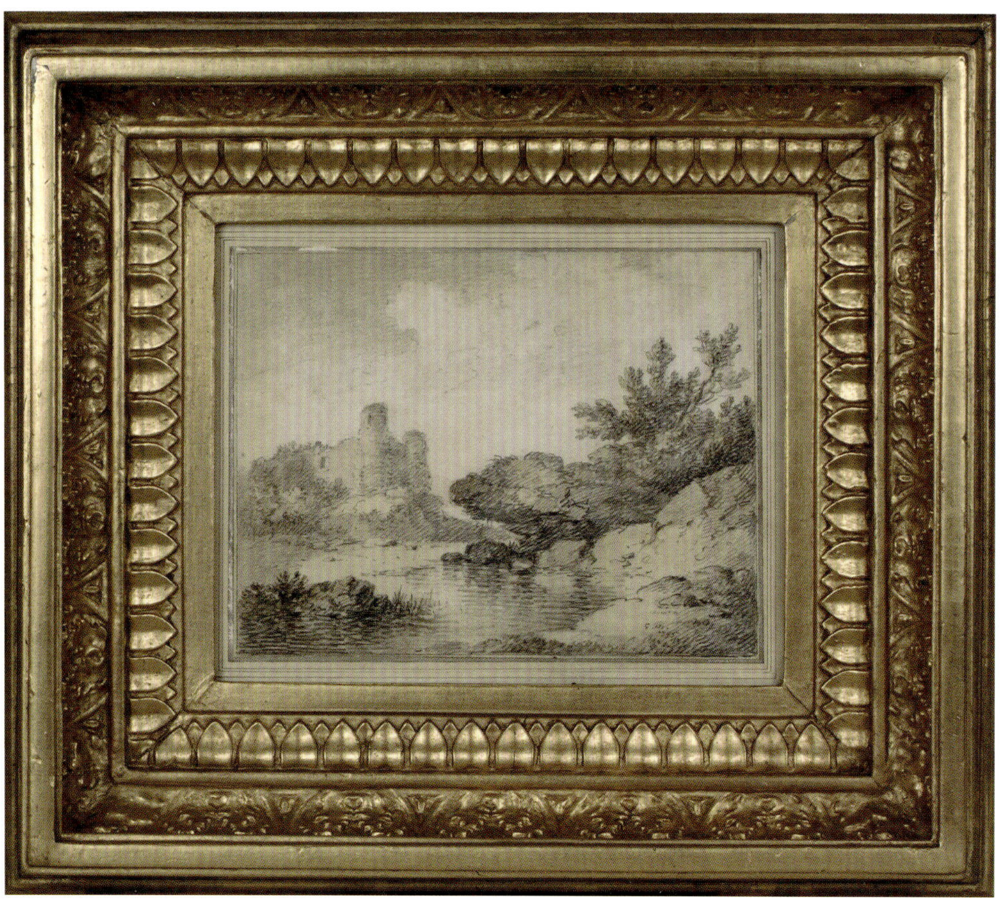

121 LANDSCAPE WITH CASTLE RUINS
signed and dated 1795
pencil with watercolour
5 ½ x 7 inches

JOHN WHITE ABBOTT
John White Abbott (1763-1851)

The reputation of John White Abbott now rests on his works on paper, in which he emulated the practice of his teacher, Francis Towne, by making use of clear outlines, flat washes and precise notation. Particularly appealing are his detailed studies of woodland, which meld the spirit of his native Devon to motifs and arrangements taken from the Old Masters.

John White Abbott was born in Exeter, Devon on 13 May 1763, and spent his entire career in that city as an apothecary and surgeon. He became an important friend and patron of Francis Towne, and as a keen amateur artist was the finest of the group who took lessons from him and worked in his manner. He established his devotion to the art of Towne in his earliest known watercolours, made in 1791 on a tour of Scotland, the Lake District, Lancashire, Derbyshire and Warwickshire.

Some of the paintings made by Abbott early in the nineteenth century suggest, by their ambitious scale, a knowledge of Thomas Girtin and J M W TURNER. Yet he remained an essentially eighteenth-century figure, who developed a classically-based sensibility by studying Towne's Italian views and prints after the Old Masters.

Between 1793 and 1812, Abbott exhibited intermittently in London, as an honorary member of the Royal Academy of Arts; but he never sold a picture, despite the fact that his oils were more highly praised than those of Towne.

In 1803, the Academician Joseph Farington reported in his diary a conversation with fellow artist John Downman who had said of Abbott, that he 'only paints by snatches, though by choice he would always be so employed'. He was able to fulfil this desire from 1825, when he inherited the Devon estate of Fordland from his uncle, James White, the prominent lawyer and another pupil of Towne. He then made sketching tours of Gloucestershire, Wiltshire and Monmouthshire (all in 1827), and made some studies of Richmond, Surrey (in 1842), but continued to work mainly in south Devon. He was appointed Deputy Lieutenant of Devonshire, in 1831, and died in Exeter twenty years later.

Having married in 1795, Abbott was father to three sons and two daughters.

His work is represented in numerous public collections, including the British Museum and the V&A; the Ashmolean Museum (Oxford), The Fitzwilliam Museum (Cambridge) and the Royal Albert Memorial Museum (Exeter); and the National Gallery of Scotland (Edinburgh).

Further reading:

Carolyn Jane Baker, *Paintings and Drawings by Francis Towne and John White Abbott*, Exeter: Royal Albert Memorial Museum, 1971

Susan Morris, 'Abbott, John White (*b* Exeter, 13 May 1764; *d* Exeter, 1851)', Jane Turner (ed), *The Dictionary of Art*, London: Macmillan, 1996, vol 1, p 24

Adolph Paul Oppé, 'John White Abbott of Exeter', *Walpole Society*, vol 13, 1924-25, pp 67 84

Iolo Aneurin Williams, 'John White Abbott: A Devonshire Artist', *Apollo*, vol 17, 1933, pp 84–86

Many thanks to Dr Toby Thorne for help in compiling this entry.

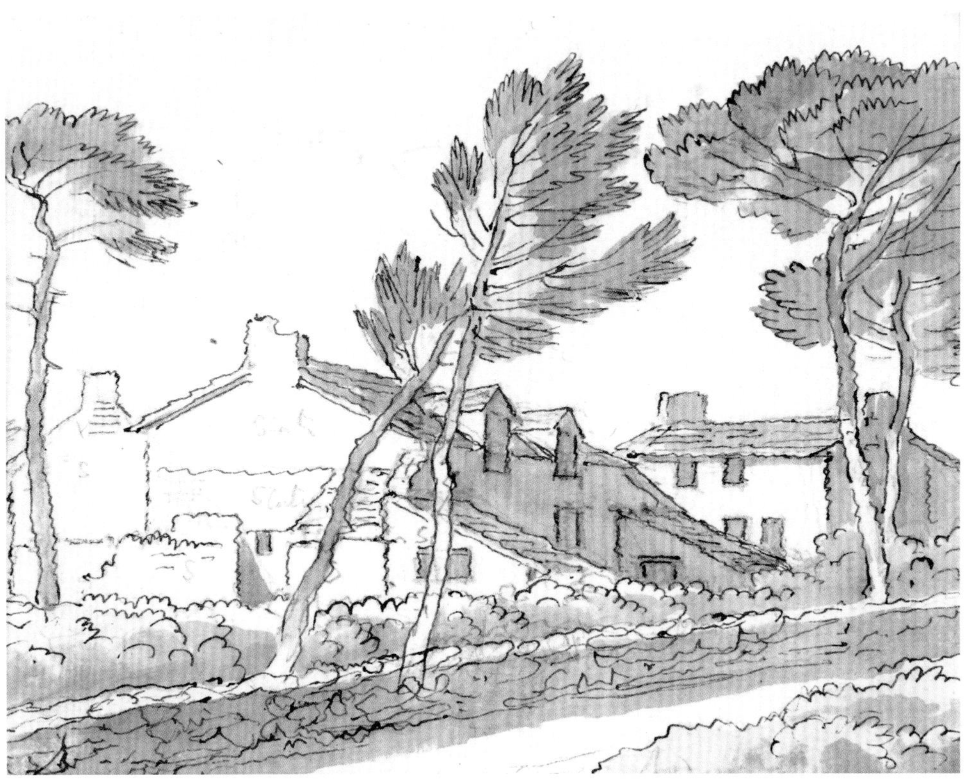

122 TWO BRIDGES
pen ink and watercolour with pencil
3 ¾ x 4 ½ inches

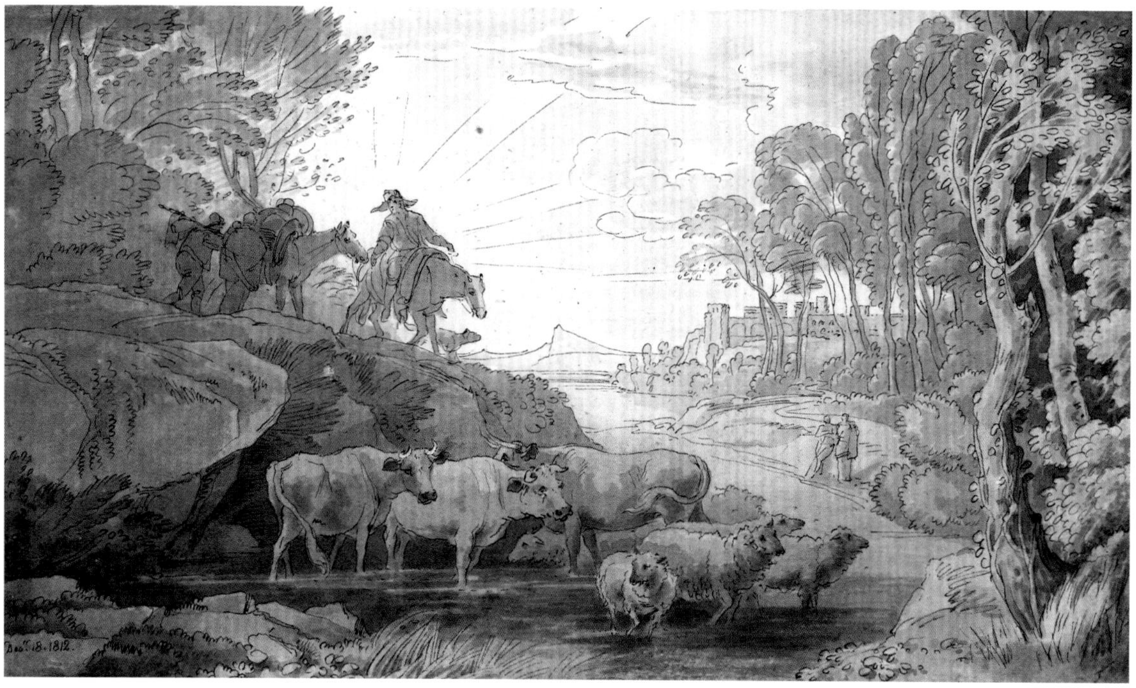

123 WATERING CATTLE AND SHEEP
dated 'Decr 18 1812'
pen ink and monochrome watercolour
7 ¼ x 12 inches

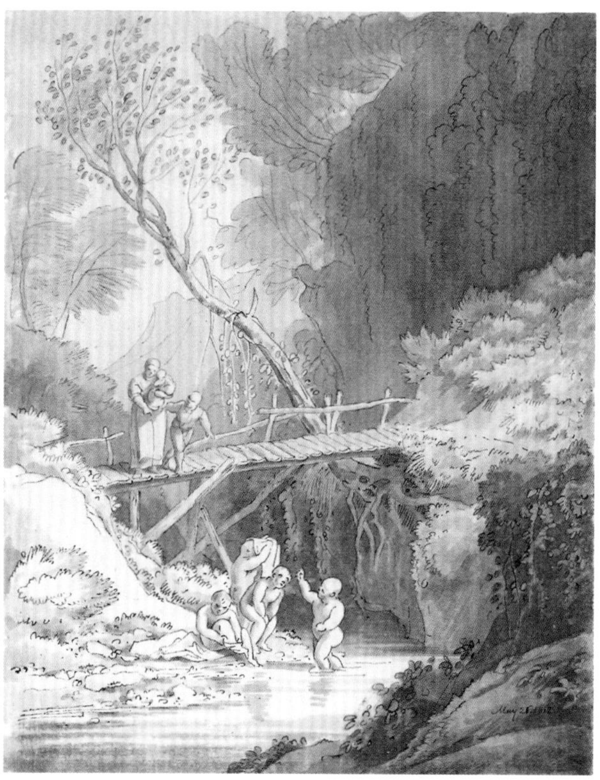

124 CHILDREN BATHING IN A MOUNTAIN STREAM
dated 'May 25 1812'
pen ink and monochrome watercolour
9 ½ x 7 ¼ inches

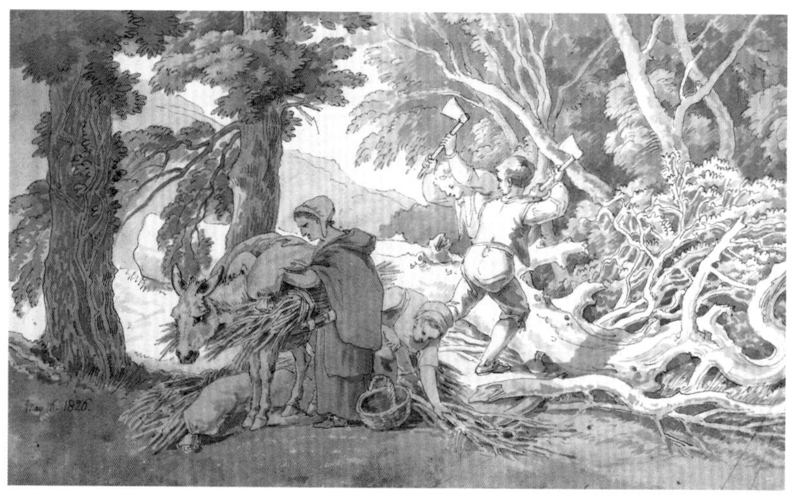

125 WOODCUTTERS
dated 'May 16 1826'
pen ink and monochrome watercolour
7 ¼ x 11 ¾ inches

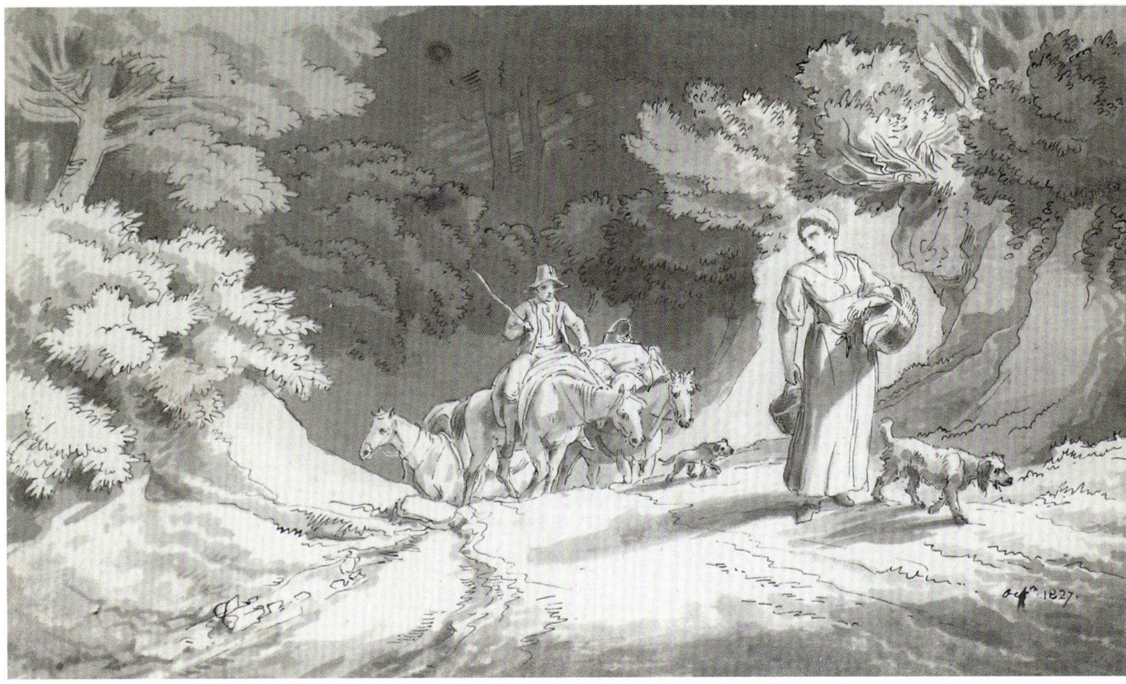

126 BRINGING THE HORSES UP THE HILL
dated 'Octr 1827'
pen ink and monochrome watercolour
7 ¼ x 12 inches

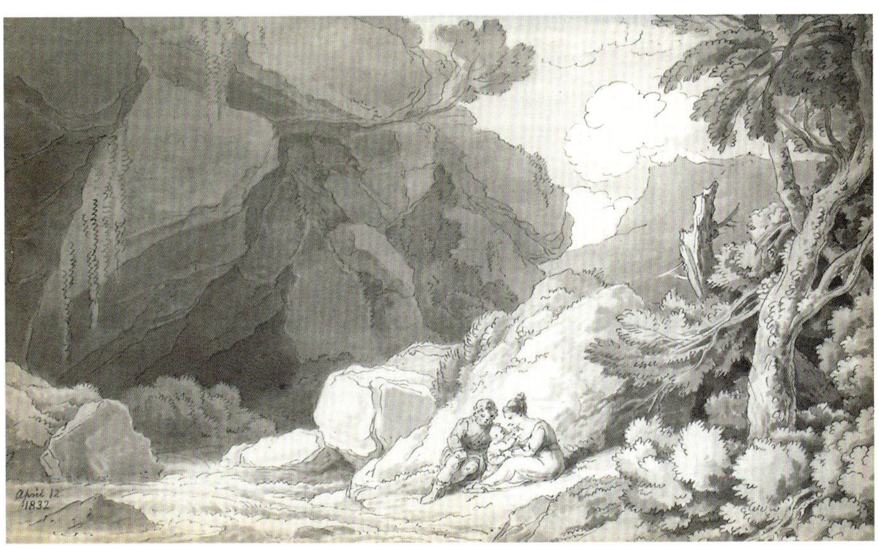

127 A FAMILY IN THE WILDERNESS
dated 'April 12 1832'
pen ink and monochrome watercolour
8 x 12 ¼ inches

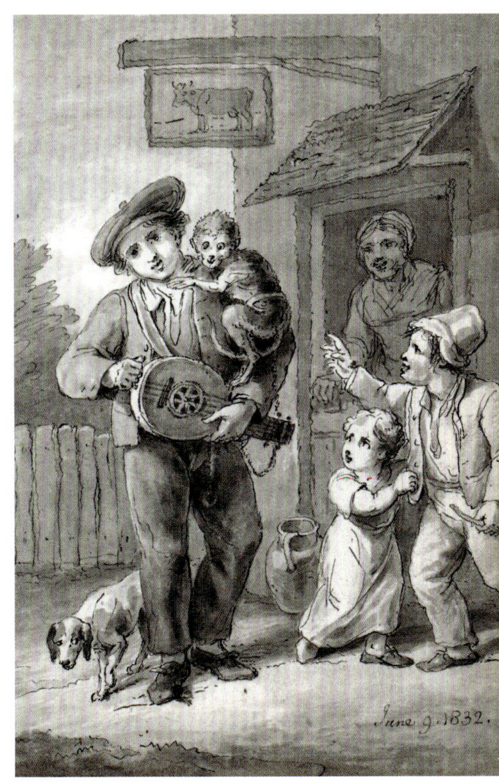

128 THE HURDY-GURDY PLAYER AND HIS MONKEY
dated 'June 9 1832'
pen ink and watercolour
7 ¾ x 5 ¼ inches

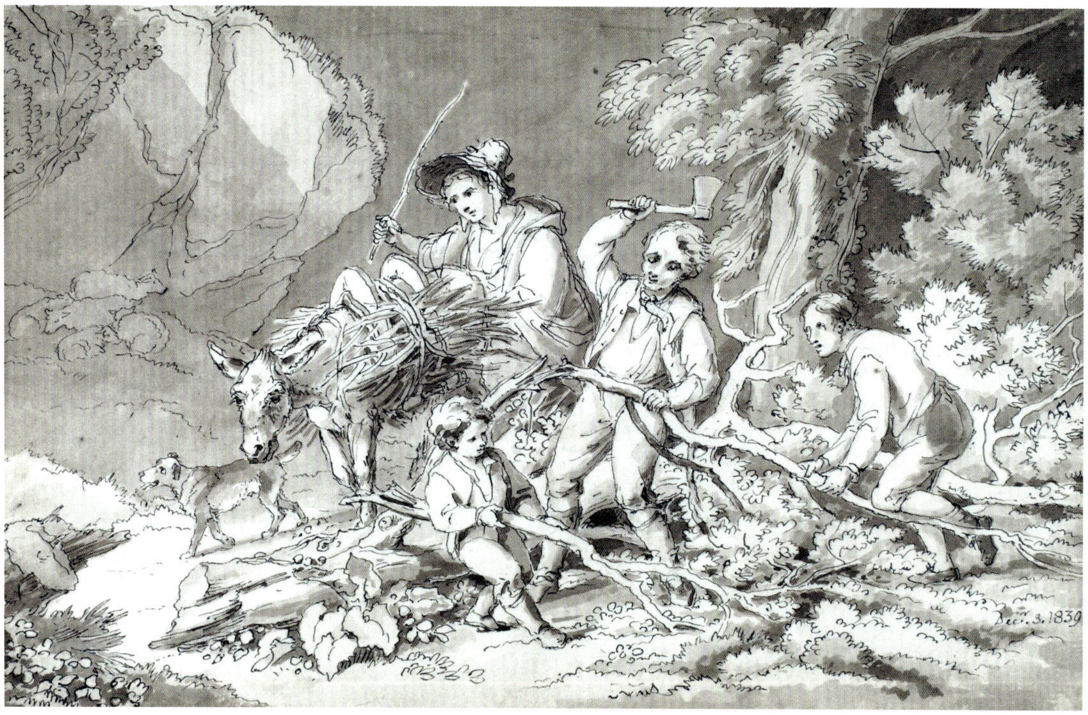

129 COLLECTING WOOD
dated 'Decr 3 1839'
pen ink and monochrome watercolour
7 ¾ x 12 ¼ inches

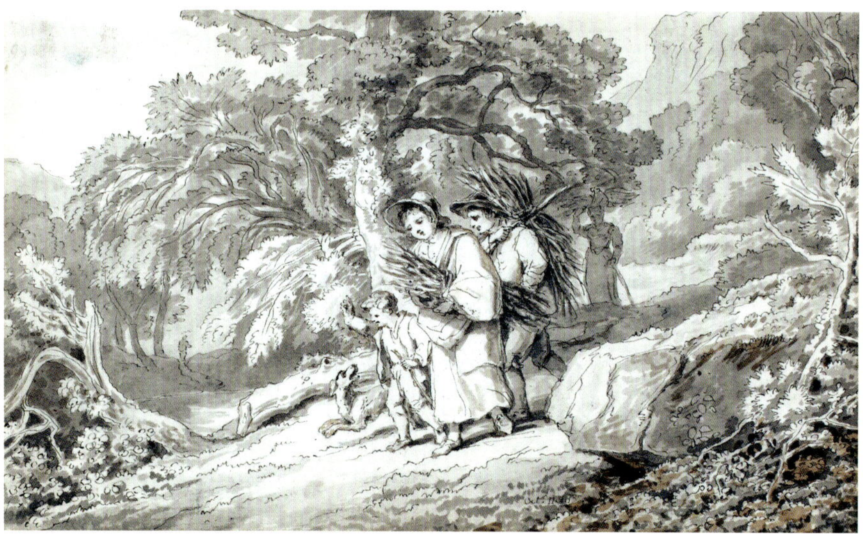

130 GATHERING FIREWOOD
dated 'Octr 11 1835'
pen ink and monochrome watercolour
7 ¼ x 12 inches

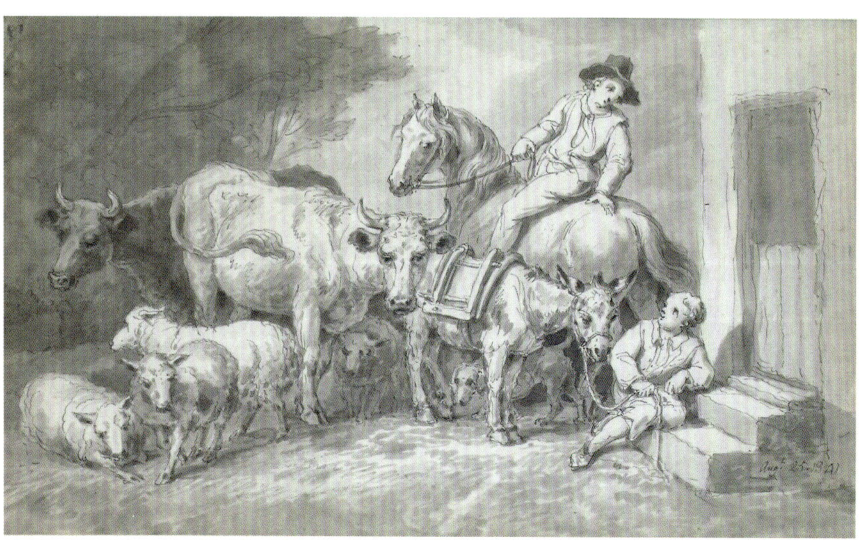

131 ANIMALS AT THE FARM DOOR
dated 'Augt 25 1841'
pen ink and monochrome watercolour
7 ½ x 12 ¼ inches

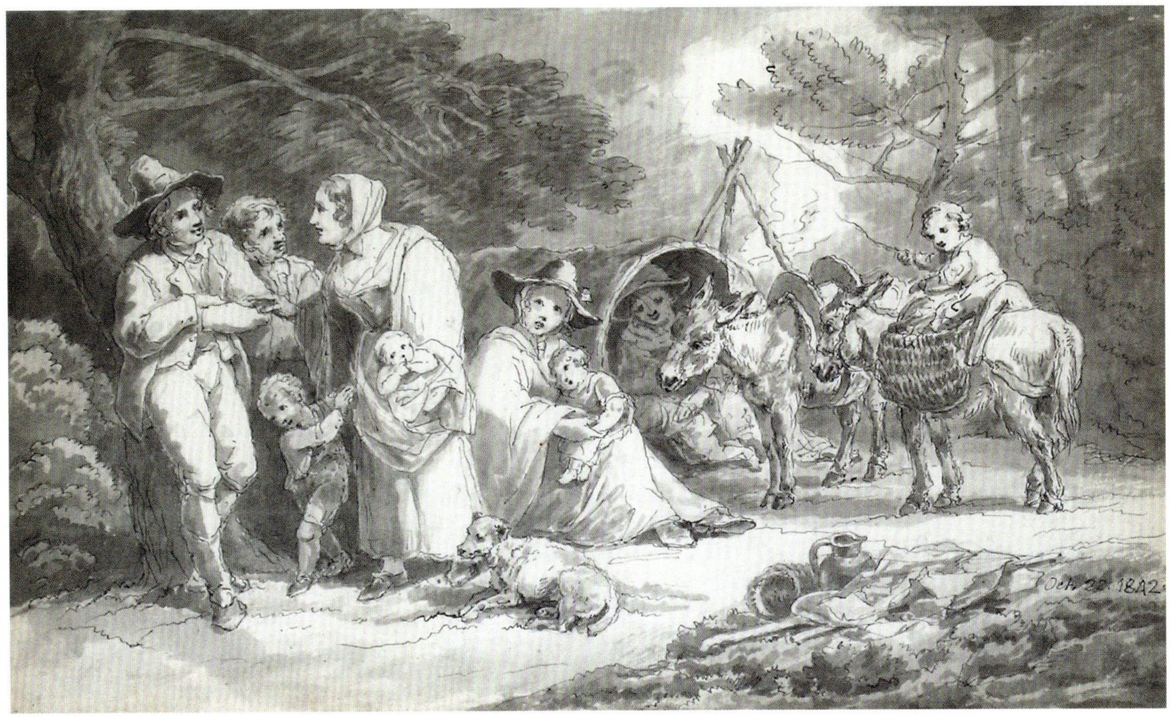

132 GYPSIES
dated 'Oct 22 1842'
pen ink and monochrome watercolour
7 ½ x 12 ¼ inches

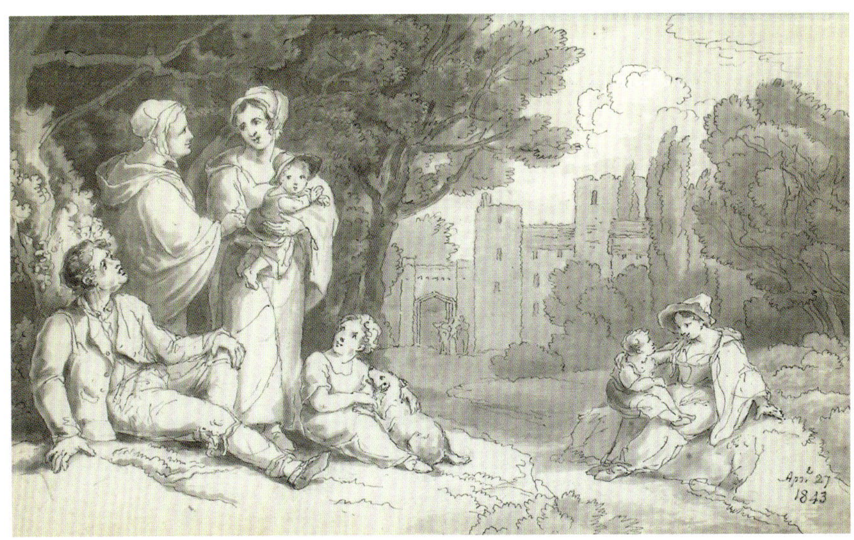

133 RESTING OUTSIDE A CASTLE
dated 'Aprl 27 1843'
pen ink and monochrome watercolour
7 ¾ x 12 ¼ inches

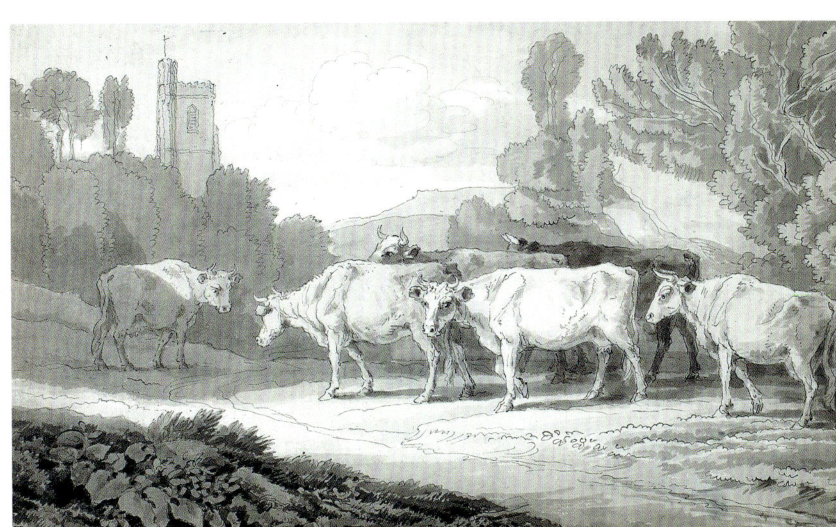

134 CATTLE ON THE VILLAGE ROAD
pen ink and watercolour
8 x 12 ¼ inches

JOHN GLOVER
John Glover, POWS SBA (1767-1849)

John Glover rose from rural obscurity to gain a reputation as a landscape painter second only to J M W Turner. He also proved highly influential, both directly as a teacher of professionals and amateurs in England, and then as an inspiration to newly-established artists in Australia. Mastering a variety of techniques, he was able to capture a wide range of atmospheric effects, though increasingly he gave watercolour the weight and intensity of oil, in order to emulate the Claudean tradition. Most characteristic – and popular – was his use of the 'split brush', in which watercolour was applied briskly with divided bristles in order to represent foliage.

The son of an impoverished farmer, John Glover was born at Houghton on the Hill, Leicestershire on 18 February 1767. He had two club feet, but worked in the fields as a youth and was extremely agile and active throughout his life. His experience of farming also instilled in him a great love of birds, animals and nature in general.

A proficient calligrapher, Glover was appointed writing-master at the Free School in Appleby, Westmoreland, in 1786. Soon, he began to paint professionally and, in order to expand his artistic horizons, made visits to London; while there, he went to exhibitions and took lessons in watercolour, certainly from William Payne and possibly from John 'Warwick' Smith.

Marrying in 1790, Glover became father of his first child, John Richardson Glover, in the same year; both John Richardson and a brother, William, would follow in their father's footsteps to become landscape painters.

In 1794, Glover set up as a drawing master in Lichfield, Staffordshire, teaching Henry Curzon Allport and Henry Salt – among others – and passing his 'split brush' technique onto them. During his time in the town, he entered the circle of the poet, Anna Seward, known as 'the Swan of Lichfield'.

Developing a reputation as a landscape watercolourist, Glover sent drawings each year for exhibition in London and, from 1795, also began to show oils at the Royal Academy of Arts. Though much of the period 1795-99 was taken up with making sketching tours through Britain, he then exhibited regularly; soon, he appeared to many contemporaries as the chief rival to J M W Turner – much to the irritation of John Constable.

A founder member of the Society of Painters in Water Colours in 1804, Glover took a house in London – at 3 Montague Square – in 1805, following the success of its first exhibition, in which his works were more highly priced than those of any competitor. He was elected President in 1807, and again in 1814-15, during the period in which he was instrumental in its short-lived reconstruction as the Society for Painters in Oil and Water-Colours. At the same time, in 1814, he became the first English artist to be awarded a gold medal at the Paris Salon. In 1817, he withdrew from the Society of Painters in Water Colours in order to make his (unsuccessful) bid for election to the Royal Academy.

Shortly after his resignation, Glover moved to Blowick Farm, a property near Patterdale, Ullswater, in the Lake District. However, a year later, he set out on a tour of Switzerland and Italy with H C Allport; and would sell the property to buy a work by Claude Lorrain.

Between 1820 and 1824, Glover held a number of solo shows in London; these emphasised the traditional nature of his work by placing it among pictures by Claude Lorrain and Richard Wilson and his own copies of seventeenth-century landscapes. In 1823, he also helped inaugurate the Society of British Artists.

In 1830, Glover decided to follow his three younger sons to Van Diemen's Land (now known as Tasmania). He was joined by his wife and eldest son, while his two married daughters remained in England. Arriving in Hobart on 1 April 1831, he used the substantial profit from the sale of both his pictures and his house (at 16 Montague Square) to purchase a large estate at Mill's Plain, at the foot of Ben Lomond, east of Launceston – an estate he nostalgically named Patterdale. Painting the local scenery and inhabitants, as well as farming sheep, he sent pictures to various London exhibitions, including a solo show. However, he probably had a greater influence on the development of Australian art. He died on his estate on 9 December 1849.

His work is represented in numerous public collections, including the British Museum, Tate and the V&A; The Fitzwilliam Museum (Cambridge), Leeds Art Gallery and Tyne & Wear Museums; and the Art Gallery of New South Wales (Sydney), the Art Gallery of South Australia (Adelaide), the Queen Victoria Museum and Art Gallery (Launceston) and the Tasmanian Museum and Art Gallery (Hobart).

Further reading:

Patrick Conner, 'Glover, John (*b* Houghton-on-the-Hill, Leics, 18 Feb 1767; *d* Launceston, Tasmania, 9 Dec 1849)', Jane Turner (ed), *The Dictionary of Art*, London: Macmillan, 1996, vol 12, pp 820-821
Robert Dingley, 'Glover, John (1767-1849)', H C G Matthew and Brian Harrison (eds), *Oxford Dictionary of National Biography*, Oxford University Press, 2004, vol 22, pp 489-490
David Hansen, *John Glover and the Colonial Picturesque*, Hobart: Tasmanian Museum and Art Gallery 2003
Basil Somerset Long, 'John Glover', *Walker's Quarterly*, no 15, April 1924
John McPhee, *The Art of John Glover*, South Melbourne: Macmillan, 1980
John McPhee, *John Glover*, Launceston: Australian Gallery Directors' Council, 1977
Hammond Smith, 'John Glover, OWCS. 1769–1849', *Old Watercolour Society's Club*, vol 57, 1982, pp 7–21

135 A VIEW IN THE LAKE DISTRICT
watercolour
11 ¾ x 16 ½ inches
Provenance: Agnew's, London

136 THE RIVER VALLEY
watercolour
11 x 15 ¾ inches

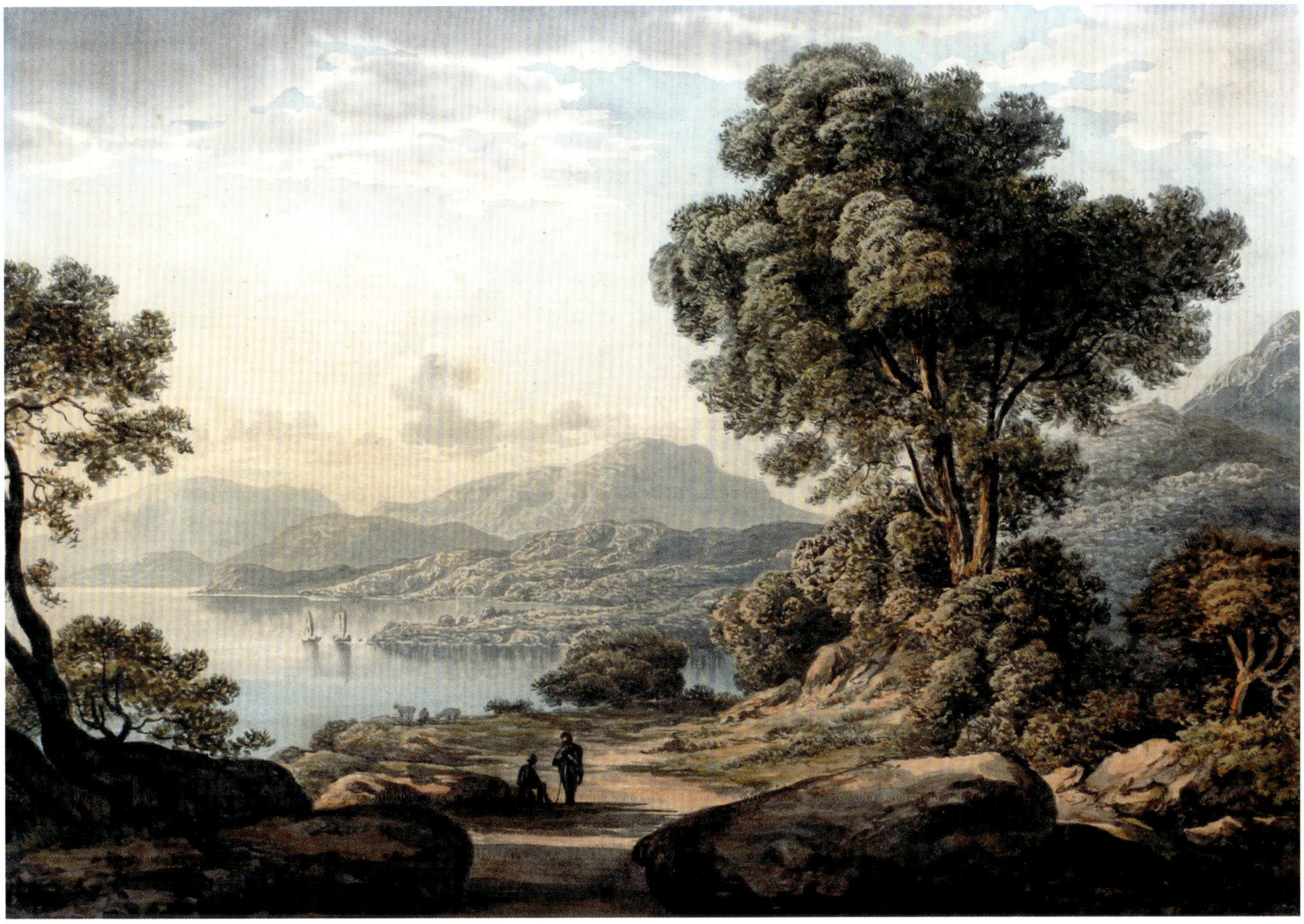

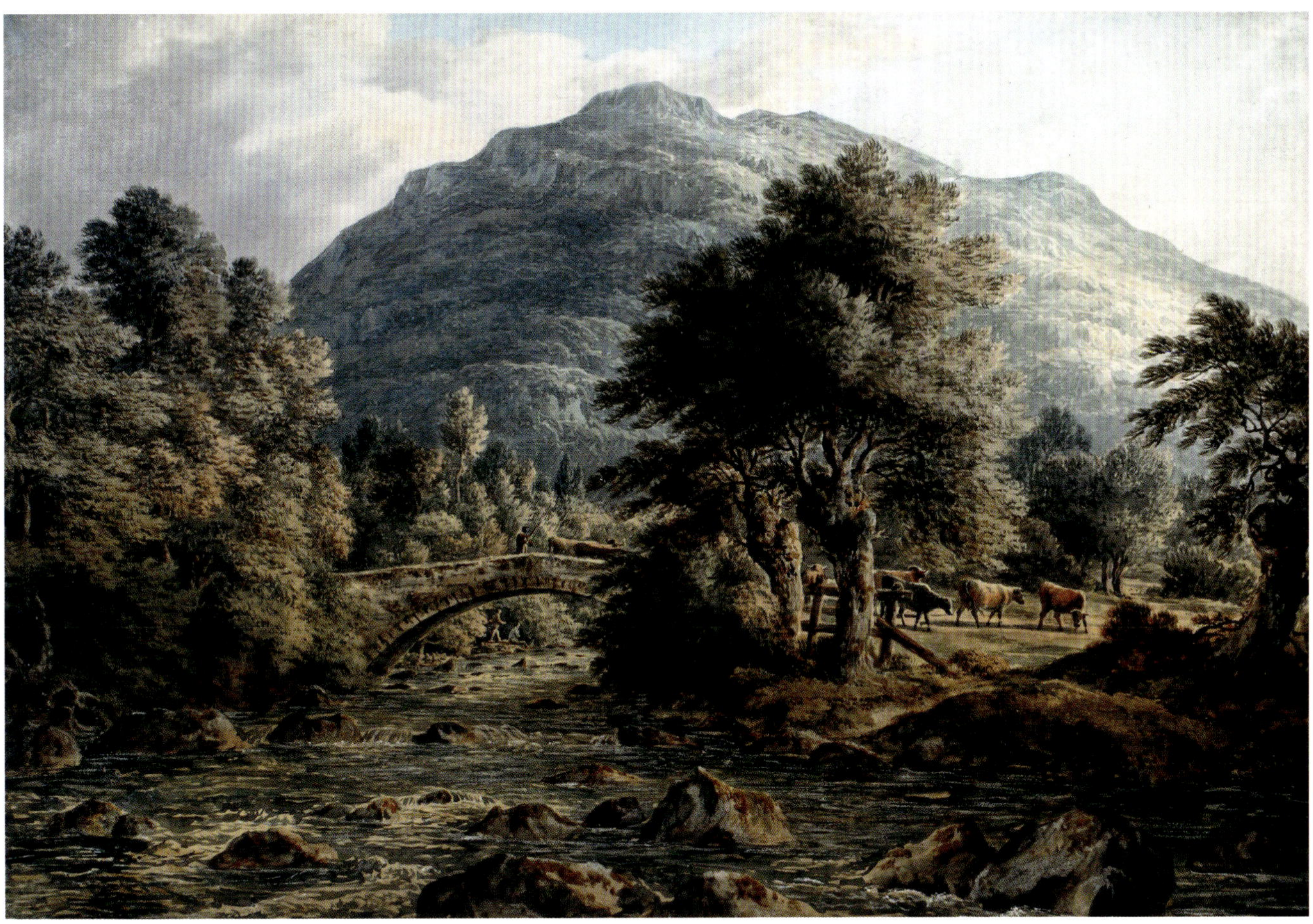

WILLIAM MARSHALL CRAIG
William Marshall Craig, AA (died *circa* 1828)

William Marshall Craig achieved great success and honour as a painter, becoming a popular drawing master, and rising to the position of painter in watercolours to Queen Charlotte. He was also a prolific illustrator of a wide range of books, including stories for children, literary classics and his own varied writings, most significantly those on art.

For an artist who achieved such success, it is surprising how much of his biography remains uncertain, and to what degree the few facts may have been misinterpreted.

There was a long-held belief that William Marshall Craig was a brother of the Edinburgh architect, James Craig, and therefore a nephew of the poet, James Thomson. However, this can now be discredited, as he is not mentioned in recent biographical studies of either figure (and is not listed as one of James Craig's five siblings in Kitty Cruft and Andrew Fraser (eds), *James Craig 1744-1795*, Edinburgh: Mercat Press, 1995, p 2).

More certainly, he was the artist who advertised in the *Manchester Chronicle* on 18 February 1786, as 'Mr Craig (Junior) Miniature Painting and Drawing. Instructed by his father & the ablest artist in London. Sets up in Manchester'. A definite record of his activities begins in 1788 when, living in Manchester, he exhibited at the Royal Academy of Arts for the first time. So he may have arrived in Manchester from London two years earlier.

The identity of his father remains a mystery; though a decade later, in 1798, when he was established in London, he exhibited *A View of Leeds* at 'Mr Craig's Sen. Providence Row. Leeds' (as advertised in *The Leeds Intelligencer*). 'Mr Craig Senior' was E W Craig, a drawing master and watercolour supplier, based in Leeds, at 5 Providence Row from 1794 (when W M Craig happened to be with Walter Fawkes at Farnley Hall, Yorkshire), and Queens Square from 1809. Additionally, a 'James Craig' was listed as a drawing master in Providence Row in 1800, and then in Queens Square, where he was joined by E W Craig (as detailed in 'British artists' suppliers, 1650-1950' on the National Portrait Gallery's website). It is possible, at least, that these were Craig's father and brother.

From about 1790, Craig lived mainly in London, while retaining contacts with Liverpool and Manchester throughout his career. He soon established himself as a painter and specialised in miniatures and other portraits, while also producing domestic and rustic scenes and landscapes. The results were exhibited at the Royal Academy (until 1827), and later at the British Institution (1806-20) and the Associated Artists in Water Colours (1808-1812). He became a member of the latter in 1810 until its demise two years later. Exhibits in the provinces included a group of works shown in Liverpool in 1812. He retained contacts with Liverpool and Manchester through much of his career.

The publication of his manual, *An Essay on the Study of Nature in Drawing Landscape*, in 1793, introduced him to the public as both a drawing master and an illustrator. Other manuals and lectures and many illustrated books would follow (see the list opposite).

In December 1802, Craig attempted to set up an art academy in Manchester, and succeeded in 1804 with the – admittedly short-lived – 'Manchester Academy for Drawing and Designing'.

By 1802, Craig had spent time at Powderham Castle, near Exeter, Devon, as drawing master to the 3rd Viscount Courtenay. He rose to the position of drawing master to Princess Charlotte of Wales, probably before he published *A Wreath for the Brow of Youth* in 1804, 'a book said to have been written for the Princess' (according to Austin Dobson in the first edition of the *Dictionary of National Biography* [London: Smith Elder & Co, vol 12, p 452]). He was appointed painter in watercolours to Queen Charlotte in 1810, and also acted as miniature painter to the Duke and Duchess of York, from 1815. His other pupils included Sarah Biffin, the miniature painter 'born without arms or legs', who was introduced to Craig by his patron, Lord Morton.

Craig was the father of at least seven children, five of whom exhibited at the Royal Academy: W Craig Junior (active 1801-6), Miss E Craig (active 1812-13), H Craig (active 1815), H D Craig (active 1816-17) and J K Craig (active 1819-21).

His work is represented in numerous public collections, including the British Museum and the V&A; and Manchester Art Gallery.

Further reading:
Austin Dobson, rev Annette Peach, 'Craig, William Marshall (*d* 1827)', H C G Matthew and Brian Harrison (eds), *Oxford Dictionary of National Biography*, Oxford University Press, 2004, vol 13, pp 961-962

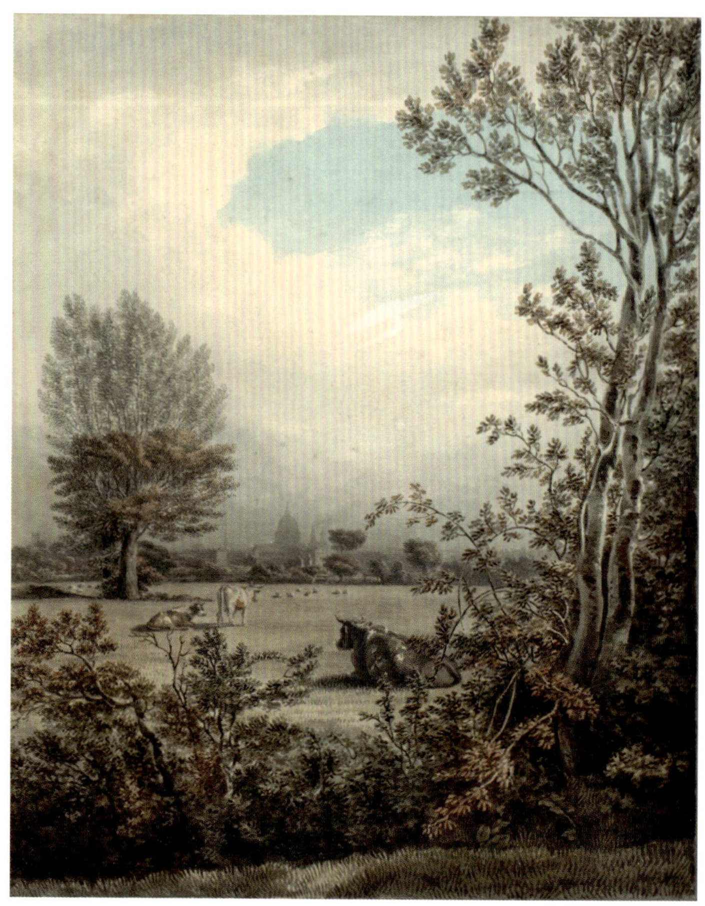

137 ST PAUL'S CATHEDRAL FROM HACKNEY
signed and dated 1797 on original mount
watercolour
11 ½ x 8 ¾ inches

A Preliminary List of Books Written and Illustrated by William Marshall Craig

1793
William Marshall Craig, *An Essay on the Study of Nature in Drawing Landscape*, London: William Bulmer & Co (with illustrative prints, engraved by the author)

1795
William Dodd, *The Beauties of History*, London: Vernor and Hood, E Newbery, J Cuthell, Darton and Harvey, J Scatchard, Lackington, Allen & Co, and J Walker (illustrated, with John Bewick and Thomas Stothard)

1797
John Bell (ed), *British Theatre*, London: George Cawthorne (34 vols) (illustrated, with others)

1800
William Marshall Craig, *The Complete Instructor in Drawing*, London (5 parts)

From 1801
John Britton, *The Beauties of England and Wales*, London: Vernor & Hood (18 vols) (illustrated, with others)

1802
Marquise de Saint-Lambert, *Sara Phillips, from the French*, Poughnill: George Nicholson (title page illustrated, engraved by Hawkins)

***Circa* 1802**
Anon, *A Funeral Oration of a Peasant; The Speech of Logan*; …, Poughnill: George Nicholson (illustrated, engraved by S Austin)

1804: Tabart's Juvenile Library
Anon, *The adventures of Andolocia, with the purse and cap of his father Fortunatus*, London: Tabart and Co (illustrated)
Anon, *The History of Goody Two-Shoes, and the adventures of Tommy Two-Shoes*, London: Tabart and Co (illustrated)
Anon, *The History of Robin Hood*, London: Tabart and Co (illustrated)
Anon, *Riquet with the Tuft*, London: Tabart and Co (illustrated)
Anon, *The Sleeping Beauty in the Wood*, London: Tabart and Co (illustrated)
Madame d'Aulnoy, *The History of the White Cat*, London: Tabart and Co (illustrated)
Charles Perrault, *Hop-o'-my-thumb*, London: Tabart and Co (illustrated)

1804: Other Publications
Anon, *The Story of the Doctor of Smiedberg* …, London: S Fisher [printer] (title page illustrated, engraved by J Nesbit)
William Marshall Craig, *The Wreath*, London: J Harris (illustrated)
William Marshall Craig, *A Wreath for the Brow of Youth*, London: William Marshall Craig (illustrated)
Oliver Goldsmith, *The Poetical Works* …, London: James Cundee (illustrated, possibly with others)
Richard Phillips, *Modern London… London Cries*, London: Richard Phillips (illustrated)
Various, *The Poetical Magazine: or The Temple of the Muses*…, London: Vernor & Hood (illustrated)

1805: Tabart's Juvenile Library
Anon, *The Voyages of Sindbad the Sailor*, London: Tabart and Co (illustrated)

1805: Other Publications
Sir Charles Morell (tr), *The Tales of Genii*, London: James Wallis (illustrated, and variously engraved)

1806: Tabart's Juvenile Library
Anon, *The History of Fortunatus*, London: Tabart and Co (illustrated)

1806: Other Publications
Anon, *Scripture Illustrated*, London (illustrated, with others)

1807
Edward Orme, *An Essay on Transparent Prints*, London: Edward Orme and others (illustrated)

1808
John Bunyan, *The Pilgrim's Progress*, Bungay: C Brightly (illustrated)
Henry Tresham & William Young Ottley, *The British Gallery of Pictures*, London (illustrated, with others)
Isaac Walton & Charles Cotton, *The Complete Angler*, London: Samuel Bagster (illustrated, with Samuel Wale)

From 1808
Elizabeth Inchbold (ed), *The British Theatre*, London: Longman & Co (25 parts) (illustrated, with others)

1809: Tabart's Juvenile Library
Anon, *The Story of Griselda*, London: Benjamin Tabart (illustrated)

1809: Other Publications
Miguel Cervantes (tr Charles Jarvis), *The Life and Exploits of the Ingenious Gentleman Don Quixote de la Mancha*, London: SA and H Oddy (2 vols) (title page illustrated, with other illustrations adapted from Charles Antoine Coypel)
Robert Dodsley, *The Economy of Human Life*, London: Sherwood, Neely & Jones (illustrated, wood-engraved by William Austin and Hole)

***Circa* 1810**
François de Salignac de La Motte-Fénelon, *Pious reflections for every day of the month. Translated from the French* …, Stourport: George Nicholson (illustrated, engraved by William Bromley)

1812
John Milton, *Paradise Lost*, Liverpool: Nuttall, Fisher & Dixon (illustrated)
Ralph Wewitzer, *The Pedigree of King George the Third*, London (illustrated, wood-engraved by J Berryman)

1813
William Cowper, *Poems*, London: S A Oddy (2 vols) (illustrated)
William Marshall Craig (tr), Jean Pierre Claris de Florian after Miguel Cervantes, *Galatea*, London: George Robinson (illustrated, wood-engraved by Francis Craig; engraved frontispiece by J Craig)
Oliver Goldsmith, Clara Reeve and Tobias Smollett, *Mirror of Amusement*, Liverpool: Nuttall, Fisher & Dixon (illustrated)
Samuel Johnson, *The History of Rasselas*, Liverpool: Nuttall, Fisher & Dixon (illustrated)

1815
Anon, *The Self Instructor*, Liverpool: Henry Fisher (illustrated)
Henry Venn, *The Whole Duty of Man* …, London: printed at the Caxton Press, by Nuttall, Fisher & Dixon (illustrated)

***Circa* 1815**
William Marshall Craig, *Instructions for Drawing Landscape*, London (illustrated)

1816
William Marshall Craig, *Instructions for Drawing and Understanding the Human Figure*, London (illustrated)

1817
William Marshall Craig (ed), Gerard de Lairesse, *A Treatise on the Art of Painting*, London: E Orme (2 vols)

1818
William Marshall Craig, *Sports of Love, in six poems and six etchings*, London: Thomas M'Lean

***Circa* 1820**
Anon, *Jack the Giant Killer*, Banbury: printed by J G Rusher (illustrated, wood-engraved by John Lee)

1821
William Marshall Craig, *A Course of Lectures on Drawing, Painting and Engraving… Delivered in the Saloon of the Royal Institution* …, London: Longman, Hurst, Rees, Orme & Brown
William Marshall Craig, *Memoir of Her Majesty Sophia Charlotte, of Mecklenburg Streletz, Queen of Great Britain* …, Liverpool: Caxton Press (illustrated)

***Circa* 1823**
Charles Atmore, *The Whole Duty of Man* ..., London: printed at the Caxton Press, by H Fisher (illustrated)

WILLIAM DANIELL
William Daniell, RA (1769-1837)

The excellent draughtsmanship of William Daniell was matched by his accomplishment as a printmaker, so that he was able to disseminate high quality images of his own drawings. Having contributed significantly to the European perception of India early in his career, he became equally expert at providing visual interpretations of Britain.

The son of the innkeeper of The Swan at Chertsey, William Daniell was orphaned at a young age, and brought up by his uncle, the topographical painter, Thomas Daniell. His brother, Samuel Daniell (1775-1811) remained independent of his uncle, but also became a topographical artist.

In 1784, Thomas decided to go to India to work as an engraver, and William went with him as his assistant. Arriving in Calcutta in 1786, uncle and nephew set about drawing and engraving a set of twelve views of the city, which they aimed at a rapidly expanding market of European inhabitants. Perhaps as a result of their inexperience as engravers, they used a camera obscura and had to enlist the help of Indian craftsmen. Nevertheless, two years later, in 1788, they launched what proved to be a successful publication.

William then joined Thomas on a series of ambitious sketching tours across India. The work that they produced during their first trip – north to Delhi, the Himalayas and Lucknow – was sold by lottery on their return to Calcutta at the end of 1791. The proceeds funded a second tour to the south, and the resulting work was sold by lottery in Madras to fund a third tour westwards to Bombay. William kept an extensive diary of these years in India.

On their return to England, in September 1794, the Daniells began to work up their drawings into colour aquatints, 144 of which were issued in the six volumes of *Oriental Scenery* (1795-1808). This publication made their name, and was highly influential, both on the development of architecture and design and, more generally, on the British perception of India. As a result, it joined the company of such pioneering projects as Stuart and Revett's *Antiquities of Athens* (1762) and Robert Wood's *Ruins of Palmyra* (1753) and *Ruins of Balbec* (1757). It provided an entirely new vision of the Indian subcontinent that was to influence British architecture and the decorative arts. Above all, it formed a popular vision of a romantic and picturesque India that to some extent persists.

William, like Thomas, worked up his drawings into exhibition oils. He showed these, which included British views, at both the Royal Academy of Arts (1795-1838) and the British Institution (1807-36, including the prize-winning *The Battle of Trafalgar* in 1826). Gradually, he distinguished himself from his uncle by producing figure subjects and small waterside scenes that are less topographic than capricious. He also expanded his artistic skills, by gaining some formal training, at the Royal Academy Schools in 1799, the year in which his uncle was elected as Royal Academician. In turn, he too would become an academician (ARA 1807, RA 1822).

In 1801, William married Mary Westall, the eldest sister of the artist Richard Westall. Continuing to develop as an accomplished and prolific printmaker, he worked both independently and in collaboration with other artists, notably his uncle, his brother and his brother-in-law. Much of his independent work was based on tours that he undertook across Britain, a process that culminated in *A Picturesque Voyage round Great Britain* (4 vols, 1814-25), with a text by his fellow traveller, Richard Ayton. The present watercolour relates to the equally fine *Views of Windsor, Eton and Virginia Water* (1827–30). Despite his topographical focus, he also made engravings after 76 of the distinctive portrait drawings made by George Dance the younger (1808-14).

William Daniell died in Camden Town, London, on 16 August 1837.

His work is represented in the collections of the British Museum, The Courtauld Gallery and the V&A; and the Victoria Memorial Hall (Calcutta).

Further reading:

Mildred Archer, 'Daniell', Jane Turner (ed), *The Dictionary of Art*, London: Macmillan, 1996, vol 8, p 505
Mildred Archer, *The Daniells in India, 1786-1793*, Washington DC: Smithsonian Institute, 1962
Mildred Archer, *Early Views of India: The Picturesque Journeys of Thomas and William Daniell, 1786–1794: The Complete Aquatints*, London: Thames & Hudson, 1980
Natasha Eaton, 'Daniell, William (1769–1837)', H C G Matthew and Brian Harrison (eds), *Oxford Dictionary of National Biography*, Oxford University Press, 2004, vol 15, p 87
Martin Hardie and Muriel Clayton, 'Thomas Daniell RA (1749-1840): William Daniell, RA (1769-1837)', *Walker's Quarterly*, nos 35-6, 1932
Maurice Shellim, *Oil Paintings of India and the East by Thomas Daniell, 1749-1840 and William Daniell, 1769-1837*, London: Spink, 1979
Thomas Sutton, *The Daniells: Artists and Travellers*, London: Bodley Head, 1954

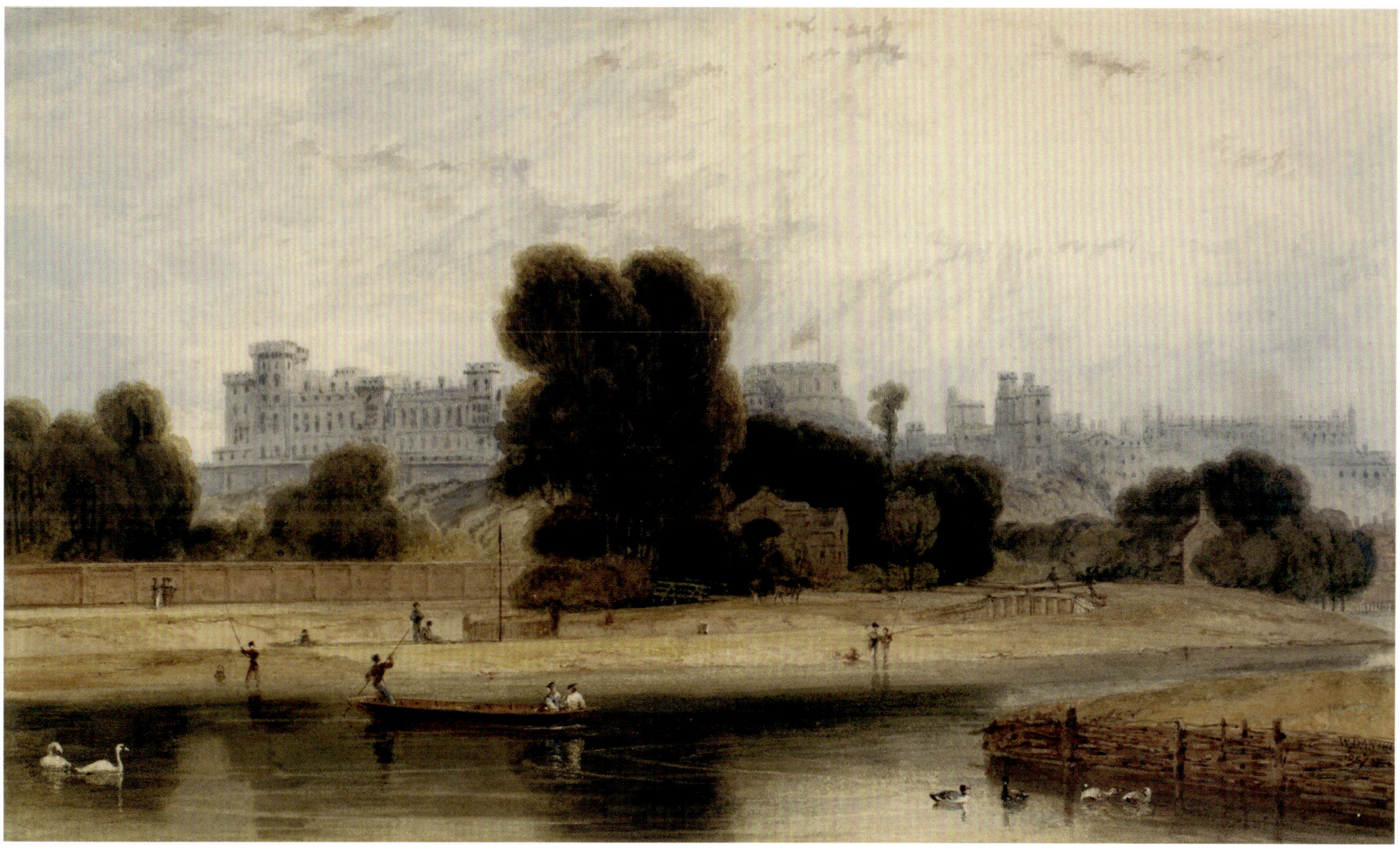

138 WINDSOR CASTLE
signed and dated 1827
watercolour with bodycolour
12 x 19 ¾ inches

WILLIAM HENRY PYNE

William Henry Pyne, OWS (1770-1843)

As a painter and illustrator, William Henry Pyne enlivened his landscapes with human and animal figures, and encouraged amateurs to do the same through volumes of images designed for copying. Instrumental in the foundation of the Society of Painters in Water Colours, he proved even more significant in publishing the first systematic record of the pioneers of watercolour painting and anecdotes about his contemporaries.

William Henry Pyne was born at 9 Exeter Court, The Strand, London on 21 April 1770, the second son of a leather dresser in Holborn. His father encouraged his early interest in art by sending him to study at Henry Pars' drawing school. Apprenticed to William Sharp from the age of fourteen, he quickly developed his facility, and two years later was inspired by the work of Philip James de Loutherbourg to introduce human and animal figures into his landscape compositions. His skill at figures was clear from the first of his twenty-two exhibits at the Royal Academy of Arts, shown in 1790, two years before he married.

In 1798, Pyne began to collaborate with the publisher Rudolph Ackermann on a series of illustrated books that catered for the need of amateur artists to improve their skills by copying. The early volumes included some of his most characteristic work as an illustrator and etcher, *Microcosm* (1803-8) and *The Costume of Great Britain* (1808) comprising well-observed figure groups in picturesque settings.

In 1804, Pyne was one of four artists to originate the idea of founding a Society of Painters in Water Colours and, a year later, contributed a total of twenty-six works to its first exhibition. He resigned four years later, when the society refused to increase its membership above twenty-four artists, though he exhbition once again, in 1815. He was also a member of the Society for the Study of Epic and Pastoral Design, a sketching society founded in 1808 by the CHALON brothers and Francis Stevens (which was later known, more demotically, as the Bread and Cheese Society).

With the wane in his influence with the Society of Painters in Water Colours, Pyne concentrated his energies in his work with Ackermann and, sociable and knowledgeable, became what John Britton called the 'Cicerone' at Ackermann's shop, the Repository of Arts. Not only did he write the text of the first two volumes of *The Microcosm of London* (1808), but he also became a principal contributor to the monthly periodical *Repository of Arts* (1809-28), publishing – anonymously – the pioneering series of articles, 'Observations on the Rise and Progress of Painting in Watercolours'.

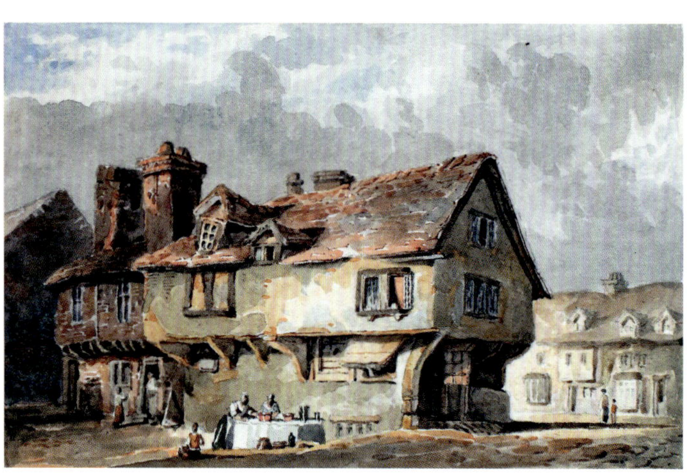

At this stage, Pyne was still as significant a draughtsman as he was a writer, his drawings featuring in a number of Ackermann's publications, including *W H Pyne on Rustic Figures in Imitation of Chalk* (1813) and *A History of the University of Oxford*, with a text by Ackermann (1814). However, by the middle of the decade, writing was becoming his principal source of income, a change signalled by *The History of the Royal Residences*. While Pyne generated this production and wrote its text, he commissioned other artists and printmakers to produce the hundred aquatints, with sumptuous results. Yet the publication of the first part in 1816 proved sobering, for Pyne was forced to dispose of the work at a loss before its completion, remaining only as its editor.

Using the pen name Ephraim Hardcastle, Pyne published a series of art historical anecdotes in the *Literary Gazette*, collecting them together in two volumes as *Wine and Walnuts* in 1823. In that year, he used the same name to launch his own weekly, *The Somerset House Gazette*, though this proved short-lived, and he contributed many articles to other periodicals. Then, in 1825, he published a historical novel, *The Twenty-Ninth of May*, but this too was unsuccessful.

Working again with Ackermann in 1827, Pyne edited the last four volumes of Ackermann's *The World in Miniature*. Yet even this collaboration could not save him from suffering the serious financial difficulties that led, in the following year, to a period of confinement in the King's Bench Prison for debtors. On his release, he painted a few watercolours and contributed to a work entitled *Lancashire Illustrated* (1832), but was confined again as a debtor in 1835.

Pyne died in obscurity at Pickering Place, Paddington, Middlesex on 29 May 1843. He was survived by his wife. His son, George Pyne was also a watercolour painter and wrote on drawing and perspective.

His work is represented in numerous public collections, including the British Museum and the V&A.

Further Reading:

Adrian Bury, 'William Henry Pyne, 1769-1843', *Old Watercolour Society's Club*, vol 28, 1950, pp 1-10
John Ford, 'Pyne, William Henry (*b* London, 1769; *d* London, 29 May 1843)', Jane Turner (ed), *The Dictionary of Art*, London: Macmillan, 1996, vol 25, pp 759-760
Harriet Myers, 'Pyne, William Henry [pseud. Ephraim Hardcastle] (1770–1843)', H C G Matthew and Brian Harrison (eds), *Oxford Dictionary of National Biography*, Oxford University Press, 2004, vol 45, pp 645-646

139 AN OLD TOWN HOUSE
watercolour
3 x 4 ¾ inches

PAUL SANDBY MUNN
Paul Sandby Munn, AOWS (1773-1845)

Paul Sandby Munn is best regarded as a watercolourist of atmospheric, even dramatic landscapes of England and Wales, though he revived his skills during European travels late in life.

Paul Sandby Munn was born at Thornton Row, Greenwich, Kent on 8 February 1773, one of at least two sons of James Munn, carriage decorator and landscape painter. His earliest works reveal the influence of Paul Sandby, and he is believed to have been Sandby's godson as well as pupil – hence his name. He may have sketched alongside such gifted contemporaries as Thomas Girtin and J M W TURNER at Dr Thomas Monro's informal academy in London. He certainly made some drawings with the Sketching Society or 'The Brothers', founded by Girtin in 1799. Following Girtin's death in 1802, JOHN SELL COTMAN became the society's guiding spirit and Munn its secretary.

Munn showed work at the Royal Academy of Arts from 1799 until 1805, when he and his pupil, Francis Stevens, were elected as two of the first associates of the Society of Painters in Water Colours. Many of Munn's best exhibits were developed from sketches made while touring with Cotman to Wales (1802) and Yorkshire (1803). In those years, Cotman was lodging at 107 New Bond Street with Munn and his brothers, William and James, who sold stationery, prints – and Paul's watercolours – from the same address. In addition to his work as a watercolourist, Munn contributed images to one of the earliest set of lithographs and to John Britton's *Beauties of England and Wales* (1801-18).

In 1811, or soon after, Munn settled in Hastings, where he became a teacher of drawing and music. Ceasing to exhibit after 1815, he had largely given up painting for music by the early 1830s. However, Continental travels to Switzerland (1835) and northern France (1836) seem to have rekindled his artistic interests.

Though married, Munn died childless at Margate, Kent on 11 February 1845 from the effects of diabetes.

His work is represented in numerous public collections, including the British Museum, The Courtauld Gallery and the V&A; and the Ashmolean Museum (Oxford) and The Fitzwilliam Museum (Cambridge).

Further reading:
Susan Sloman, 'Munn, Paul Sandby (1773–1845)', H C G Matthew Harrison and Brian Harrison (eds), *Oxford Dictionary of National Biography*, Oxford University Press, 2004, vol 39, pp 759-760

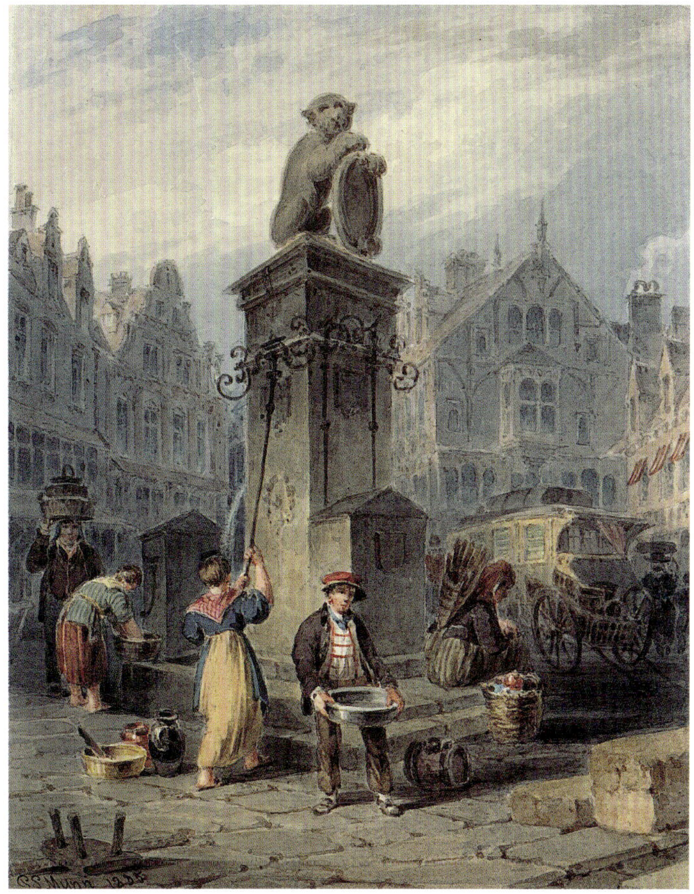

140 BERNE
signed and dated 1835 and inscribed with title on original mount
watercolour
7 ¾ x 6 inches

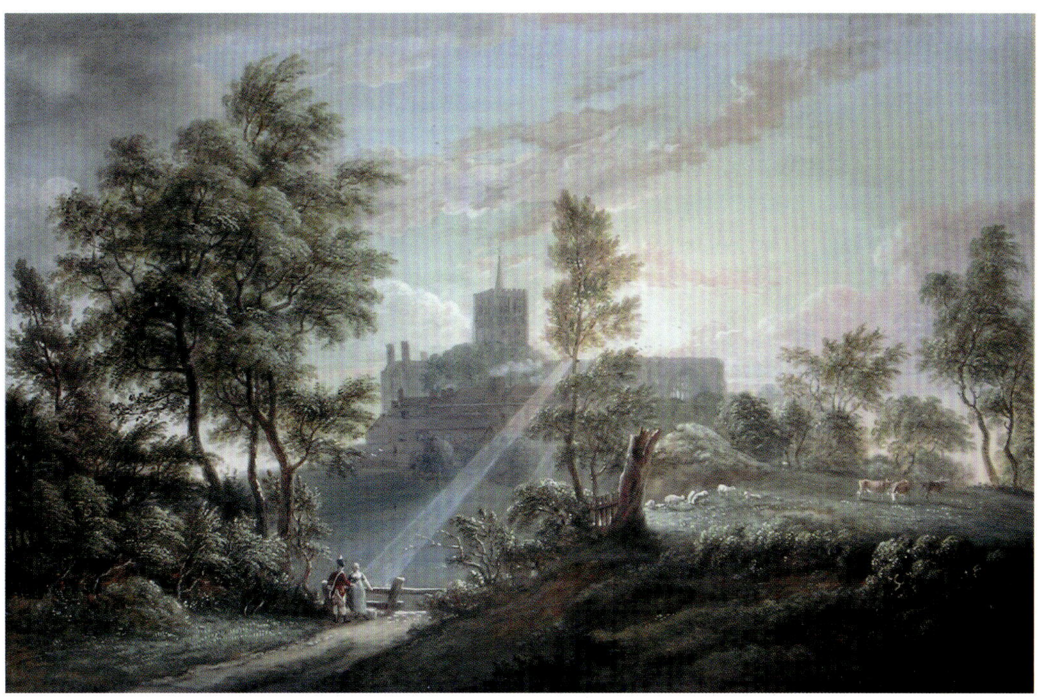

141 BY EVENING LIGHT
watercolour and bodycolour
21 ½ x 31 inches

JAMES BOURNE
The Reverend James Bourne (1773-1854)

During the first three decades of the nineteenth century, James Bourne was a leading London drawing master, numbering members of the aristocracy among his clients and mixing with some of the most innovative watercolourists of his generation.

James Bourne was born in Dalby, near Spilsby, Lincolnshire on 24 April 1773, the son of a landed gentleman. When his father remarried four years later, he was sent away to Louth Grammar School. While there, he suffered from such harsh conditions that, on the death of his father in 1788, he persuaded friends to transfer him to another school.

While in Louth, Bourne was influenced by one of his brothers, a solicitor, to join the Methodists. However, he was at once too free to observe its strict principles yet too conscientious to make a complete break, with the result that he developed a highly melancholic temperament.

In his early years, Bourne seems to have been uncertain as to which direction his life should take. Though he went to London to find work in 1789, he moved to Manchester eighteen months later. Either there, or soon after, he received offers of both a commission in the army and a place at St John's College, Cambridge, but took up neither. Eventually, a relative gave him some financial support, and this allowed him to take up drawing, and then set up as a drawing master.

In 1796, Bourne returned to London, where an old schoolfriend introduced him to two of his first clients, Lord Spencer and the Countess of Sutherland. Through Lady Sutherland, it is likely that he met Thomas Girtin and J M W TURNER. From 1799, he made regular summer sketching tours, probably including one to Wales with Sir George Beaumont, in 1800, and several to Lincolnshire. He exhibited thirteen drawings at the Royal Academy of Arts from 1800 to 1809, and contributed others to *A Selection of Views in the County of Lincoln* (1797-1801).

According to entries in the Royal Academy catalogues, Bourne lived at 30 Park Street, Grosvenor Square, (1801) and 20 Prince's Street, Cavendish Square (1806); and then, following his marriage in 1810, at 41 Margaret Street, Cavendish Square (by 1817) and 7 Somerset Street, Portman Square (1820).

In 1827, Bourne exhibited eleven of his works at the first exhibition of the Royal Manchester Institution. Yet, despite his growing reputation, his health declined, so that, once again, he became preoccupied by his faith. He gave up his profession for the Methodist ministry in 1838 and, eight years later, left London for the provinces, where he developed into an experiential preacher of some note. He worked at Pulverbach (Shropshire), Hertford, and Maney, Sutton Coldfield (Warwickshire), dying in the last on 11 June 1854. He was survived by his widow and seven of his eight children. His many imitators included his three daughters: Edmunda, Henrietta and Elizabeth.

His *Letters … With Outlines of his Life*, detailing the spiritual dimension of his life, was edited by his son-in-law, William Benson, and published in 1861.

The V&A possesses a copy of Bourne's *Interesting Views of the Lakes of Cumberland, Westmoreland and Lancashire* (*circa* 1810), which is dedicated to Lord Yarborough, and includes nine original watercolours bound into the volume. His work is also represented in the collections of the British Museum; Birmingham Museum & Art Gallery, The Fitzwilliam Museum (Cambridge), Manchester Art Gallery, the Usher Gallery (Lincoln) and the Whitworth Art Gallery (Manchester); and the Glynn Vivian Art Gallery (Swansea) and National Museum Wales (Cardiff).

Further reading:

M J H Liversidge, 'James Bourne (1773-1854). an assessment of his life and work', *The Connoisseur*, vol 163, November 1966, pp 161-165

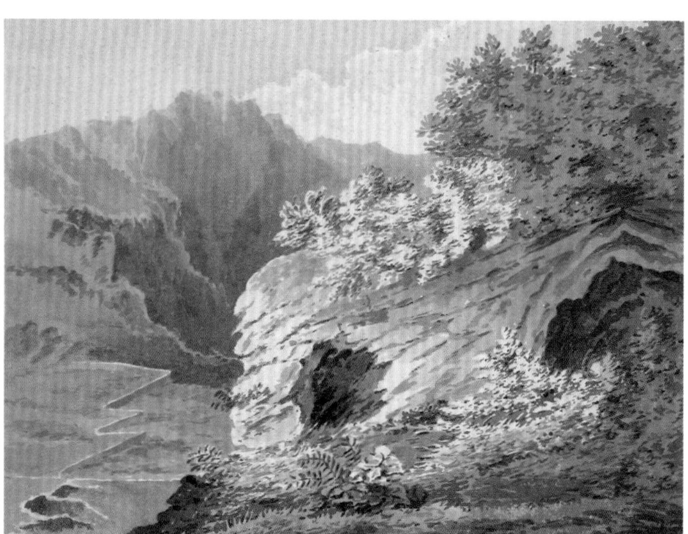

142 MOUNTAINOUS LANDSCAPE
monochrome watercolour
8 ¼ x 10 ½ inches

JOSEPH MALLORD WILLIAM TURNER
Joseph Mallord William Turner, RA (1775-1851)

From the 1790s, J M W Turner competed with his friend, Thomas Girtin, to revolutionise the art of watercolour. Then, following Girtin's death in 1802, he rose to become the foremost English landscape painter of the nineteenth century, who had the vision and energy to exploit many media and genres to his own virtuosic ends.

J M W Turner was born on 23 April 1775 at 21 Maiden Lane, Covent Garden, to William Turner, a barber and wig-maker from South Molton, Devon. Probably because of his mother's mental instability, he spent periods away from London. In 1785, he stayed with his mother's brother, J M W Marshall, a butcher in Brentford, Middlesex, where he attended John White's School; while, in the following year, he stayed in Margate, Kent, with another Marshall relative, a fishmonger, and attended the school run by Thomas Coleman, a Methodist preacher.

Turner drew from an early age and his father hung the results around the entrance to his shop (following the family's move across the road to 26 Maiden Lane in the early 1780s). It seems likely that he gained some experience as a draughtsman in the office of the architect, Thomas Hardwick, before working with the architectural draughtsman, Thomas Malton the younger, in 1789. By the end of that year, his father had entered him into the Royal Academy Schools, and he exhibited his first work, a watercolour of Lambeth Palace (Indianapolis Museum of Art), at the Royal Academy of Arts in 1790. He last signed the register of the life academy in November 1799.

During the early 1790s, Turner followed the eighteenth-century topographical tradition, and was inspired by his first sketching tours in England and Wales to make many drawings and watercolours. As landscape was not taught at the Royal Academy, he spent valuable time at Dr Thomas Monro's informal academy, copying drawings by J R Cozens, EDWARD DAYES, Thomas Hearne and others, sometimes in collaboration with Thomas Girtin.

Turning to oils in the mid 1790s, Turner exhibited his first painting in that medium – *Fishermen at Sea* (Tate) – at the Royal Academy in 1796. While his watercolours reflected direct observation and awareness of contemporaries, his oils reinterpreted popular styles of the past, including the Classical landscapes of Claude Lorrain and Richard Wilson, and seascapes in the Dutch tradition, seen in the collections of his patrons. However, his experiments in oil and his experience of Britain's mountains (the Lake District, Snowdonia, and then Scotland from 1801) together fuelled his ambitions in watercolour. So, during the first decade of the nineteenth century, he would begin to produce the highly powerful and atmospheric works on paper that are now synonymous with Romanticism.

Turner was also a Romantic in his constant attempts to parallel the visual and the verbal. Inspired by the example of eighteenth-century poets, including James Thomson, he began to write his own poetry, and use quotations from his and others' writings as titles for his paintings. At the same time, his images had begun to appear in engraved form in *The Copper-Plate Magazine*, *The Pocket Magazine* and similar illustrated albums.

Encouraged by his election as an associate of the Royal Academy in 1799, Turner left home and rented rooms at 64 Harley Street. He may have done so in part to free himself from his mother, who was committed to the Royal Bethlehem Hospital, Moorfields, in 1800, and died there four years later. However, it also gave him the opportunity to install his mistress, Sarah, widow of the glee composer, John Danby, in a studio nearby. She gave birth to the first of Turner's daughters, Evelina, a year later.

Elected a Royal Academician in February 1802, Turner made his first tour of the Continent from July to October, taking in Paris and travelling as far as Switzerland. Soon after his return, he attended the funeral of Girtin, his friend but also his rival. He would later remark that, 'if Tom had lived, I should have starved' and, though this now seems an exaggeration, Girtin was certainly considered the greater watercolourist at the time, Turner being more appreciated for his oils.

Thus Girtin's death acted as a kind of release for Turner, and the Swiss watercolours that he began to exhibit demonstrated his new predominance in the field. Indeed, his watercolours began to be more favourably received than his oils, and he was treated as a leader by fellow watercolourists, though his status as an academician disqualified him from joining the Society of Painters in Water Colours, which was founded in 1804 by, among others, his close friend, William Frederick Wells.

From this time, Turner exhibited most of his watercolours at the gallery he had built in 1803 at Harley Street. A year later, his widowed father joined him there, becoming a close companion and studio assistant. Around the same time, he rented a second home on the Thames, first at Isleworth, and then – from 1806 to 1811 – at Hammersmith.

It was W F Wells who suggested that Turner produce his *Liber Studiorum* (1807-19), a large-scale series of mezzotint engravings intended to demonstrate the various categories of landscape. Turner not only etched the plates, but oversaw the entire project, to the degree that he trained a whole school of engravers, notably Thomas Lupton, Charles Say and Charles Turner.

While spreading his reputation through the *Liber Studiorum*, Turner also developed close personal relationships with three of his most significant patrons: Sir John Leicester, 1st Lord de Tabley, of Tabley House, Cheshire; George O'Brien Wyndham, 3rd Earl of Egremont of Petworth, Sussex; and, particularly, Walter Fawkes of Farnley Hall, Yorkshire. Until Fawkes' death in 1825, Turner made annual visits to his estate and many of his works entered his patron's collection.

In 1810, Turner moved to 47 Queen Anne Street West (around the corner from Harley Street), and a year later Sarah Danby gave birth to Georgiana, his second child. During this time he also designed a second home, possibly with the help of his architect friend, John Soane. This modest house was built in Twickenham as Solus Lodge, though was later renamed Sandycombe Lodge. The house was sold in 1826, when Turner's father 'was no longer able to enjoy working in the garden' (Luke Herrmann, in Matthew Harrison 2004, vol 55, p 637).

Having been Professor of Perspective at the Royal Academy Schools since 1807, he began to lecture there in 1811, and would continue to offer his course until 1828 (resigning the Professorship in 1837). He prepared his lectures with care, and produced many fine large drawings to illustrate them, but his delivery was poor, so making them difficult to hear and understand. Patently, Turner communicated better visually than verbally (his attempts at poetry consisting, at best, of resonant fragments). Through the second decade of the nineteenth century, he produced an increasing number of images for publication, while developing into the greatest force in British painting.

The volumes of engravings on which Turner worked during the second decade of the nineteenth century give an indication of his travels within Britain: W B Cooke's *Picturesque Views of the Southern Coast of England* (1814-26), Thomas Dunham Whitaker's *A History of Richmondshire* (1818-23) and Sir Walter Scott's *Provincial Antiquities and Picturesque Scenery of Scotland* (1819-26). However, following the end of the Napoleonic Wars in 1815, he was as likely to be found travelling and sketching abroad. He toured Belgium and the Rhine in 1817, and two years later made his first visit to Italy, armed with advice from James Hakewill, whose drawings he worked up for *A Picturesque Tour of Italy* (1818-20). His experience of Italy, and especially Venice, would have an enormous effect on Turner's approach to light and colour.

During the 1820s, Turner continued to travel extensively, both in Britain and on the Continent. He made repeated visits to France, toured Holland, Belgium and the Rhine (1825), and even set up a studio in Rome (1828). In addition innumerable paintings and drawings, the fruits of his native travels included the mezzotints published in W B Cooke's *Rivers of England and Wales* (1823-27) and line engravings published in Charles Heath's *Picturesque Views of England and Wales* (1827-38), the last of the artist's large-scale topographical projects. During the same period, he also produced – almost single-handedly – his own set of twelve mezzotints, known as the 'Little Liber'.

Following the death of Walter Fawkes, Turner made regular visits to Petworth to stay with Lord Egremont and, in 1828, he received a commission to paint four decorative panels for the dining room.

The death of his father in 1829 had a profound effect on Turner. Returning to Margate, where he had attended Colman's School, he began to spend frequent weekends at the Cold Harbour lodgings of Mrs Sophia Caroline Booth, and became her lover after her husband's death in 1833. Yet, ever restless, he continued to make extensive tours in order to gain inspiration and gather material for his paintings and illustrations.

In the summer of 1831, Turner returned to Scotland, staying with Sir Walter Scott at Abbotsford in order to prepare for *The Poetical Works of Sir Walter Scott* (1832-34) and *Miscellaneous Prose Works of Sir Walter Scott* (1834-36). Then, two years later, he made an extensive tour of Europe, culminating in a second visit to Venice. This gave rise to an enormous number of watercolours, and also influenced his illustrations to Finden's *Landscape and Portrait Illustrations to the Life and Work of Lord Byron* (1832-34) and Samuel Rogers' *Poems* (1834). Elsewhere, his travels were rehearsed more directly in print, through the publication of 'Turner's Annual Tours': *Wanderings by the Loire* (1833) and *Wanderings by the Seine* (1834-35).

Turner's developing relationship with a new patron, H A J Munro of Novar, gave rise to a tour of France, Switzerland and the Val d'Aosta in 1836; and the creativity generated by the Alpine landscape, seen especially in a series of watercolours, ensured that he revisited Switzerland annually between 1841 and 1844.

Through the 1830s and 1840s, Turner increasingly sustained the immediacy of his studies from nature into his large-scale canvases, becoming famous for substantially completing his exhibits once they were hanging in the Royal Academy. However, this practice often led to bewildered responses, as when one newspaper critic described *Snow Storm: Steam-Boat off a Harbour's Mouth* (exhibited 1842; Tate) as 'soapsuds and whitewash'. John Ruskin came to the artist's defence, writing the five volumes of *Modern Painters* (1843-60) to explain his supremacy.

By the mid 1840s, Turner was at the same time an experimental painter and an establishment figure, acting as President of the Royal Academy in summer 1845, during the illness of Sir Martin Archer Shee. He himself became ill soon after, and his activity began to wane, his last Continental trip – to Normandy and Picardy – taking place in autumn 1845.

By 1846, Turner had taken 6 Davis Place, Cremorne New Road, Chelsea, under the assumed name of Admiral Booth, and brought Mrs Booth from Margate to act as his housekeeper. Meanwhile, his London home, at 47 Queen Anne Street West, was presided over by Hannah Danby, niece to his mistress, Sarah. His last dated watercolours were produced in 1846, though he continued to exhibit oils at the Royal Academy until 1850.

Though dying obscurely in Chelsea on 19 December 1851, Turner was buried with great ceremony in the crypt of St Paul's Cathedral at the end of the same month.

At his death, Turner bequeathed nearly 300 paintings and over 30,000 watercolours and drawings to the nation. They are mainly housed in the Clore Gallery at Tate Britain, though some of the oils are on show at the National Gallery.

His work is also represented in numerous public collections, including the British Museum, The Courtauld Gallery, the V&A and the Wallace Collection (London); the Ashmolean Museum (Oxford), Birmingham Museum & Art Gallery, The Fitzwilliam Museum (Cambridge), the Lady Lever Art Gallery (Port Sunlight), Manchester Art Gallery, Sudley House (Liverpool), Tyne & Wear Museums, the Walker Art Gallery (Liverpool) and The Whitworth Art Gallery (Manchester); National Museum Wales (Cardiff); Aberdeen Art Gallery & Museums and the National Gallery of Scotland (Edinburgh); the National Gallery of Ireland (Dublin); Musée du Louvre (Paris); The Frick Collection (New York), the Getty Center (Los Angeles), Harvard University Art Museums (Cambridge MA), the Metropolitan Museum of Art (New York), The Morgan Library & Museum (New York), the Museum of Fine Arts (Boston), the National Gallery of Art (Washington) and the Yale Center for British Art (Newhaven); The National Gallery of Canada (Ottawa); and the National Gallery of Victoria (Melbourne).

Further reading:
Martin Butlin and Evelyn Joll, *The Paintings of J M W Turner*, London: 1977, rev 1984 (2 vols)
Martin Butlin, Andrew Wilton and John Gage, *Turner, 1775-1851*, London: Royal Academy of Arts, 1974
John Gage, *J M W Turner, 'A Wonderful Range of Mind'*, London, 1987
Luke Herrmann, *J M W Turner, 1775-1851*, London: Methuen & Co, 1963
Luke Hermann, 'Turner, Joseph Mallord William (1775-1851)', H C G Matthew and Brian Harrison (eds), *Oxford Dictionary of National Biography*, Oxford University Press, 2004, vol 55, pp 632-648
Jack Lindsay, *J M W Turner. His Life and Work*, London: Cory, Adams & Mackay, 1966
Andrew Wilton, *The Life and Work of J M W Turner*, London: Academy Editions, 1979
Andrew Wilton, *Turner in his Time*, London: Thames and Hudson, 1987
Andrew Wilton, 'Turner, J(oseph) M(allord) W(illiam) (*b* London, 23 April 1775, *d* Chelsea [now in London], 19 December 1851)', Jane Turner (ed), *The Dictionary of Art*, London: Macmillan, 1996, vol 31, pp 466-476

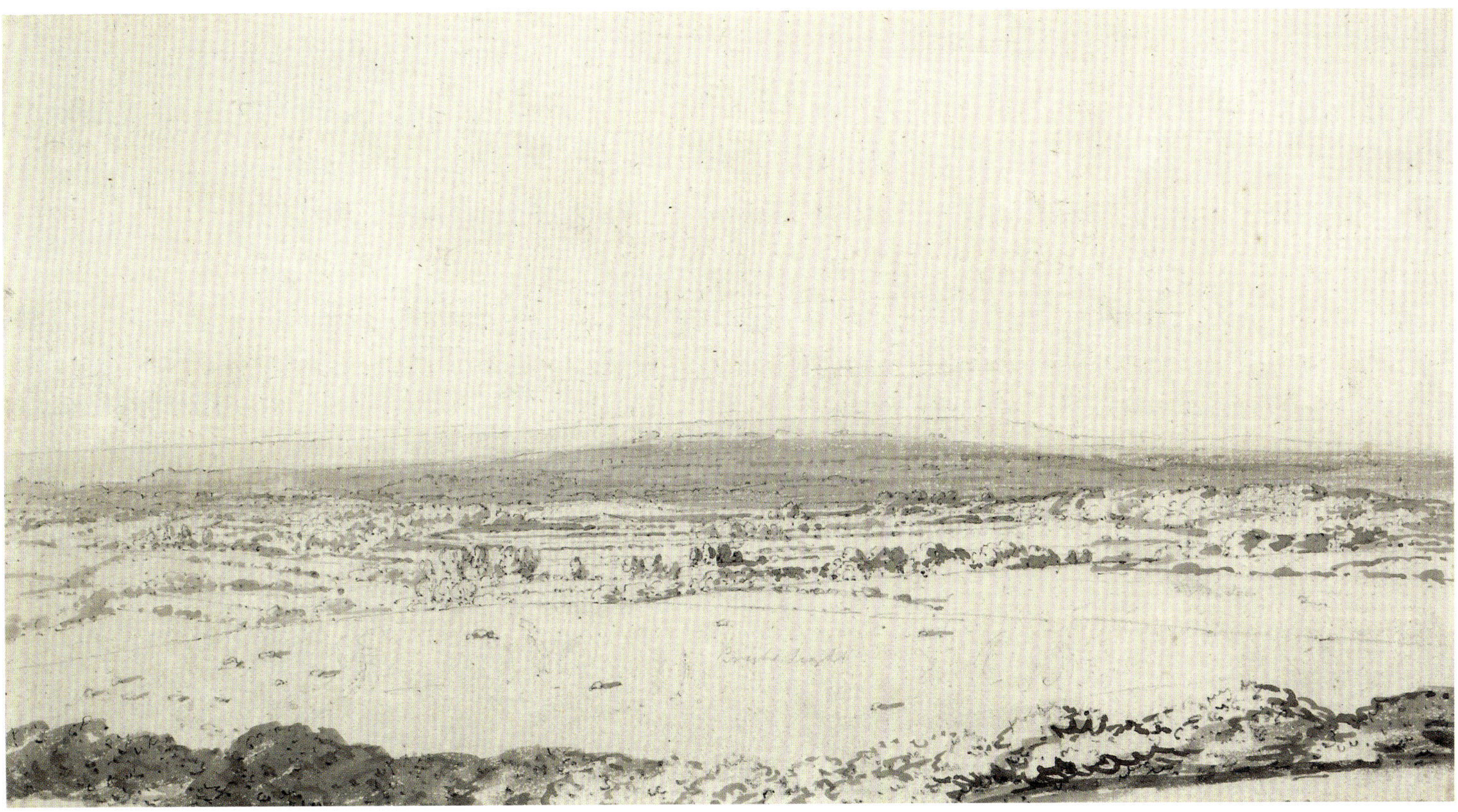

143 NORBURY PARK
inscribed with title on reverse
pen ink and monochrome watercolour
5 ½ x 10 ¼ inches

Norbury Park
It was probably Dr Thomas Monro who introduced J M W Turner to the banker, William Lock (1732-1810), of Norbury Park, between Leatherhead and Dorking, Surrey.

From 1794, Turner had worked in Dr Monro's informal academy at 8 Adelphi Terrace, London, and would join him at the cottage that he rented at Fetcham, also near Leatherhead, from 1795. Monro introduced Turner to a number of collectors and patrons, of whom Lock is likely to have been the first.

Lock was a significant connoisseur, who had befriended and patronised the landscape painter, Richard Wilson, while on the Grand Tour in 1749, and also became a friend of Henry Fuseli and Thomas Lawrence. His dining room at Norbury Park was famously painted with landscapes and trompe-l'oeil effects by George Barret the elder, Giambattista Cipriani and Benedetto Pastorini.

On returning from his first tour of the north of England in summer 1797, Turner visited Lock, and produced a number of watercolours of the estate, including the present image and one of the fern-house that was exhibited at the Royal Academy in the following year.

Monro continued to patronise Turner into the 1830s, and probably introduced him to his friend (and relative by marriage), John Julius Angerstein, whose art collection, including works by Claude Lorrain, would prove such an influence on the artist.

WILLIAM DELAMOTTE
William Alfred Delamotte, AOWS (1775-1863)

A drawing master at the Royal Military College for forty years, William Delamotte developed a reputation as a skilful topographic painter and printmaker, known especially for his views of Oxford and the Thames Valley.

William Delamotte was born in Weymouth, Dorset, on 2 August 1775, the eldest son of Peter Delamotte. Peter Delamotte was a postal agent of Huguenot extraction who established Delamotte's Circulating Library on the esplanade, and produced *The Weymouth Guide* from 1785.

George III was a frequent visitor to Weymouth during this period, and it is said that he first encouraged the young Delamotte to draw and then sent him to London to study under his favourite artist, Benjamin West, President of the Royal Academy of Arts. Certainly, Delamotte exhibited at the Royal Academy from 1793 (until 1850), and entered the Royal Academy Schools in March 1794. Working in watercolour as well as oil, he was influenced first by WILLIAM TAVERNER, and then by Thomas Girtin, though he soon established his own manner of outline enlivened by light wash.

In 1798, Delamotte moved to Oxford, where he succeeded John Baptist Malchair as drawing master to the undergraduates (being succeeded, in 1803, by William Crotch). Following the signing of the Treaty of Amiens between Britain and France in 1802, he joined many other artists in visiting Paris, and stayed in the city for ten weeks. On his return to Oxford, he restored Robert Streater's ceiling decoration in the Sheldonian Theatre. (In 1805, he would restore a triptych by William Hogarth in St Mary Redcliffe, Bristol.)

In 1803, Delamotte was appointed second drawing master at the Junior Department of the Royal Military College in Great Marlow, Buckinghamshire (being subordinate to WILLIAM ALEXANDER until his resignation in 1808). Marrying in 1804, and eventually becoming the father of nine children, he entered a settled lifestyle. Following the college's move to Sandhurst, Surrey, in 1812, he remained as its drawing master for another three decades, while developing his own oeuvre.

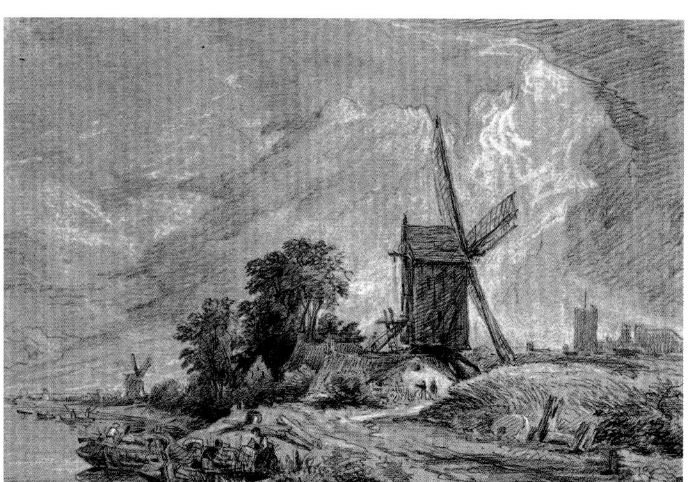

In the years 1805-7, Delamotte made a number of pioneering oil sketches in the open air along the Thames, sometimes working with William Havell, and absorbing the influence of another friend, J M W TURNER. He also took a number of sketching tours in England and Wales and, following the fall of Napoleon, on the Continent. As a result of these travels, he increased the number and range of his exhibits. He became an associate of the Society of Painters in Water Colours in 1806 (for just three years), and also showed at the British Institution (1808-46) and, later, at the Society of British Artists (1829-31).

Like many artists of the day, Delamotte contributed to John Britton and E W Brayley's series, *The Beauties of England and Wales* (*Oxfordshire*, 1813). He soon followed this with his set of *Thirty Etchings of Rural Subjects* (1816). However, his landscapes were not regularly disseminated as prints and illustrations until the late 1830s, when he published his *Picnic Set of Etchings* and contributed to James Ingram's *Memorials of Oxford* (both 1837). In the 1840s, his publications were many and varied. He contributed illustrations to *Ainsworth's Magazine* (1842) and Harrison Ainsworth's *Windsor Castle* (1843); illustrated his own compilation, *An Historical Sketch of the Priory and Royal Hospital of St Bartholomew* (1844) and also George T Fisher's *Smoking & Smokers* (1845); produced *Original Views of Oxford* (as lithographed by William Gauci, 1843) and worked up sketches by Frances Broughton as *Views of the Overland Journey to India* (1847).

On leaving Sandhurst, Delamotte seems to have lived in Oxford. He died at the home of one of his four daughters, The Lawn, St Giles' Fields, near Oxford, on 13 March 1863. A sale of his drawings and sketches took place at Sotheby's in the following May.

His brother George Orleans Delamotte was also a landscape painter, who taught at Sandhurst and elsewhere, and sketched in Wales.

Of William's five sons, three became artists: William Alfred Delamotte, a watercolour artist who is often confused with his father; Freeman Gage Delamotte, a wood-engraver who compiled works on lettering and illumination; and Philip Henry Delamotte, a photographer and drawing master, who became Professor of Fine art at King's College, London, in 1879.

His work is represented in Canterbury Cathedral Library, and numerous public collections, including the British Museum and the V&A; and the Ashmolean Museum (Oxford) and The Fitzwilliam Museum (Cambridge).

Further reading:

Patrick Conner, 'Delamotte: (1) William Delamotte (*b* Weymouth, Dorset, 2 Aug 1775; *d* Oxford, 2 Feb 1863)', Jane Turner (ed), *The Dictionary of Art*, London: Macmillan, 1996, vol 8, p 652
Luke Herrmann, 'Delamotte [de la Motte], William (1775–1863)', H C G Matthew and Brian Harrison (eds), *Oxford Dictionary of National Biography*, Oxford University Press, 2004, vol 15, pp 705-706

144 LANDSCAPE WITH A WINDMILL
signed and dated 1819
pencil and bodycolour on tinted paper
8 ¼ x 11 ½ inches

JOHN SAMUEL HAYWARD
John Samuel Hayward (1778-1822)

While remaining an amateur artist, John Samuel Hayward had a surprisingly high status in the London art world of the first two decades of the nineteenth century, befriending Joshua Cristall and Thomas Girtin among others. As a floor cloth manufacturer, he provided canvas for the large-scale panoramic paintings that were popular at the time. As an artist, he produced his own – collaborative – panoramas, exhibited watercolours at the Royal Academy of Arts, and took an active part in the pioneering Sketching Society.

John Samuel Hayward was the eldest of the five surviving children of John and Elizabeth Hayward. John Hayward had been a tobacconist until his marriage, in 1770, to Elizabeth, the only daughter of Samuel Barnes, a carpet and floor cloth manufacturer of 37 Newington Causeway, Southwark. John was then taken into the business and, on the death of his father-in-law in 1778, became its proprietor. When John Hayward died in 1794, he was succeeded by Thomas Hayward, who may have been a brother. A decade later, Thomas Hayward also had a floor cloth manufactory at 195 Whitechapel Road, Tower Hamlets. (Thomas was a musical amateur, and made these premises available for the first British concert performance of Mozart's *Don Giovanni* in 1805.) Southwark and Tower Hamlets, to the south and east of London, were both important centres for the production of 'floor cloth', the precursor to oilcloth and linoleum.

John Samuel Hayward seems to have been well educated – for he was fluent in French and Italian – and brought up to work in the family business. Eventually, he was able to describe himself on his business card as a 'Floor Cloth and Canvas Manufacturer, House Painter and Decorator, and Supplier of Portable Temples, Ball Rooms, Pavillions, Domes, Treillage Balconies, Awnings and Covered Ways, any of which could be erected in any part of the kingdom'. So he came to combine art and commerce.

The young Hayward spent some time studying pattern design at a calico print works at Old Ford, Tower Hamlets, and there he befriended the budding young artist, Joshua Cristall. Later, Cristall moved in with Mr Lacklan, a print designer, who lived at 28 Surrey Street (now Blackfriars Street), Southwark – close to Hayward's home in Newington Causeway. Cristall received some support from Lacklan during his formative years as an artist, a period that included the production of a panorama of Constantinople, painted in collaboration with Hayward and others, and displayed at the Great Room, Spring Gardens (near what is now Trafalgar Square). Panoramas had become the rage in 1792, when the Scottish painter, Robert Barker, displayed his all-encompassing paintings of Edinburgh in Castle Street, off Leicester Square.

Painting mainly in watercolour in his spare time, Hayward exhibited figure subjects and especially landscapes at the Royal Academy from 1798 to 1816. His early style (before 1880) has been compared to that of SAMUEL HIERONYMUS GRIMM (Mallalieu 1986, p 170), while his subjects were informed by his extensive travels, which seem to have begun with a visit to the Isle of Wight in 1799.

By 1800, Hayward had made the acquaintance of Thomas Girtin. They certainly spent time together in North Wales in July 1800, in the company of Sir George Beaumont, and again in Paris in the winter of

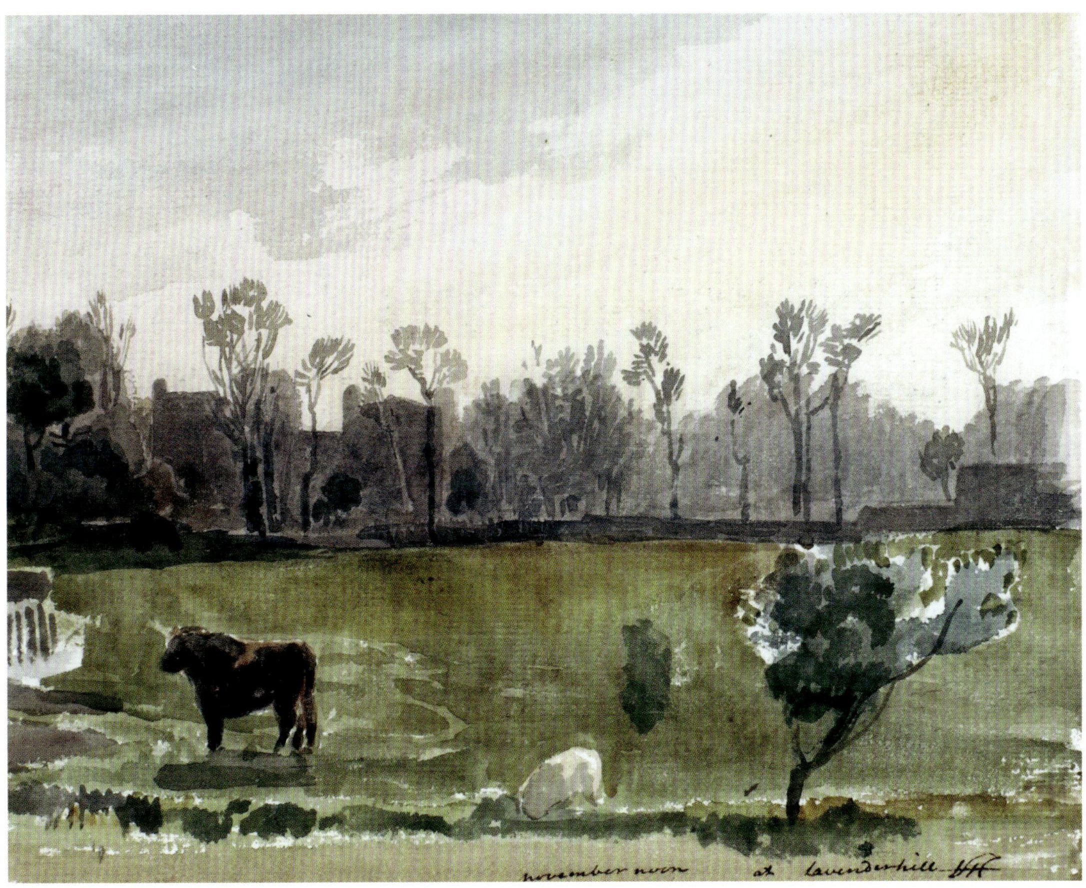

145 NOVEMBER NOON AT LAVENDER HILL
signed with initials and inscribed with title
watercolour
7 x 8 ½ inches
Exhibited: 'John Samuel Hayward 1778-1822', Manning Gallery, London, 1974

JOHN SAMUEL HAYWARD

1801-2, while Hayward was on business (and where he saw panoramas of Paris and Lyons). Soon after, Girtin made use of Hayward's premises in Newington Causeway to paint his panorama of London, known as the Eidometropolis, which was exhibited at the Great Room, Spring Gardens. Hayward is likely to have supplied the canvas for Girtin's panorama, and may also have given him assistance in painting it. Certainly, he would go on to work on other panoramas with James Demaria, the scene painter, who had trained with Thomas Malton at Drury Lane and in turn trained DAVID COX at the Birmingham Theatre. A panorama of Paris by Demaria and Hayward was displayed at the Haymarket in spring 1802.

A year after his return from his first trip to Italy in 1802, Hayward was elected to the Sketching Society, becoming its Secretary. Originally founded in 1799 by Girtin (who died in 1803), and known initially as 'The Brothers', the society was under the Presidency of JOHN SELL COTMAN at the time of Hayward's election. As Girtin had influenced Cotman, so Cotman now influenced Hayward, though Hayward's drawings, of – for instance – Tivoli, also proved inspiring to Cotman. Cristall was another member of the society, and he too influenced Hayward's artistic development.

Through the opening decade of the nineteenth century, Hayward made frequent travels, which he recorded in sketchbooks. In June 1803, he visited Scotland, taking in the Lake District and Liverpool on the return journey. A year later, he returned to Paris, going out from Southampton and returning by way of the Isle of Wight. In August 1805, he travelled to Ireland, staying in Dublin, and exploring County Wicklow and County Kildare. Then, two years later, in autumn 1807, a trip through the West Country, as far west as Penzance, inspired some of his most attractive watercolour sketches.

From 1810, when he returned to North Wales, Hayward seemed to focus on favourite haunts; for, in September 1811, he made drawings in and around Plymouth, while in August 1816, he set off on his last long tour, travelling through France and Italy to Rome, despite suffering from gout. He was accompanied on this five-month journey by the architect, Joseph Gwilt, who produced *Notitia architectonica italiana* (1818) as a result.

Hayward had continued as a member of the Sketching Society following its reconstitution – by Francis Stevens and the CHALON brothers in 1808 – as the Society for the Study of Epic and Pastoral Design. Attending meetings until 1820, he died two years later. His collection and library were sold in auction at Christie's on 27 June 1822 and 26-28 February 1823.

His work is represented in the collections of the British Museum, while the V&A holds an archive of manuscripts, including Hayward's illustrated journal of his 1816-17 tour of France and Italy, and biographical material compiled by Robert and Joseph Howard Barnes. The V&A also holds 'Papers in connection with the early floor cloth manufacture' as arranged by Robert Barnes.

Further reading:
[Anthony Reed], *John Samuel Hayward 1778-1822*, London: Andrew Wyld/Manning Gallery, 1974

Many thanks to Andrew Wyld for help in compiling this entry.

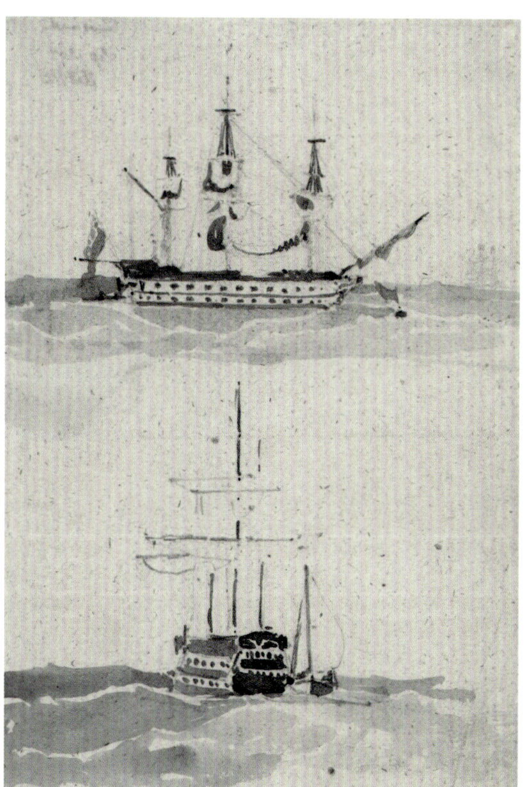

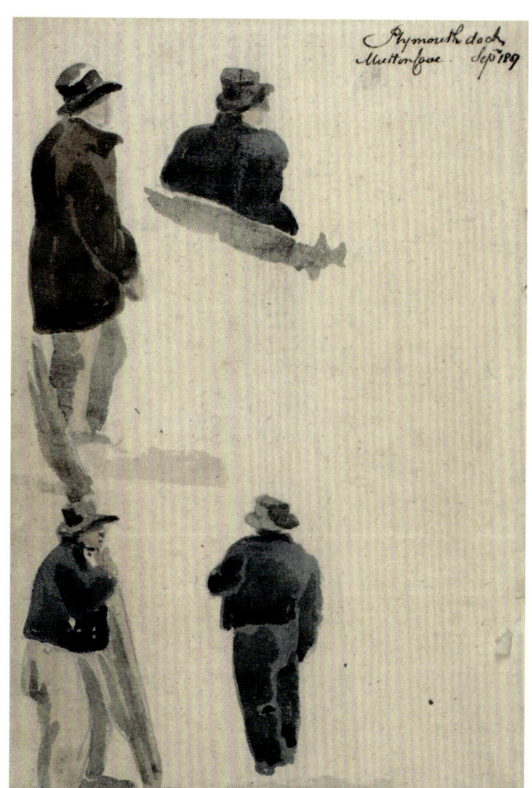

146 LAWSAND
signed with initials, inscribed with title, and dated 'Sept 1807' on reverse
monochrome watercolour
7 ¾ x 5 inches
Exhibited: 'John Samuel Hayward 1778-1822', Manning Gallery, London, 1974

147 PLYMOUTH DOCK
inscribed with title and dated 'Sept 1807'
watercolour
8 x 5 ½ inches
Exhibited: 'John Samuel Hayward 1778-1822', Manning Gallery, London, 1974

JOHN SELL COTMAN
John Sell Cotman, AOWS (1782-1842)

Though working in oils and as an etcher, John Sell Cotman is best remembered as a watercolourist of great originality, who rivalled the achievement of J M W Turner and remains an inspiration to artists today. In combining strong draughtsmanship and a confident application of flat washes, he managed to 'translate the patterns of nature into exquisite two-dimensional designs' (Andrew W Moore, in Jane Turner 1996, vol 8 p 27).

John Sell Cotman was born in the parish of St Mary Coslany, Norwich on 16 May 1782, the son of a hairdresser, who later became a haberdasher. At the age of eleven, he gained a free place at Norwich Grammar School.

In 1798, Cotman moved to London, where he worked as an assistant to printseller and publisher, Rudolph Ackermann. In the following year, he left Ackermann's service and received the patronage of Dr Thomas Monro, so gaining the same opportunity as J M W TURNER and Thomas Girtin to study and copy examples from a significant collection of English watercolours.

While living at 28 Gerrard Street, Soho, in 1800, Cotman exhibited at the Royal Academy of Arts for the first time and, in the same year, was awarded a large silver palette by the Society of Arts for his drawing of a mill. During this period, he supported himself by selling his drawings to local print-sellers, one of which – Peter Norton – sent him to Bristol with an introduction to his brother, a bookseller. This experience led Cotman to make the first of the series of sketching tours – to Wales in summer 1800 – that had such a dramatic effect on his development. While in Conway, he may have worked alongside Girtin. Certainly, by the following year, he had become a member of 'The Brothers', the sketching society that Girtin had founded, and was its President in 1802. Girtin's influence was strong at this time.

Between 1802 and 1804, Cotman lodged with the Munn brothers, above their print shop at 107 New Bond Street. In 1802, PAUL SANDBY MUNN accompanied him on his second tour of Wales, during which they travelled light and worked mainly in pencil. Cotman's resulting watercolours, produced subsequently, displayed a new confidence of design and handling, a confidence that the artist was able to exploit further in responding to new experiences. A year later, Cotman and Munn went travelling again – to Yorkshire, where they were taken up by the Cholmeley family of Brandsby Hall. Yorkshire proved as important to Cotman as to Girtin and Turner, so that he returned to the county in both 1804 and 1805 (by which time he was living at 20 Woodstock Street, off Bond Street).

On the last trip, while staying on the River Greta – at Rokeby Park and then Greta Bridge – Cotman produced a series of watercolours that have later been described as 'the most perfect examples of pure water-colour ever made in Europe' (Binyon 1931, p 132). Yet at the time, his contemporaries failed to recognise his distinction. This failure was epitomised, in 1806, by the decision taken by the recently formed Society of Painters in Water Colours not to elect him to its membership. So, having exhibited at the Royal Academy for one last time, he left his London address (71 Charlotte Street) and returned to Norwich before the end of the year.

Cotman seems to have been determined to establish himself as an artistic force in his native city. He set up a 'School of Drawing and Design' at his home at Luckett's Court, Wymer Street, St Andrew's, and advertised its foundation by holding a large retrospective exhibition. He also broadened his ambitions, experimenting with oils and painting portraits. Indeed, a year after he first exhibited with the Norwich Society of Artists in 1807, he described himself in its catalogues as a portrait painter. At the same time, he remained at heart a landscape watercolourist, using pure, often bright washes to render his environment in simplified, even abstracted, forms. Yet, despite these manifold activities, the local public was slow to purchase his work, and at a time when he needed financial security; in 1809, he married the daughter of a tenant farmer from Fellbrigg.

Undeterred, Cotman expanded his enterprises as an educator, in 1810, by establishing a Circulating Library of drawings that pupils could borrow to copy. At the same time, he was elected Vice-President (1810) and then President (1811) of the Norwich Society of Artists, and also exhibited in London, with the Associated Artists in Water Colours and at the British Institution.

In 1812, Cotman accepted the invitation of Dawson Turner – banker, botanist and antiquary – to move to Great Yarmouth, and settled at what is now 83-84 Southdown Road. He acted as the drawing master to Turner's family, as well as contributing etched illustrations to Turner's antiquarian projects. Having established himself as a printmaker with his *Miscellaneous Etchings of Architectural Antiquities in Yorkshire* (1812), Cotman produced over 600 etched plates for the six volumes of *Architectural Antiquities in Norfolk*, for which Turner provided the commentaries (1812-18).

Dawson Turner probably instigated, and certainly facilitated, Cotman's three tours of Normandy, in 1817, 1819 and 1820. During his time there he worked hard, making many, often precise drawings in preparation for the two-volume *Architectural Antiquities of Normandy*, again with commentaries by Turner. On the appearance of these volumes in 1822, their ninety-seven etchings would bring Cotman wide acclaim.

In 1823, Cotman returned to Norwich and took a house in St Martin-at-Palace Plain. In the following year, he set up a School for Drawing in his home, and began to capitalise on his new-found success, exhibiting in London and organising a large sale of his drawings at Christie's. In 1825, he was finally elected an associate of the Society of Painters in Water Colours, without having to submit drawings for approval, and showed work at its exhibitions for the first time (continuing to do so until 1839). Despite, or perhaps because of, his industry, he was prone to suffer from depression, and had a particularly serious bout in 1826.

At the opening of the 1830s, Cotman was again elected Vice-President (1831) and then President (1833) of the Norwich Society of Artists, under its new name of the Norfolk and Suffolk Institution for the Promotion of the Fine Arts. However, the society was disbanded later that year, during a meeting at his house and, in 1834, Cotman accepted the position of drawing master at King's College School, London. He organised a sale of his large collection at his house, with the aid of the auctioneer, Spelman, on 10-12 September, and moved to 42 Hunter Street, Brunswick Square, Bloomsbury, which remained his home for the rest of his life. MILES EDMUND COTMAN, his eldest son, acted as his assistant at the school, while his pupils included William and Dante Gabriel Rossetti (from 1837) and William Burges (from 1839).

His last publications, of 1838, were the *Liber Studiorum* and the retrospective collection, *Specimens of Architectural Remains in Various Counties in England, but Especially in Norfolk*.

He died at home in London on 24 July 1842, and his collection was sold through four auctions: two at Christie's in 1843, and two in Norwich in the 1860s.

Of his five children, three became artists: Miles Edmund Cotman, Ann Cotman and John Joseph Cotman, the last continuing the family drawing practice in Norwich.

His work is represented in numerous public collections, including the British Museum, The Courtauld Gallery, Tate and the V&A; the Ashmolean Museum (Oxford), The Fitzwilliam Museum (Cambridge), Leeds Art Gallery, Manchester Art Gallery and Norwich Castle Museum & Art Gallery; and the Museum of Fine Arts (Boston).

Further reading:

Adele M Holcomb, *John Sell Cotman*, London: British Museum Publications, 1978
Sydney D Kitson, *The Life of John Sell Cotman*, London: Faber and Faber, 1937
Andrew W Moore, 'Cotman, John Sell (*b* Norwich, 16 May 1782; *d* London, 24 July 1842)', Jane Turner (ed), *The Dictionary of Art*, London: Macmillan, 1996, vol 8, pp 27-30
Andrew W Moore, 'Cotman, John Sell (1782–1842)', H C G Matthew and Brian Harrison (eds), *Oxford Dictionary of National Biography*, Oxford University Press, 2004, vol 13, pp 574-577
Andrew W Moore, *John Sell Cotman 1782-1842*, Norwich: Castle Museum, 1982
Miklós Rajnai, *John Sell Cotman, 1782-1842*, London: Arts Council of Great Britain, 1982
Victor Rienaecker, *John Sell Cotman, 1782-1842*, Leigh-on-Sea: F Lewis, 1953

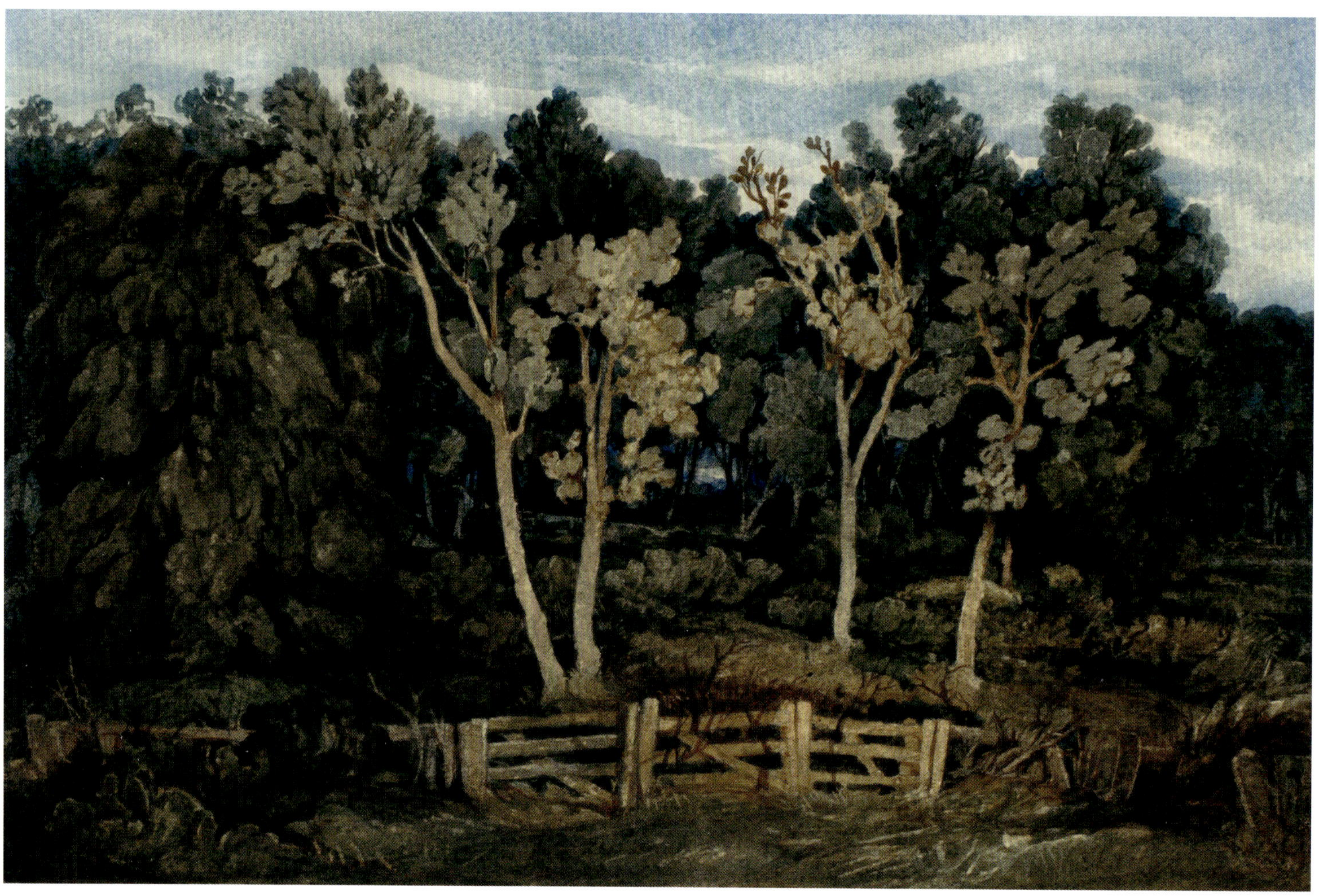

148 STRATTON WOODS, NEAR NORWICH
watercolour
7 x 10 ½ inches

Provenance: P & D Colnaghi & Co, London; The Graham Watson Collection

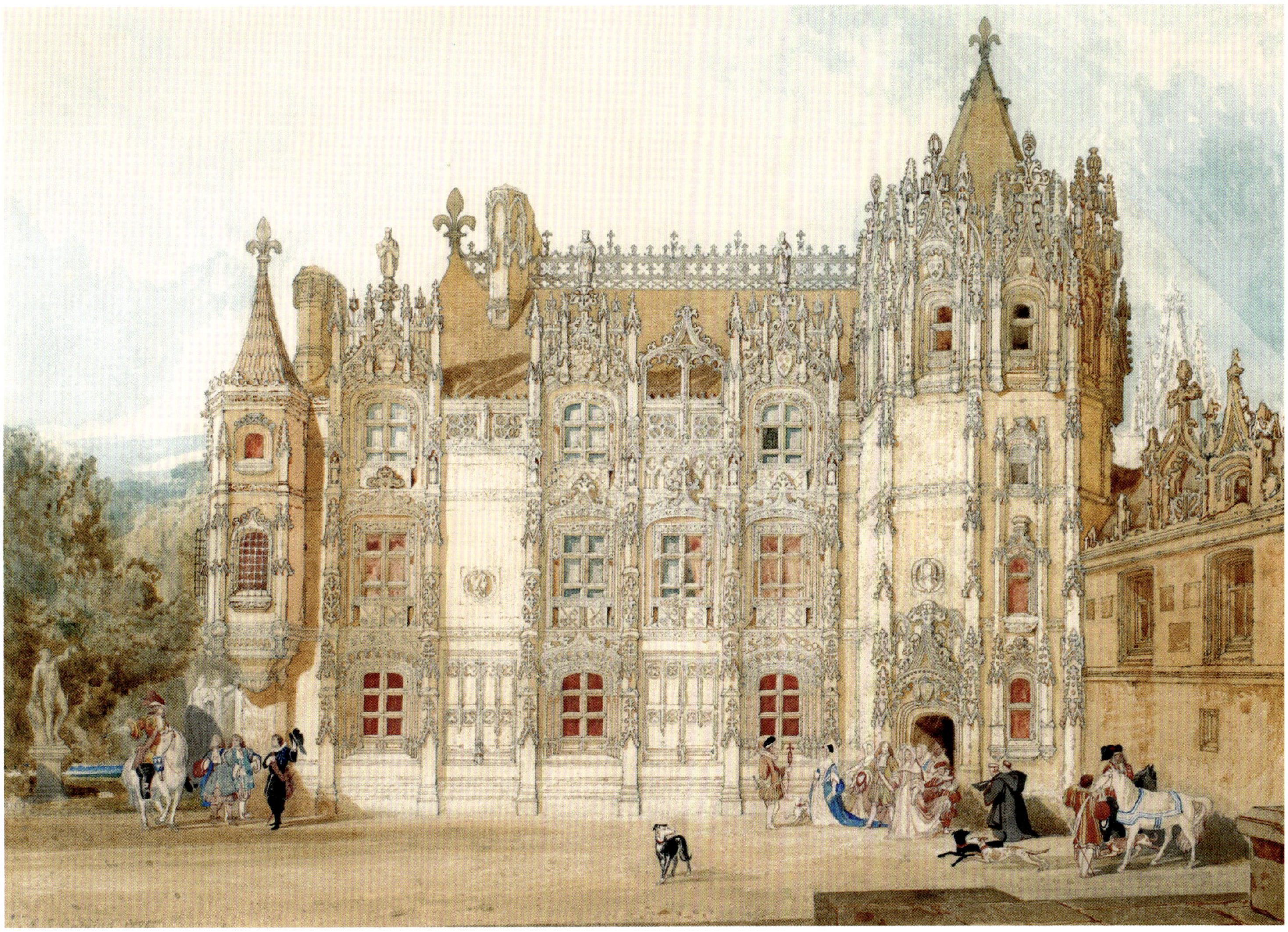

149 ABBATIAL HOUSE OF ST OUEN
watercolour with pencil and ink
16 ¼ x 22 ½ inches

Provenance:
Painted for the Reverend C P Burney, but retained by the artist;
Purchased from the artist by Charles Turner of Norwich;
A E Alston and by descent to J D Alstom;
Spink-Leger

Exhibited:
Norwich Society of Artists, 1824, no 94;
Society of Painters in Water Colours, 1825, no 105;
'John Sell Cotman, Drawings of Normandy in Norwich Castle Museum', Norwich Castle Museum, 1975

JOHN SELL COTMAN

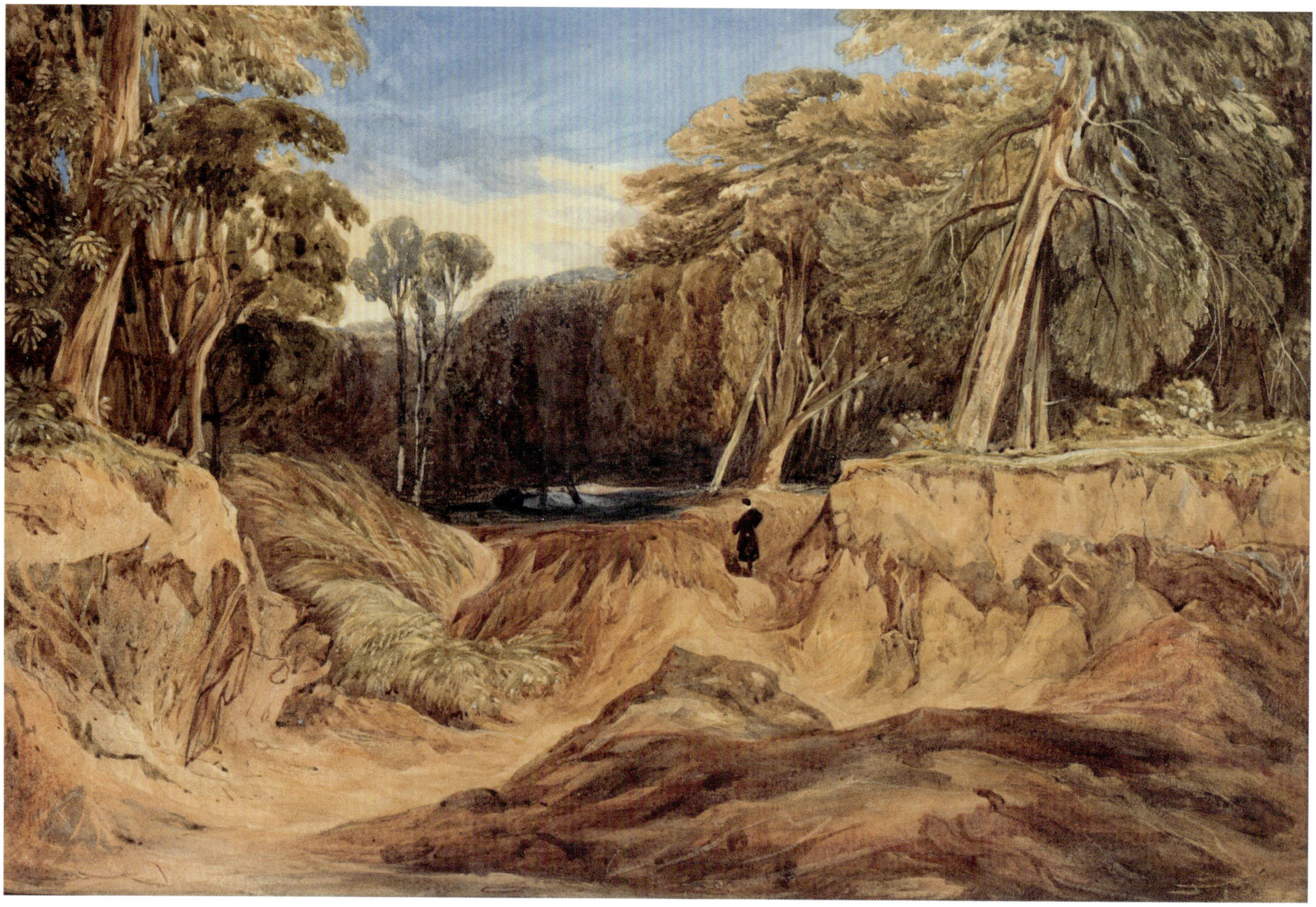

150 LEIGH HIGH WOODS
WITH THE REV JAMES BULWER IN THE FOREGROUND
watercolour
12 ¾ x 18 ¾ inches
(also illustrated back endpaper, detail)

Leigh High Woods with the Rev James Bulwer in the foreground
Norfolk born James Bulwer (1794-1879) became a drawing pupil of John Sell Cotman while studying Divinity at Jesus College, Cambridge between 1814 and 1823. They became firm friends and, throughout his subsequent career in the priesthood, Bulwer acted as a fervent supporter and patron of Cotman and other artists of the Norwich School. A noted antiquarian, naturalist, collector and patron, he liked to move in creative circles and became close to several other artists, including Frederick Sandys and William James Müller.

A talented artist himself, Bulwer sketched with Müller in various spots around Bristol, including Leigh High Woods, in the early 1830s, while he was curate of St Mary Redcliffe in Bristol.

Bulwer's drawings of places and buildings were published in a number of books, examples of which were even used as models by Cotman. He also embarked on sketching tours abroad to Spain, Portugal and Madeira with the philosopher Alfred Lyall.

Cotman's last sketching holiday was in the company of Bulwer – they toured Norfolk together in 1841, a year before Cotman's death.

Bulwer is particularly remembered by ornithologists for discovering the 'Bulwer's Petrel' off the coast of Madeira in 1825.

Note by Giles Huxley-Parlour

JOHN SELL COTMAN

Thornton College, Lincolnshire
Henry VIII founded Thornton College, Lincolnshire, as a charitable and educational institution in 1542, following the dissolution of his twelfth-century Thornton Abbey. However, the foundation was suppressed at the beginning of the reign of Edward VI, and the building passed to the Skynner family.

Cotman travelled through Lincoln in 1804, and it is likely that this drawing, of the gatehouse, was produced at that time.

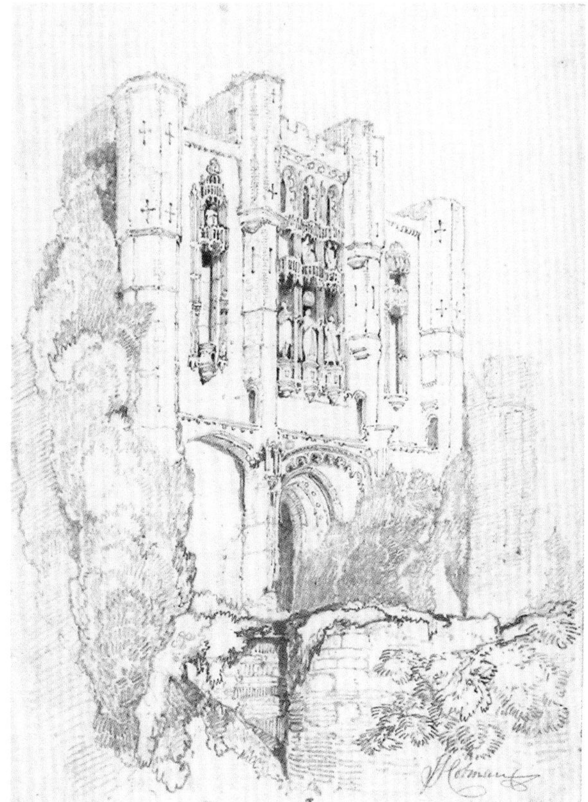

151 THORNTON COLLEGE, LINCOLNSHIRE
signed
inscribed with title on label below mount
pencil
12 ¾ x 9 ½ inches

MILES EDMUND COTMAN
Miles Edmund Cotman (1810-1858)

The eldest child of John Sell Cotman, Miles Edmund Cotman became his father's closest associate and collaborator. Indeed, he produced work so close in style and high in quality that his father sometimes signed it as his own. However, he developed into an artist of some individuality, being known for his seascapes as well as his architectural studies.

Miles Edmund Cotman was born in Wymer Street, Norwich on 5 February 1810, though he spent most of his early years in Great Yarmouth, and studied there under his father, JOHN SELL COTMAN. In 1823, when the Cotmans returned to Norwich and took a house at St Martin-at-Palace Plain, Miles began to exhibit with the Norwich Society of Artists (continuing to show there for a decade). In the following year, he became his father's assistant when a School of Drawing was set up in their house.

A decade later, John Sell Cotman was appointed drawing master at King's College School, London, and Miles Edmund became his assistant, a position that was officially recognised two years later. Then, on the death of his father, in 1842, he became the drawing master. He remained in the Cotman family home, at 42 Hunter Street, near Brunswick Square, until 1843. In London, he exhibited with the Royal Academy, the British Institution and the Society of British Artists between 1835 and 1856.

Specialising in seascapes, landscapes and buildings, Miles Edmund worked mainly in watercolour, while also producing oils, etchings and lithographs. Initially influenced by his father, and also William James Müller and Richard Parkes Bonington, he gradually developed a distinctive style of increasing fluidity.

On 16 May 1842, Miles Edmund married a widow, Mrs Elizabeth Juby (née Worts); together they would have a son and two daughters. By 1851, the family was living at 9 Hollis Place, Haverstock Hill. However, ill health brought on by overwork led him to return to Norfolk by 1854. After living for a period with his brother, John Joseph Cotman, he finally removed to North Walsham, where he taught and painted, though he was often in poverty.

Eventually Miles Edmund was admitted to the Norfolk and Norwich Hospital with a diseased ankle, and died on 23 January 1858.

His work is represented in numerous public collections, including the British Museum and the V&A; and Norwich Castle Museum & Art Gallery.

Further reading:
Charles Francis Bell, 'Miles Edmund Cotman (1810-1858) with a catalogue of fifty drawings by him selected from the Bulwer collection', *Walker's Quarterly*, no 21, 1927, pp 3-43
Norma Watt, 'Cotman, Miles Edmund (1810-1858)', H C G Matthew and Brian Harrison (eds), *Oxford Dictionary of National Biography*, Oxford University Press, 2004, vol 13, p 577

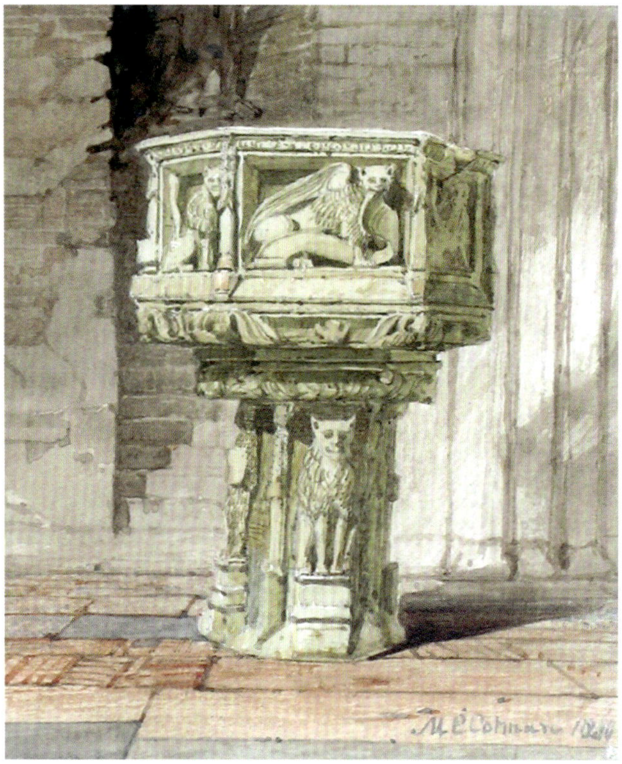

152 LUDHAM FONT
signed and dated 1850
inscribed 'the Ludham Church' on reverse
watercolour
5 x 4 ¾ inches

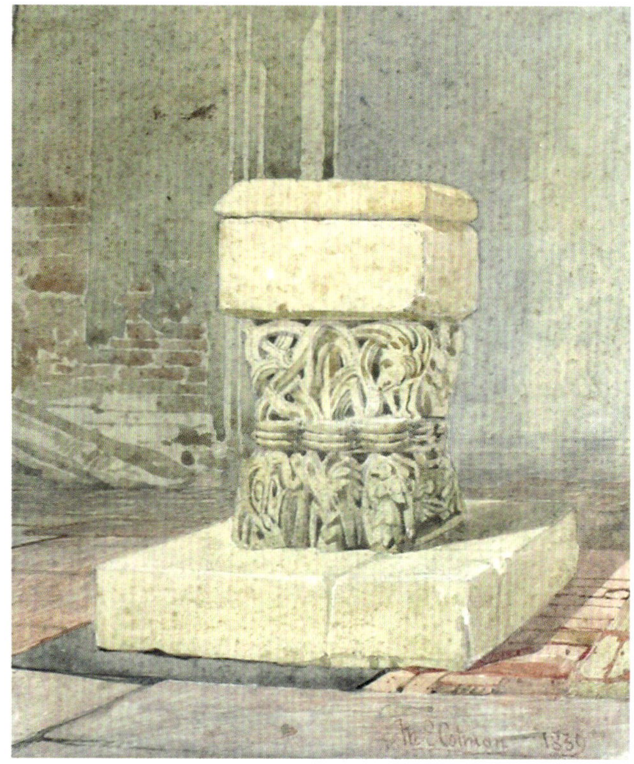

153 HAUTBOIS FONT
signed and dated 1839
inscribed with title on reverse
watercolour
6 ¼ x 5 ¼ inches

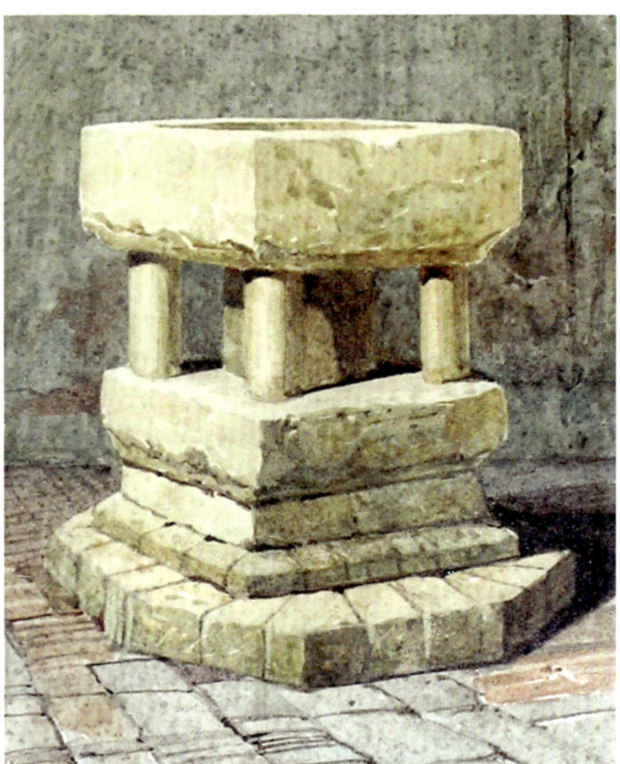

154 CHEDGRAVE FONT
inscribed 'a font in Chedgrave Ch. Norfolk' on reverse
watercolour
5 x 4 ¼ inches

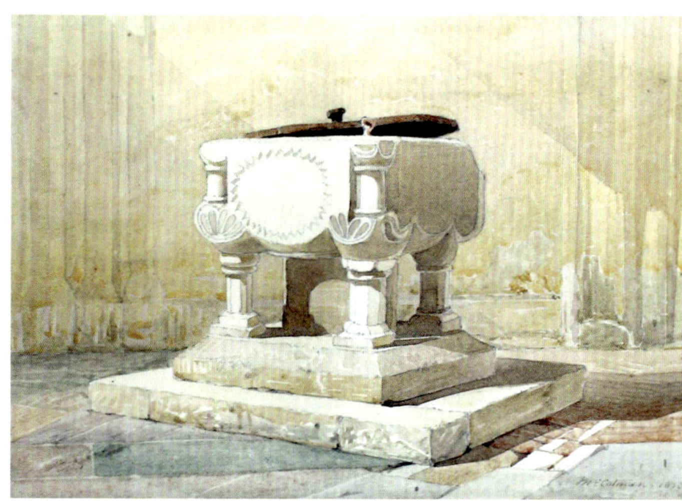

155 HUNSTANTON FONT
signed and dated 1838
inscribed 'Hunstanton Ch.' on reverse
watercolour
6 x 8 ¾ inches

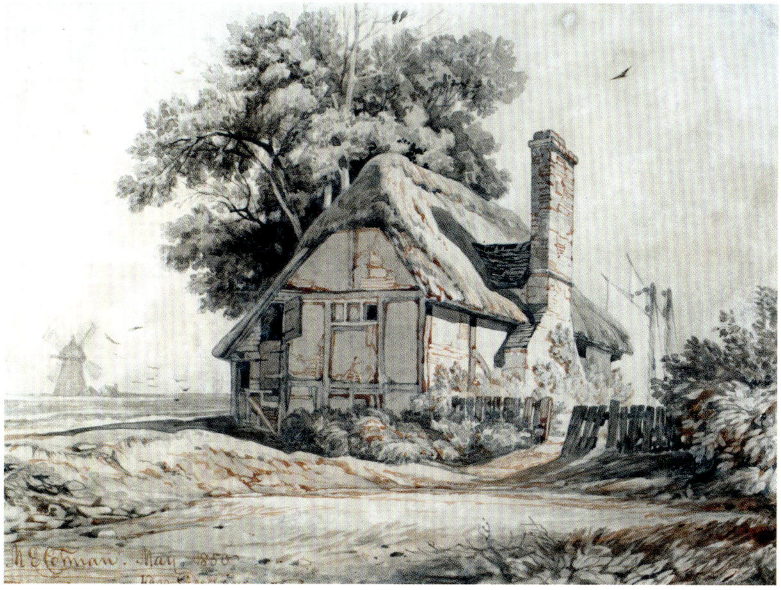

156 NEAR DEDHAM
signed, inscribed with title and dated 'May 1850'
watercolour and pencil
9 ¼ x 12 inches
Provenance: Mandells Gallery, Norwich

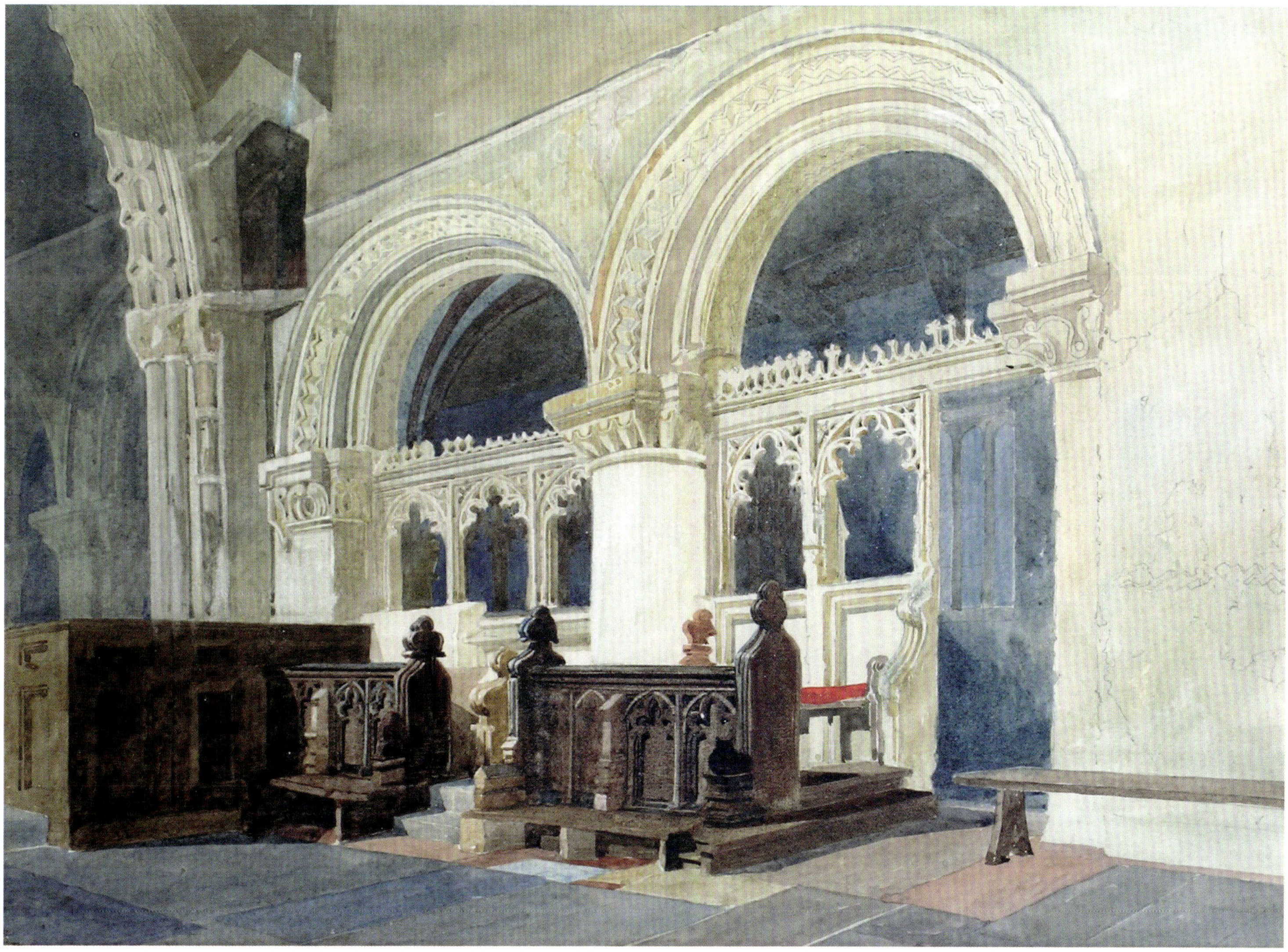

157 CHANCEL, WALSAKEN CHURCH
watercolour
10 x 13 ¼ inches
Exhibited: '88th Annual Exhibition Of Watercolour Drawings', Thos Agnew And Sons, London, February-March 1961

JOHN MIDDLETON
John Middleton (1827-1856)

During his brief career, John Middleton developed into a landscape painter of great freshness and acute observation. His works show a particular interest in such details of nature as rocky streams and plants and grasses.

John Middleton was born in the Parish of St Stephen, Norwich on 9 January 1827. His father was a painter and decorator and his mother an amateur flower painter who exhibited at the Norwich Society of Artists. Studying art under John Berney Ladbrooke, John Crome and Henry Bright, he befriended a number of local artists. During a sketching tour with Bright – to Kent in 1847 – he produced watercolours of such confidence and freedom that he influenced his own teacher. In the same year, he moved to London, and began to exhibit at the Royal Academy of Arts and the British Institution. On the death of his father in 1848, he was called back to Norwich to take over the family business. Nevertheless, he continued to work as an artist – painting in oil and watercolour, undertaking sketching trips (to Devon, Wales and Scotland), and exhibiting in London and Norwich. His later work can be identified by a greater degree of finish. He also produced etchings – after his own paintings – and took an active interest in photography.

John Middleton died of consumption on 11 November 1856 in Surrey Street, Norwich.

His work is represented in the collections of the British Museum and Norwich Castle Museum & Art Gallery.

Further reading:

Anne Pimlott Baker, 'Middleton, John (1827–1856)', H C G Matthew and Brian Harrison (eds), *Oxford Dictionary of National Biography*, Oxford University Press, 2004, vol 38, pp 69-70
F W Hawcroft, 'John Middleton: A Sketch of his Life and Work', *The Saturday Book*, no 16, London: Hutchinson, 1956, pp 37-41
Andrew W Moore, 'Middleton, John (*b* Norwich, 9 Jan 1827; *d* Norwich, 11 Nov 1856)', Jane Turner (ed), *The Dictionary of Art*, London: Macmillan, 1996, vol 21, p 482

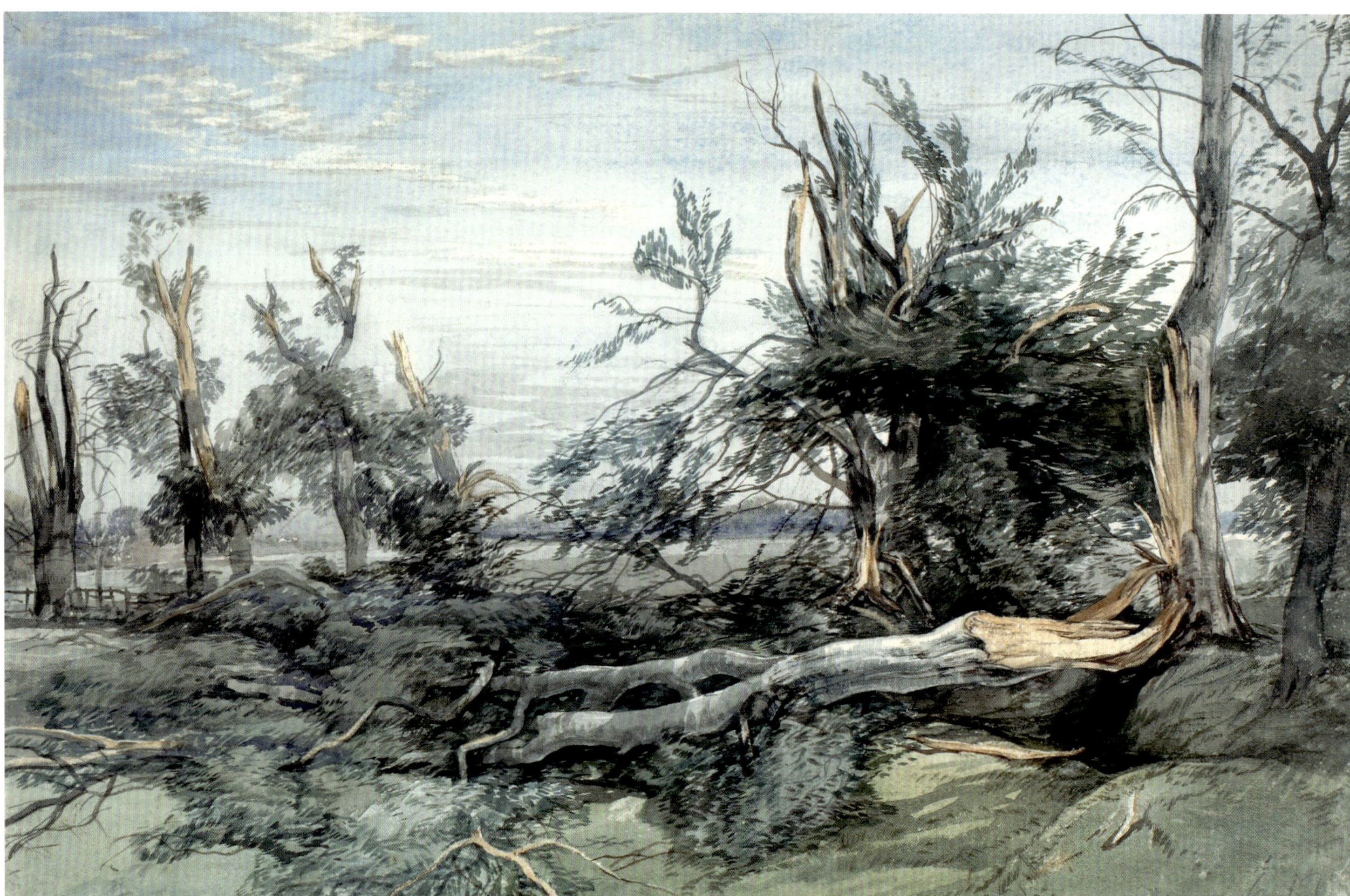

158 THE BLOWN WOOD
watercolour
13 ¼ x 17 ¼ inches

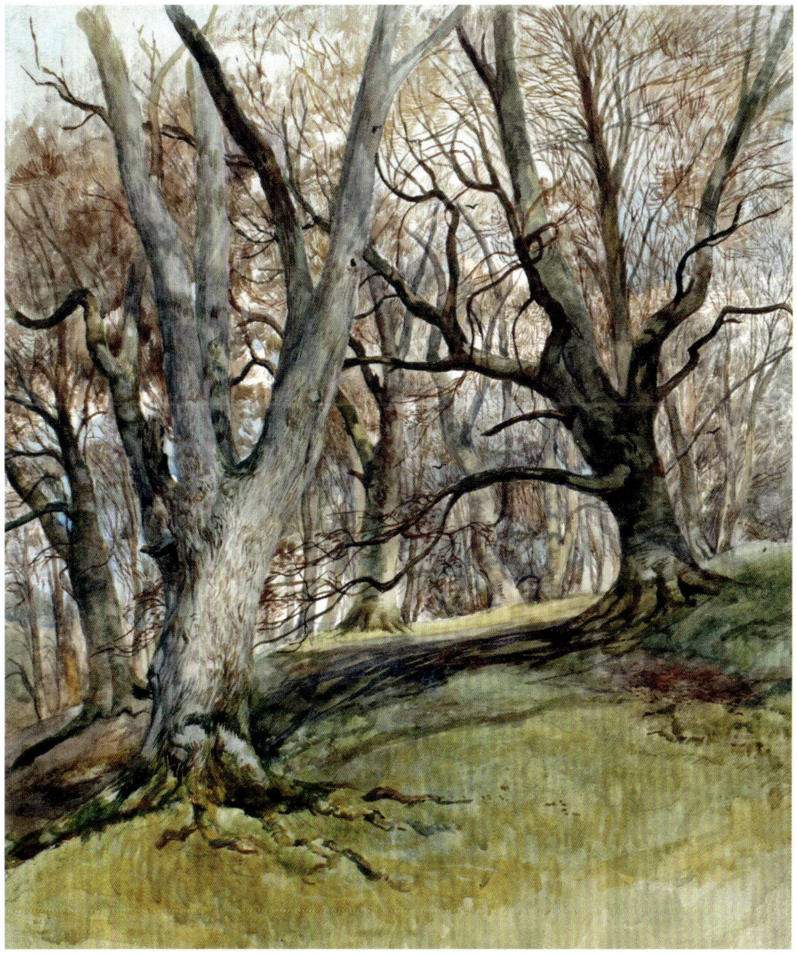

159 A WOODED LANDSCAPE IN WINTER
watercolour
12 x 9 ¾ inches

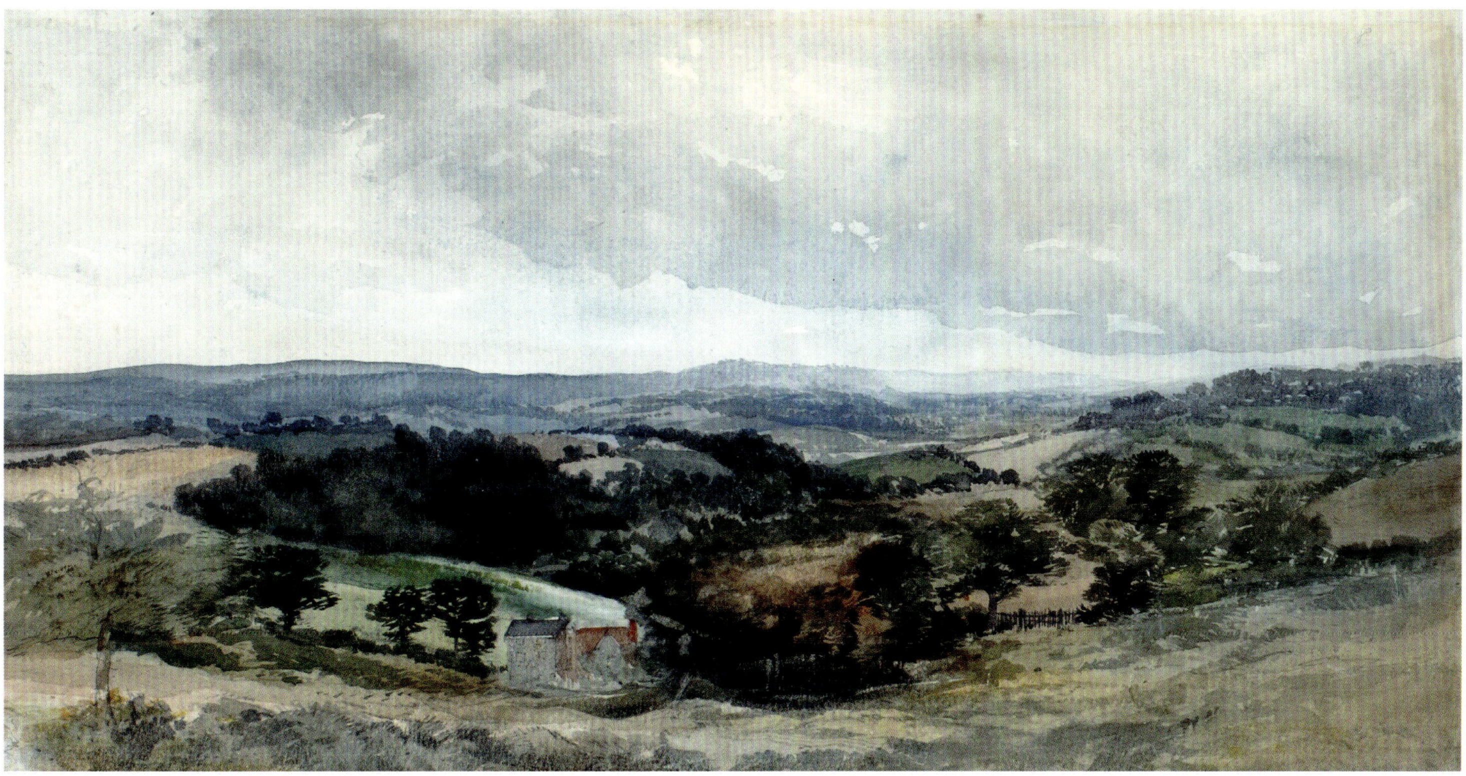

160 VALLEY FARM
watercolour
8 ½ x 16 ½ inches

4: PORTRAITS AND FIGURE SUBJECTS

THOMAS STOTHARD
Thomas Stothard, RA (1755-1834)

Thomas Stothard was the most successful illustrator, and one of the most foremost history painters, of his time.

Thomas Stothard was born at the Black Horse Inn, Long Acre, London on 17 August 1755, the only child of a prosperous publican from Yorkshire. At the age of five, he was sent away, first to an uncle at Acomb, near York, and then to a boarding school in Ilford, Essex.

On the death of his father in 1770, Stothard returned to London and took up an apprenticeship with the silk weaver, John Vansommer of Spital Square. When his master died in 1774, he completed the final three years of his apprenticeship with his wife, Ann Vansommer. It seems that he then embarked on a trip to North Wales, as he exhibited two views of Caernarfon, as well as a scene from Homer, at the Society of Arts in 1777. Though beginning a career as a silk pattern designer, he entered the Royal Academy Schools at the end of that year.

In 1779, while still a student, Stothard began to work as an illustrator, by contributing to the *Town and Country Magazine*, *Harrison's Novelists Magazines* (1780-86) and *Bell's British Poets* (1782-83). A friend of fellow students William Blake and John Flaxman, he shared their economical approach to draughtsmanship, though he was neither as visionary as the former or as austere as the latter. Instead, he developed an elegant style through which he was able to tease out the subtleties of human sentiment, in keeping with the contemporary concept of 'sensibility'. As a result, he became an ideal illustrator of such novels as Samuel Richardson's *Clarissa Harlowe* (1784) and Oliver Goldsmith's *The Vicar of Wakefield* (1792). His other important sets of illustrations include Daniel Defoe's *Robinson Crusoe* (1790), and Samuel Rogers' *Italy* (1830, produced in collaboration with J M W TURNER).

Stothard developed a parallel career as a painter and designer, spurred on by his election to the membership of the Royal Academy of Arts (ARA 1791, RA 1794, Librarian to the Royal Academy 1812-34). He undertook important decorative commissions, painting the staircase at Burghley House, Cambridgeshire (1799-1803) and the cupola of the Advocates' Library, Edinburgh (1822), and winning the competition for the design of the Wellington Shield (1814). He also produced landscapes and scenes of historical genre, as exemplified by his most celebrated canvas, the Chaucerian subject *Pilgrimage to Canterbury* (1806, Tate), which was commissioned by Robert Cromek, the engraver. About 1805, he was employed by Colonel Thomas Johnes of Hafod House, Cardigan, to teach drawing to his daughter Mariamne.

In 1783, Stothard had married Rebecca Watkins, an Anabaptist, and moved into Henrietta Street, Covent Garden. Together, they had six children that survived infancy. In 1793, he bought 28 Newman Street, and lived there until his death on 27 April 1834, as a result of a carriage accident. He outlived not only his wife but also two of his sons.

His work is represented in the collections of the British Museum, The Courtauld Gallery, the National Portrait Gallery and Tate; and Manchester Art Gallery.

Further reading:

Shelley M Bennett, *Thomas Stothard: The Mechanisms of Art Patronage in England Circa 1800*, Columbia: University of Missouri Press, 1988

Mark Stocker, 'Stothard (1) Thomas Stothard (*b* London, 17 Aug 1755; *d* London, 27 April 1834)', Jane Turner (ed), *The Dictionary of Art*, London: Macmillan, 1996, vol 29, pp 731-732

M G Sullivan, 'Stothard, Thomas (1755-1834)', H C G Matthew and Brian Harrison (eds), *Oxford Dictionary of National Biography*, Oxford University Press, 2004, vol 52, pp 964-967

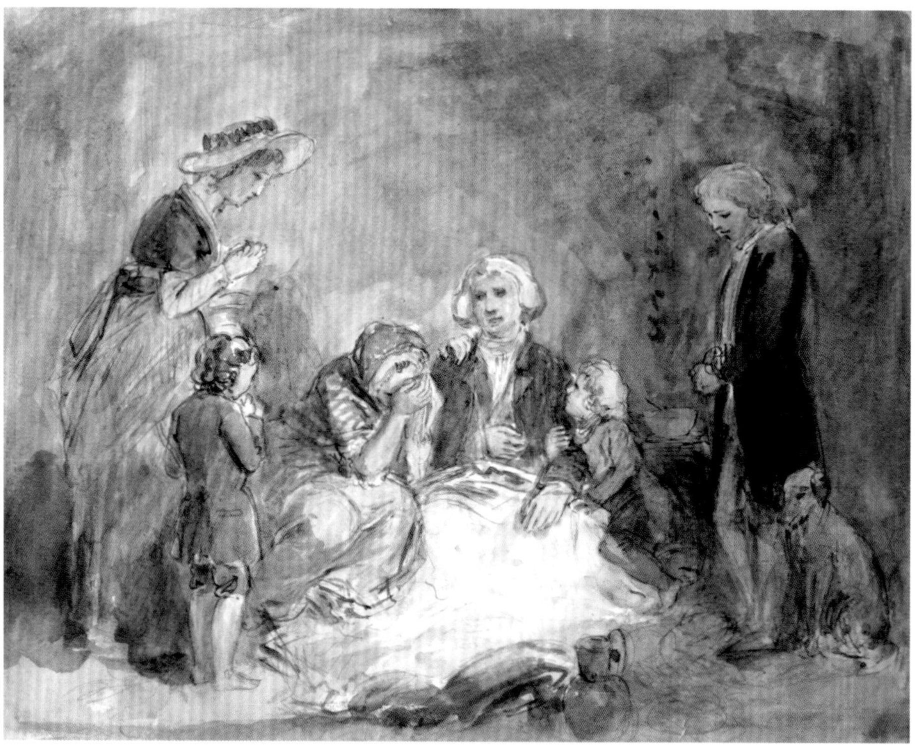

161 BAD NEWS
monochrome watercolour
8 ½ x 10 ¾ inches

RICHARD CORBOULD
Richard Corbould (1757-1831)

Though Richard Corbould was a wide-ranging painter and occasional etcher, he is best remembered as an illustrator, able to interpret a text with precision and sensitivity.

Richard Corbould was born in the Parish of St Edmund Lombard Street, London, on 18 April 1857. He studied under the landscape draughtsman, Robert Marris, the son-in-law of Arthur Devis, and lodged with him in the early 1770s. A versatile artist who tried his hand at many media and subjects, he first developed a specialism as a painter of English and Welsh landscapes in oil and watercolour. He exhibited from 1776, when he showed three works at the Free Society, and from the following year began to exhibit regularly at the Royal Academy of Arts (1777-1811), later showing also at the British Institution (1806-17).

From the early 1780s, Corbould was employed mainly as a book illustrator. He contributed to numerous periodicals – including *The Tatler*, *The Spectator* and the *Guardian* – and principally to Cooke's 'pocket editions' (1793-1802), of which the illustrations to Fielding's *Amelia* are representative. The delicate and detailed results, presented within decorative frames, are fine and characteristic examples of illustration in the Age of Sensibility.

For some years, Corbould lived in John Street, off Tottenham Court Road. He died in Highgate on 26 July 1831, and was buried in the Churchyard of St Andrew's, Holborn. His two sons, George and Henry, had become artists under his tutelage, while Henry's son, Edward Henry Corbould, would become an illustrator.

His work is represented in the collections of the British Museum and the V&A; and Birmingham Museum & Art Gallery.

Further reading:
L H Cust, (rev Ruth Stewart), 'Corbould, Richard (1757–1831)', H C G Matthew and Brian Harrison (eds), *Oxford Dictionary of National Biography*, Oxford University Press, 2004, vol 42, pp 904-905
Richard Corbould, 1757-1831, illustrator: a glimpse of the common life of Georgian Society, London: Spink & Son, 1984

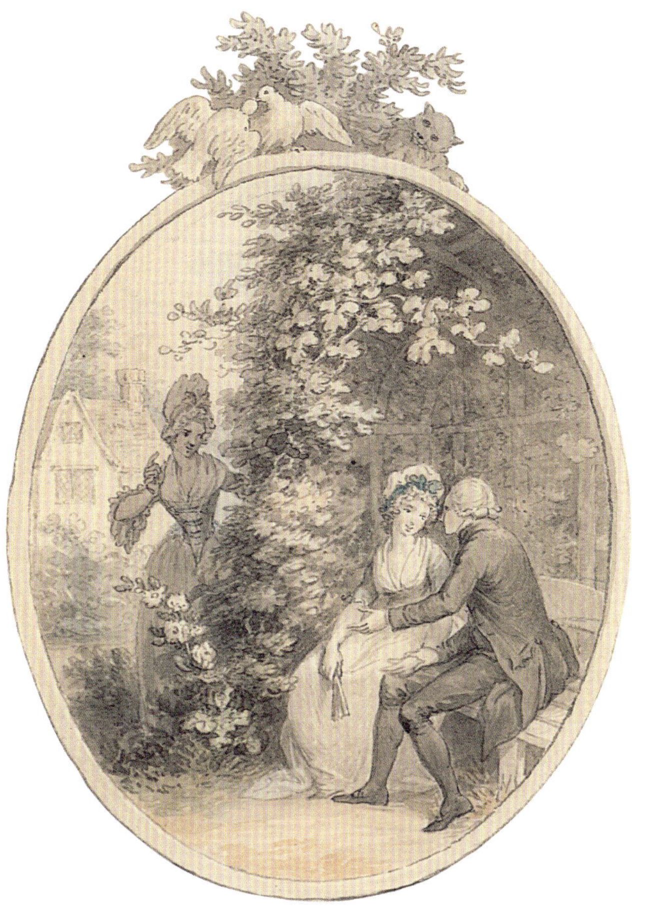

162 MR BENNET INTERRUPTED IN HIS COURTSHIP BY THE AUNT OF HIS FAVOURITE
inscribed 'Mr and Mrs Bennet's conversation overheard by her aunt' and 'V2. p115'
pen ink and watercolour, 4 ½ x 2 ½ inches
Illustrated: (in reverse) Henry Fielding, *Amelia*, 1797; Henry Fielding, *Amelia*, New York: Croscup & Sterling Company, 1902, vol 2 (The Drury Lane Edition of The Complete Works of Henry Fielding, Esq in Sixteen Volumes, vol 7), frontispiece

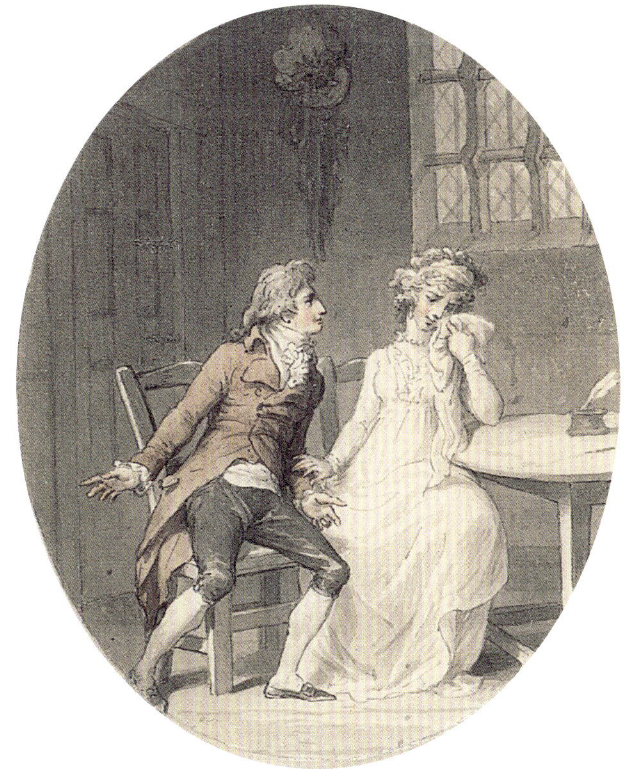

163 BOOTH CONSOLING MISS MATTHEWS IN HER IMPRISONMENT
inscribed 'Mr Booth endeavouring to soothe Miss Mathews' and 'p.29 V1'
pen ink and watercolour, 4 ¼ x 2 ½ inches
Illustrated: Henry Fielding, *Amelia*, 1797; Henry Fielding, *Amelia*, New York: Croscup & Sterling Company, 1902, vol 1 (The Drury Lane Edition of The Complete Works of Henry Fielding, Esq in Sixteen Volumes, vol 6), facing p 36

RICHARD CORBOULD

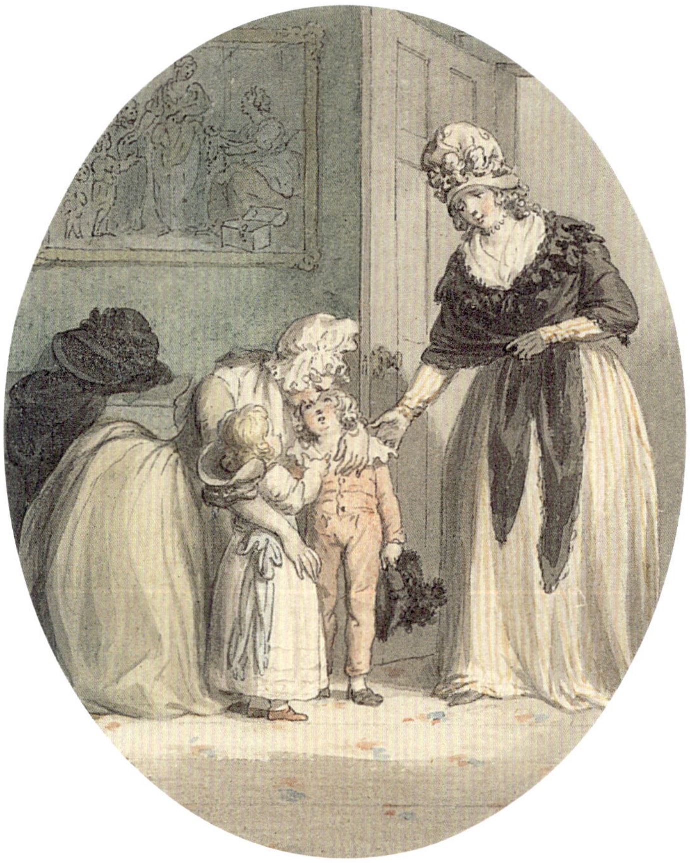

Amelia

Henry Fielding's last novel, *Amelia*, was published in 1751. The best selling of his books in his lifetime, it was also his own favourite, being based in spirit on his loving marriage:

Captain William Booth has married the beautiful and virtuous Amelia against his mother's wishes, but with the assistance of the good parson Dr Harrison. The couple run away and, in so doing, become victims of unscrupulous London society. Careless rather than guilty, Booth is thrown into Newgate prison, and there shares a cell with Miss Matthews, a courtesan of his acquaintance. He is released on bail by the seemingly friendly Colonel James, who takes Miss Matthews as his mistress. However, while hoping to receive a commission from the rich and powerful, he enters a life of gambling, and is supported only by the faithfulness of Amelia. In turn, she is threatened by the machinations of Colonel James and a character known only as 'My Lord', but saved by the warning of Mrs Bennet, who 'My Lord' has already ravished. Eventually, Booth is saved by Dr Harrison, who pays his debts, while Amelia discovers that she and not her sister is rightly heiress to her mother's fortune. They retire to the country to a happy life of farming.

164 THE AFFECTING INTERVIEW BETWEEN AMELIA, AND HER TWO CHILDREN
inscribed 'Amelia' and 'V2 138 C3 p177'
pen ink and watercolour, 4 x 2 ¾ inches
Illustrated: Henry Fielding, *Amelia*, London: C Cooke,1793, vol 2, facing p 152; Henry Fielding, *Amelia*, New York: Croscup & Sterling Company, 1902, vol 2 (The Drury Lane Edition of The Complete Works of Henry Fielding, Esq in Sixteen Volumes, vol 7), facing p 72

WILLIAM ALEXANDER
William Alexander (1767-1816)

William Alexander was the only English artist of the late eighteenth century to penetrate the interior of China. As a result, he became well known for his images of the country at a time when Chinoiserie was all the rage. Admired as a technician, he worked as drawing master until 1808, when he accepted a position as one of the first curators at the British Museum.

William Alexander was born in Maidstone, Kent, on 10 April 1767, the son of a coachbuilder. Educated at Maidstone Grammar School, he showed a talent for drawing at an early age. In 1782, he moved to London to study art, and may have taken lessons with Julius Caesar Ibbetson before entering the Royal Academy Schools two years later.

Ibbetson had taken part on the first – abortive – British mission to Beijing. It is therefore likely that he recommended Alexander for the post of junior draughtsman in the embassy of Lord Macartney to China (1792-94), for which the senior draughtsman was the Irish artist, Thomas Hickey. The embassy itself proved a failure, as the Emperor Qianlong was uninterested in trade and communication, but the experience provided an inspiration and springboard for Alexander in his career as a painter and illustrator.

On his return from China, Alexander married on 10 April 1795, but his wife died shortly afterwards, and left no children.

During the ensuing decade, Alexander worked up many of his Chinese sketches into finished watercolours, and exhibited the results at the Royal Academy of Arts. In providing highly skilled representations of unusual subjects, they attracted great interest. In turn, his images were engraved for the official record of the embassy (1797) and other publications, including his own *View of the headlands, islands, etc, taken during a voyage to, and along the eastern coast of China, in the years 1792 & 1793* (1798), and John Barrow's *A Voyage to Cochin China, in the Years 1792, and 1793* (1806).

In the same period, Alexander attended Dr Monro's unofficial academy at his house in Fetcham, Surrey; there he had the opportunity to work alongside such leading contemporaries as Thomas Girtin, in copying exemplars of the art of watercolour collected by Monro and drawing *en plein air* in the surrounding countryside. He was also an active member of Girtin's Sketching Club, 'The Brothers'.

In 1802, Alexander was appointed Professor of Landscape Drawing at the Junior Department of the Royal Military Academy in Great Marlow, Buckinghamshire (the forerunner of Sandhurst). WILLIAM DELAMOTTE and William Gilpin were the second and third masters.

Six years later, in 1808, Alexander resigned from his professorship in order to become first Keeper of Prints and Drawings, and Assistant Librarian, at the British Museum. In 1810, he began to produce the first inventory of the museum's collection of prints and drawings. The trustees also commissioned him to illustrate items from the Townley collection, in Taylor Combe's *A Description of the Collection of Ancient Terra-cottas in the British Museum* (1810) and a *Description of the Collection of Ancient Marbles in the British Museum* (1812-18). He was a member of the Society of Antiquaries.

Later in life, Alexander produced a number of picturesque landscapes as well as drawings of antiquities.

Alexander died of a brain fever on 23 July 1816 at his uncle's house in Maidstone. He was buried at Boxley, Kent. Some of his collection of contemporary British paintings and drawings was sold at Sotheby's in the following year.

His work is represented in numerous public collections, including the British Library, the British Museum, Tate and the V&A.

Further reading:

Patrick Conner, 'Alexander, William', Jane Turner (ed), *The Dictionary of Art*, London: Macmillan, 1996, vol 1, p 612
Patrick Conner and Susan Sloman, *William Alexander: An English Artist in Imperial China*, Brighton Museum and Art Gallery, 1981
Richard Garnett (rev Heather M MacLennan), 'Alexander, William (1767–1816)', H C G Matthew and Brian Harrison (eds), *Oxford Dictionary of National Biography*, Oxford University Press, 2004, vol 1, pp 695-696
Susan Sloman, *Image of China: William Alexander*, London: Jupiter Books, 1980

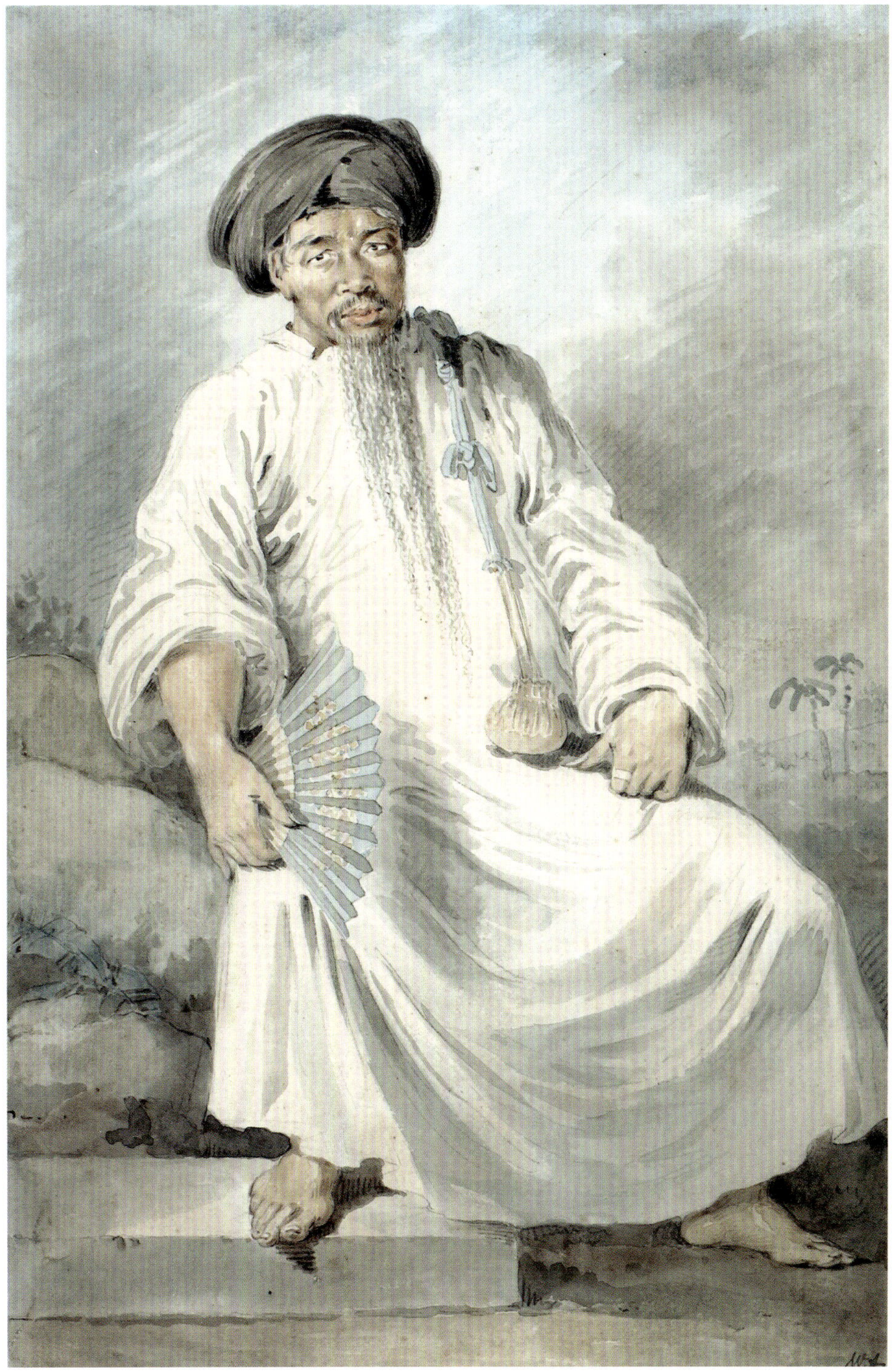

165 PORTRAIT OF A CHINESE MAN
signed with initials
watercolour with bodycolour
14 ¾ x 9 ½ inches

ROBERT HILLS
Robert Hills, OWS (1769-1844)

A painter, etcher and modeller in clay, Robert Hills developed a significant reputation for his accurate and evocative representations of animals in rural settings. A founder member of the Society of Painters in Water Colours, he worked mostly in watercolour, making fresh colour sketches in the open air, and using a stippling technique in the studio to develop exhibits of great intensity.

Robert Hills was born in Islington, Middlesex (now in London) on 26 June 1769. He received some drawing lessons from John Alexander Gresse, possibly at Mrs Broadbelt's School in Queen's Square, Bloomsbury, where Gresse was drawing master. Though he entered the Royal Academy Schools in 1789, he seems not to have stayed long as, in the same year, he advertised his services as a 'stained glass' painter of landscapes. From then until he began to exhibit at the Royal Academy of Arts in 1791, he lived at 4 Keppel Row, New Road (now the Marylebone Road).

Hills made intensive studies from nature, including anatomical drawings, in order to develop as a draughtsman and painter of animals. Between 1798 and 1815, he produced and issued an extensive series of *Etchings of Quadruped*, intended as an aid for other artists, both amateur and professional. By the turn of the century, when he was living in Upper Grafton Street, he was also giving direct instruction as a drawing master.

From 1800 to 1806, Hills was a regular member of a sketching society, at which artists met on a weekly basis to sketch and talk about art, as well as share modest refreshments. In the winter months, they met in each other's houses, while in the summer they went on sketching expeditions to such places as Windsor. Fellow members included J C Nattes and James Ward (friends), WILLIAM HENRY PYNE and Samuel Shelley (neighbours, living in George Street, Hanover Square), and Sir George Beaumont and James Green. They were sometimes joined by numerous guests.

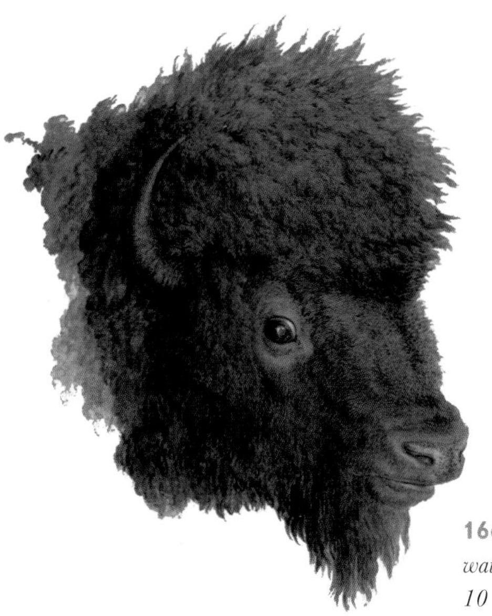

166 HEAD OF A BISON
watercolour
10 x 8 ¼ inches

The ambitions of this society found fruit in 1804, in the foundation of the Society of Painters in Water Colours, of which Hills was appointed the first secretary. He would become one of its most prolific exhibitors, showing over six hundred works, ranging from tinted drawings to virtuosic watercolours, and including collaborations with fellow members (notably, the addition of deer or cattle to the landscapes of George Barret junior, DAVID COX, William Andrews Nesfield and George Fennel Robson).

In about 1805, Hills moved to the artistic quarter north of Oxford Street, living first in Newman Street and then, from 1812, in London Street, Fitzroy Square. In 1812, he retired temporarily from the society, when it was reformed as the Society of Painters in Oil and Water-Colours, though he continued to exhibit until 1818. Following its return to its original constitution, he was re-elected to the membership in 1823, and acted as Treasurer (in 1823) and Secretary (from 1831 until his death).

Hills often sketched in Surrey and in western Kent, near to the home of his leading patron, John Garle. Locations included Dorking and Box Hill (1811-12), Sevenoaks, Knole and Underriver (1817-18), and Penshurst Park and Chiddingstone. He may also have worked in and around Shoreham with members of The Ancients, a group of admirers of William Blake (see Martin Hardie's article, listed below in Further Reading). Interestingly, there were people with the surname Hills living in Shoreham from the seventeenth century or earlier.

Hills also travelled further afield, sometimes in the company of such fellow artists as James Ward and JOHN GLOVER (for instance, going to the Lake District with Glover in 1805). He visited Paris in 1814, and returned to the Continent in the following year to see the site of the Battle of Waterloo, a trip that gave rise to a set of aquatints, *Sketches of Flanders and Holland*.

In or before 1831, Hills went to Jersey, returning there two years later with Robson. (According to Martin Hardie, Hills had a brother, now known only as 'T Hills', who died in Jersey in 1828, and was buried in St Saviour's Church Yard.)

In 1833, Hills moved from an address in Margaret Street to 17 Golden Square, dying there on 14 May 1844. He was the last surviving foundation member of the Society of Painters in Water Colours. Though unmarried, he was highly sociable, and known for his generosity.

Among his benefactors was Isaac Mendes Belisario (1795-1849). Belisario was a Jewish Jamaican-born artist who studied under Hills and developed a style close to his master. While working as a stockbroker, he exhibited works at the Society of Painters in Water Colours from 1815 to 1831. He then settled in Kingston, Jamaica, where he established an artistic reputation.

His work is represented in numerous public collections, including the British Museum, The Courtauld Gallery, Tate and the V&A; and Birmingham Museum & Art Gallery.

Further reading:

Patrick Conner, 'Hills, Robert (*b* Islington [now in London], 26 June 1769; *d* London, 14 May 1844)', Jane Turner (ed), *The Dictionary of Art*, London: Macmillan, 1996, vol 14, pp 548-549
Nicola Gauld, *'The fields calls me to labour'. Watercolours of nineteenth-century rural Britain by Robert Hills (1769-1844) and his contemporaries*, Cambridge: The Fitzwilliam Museum, 2008
Martin Hardie, 'Robert Hills: Extollager (1769-1844)', *The Old Water-Colour Society's Club*, vol 25, 1947, pp 38-40

Luke Herrmann, 'Robert Hills at Waterloo', *The Connoisseur*, 1962, vol 150, pp 174–177
Maureen Lambourne, 'A Watercolourist's Countryside: The Art of Robert Hills', *Country Life*, 25 July 1968, pp 235-238
Basil Somerset Long, 'Robert Hills, Water-colour Painter and Etcher', *Walker's Quarterly*, no 12, 1923
Greg Smith, 'Hills, Robert (1769–1844)', H C G Matthew and Brian Harrison (eds), *Oxford Dictionary of National Biography*, Oxford University Press, 2004, vol 27, p 238
Watercolours by Robert Hills, London: Albany Gallery, 1968
Iolo Aneurin Williams, 'Robert Hills (1779-1844)', *Burlington Magazine*, February 1945, pp 39-45

JOHN MASEY WRIGHT
John Masey Wright, OWS (1777-1866)

John Masey Wright was best known for his contributions to the Society of Painters in Water Colours, notably subjects taken from Shakespeare. While revealing the influence of Wright's teacher, Thomas Stothard, they have a distinct – and authentic – charm of their own, as a result of the artist's experience as a theatrical painter.

John Masey Wright was born in Pentonville, London on 14 October 1777. The son of an organ builder, he trained in the same business and began work as a piano-tuner for Broadwood. During his boyhood, however, he spent time in the studio of THOMAS STOTHARD, and developed his own artistic skills under the older artist's influence. The most prolific and distinguished illustrator of his day, Stothard contributed extensively to the fashionable anthologies of verse and prose, such as pocket-books, almanacs and 'galleries'. Wright's ability to summarise character and action of a work of literature in a single image was rooted in this kind of work and, not surprisingly, he later made a number of his best drawings for the similarly occasional 'annuals', *The Literary Souvenir* (1825-26), *The Amulet* (1826-27) and *Heath's Gallery* (1836).

In 1810, at the age of thirty-three, Wright married and moved to Lambeth, where he shared a house near the Thames, in Bishop's Walk, with the Scots marine painter, John ('Jock') Wilson. Lambeth was then a theatrical quarter, and Wilson – who painted scenery for Astley's circus theatre – introduced Wright into a circle of notable managers and designers, including T E Barker and David Roberts, who frequented Bent's public house. In turn, Wright contributed figures for reconstructions of famous battles at Barker's Panorama in the Strand, and painted scenery at Covent Garden and at His Majesty's Theatre. Through this work, he gained the first-hand knowledge of the stage, which affected both the structure of his literary watercolours – distinguishing them from Stothard's more frieze-like compositions – and the expansiveness of the rare historical set-pieces in oil that he exhibited at the Royal Academy of Arts between 1812-18. During this period he gave his address as 24 Great Pulteney Street in Soho, an area frequented by writers.

Wright was elected an associate of the Society of Painters in Water Colours in 1824, and became a full member in the following year. From that time, he made his living as an exhibiting watercolourist and illustrator of literary subjects (Burns, Cervantes, Goldsmith, Milton, Scott, Shakespeare) and as the teacher of such aristocratic clients as Lady Craven, the Marquess of Lansdowne and the daughters of the Earl de Grey. Despite this apparent success, however, he never gained financial security and, until his death at Twickenham Common, on 13 May 1866, was dependent upon charitable payments from the 'Old' Watercolour Society (1849 and 1860) and a small life annuity from the Royal Academy (1858). He was survived by four daughters and a son.

The particular devotion of Wright to Shakespeare, is indicated by the anecdote, told by his son, that 'during an illness, [he] loudly and repeatedly recited passages from his favourite Shakespeare plays while asleep' (F G Burnett).

His work is represented in the collections of the British Museum and the V&A; and the Folger Shakespeare Library (Washington).

Further reading:

F G Burnett, 'John Massey Wright (1777-1866)', *The Old Water-Colour Society's Club*, vol 54, 1979, pp 42-47
Simon Fenwick, 'Wright, John Masey (1777–1866)', H C G Matthew and Brian Harrison (eds), *Oxford Dictionary of National Biography*, Oxford University Press, 2004, vol 60, pp 455-456

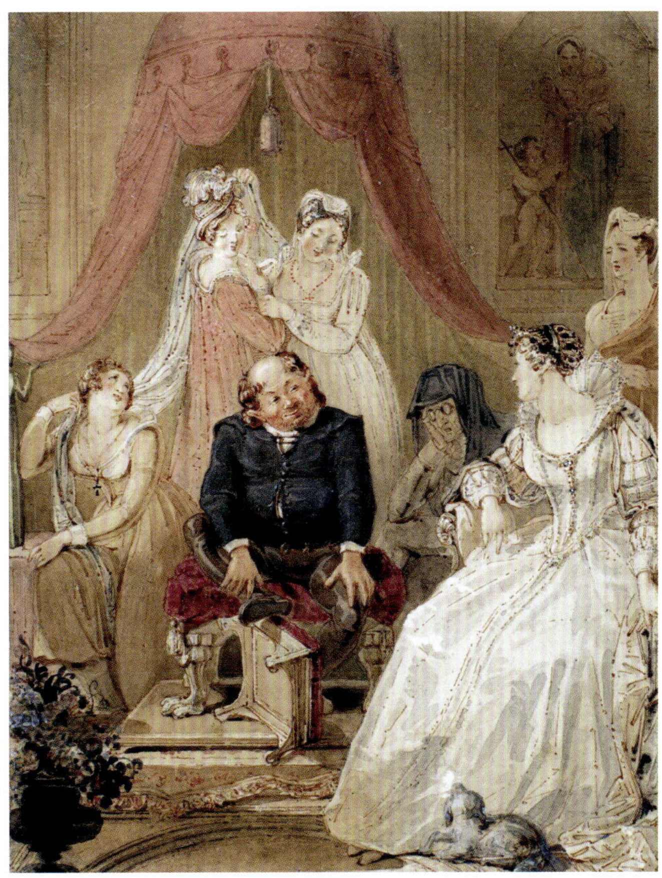

167 SANCHO PANZA
watercolour
6 ½ x 5 inches

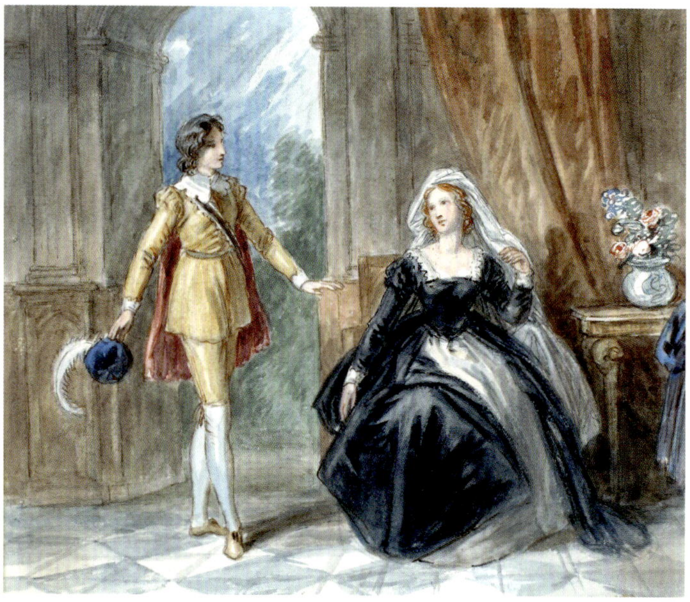

168 TWELFTH NIGHT
ACT THREE, SCENE IV, MALVOLIO, OLIVIA
OLIVIA SMIL'ST THOU? I SENT THEE FOR A SAD OCCASION
inscribed 'Twelfth Night' below mount
inscribed 'Malvolio, Olivia' on reverse
watercolour with pen and ink
6 ½ x 7 ½ inches

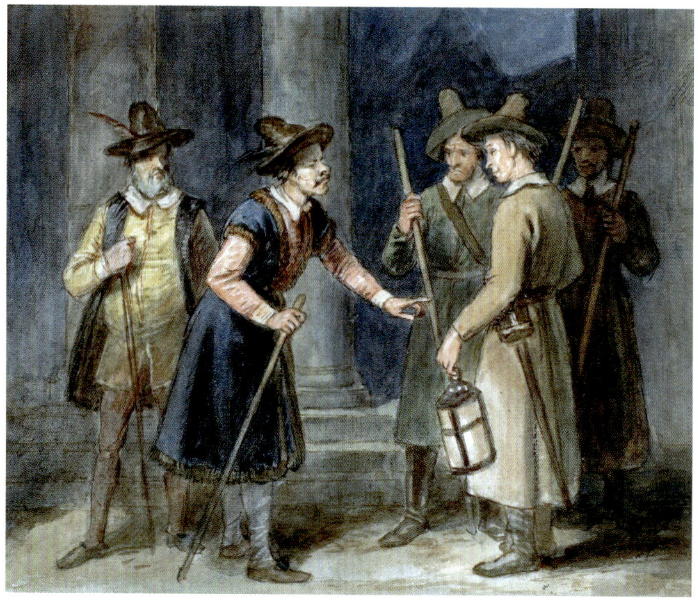

169 MUCH ADO ABOUT NOTHING
ACT FOUR, SCENE II, A PRISON, ENTER DOGBERRY, VERGES AND SEXTON IN GOWNS; AND THE WATCH WITH CONRADE AND BORACHIO
inscribed 'Much Ado About Nothing' below mount
inscribed with title on reverse
watercolour with pen and ink
6 ¾ x 7 ½ inches

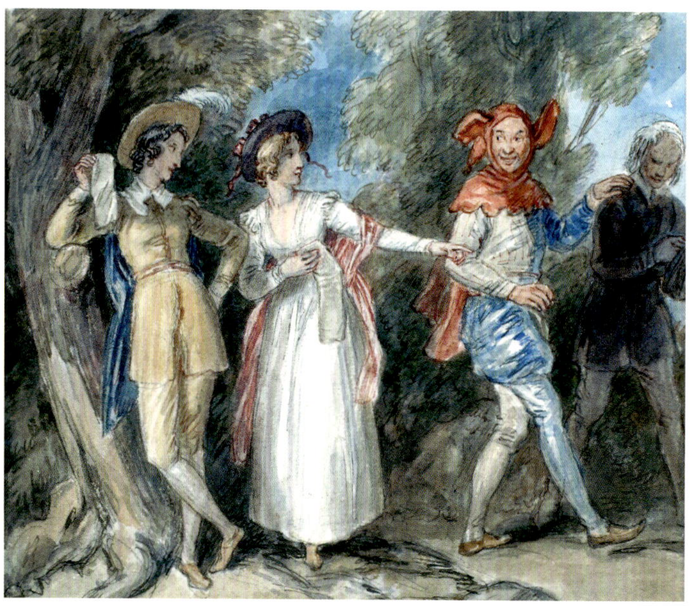

170 AS YOU LIKE IT
ACT TWO, SCENE IV, ENTER ROSALIND FOR GANYMEDE, CELIA FOR ALIENA AND CLOWN ALIAS TOUCHSTONE
inscribed 'As You Like It' below mount
inscribed with title on reverse
watercolour with pen and ink
6 ¾ x 7 ½ inches

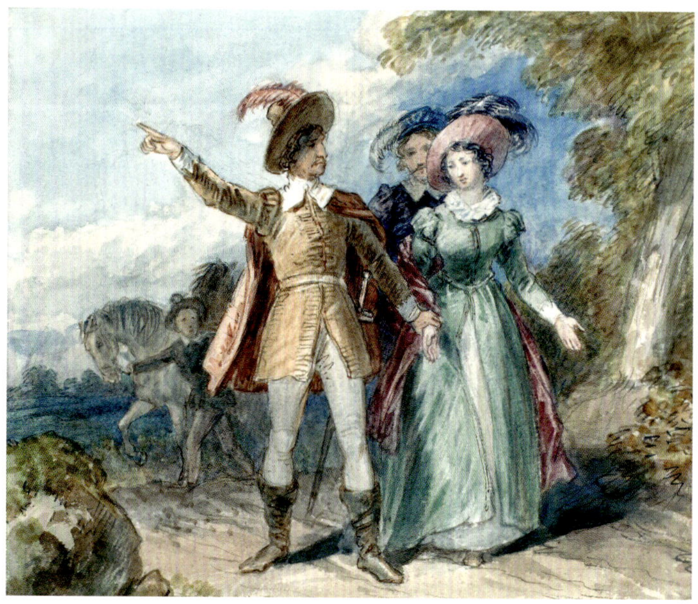

171 THE TAMING OF THE SHREW
ACT FOUR, SCENE V, A PUBLIC ROAD, PETRUCHIO, KATHERINE, HORTENSIO AND SERVANTS
PETRUCHIO GOOD LORD, HOW BRIGHT AND GOODLY SHINES THE MOON!
inscribed 'Taming of the Shrew' below mount
inscribed 'Petruchio, Katherine and Hortensio' on reverse
watercolour with pen and ink
6 ¾ x 7 ½ inches

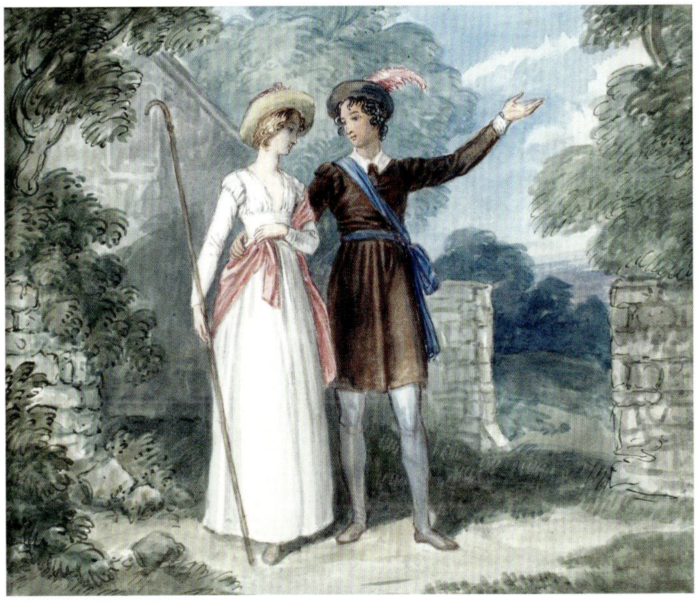

172 THE WINTER'S TALE
ACT FOUR, SCENE IV, BOHEMIA, THE SHEPHERD'S COTTAGE
FLORIZEL AND PERDITA
inscribed 'Winter's Tale' below mount
inscribed with title on reverse
watercolour with pen and ink
6 ¾ x 7 ½ inches

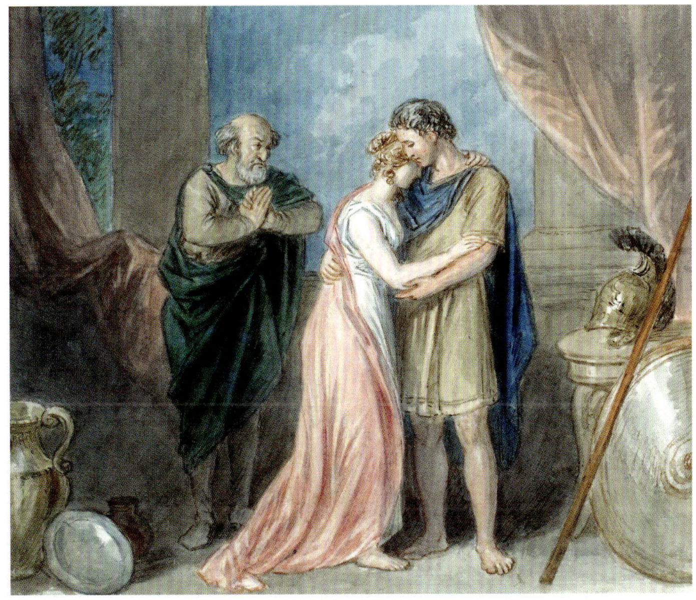

173 TROILUS AND CRESSIDA
ACT FOUR, SCENE IV, TROY, PANDARUS' HOUSE
CRESSIDA O TROILUS! TROILUS [EMBRACING HIM]
PANDARUS WHAT A PAIR OF SPECTACLES IS HERE
inscribed 'Troilus and Crysida' below mount
watercolour with pen and ink
6 ¾ x 7 ½ inches

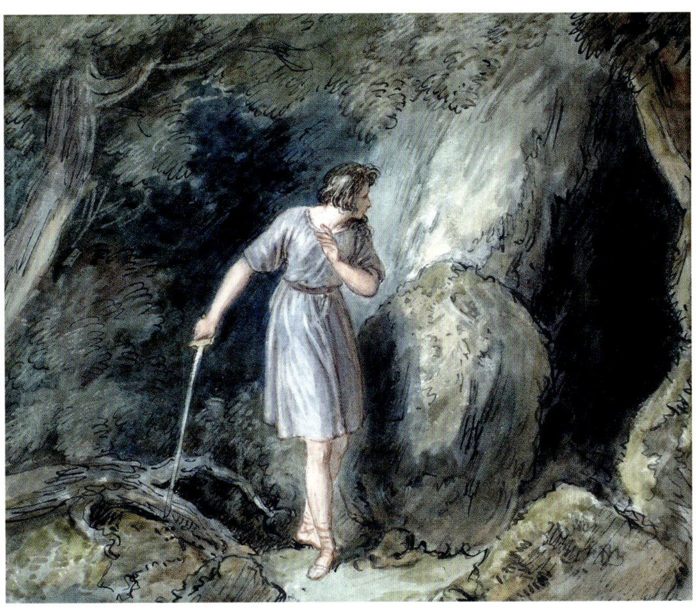

174 CYMBELINE
ACT THREE, SCENE VI, BEFORE THE CAVE OF BELARIUS
ENTER IMOGEN ALONE, IN BOY'S CLOTHES
inscribed 'Cymbeline' below mount
watercolour with pen and ink
6 ¾ x 7 ½ inches

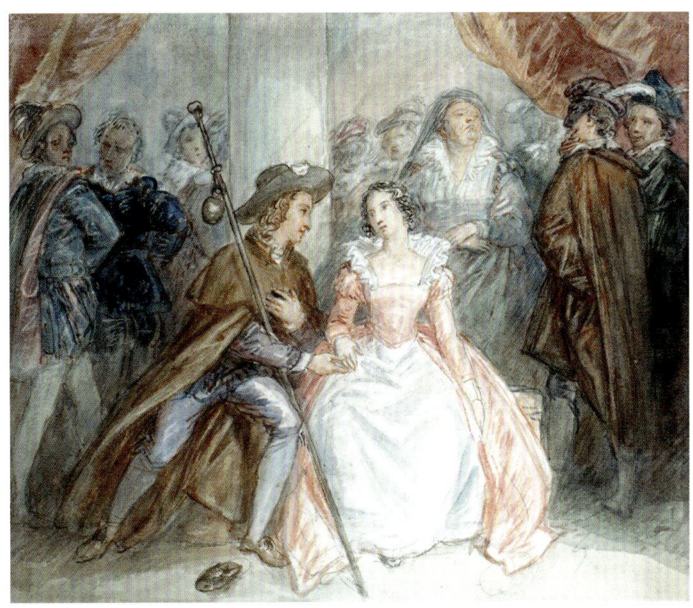

175 ROMEO AND JULIET
ACT ONE, SCENE V, CAPULET'S HOUSE
ROMEO [TO JULIET] IF I PROFANE WITH MY UNWORTHIEST HAND THIS HOLY SHRINE,
inscribed 'Romeo and Juliet' below mount
watercolour with pen and ink
6 ¾ x 7 ½ inches

ALFRED EDWARD CHALON
Alfred Edward Chalon, RA AA (1780-1860), christened Alfred-Edouard Chalon

Alfred Edward Chalon became synonymous with a particular format of elegant female portraiture, representing society ladies and fashionable performers, especially ballerinas. They prompted his friend and fellow artist, C R Leslie to state that, 'to my mind Alfred Chalon has long been the first among painters in watercolours'.

Alfred Edward Chalon was born in Geneva, Switzerland, on 15 February 1780, the son of Jean-Jacques Chalon, a Huguenot watchmaker. Leaving Switzerland in 1794, during troubles arising from the French Revolution, the family moved first to Ireland before settling in England. Jean-Jacques Chalon was appointed Professor of French at the Royal Military Academy – probably at Marlow, and then certainly at Sandhurst – retiring in 1817.

The Chalon family lived at 8 Church Lane, Kensington, and played host to a number of Swiss artists visiting or settling in England. These included François Ferrière and Jacques-Laurent Agasse, the latter arriving in London in 1800, and becoming a close friend of Alfred Edward and his brother, John James (Jean-Jacques). (See Agasse's group portrait, *The Chalon Family*, in the collections of Yale Center for British Art, for a record of his stay in Kensington.)

Jean-Jacques Chalon wanted his sons to enter a career in trade, and so placed each in a large commercial establishment. However, his plan did not succeed, and they soon entered the Royal Academy Schools, John in 1796 and Alfred in 1797. The artists would live together and, sharing a close fraternal bond, never marry.

Exhibiting at the Royal Academy of Arts from 1801, A E Chalon established himself with watercolour portraits, including miniatures, of fashionable performers and society ladies, which gained great currency through their reproduction in periodicals and albums, and on the covers of sheet music. In particular, his images of such prima ballerinas as Carlotta Grisi and Marie Taglioni did much to disseminate the poetic character of the contemporary Romantic ballet. He also produced occasional oils of a more ambitious character, and a number of unpublished theatrical caricatures in brown ink wash (a group of which is now in the V&A).

Becoming a member of the short-lived Associated Artists in Water Colours in 1808, A E Chalon helped found the Society for the Study of Epic and Pastoral Design in the same year, with his brother, J J Chalon, and Francis Stevens. The other founder members were Michael Sharp, WILLIAM TURNER of Oxford and Cornelius Varley, with Henry Pierce Bone joining them at the second meeting. The society was later known as the Bread and Cheese Society and then the Chalon Sketching Society, until its demise in 1851. Later members – at various stages – included Henry Pierce Bone, Decimus Burton, Joshua Christall, Charles Lock Eastlake, JOHN SAMUEL HAYWARD, C R LESLIE, Daniel Maclise, John Partridge, WILLIAM HENRY PYNE, David Roberts, Clarkson Stanfield, S J Stump and Thomas Uwins. Agasse, John Constable and Washington Irvin were among the visitors and exhibitors.

As his reputation developed, A E Chalon also became an associate of the Royal Academy in 1812 and a full Academician in 1816, and later a member of the Society of Arts of Geneva. Proving very popular in court circles, he was the first artist to paint a portrait of Queen Victoria following her accession, and was appointed Portrait Painter in Water Colour to Her Majesty. In 1842, the Queen twice provided the subject for meetings of the Chalon Sketching Society ('Desire' and 'Elevation'). From 1851, the head in Chalon's portrait of Queen Victoria was used as the basis of the design of postage stamps in the British colonies.

Between 1806 and 1853, the Chalon brothers lived in the artistic quarter north of Oxford Street, with addresses at 23 Charles Street, north of the present Berners Street (1806-8); 43 Great Titchfield Street (1809-11); 71 Great Titchfield Street (1812-16); 11 Great Marlborough Street (1817-25); 42 Great Marlborough Street (1826-39) and 10 Wimpole Street (1840-53). For some periods, they shared their accommodation with their father and unmarried sister.

In 1847, J-J Chalon suffered a paralytic seizure, and began to decline both physically and mentally. A E Chalon nursed him throughout until he died on 14 November 1854. Earlier that year, the brothers had moved to El Retiro, Campden Hill, Kensington.

In 1855, A E Chalon mounted an exhibition of his and his brother's work at the Society of Arts in the Adelphi. Within the next few years, he offered a collection of their work to the people of Hampstead, on condition that they provide a gallery to house it. As they failed to do so, he then intended to offer it either to the University of Cambridge or to the nation, but died before the plan could be properly developed. He died at Campden Hill, Kensington, on 3 October 1860 and was buried at Highgate cemetery in the same grave as his brother. The collection was auctioned after his death at Christie's on 11-15 March 1860.

His work is represented in the collections of the British Museum, The Courtauld Gallery, the National Portrait Gallery and the V&A.

Further reading:

Patrick Conner, 'Chalon', Jane Turner (ed), *The Dictionary of Art*, London: Macmillan, 1996, vol 6, p 402
Lionel Lambourne, *The Chalon Brothers*, London: Victoria and Albert Museum, 1981
Raymond Lister, 'Chalon, Alfred Edward (1780-1860)', H C G Matthew and Brian Harrison (eds), *Oxford Dictionary of National Biography*, Oxford University Press, 2004, vol 10, pp 888-889

Bliss Was It In That Dawn To Be Alive

British Drawings and Watercolours 1750-1850

William Taverner (1700-1772)
1 Figure in a Wooded Landscape £3500

Anthony Devis (1729-1816)
2 Old Castle Ruins £2250
3 Distant View of Coastal Village £1250
4 Above Mr Callings Hop Grounds £850
5 View of a Hamlet £1250
6 Green Hythe £950
7 In Mr Malthus's Woods £750
8 Deer Park £750
9 Sheep in a Romantic Valley Landscape £750
10 In the Footway to Cleve £550
11 Yonder Spire £850
12 Old Mill at Albury £850
13 Salanche on R Arve Savoy £850
14 Goatherds Below Mountain Ruins £950
15 Between the Chartruse & Preppe £850
16 Pastoral Scene in an Italianate Landscape £1250

Samuel Hieronymus Grimm (1733-1794)
17 Village with a Ruined Tower £3500

Nicholas Pocock (1740-1821)
18 The Strait of Menai £4500
19 Entrance into Borodale £1250

William Pars, ARA (1742-1782)
20 Ruin at Adare £4500
21 The Imperial Palaces, The Palatine, Rome £7500

George Cuit (1743-1818)
22 Tanfield Yorks £3500

Thomas Sunderland (1744-1823)
23 Perugia £1450
24 The Lake of Perugia £950
25 Terni £850
26 Italian Scene £850
27 Aqueduct of Spoletta £950

George Frost (circa 1745-1821)
28 A Woodland Walk £3500

Michael Angelo Rooker, ARA (1746-1801)
29 The Country Halt £2750

Moses Griffith (1747-1819)
30 Kirkstall Abbey Yorkshire £4500

Joseph Halfpenny (1748-1811)
31 Wycliffe in Yorkshire £2750

John 'Warwick' Smith, OWS (1749-1831)
32 Look into the Glen of the Rheidol £4500

Samuel Howitt (1756/57-1822)
33 S Ethiopicus £850
34 A Brief Salutation on the Road £1750

Thomas Rowlandson (1756/57-1827)
35 The Virtuous Chambermaid £14500
36 Harvesters Merrymaking £4750
37 The Highwayman £6500
38 A Meeting of Class £9500
39 Invitation to Dance £2750
40 Taking her Pulse £5500
41 The Alchemy of Love £4500
42 Lord Fellamar £4500
43 A Plate of Oysters £8500
44 The Tradesman £2250
45 The Soldier's Departure £5500
46 Give Point, and Left Parry £6500
47 The Duel £5500
48 Portrait of Doctor Guise £12500
49 Crossing the Ford £4750
50 Chelsea Pensioners £2750
51 Idle Spinning £7500
52 A Peasant Family £2250
53 Picnic at the Roadside £2750
54 Unloading the Shipping £9500
55 Nymphs Bathing £3750
56 A Sylvan Idyll £6500
57 Lovers' Recreation £12500
58 The Courtyard of a Monastery £9500
59 Packing a Coach £22500
60 Dr Sangrado and his Patient £6500
61 A Fall in Beer £12500
62 The Long Room, Custom House £4500
63 Quarterly Duns £14500
64 The Baron Makes a Speech £1750
65 A Picture of Misery £5500
66 Susannah and the Elders £4750
67 Ugolino and his Family £850
68 At the Tailor's £9500
69 Parson's Pleasure £950
70 A Hit at Backgammon £22500
71 The Gamesters £12500
72 Male Face Studies £1750
73 A Close Shave £4250
74 Tripe and Trollebobs £6500
75 Laughing Grotesques £3750
76 Sea Stores £12500
77 The Coquette £5500
78 The Parson and Milkmaids £17500
79 The Artificial Flower Makers £12500
80 Drawing from Life £4750
81 Madame Callee (Culloni) and M Renault in a Fencing Contest £9500

John Nixon (before 1759-1818)
82 Doctor Benemar the Magnitiser £2750
83 The Naumacia £6500

George Moutard Woodward (1760-1809)
84 Indeed Sir Jacob £850
85 Keeping!!! £850
86 At the Theatre £3250
87 A Consul and a Consultation £3250
88 Comfort in the Gout £2750

Isaac Cruikshank (1764-1811)
89 The Road to Ruin £2750

Henry Alken (1785-1851)
90 Persian with Horse £3500
91 Whipping It £2750
92 Tally Ho £2750
93 Trotting On £2250
94 View Hallo £2450
95 Arab With Stallion £3500

George Cruikshank (1792-1878)
96 Dancing with Crutches £2250

Phiz (Hablot Knight Browne) (1815-1882)
97 Woa! Emma! £1450
98 Beggars Outside The Imperial Hotel £2250

John Frederick Herring (1815/21-1907)
99 The Jump £1750
100 The Stable £2250
101 A Request for Help £1450
102 Farmer O'phat and Squire M'lean £1250
103 Hats Off! £2750
104 Tally Ho! £1450

John Leech (1817-1864)
105 Mr and Mrs Joys out Hunting £1450

Rev John Swete (circa 1752-1821)
106 A Devon Cottage £950
107 Old Gateway, Tor Abbey £1450
108 The Light House, at Ilfracomb £3250

Francis Nicholson, OWS (1753-1844)
109 Rudding House, Yorkshire £9500
110 Ripon £4500

Rev William Thomas Bree (1754-1822)
111 Maxstoke Priory £1250

Julius Caesar Ibbetson (1759-1817)
112 The Waterfall £5500

John Thomas Serres (1759-1825)
113 The Village Carrier £4500

William Payne (1760-1830)
114 Across the Tiber Plain £5500
115 A Rest at Sunset £3750
116 Cowes Castle £2250
117 Brockwear Quay – On The Wye £4500

John Laporte (1761-1839)
118 View of Eastbourne, Sussex £3500

Edward Dayes (1763-1804)
119 Binham Priory, Norfolk £4500

George Morland (1763-1804)
120 Figures on a Horse £3500
121 Landscape with Castle Ruins £3500

John White Abbott (1763-1851)
122 Two Bridges £950
123 Watering Cattle and Sheep £1750
124 Children Bathing £2450
125 Woodcutters £2250
126 Bringing the Horses up the Hill £1750
127 A Family in the Wilderness £1750
128 The Hurdy-Gurdy Player £2250
129 Collecting Wood £2250
130 Gathering Firewood £2750
131 Animals at the Farm Door £2450
132 Gypsies £1850
133 Resting Outside a Castle £1750
134 Cattle on the Village Road £1250

John Glover, OWS (1767-1849)
135 A View in the Lake District £7500
136 The River Valley £9500

William Marshall Craig (died circa 1828)
137 St Paul's Cathedral From Hackney £2750

William Daniell, RA (1769-1837)
138 Windsor Castle £9500

William Henry Pyne, OWS (1769-1843)
139 An Old Town House £650

Paul Sandby Munn (1773-1845)
140 Berne £2750
141 By Evening Light £4500

James Bourne (1773-1854)
142 Mountainous Landscape £650

J M W Turner, RA (1775-1851)
143 Norbury Park £8500

William Delamotte (1775-1863)
144 Landscape with a Windmill £1750

John Samuel Hayward (1788-1822)
145 November Noon at Lavender Hill £3500
146 Lawsand £950
147 Plymouth Dock £850

John Sell Cotman (1782-1842)
148 Stratton Woods, Near Norwich £7500
149 Abbatial House of St Ouen £14500
150 Leigh High Woods £12500
151 Thornton College, Lincolnshire £5500

Miles Edmund Cotman (1810-1858)
152 Ludham Font £1750
153 Hautbois Font £1750
154 Chedgrave Font £1750
155 Hunstanton Font £1750
156 Near Dedham £2750
157 Chancel, Walsaken Church £4500

John Middleton (1827-1856)
158 The Blown Wood £6500
159 A Wooded Landscape in Winter £4500
160 Valley Farm £3500

Thomas Stothard, RI (1755-1834)
161 Bad News £650

Richard Corbould (1757-1831)
162 Mr Bennet Interrupted £950
163 Booth Consoling Miss Matthews £950
164 The Affecting Interview £950

William Alexander (1767-1816)
165 Portrait of a Chinese Man £6750

Robert Hills, OWS (1769-1844)
166 Head of a Bison £1750

John Masey Wright, OWS (1777-1866)
167 Sancho Panza £1250
168 Twelfth Night £950
169 Much Ado About Nothing £650
170 As You Like It £950
171 The Taming of the Shrew £950
172 The Winter's Tale £850
173 Troilus and Cressida £650
174 Cymbeline £750
175 Romeo and Juliet £950

Alfred Edward Chalon, RA (1780-1860)
176 An Opera Box £1250

William Henry Hunt, OWS (1790-1864)
177 Negro Boxer £7500
178 An Unwelcome Visitor £2750
179 Below the Cliff £750
180 Still Life with Rabbit & Lobster £4500

Charles Robert Leslie, RA (1794-1859)
181 King Henry the Fourth £1250

Henry Perlee Parker (1795-1873)
182 Smugglers £3500

George Richmond, RA (1809-1896)
183 The Young Cricketer £3500

Joseph Nash, OWS (1809-1878)
184 In the Gatehouse, Kenilworth £3500

William Edward Frost, RA (1810-1877)
185 Three Graces £2750
186 Love £1750

Theodor Von Holst (1810-1844)
187 My Lady's Pleasure £7500

John Varley, OWS (1778-1842)
188 The Ruins £4750
189 Bolton Abbey £3250
190 Castle on the Lake £3250
191 The Wooded Dell £3750
192 Thatched Cottage £8500
193 Beddgellert Bridge, Wales £5500
194 By the River £2250
195 Sheep Grazing £2750
196 Dolgelly from the Road to Barmouth, Merioneshire £12500
197 Conway Castle £12500
198 Near Dolgelly, Wales £12500
199 Tintern Abbey, Wales £12500
200 Town in North Wales £7500
201 Kilchurn Castle on Loch Awe £8500
202 Berry Pomeroy Castle £8500

Samuel Prout, OWS (1783-1852)
203 Arthur's Castle at Tintagel £2750
204 Old Boats £4500
205 Charles Bridge, Prague £2750

David Cox, OWS (1783-1859)
206 Old Calais Fortifications, France £2250
207 Richmond Castle, Yorkshire £1750
208 By the Mill Stream £8500
209 Pont-y-Pair, Glaslyn £2750
210 Figures by an Old Castle £4500

George Sidney Shepherd, NWS (1784-1862)
211 Winchester House, Austin Friars £4500

Copley Fielding, POWS (1787-1855)
212 The Cattle Pool £4500
213 Derwentwater £3500
214 Benares £4500

William Turner Of Oxford, OWS (1789-1862)
215 Sheep Grazing at Stonehenge £12500
216 Oxford from Iffley £1750

Thomas Churchyard (1798-1865)
217 A Woodbridge Walk £1450
218 The House Beyond the Trees £750
219 A Bird's Nest £3500

James Baker Pyne (1800-1870)
220 View Near Clifton £2250

George Pyne (1800-1884)
221 Hilton House £2750
222 Christ's College, Cambridge £3500
223 Eton College £4250

Henry Barlow Carter (1795-1867)
224 Barton-On-Humber £850
225 Off Scarborough £3500
226 North View Scarborough £1750
227 Kingskerswell Church £6500

Joseph Murray Ince (1806-1859)
228 May Day £1450
229 Trinity Gate, Cambridge £4500

Thomas Hosmer Shepherd (1793-1864)
230 St Mary's, Aldermanbury £2750
231 St Paul's Cathedral £4000
232 Westminster Abbey West Front £3500
233 St Paul's Church, Covent Garden £3500
234 Lincoln's Inn £4500
235 Cordwainers' Hall, Distaff Lane £4000
236 Stationers' Hall £3500
237 Town Hall, Borough, Southwark £3500
238 Newgate Prison, Old Bailey £3500
239 St Michael, Crooked Lane £3000
240 St Mary Somerset £3000
241 Duke of York's School, Chelsea £3750
242 All Hallows, Bread Street £3000
243 St James's, Garlick Hill £3000
244 Temple Bar from the Strand £3250
245 All Hallows, London Wall £2750
246 St Nicholas, Cole Abbey £3000
247 Piccadilly, from Coventry Street £4250
248 St Martin Outwich £3750
249 Shaftesbury House £3500
250 The New Opening to St Martin's Church from Pall Mall East £3500
251 United Service Military Club £4500
252 The Temple Church £3500
253 Theatre Royal, Drury Lane £4500
254 The King's Entrance £3750
255 The Russell Institution £3500
256 The Royal College of Surgeons £4500
257 Asylum for the Indigent Blind £3750
258 The Bank of England £4500
259 St Barnabas, King's Square £2750
260 New Church, Camden Town £2750
261 Coal Exchange, Thames Street £3750

Louis Francia (1772-1839)
262 Uzerche £3500

Newton Fielding (1799-1856)
263 Sunset £3500

George Cattermole (1800-1868)
264 Shipwreck £3250

Frederick Tayler, PRWS (1806-1889)
265 Sophia and Squire Western £4500

Thomas Shotter Boys, NWS (1803-1874)
266 Rue Maritaine, Rouen £4500
267 Elegant Figures in the Grounds of a Stately Home £6500

Charles Bentley, OWS (1806-1854)
268 A Couple in Courtly Dress £3250
269 Travellers near a Town £3500

William Wyld, RI (1806-1889)
270 A Chateau by the River £2750
271 Landscape in Northern France £4500

William Callow, RWS (1812-1908)
272 A Ride in the Country £3500
273 Rouen £15000
274 Cleaning the Nets, Rouen £8500
275 Boulogne £8500
276 Rheinfels £35000
277 In The Park at Royaumont £3750

All images are available to view on our website

www.chrisbeetles.com

Chris Beetles Ltd
8 & 10 Ryder St
London
SW1Y 6QB
0207 839 7551
gallery@chrisbeetles.com

ALFRED EDWARD CHALON

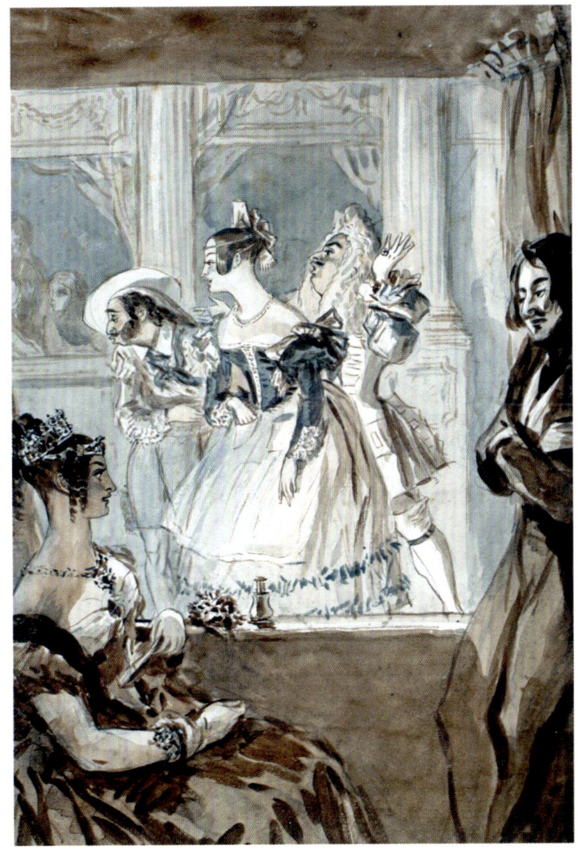

The Opera Box
The appearance of the figures on stage in this watercolour by A E Chalon suggest Rossini's *Il Barbiere di Siviglia*, which received it's first London performance at the King's Theatre, Haymarket, on 10 March 1818.

A watercolour by Chalon with the same title is in the collections of the British Museum. Dated 1838, it is similar in composition, though the performer is a prima ballerina, while the treatment is more detailed but less lively. According to Raymond Lister (Matthew and Harrison 2004, vol 10, p 889), it was 'originally painted as an illustration to Lady Blessington's poem *The Belle of the Season* (1839)'.

Charles Robert Leslie also produced a watercolour entitled *The Opera Box*, which suggests that it may have been the set subject at a meeting of the Chalon Sketching Society.

176 AN OPERA BOX
signed and inscribed with title below mount
watercolour
17 x 11 ½ inches

WILLIAM HENRY HUNT
William Henry Hunt, OWS (1790-1864)

William Henry Hunt was one of the most distinctive and influential of early Victorian watercolourists, who became synonymous with his naturalistic still life compositions executed in detailed stippling.

The son of a tin-plate worker and japanner, William Henry Hunt was baptised in London on 28 March 1790, and grew up at 8 Old Belton Street (now Endell Street), Covent Garden. As a result of his deformed legs and stunted growth, he was encouraged by his parents to pursue a career in art, and at the age of sixteen he was placed with JOHN VARLEY (living with him for a time at 18 Broad Street, Golden Square). There he made friends with William Mulready and John Linnell; Linnell and Hunt exerted a positive influence on each other's work and made a number of sketching tours together in southern England. While still a pupil of Varley, he began to exhibit at the Royal Academy of Arts (1807-25) and spent a short time in the Royal Academy Schools (1808-09), during which he helped to re-decorate Drury Lane Theatre. His earliest important private patrons were the Duke of Devonshire and the Earl of Essex, who respectively commissioned drawings of the staterooms at Chatsworth and Cassiobury. It was at the latter place that he met Dr Monro, who then employed him in his informal academy.

By 1815, Hunt had established himself as an independent architectural and landscape painter, working in the eighteenth-century manner in pen and wash. He first exhibited with the Society of Painters in Water Colours during its phase as the Society of Painters in Oil and Water-Colours, and became an associate in 1824, and a full member two years later. In 1822, he moved to 36 Brownlow Street, Drury Lane, and in 1825 to 6 Marchmont Street, Brunswick Square. For a number of years, he wintered in Hastings, Sussex.

By this time, Hunt was turning to genre scenes and still life compositions, which he depicted with a new found meticulousness. In these works, he was able to create fine atmospheric detail by building up coloured tints in hatch and stipple over a ground of white bodycolour. In 1830, he exhibited his first still life containing details of nature against a mossy bank, and became so well known for the type that he was soon dubbed 'Bird's Nest Hunt'. However, he also painted a number of figures, some being humorous rustics, while others were set in candlelit interiors.

On 13 September 1830, Hunt married his eighteen-year-old cousin, Sarah Holloway, the daughter of a farmer and miller in Bramley, Hampshire. A daughter was born in 1832. In 1845, they moved to 62 Stanhope Street, Hampstead Road, London and, from 1851, took a second home at Park Gate, Bramley.

Hunt's approach to picture making proved very popular with both oil and watercolour painters, and became even more influential through the advocacy of John Ruskin. Hunt gave Ruskin lessons between 1854 and 1861, and in turn Ruskin recommended study of his work in *The Elements of Drawing* (1857) and *Notes on Prout and Hunt* (1879).

In the 1850s, Hunt developed an international reputation, being awarded a certificate of merit at the Paris Universal Exhibition of 1855, and becoming an honorary member of the Koninklijke Academie van Beeldende Kunsten in Amsterdam in the following year. In 1857, his work was well represented in the Manchester Art Treasures Exhibition.

Hunt died of a stroke at home in London on 10 February 1864. The contents of his studio were sold at Christie's on 16 and 17 May 1864.

His manner of painting still life subjects was continued by John Sherrin (1819-1896), William Hull (1820-1880), John Jessop Hardwick (1831-1917), William Hough (active 1857-1894) and Thomas Collier (1840-1891).

His work is represented in numerous public collections, including the British Museum and the V&A; and Yale Center for British Art (New Haven).

Further reading:

Simon Fenwick, 'Hunt, William Henry (1790–1864)', H C G Matthew and Brian Harrison (eds), *Oxford Dictionary of National Biography*, Oxford University Press, 2004, vol 28, pp 878-880
Tom Jones, *William Henry Hunt, 1790–1864*, Wolverhampton Art Gallery, 1981
Scott Wilcox, 'Hunt, William Henry (*b* London, 28 March 1790; *d* London, 10 Feb 1864)', Jane Turner (ed), *The Dictionary of Art*, London: Macmillan, 1996, vol 15, p 24
Sir John Witt, *William Henry Hunt (1790-1864): Life and Work, with a Catalogue*, London: Barrie and Jenkins, 1982

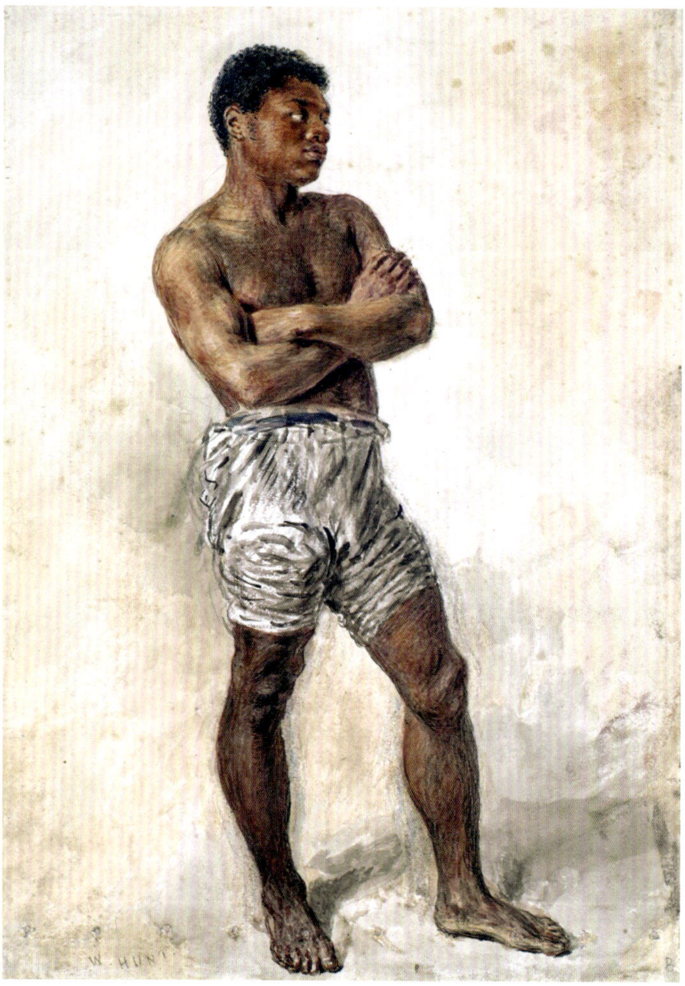

177 NEGRO BOXER
watercolour with bodycolour
14 x 9 ½ inches
Provenance: David Daniels, New York
Literature: John Witt, *William Henry Hunt (1790-1864), Life and Work*, with a catalogue, London: Barrie & Jenkins, 1982, no 329, plate 10

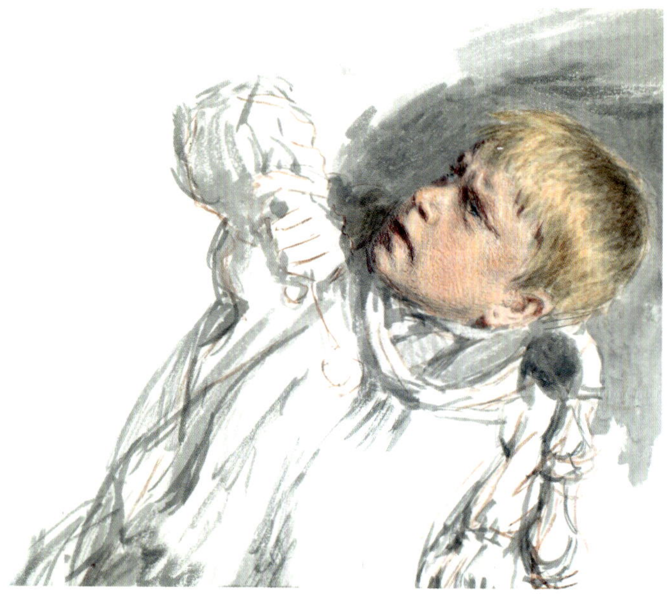

178 AN UNWELCOME VISITOR
watercolour
9 x 10 ¾ inches
Exhibited: Society of Painters in Water Colours, 1842
Study for the figure in 'The Boy and the Wasp', originally exhibited at the Society of Painters in Water Colours, 1845, no 55, as 'An Unwelcome Visitor'

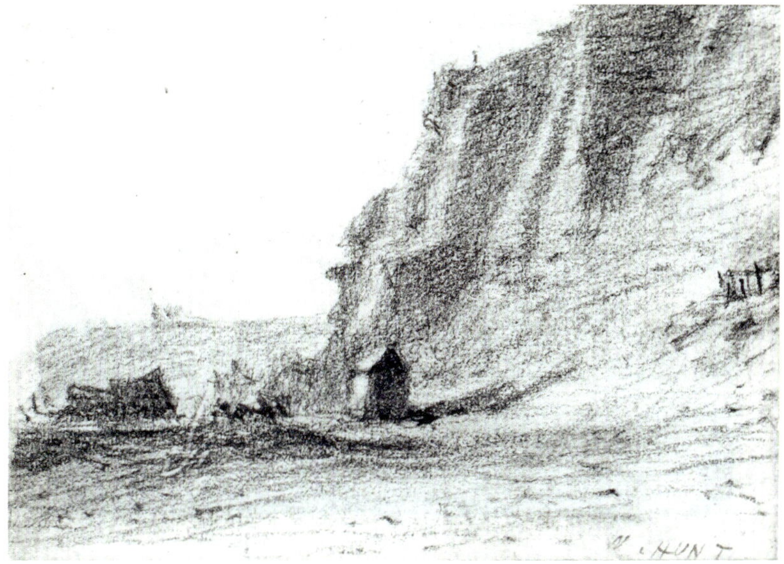

179 BELOW THE CLIFF
signed
pencil
2 ½ x 3 ½ inches
Provenance: Walker Galleries, London, January 1960

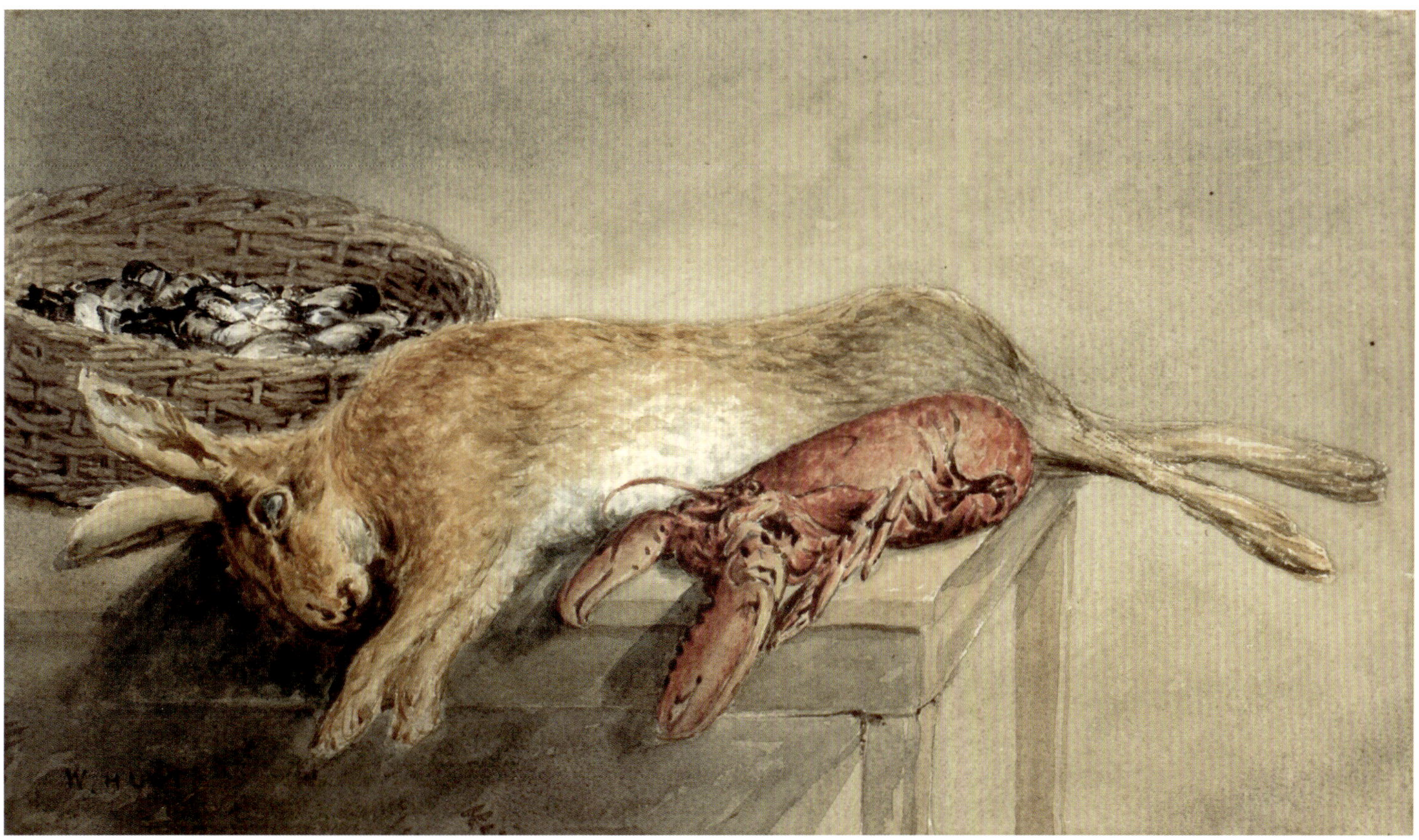

180 STILL LIFE WITH RABBIT AND LOBSTER
signed
watercolour
5 ½ x 9 ¼ inches
Exhibited: Society of Painters in Water Colours, 1827, no 216
A preparatory sketch for this watercolour is in the collection of the Yale Center for British Art (New Haven). See John Witt, *William Henry Hunt (1790-1864), Life and Work*, with a catalogue, London: Barrie & Jenkins, 1982, no 774, plate 55. On p 215, Witt suggests that it is the preparatory sketch that was exhibited in 1827.

CHARLES ROBERT LESLIE

Charles Robert Leslie, RA (1794-1859)

Interested in literature from an early age, Charles Robert Leslie became a leading exponent of literary genre painting, and later a writer on art, proving a crucial source of information on his friend, John Constable.

Charles Robert Leslie was born in Clerkenwell, London, on 19 October 1794, the son of a Philadelphian clockmaker of Scottish descent. At the age of six, he left for Philadelphia, Pennsylvania, with his parents and sisters. From this time, he showed a great interest in drawing, and the activity dominated his education, at a school in nearby New Jersey and at the University of Pennsylvania, which he attended at the age of ten. Following his father's death in 1804, he became apprenticed to the Philadelphia publishers, Bradford and Inskeep, where his artistic talent was soon discovered and encouraged by Samuel T Bradford, a senior partner. As a director of the Pennsylvania Academy of Fine Arts, Bradford was in a good position to forward Leslie's artistic development: by ensuring that the academy took him on as a pupil and exhibited his work at its annual exhibition, as well as contributing financially to his studying abroad. In addition, Bradford published engravings after some of Leslie's theatrical subjects in the firm's monthly, *The Mirror of Taste*. Before he left for England in 1811, Leslie took some lessons in oil painting from the portraitist, Thomas Sully.

With a letter of introduction from Sully, Leslie entered the circle of American-born history painters, studying first with Benjamin West, the President of the Royal Academy, and West's former pupil, Washington Allston; and also lodging with their student, Samuel F B Morse. He then entered the Royal Academy Schools in March 1813 and exhibited history paintings at the Royal Academy of Arts from that year, while making a living from portrait commissions. (He would be elected an associate in 1821, and a full Academician in 1826.)

Leslie married in 1825, and became the father of six children during the following decade. With the exception of a year spent as Drawing Master to the American Military Academy at West Point (1833), he based himself in England. Becoming an essential part of its artistic life, as a teacher and historian as well as a painter and illustrator, he also provided an exemplar to the younger generation of American artists.

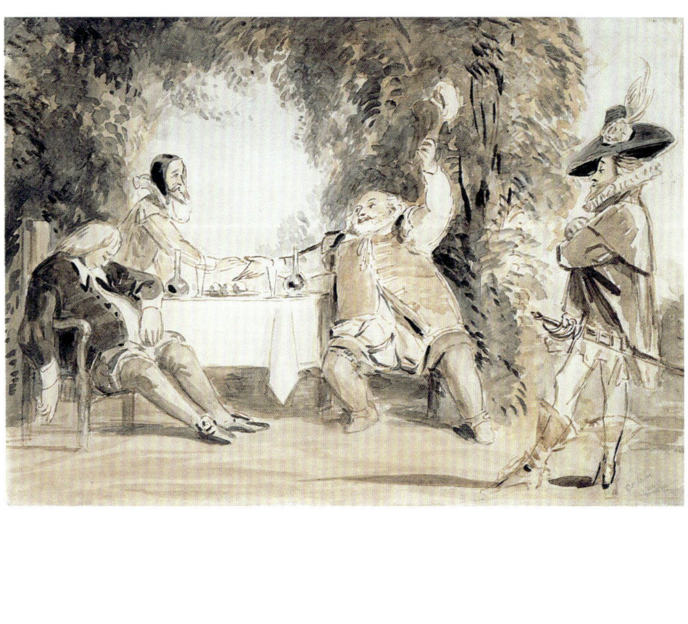

Leslie's residence in London sharpened his pronounced taste for literature. He fell into the company of Washington Irving and made the acquaintance of the poet, Samuel Taylor Coleridge, a friend of Washington Allston. Fuelling his love for the stage, he attended, and was greatly inspired by, a number of Coleridge's lectures on Shakespeare (first given in 1811-12 at the London Philosophical Society).

Directly influenced by West, Leslie's early work stands in the grand tradition of Joshua Reynolds and parallels contributions to John Boydell's Shakespeare Gallery. His later work was more akin to that of David Wilkie and William Mulready, though his highly finished, small-scale genre pieces tend to focus on humorous episodes from popular literary classics, from Cervantes to Sterne, rather than on contemporary life. His contributions to the depiction of the works of Shakespeare included illustrations for Charles Heath's The Shakespeare Gallery (1836) and two paintings for Isambard Kingdom Brunel's 'Shakespeare Room' at his house at 17-18 Duke Street, St James's (1848-50). He also proved to be an ideal illustrator for the work of his friend Sir Walter Scott (in the 1820s and 1830s).

From 1829, Leslie was a member of the Sketching Society that had been founded by the CHALON brothers, and Francis Stevens (see page 110). Visitors to the society included his friends, Washington Irving and John Constable.

Following Constable's death in 1837, Leslie embarked on the first biography of the landscape painter, which proved the definitive source of information on his life for a century. His subsequent writings comprised a *Handbook for Young Painters* (1854), based on his lectures as Professor of Painting at the Royal Academy (1847-52), and two volumes published posthumously, in editions by Tom Taylor: *Autobiographical Recollections of the late Charles Robert Leslie* (1860) and *The Life and Times of Joshua Reynolds* (1865).

Leslie died at his home at 2 Abercorn Place, St John's Wood, London on 5 May 1859. Seven years after his death, the brothers Redgrave declared, in *A Century of British Painters*, that the key to his success was due to his 'entering into the true spirit of the poet or writer'.

His sons Robert Charles Leslie and George Dunlop Leslie were also painters.

His work is represented in numerous public collections, including the National Portrait Gallery, Tate and the V&A; and the Metropolitan Museum of Art (New York), the Museum of Fine Arts (Boston) and Pennsylvania Academy of Fine Arts (Philadelphia).

Further reading:

Dorinda Evans, 'Leslie, Charles Robert (1794–1859)', H C G Matthew and Brian Harrison (eds), *Oxford Dictionary of National Biography*, Oxford University Press, 2004, vol 32, pp 438-441

Robin Hamlyn, 'Leslie, C(harles) R(obert) (*b* Clerkenwell, London, 19 Oct 1794; *d* London, 5 May 1859)', Jane Turner (ed), *The Dictionary of Art*, London: Macmillan, 1996, vol 19, pp 239-241

181 KING HENRY THE FOURTH, PART ONE
FALSTAFF
signed
watercolour
12 x 17 ½ inches

HENRY PERLEE PARKER
Henry Perlee Parker (1795-1873)

One of the best-known painters working in north-east England during the early nineteenth century, Henry Perlee Parker contributed greatly to the development of the region's cultural life. While producing a variety of portraits and genre subjects, he became synonymous with scenes of smuggling life.

Henry Perlee Parker was born at Plymouth Dock (now Devonport), Devon on 15 March 1795. He was the son of Robert Parker, a teacher of marine and mechanical drawing to the Royal Navy, who has also been described as 'a painter, carver and gilder' (Wood 1978, p 356).

Though he worked briefly as both a tailor and a coachman, Parker soon turned to art, painting portraits and producing drawings for his father's pupils to copy. In about 1813, he was commissioned by C T Gilbert to illustrate his *Historical Survey of the County of Cornwall* (1815), and travelled with him through Cornwall in order to make preparatory drawings. This gave him the opportunity to see paintings in the private collections of county families.

In 1815, Parker married a Suffolk-born woman at Maker, Cornwall, and returned to Plymouth to establish himself as a portrait painter. However, while his work was admired, little of it sold, so he decided to try his luck in Sunderland, Co Durham, where he and his wife were able to stay with relatives. Initially, he gave drawing lessons.

Settling in Newcastle upon Tyne before the end of the year, Parker developed as one of the best-known artists in north-east England during the following quarter of a century. He made his name with a portrait of George Gray, a local fruit painter, and the group portrait, *Principal Eccentric Characters of Newcastle*, selling the latter to Charles John Brandling, the local member of parliament. As a result, he received many prestigious commissions, and was able to move into a house in one of the town's most fashionable streets.

Parker engaged fully in Newcastle's artistic life, taking on a number of pupils and befriending some significant local artists. Most notable among these was Thomas Miles Richardson, with whom he founded two exhibiting societies: the Northumberland Institution for the Promotion of the Fine Arts (1822) and the Northern Academy of Arts (1828). He also gained a wider reputation, exhibiting in London, at the Royal Academy of Arts (from 1817), the British Institution (from 1822), the Society of British Artists (from 1827) and the New Society of Painters in Water Colours; and also in Carlisle and Edinburgh (both 1823). In addition, details of his work were disseminated through the publication of *Critiques on paintings by H P Parker … together with … etchings shewing the compositions, &c* (1835).

Parker became so well known for his many smuggling subjects that he was given the nickname 'Smuggler Parker'. However, he painted a wide variety of genre scenes; these included the famous *William and Grace Darling Going to Rescue the Forfarshire Survivors* (1838, in collaboration with the Newcastle artist, John Wilson Carmichael) and the *Historical Wesleyan Centenary Picture, Representing the Rescue of the Founder of Methodism…* (1839). The second of these was produced in anticipation of the John Wesley conference held in Newcastle in 1840, and proved so popular that he was offered the post of drawing master at Wesley College, Sheffield. Accepting the position, he moved to Sheffield with his family.

During his time at Wesley College, Parker continued to take private pupils, and to produce and exhibit his own work. He also became increasingly absorbed in plans to establish a School of Design for Sheffield. However, when it was finally established in 1845, he was not offered a post at the school. His wife having died in the previous year, he became increasingly disillusioned with the town and moved to London in 1847.

His son, Raphael Hyde Parker, succeeded him as drawing master at Wesley College while still in his teens, and exhibited at the Society of British Artists and the Royal Academy.

Following his move to London, Parker remarried. He continued to exhibit his work, but struggled to make a living, and died in poverty at his home – 1 Blenheim Villas, Goldhawk Road, Shepherd's Bush – on 9 November 1873.

His work is represented in numerous public collections, including the Grace Darling Museum (Bamburgh) and Tyne & Wear Museums. The manuscript, 'An artist's narrative', is held by Newcastle Central Library.

Further reading:
Marshall Hall, 'Parker, Henry Perlee (1795–1873)', H C G Matthew and Brian Harrison (eds), *Oxford Dictionary of National Biography*, Oxford University Press, 2004, vol 42, pp 680-681
N Johnson, 'Henry Perlee Parker', *Newcastle Life*, September 1969,
N Johnson (ed), *Henry Perlee Parker*, Newcastle: Laing Art Gallery, 1969

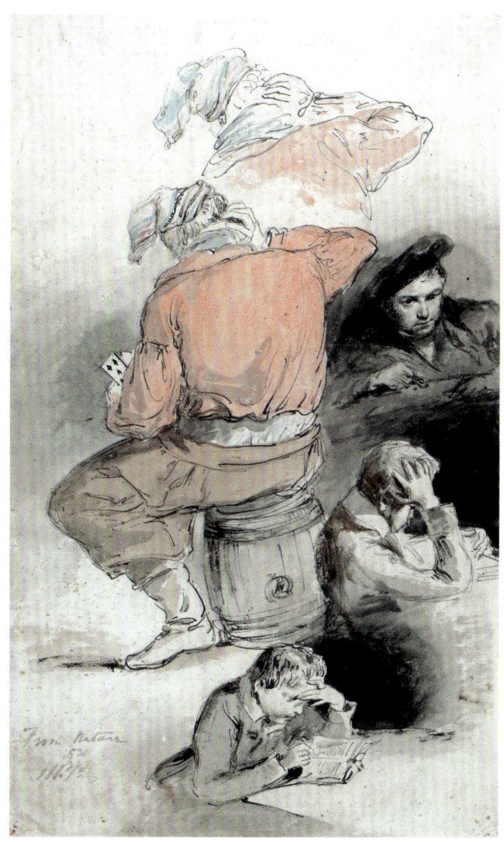

182 SMUGGLERS
signed with initials, inscribed 'from nature' and dated 1830
pen ink and watercolour
19 ½ x 11 ½ inches

GEORGE RICHMOND
George Richmond, RA HARIBA (1809-1896)

George Richmond was one of the most sensitive – and successful – of Victorian portrait painters, as is evidenced by the work included here. His success was due in great part to a thorough and sustained artistic training, and his ability to respond to a range of commissions. Establishing himself at first as a follower of William Blake, he produced figure subjects and landscapes as well as portraits, and turned his hand to engraving, carving and the restoration of paintings, while working in oil, watercolour, tempera and pencil.

George Richmond was the great-grandson of George Engleheart and the son of Thomas Richmond, both miniaturists. He was born on 28 March 1809, probably at Brompton (then a country village), and grew up at 42 Half Moon Street, Mayfair, London. Educated at a dame school in Soho, he revealed a gift for draughtsmanship by the age of twelve, and set himself on an almost lifelong course of study, by making regular visits to the British Museum to draw from the antique.

On 23 December 1824, Richmond entered the Royal Academy Schools, where he worked alongside Edward Calvert and Joseph Severn, the latter being a part-time student. (Sixteen years older than Richmond, Severn had been a friend of John Keats, and had attended him at his death bed in Rome in 1821). Influenced by Henry Fuseli, the Professor of Painting, he began to exhibit figure works at the Royal Academy of Arts in 1825.

In the same year, Richmond met William Blake in the Hampstead house of John Linnell. Falling under Blake's spell, he joined the group of his followers, The Ancients, that also included Calvert, and became a close friend of its pivotal member, Samuel Palmer. He was at Blake's home, 12 Fountain Court, the Strand, on 12 August 1827, when the artist died, and it was he who closed Blake's eyes.

Richmond met with the Ancients regularly, both in London and Shoreham, Kent, the village in which Palmer's father lived and Palmer himself owned property. The work that he produced at this time reflected the ideals of the group, in being Christian or literary in subject and archaic in treatment. (For a list of the members of the Ancients, see opposite.)

In an attempt to broaden his artistic horizons, Richmond visited Paris in the period August 1828 to May 1829. While drawing in the Louvre and studying anatomy in the hospitals, he supported himself by painting miniatures.

In 1826, Richmond had fallen in love with his pupil, Julia Tatham, the fourteen year-old daughter of Charles Heathcote Tatham, and sister to two members of the Ancients. Against her father's wishes, he married Julia at Gretna Green on 24 January 1831 and – once Tatham's anger had subsided – they set up home at 27 Northumberland Street, New Road, London. Two years later, they moved to 16 Beaumont Street.

Richmond concentrated on portraiture in order to support his family (which eventually comprised ten children to survive infancy). He produced seventy-three portraits during the first year of marriage and within five years earned an annual income of £1000 from portraiture. Intensely ambitious, he pursued potential sitters and painted many notable figures, his portraits of the 1830s including likenesses of Charles Darwin, Rowland Hill and William Wilberforce.

In 1837, Richmond and his wife left for Rome in the company of Samuel Palmer and his wife Hannah, the daughter of John Linnell, who were celebrating their honeymoon. During his time there, he visited his former fellow student, Joseph Severn, who provided him with an entrée into British society in the city. Characteristically, he threw himself into his work: copying murals, including Michelangelo's Sistine Chapel frescoes, attending life classes at the Rome Academy and experimenting with technical devices. He also travelled further afield, visiting Naples, Pompeii, and Herculaneum, and going with Julia to Florence. Finally leaving Rome in June 1839, he and Julia returned to England via Florence and Venice.

Richmond returned to Rome for a shorter visit of four months, during the winter of 1840-41. While there, Joseph Severn introduced him to the young John Ruskin, who became a friend and described his portraits as 'the truth lovingly told'. Later travels included visits to Italy (1843 and 1845) and France (1859).

Richmond's career as a portrait painter flourished, greatly helped by a series of commissions from the exclusive Grillion Club. Following the success of his portrait of Thomas Dyke Acland, in 1840, he became the club's regular portraitist, painting each new member, and producing seventy such portraits in all. In 1861, he was made an honorary member of the club.

From 1843, until the end of his life, Richmond lived at 10 York Street, near Portman Square (later renumbered 20). At this stage, he began to engage fully with the social opportunities afforded by being a successful artist. He was appointed to a seat on the School of Design (1841) and served on the royal commission for determining the site of the National Gallery, London (1856); he was elected to the Royal Academy (ARA 1857; RA 1860); and he became a member of the Athenaeum (1856), the Club of Nobody's Friends (1856) and Johnson's Club (1860). However, he refused the directorship of the National Gallery, when it was offered to him in 1871. He also received a number of honorary doctorates and an honorary associate membership of the Royal Institute of British Architects.

Richmond produced occasional sculptures, most notably a recumbent effigy of his friend Charles James Blomfield, Bishop of London, for his tomb in St Paul's Cathedral (completed in 1859). From 1866, he also undertook restoration work, scoring a particular success with his work on Daniel Maclise's mural in the Palace of Westminster during the years 1872 to 1875.

Though a hypochondriac, Richmond suffered from constant and increasing bouts of illness, exacerbated by constant overwork. He died at his home, a few days before his eighty-seventh birthday, on 19 March 1896. Among his children was the artist, William Blake Richmond.

His work is represented in numerous public collections, including the British Museum, the National Portrait Gallery, Tate and the V&A; The Fitzwilliam Museum (Cambridge); the Cleveland Museum of Art; and the Art Gallery of Greater Victoria (Victoria, Canada).

The Ancients (also known as the Shoreham Ancients or Extollagers)

The members of this group of British painters and engravers were drawn together by their admiration for William Blake and his influences. All produced elaborate work on a small-scale, and some used primitive styles and techniques. Though they had no manifesto, their motto was 'Poetry and Sentiment'. They comprised:

Henry Walter (1799-1849), portrait and animal painter
Edward Calvert (1799-1883), wood engraver and painter
Francis Oliver Finch (1802-1862), landscape watercolourist
Frederick Tatham (1805-1878), sculptor and miniature painter (son of the architect, Charles Heathcote Tatham; later brother-in-law to George Richmond)
Samuel Palmer (1805-1881), landscape painter, draughtsman and etcher
Welby Sherman (active 1827-1836), engraver
Arthur Tatham (1808-1874), later rector of Broadoak and Boconoc, Cornwall (son of the architect, Charles Heathcote Tatham; later brother-in-law to George Richmond)
George Richmond (1809-1896), painter, draughtsman and engraver
John Giles (1810-1880), stockbroker (cousin of Samuel Palmer)

Associates included John Linnell (1792-1882), painter (later Samuel Palmer's father-in-law) and William Palmer (1810-1866), later a warder at the British Museum (Samuel Palmer's brother).

Robert Hills (1769-1844), animal painter and etcher, has also been suggested as a member by Martin Hardie (see Further Reading to Robert Hills on p 106). His evidence is that Hills signed a drawing, on paper watermarked '1826', with the peculiar term 'Extollager' (a rustic corruption of the word 'astrologer', referring to the Ancients' habit of taking nocturnal walks).

Further reading:

David Blayney Brown, 'Richmond (ii): (1) George Richmond (*b* London, 28 March 1809; *d* London, 19 March 1896)', Jane Turner (ed), *The Dictionary of Art*, London: Macmillan, 1996, vol 26, pp 353-354
Raymond Lister, *George Richmond: A Critical Biography*, London: Garton, 1981
Raymond Lister, 'Richmond, George (1809-1896)' H C G Matthew and Brian Harrison (eds), *Oxford Dictionary of National Biography*, Oxford University Press, 2004, vol 46, pp 872-875
Susan Sloman, *Missing Pages. George Richmond RA 1809-1896*, London: Agnew's/W/S Fine Art, 2001

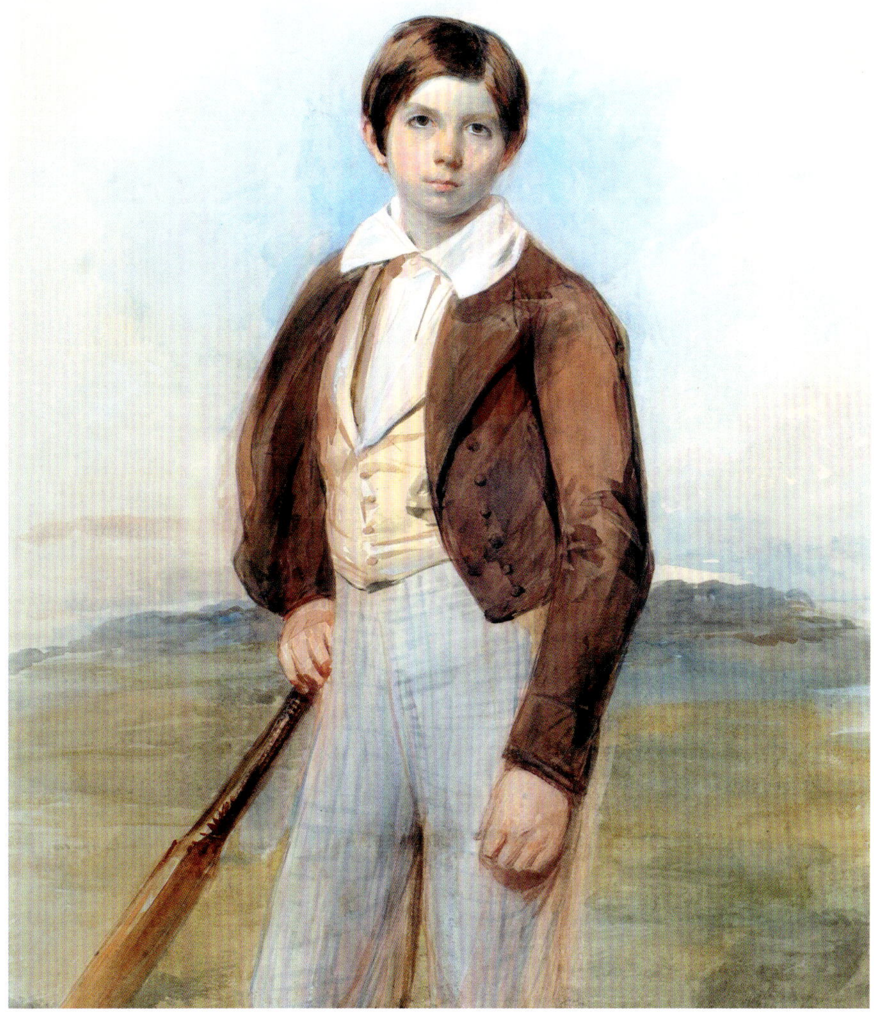

183 THE YOUNG CRICKETER
watercolour
20 ½ x 14 ½ inches

JOSEPH NASH
Joseph Nash, OWS (1809-1878)

Joseph Nash gathered together his skills as architectural draughtsman, genre painter and lithographer to produce his highly popular and influential publication, *The Mansions of England in Olden Time* (1839-49).

Joseph Nash was born in Great Marlow, Buckinghamshire, on 17 December 1809. He was the eldest son of Okey Nash, who took holy orders and became the proprietor of the Manor House School, North End, Croydon. Joseph Nash was educated at the school, but 'showed his bent by covering his lesson books with sketches' (Roget 1891, vol 2, p 242).

In about 1827, Nash entered the architect's office of Augustus Charles Pugin, at 105 (now 106) Great Russell Street, Bloomsbury, London, in order to learn the art of architectural drawing. Two years later, he and his fellow apprentices accompanied Pugin on a trip to France to produce drawings for *Paris and its Environs* (1830). Becoming interested, and then skilled, in lithography, he also prepared Pugin's drawings for *Views Illustrative of the Examples of Gothic Architecture* (1830).

After his marriage to 'a lady of property' in 1831, Nash developed as a painter and illustrator of genre, contributing to keepsake annuals and exhibiting at the Society of Painters in Water Colours, of which he became an associate in 1834.

However, following in the tradition of Pugin, Nash became best known for 'recreating the original state of old buildings and peopling them with picturesque tableaux' (Peter Mandler, in Matthew and Harrison 2004, vol 40, p 222). He established this reputation in 1838 with *Architecture of the Middle Ages: drawn from nature and on stone*; this folio of twenty-five lithographs featured English and French ecclesiastical buildings of the late Gothic and Renaissance periods.

A year later, in 1839, Nash embarked on his four-volume *magnum opus*, *The Mansions of England in the Olden Time*. He toured the country in order to sketch both the exteriors and interiors of many of the surviving country houses of the fifteenth to seventeenth centuries. He also researched the social life of the same period, by reading the writings of the antiquarian, Joseph Strutt, in order to populate his images of buildings with appropriate figures. The highly Romantic results comprised 100 lithographs, the quality of which reflected Nash's collaboration with Charles Joseph Hullmandel, the pioneering lithographer.

Nash's plates for *The Mansions of England* proved extremely influential, especially from their authorised appearance as engravings in the *Saturday Magazine*, and on their subsequent unauthorised appearance in other periodicals. They provided a source for architects and affected the popularity of certain tourist sites, even being reproduced on advertising placards. However, William Makepeace Thackeray dismissed Nash as 'a miniature scene-painter' in preference to GEORGE CATTERMOLE, a rival painter of historical genre (*Fraser's Magazine*, 1839, vol 19, p 749, as cited by Peter Mandler).

The project brought Nash more esteem than wealth, though it also attracted further commissions. So following his election to full membership of the Society of Painters in Water Colours, in 1842, he translated drawings by the late David Wilkie into lithographs (*Sketches in Turkey, Syria & Egypt...*, 1843 and *Sketches, Spanish & Oriental...*, 1846), and produced *Views of the Interior and Exterior of Windsor Castle* (1848) under royal patronage. Eventually, in 1849, he was able to bring work on *The Mansions of England* to a close.

Gradually withdrawing from public attention, Nash suffered from an attack of brain fever in 1854, and sold the contents of his studio at the end of that year. However, while accusing the Society of Painters in Water Colours of neglecting his work, and that of his son, he continued to produce and exhibit drawings until the end of his life. He died a widower at home, at 84 Hereford Road, Kensington, on 19 December 1878. His son and a daughter survived him.

His work is represented in The Royal Collection, and numerous public collections, including the British Museum and the V&A.

Further reading:

Peter Mandler, 'Nash, Joseph (1809-1878)', H C G Matthew and Brian Harrison (eds), *Oxford Dictionary of National Biography*, Oxford University Press, 2004, vol 40, pp 221-222

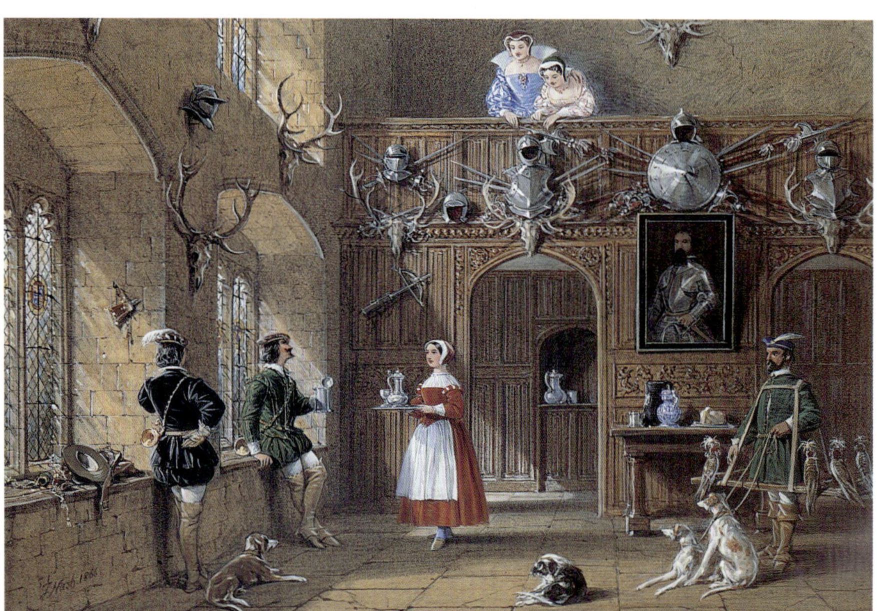

184 IN THE GATEHOUSE, KENILWORTH, WARWICKSHIRE
signed and dated 1866
watercolour with bodycolour
13 x 18 ¾ inches

WILLIAM EDWARD FROST
William Edward Frost, RA (1810-1877)

William Edward Frost was one of the most popular Victorian painters of the nude, appreciated for a purity of approach and elegance of execution. His subjects ranged from generalised recreations of the ancient world to representations of specific episodes from classic English poetry.

William Edward Frost was born in Wandsworth, then in Surrey, in September 1810. He showed an artistic talent from an early age, and was encouraged in this by his father: first by his arranging drawing lessons with a Miss Evatt, a neighbouring amateur, and then, in 1825, by his introducing him to William Etty, who became his mentor. On Etty's recommendation, he entered Henry Sass's School for Drawing and Painting at 6 Charlotte Street, in 1826, and spent three years there, while also studying at the British Museum each winter. He was then accepted into the Royal Academy Schools and, as a diligent student, gained first medals in every class except the Antique, in which Daniel Maclise was a competitor.

Initially specialising in portraiture, from about 1830, Frost painted more than 300 portraits during a fifteen-year period, and showed some as his first exhibits from 1836. However, a series of successes with mythological and allegorical subjects, often inspired by Spenser and Milton, led him to change his focus. In December 1839, he received the Academy's Gold Medal for *Prometheus Bound by Force and Strength* (exhibited at the RA in 1840). Four years later, he won a third-prize premium for *Una Alarmed by the Fauns and Satyrs* (V&A), his entry for the competition to decorate the New Palace of Westminster, while his academy exhibition picture, *Christ Crowned with Thorns*, was selected by a prize-holder of the Art Union Society. This early development of his reputation culminated in his election as an associate of the Royal Academy of Arts in November 1846.

Frost attracted a ready patronage among middle-class industrials and aristocrats and, indeed, from Queen Victoria, who paid £420 for *Una Among the Fairies and Wood Nymphs* (1847), and subsequently commissioned two more pictures. However, his work was popular with all levels of society, as a result of the wide circulation of engravings of his paintings made by Peter Lightfoot, among others.

Frost shared several of his patrons with Etty, and his work was inevitably compared to that of his mentor. However, some contemporary critics did distinguish between the two, William Sandby writing that Frost differed materially from Etty,

> in the chastely correct and highly-finished manner in which he depicts the undraped nymphs in his pictures. They are always full of grace and refinement, of beauty and feminine simplicity; and there is nothing in his pictures which the most delicate and highly-cultivated taste could disapprove. (Sandby 1862, vol 2, p 221)

As Frost was intimately familiar with Etty's methods and ideas, he became a principal source for the older artist's biography. He was also knowledgeable about the work of THOMAS STOTHARD, collecting a large number of engravings of the artist's work. In addition, he collaborated with Henry Reeve on a catalogue of the art collection of Hugh Munro of Novar, which was privately printed in 1865.

After a gap that surprised and irritated him, Frost was elected a full academician in 1870. Yet, at the time of the exhibition of his diploma work, *Nymphs and Cupid*, two years later, he voluntarily retired from the RA. He had also exhibited regularly at the British Institution.

Never marrying, Frost lived with Elizabeth, his unmarried sister, latterly at 40 Fitzroy Square. On his death on 4 June 1877, she became his sole executor.

Almost a year later, on 14 March 1878, Christie's held a sale of the remains of Frost's studio, including a hundred of his works, as well as his copies after old masters.

His work is represented in numerous public collections, including the British Museum; and the Ashmolean Museum (Oxford) and The Fitzwilliam Museum (Cambridge).

Further reading:

Robyn Asleson, 'Frost, William Edward (1810–1877)', H C G Matthew and Brian Harrison (eds), *Oxford Dictionary of National Biography*, Oxford University Press, 2004, vol 21, pp 70-71

Philip McEvansoneya, 'Frost, William Edward (*b* London, Sept 1810; *d* London, 4 June 1877)', Jane Turner (ed), *The Dictionary of Art*, London: Macmillan, 1996, vol 11, pp 804-805

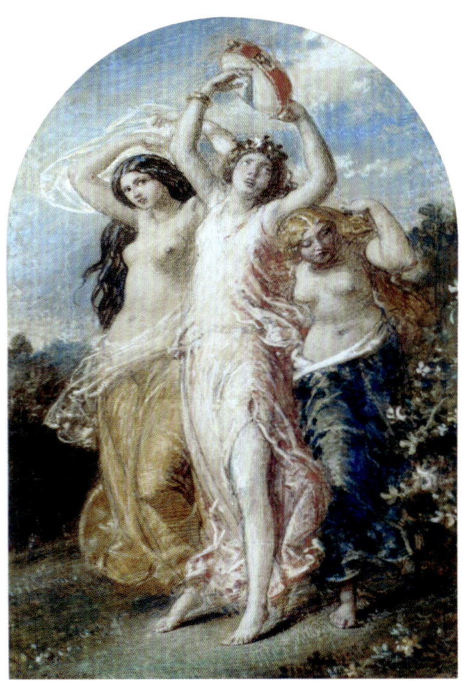

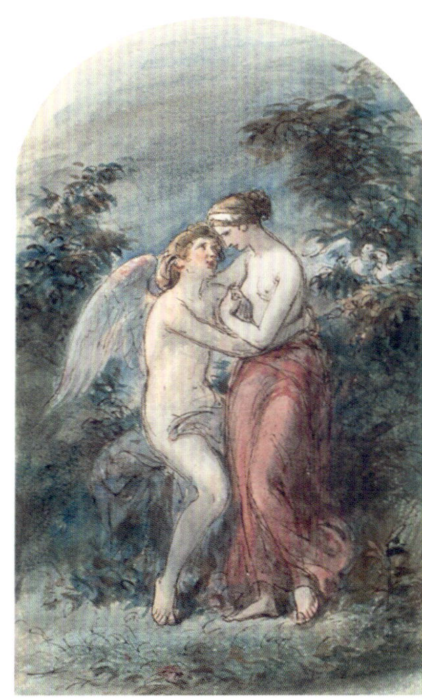

185 THREE GRACES
watercolour with bodycolour
6 x 4 inches

186 LOVE
pen ink and watercolour
7 x 4 ½ inches

THEODOR VON HOLST
Theodor Richard Edward von Holst
(1810-1844)

Developing his fascination with the supernatural and erotic, Theodor von Holst became the most prolific English painter-illustrator of German romance.

Theodor von Holst was born in London on 3 September 1810, his parents having emigrated from Riga to flee the troubles created by the Napoleonic wars. The family was very musical, Holst's father being a composer and professor of music (while his great-nephew was the composer, Gustav Holst).

Holst's precocious artistic talents were recognised by 1820, when Sir Thomas Lawrence bought a drawing from him, and Henry Fuseli became a family friend. He soon proved Fuseli's favourite disciple and, after copying from the antique at the British Museum, became his formal pupil at the Royal Academy Schools during 1824, the last year of Fuseli's life. As a result of this experience, he befriended the artist – and infamous poisoner – Thomas Griffiths Wainewright, who was also a pupil of Fuseli. The influence of Fuseli remained with him throughout his short career, though his work tends to be more highly coloured.

Like Fuseli, Holst was inspired by bizarre and fantastic literary subjects, especially the tales of E T A Hoffmann, Le Motte Fouqué's *Undine* and Goethe's *Faust*. He abandoned his plan to illustrate *Faust*, when he became aware of Eugène Delacroix's intention to do the same. However, he did illustrate other key works, producing two designs for *Frankenstein*, in the edition of 1831, in which Mary Shelley was first identified as the author. He also exhibited works at the Royal Academy of Arts (1827-43) and the Society of British Artists (1838-40), in Liverpool (1837-41), and at the British Institution (where he was awarded a premium of 50 guineas for *The Raising of Jairus's Daughter* in 1841).

Holst lived at 46 Upper Charlotte Street, Fitzroy Square in the late 1830s and then at 19 Nassau Street, Middlesex Hospital. He died of liver disease on 14 February 1844 at his home at 2 Percy Street, Bedford Square.

Holst was an important influence on the Pre-Raphaelites, notably Dante Gabriel Rossetti, who called him 'the Edgar Poe of painting'. The Pre-Raphaelites frequented Campbell's Scotch Stores restaurant in Soho because it was hung with works by Holst.

His work is represented in the collections of the British Museum and the V&A; the Gustav Holst Birthplace Museum, Cheltenham; and Indiana University Art Museum.

Further reading:

Max Browne, 'Holst, Theodor Richard Edward von (1810-1844)', H C G Matthew and Brian Harrison (eds), *Oxford Dictionary of National Biography*, Oxford University Press, 2004, vol 27, pp 821-822
Max Browne, *The Romantic Art of Theodor von Holst 1810-44*, London: Lund Humphries, 1994
Gert Schiff, 'Theodore Matthias von Holst', *Burlington Magazine*, 1963, vol 105, pp 23-32

My Lady's Pleasure

According to his obituary in the *Art-Union*, Theodor von Holst was employed by Sir Thomas Lawrence, President of the Royal Academy, to provide erotic drawings for King George IV, 'and these were of a class that a youth with very limited means may have been tempted to execute; but the subjects selected were little to the credit of the President or his Royal employer'.

This youthful drawing by Holst (*circa* 1824-30) shows the strong influence of his master Henry Fuseli. In erotic content and stylistic detail, such as the elongated neck and elaborate hairstyle of the young courtesan portrayed here, Holst imitates, perhaps even copies, the private obsessions of his RA professor but with a softer, more sensual execution. Such a bold centrally placed figure is a favourite of the artist, one which can be seen repeatedly in his oeuvre and most potently in his later, more highly finished, portraits of romanticised women that Dante Gabriel Rossetti so admired and was later to develop into his own 'sensual stunners'.

One of Holst's closest friends was the notorious forger, poisoner, writer and fellow Fuseli disciple, Thomas Griffiths Wainewright, who also produced similar work and reportedly possessed a private portfolio of 'exquisite delineations of the female human form'. All three artists contributed to this fascinating backwater of Georgian draughtsmanship, which will, no doubt, take some time to fully emerge.

Note by Max Browne

187 MY LADY'S PLEASURE
watercolour with pencil
on laid paper watermarked 'Golding and Snelgrove 1815'
10 ½ x 8 inches
Exhibited: 'The Romantic Art of Theodor Von Holst (1810-1844)', Hazlitt, Gooden & Fox, London, May 1994; Cheltenham Art Gallery & Museum, June-July 1994, No 24, as 'Seated Courtesan Holding a Phallic Object'

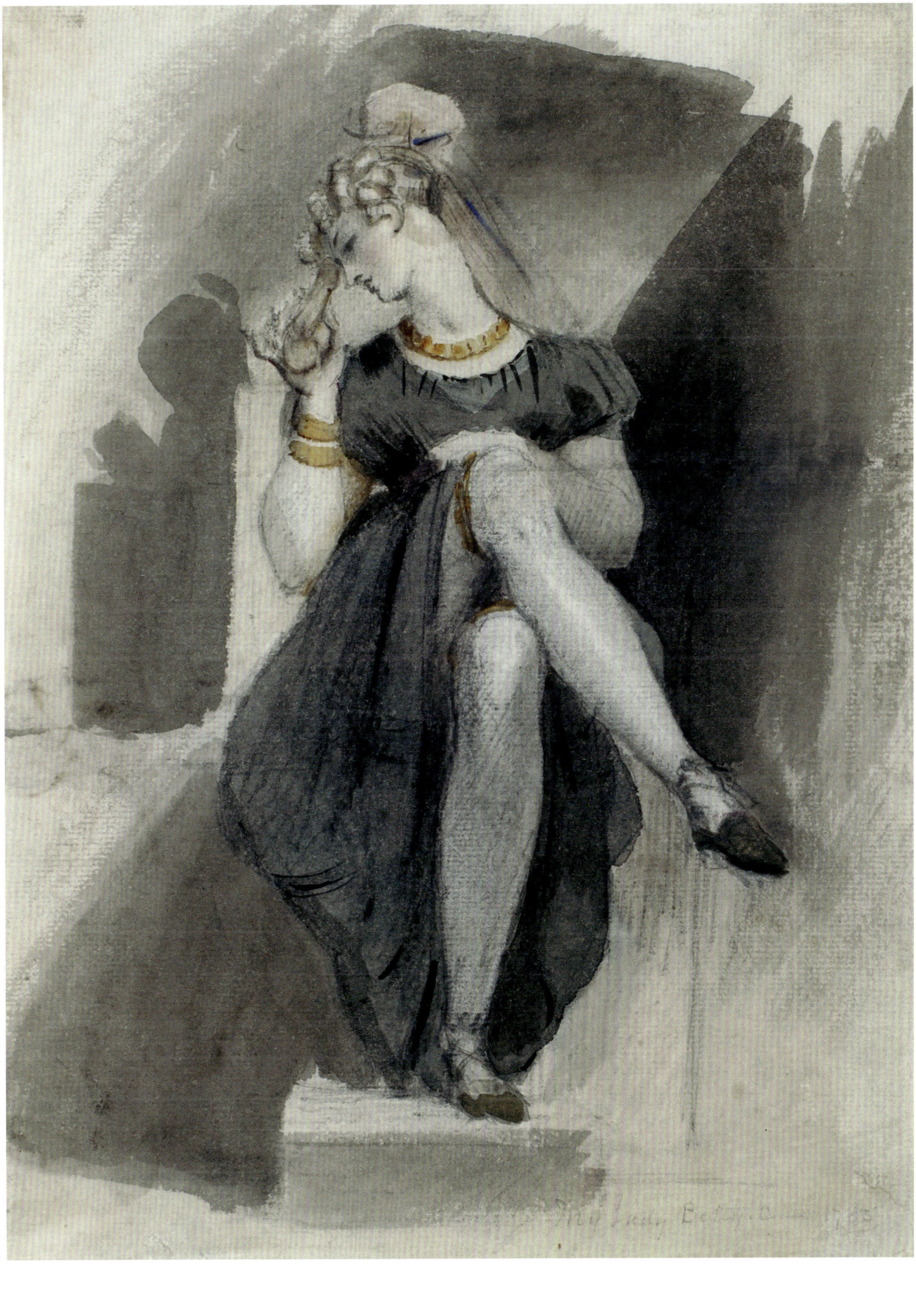

5: THE WATERCOLOUR SOCIETIES

JOHN VARLEY
John Varley, OWS (1778-1842)

John Varley was a central figure for the watercolourists of the early nineteenth century. A founder member of the Society of Painters in Water Colours, and its most prolific exhibitor, he was also a highly significant teacher of both professionals and amateurs, and a writer of instruction manuals. He encouraged his students to paint in the open air, but also promoted the Picturesqure theory of adapting nature to the requirements of composition.

Of Lincolnshire descent, John Varley was born in Hackney, Middlesex on 17 August 1778. He and his brothers 'were said to have been born at the Blue Posts (formerly the Templars' house), after their father had converted it to private use, although the building was still an inn in 1785' (T F T Baker (ed), *A History of the County of Middlesex: Volume 10: Hackney*, London: Oxford University Press for the Institute of Historical Research, 1995, pp 10-14).

Despite parental disapproval, three of his siblings would also become artists: Cornelius Varley, William Fleetwood Varley and Elizabeth Robinson Varley.

The death of Varley's father in 1791 left the family in poverty, and forced a move to a more modest dwelling, off Old Street, Hoxton. Varley's early attempts to undertake an apprenticeship – first as a silversmith and then as a law stationer – did not suppress his desire to become an artist. So he spent a brief time working with a portrait painter in Holborn before becoming a pupil and assistant to Joseph Charles Barrow at the age of fifteen or sixteen. Barrow ran an evening drawing school at his house – 12 Furnival's Inn Court, Holborn – where he was assisted by LOUIS FRANCIA, and the young Varley had to undertake the more menial tasks when he was not receiving lessons.

While drawing in Hornsey Wood in spring 1796, John Varley met John Preston Neale and, forming a lasting friendship, would often accompany him on sketching expeditions to villages north-east of London. In the following year, he was lucky enough to accompany Barrow on a more distant journey, to Peterborough, in Cambridgeshire, and while there produced a pencil drawing of the cathedral. This became his first exhibit at the Royal Academy of Arts in 1798, and he then showed there regularly until 1804.

Either in 1798 or 1799, Varley made his first sketching tour to Wales, in the company of George Arnald, an experience that would prove decisive in the direction of his art. He returned there in 1800, and again in 1802, when he was joined by his brother, Cornelius. (John moved from Hoxton to live with Cornelius in Charles Street, Covent Garden, in 1800; then, a year later, moved again, to live with his other brother, William, at 2 Harris Place, an alley near the Pantheon, the entrance to which stood on the eastern section of Oxford Street.)

During the same period, Varley began to study at Dr Thomas Monro's informal academy at his home in Adelphi Terrace, and he also visited him at his country cottage in Fetcham, Surrey. The association would last for twenty years and prove very useful to Varley, for Monro kindly introduced him to patrons and pupils. One early patron, Edward, Viscount Lascelles, invited Varley to his Yorkshire home, Harewood House, in 1803.

If he did not meet Thomas Girtin at Monro's academy, Varley would certainly have copied examples of his watercolours, and the influence of Girtin soon showed in his work. At the time of Girtin's death, in 1802, he joined the Sketching Society that Girtin had founded, which was then chaired by JOHN SELL COTMAN. In turn, Cotman's use of clear, flat washes would also influence Varley.

Following his marriage to Esther Gisborne in 1803, Varley began to father a family of eight children, and so needed to combine his development as an exhibiting watercolourist with a settled career as a drawing master. While proving a mainstay of the Society for Painters in Water Colours, which he helped to found in 1804, he trained many of the leading watercolourists of the following generation. Two of the earliest were WILLIAM TURNER of Oxford and William Mulready, the latter becoming his assistant (and also his brother-in-law, marrying his sister, Elizabeth, in 1803).

In 1806, the Varleys moved to 5 Broad Street, Golden Square, Soho, which allowed more room for a growing family and an increasing number of pupils, including WILLIAM HENRY HUNT and John Linnell. In the same year, Peter DeWint became a neighbour of Varley in Broad Street, and took lessons from him. From 1809, COPLEY FIELDING also became a pupil (and four years later would marry the sister of Varley's wife).

From the time of his move to Broad Street, Varley also rented a house in the summer months at Twickenham so that he and his pupils could sketch along the River Thames. However, he still found time to make more ambitious trips in order to inspire his art, notably a visit to the Northumberland coast in 1808.

From 1812, Varley altered the style of his work and exhibited fewer watercolours, a response to his commitments as a teacher and family man. By this time, he was charging amateurs a guinea a lesson and apprentices £200 for the seven years, so that his income would soon rise to £3000 a year (putting him on a par with those in the higher echelon of the mercantile class). At some point, the Varleys moved to Great Titchfield Street, in the artistic quarter north of Oxford Street.

Practising what he preached, Varley increasingly employed compositions that reveal the inspiration of the Classical tradition and of J M W TURNER'S *Liber Studiorum*. He also made use of the Patent Graphic Telescope, invented as an artistic aid by his brother, Cornelius (who had trained under their uncle, Samuel Varley, a watchmaker and jeweller).

Varley disseminated his systematic approach to art through a series of manuals that were mainly intended for amateurs, including *A Practical Treatise on the Art of Drawing in Perspective* (1815-20), *Treatise on the Principles of Landscape Design* (in eight parts, 1816-21) and *Precepts of Landscape Drawing* (*circa* 1818).

In 1818, Linnell, a former pupil, introduced Varley to William Blake. He entered Blake's circle of admirers, known as the Ancients (see p 117), and gave lessons to at least two of its members: Francis Oliver Finch and Samuel Palmer. As Varley believed strongly in astrology, he was attracted to Blake's propensity for visions and excited by the spiritual portraits that Blake drew on visits to Varley's house at Great Titchfield Street between 1819 and 1825. Linnell would engrave some of these as illustrations to Varley's *Treatise on Zodiacal Physiognomy* (1828).

From 1818, Varley began to ask Linnell repeatedly to lend him money but, still unable to manage his finances two years later, he was declared bankrupt and gaoled. Remaining insolvent throughout the 1820s and 1830s, he attempted to improve his situation by exhibiting an increased number of works at the Society of Painters in Water Colours, in the years 1823-26, and opening a gallery at his home. However, a fire in Great Titchfield Street in June 1825 – that started in the workshops of Crozet, a carver and guilder – spread to Varley's address, and the damage must have affected the artist's chances of recovery.

Having lost his first wife in 1824, Varley married Delvalle Lowry, the daughter of his friend, the engraver Wilson Lowry, in the following year. They would have two children.

During the 1830s, Varley began to recapture the power of his early watercolours and, by the end of the decade, was inspired by the work of Samuel Palmer to paint dense washes in a glowing tonality on coarse paper. His imaginative compositions were received with enthusiasm, not least by the dealers, Samuel Woodburn and William Vokins, the second becoming a friend. He spent his last days with Vokins at his house at 5 John Street, off Oxford Street, dying there on 17 November 1842. He was survived by his second wife.

In 1843, the Society of Painters in Water Colours showed a posthumous group of Varley's watercolours, 'an unusual concession made…for the sake of his penurious family' (Wilcox 2005, pp 112-113); one was bought by Albert, the Prince Consort.

Of John Varley's ten children, two became professional painters: Albert Fleetwood Varley and Charles Smith Varley.

His work is represented in the Government Art Collection and numerous public collections, including the British Museum, The Courtauld Gallery, Tate and the V&A; Dove Cottage and the Wordsworth Museum (Grasmere), Hereford Art Gallery, Manchester Art Gallery and Tyne and Wear Museums; the Fine Arts Museums of San Francisco; and the Art Gallery of Greater Victoria (Victoria, Canada).

Further reading:

Adrian Bury, *John Varley of the Old Society*, Leigh-on-Sea: F Lewis, 1946
Claus Michael Kauffmann, *John Varley, 1778–1842*, London: Batsford/Victoria and Albert Museum, 1984
Claus Michael Kauffmann, 'Varley, John (1778-1842)', H C G Matthew and Brian Harrison (eds), *Oxford Dictionary of National Biography*, Oxford University Press, 2004, vol 56, pp 148-149
Anne Lyles, 'John Varley's early work', *Old Water-Colour Society's Club*, vol 59, 1984, pp 1-22
Anne Lyles, 'Varley (1) John Varley', Jane Turner (ed), *The Dictionary of Art*, London: Macmillan, 1996, vol 31, pp 908-909

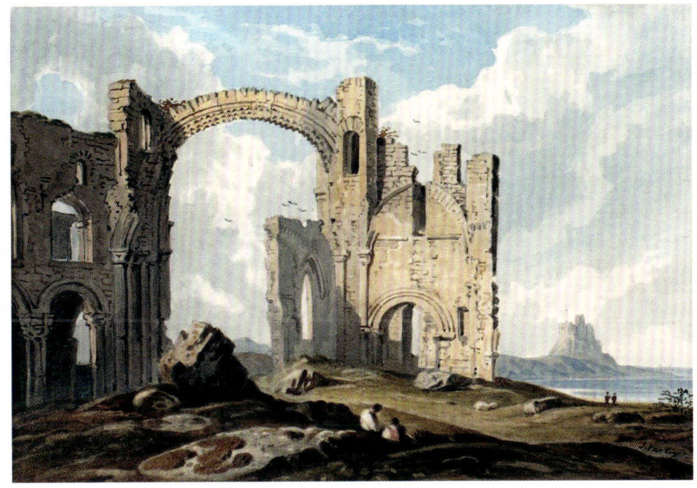

188 THE RUINS, BY HOLY ISLAND, LINDISFARNE
signed
watercolour
5 ¾ x 8 ¼ inches

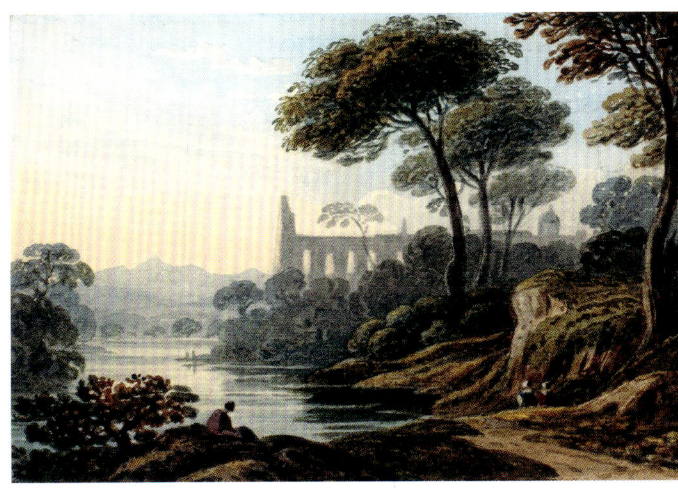

189 BOLTON ABBEY
watercolour
3 ¼ x 4 ½ inches

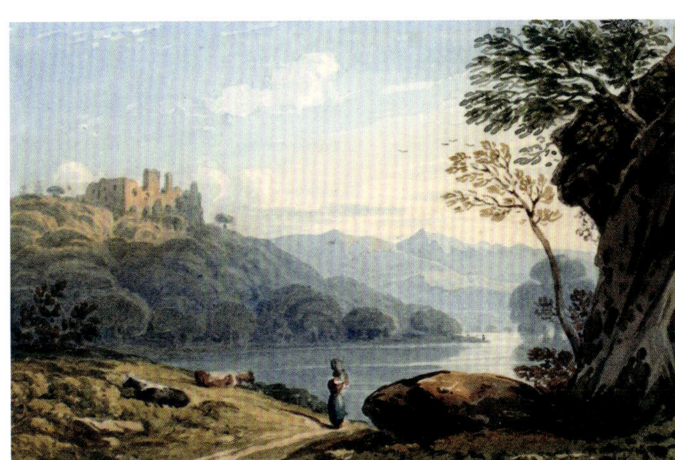

190 CASTLE ON THE LAKE
watercolour
3 ¼ x 5 inches

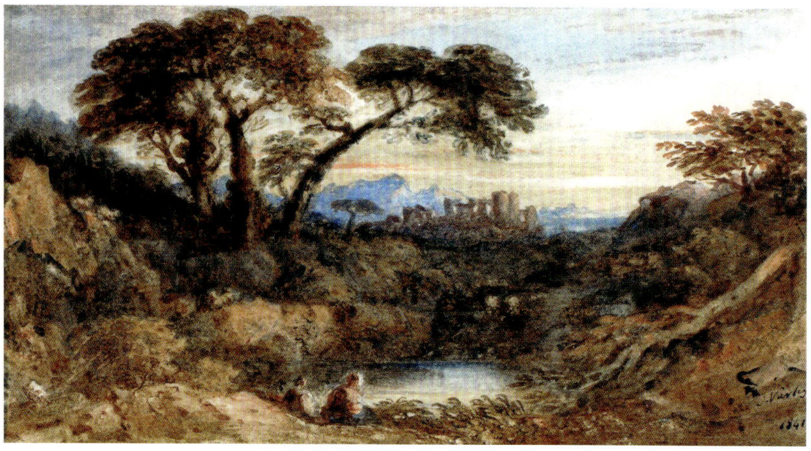

191 THE WOODED DELL
signed and dated 1841
watercolour
6 x 10 ¾ inches

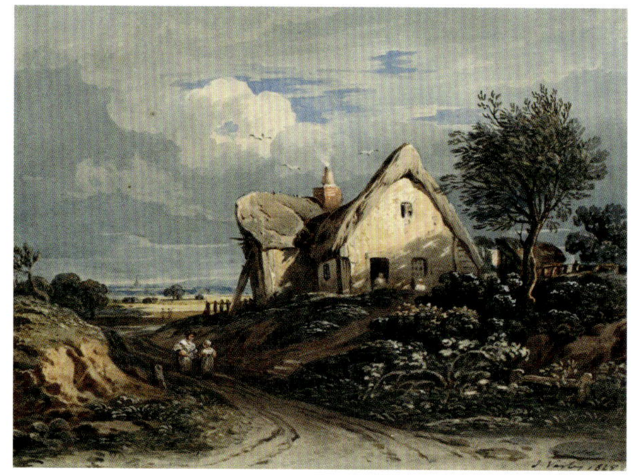

192 THATCHED COTTAGE
signed and dated 1825
watercolour
6 ½ x 8 ½ inches

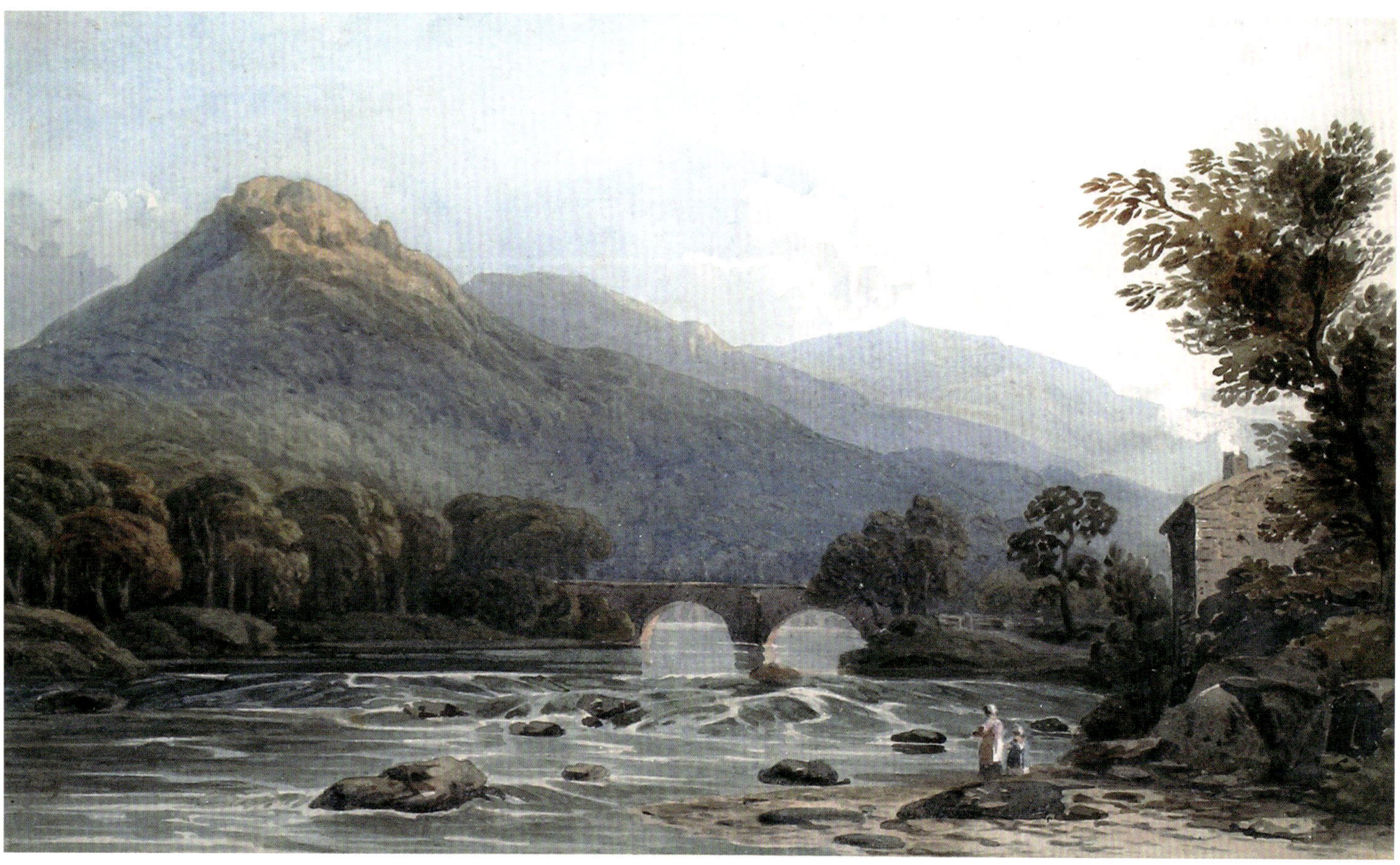

193 BEDDGELERT BRIDGE, WALES
watercolour
9 x 14 ½ inches

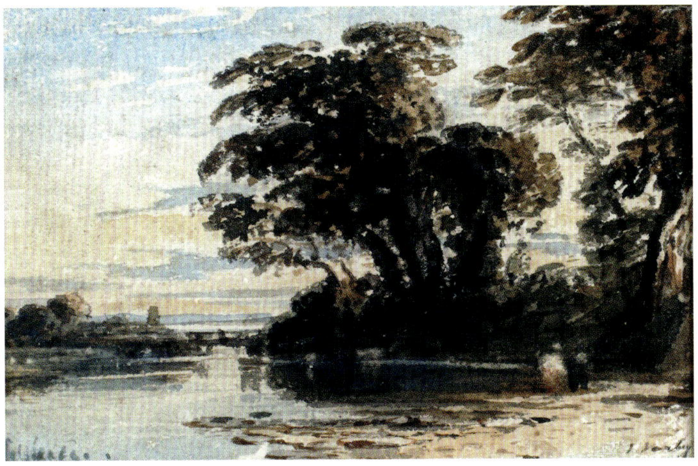

194 BY THE RIVER
signed
watercolour
3 ½ x 5 ½ inches

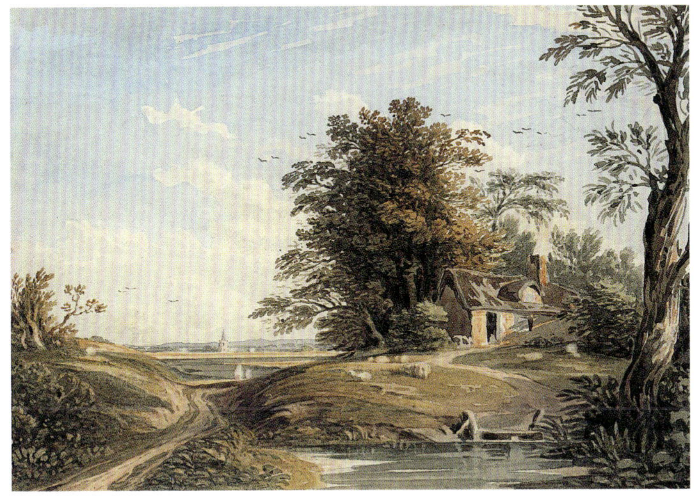

195 SHEEP GRAZING
watercolour
5 ½ x 7 ¾ inches

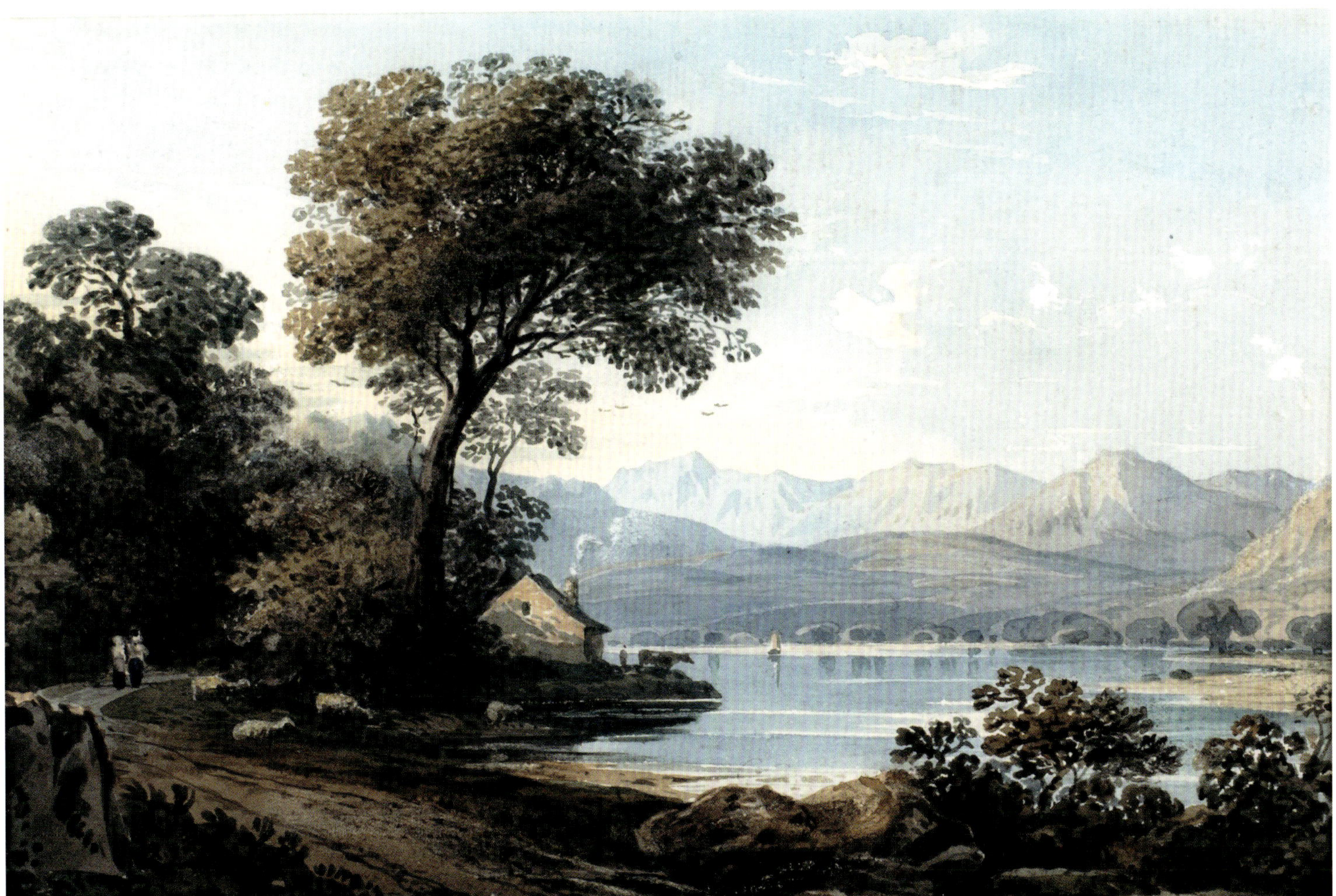

196 DOLGELLY FROM THE ROAD TO BARMOUTH, MERIONESHIRE N.W. (AT THE FOOT OF CADER IDRIS)
signed
signed and inscribed with title on reverse
watercolour
5 ½ x 8 ½ inches

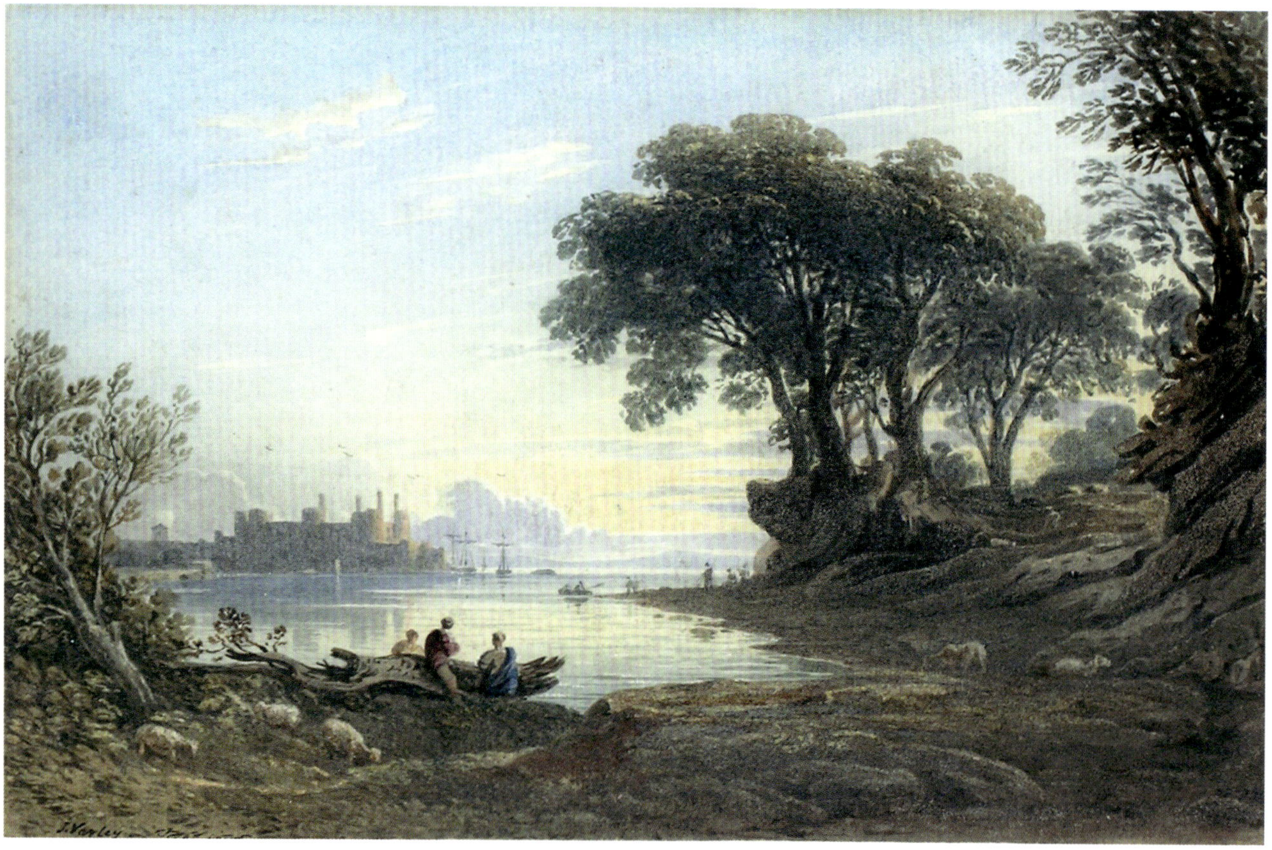

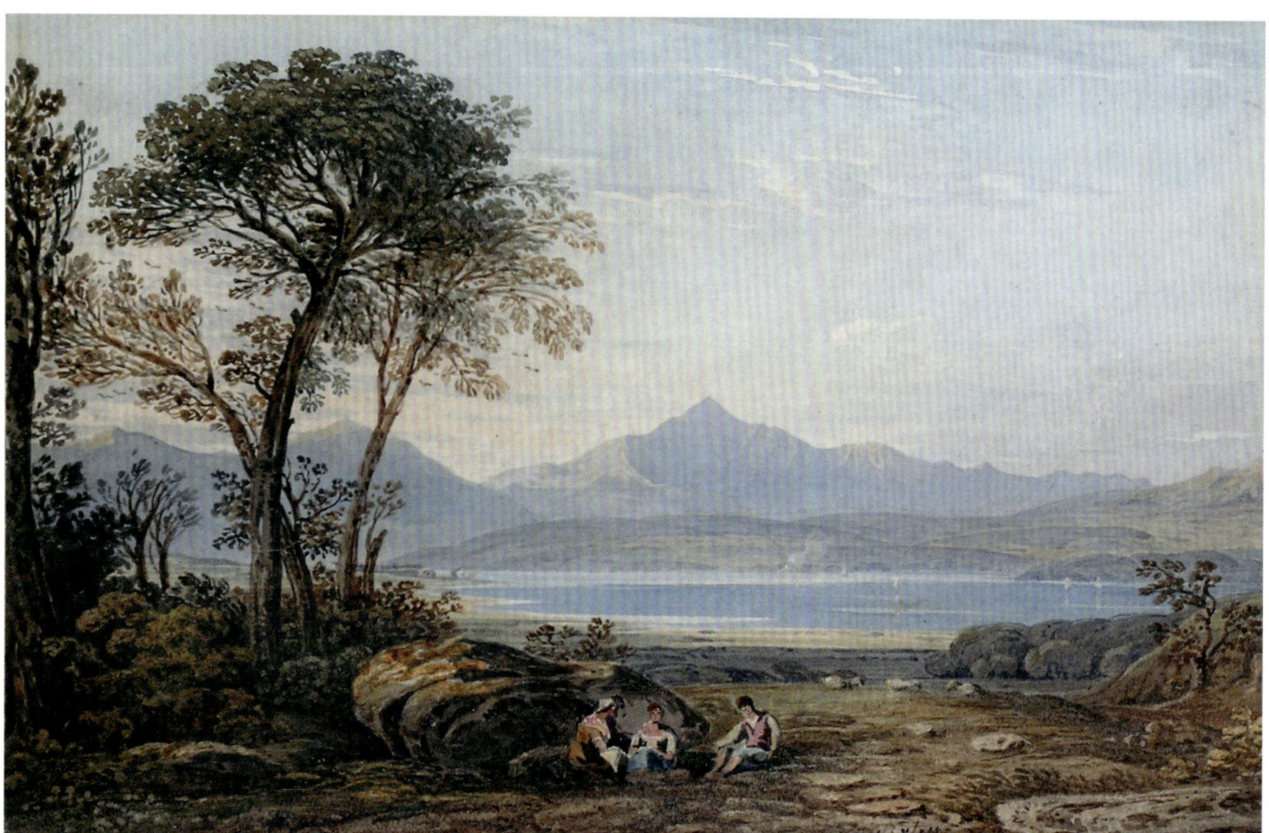

197 CONWAY CASTLE
signed
watercolour
5 ¾ x 8 ½ inches

198 NEAR DOLGELLY, WALES
signed
watercolour
5 ½ x 8 ½

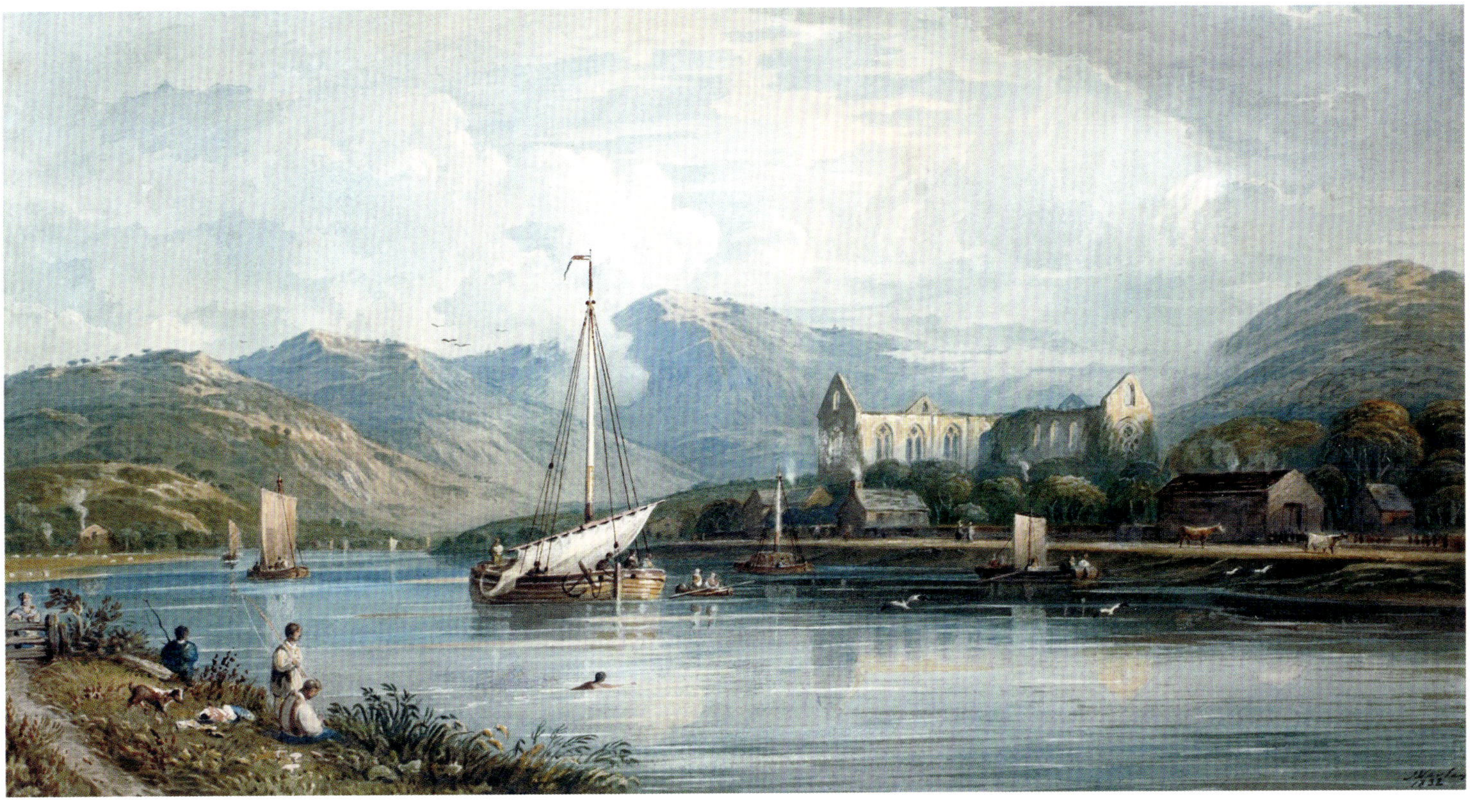

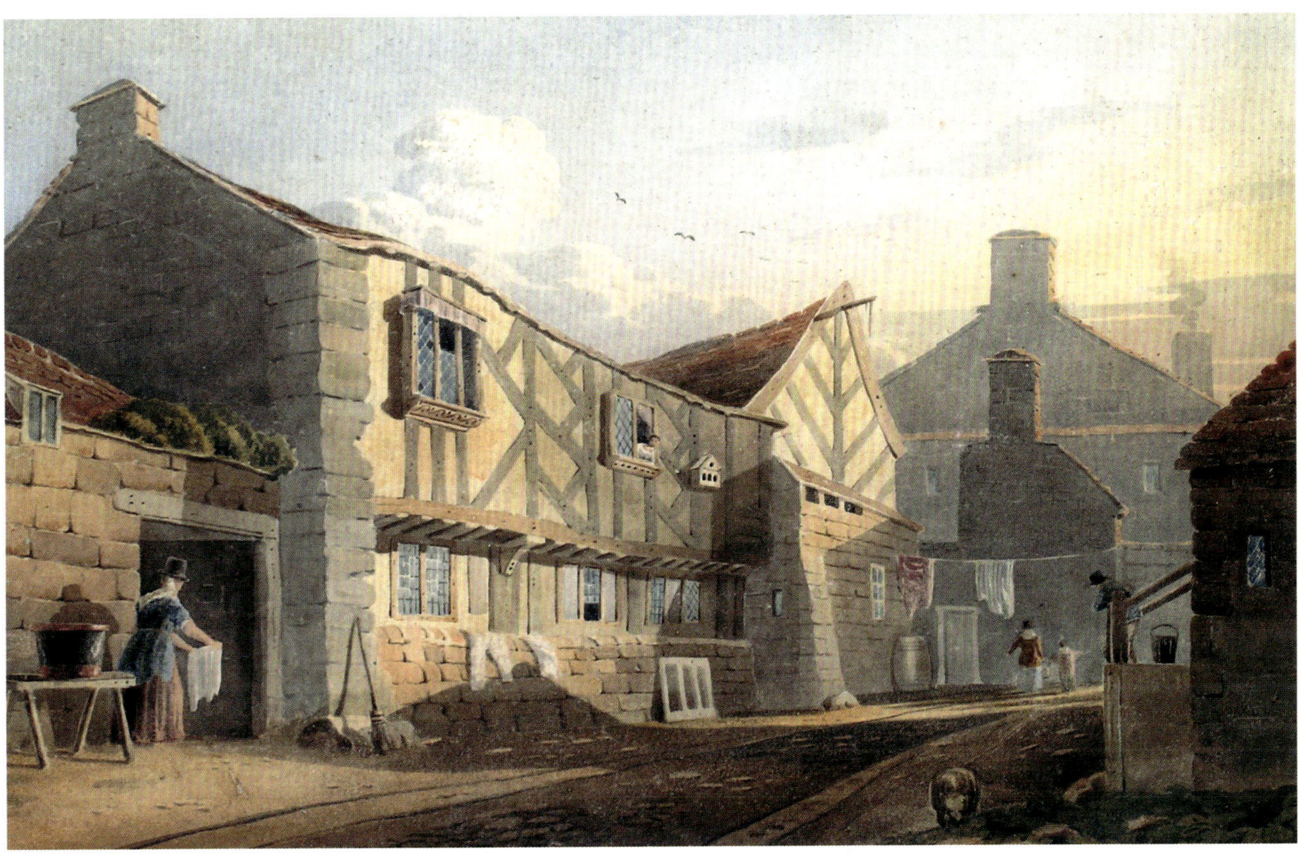

199 TINTERN ABBEY, WALES
signed and dated 1832
watercolour
12 x 21 ¾ inches
(also illustrated cover, detail)

200 TOWN IN NORTH WALES
watercolour
10 ¾ x 16 ½ inches

JOHN VARLEY

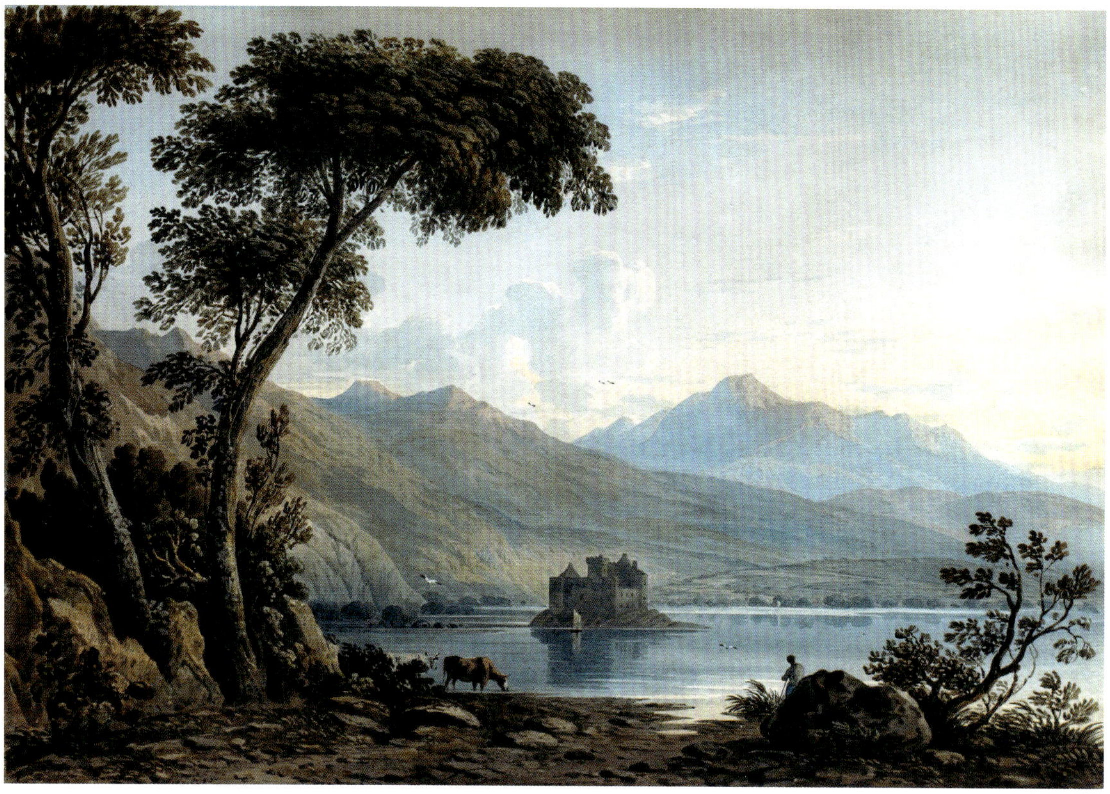

201 KILCHURN CASTLE ON LOCH AWE, ARGYLLSHIRE
signed
watercolour
14 ½ x 20 ¼ inches

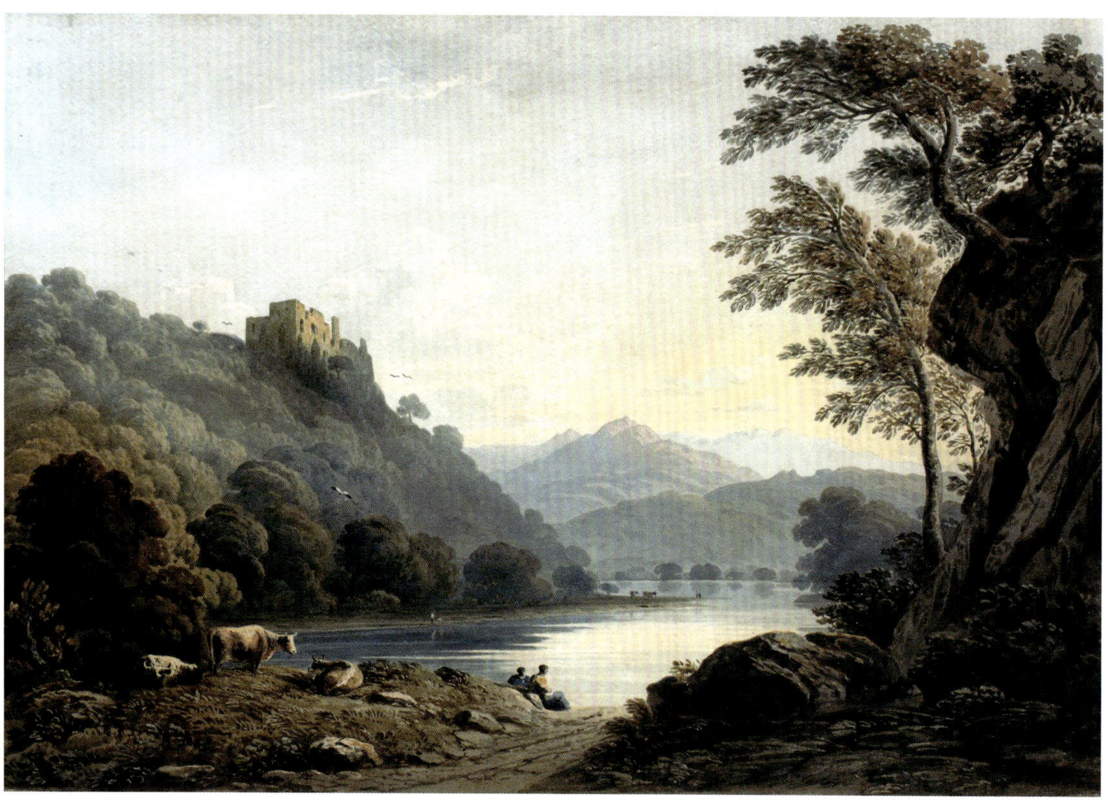

202 BERRY POMEROY CASTLE, DEVONSHIRE
signed
watercolour
14 ¼ x 20 inches

SAMUEL PROUT

Samuel Prout, AA OWS (1783-1852)

Despite persistent ill health, Samuel Prout developed as a highly distinctive topographical artist and undertook regular sketching tours, first in Britain and later on the Continent. The resulting images of ancient buildings at their most picturesque were highly popular and influential – as exhibition watercolours and, especially, lithographic illustrations.

Samuel Prout was born at Trevil Street, Plymouth, Devon, on 17 September 1783, the fourth of fourteen children of a shopkeeper and naval outfitter. As a child, he suffered from severe sunstroke, which gave him violent headaches for the remainder of his life. They were so debilitating that he had to take to his bed once or twice a week until his marriage in 1810. He was also victim to chronic lung congestion.

Prout made sketches and copied prints as a young child, and received encouragement from his headmaster, the Rev John Bidlake, when he attended Plymouth Grammar School. He was also given some lessons from Thomas H Williams. The Plymouth area became well known to him through the many sketching expeditions he undertook with his friend and fellow pupil, Benjamin Robert Haydon, who became a history painter.

Haydon's father was a printer, publisher and bookseller, who kept a shop in the Market Place in Plymouth. There, in 1801, Prout met the budding antiquary, John Britton, who was in town to look for materials for the projected topographical survey, *Beauties of England and Wales*. (This collaboration with E W Brayley was published in parts between 1803 and 1815).

Prout joined Britton on a tour of Cornwall, in order to make drawings for *Beauties*, but he had problems with the perspective of the buildings, and had to work hard through the following year in order to improve his skills.

Aware of the artist's potential, Britton persuaded Prout to move to London in 1802, and live with him at his home, 21 Wilderness Row, Clerkenwell. There he entered a circle of topographical illustrators that included Frederick Mackenzie and GEORGE SIDNEY SHEPHERD. He was set to copy the work of leading contemporary watercolourists, including WILLIAM ALEXANDER, J M W TURNER, JOHN SELL COTMAN, Thomas Girtin and Thomas Hearne, the last three having a particular influence on his early style. He was also sent on sketching tours of Cambridgeshire, Essex and Wiltshire during the years 1803 and 1804, as preparation for work on *Beauties* and *The Architectural Antiquities of Great Britain* (5 vols, 1806-26). During the same period, he began to exhibit at the Royal Academy of Arts and make useful contacts with dealers, including Thomas Palser of Surrey Side, Westminster Bridge, who was the earliest purchaser of his work.

In 1805, Prout became so ill that he had to return to Plymouth, though he was well enough to make a sketching tour of Devon and Cornwall in the October of that year. During his prolonged stay at home, he gave Charles Lock Eastlake his first drawing lessons.

By 1808, Prout had returned to London, and was living at 55 Poland Street, Soho. He brought with him many West Country coastal scenes, which he exhibited at the Royal Academy, the British Institution and the Associated Artists in Water Colours (becoming a member of the last in 1810, and remaining so until its demise in 1812). These scenes would also provide the basis for *Picturesque Delineations in the Counties of Devon and Cornwall*, published by Palser in 1812.

Establishing himself as a drawing master, Prout taught at Dr William Glennie's academy in Dulwich Grove, from 1809 to 1821, during which time his pupils included (the Rev) J D Glennie and William Henry Harriott, two future amateur artists. He also attracted a private clientele of about thirty, one of his first pupils being James Duffield Harding (who followed Prout to become a landscape painter and lithographer).

Marrying in Brixton in 1810, Prout and his wife moved into 4 Brixton Place (now part of Brixton Road) in the following year. (Together, they would have four children.) Once settled, he began to capitalise on his teaching, by producing a series of drawing books for the use of the beginners, starting with *Rudiments of Landscape in Progressive Studies* (1813, containing 16 aquatints). Over three decades, Prout issued fourteen publications, which, while falling into either drawing manuals or volumes of topographical plates, together promoted the taste for the Picturesque.

Not neglecting his career as an exhibiting artist, Prout began to show work at the Society of Painters in Oil and Water-Colours in 1815, becoming an associate in 1817 and a member in 1819. (The society returned to its former name of the Society of Painters in Water Colours in 1821.)

Prout's style and subject matter were profoundly affected by his first Continental sketching tour, to Northern France in 1819. Keen to meet the challenge of recording the ancient architecture in all its atmospheric detail, he found inspiration in the recent drawings of Norman buildings by Henry Edridge. The death of Edridge in 1821 left the way free for Prout to exploit the genre, and his regular travels (until 1846) provided him with constant material.

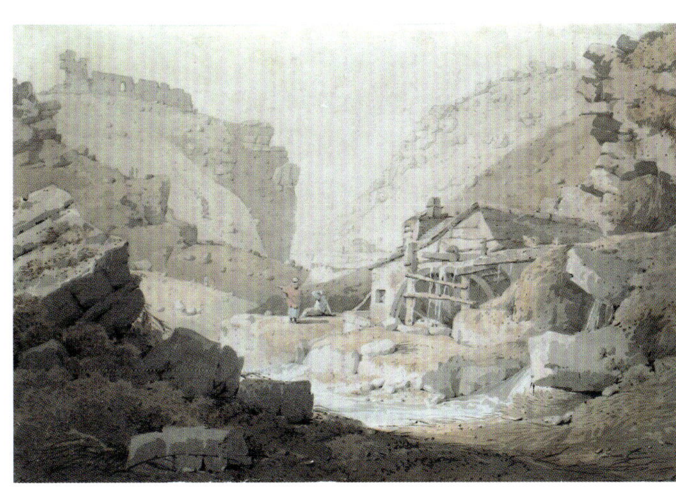

203 ARTHUR'S CASTLE AT TINTAGEL, CORNWALL
watercolour
10 x 15 inches

Through the 1820s, Prout took in France, the Low Countries, Germany (including the Rhineland and Bavaria), and Italy (of which Venice proved an inevitable highlight). Sometimes, he travelled and sketched in the company of other artists, as with Richard Parkes Bonington in St Omer (1822).

In order to reproduce his graphic responses accurately and vividly, Prout turned from aquatint to lithography, as is seen to great effect in *Picturesque Buildings in Normandy* (1821, printed by Charles Hullmandel) and *Illustrations of the Rhine* (1822-26). The most notable later volumes included *Facsimiles of Sketches made in Flanders and Germany* (1833) and *Facsimiles of Sketches made in France, Switzerland and Italy* (1839).

The breadth of his travels, and the resulting range of images, ensured Prout a strong reputation on both sides of the Channel, a reputation that reached its height around 1830. His contacts in the Parisian art world included Baron Isidore Taylor, who helped him to show watercolours at the Paris Salon of 1824, and who, in the following year, included lithographs of his work in the third volume of *Voyages pittoresques et romantiques dans l'ancienne France* (produced by Taylor in collaboration with Charles Nodier).

Back in England, Prout received a number of honours and mixed freely with fellow leading artists. In 1829, George IV appointed him 'Painter in Water-Colours in Ordinary to His Majesty', an honour renewed by both William IV and Queen Victoria; while, a year later, he became a fellow of the Society of Antiquaries. During the early 1830s, he regularly attended the Artists' and Amateurs' Conversazione, where he met with THOMAS SHOTTER BOYS, JOHN SELL COTMAN, DAVID COX, David Roberts and Clarkson Stanfield.

However, in 1836, ill health drove Prout from London to Hastings, where he spent eight years in what he regarded as exile. On his return to the capital, in 1845, he settled at 5 De Crespigny Terrace, where he became a neighbour of the young critic, John Ruskin, who was a great admirer of his work. Making his last Continental tour, to Normandy, in 1846, he then produced gradually less work until his death at home on 10 February 1852. His studio sale was held at Sotheby's on 19-22 May 1852.

Prout's distinctive style, and Ruskin's promotion of it, continued to prove highly influential. What may be termed the Prout effect was sustained into the late nineteenth century by Samuel Gillespie Prout and John Skinner Prout (respectively his son and nephew), and also through aspects of the work of T R C Dibdin and Louis Haghe. In 1879, the Fine Art Society published *Notes by Ruskin on Samuel Prout and William Hunt illustrated by A Loan Collection of Drawings*.

His work is represented in numerous public collections, including the British Museum, The Courtauld Gallery, Tate and the V&A; The Fitzwilliam Museum (Cambridge), Manchester Art Gallery, Plymouth City Museum and Art Gallery, Royal Cornwall Museum (Truro), Southampton Art Gallery and The Whitworth Art Gallery (Manchester).

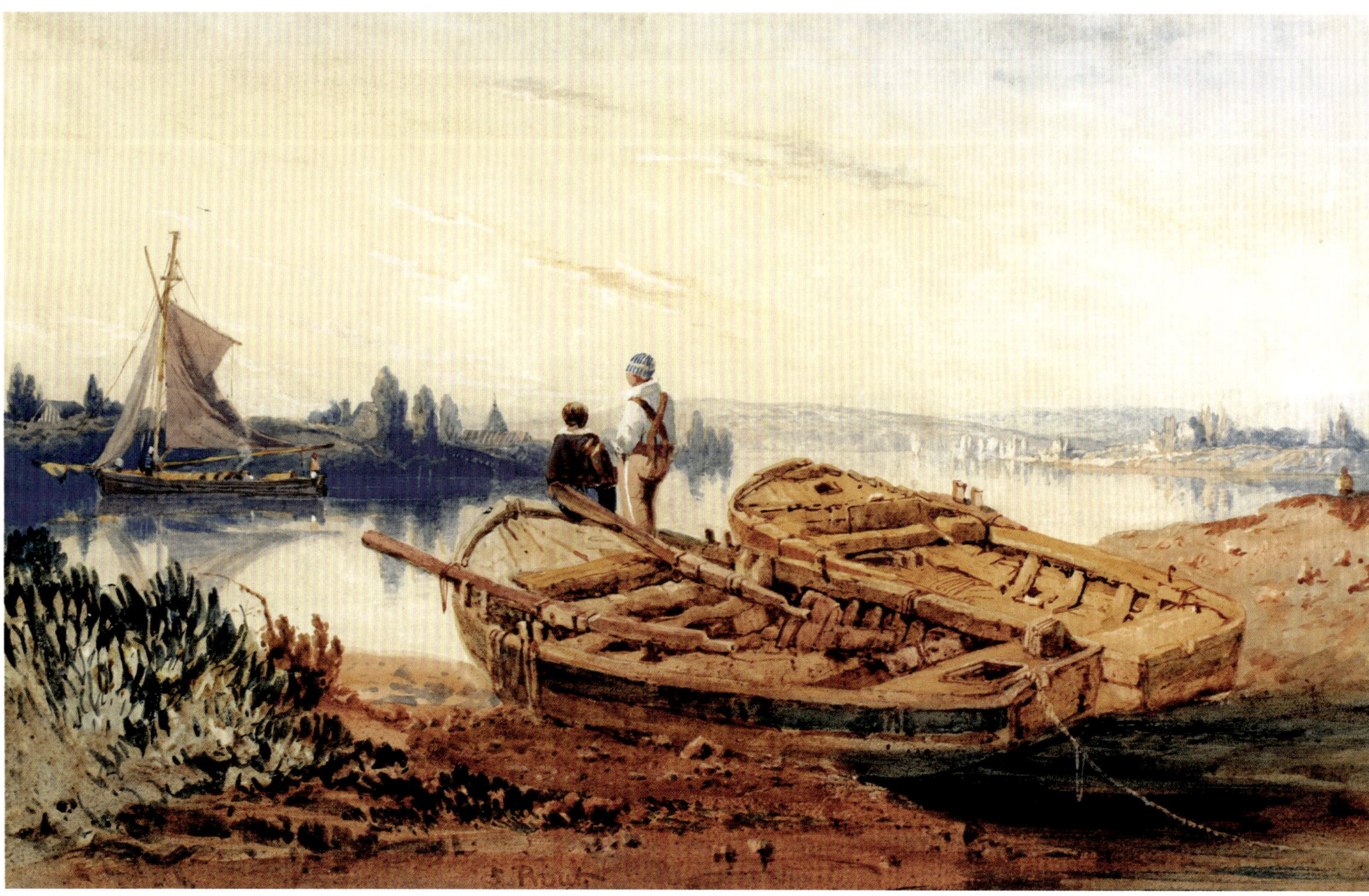

204 OLD BOATS
signed
watercolour
10 ½ x 16 ¼ inches

Further reading:
Richard Lockett, 'Samuel Prout (1753-1852)', H C G Matthew and Brian Harrison (eds), *Oxford Dictionary of National Biography*, Oxford University Press, 2004, vol 45, pp 477-480
Richard Lockett, *Samuel Prout, 1783-1852*, London: Batsford/Victoria and Albert Museum, 1985
Scott Wilcox, 'Prout: (1) Samuel Prout (*b* Plymouth, 17 Sept 1783; *d* London, 10 Feb 1852)', Jane Turner (ed), *The Dictionary of Art*, London: Macmillan, 1996, vol 25, p 661-662

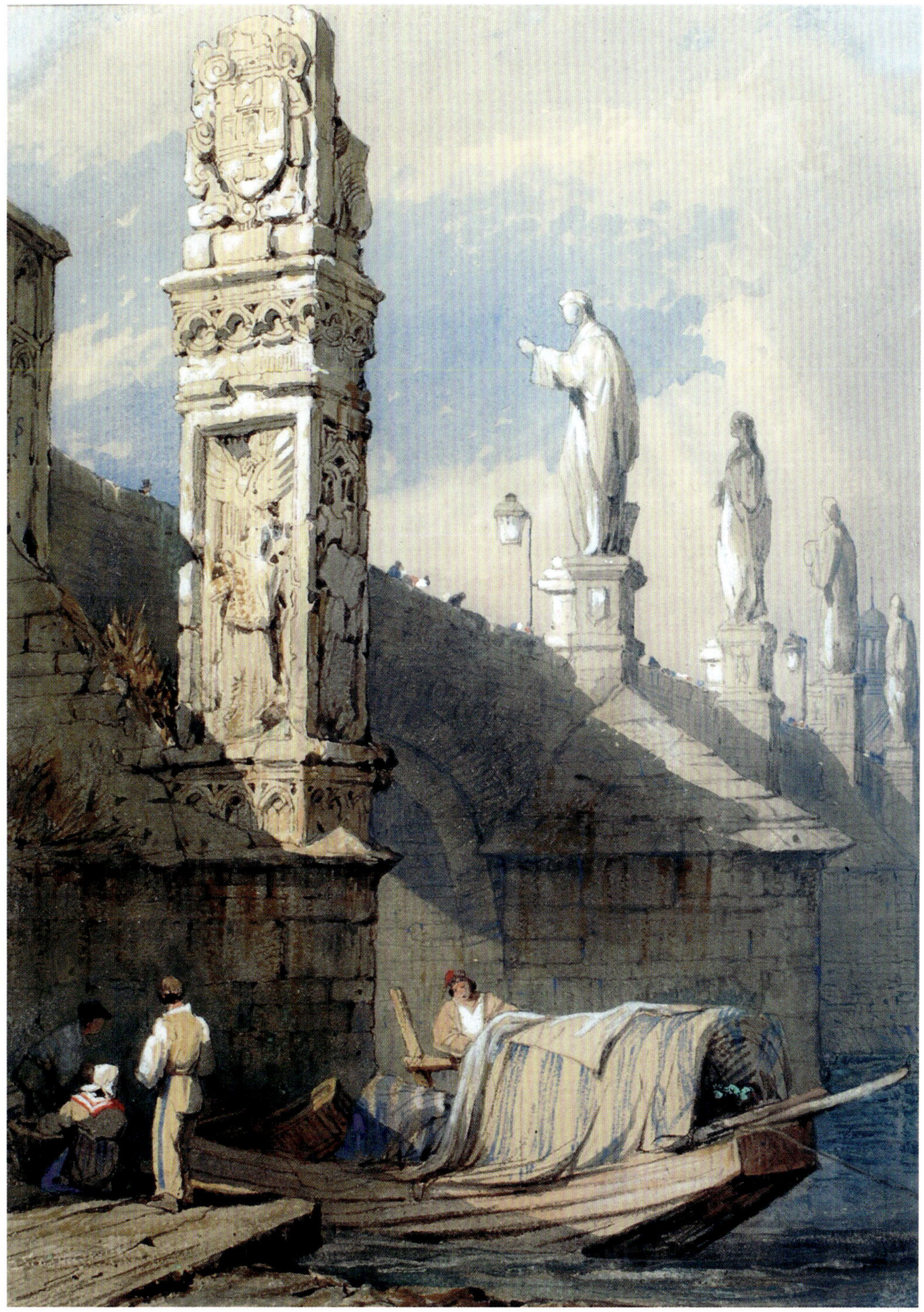

205 CHARLES BRIDGE, PRAGUE
watercolour with bodycolour
11 x 8 inches

Charles Bridge
From 1819, Samuel Prout made regular sketching tours of the Continent, evolving his characteristic picturesque style in response to the old architecture that attracted his attention. While he shared such topographical interests with a number of contemporary British artists, he was almost unique in his exploration and depiction of the more distant cities of Germany. At the time those cities included Prague, which he visited in September 1829, as part of a tour mainly of Germany and, according to Richard Lockett, 'made at least seventeen drawings while he was there' (Richard Lockett, *Samuel Prout, 1783-1852*, London: Batsford/Victoria and Albert Museum, 1985, p 143).

Prout first presented views of the city to the public five years later in the volume of lithographs, *Facsimiles of Sketches made in Flanders and Germany* (1833). Other views of the Bridge at Prague are in the collections of the British Museum and Plymouth City Museum and Art Gallery.

DAVID COX

David Cox, OWS PAA (1783-1859)

The freedom and atmosphere of his mature landscapes of England and Wales made David Cox one of the most influential of Victorian watercolourists.

David Cox was born at Heath Mill Lane, Deritend, on the edge of Birmingham, on 29 April 1783. He was educated at a basic local day school and, from an early age, worked in his father's smithy. But, encouraged to paint by a cousin, he took drawing lessons from the drawing master, Joseph Barber, and began an apprenticeship with Fieldler, a painter of lockets and trinkets.

When Fieldler committed suicide, in about 1800, Cox became a scenery painter, under James Demaria, at the New Theatre and, in 1804, travelled to London on the promise of similar work. When this came to little, he decided to become a watercolour painter. He was helped in this decision by John Varley who, before 1808, may have given him some lessons; however, he had begun to exhibit landscapes at the Royal Academy of Arts as early as 1805. In this same period, he made his first journeys into Wales (1805, 1806), in the company of Joseph Barber's son, Charles. So, at the outset, he established one of his most characteristic sketching grounds.

In 1808, Cox settled into married life with the daughter of his first landlady at 16 Bridge Row, Lambeth; their only child, David junior, would be born in the following year. They rented a cottage on the edge of Dulwich Common, south of London, and he established himself as a drawing master. He soon became a notable contributor to the development of watercolour as a distinguished independent medium. Exhibiting at the Associated Artists in Water Colours from 1809 (until its closure in 1812), he became both member and President in the following year. Then transferring allegiance to the Society of Painters in Water Colours (during its reconstitution as the Society of Painters in Oil and Water-Colours), he rose almost immediately from the position of associate to that of member. He worked for a brief period as drawing master at the Military Staff College, Farnham, Surrey, and published drawing manuals, including *A Treatise on Landscape Painting and Effect in Water Colours* (1813-14).

In 1814, Cox took up a teaching position at Miss Croucher's School for Young Ladies at the Gate House, Widmarsh Street, Hereford; while, a year later, he also began to teach at Hereford Grammar School. Notable among the private pupils that he accepted while in Hereford was JOSEPH MURRAY INCE, who received lessons in the mid 1820s.

The move to Hereford gave Cox close access to some of his favourite sketching sites, at a time when the London art market was depressed. He travelled in Wales (1818, 1825), and made exploratory visits to Devon (1819) and to the Low Countries in the company of his son, David, who was also becoming a painter (1826). These experiences, coupled to the influence of J M W TURNER and Richard Parkes Bonington, helped him to develop his art; he tackled new subjects and employed both a brighter palette and more varied handling. This he sustained on returning to London in 1827, soon after he had illustrated *The Hereford Guide*. The family then lived at 9 Foxley Cottages (later known as 34 Foxley Road), Kennington.

Cox made two further visits to the Continent: a six-week tour of northern France with his son (1829), and a shorter visit along the north coast of France (1832). Yet more important to the direction of his art were his first visits north to Bolton Abbey, Yorkshire and Ulverston Sands, Lancashire (1834), and to the stately homes of Derbyshire: Haddon Hall (1831) and Hardwick Hall (1838). Ulverston provided him with his highly popular motif of marketeers crossing the sands, while Haddon and Hardwick were used as settings for historical costume genre. He capitalised on this increasing range of subjects by exhibiting at new venues, the revived Birmingham Society of Artists (from 1829) and the Liverpool Academy (from 1831). He also rehearsed his extensive knowledge of Wales, in providing illustrations for Thomas Roscoe's *Wanderings and Excursions in North Wales* (1836) and its companion, *South Wales* (1837).

Late in the 1830s, Cox began to experiment with oil painting, receiving advice and inspiration from William James Müller (1839). In order to devote more time to this new medium, he retired from teaching and moved to Greenfield House, Harborne, near Birmingham (1841). This return to his birthplace gave him easy access to both established sketching spots and to the mountainous vicinity of Bettwys-y-Coed, north Wales, (visited annually between 1844 and 1856). It also brought him close to the provincial markets that showed greater appreciation of his oils than did London. More generally, critics were ambivalent about the boldness of his later work, praising its depth and power, but regretting the loose handling. Its intensity was if anything emphasised, after June 1853, when Cox suffered a stroke. He was represented by a group of watercolours at the Paris Exposition Universelle (1855), and honoured by a well-received retrospective at the German Gallery, Bond Street, London (April 1859). He died in Harborne on 7 June 1859.

Most of his remaining works were sold at Christie's on 3 and 5 May 1873.

His work is represented in numerous public collections, including the British Museum, The Courtauld Gallery, Tate and the V&A; the Ashmolean Museum (Oxford), Birmingham Museum & Art Gallery, The Fitzwilliam Museum (Cambridge), Manchester Art Gallery and Tyne & Wear Museums; National Museum Wales (Cardiff); the National Gallery of Scotland (Edinburgh); Harvard University Art Museums (Cambridge MA) and Fine Art Museums of San Francisco; and Art Gallery of Greater Victoria (Victoria, Canada).

Further reading:

George Trenchard Cox, *David Cox*, London: Phoenix House, 1947
Frederic Gordon Roe, *The Life and Art of David Cox, 1783-1859,* Leigh-on-Sea: F Lewis, 1946
Scott Wilcox, 'David Cox', Jane Turner (ed), *The Dictionary of Art*, London: Macmillan, 1996, vol 8, pp 83-85
Stephen Wildman, 'Cox, David (1783-1859)', H C G Matthew and Brian Harrison (eds), *Oxford Dictionary of National Biography*, Oxford University Press, 2004, vol 13, pp 837-841
Stephen Wildman (ed), *David Cox, 1783-1859*, Birmingham Museum and Art Gallery, 1983

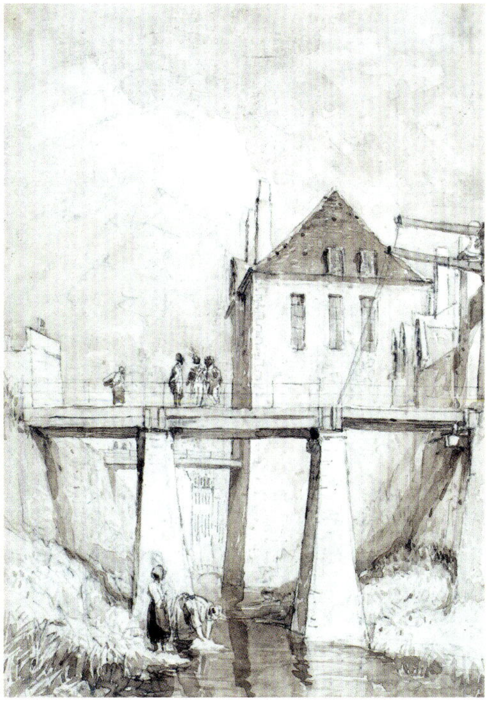

206 OLD CALAIS FORTIFICATIONS, FRANCE
monochrome watercolour with pencil
8 ½ x 7 inches

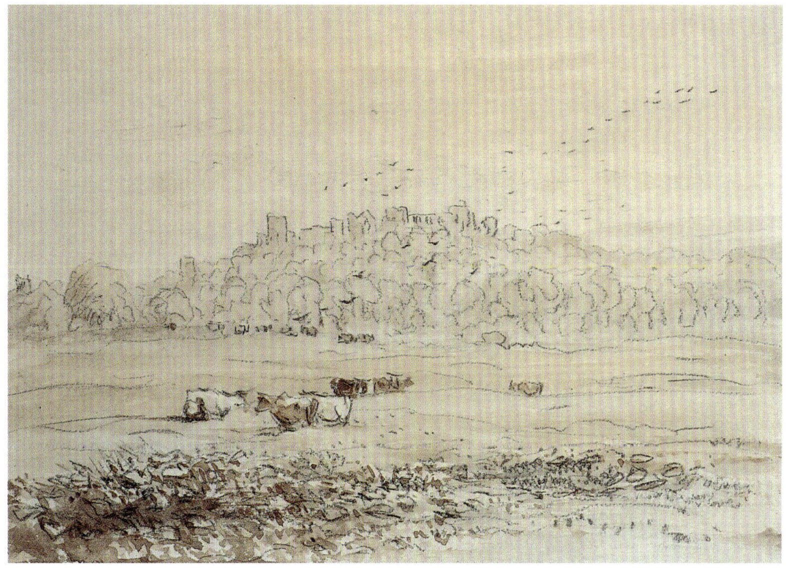

207 RICHMOND CASTLE, YORKSHIRE FROM THE MEADOWS
pen ink and pencil
7 ½ x 10 ¼ inches

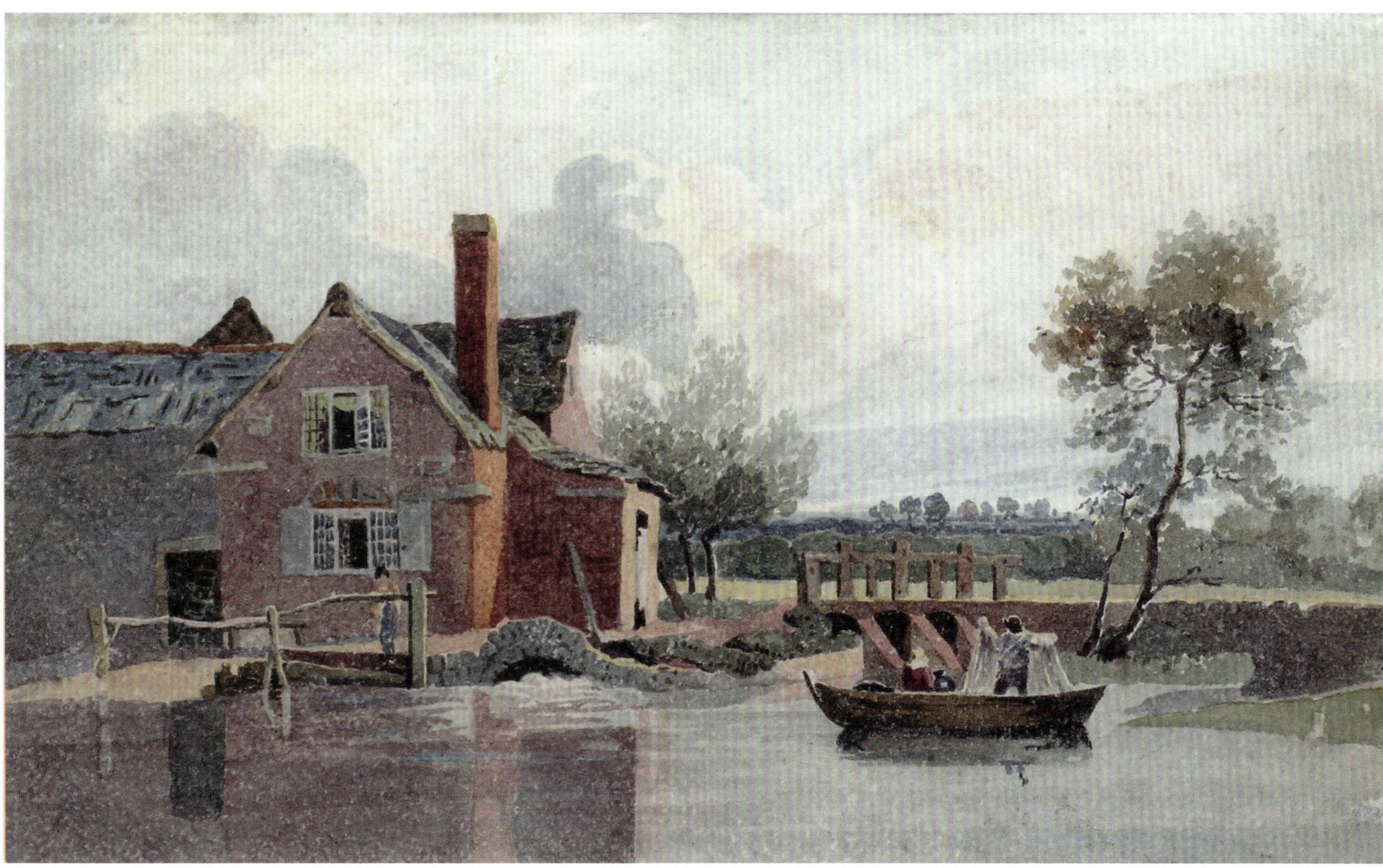

208 BY THE MILL STREAM
watercolour
6 ¾ x 11 inches

DAVID COX

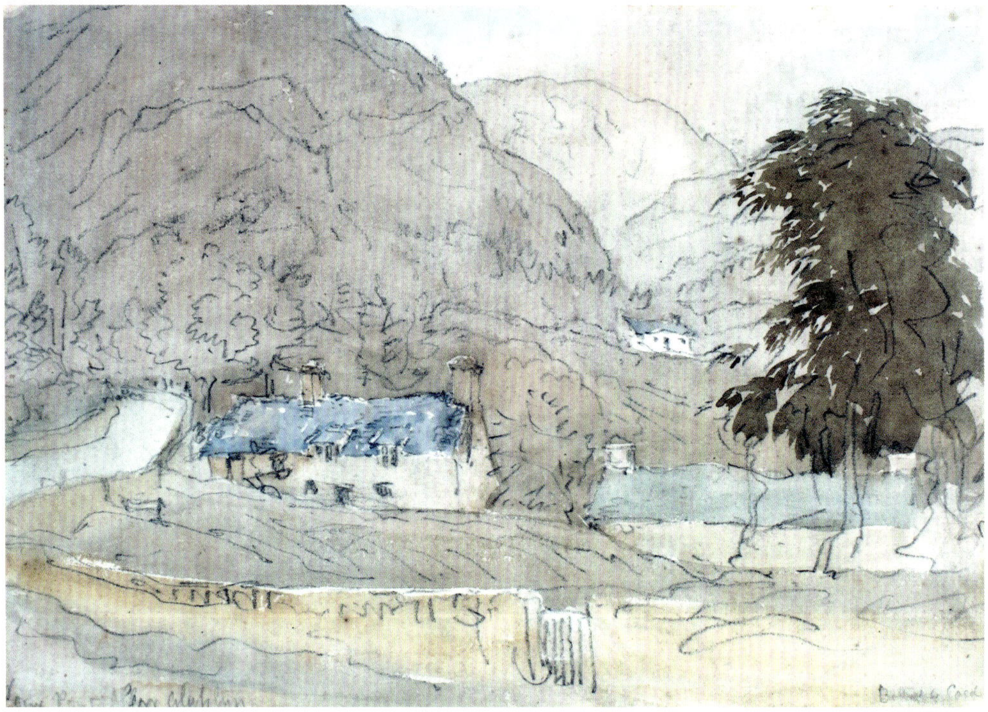

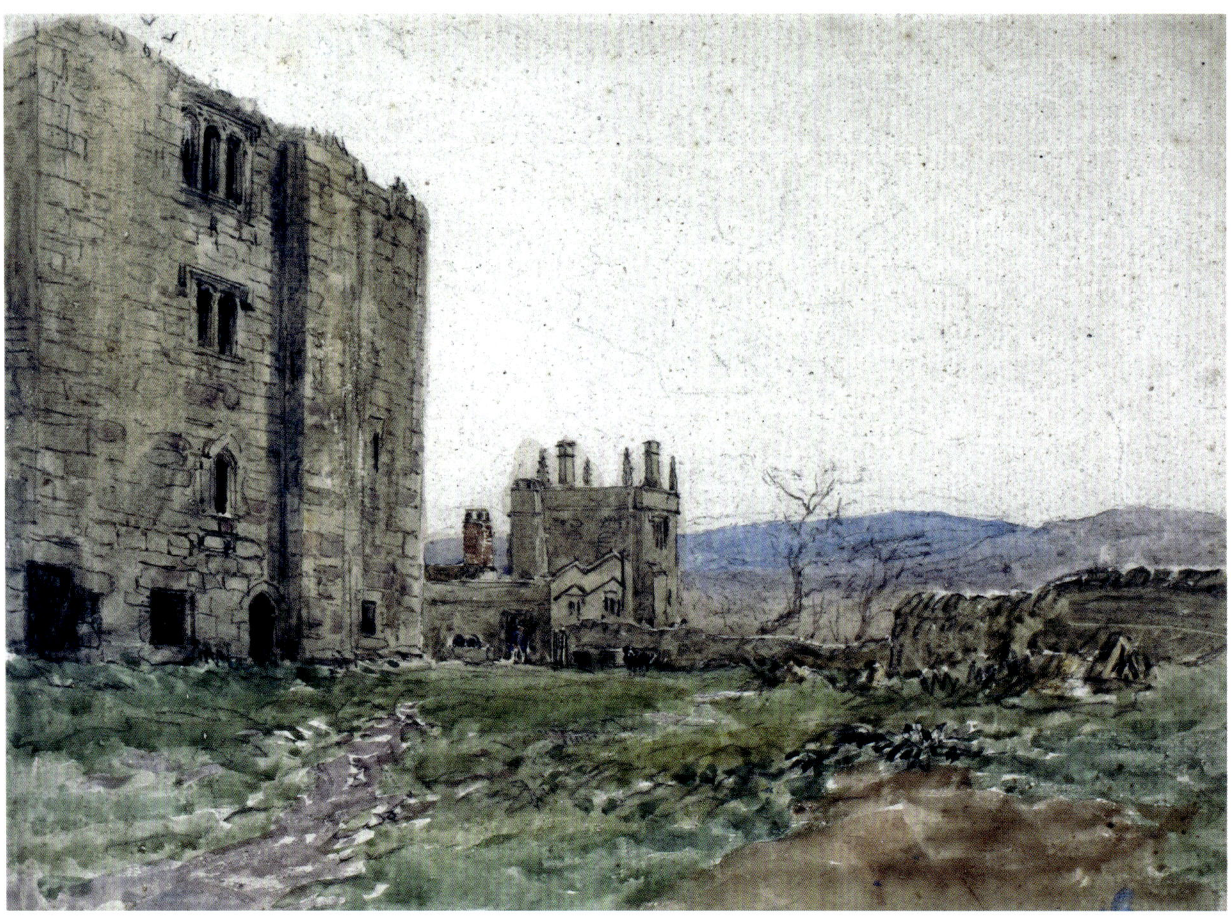

209 PONT-Y-PAIR, GLASLYN
inscribed with title and 'Bettws Y Coed'
watercolour and pencil
7 ¼ x 10 inches
pencil sketch on reverse

210 FIGURES BY AN OLD CASTLE
pencil and watercolour
17 ¾ x 21 ¼ inches

GEORGE SIDNEY SHEPHERD
George Sidney Shepherd, NWS (1784-1862)

Establishing himself with his excellent topographical views of London, George Sidney Shepherd became a founder member of the New Society of Painters in Water Colours, and one of its most prolific exhibitors.

George Sidney Shepherd was born in Old Street, Finsbury, London, the son of a watchcase maker. He probably studied at Dr Monro's informal academy and, by 1800, had begun to exhibit watercolours at various London venues, including the Royal Academy of Arts. He was awarded a silver palette by the Society of Arts in both 1803 and 1804.

While his earliest subjects were close to his home, off the City Road in rural Islington, Shepherd began to travel further afield by 1807, when he produced sketches of Cambridge and Northampton for John Britton's *Architectural Antiquities of Great Britain* (1807). His range encompassed rural and natural landscapes, including some of Bedfordshire, the home county of his first wife, whom he married in 1812. Yet, increasingly, he specialised in townscapes and, in particular, scenes of London. Many of his images were engraved for such publications as John Booth's *Architectural Series of London Churches* (1818), Charles Clarke's *Architectura ecclesiastica Londini* (1819) and Robert Wilkinson's *Londina illustrata* (1825-34). Sometimes he worked in collaboration with his brother, THOMAS HOSMER SHEPHERD.

In the mid 1820s, Shepherd changed his style from the precise and delicate to the painterly and impressionistic, signalling the start of this new phase in 1824 by altering his signature from 'George Shepherd' to 'George Sidney Shepherd'. (One of his eight children was given the middle name of 'Sidney' in the same year.)

In 1831, Shepherd helped to found the New Society of Painters in Water Colours, and during the next two decades exhibited nearly 225 works. Almost expelled for non-payment of dues, he was found to be in dire poverty and instead made an honorary member. Following his confinement to bed, in 1860, he was granted a pension by the society until February 1861. A year later, he died in St Pancras Workhouse.

His work is represented in numerous public collections, including the British Museum and the V&A; and Cecil Higgins Art Gallery (Bedford).

Further reading:

Lucy Peltz, 'Shepherd, George Sidney (1784-1862)', H C G Matthew and Brian Harrison (eds), *Oxford Dictionary of National Biography*, Oxford University Press, 2004, vol 50, pp 244-245

J F C Phillips, *George Shepherd (1784-1862): a double career?*, privately issued, 1984

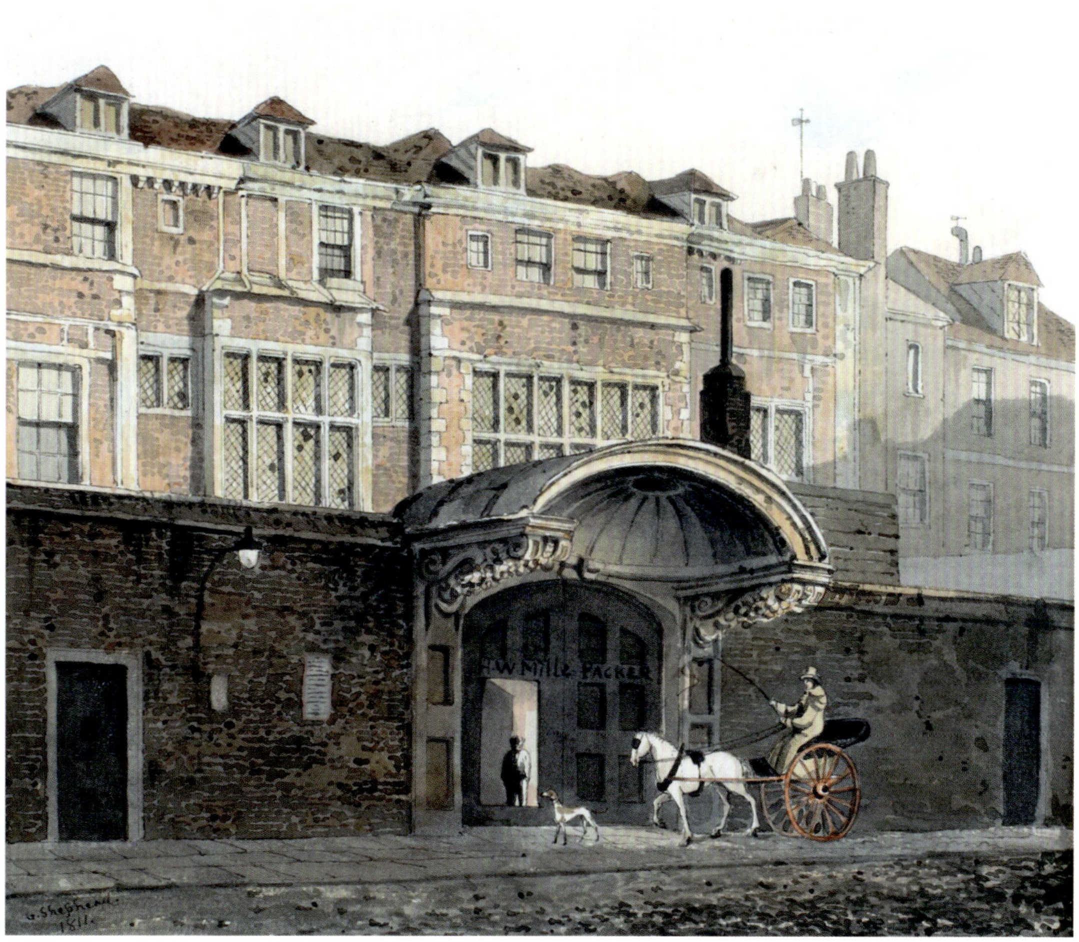

211 WINCHESTER HOUSE, AUSTIN FRIARS
signed and dated 1811
watercolour
8 ¼ x 7 inches

COPLEY FIELDING
Anthony Vandyke Copley Fielding, POWS (1787-1855)

Copley Fielding was one of the most technically impressive watercolourists of his day, both popular as an artist and influential as a teacher.

Copley Fielding was born in Sowerby, near Halifax, Yorkshire, on 22 November 1787. He was the third, and best known, of the five artist sons of Nathan Theodore Fielding, a Yorkshire portrait and landscape painter. His full name suggests his father's ambitions for him, as it combines those of Anthony Van Dyck and the history painter, John Singleton Copley RA (though Copley was also a neighbouring hamlet to Sowerby).

In 1788, the Fielding family moved to Acton, Middlesex (now in London). Copley attended a local school and, like his brother Frederick, worked as 'an engrossing clerk in the enrolment office of the court of chancery' (Mallalieu, in Matthew and Harrison 2004, vol 19, p 498). After periods in Durham and London, the Fieldings settled in the Lake District in around 1804, first at a cottage in Ambleside and later in Keswick.

Given his first lessons in art by his father, Copley was soon working in a very similar style, though he was sent out each morning to draw from nature. In 1807, he accompanied his father to Liverpool, in order to sell his drawings, and while there began to give drawing lessons. Father and son toured north Wales together in the following year.

In 1809, Copley Fielding settled in London, and lodged at Wells Street, in the artistic quarter north of Oxford Street. He took advice and lessons from JOHN VARLEY, who may have suggested that he look at the work of Thomas Girtin, which he could have seen at Dr Monro's informal academy. His election as an associate of the Society of Painters in Water Colours in January 1810 indicates the speed of his development.

During the summer, Fielding toured the Borders (visiting his brothers Theodore, in Penrith, and Frederick, in Carlisle), while, in the following year, he revisited Liverpool and north Wales. Further sketching tours in Britain followed through the decade. Though exhibiting eleven oils at the Royal Academy of Arts (1811-42), Fielding strengthened his allegiance to watercolour in becoming a member of the Society of Painters in Water Colours in 1811, its Treasurer in 1813 and its Secretary in 1815. Hugely prolific, he would average over forty exhibits a year there for forty-three years, a total of 1,748 works.

In 1813, Fielding married Susannah Gisborne, the sister of John Varley's wife, and two years later they rented Capo di Monte, a house in Judges Walk, Hampstead (previously occupied by Sarah Siddons, the great tragedienne). In 1817, he also bought a house at 26 Newman Street, north of Oxford Street, 'which was to be the London base of the family business for the next thirty years' (Mallalieu, op cit, p 499) and, particularly, his highly successful practice as a drawing master. His pupils would include William Leighton Leitch, William Andrews Nesfield and John Ruskin, the last a lifelong admirer.

Yet, despite this activity, the ill health of both his wife and elder daughter necessitated a home on the coast, and the family settled at Sandgate, Kent, in 1817. From this time, Fielding not only painted many views of the southern counties, but also many seascapes, especially through the 1820s. At the close of that decade, the family moved to Brighton, living first at 41 Regency Square and, by 1840, at 2 Lansdowne Place. Views of the South Downs then became common to Fielding's repertoire.

Remaining popular and successful throughout his career, Fielding was elected Deputy President of the Society of Painters in Water Colours in 1823, and President in 1831. In 1824, he was awarded a gold medal at the Paris Salon, in the same year as Richard Parkes Bonington and John Constable, although he was the only Fielding brother never to visit France or, indeed travel abroad. His foreign views, such as *Benares* [**214**], were developed from the sketches of other artists.

Having made a final move, to 5 Park Crescent, Worthing, in 1847, Copley Fielding died there on 3 March 1855.

His work is represented in numerous public collections, including the British Museum, Tate, the V&A and the Wallace Collection; Brighton & Hove Museums, The Fitzwilliam Museum (Cambridge), Manchester Art Gallery, Southampton Art Gallery and Tyne & Wear Museums; and the Art Gallery of New South Wales (Sydney).

Further reading:

Solomon Charles Kaines-Smith, 'Anthony Vandyke Copley Fielding', *Old Water-Colour Society's Club*, 1925, vol 3, pp 8-30

Huon Mallalieu, 'Fielding (Anthony Vandyke) Copley (1787-1855)', H C G Matthew and Brian Harrison (eds), *Oxford Dictionary of National Biography*, Oxford University Press, 2004, vol 19, pp 498-499

Terence Mullaly, 'Copley Fielding, *The Sussex County Magazine*, 1952, vol 26, pp 574-578

Marcia Pointon, 'Fielding (3) (Anthony Van Dyck) Copley Fielding', Jane Turner (ed), *The Dictionary of Art*, London: Macmillan, 1996, vol 11, p 60

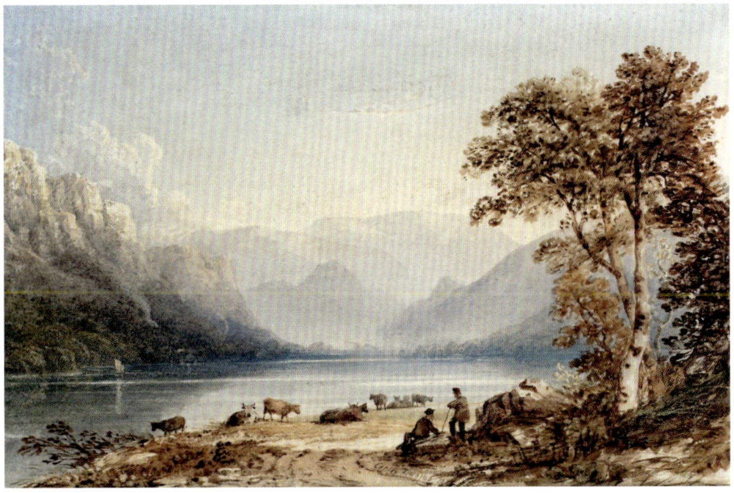

212 THE CATTLE POOL
signed
watercolour
10 ¾ x 15 inches

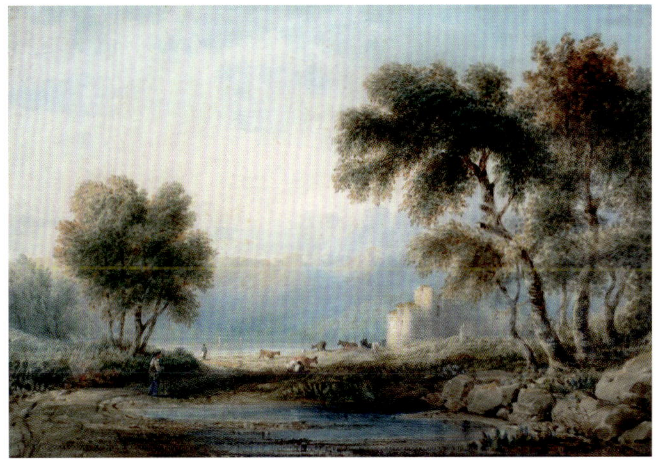

213 DERWENTWATER LOOKING TOWARDS BORROWDALE
signed and dated 1837
watercolour
7 ¼ x 10 ½ inches

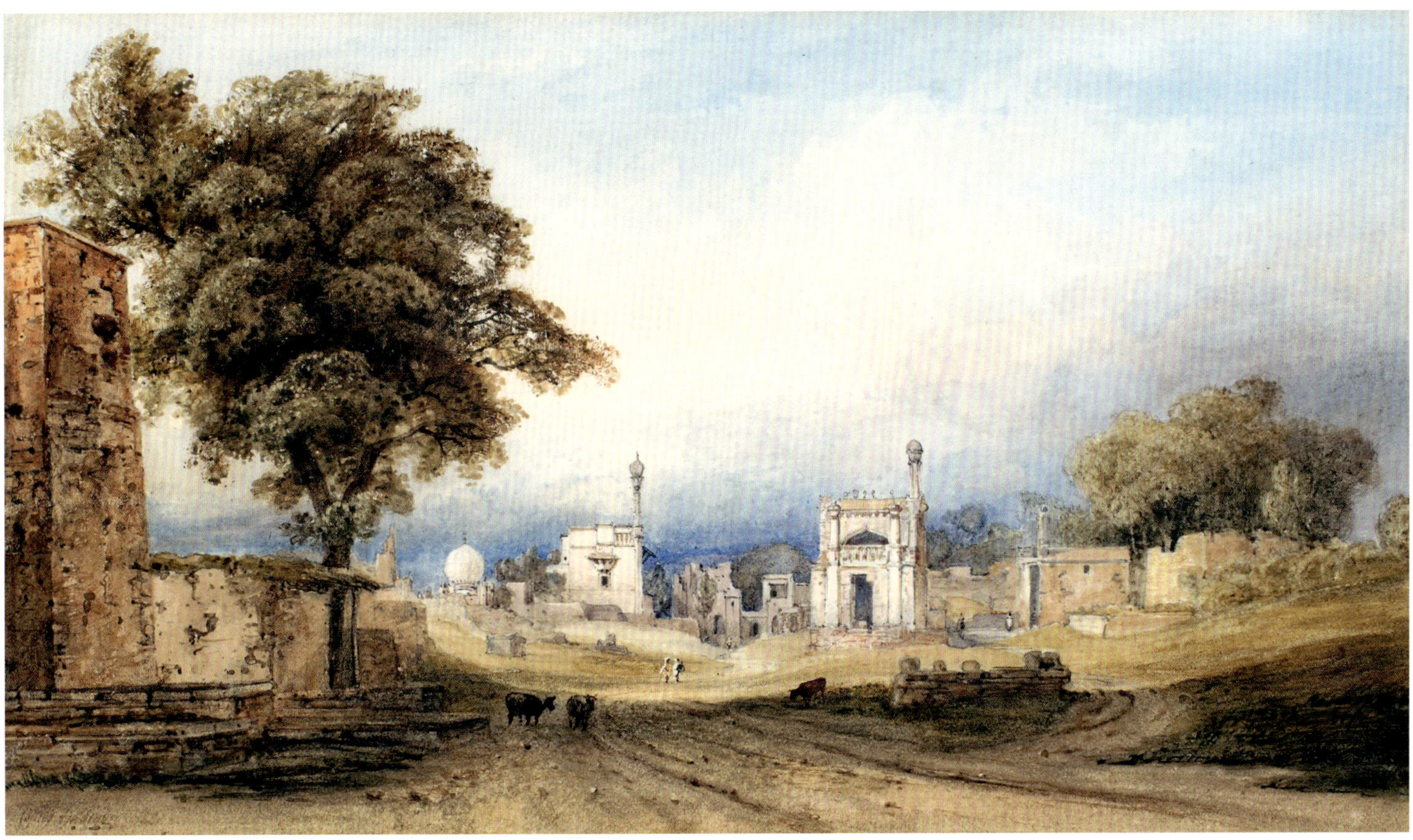

214 BENARES
signed and dated 1832
watercolour
6 ¼ x 10 inches

WILLIAM TURNER

William Turner, OWS (1789-1862), known as William Turner of Oxford

Though William Turner became known as 'Turner of Oxford' to distinguish him from J M W Turner, his work is very different from that of his better-known namesake. While J M W Turner presented the natural world in all its dramatic variety, Turner of Oxford captured its intense stillness.

William Turner was born at Black Bourton, near Bampton, Oxfordshire on 12 November 1789. From 1803, he lived with his uncle, William Turner, at the manor house of Shipton-on-Cherwell, near Woodstock, and probably received his first drawing lessons from WILLIAM DELAMOTTE in Oxford. Following his move to London in 1804, he became one of the earliest apprentices of JOHN VARLEY, living at his house in Broad Street, Soho, and working alongside WILLIAM HENRY HUNT, John Linnell and William Mulready.

Turner began to exhibit at the Royal Academy of Arts in 1807, and in the following year became the youngest member of the Society of Painters in Water Colours, to which he remained faithful until his death. He was also an early member of the Society for the Study of Epic and Pastoral Design (founded in 1808 by the CHALON brothers and Francis Stevens), though he resigned after thirteen meetings.

About 1812, Turner returned to Oxfordshire, and probably lived with his uncle at Shipton. He soon established himself as a drawing master, giving lessons at the University of Oxford and around the county. His method was to take a watercolour through all its stages, giving it to the pupil to copy after each lesson. He often sketched the local countryside, in particular the meadows along the River Cherwell, and also anticipated artists of the Bristol School by working in the Leigh Woods in the Bristol area.

From the middle of the decade, Turner began to travel more widely, visiting Salisbury Plain, north Devon, north Wales, the Peak District and the Lakes; and then the New Forest (in the late 1820s), and the Sussex Downs, the Isle of Wight and the west coast of Scotland (in the 1830s). He never went abroad, and the Italian and Swiss scenes that he produced were worked up from sketches made by other artists.

From 1833, Turner lived at 16 John Street, near Worcester College, Oxford. In 1836, he began to exhibit watercolours that depicted the River Cherwell covered with water lilies; he continued in this attractive vein for two decades. He died in Oxford on 7 August 1862, and was buried at Shipton-on-Cherwell. Though he had married in 1824, his wife had died in 1851, and they had no children.

His studio sale was held at Christie's on 9 March 1863.

His work is represented in the Government Art Collection and numerous public collections, including the British Museum, The Courtauld Gallery, Tate and the V&A; and the Ashmolean Museum (Oxford), The Fitzwilliam Museum (Cambridge) and The Oxfordshire Museum (Woodstock).

Further reading:
Martin Hardie, 'William Turner of Oxford', *Old Water-Colour Society's Club*, 1931-32, vol 9, pp 1-23
Luke Herrmann, '"This Patient and Unassuming Master": William Turner of Oxford', *Connoisseur*, vol 162, 1966, pp 242-247
Christopher Titterington and Timothy Wilcox, *William Turner of Oxford (1789-1862)*, Woodstock: Oxfordshire County Museum, 1984
Timothy Wilcox, 'Turner, William [*known as* William Turner of Oxford] (1789-1862)', H C G Matthew and Brian Harrison (eds), *Oxford Dictionary of National Biography*, Oxford University Press, 2004, vol 55, ppp 681-682
Timothy Wilcox, 'Turner, William [Turner of Oxford] (*b* Black Bourton, Oxon, 12 Nov 1789; *d* Oxford, 7 Aug 1862)', Jane Turner (ed), *The Dictionary of Art*, London: Macmillan, 1996, vol 31, p 477

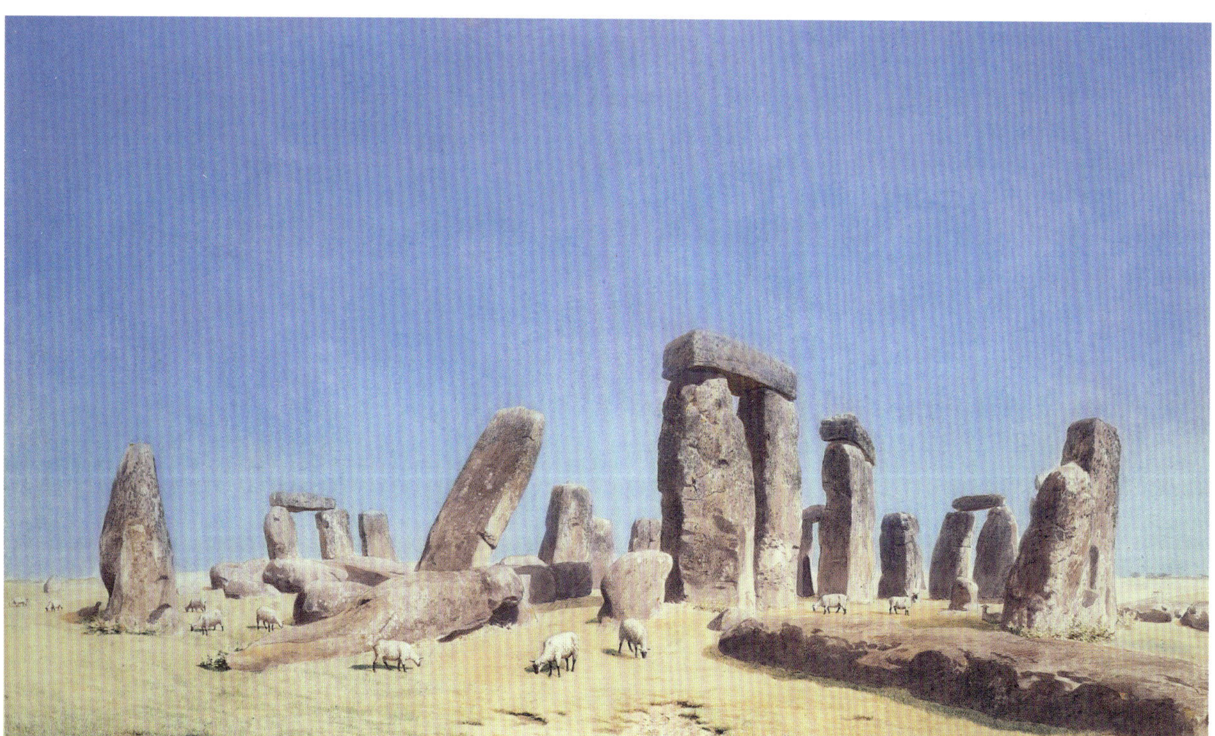

215 SHEEP GRAZING AT STONEHENGE
watercolour
19 ½ x 31 ½ inches

WILLIAM TURNER

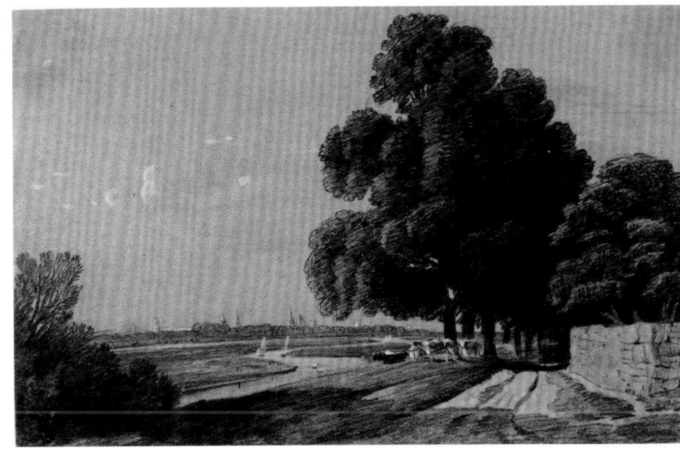

216 OXFORD FROM IFFLEY
inscribed with title on original mount
pencil and chalk on tinted paper
6 ¾ x 10 ½ inches
Exhibited: Thomas Agnew

THOMAS CHURCHYARD
Thomas Churchyard (1798-1865)

Often mistaken for those of John Constable, the Suffolk landscapes of Thomas Churchyard are as fresh and lyrical as any of the period.

Thomas Churchyard was born in Melton, Suffolk on 22 January 1798, the only child of a cattle dealer, grazier and butcher. He was educated at Queen Elizabeth's Free Grammar School in Dedham, Essex, and articled to a firm of solicitors at Halesworth, north of Woodbridge, Suffolk. By 1822, he was established as an attorney in Woodbridge, and would develop a reputation for being 'liberal and humane' (Denis Thomas, in Matthew and Harrison 2004, vol 11, p 690), though would devote most of his energy to painting.

Marrying in January 1825, Churchyard and his wife rented 29 Well Street (now called Seckford Street), Woodbridge. During the following fifteen years, they had two sons and seven daughters, most of the daughters showing a talent for art.

An early admirer and collector of paintings by members of the Norwich School, Churchyard was particularly influenced by John Crome, and made convincing copies of his works, as well as those by John Constable. In 1831, he exhibited his first landscapes at the Norfolk and Suffolk Institution, in Norwich, and was elected an honorary member. He also exhibited in London, at the Royal Academy of Arts and the Society of British Artists. As a result of this success, he decided to devote himself to painting, and settled his family at The Beeches, Melton, in 1832, so that he could try his luck in the capital. However, he failed to have any pictures accepted by the Royal Academy that year, and soon returned to his family and his legal practice. Though continuing to paint – and develop as an artist – he did not exhibit publicly again for another twenty years. And, while he made visits to Bury St Edmunds and London, his oil and watercolour sketches were almost exclusively of the fields and rivers of his native area.

Churchyard the solicitor took on Edwin Church Everitt as a partner and moved his business into part of Marston House, Cumberland Street, Woodbridge (Everitt living in the remainder). Later, they took on Daniel Charles Meadows as a further partner, and moved the business to Market Hill. However, by 1841, Churchyard was working alone again, and moved his family into Marston House.

Churchyard became a focus of local artistic and literary life. He formed a close friendship with the poets, Bernard Barton and Edward Fitzgerald, and also the son of the poet, George Crabbe. Fitzgerald described the group – initially ironically – as 'the wits of Woodbridge'. Both Churchyard and Fitzgerald were members of Ipswich Society of Professional and Amateur Artists (founded in 1832).

When Churchyard did exhibit again, in 1850, it was alongside painters of the Norwich School at the inaugural exhibition of the Suffolk Fine Arts Association, of which Churchyard was acting local secretary.

Though Churchyard was professionally and financially successful, he spent much money on building up his art collection, as well as supporting his large family. Expectations of a large inheritance from his uncle, Isaac Churchyard of Byng Hall, came to nothing; for, when Isaac died in 1858, he did so intestate and in debt. Becoming concerned about the future of his daughters, Churchyard divided his own works between them so that they could not be considered part of his estate (see inscription to reverse of **219**). When he died, of heart failure, on 19 August 1865, he too was insolvent, but he left behind him a great collection of pictures (including examples by Constable, John Sell Cotman, Crome, Gainsborough and Wilson).

His work is represented in numerous public collections, including the British Museum, Tate and the V&A; and the Ashmolean Museum (Oxford), Ipswich Museums Service and Woodbridge Museum.

Further reading:

Hugh Belsey, *Thomas Churchyard, 1798-1865: from the collection of Ipswich Borough Council Museums and Galleries*, Ipswich: Wolsey Art Gallery, 1998
Robert Blake, *The Search for Thomas Churchyard, 1798-1865*, Brightlingsea, 1997 (privately printed)
Denis Thomas, 'Churchyard, Thomas (1798-1865)', H C G Matthew and Brian Harrison (eds), *Oxford Dictionary of National Biography*, Oxford University Press, 2004, vol 11, pp 690-691
Denis Thomas, *Thomas Churchyard of Woodbridge*, Chislehurst: Quadrangle Books, 1966

THOMAS CHURCHYARD

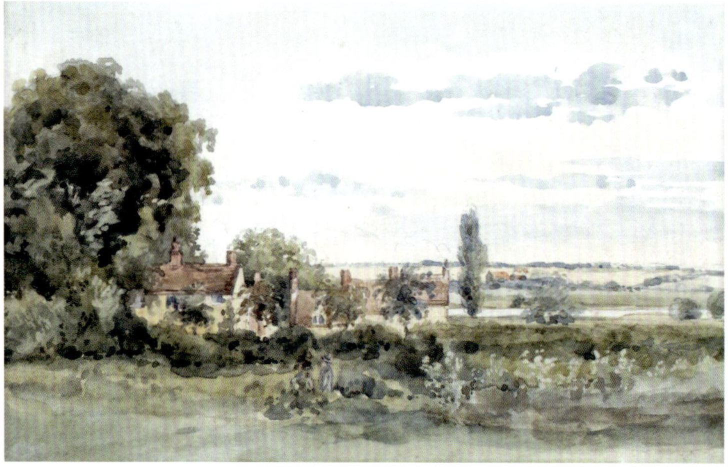

217 A WOODBRIDGE WALK
watercolour
5 ¾ x 9 inches

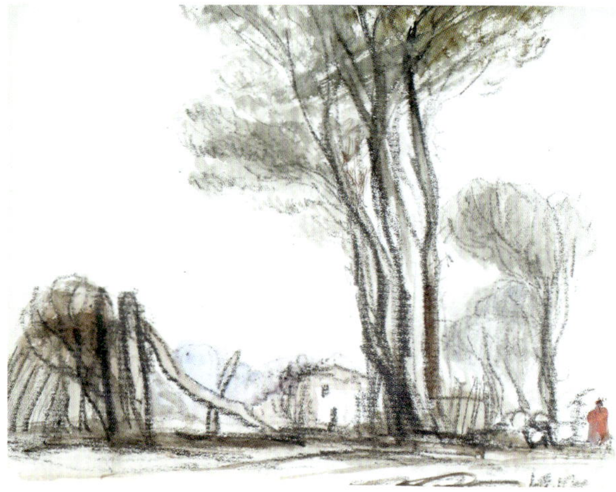

218 THE HOUSE BEYOND THE TREES
charcoal and watercolour
6 ¾ x 9 ½ inches

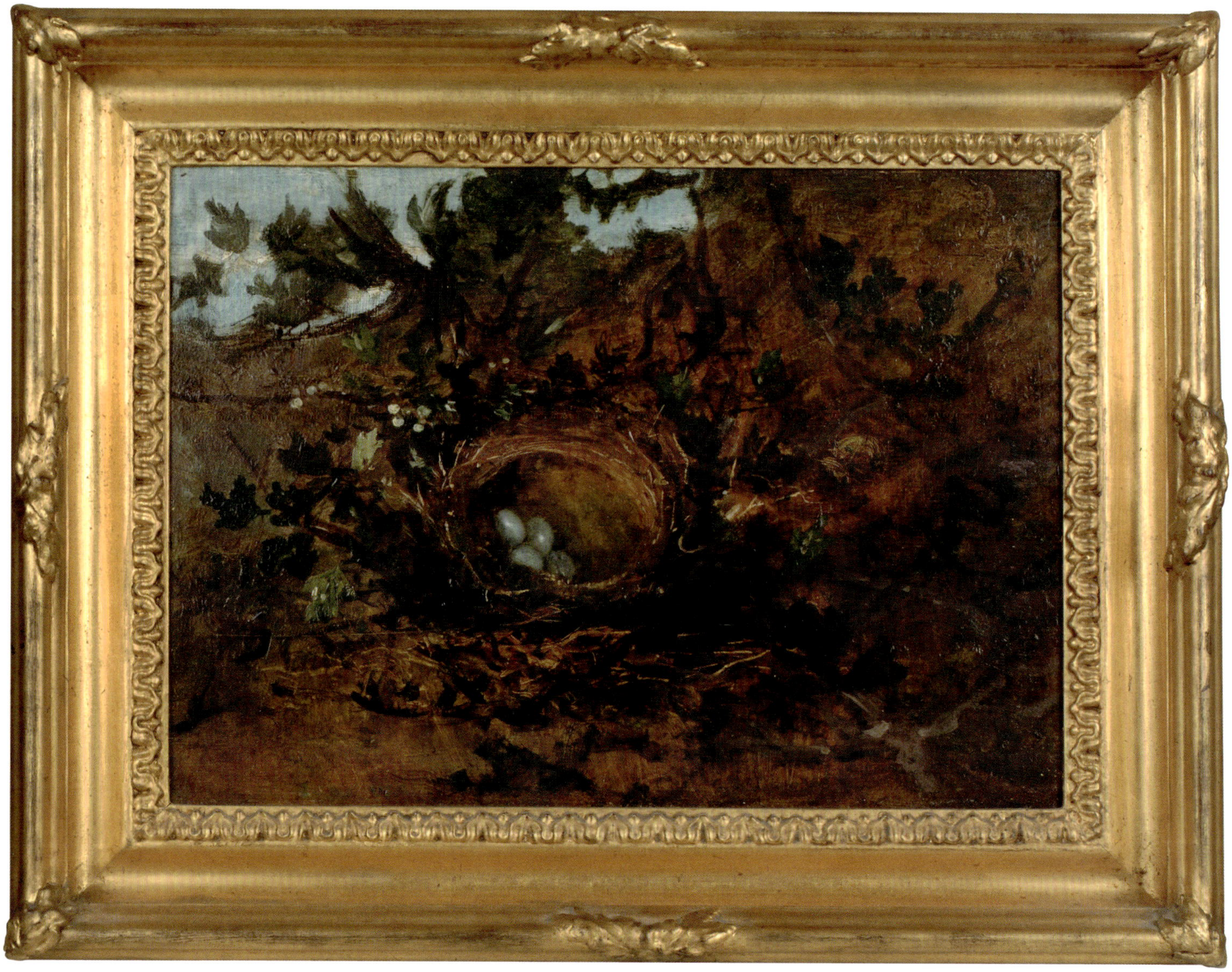

219 A BIRD'S NEST
signed and inscribed with title and 'No 8, Emma Churchyard' on label on reverse
oil on board
10 x 13 ¾ inches

JAMES BAKER PYNE

James Baker Pyne, VPSBA (1800-1870)

Though he seems to have taught himself to paint, James Baker Pyne developed into a significant landscape painter, first as a member of the Bristol School, and then as a spirited follower of J M W Turner.

James Baker Pyne was born in Bristol on 5 December 1800. In accordance with his parents' wishes, he was articled to an attorney, but abandoned law at the age of twenty-one to pursue his interest in art. Apparently self-taught, he absorbed the influence of other Bristol painters, especially Francis Danby, whose characteristic dark, poetic tones reappear in Pyne's early landscapes of the local area.

Pyne's artistic development was supported by an increasing local interest in the visual arts. The Bristol Institution for the Promotion of Literature, Science and the Fine Arts, in Park Street, was founded in 1823, and held inaugural exhibitions of Old Masters and contemporary artists in 1824. The contemporary exhibition – called in some sources the 'Bristol Gallery of Arts' – was organised by a number of leading artists, including Edward Villiers Rippingille and Samuel Jackson, the latter taking responsibility for its hanging. A landmark in the establishment of a Bristol School of Artists, it also provided Pyne with his first opportunity to show his work in public.

By the late 1820s, Pyne was living at 6 Dove Street, Kingsdown, near the centre of Bristol, and supplementing his income by working as a drawing master and, possibly, a picture restorer. In 1827, William James Müller became his apprentice, and had lessons in oil and watercolour, though amicably cancelled his indentures after two years (and never took another teacher). At some point, Müller's friend, George Arthur Fripp, also took lessons in oils from Pyne.

Though 'he enjoyed little of the social life of Bristol's other artists' (Greenacre, in Matthew and Harrison 2004, vol 45, p 643), Pyne briefly shared a studio with Samuel Jackson in 1829, and three years later spent six weeks in France with E V Rippingille.

In 1831, when he first exhibited in Liverpool, Pyne was living at 11 Wellington Place, Stapleton Road, Bristol. Two years later, he gave his address as 33 New Church Street, Edgware Road, Paddington, London, and exhibited for the first time at both the British Institution (until 1844) and the Society of British Artists. Between 1836 and 1841, he also exhibited seven works at the Royal Academy of Arts. During this period, he moved fairly frequently, living at 89 Milton Street, Dorset Square (1836) and 6 Earl's Court Terrace, Old Brompton (1840), before settling at York Cottage, North End, Walham Green, Fulham, in 1841. This probably coincided with his marriage.

From the 1830s, Pyne's works showed the influence of J M W TURNER, through their use of dramatic effects and increasingly restricted palette, often dominated by pale yellow. The artist passed this influence onto his pupil, James Astbury Hammersley, who would have an important role in the artistic life of Manchester. From 1840, Pyne followed Turner in producing the first of a series of volumes of lithographed illustrations, *Windsor and its Surrounding Scenery*.

In 1842, Pyne was elected a member of the Society of British Artists, and soon showed exclusively at its gallery in Suffolk Street, off Pall Mall East (206 pictures in all). For some years, he also acted as its Vice-President. Occasionally, he collaborated with other artists, notably William Shayer SBA, who added figures to his landscapes, and Thomas Sidney Cooper RA, who added animals.

In 1846, Pyne travelled through Germany and Switzerland to Italy, in order to gather material to work up into finished pictures. The initial results appeared at the Suffolk Street Galleries in the following year: two views of the Rhine and three of the Italian Lakes. It is perhaps these pictures that prompted the Manchester art dealer, William Agnew, to commission Pyne to paint the English Lake District, between 1848 and 1851, and then to revisit Italy, between 1851 and 1854 (partly in the company of the watercolourist, William Evans of Bristol). His paintings of the Lake District resulted in an exhibition in 1852, and two volumes of lithographs: *The English Lake District* (1853, published by Agnew, lithographed by W Gauci) and *Lake Scenery of England* (1859, published by Day & Son, lithographed by Thomas Picken). He also contributed frequently to the *Art Journal* between 1856 and 1870. Several of his Continental subjects were included in the Manchester Art Treasures Exhibition in 1857.

By 1855, Pyne had moved from Fulham to Camden Town, living first at 43 Camden Villas and, by 1863, at 203 Camden Road. He died at this last address on 29 July 1870. His sons, James Baker Pyne, a photographer, and Charles Pyne, an artist, survived him.

His studio sale took place at Christie's on 25 February 1871.

His work is represented in numerous public collections, including the British Museum and the V&A; Manchester Art Gallery and Wolverhampton Art Gallery; and Indianapolis Museum of Art.

The V&A also holds his Picture Memoranda, two manuscript volumes recording the oil paintings that he produced between 1840 and 1868.

Further reading:

David Cordingly, 'Pyne, James Baker (*b* Bristol, 5 Dec 1800; *d* London, 29 July 1870)', Jane Turner (ed), *The Dictionary of Art*, London: Macmillan, 1996, vol 25, p 759

Francis Greenacre, 'Pyne, James Baker (1800-1870)', H C G Matthew and Brian Harrison (eds), *Oxford Dictionary of National Biography*, Oxford University Press, 2004, vol 45, p 643

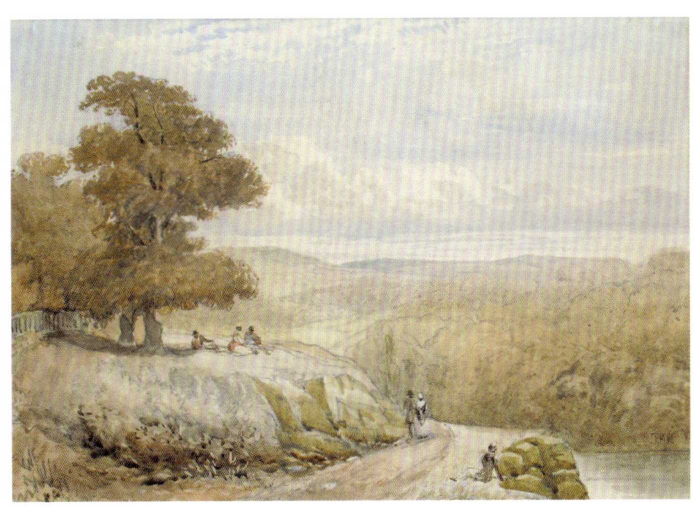

220 VIEW NEAR CLIFTON
signed
inscribed with title and dated 'September 27. 1844' on reverse
9 ½ x 13 ½ inches

GEORGE PYNE
George Pyne, AOWS (1800-1884)

Though overshadowed in his early career, by the artistic achievements of his father and father-in-law, George Pyne came into his own as a precise, and sometimes intense, architectural draughtsman.

George Pyne was influenced by his father WILLIAM HENRY PYNE, and his father-in-law JOHN VARLEY, both founder members of the Society of Painters in Water Colours. He exhibited landscapes, particularly of Kent, at the Society of British Artists and the Society of Painters in Water Colours, becoming an associate member of the latter in 1827. He gradually widened the range of his subject matter, by contributing with his father and his younger brother, Charles Claude Pyne, to *Lancashire Illustrated* (1831), and by living and working in Tavistock, Devon (1837-39). His relationship with the Varleys ended in 1842, when his wife obtained a divorce, and a year later he resigned from the Society of Painters in Water Colours.

From the later 1840s, Pyne worked increasingly as an architectural draughtsman, specialising in depictions of the colleges of Oxford and Cambridge, and also Eton, and publishing related drawing manuals: *A Rudimentary and Practical Treatise on Perspective for Beginners* (1848) and *Practical Rules on Drawing for the Operative Builder, and Young Student in Architecture* (1854).

His work is represented in the collections of the V&A.

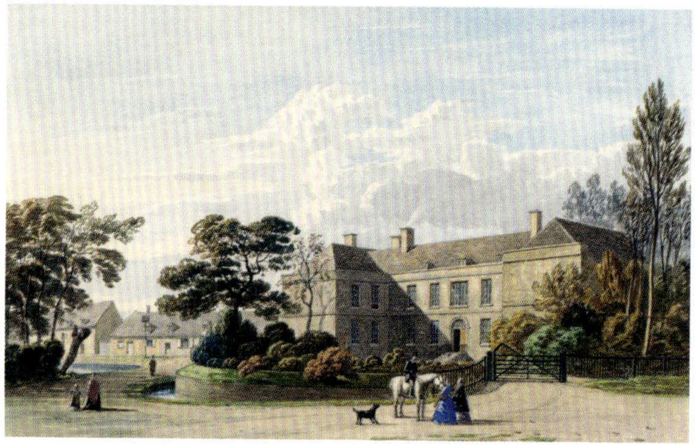

221 HILTON HOUSE
watercolour
9 x 13 inches

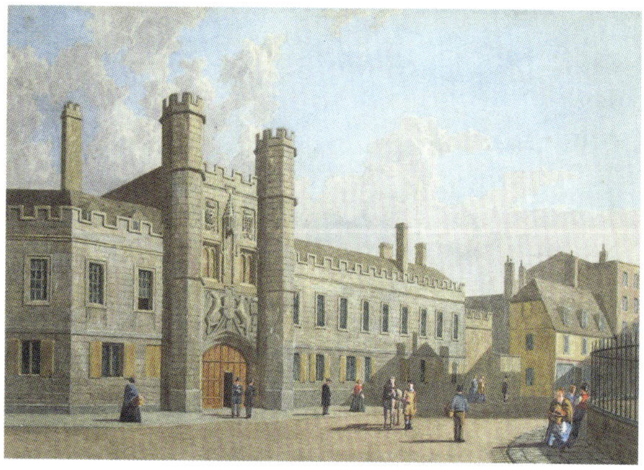

222 CHRIST'S COLLEGE, CAMBRIDGE
watercolour
8 x 11 inches

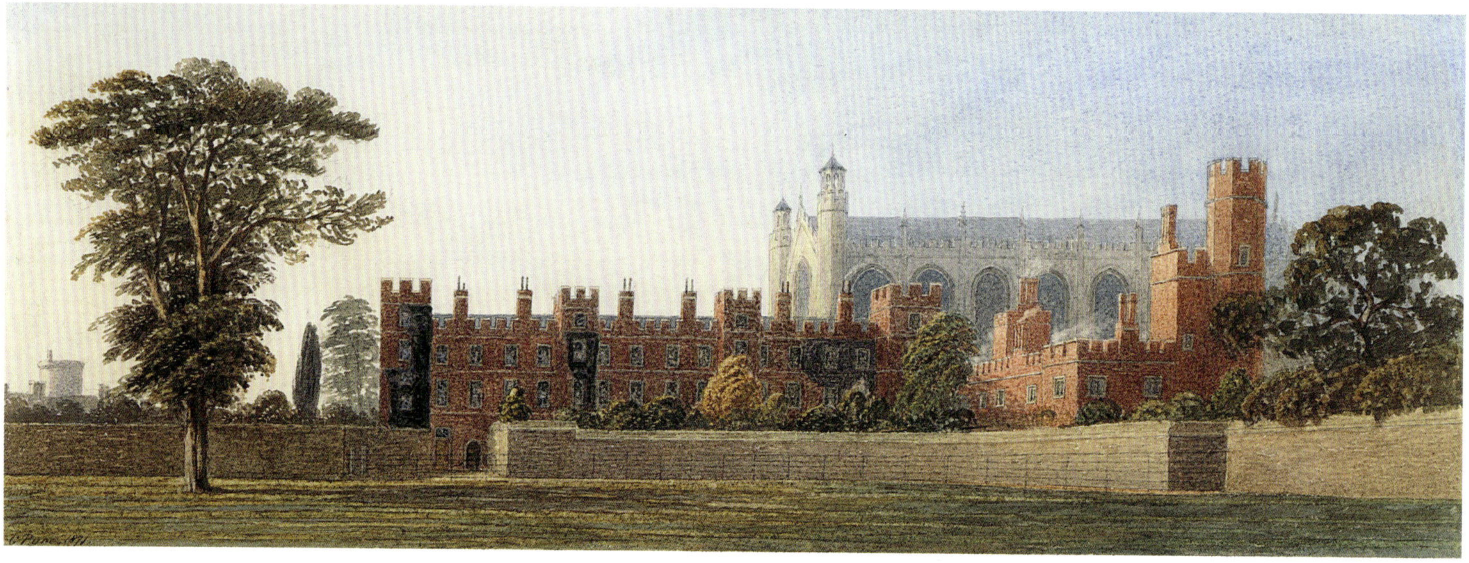

223 ETON COLLEGE
signed and dated 1871
watercolour
7 ½ x 20 inches

Eton College
Eton College, Buckinghamshire, was founded by Henry VI in 1440. The institution was originally modelled on Winchester, founded in 1387, as a charity school for seventy less privileged boys. A fine grey-stone chapel in the Perpendicular style was constructed between 1449-1483, giving an air of grandeur to the surrounding red brick buildings. The upper school was added in 1694, when the school first became fashionable for sons of the nobility. Further expansion occurred as both the fame of the school and its population grew.

When Pyne painted his view of Eton, in 1871, the Head Master was the highly influential James John Hornby. He increased the number of pupils to 894, doubled the number of school rooms and reformed the curriculum. Famous Old Etonians of the 1870s include A C Benson (writer and Master of Magdalen College, Cambridge) and M R James (Director of The Fitzwilliam Museum, Cambridge; Vice-Chancellor of Cambridge University; Provost of Eton; and writer of spine-tingling ghost stories).

HENRY BARLOW CARTER
Henry Barlow Carter (1804-1868)

Inspired by the seascapes of J M W Turner, Henry Barlow Carter specialised in bracing coastal scenes, especially of Yorkshire. His watercolours – and the prints made from them – made ideal souvenirs for the discerning tourist to the resort of Scarborough.

Henry Barlow Carter was born in Bermondsey, south London, and probably named after an uncle, Henry Barlow, who lived close to the west, in Church Yard Row, Newington Butts. Barlow 'had served in the British East India Company and had been involved in action in the China seas with the French navy' (Gordon Bell, 'Chester and the Art of Watercolour', *The Collegian*, 2005, p 26). However, there is no record that Henry Barlow Carter followed in his uncle's footsteps and served in the navy, as has long been believed.

Two watercolours in the British Museum dated 1824, of the breakwaters of Plymouth Dock, provide the starting point for tracing Carter's artistic development, which was influenced by the example of J M W TURNER (and also Peter DeWint, whose work he collected). While living in Plymouth, he exhibited at the Royal Academy of Arts (1827-30), and would also show at the British Institution and the Society of British Artists.

By 1830, Carter had moved to Kingston upon Hull, in Yorkshire, to work as a drawing master. Making contact with relatives in County Durham, he fell in love with his cousin Eliza. They married at St Mary's Parish Church, Scarborough, Yorkshire, in July 1830, and settled in the developing coastal resort, Carter establishing himself as a drawing master. They lived at increasingly better addresses: Auborough Street, Queen Street and then, from 1845, 16 York Place.

Carter continued to paint in Hull through the 1830s. The Carters' first son, Henry Vandyke Carter, was born there in 1831 and, though christened and raised in Scarborough, would be educated at Hull Grammar School.

Both Henry Vandyke and his brother, Joseph Newington, received lessons from their father. While J N Carter developed as a painter, H V Carter studied medicine, and produced the illustrations for the first edition of *Gray's Anatomy* (1858), before becoming a pioneer in tropical epidemiology.

Henry Barlow Carter worked closely with Solomon Wilkinson Theakston, the Scarborough bookseller, stationer and printer, who was based in Long Room Street during the 1830s, and later in St Nicholas Street. In 1840, Theakston produced his first *Guide to Scarborough*, with twenty-two illustrations, drawn by Carter and wood-engraved by Stephen Sly, a publication that would be expanded over the years. Theakston also published souvenir images by Carter as *Sixteen Views of Scarborough* (wood-engraved by Sly) and *Four Views of Scarborough* (lithographed by Day & Haghe). The enterprising Mr Theakston would go on to set up a circulating library, a news room and an art gallery and, in 1845, found the *Scarborough Gazette*.

Carter's circle of friends also included the miniaturist, Edward Westoby, who lived in Scarborough during the 1840s and 1850s.

Five years after the death of his wife in 1857, Carter left Scarborough and moved – via Bath – to Torquay. His known addresses there were Geneva Cottages (1862) and Scarborough Lodge (1863). He died in Torquay of bronchitis in 1868.

His work is represented in numerous public collections, including the British Museum and the V&A; and Hull Maritime Museum and Scarborough Art Gallery.

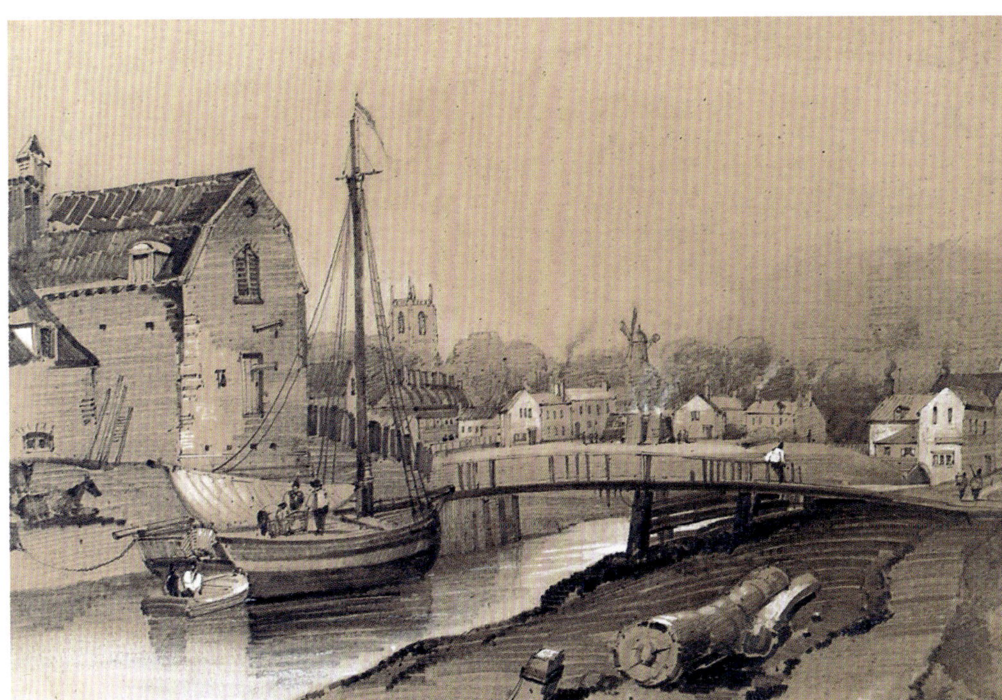

224 BARTON-ON-HUMBER
signed
pencil and bodycolour on tinted paper
10 ¼ x 14 ¼ inches

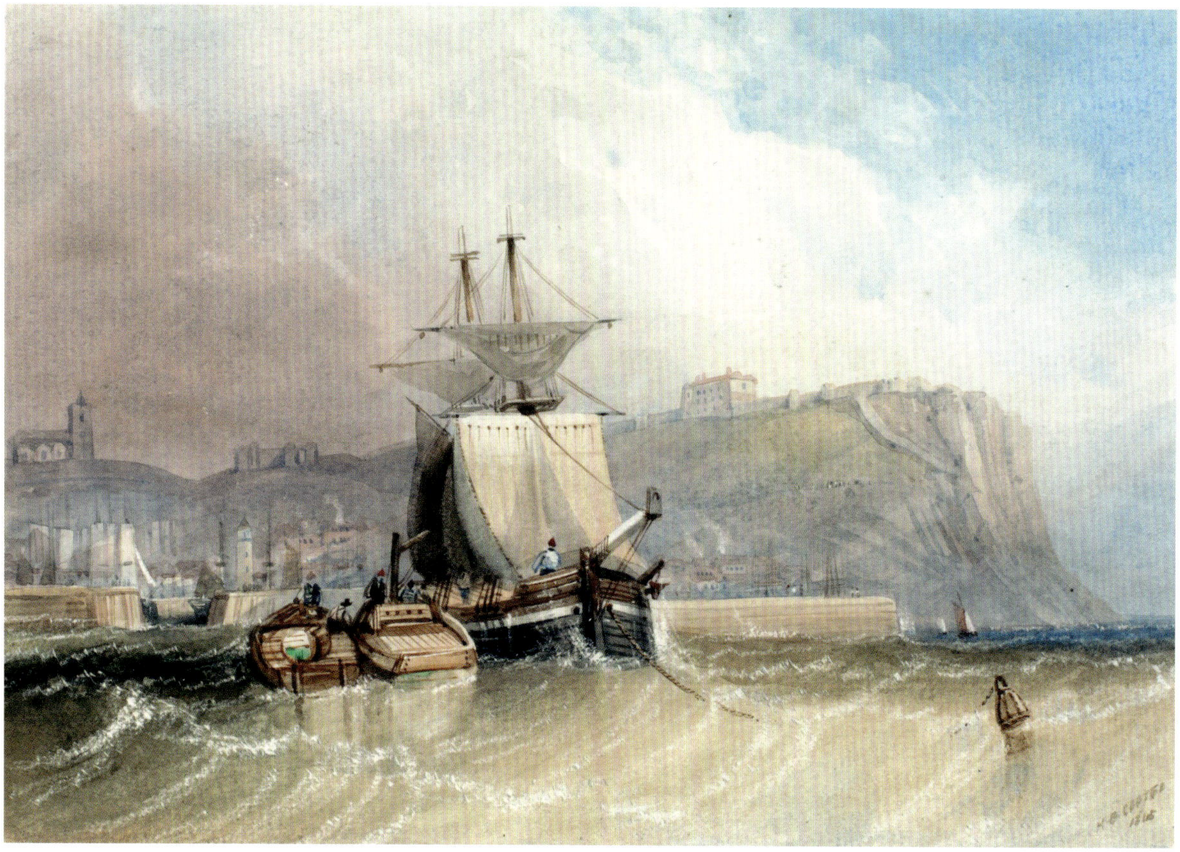

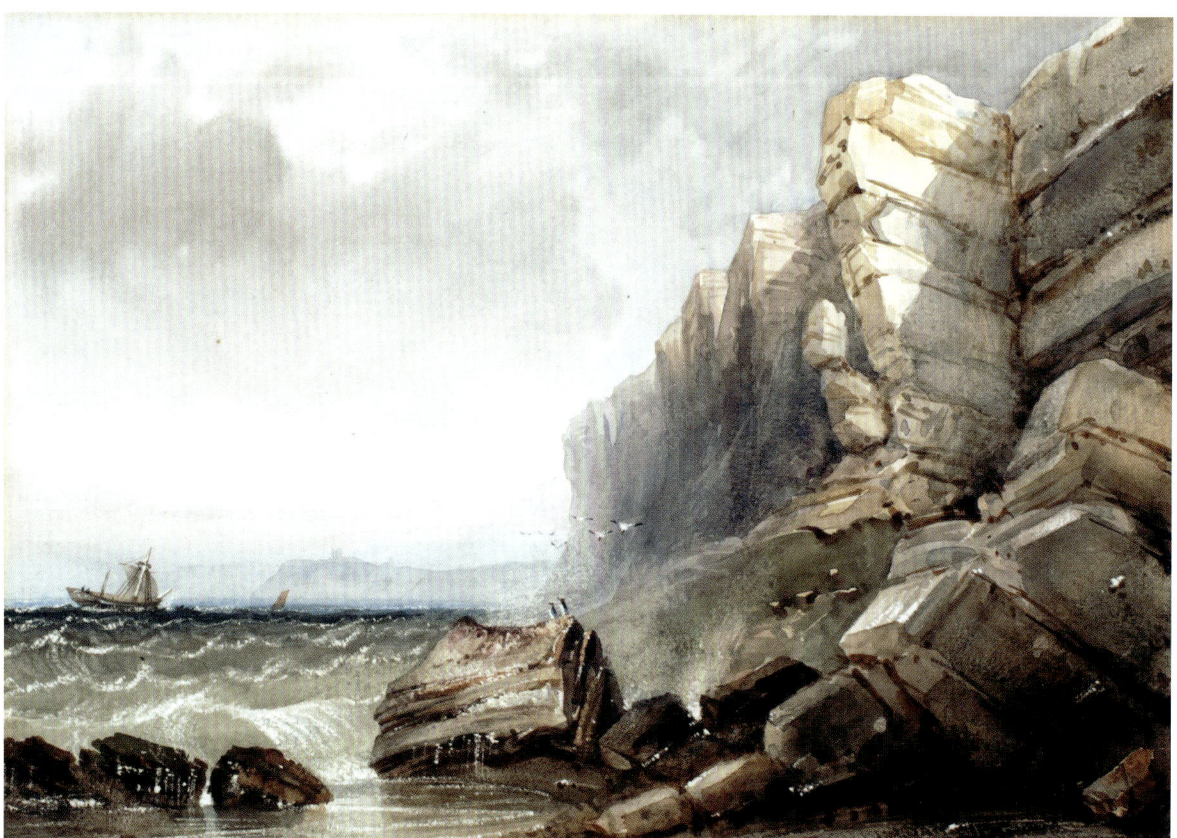

225 OFF SCARBOROUGH
signed and dated 1845
watercolour with bodycolour
6 ¾ x 9 ½ inches

226 NORTH VIEW SCARBOROUGH
watercolour
6 ¾ x 9 ½ inches

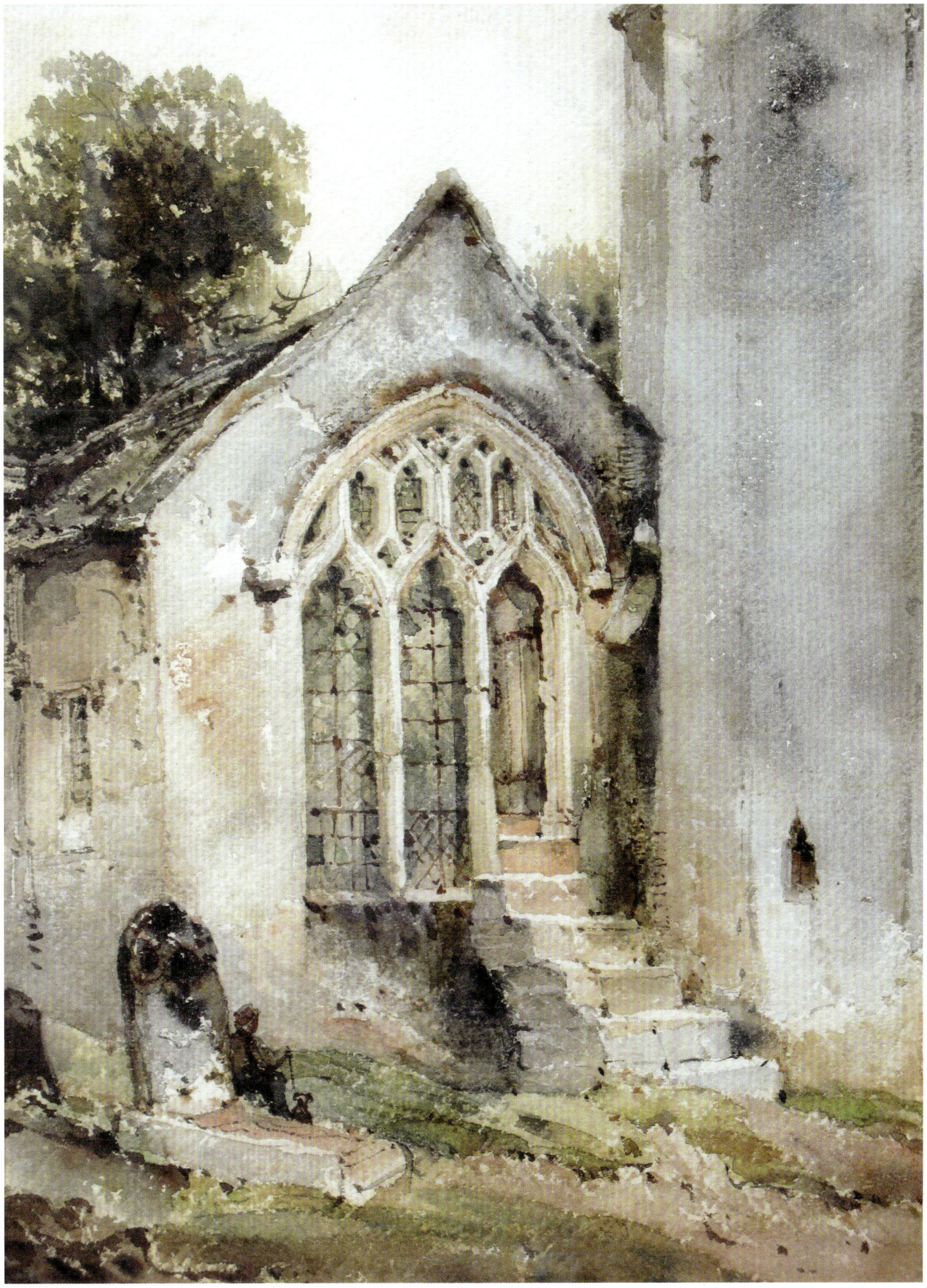

227 KINGSKERSWELL CHURCH
inscribed with title and 'Sketch from nature by H B Carter 1857' by a contemporary hand on reverse
watercolour
14 ½ x 10 ½ inches
in a frame by John Limb of Scarborough
Exhibited: 'Peter De Wint. 1784-1849. A Bicentenary Exhibition', Stoke-on Trent City Museum and Art Gallery, November 1984–January 1985, no 97

JOSEPH MURRAY INCE
Joseph Murray Ince (1806-1859), christened Josef-Marie Ince

A pupil of David Cox during his time in Hereford, Joseph Murray Ince became a painter in oil and watercolour and produced native landscapes and coastal scenes, as well as views of towns both British and Continental. Though Ince was long considered to be of Welsh birth, recent researches confirm that both his birth and his outlook were more cosmopolitan.

Joseph Murray Ince was born in London in April 1806 and christened Josef-Marie Ince. His father was Dr Henry Robert Ince, who came from a family of skilled craftsmen, though he trained as a doctor and worked as a military surgeon; while his mother was Anne-Elisabeth, daughter of Comte le Jeune, an émigré from Revolutionary Paris. At the time of his birth, the family was living at Upper Grafton Street.

Soon after Ince was born, his father was invited by an old friend to set up as a general practitioner in Presteign, Radnorshire, Wales. The family rented Roseland, Broad Street, and Ince attended John Beddoes Free Grammar School. During his childhood, he befriended John Scarlett Davis of Leominster who, like him, shared his passions for fishing and painting and would develop as an artist.

Ince studied under DAVID COX in Hereford from December 1823 until early 1826 – and his watercolours of the 1830s and 1840s show his teacher's influence.

In 1826, Ince moved to London and lived at 31 King's Street, off the Edgware Road, possibly lodging with his uncle, Charles Ince, a former cabinet-maker. Almost immediately, he became an occasional exhibitor at the Royal Academy of Arts (1826-47) and the British Institution, and a frequent exhibitor at the Society of British Artists (showing 138 works in its Suffolk Street galleries between 1826 and 1858). Early exhibits included south-coast seascapes (from 1828) and views of Stockholm (from 1829), as well as scenes of Herefordshire and Radnorshire, suggesting that he had opportunities to travel.

Ince decided to build on some good sales and a developing reputation by publishing a set of seven lithographs, which appeared in 1832 as *Views Illustrating the County of Radnor*. The original paintings on which these were based appeared among his exhibits at the Society of British Artists in 1833.

On 12 June 1834, Ince married Sarah Phillips (the daughter of a Presteign painter and decorator) at St Mary's Church, Marylebone, the parish in which he was residing. They celebrated their marriage with a honeymoon-cum-sketching trip that seems to have taken in Devon, Bristol, Oxford and Cambridge, as well as a visit home to Presteign. When Sarah became pregnant in the autumn, they travelled back to Presteign but, unfortunately, both she and their premature son died the following summer.

From that time, and for more than a decade, Ince shared his time between London and Presteign, while travelling widely. His London addresses were 48 George Street, near Portman Square – until 1841 – and then 9 George Street. He visited Oxford (1836), Wales (1839-40), possibly Holland and Germany (1839-40) and certainly Cambridge (1842-43). *The Cambridge Portfolio*, edited by the Reverend J J Smith, and published in parts between 1838 and 1840, included illustrations by Ince, probably based on drawings he had made during his first visit to the town.

On the death of his father in 1849, Ince became executor of his estate, and organised the sale of the contents of Roseland (including a number of significant paintings by John Crome and other artists). He also became legal guardian of his young half-brother, Edward Ince Young.

On leaving Presteign, Ince seems to have travelled in Italy and Spain (again suggested by exhibited paintings). He then took up residence at 12 King's Parade, Cambridge, while retaining an address in London. He would die at his London home on 24 September 1859.

His work is represented in numerous public collections including the British Museum and the V&A; and The Fitzwilliam Museum (Cambridge).

Further reading:

L H Cust, rev Patricia Morales, 'Ince, Joseph Murray (1806–1859)', H C G Matthew and Brian Harrison (eds), *Oxford Dictionary of National Biography*, Oxford University Press, 2004, vol 29, p 220

Margaret Newman Turner, *Joseph Murray Ince 1806-1859. The Painter of Presteigne*, Little Logaston: Logaston Press, 2006

Scott Wilcox, 'Ince, Joseph Murray (*b* Presteign, Powys, 1806; *d* London, 24 Sept 1859)', Jane Turner (ed), *The Dictionary of Art*, London: Macmillan, 1996, vol 15, p 164

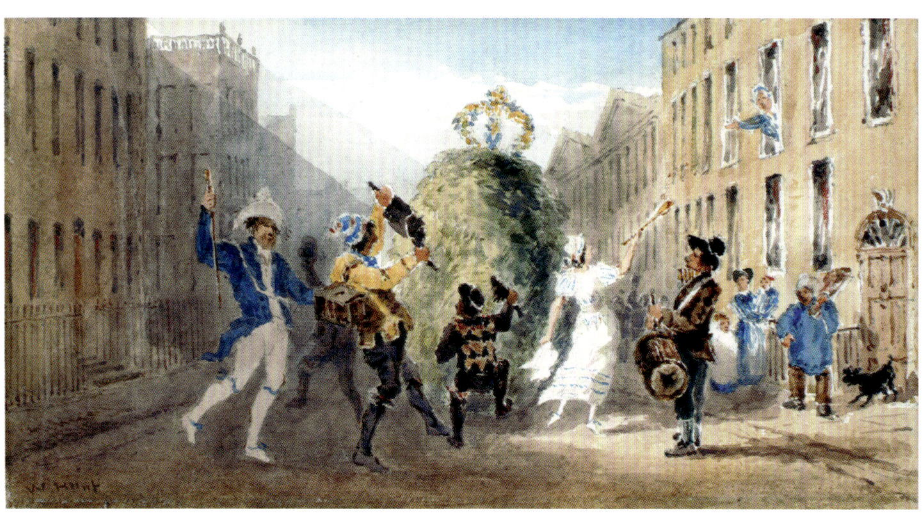

228 MAY DAY
watercolour with pencil
4 x 8 inches
Joseph Murray Ince reversed this composition for *Jack in the Green*, a watercolour of circa 1850, now in the collection of Hereford Museum.

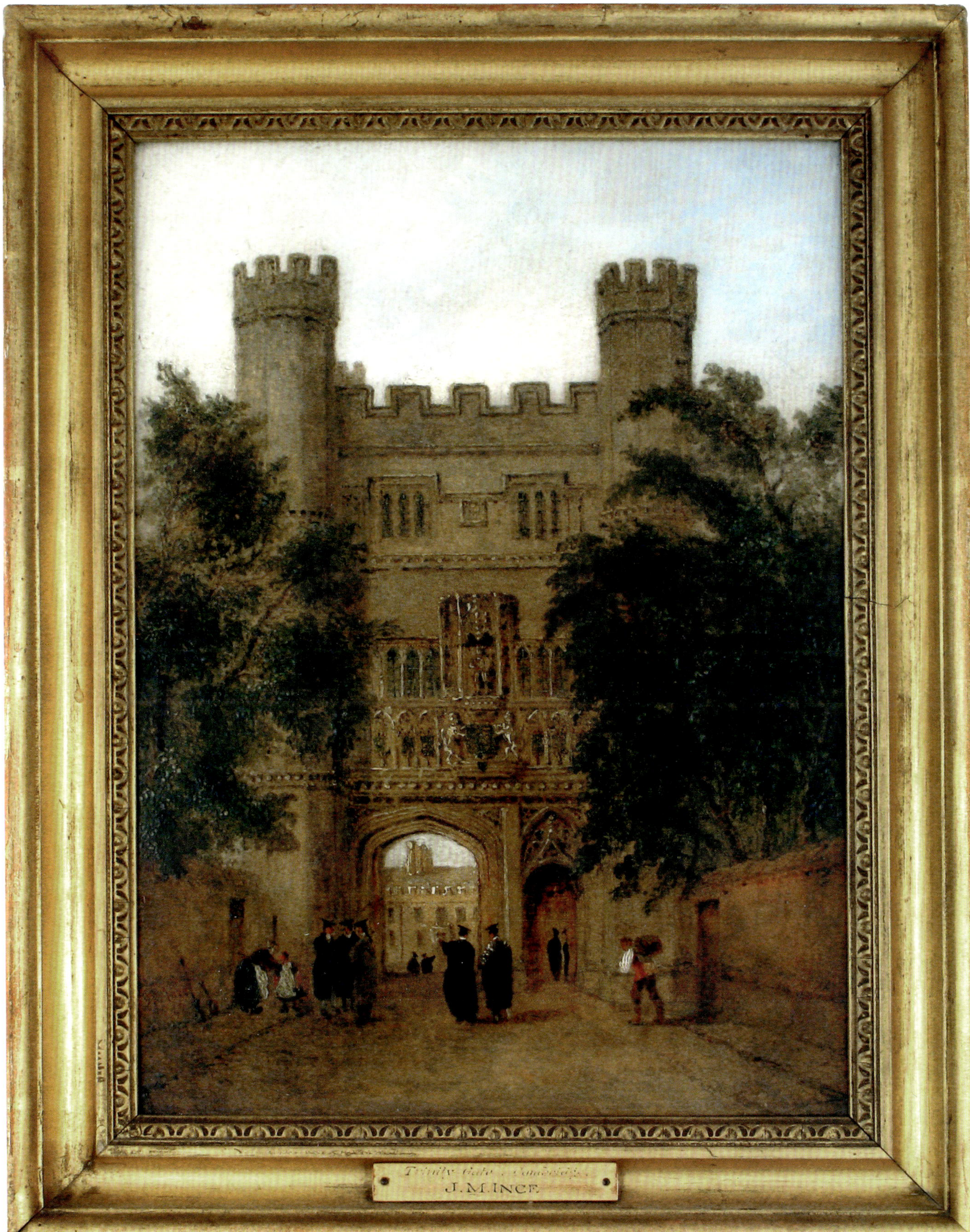

229 TRINITY GATE, CAMBRIDGE
signed and dated 1847
oil on board
14 x 10 ¼ inches

6: AN URBAN TOPOGRAPHER

THOMAS HOSMER SHEPHERD
Thomas Hosmer Shepherd (1793-1864)

Thomas Hosmer Shepherd was probably the most talented member of a family of London topographers, his once famous images outstanding in their vivacious detail.

Thomas Hosmer Shepherd was born in France on 16 January 1793, the son of a watchcase maker. On returning to England, the Shepherd family settled in a neighbourhood close to the City Road, and Thomas was baptised at St Luke Old Street, on 24 February.

Throughout his career, from 1809 to 1859, Shepherd was patronised by the celebrated interior designer, Frederick Crace, who became equally famous as a collector of views and maps of London. Crace commissioned him to produce watercolours of specific London buildings and locations, and also bought others from him. The fame of the Crace Collection then acted as a springboard for Shepherd's career, as he began to receive commissions from others, including Rudolph Ackermann. From around the time of its foundation in 1809, until its demise in 1828, Shepherd produced a series of street views for Ackermann's magazine, *The Repository of Arts*, sometimes in collaboration with his elder brother, GEORGE SIDNEY SHEPHERD.

Though he became virtually synonymous with the modern city, Shepherd was equally skilful in representing the countryside. To this end, he made a number of sketching tours, the first in 1810.

Eight years later, Shepherd visited France, probably on his honeymoon, an event apparently commemorated in the naming of the first of his seven children, Frederick Napoleon Shepherd, who was born in June 1819. By 1820, the family had settled at 26 Chapman Street (now Batchelor Street), Islington, one of the new streets on the west side of the Liverpool Road, on the edge of the built up area of the city. He used his home address when advertising as a drawing master.

From this time, Shepherd established himself as a book illustrator, with contributions to the part work, *Londina Illustrata* (1819-25), again in collaboration with his brother, George, among others. Security and success soon arrived, with his first commission from the publisher, Jones & Co, based at the Temple of the Muses, Finsbury Square. The first part of *Metropolitan Improvements* appeared in 1827, and comprised numerous steel engravings after drawings by Shepherd, with a commentary by the architect, James Elmes. Its popularity not only ensured further commissions for Shepherd from Jones but 'induced many publishers to embark on similar works' (an unsigned review in the *Gentleman's Magazine* for March 1829, cited by J F C Phillips, *Shepherd's London*, London: Cassell 1976, p 11).

The sequel to *Metropolitan Improvements*, entitled *London and its Environs*, would begin to appear in 1828.

During 1827, Shepherd made sketching tours of the West Country and Scotland in order to prepare his drawings for *Modern Athens!* (1829) and *Bath and Bristol* (1829-31), published by Jones with commentaries by the well-known antiquarian, John Britton. Yet, while Jones and Shepherd planned other volumes about parts of Great Britain (and Shepherd responded by travelling to Ireland in 1828), no further such publication materialised.

Shepherd began to work with other publishers, often reworking images of London that he had drawn for Jones, while also broadening his horizons. So he exhibited four watercolours of Scotland at the Society of British Artists, in 1831 and 1832, and produced illustrations of Westmorland and the Rhine, by 1832 (though not necessarily on location).

A decade later, Shepherd moved to 2 Bird's Buildings (now part of Colebrooke Row), north of Camden Passage, Islington – probably to better accommodate his growing family. From that time, he provided some images for the *Illustrated London News*, but became very poor, and was sustained only by the continuing patronage of Crace, who died in 1859.

Shepherd himself died in Islington on 4 July 1864. His wife and at least three of his children survived him, including Frederick Napoleon Shepherd, who carried on the family tradition of topography, and Valentine Claude Shepherd, a wood engraver.

The Crace Collection in the British Museum contains nearly 500 images by Shepherd, including thirty-eight views of Edinburgh for *Modern Athens!*

His work is also represented in numerous other public collections, including Kensington & Chelsea Library and the V&A.

Further reading:

Brian Reginald Curle and Patricia Meara, *Thomas Hosmer Shepherd, 1793-1864: a descriptive catalogue of watercolours and drawings in the local collections of Kensington and Chelsea libraries*, London: Kensington and Chelsea Public Libraries, 1973
Lucy Peltz, 'Thomas Hosmer Shepherd (1784-1862)', H C G Matthew and Brian Harrison (eds), *Oxford Dictionary of National Biography*, Oxford University Press, 2004, vol 50, p 245
J F C Phillips, *Shepherd's London*, London: Cassell, 1976

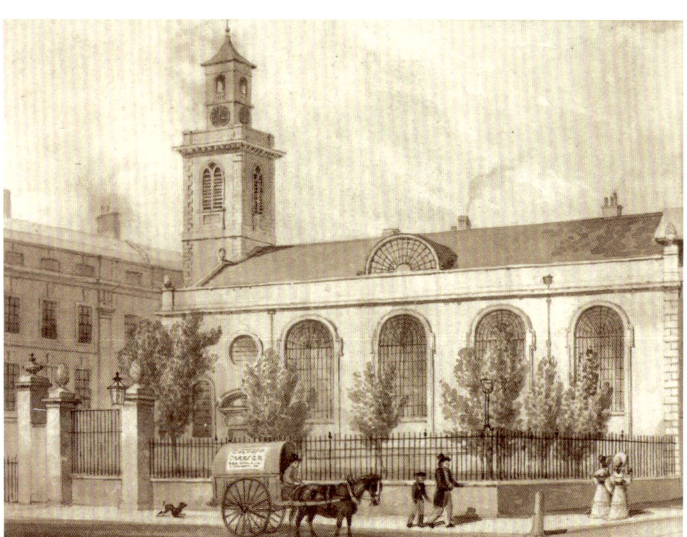

230 ST MARY'S, ALDERMANBURY
signed and inscribed indistinctly with a poem on reverse
monochrome watercolour with pencil
4 ½ x 5 ¾ inches

A Preliminary List of Books Illustrated by Thomas Hosmer Shepherd

1819-25
William Herbert, *Londina Illustrata. Graphic and Historical Memorials of Monasteries, Churches, Chapels, Schools, Charitable Foundations, Palaces, Halls, Courts, Processions, places of Early Amusement and Modern and present Theatres in the Cities and Suburbs of London & Westminster*, London: Robert Wilkinson (36 nos) (illustrated in collaboration with George Samuel, Jacob Schnebbelie, George Sidney Shepherd, C J M Whichelo and others)

1821
Count Lorenzo Magalotti, *Travels of Cosmo the Third, Grand Duke of Tuscany, through England during the reign of King Charles II (1669). Translated from the Italian Manuscript … to which is prefixed a memoir of his life … With … views of the Metropolis*, etc, London: J Mawman

1823
John Hassell, *Excursions of Pleasure and Sports on the Thames, Illustrated in a Series of Engravings in Aqua-tinta, Coloured after Nature, Accompanied by a descriptive and historical account of Every Town, Villa, Mansion, and the Adjacent Country on the Banks of that River…*, London: W Simpkin and R Marshall (12 parts)

1827-31
James Elmes, *Metropolitan Improvements; or, London in the Nineteenth Century: Being a Series of Views of the New and Most Interesting Objects in the British Metropolis & its Vicinity; from original drawings, with historical, topographical & critical illustrations*, London: Jones & Co (41 parts) (steel engravings)

1828-31
[James Elmes], *London and its Environs in the Nineteenth Century: with historical, topographical and critical notices. illustrated by a series of views from original drawings by Thomas H Shepherd. With historical, topographical and critical notices*, London: Jones & Co (2 vols)

1829
John Britton, *Modern Athens! displayed in a series of views; or, Edinburgh in the nineteenth century; exhibiting the whole of the new buildings, modern improvements, antiquities, & picturesque scenery, of the Scottish metropolis & its environs, from original drawings by Mr Thomas H Shepherd*, London: Jones & Co

1829-31
John Britton, *Bath and Bristol, with the Counties of Somerset and Gloucester, displayed in a series of views; including the modern improvements, picturesque scenery, antiquities, etc. From original drawings by Thos H Shepherd; with historical and descriptive illustrations*, London: Jones & Co

1831
Christian Isobel Johnstone, *The Public Buildings of the City of London Described* (The Little Library), London: John Harris (12 engravings, engraved by James Sands)

1832
William Gray Fearnside (ed), *Tombleson's Views of the Rhine*, London: W Tombleson & Co (3 vols) (steel engravings)

1832-34
Charles Frederick Partington (ed), *National history and views of London and its environs: embracing their antiquities, modern improvements, &c &c from original drawings by eminent artists*, London: Alan Bell & Co, Simpkin and Marshall (2 vols)

1832-35
Thomas Rose, *Westmorland, Cumberland, Durham and Northumberland*, London: Fisher, Son & Co (3 vols) (illustrated in collaboration with Thomas Allom, G Pickering and others)

1834
William Gray Fearnside, *Tombleson's Thames*, London: Tombleson

1838
William Gray Fearnside and Thomas Harral (eds), *The History of London. Illustrated by views in London and Westminster engraved by John Woods*, London: Orr & Co, Simpkin Marshall & Co, Ackermann & Co, J Woods

1838-60
Thomas Dugdale, *The Curiosities of Great Britain, England and Wales: Delineated Historical, entertaining & commercial Alphabetically arranged*, London: Tallis (11 vols)

1841-44
Charles Knight (ed), *London*, London: Charles Knight & Co (6 vols) (44 wood engravings);
London Interiors: A grand national exhibition of the religious, regal and civic solemnities, public amusements, scientific meetings, and commercial scenes of the British capital; beautifully engraved on steel, from drawings made expressly for this work, by Command of Her Majesty, and with permission of the proprietors and trustees of the metropolitan edifices. With descriptions written by official authorities, London: Joseph Mead (2 vols) (steel engravings)

1851
William Gray Fearnside and Thomas Harral (eds), *Holmes's Great Metropolis: or, Views and History of London in the Nineteenth Century. Being a Grand National Exhibition of the British Capital. With Historical and Topographical Notices of Each Place*, London: Thomas Holmes (steel engravings)

***Circa* 1854**
Thomas Hosmer Shepherd, *The World's Metropolis, Or, Mighty London: Palaces, Public Buildings, Monuments & Streets; from Original Drawings by Thomas H Shepherd, to which is Added a Comprehensive History from the Earliest Period to the Present Day; Illustrated by a Series of Views Beautifully Engraved on Steel*, London: Read and Co (2 parts) (steel engravings)

Nos 232-248 are illustrated in [James Elmes], *London and its Environs in the Nineteenth Century… illustrated … by Thomas H Shepherd*, London: Jones & Co, 1828-31

Nos 250-260 are illustrated in James Elmes, *Metropolitan Improvements; or, London in the Nineteenth Century…* from original drawings, London: Jones & Co, 1827-31

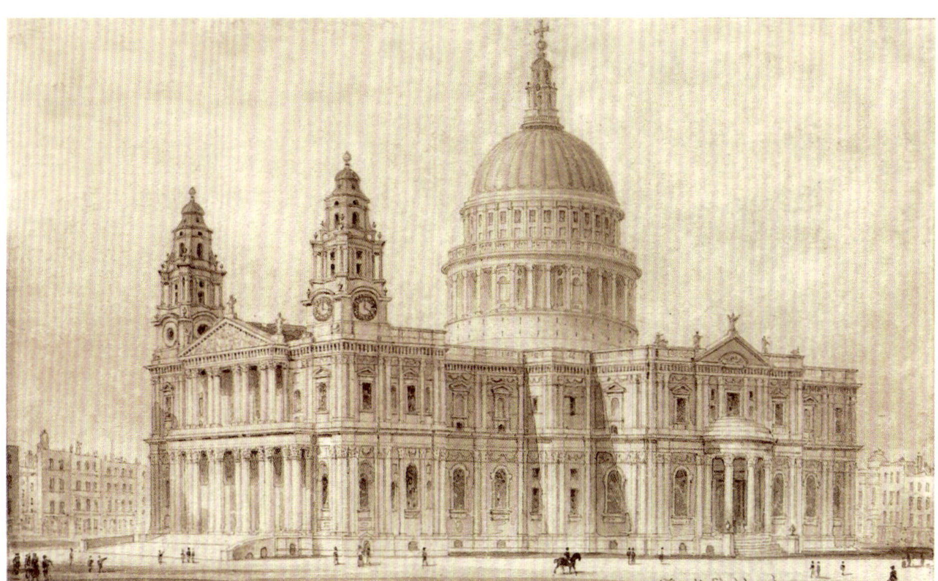

231 ST PAUL'S CATHEDRAL
signed
pencil with monochrome watercolour
4 ¼ x 6 ¼ inches

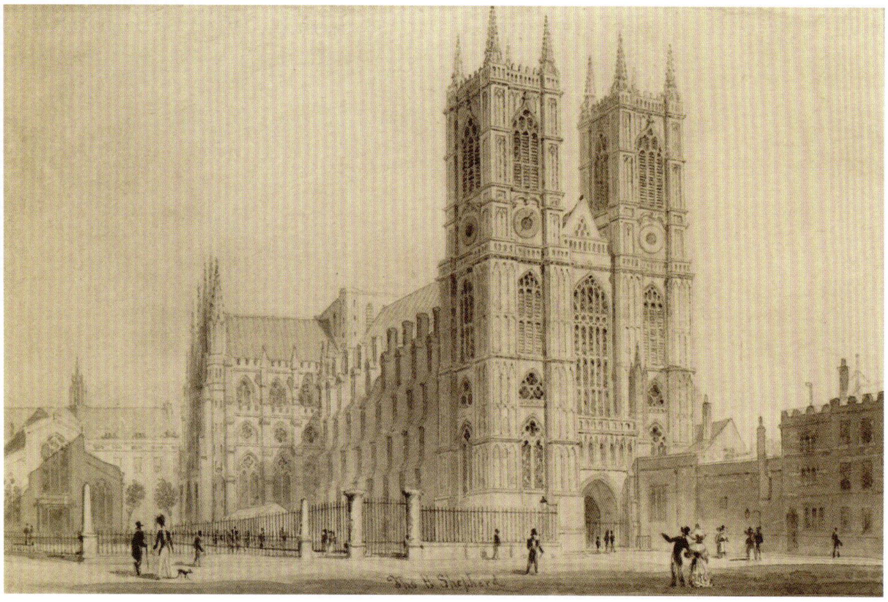

Westminster Abbey, West Front
This view of Westminster Abbey shows the west front, eighty years or so after the architect Nicholas Hawksmoor (1661-1736) erected the two major towers. Whilst this was the last major addition to the original medieval structure, the western façade seen by Shepherd was very different from that of today. In particular, its crumbling stonework was heavily restored by Sir George Gilbert Scott (1811-1878) when he was surveyor to Westminster Abbey (1849-78). Scott added a considerable quantity of Gothic Revival motifs that purists consider inappropriate, including a new west window.

232 WESTMINSTER ABBEY, WEST FRONT
signed
monochrome watercolour with pencil
4 x 6 inches
Illustrated: *London and its Environs*, 1828-31
(engraved by James Tingle)

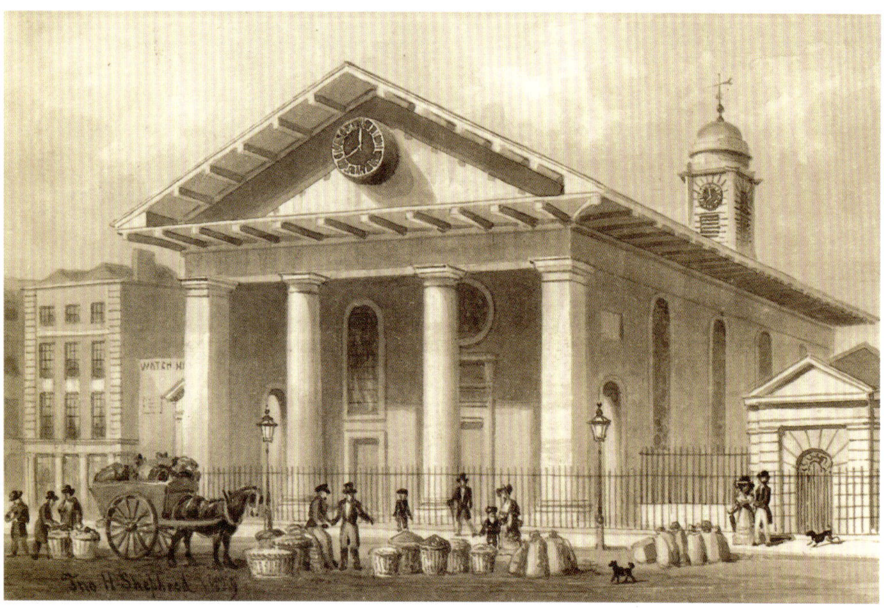

St Paul's Church, Covent Garden
Also known as the Actors' Church, St Paul's Church, Covent Garden was built in 1631 by the famous architect Inigo Jones (1573-1652) and has played a colourful part in Covent Garden life ever since. The building is rich in theatrical association – many performances have been played out in the shadow of its portico, including the first ever 'Punch and Judy' puppet show in 1662.

233 ST PAUL'S CHURCH, COVENT GARDEN
signed and dated 1829
inscribed with title on reverse
monochrome watercolour with pencil
3 ¾ x 5 ¾ inches
Illustrated: *London and its Environs*, 1828-31
(engraved by James Tingle)

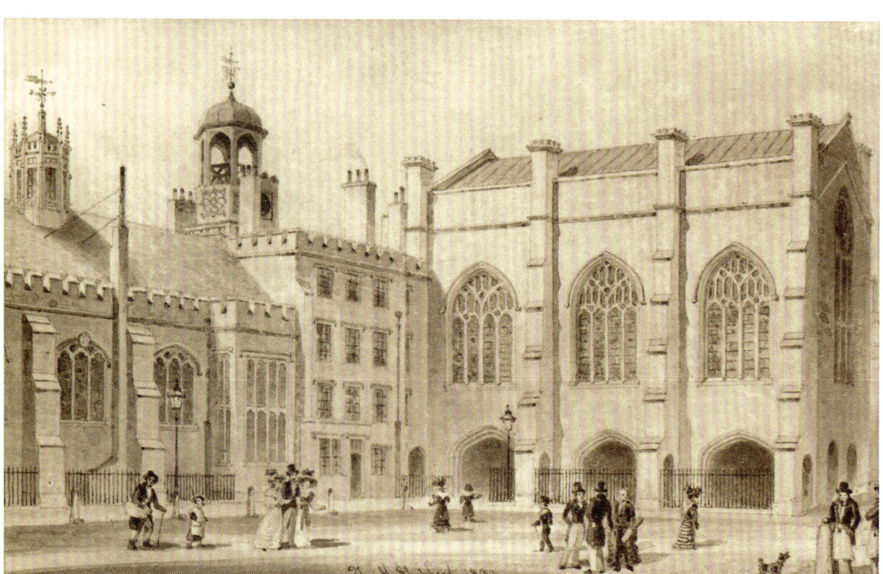

Lincoln's Inn Hall, Chapel and Chancery Court
The buildings and grounds of Lincoln's Inn were first established in the early fourteenth century to provide a complete working environment for those studying and practising law. It is now one of the four Inns of Court at which all English and Welsh barristers are first called to the bar, and then given membership. The hall pictured here is now known as the 'Old Hall', and is an original Tudor building, built in 1490. The current Chapel, seen in this picture, was consecrated in 1623 and is an improvement on earlier fifteenth century building.

234 LINCOLN'S INN HALL, CHAPEL AND CHANCERY COURT
signed and dated 1830
monochrome watercolour with pencil
4 x 6 inches, sketch of a figure on reverse
Illustrated: *London and its Environs*, 1828-31
(engraved by William Watkins)

The notes to the watercolours by Thomas Hosmer Shepherd are written by Giles Huxley-Parlour.

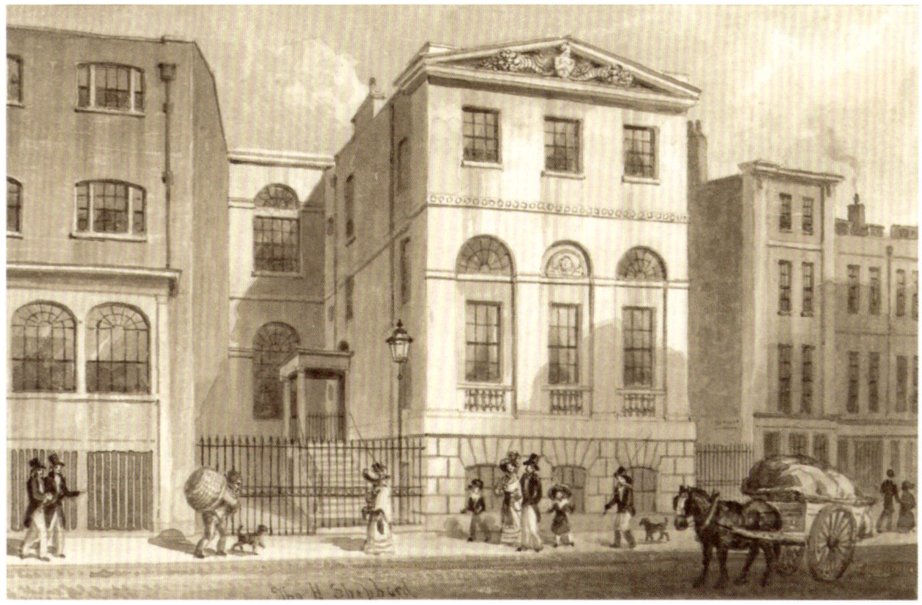

235 CORDWAINERS' HALL, DISTAFF LANE
signed
monochrome watercolour with pencil
3 ¾ x 5 ¾ inches
Illustrated: *London and its Environs*, 1828-31
(engraved by John Greig)

Stationers' Hall
The Worshipful Company of Stationers and Newspaper Makers is one of the oldest guilds in England, with over six hundred years of commercial history. The company was officially responsible for enforcing copyright regulations until the Statute of St Anne in 1709, which significantly reduced its power. The original wooden Hall, which the company secured from Lord Abergaveny in the seventeenth century, burned down in 1666, during the Great Fire of London, and was rebuilt in 1673. The building was then refronted in 1800 by the architect Robert Mylne (1733-1811).

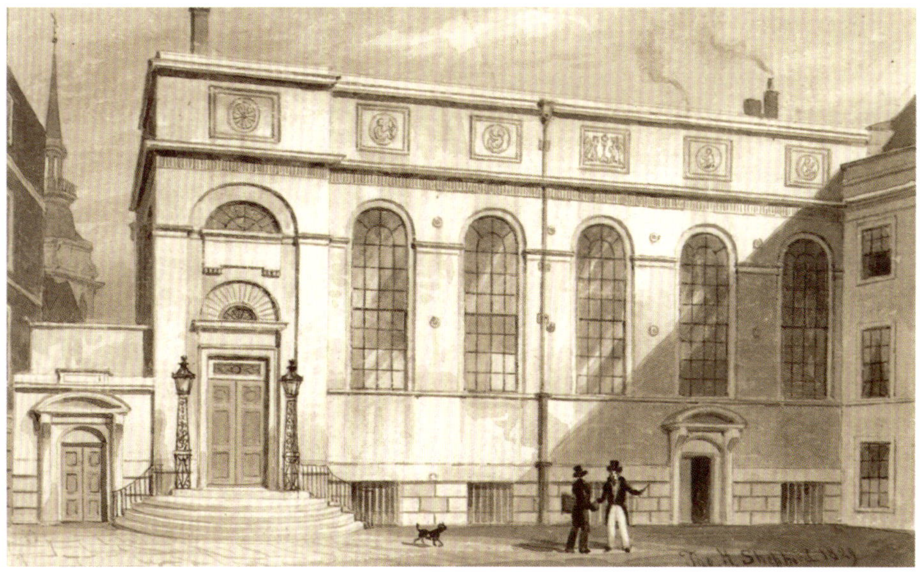

236 STATIONERS' HALL
signed and dated 1829
monochrome watercolour with pencil
3 ¾ x 5 ¾ inches
Illustrated: *London and its Environs*, 1828-31
(engraved by W Watkins)

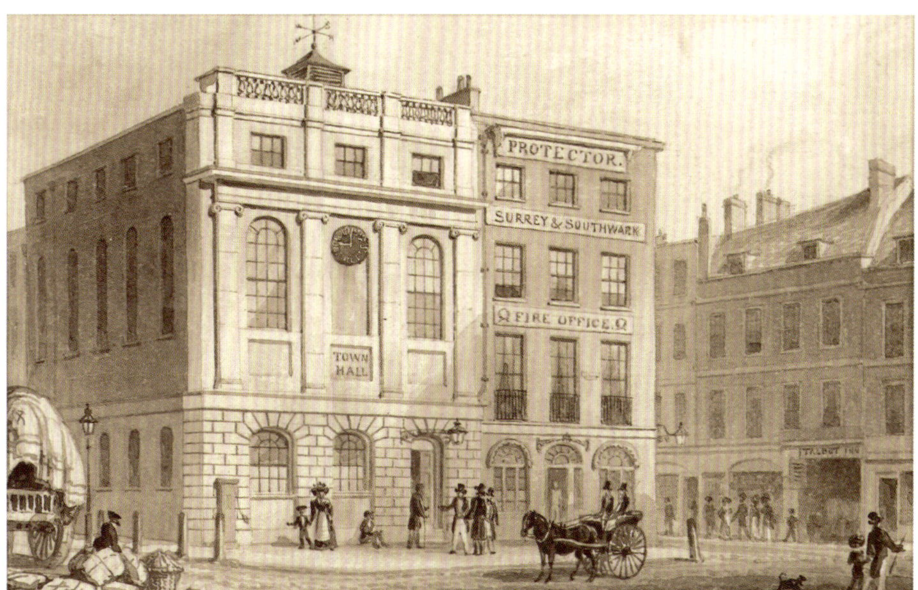

237 TOWN HALL, BOROUGH, SOUTHWARK
signed and dated 1829
inscribed 'Town Hall Boro Southwark' on reverse
monochrome watercolour with pencil
3 ¾ x 5 ¾ inches
Illustrated: *London and its Environs*, 1828-31
(engraved by R Winkles)

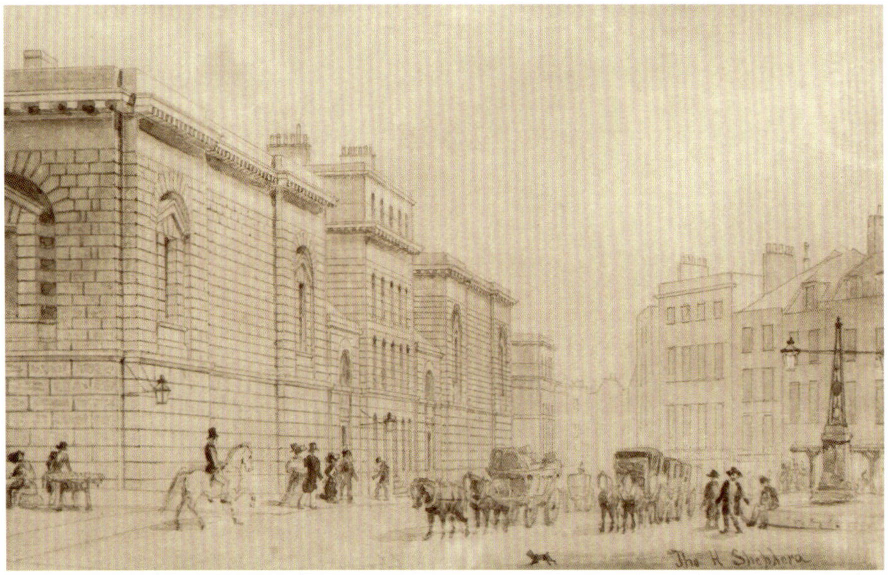

Newgate Prison, Old Bailey
Newgate Prison was demolished in 1904 after nearly seven hundred years of use. During this time it was used to incarcerate some of England's most notorious criminals, many of whom went on to be executed in public outside its gates when it became London's main prison in the 1780s. The building in Shepherd's drawing was built in 1782, after a previous version was burnt down during the infamous Gordon Riots of 1780. The Old Bailey now stands on the site.

238 NEWGATE PRISON, OLD BAILEY
signed
inscribed with title below mount
pencil with monochrome watercolour
3 ½ x 5 ¾ inches
Illustrated: *London and its Environs*, 1828-31
(engraved by Robert Acon)

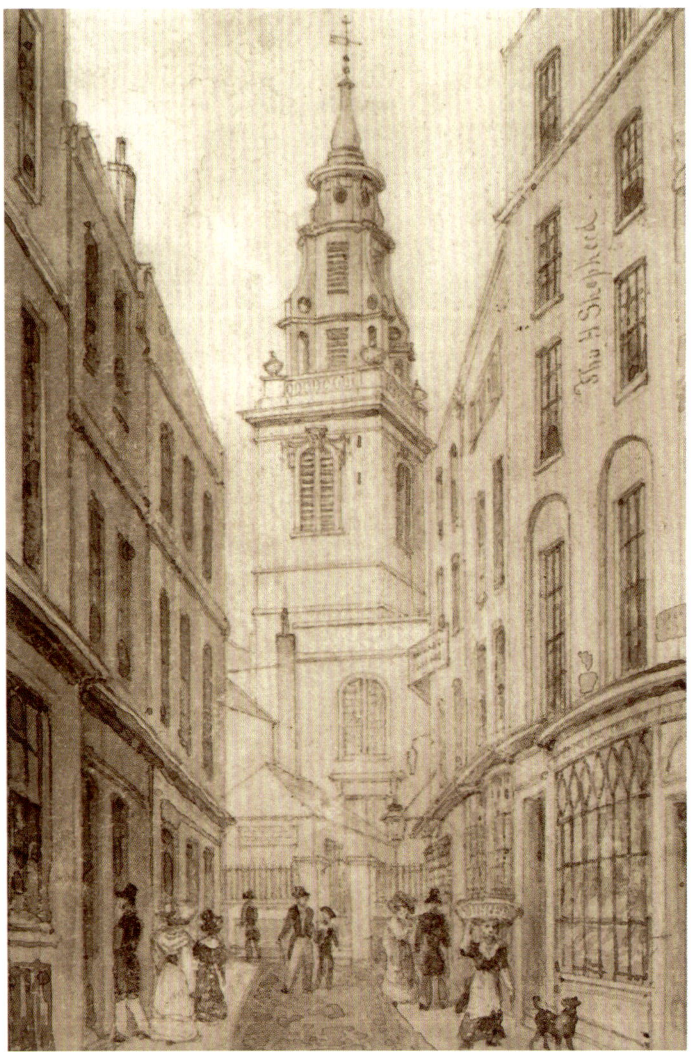

239 ST MICHAEL, CROOKED LANE
signed
pencil with monochrome watercolour
4 x 2 ½ inches
Illustrated: *London and its Environs*, 1828-31
(engraved by Edward John Roberts)

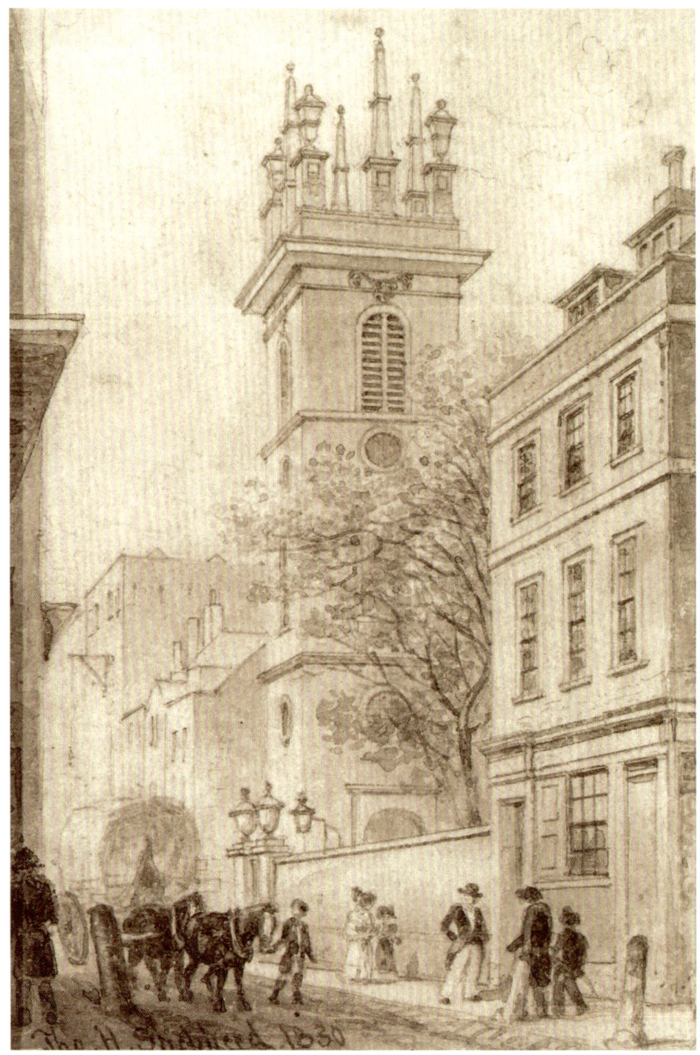

240 ST MARY SOMERSET, UPPER THAMES STREET
signed and dated 1830
pencil with monochrome watercolour
4 x 2 ½ inches
Illustrated: *London and its Environs*, 1828-31
(engraved by Edward John Roberts)

Duke of York's School, Chelsea
The Duke of York's School, Chelsea, was founded to provide an education for the children of soldiers that had been killed in service. The building was designed by John Sanders in 1801, and the foundation stone laid that same year. The school itself moved to Dover in 1909, leaving the building for use by the Territorial Army. After two hundred years of ownership by the Ministry of Defence, it was sold in 2000, reopening for a very different purpose in 2008 as the new Saatchi Gallery of contemporary art.

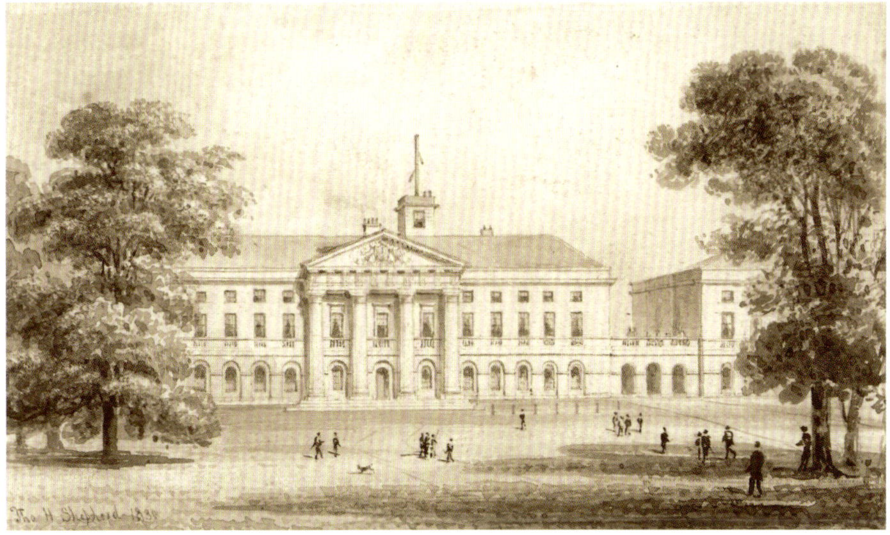

241 DUKE OF YORK'S SCHOOL, CHELSEA
signed and dated 1830
inscribed with title below mount
monochrome watercolour with pencil
3 ½ x 5 ¾ inches
Illustrated: *London and its Environs*, 1828-31
(engraved by Thomas Barber)

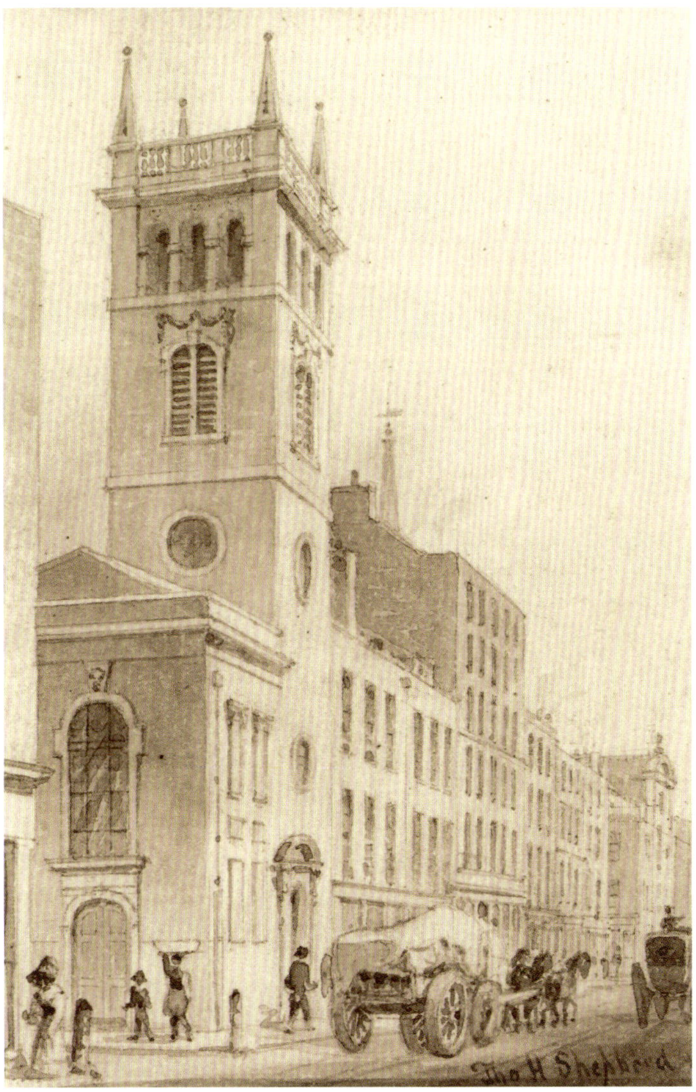

242 ALL HALLOWS, BREAD STREET
signed
monochrome watercolour with pencil
4 x 2 ¾ inches
Illustrated: *London and its Environs*, 1828-31
(engraved by Archileus Cruse)

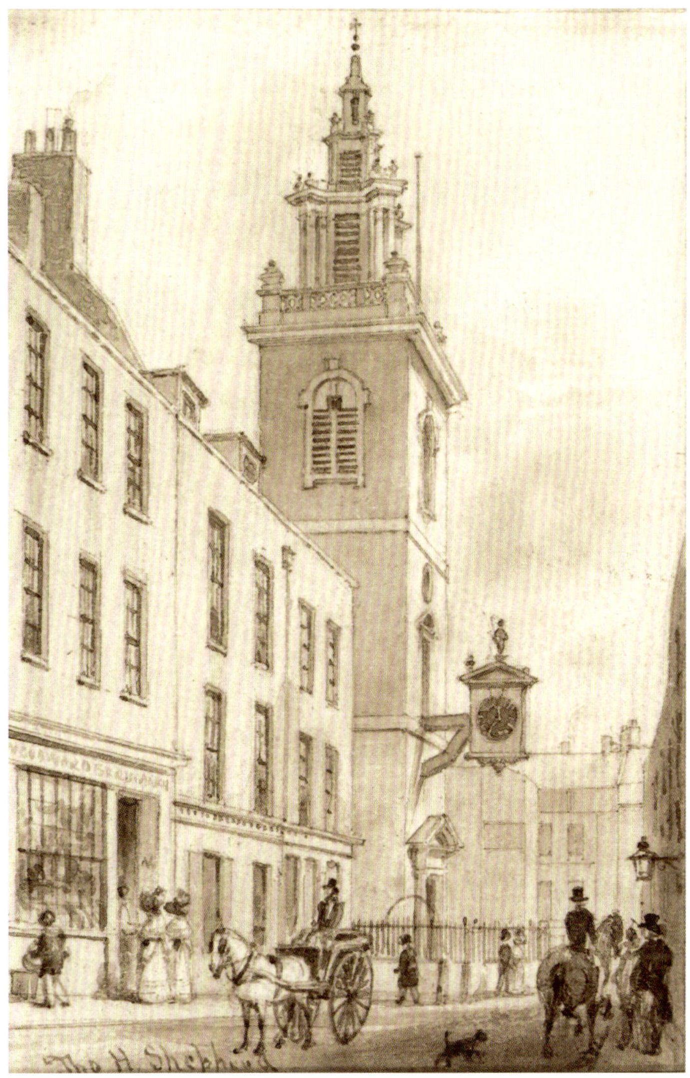

243 ST JAMES'S, GARLICK HILL
signed
monochrome watercolour with pencil
4 x 2 ¾ inches
Illustrated: *London and its Environs*, 1828-31
(engraved by Robert Acon)

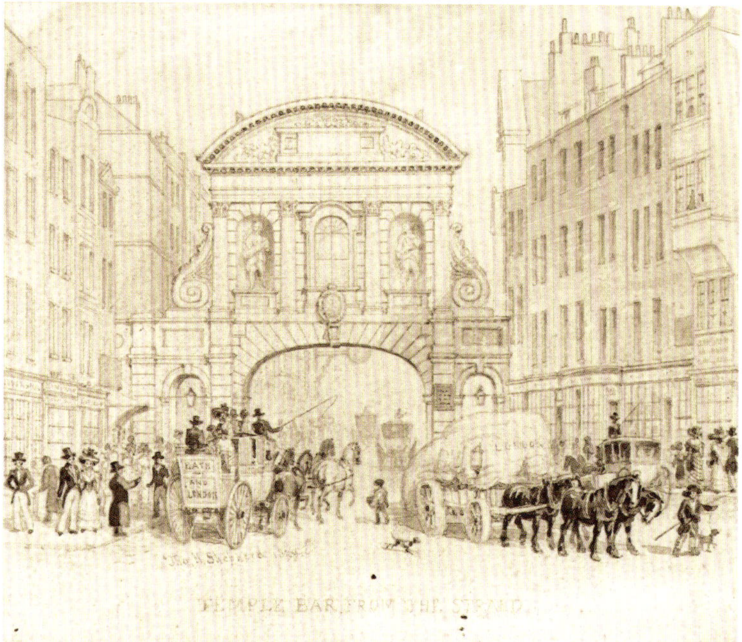

Temple Bar from the Strand

The barrier marking the westernmost extent of the City of London on the road to Westminster was demarcated by a stone gateway, known as Temple Bar. The only gateway to London still standing by 1800, it remained in place until 1878. The Corporation of London then dismantled it in order to widen the road, and stored away its 2,700 stones. In 1880, the brewer, Sir Henry Meux, bought them and re-erected the arch as a gateway at his house, Theobalds Park, Hertfordshire, where it remained until 2003. It has now been re-erected as an entrance to Paternoster Square north of St Paul's Cathedral.

244 TEMPLE BAR FROM THE STRAND
signed, inscribed with title and dated 1829
inscribed 'With historical and topographical illustrations by John Britton Esq FSA' on reverse
pencil with monochrome watercolour
4 ½ x 5 inches
Illustrated: *London and its Environs*, 1828-31
(engraved by William Wallis)

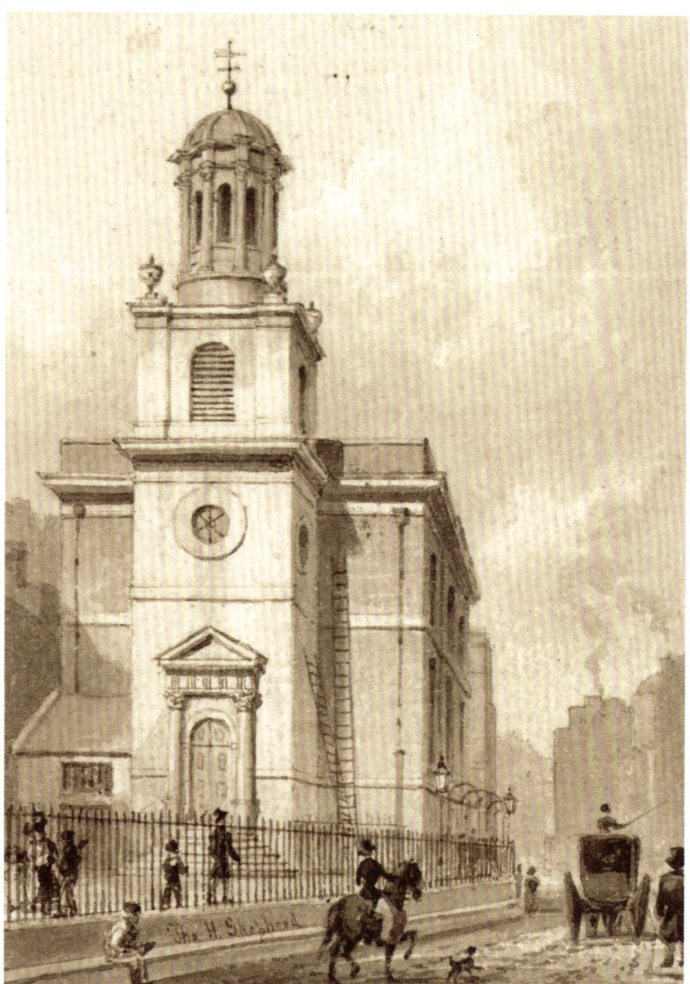

245 ALL HALLOWS, LONDON WALL
inscribed with title below mount
monochrome watercolour with pencil
3 ¾ x 2 ½ inches
Illustrated: *London and its Environs* , 1828-31
(engraved by Archileus Cruse)

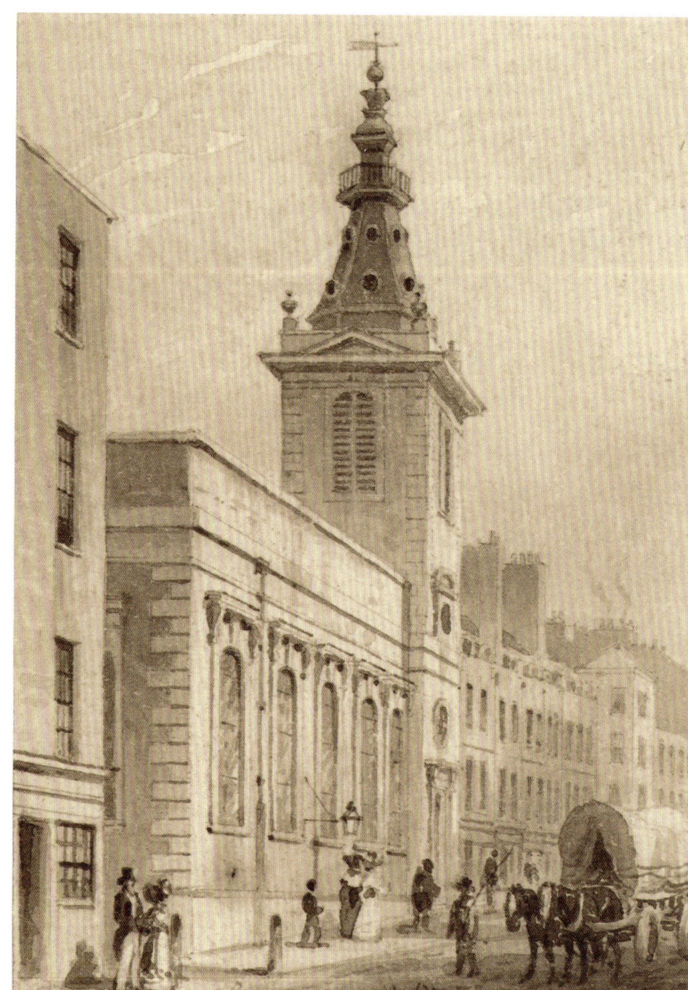

246 ST NICHOLAS, COLE ABBEY, FISH STREET
signed
monochrome watercolour with pencil
3 ¾ x 2 ½ inches
Illustrated: *London and its Environs*, 1828-31

Piccadilly, from Coventry Street
The name 'Piccadilly' comes from a seventeenth-century tailor called Robert Baker, who made his fortune making stiff collars called 'Piccadils'. He bought up a large plot of land in the open country, west of London, and there built a house that became known as 'Piccadilly Hall'. Over the next century considerable development occurred in the surrounding area, which, in turn, created a major thoroughfare between Hyde Park Corner and the Haymarket area. This road quickly gained the moniker 'Piccadilly'. Shepherd's view was drawn in 1820, from the spot still known today as Piccadilly Circus. This famous landmark was created one year earlier by John Nash (1752-1835) as a junction between Piccadilly and his newly built Regent's Street.

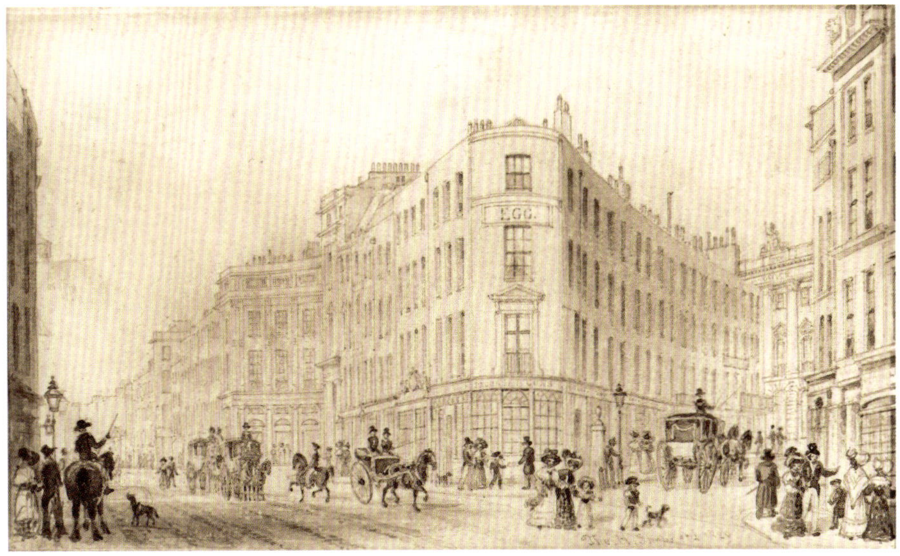

247 PICCADILLY, FROM COVENTRY STREET
signed and faintly dated 1820
pencil with monochrome watercolour
3 ½ x 5 ¾ inches
Illustrated: *London and its Environs*, 1828-31

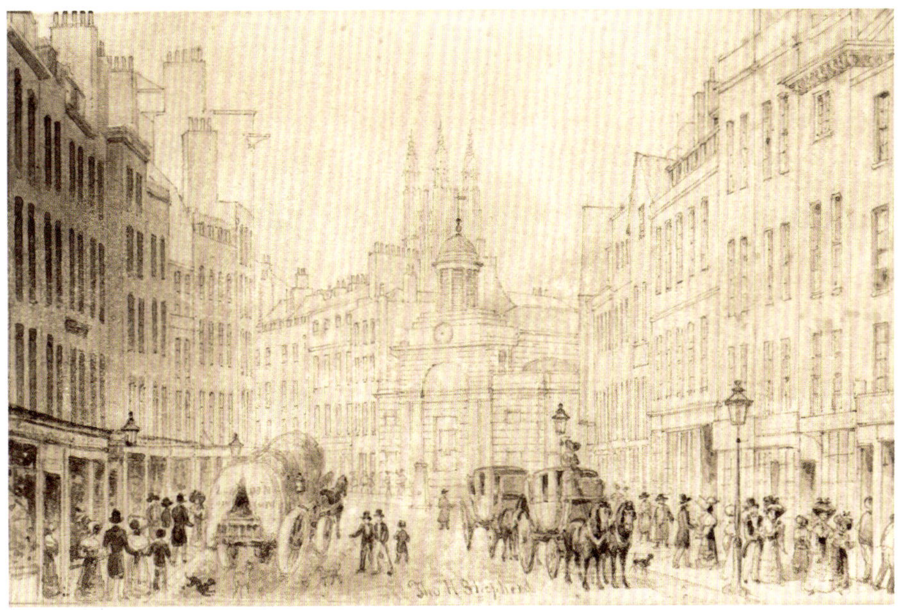

248 ST MARTIN OUTWICH, BISHOPSGATE STREET
signed
inscribed 'Bishopsgate St to the corner of Threadneedle Street' on reverse
pencil with monochrome watercolour
4 x 5 ¾ inches
Illustrated: *London and its Environs*, 1828-31 (engraved by Archileus Cruse)

Shaftesbury House, Aldersgate Street
Originally known as Thanet House, Shaftesbury House was built in 1644 by Inigo Jones), as the London home to the Earls of Thanet, before then passing to the Earls of Shaftesbury. Following a period of decline, the building briefly became a hospital in the 1750s, and then both a general dispensary and units for respectable shopkeepers during the Regency period. The building was demolished in the 1880s.

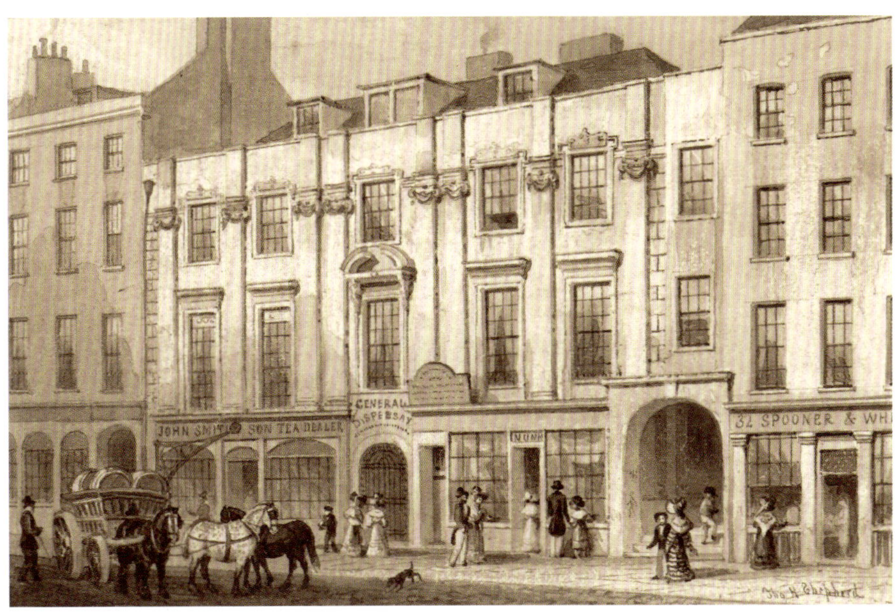

249 SHAFTESBURY HOUSE, ALDERSGATE STREET
signed
dated 'July.26.1830' below mount
monochrome watercolour with pencil
3 ¾ x 5 ¾ inches
pencil drawing of the capital of a column below mount
Originally published as an engraving by Jones & Co on 5 March 1831 (engraved by Major Samuel Barenger)

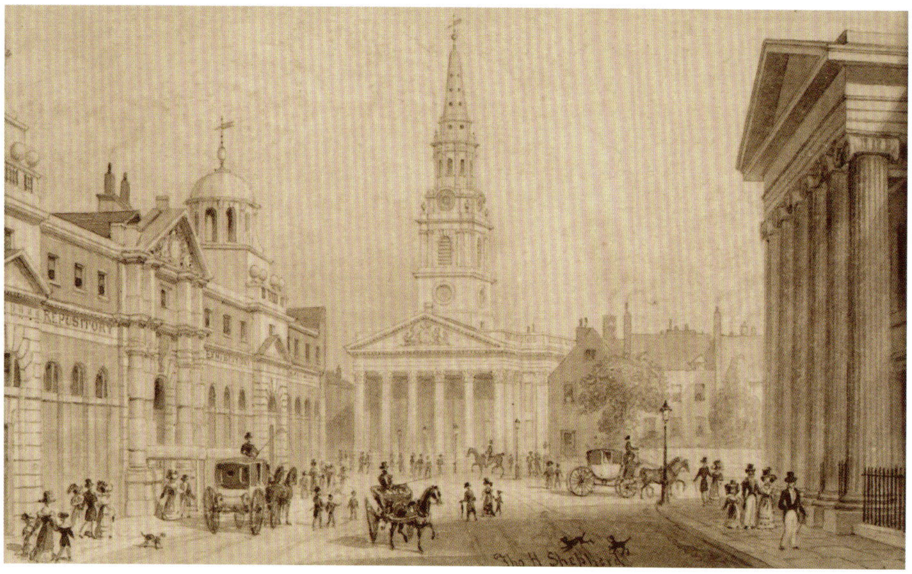

The New Opening to St Martin's Church from Pall Mall East

The new opening to St Martin's Church was conceived and built by the great architect John Nash, as part of his plan to redesign Trafalgar Square and its surrounding area during the 1820s.

250 THE NEW OPENING TO ST MARTIN'S CHURCH FROM PALL MALL EAST

signed

inscribed with title and 'The Old King's Mews now 1860 The National Gallery' on reverse

monochrome watercolour with pencil

3 ¾ x 5 ¾ inches

Originally published as an engraving by Jones & Co on 10 January 1829 (engraved by H W Bond)

Illustrated: *Metropolitan Improvements*, 1827-31

Thomas Dugdale, *The Curiosities of Great Britain, England and Wales*, J & F Tallis, 1838-60

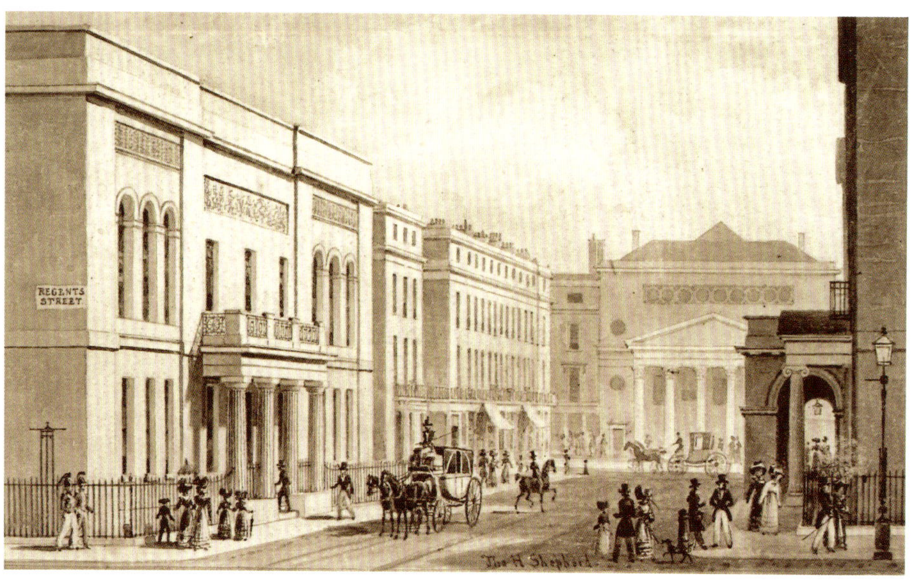

Haymarket Theatre from Regent Street

First built in 1720 by John Potter, a carpenter, the Haymarket Theatre is one of the oldest theatres in London that is still currently in use. John Nash redesigned it as part of his regeneration of the area in the early 1820s, and his classical portico seen in this picture still dominates the Haymarket today.

251 UNITED SERVICE MILITARY CLUB HOUSE, HAYMARKET THEATRE, & PART OF THE OPERA COLONADE, FROM REGENT STREET

signed

inscribed 'The United Service Military Club House, Haymarket Theatre and part of the Opera Colonade, from Regents Street' on reverse

monochrome watercolour with pencil

3 ¼ x 5 ¼ inches

pencil drawing of the capital of a column on reverse

Originally published as an engraving by Jones & Co on 10 September 1829 (engraved by William Wallis)

Illustrated: *Metropolitan Improvements*, 1827-31

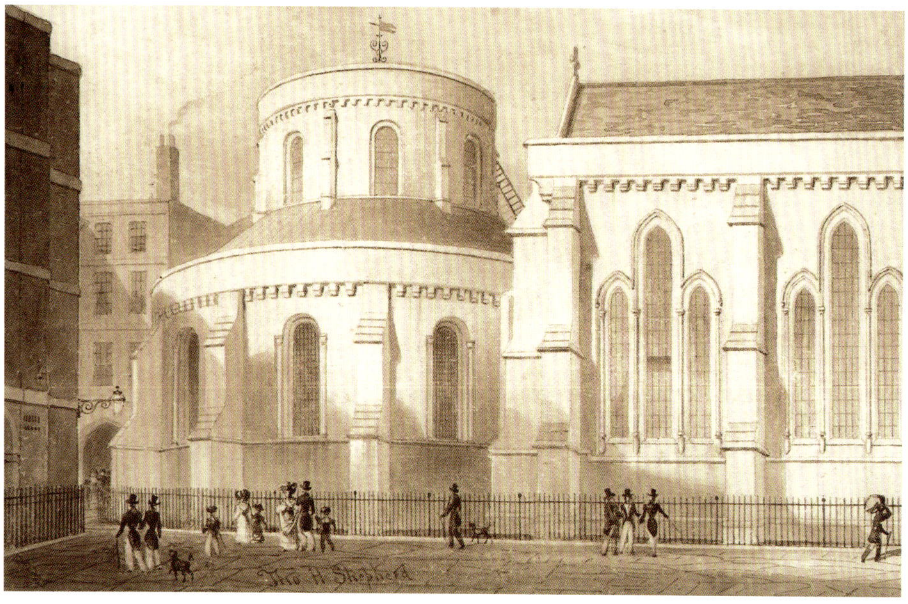

252 THE TEMPLE CHURCH, AS RESTORED

signed

monochrome watercolour with pencil

3 ¾ x 5 ¾ inches

Originally published as an engraving by Jones & Co on 16 August 1828 (engraved by J Carter)

Illustrated: *Metropolitan Improvements*, 1827-31

Theatre Royal, Drury Lane

The Theatre Royal, Drury Lane, can lay claim to being London's oldest surviving theatre, as records show one on the site as early as 1663. The present building, the fourth, was opened in 1812 after the previous three had either burned down or been demolished. Benjamin Dean Wyatt (1775-1852) designed it in a strictly neoclassical style, with seating for 3,060 people. A portico was added in 1820, and a colonnade in 1822. Each successive theatre has been run by celebrated theatrical names, from the King's Company (1663-1682) to Andrew Lloyd Webber (1999-present), and it still remains central to London's vibrant theatre scene.

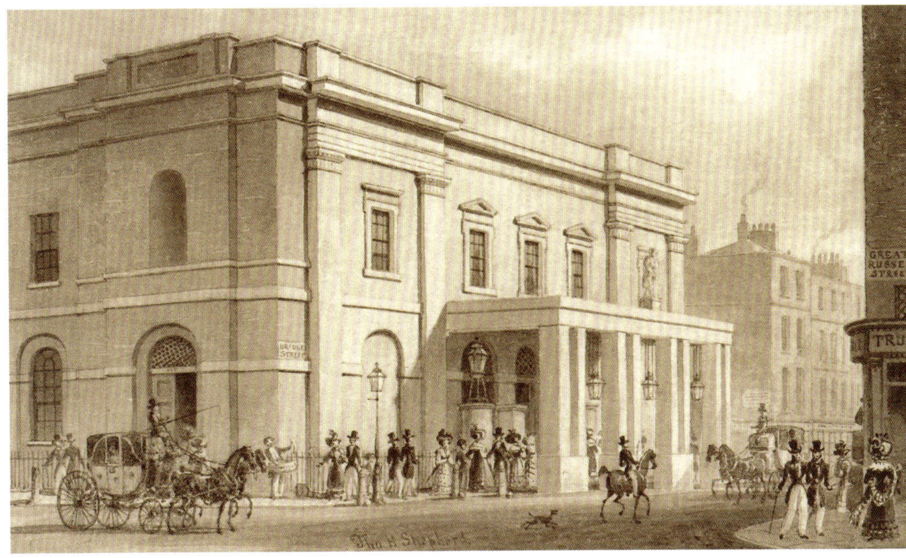

253 THEATRE ROYAL, DRURY LANE
signed
inscribed with title on reverse
monochrome watercolour and pencil
3 ½ x 5 ¾ inches
Originally published as an engraving by Jones & Co on 16 February 1828 (engraved by Thomas Dale)
Illustrated: *Metropolitan Improvements*, 1827-31

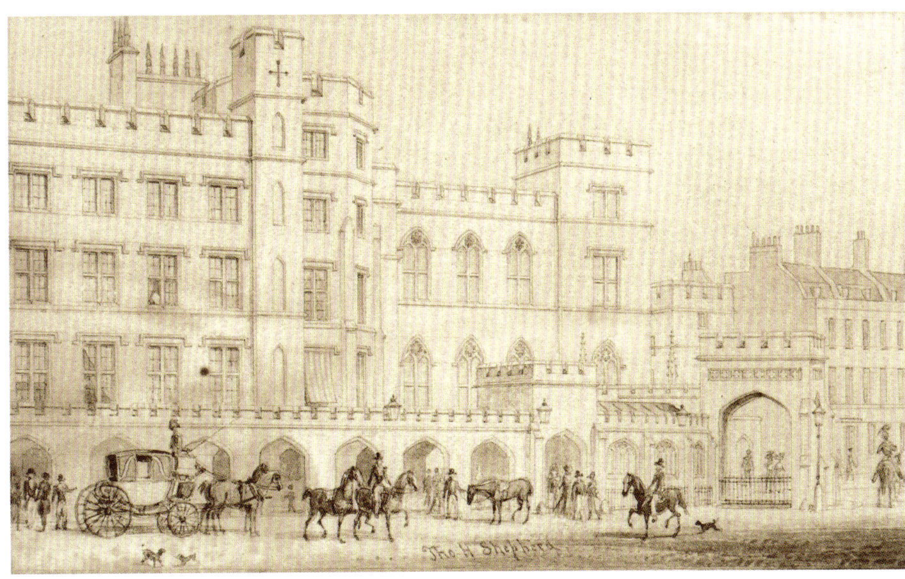

254 THE KING'S ENTRANCE TO THE HOUSE OF LORDS FROM POET'S CORNER
signed
inscribed 'The King's entrance to the House of Lords / Old Palace Yard' on reverse
pencil with monochrome watercolour
4 x 6 inches
Originally published as an engraving by Jones & Co on 21 February 1829 (engraved by William Deeble)
Illustrated: *Metropolitan Improvements*, 1827-31

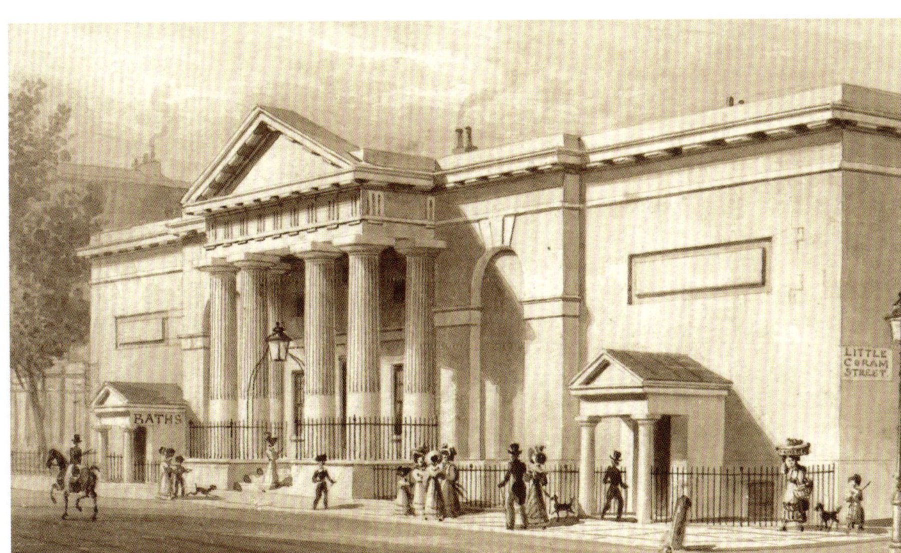

255 THE RUSSELL INSTITUTION, GREAT CORAM STREET
signed and dated 1827
inscribed 'Public Baths Great Coram St' and 'Russell Institn / Gt Coram St' on reverse
monochrome watercolour with pencil
3 ½ x 5 ¾ inches
Originally published as an engraving by Jones & Co on 16 August 1828 (engraved by James Carter)
Illustrated: *Metropolitan Improvements*, 1827-31

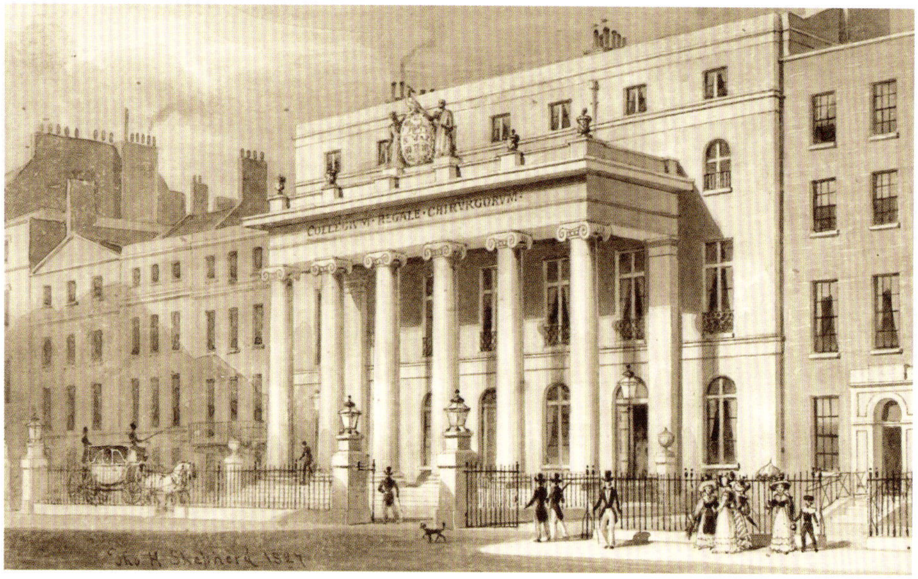

The Royal College of Surgeons, Lincolns Inn Fields

The College of Surgeons was formed in 1745 in response to anatomical and surgical advances that finally rendered inappropriate their long association with barbers. Its Royal charter was granted in 1800. The original building at Lincoln's Inn Fields was built by George Dance the Younger (1741-1825), but was rebuilt by Sir Charles Barry (1795-1860) from 1833 after the discovery of structural defects.

256 THE ROYAL COLLEGE OF SURGEONS, LINCOLNS INN FIELDS
signed and dated 1827
inscribed with title on reverse
monochrome watercolour with pencil
3 ¾ x 5 ¾ inches
Originally published as an engraving by Jones & Co on 9 February 1828 (engraved by William Deeble)
Illustrated: *Metropolitan Improvements*, 1827-31

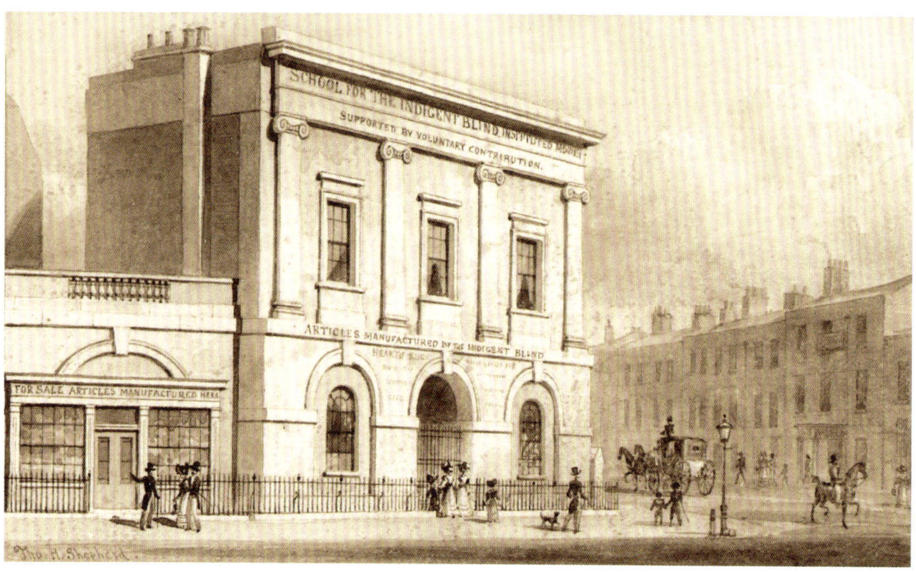

257 ASYLUM FOR THE INDIGENT BLIND, WESTMINSTER ROAD
signed
monochrome watercolour with pencil
3 ½ x 6 inches
Originally published as an engraving by Jones & Co on 28 March 1829 (engraved by Robert Acon)
Illustrated: *Metropolitan Improvements*, 1827-31

The Bank of England

When the Bank of England moved to its current premises on Threadneedle Street in 1734, it grew organically into its current three-acre site by constructing more and more adjacent buildings. Eventually the architect Sir John Soane (1753-1837) was employed to enclose the sprawling site within a beautiful, neo-classical curtain wall in 1788, a project that would consume him until his retirement in 1833. This design, along with its palatial façade, made the Bank one of the grandest buildings in the country. Unbelievably it was demolished in between the two World Wars, provoking Sir Nikolaus Pevsner to describe the process as 'the greatest architectural crime, in the City of London, of the twentieth century'. The present, equally grand, building is therefore deceptively modern, built by Sir Herbert Baker (1862-1946) between 1925 and 1942.

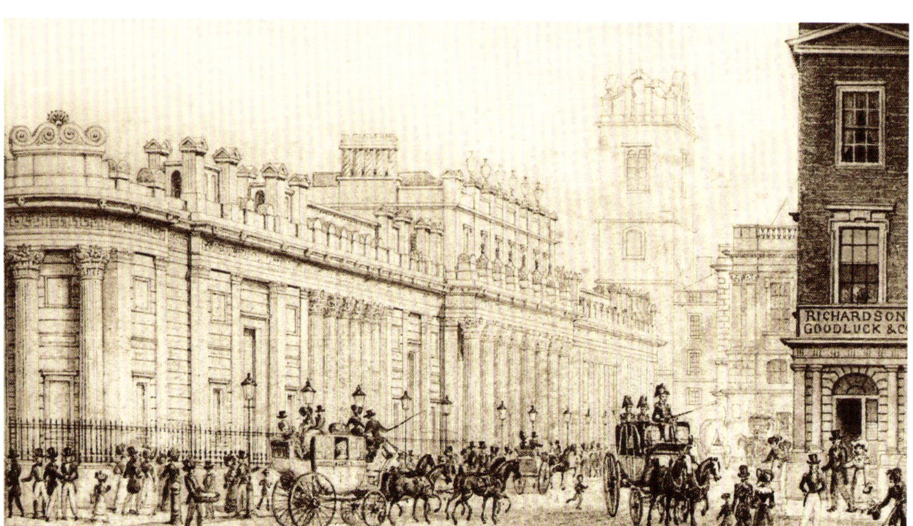

258 THE BANK OF ENGLAND
signed and dated 1827
inscribed with title on reverse
pencil with watercolour
3 ¾ x 6 ¼ inches
Originally published as an engraving by Jones & Co on 5 July 1828 (engraved by Robert Acon)
Illustrated: *Metropolitan Improvements*, 1827-31

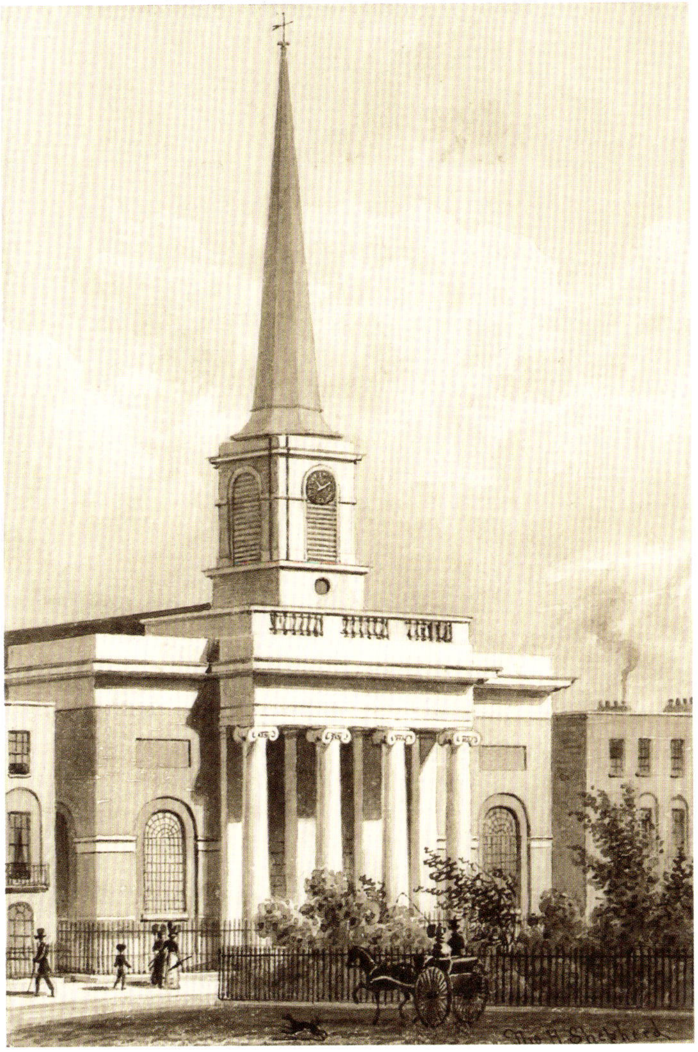

259 ST BARNABAS, KING'S SQUARE
signed
monochrome watercolour and pencil
5 ½ x 3 ½ inches
Originally published as an engraving by Jones & Co on 5 July 1828 (engraved by John Cleghorn)
Illustrated: *Metropolitan Improvements*, 1827-31

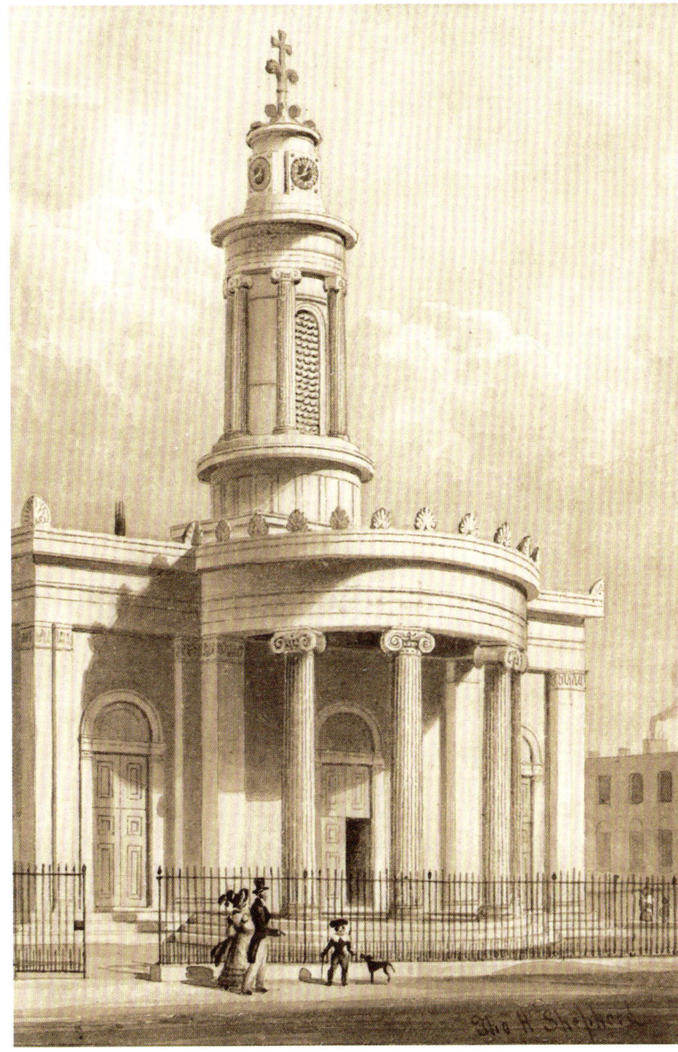

260 NEW CHURCH, CAMDEN TOWN
signed
inscribed with title on reverse
monochrome watercolour and pencil
5 ½ x 3 ¾ inches
Originally published as an engraving by Jones & Co on 5 July 1828 (engraved by John Cleghorn)
Illustrated: *Metropolitan Improvements*, 1827-31

Coal Exchange, Thames Street

The London Coal Exchange was erected in 1805 as the official trading venue for coal merchants. Despite its good, regulatory intentions, a monopoly of the biggest players quickly dominated the market place and swamped the trading. This building, although charmingly adorned with a receding portico and small Doric pillars, has been overshadowed in the history of London architecture by its grander replacement, opened in 1849.

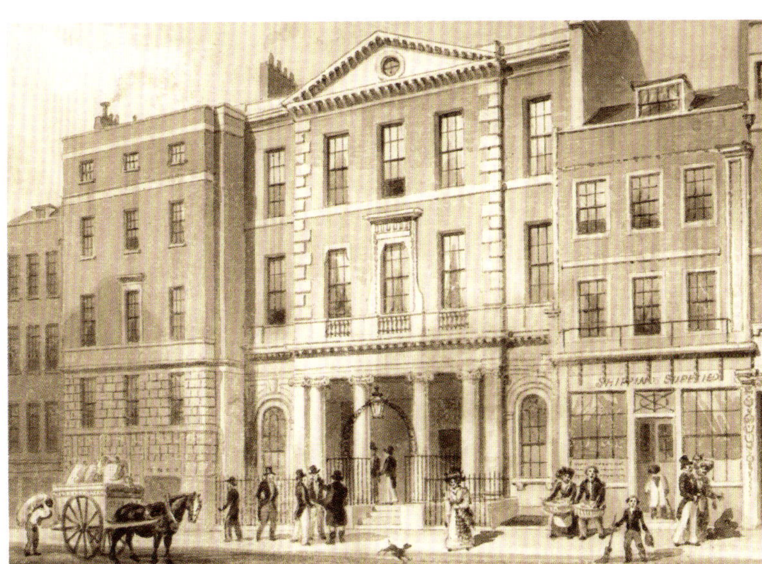

261 COAL EXCHANGE, THAMES STREET
signed
indistinctly inscribed with place names and the opening of the Lord's Prayer on reverse
monochrome watercolour with pencil
4 ¼ x 6 inches
Originally published as an engraving by Jones & Co on 25 September 1830 (engraved by Robert Acon)

7: THE BONNINGTON CIRCLE

LOUIS FRANCIA
François-Louis-Thomas Francia, AA (1772-1839)

The French painter and printmaker, Louis Francia was influential as a drawing master on both sides of the English Channel, passing on his astonishing skill at handling fluid watercolour. Famous among his pupils was Richard Parkes Bonington, and for a few months of Bonington's short life, the artists were very close.

Louis Francia was born in Calais on 21 December 1772, the son of the director of its military hospital. Though intended for the legal profession, he was permitted to take classes at the local Académie de Dessin where, at the age of sixteen, he was awarded all the prizes.

In order to avoid the political disruption created by revolution, Francia moved to London in 1790. Though he spoke little English, he managed to find employment as a drawing master in a Hampstead school. Befriended by Joseph Charles Barrow, he was invited to become his assistant when Barrow set up a drawing school in Holborn in 1792. (JOHN VARLEY became Barrow's second assistant in the following year.)

Producing a number of topographical watercolours, some intended as illustrations, Francia began to show them at the Royal Academy of Arts in 1795 (and would exhibit there regularly until 1821). At the same time, he became a member of Dr Thomas Monro's informal academy at his home in the Adelphi, where he worked alongside Thomas Girtin, who proved an important early influence. Four years later, he helped Girtin found the sketching club, 'The Brothers', and became its secretary.

By 1805, Francia was working in London as a drawing master. Three years later, he began to exhibit at the newly founded Associated Artists in Water Colours, becoming a member in 1810, and acting as its secretary from 1811 until its demise in 1812. During this period, he turned increasingly to marine subjects, often enlivened by dramatic effects of light. He also combined his skills as teacher and printmaker in publishing *Studies in Landscape* (1810), a manual comprising a series of soft-ground etchings after his own sketches and those by other artists, including Gainsborough, Girtin and Varley. *Progressive Lessons* followed in 1813, while a volume of lithographs, entitled *Marine Studies*, would apear in 1822.

It is believed that, by 1816, Francia was given the prestigious appointment of Painter in Watercolours to the Duchess of York. However, his failure to gain election to the Royal Academy in that year must have led him to reflect on his career in England, and undoubtedly contributed to his decision to return to Calais in 1817. Acting briefly as secretary to the British Consul in Calais, he soon found a patron in the expatriate Beau Brummell, and set up as a drawing master.

Francia became the centre of a significant artistic circle in Calais, and a contact for visiting British painters. His pupils included Olivier Isaac, WILLIAM WYLD, his own son, Alexandre, and, most famously, Richard Parkes Bonington, while Eugène Isabey, Jules Collignon and Louis Tesson were numbered among his associates. So he came to affect many of the younger generation of watercolourists on both sides of the Channel. And, though Bonington was in Calais for only a short time, he and Francia remained close friends and were mutually influential. (Bonington died in London in 1828, at the age of twenty-five.)

Francia continued to tour and exhibit, mounting a solo show in Calais in 1828, and visiting Brittany in 1830. Remaining interested and active in many fields until late in life, he protested against plans, in 1835, to exclude pupils under ten years of age from the drawing class of the art school.

Francia died at home in the rue de la Poissonerie on 6 February 1839.

His work is represented in numerous public collections, including the British Museum and the V&A; and The Fitzwilliam Museum (Cambridge).

Further reading:

Marcia Pointon, *Bonington, Francia and Wyld*, London: Batsford/Victoria & Albert Museum, 1985
Marcia Pointon, 'Francia (François-)Louis(-Thomas) (*b* Calais, 21 Dec 1772; *d* Calais, 6 Feb 1839)', Jane Turner (ed), *The Dictionary of Art*, London: Macmillan, 1996, vol 11, pp 702-703
Anthony Reed and Shaw Smith, *Louis Francia (1772-1839) and his son Alexandre*, London: Anthony Reed, 1985
Greg Smith, 'Francia, François Louis Thomas (1772-1839)', H C G Matthew and Brian Harrison (eds), *Oxford Dictionary of National Biography*, Oxford University Press, 2004, vol 20, pp 732-733

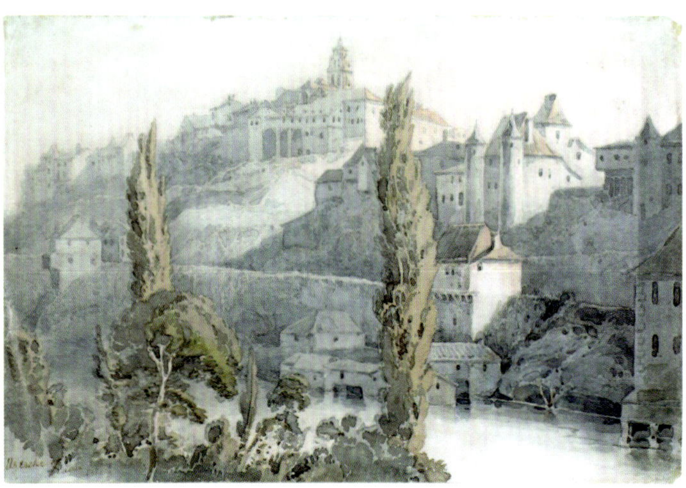

262 UZERCHE
signed, inscribed with title and dated 1814
inscribed 'Uzerche France' on reverse
watercolour
7 x 10 inches

NEWTON FIELDING
Newton Smith Limbird Fielding (1799-1856)

The youngest of the highly productive Fielding brothers, Newton Fielding shared his time between London and Paris, and worked in both cities as a painter, printmaker and drawing master. During the 1820s, he was close to Richard Parkes Bonington and his Anglo-French circle.

Newton Fielding was the youngest of the five artists sons of the Yorkshire painter, Nathan Theodore Fielding, of whom the best known was COPLEY FIELDING. Probably born in London, he became apprenticed to a doctor in the capital in 1815, while exhibiting at the Society of Painters in Water Colours for the first time in the same year (during its reconstitution as the Society of Painters in Oil and Water-Colours). Exhibiting there for a second time in 1818, he abandoned his articles and turned to art, joining the family business at 26 Newman Street, in the artists' quarter north of Oxford Street. He made his name with brightly-coloured watercolours of animals and birds in natural settings, partly inspired by the sporting tradition of the ALKEN family. Also working as a printmaker, he produced *British Game Illustrated in Twelve Spirited Etchings* in 1821.

Soon after, Fielding moved to Paris to work with his brother Thales for the publisher, J F d'Ostervald. Through the 1820s, the brothers played an important role in disseminating images by the Anglo-French school of watercolourists, centring on Eugène Delacroix and Richard Parkes Bonington. In the summer of 1824, Newton Fielding accompanied Bonington on a sketching tour of the Normandy coast. He became well known for his own albums of lithographs.

Fielding also developed an extensive teaching practice, becoming drawing master to the family of King Louis-Philippe in 1827, and taking WILLIAM CALLOW as a pupil in 1829. He and Callow would collaborate, with Fielding introducing figures into Callow's landscapes.

When revolution broke out in Paris in 1830, Fielding abandoned the family atelier and returned to London, where he worked with Thales and their brother, Theodore. Marrying a French woman in 1833, he and his wife then divided their time between Paris and London. In 1838, when he exhibited two French views in Liverpool, he gave his London address as 2 Gothic Cottages, Park Village East, Regent's Park.

However, illness from bronchitis in 1845 led Fielding to settle permanently in Paris. As an experienced drawing master, he published a series of manuals during the early 1850s, but found the market too competitive, and suffered hardship as a result. He died in Paris on 12 January 1856.

His work is represented in the collections of the British Museum.

Further reading:

L H Cust (rev Huon Mallalieu), 'Fielding, Newton Smith Limbird' (1799-1856)', H C G Matthew and Brian Harrison (eds), *Oxford Dictionary of National Biography*, Oxford University Press, 2004, vol 19, p 511
Marcia Pointon, 'Fielding: (5) Newton (Limbird Smith) Fielding (*b* Durham, 1797; *d* Paris, 1856)', Jane Turner (ed), *The Dictionary of Art*, London: Macmillan, 1996, vol 11, pp 60-61

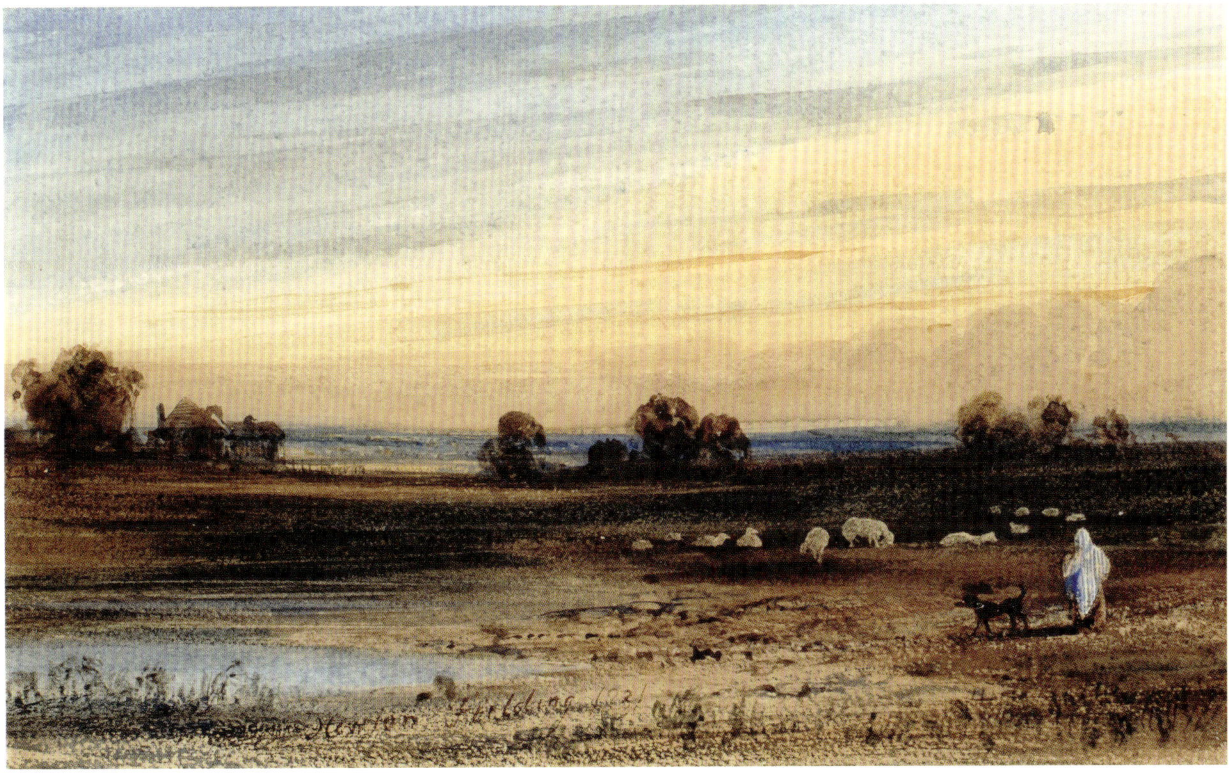

263 SUNSET
signed and dated 1831
watercolour
4 ¾ x 7 inches

GEORGE CATTERMOLE
George Cattermole, OWS (1800-1868)

Inspired by the example of Richard Parkes Bonington, George Cattermole became the foremost watercolourist of historical subjects during the early Victorian period, and developed an impressive international reputation. Equally successful as an exhibiting artist and an illustrator, he ranged in his work from the Middle Ages to the Seventeenth Century, but had a particular affinity with the imagination of Walter Scott. Civilised and sociable in his earlier years, he moved in fashionable circles, and became a close friend of many artists and writers, including Charles Dickens.

George Cattermole was born in the village of Dickleburgh, near Diss, Norfolk, on 10 August 1800, the youngest of seven children of a man of independent means. Educated by his father, he gained a love of literature and history, and developed a style of writing that has been called 'correct and classic' (Roget 1891, vol 1, p 496). He may have spent some time as an assistant schoolteacher before leaving for London in 1819.

In London, George Cattermole worked alongside his elder brother, Richard, for the antiquarian, John Britton. While Richard would abandon 'art for the Church' (Mallalieu 1986, vol 1, p 73), George became 'right hand man' on John Britton's series, *Cathedral Antiquities of Great Britain*, and so developed as an architectural draughtsman and illustrator. Almost immediately, he began to exhibit architectural compositions at the Royal Academy of Arts (1819-27) and the Society of Painters in Water Colours (1821-50), and was made an associate of the latter in 1822. Though pressure of work for Britton resulted in a lapse in his associate membership, he was re-elected in 1829 and became a full member in 1833.

In all, Cattermole would exhibit about a hundred watercolours with the Society of Painters in Water Colours over three decades. Technically, he sustained a relaxed and confident approach to handling, derived from fellow member, DAVID COX, while moving from transparent watercolour to bodycolour. Thematically, he focussed increasingly on romanticised historical narrative, in emulation of Richard Parkes Bonington, and became the foremost watercolourist in the genre. Developing an expertise in the long period from the Middle Ages to the late seventeenth century, the artist was particularly inspired by Walter Scott and, in the 1830s, travelled to Scotland to sketch the settings for many of his Waverley novels. Some of the resulting drawings were worked up for exhibition, while others were engraved as illustrations for various volumes, including keepsake annuals.

Success as an artist helped Cattermole enter distinguished social circles, notably that of Lady Blessington and the Comte d'Orsay at Gore House, Kensington. He moved from Brixton Hill to 36 Gerrard Street, Soho (by 1833), and then into a suite of private chambers at the Albany (in 1838), which had once been occupied by Lord Byron and more recently by Edward Bulwer-Lytton. At that time, he had a studio at 68 Welbeck Street, Marylebone. He was also a member of the Garrick Club, the Athenaeum and the short-lived Shakespeare Club. In July 1839, he was offered a knighthood, mainly as a result of his successful response to Queen Victoria's idea that he produce a representation of Martin Luther at the Diet of Spires (V&A); however, he believed the work to be laboured and modestly declined the honour.

On 20 August 1839, at St Marylebone Church, Cattermole married Clarissa Hester Elderton, the daughter of James Elderton, a Deputy Remembrancer of the Court of Exchequer, and a distant marital relation of Charles Dickens. Settling into a grand house in Clapham Rise, they brought up their nine children in an affectionate atmosphere, while also entertaining in extravagant style. Known collectively as the Portwiners, Cattermole's regular male guests included novelists (Dickens, Thackeray and Bulwer-Lytton), journalists (John Forster and Mark Lemon), painters (the Landseer Brothers and Daniel Maclise) and the actor Charles Macready.

During the early 1840s, Cattermole contributed illustrations to some of Dickens' writings, notably *The Old Curiosity Shop* (1840-41) and *Barnaby Rudge*, and then responded to commissions from Dickens for a pair of watercolours inspired by the former: *Little Nell's Home* (Dickens House Museum) and *Little Nell's Grave* (V&A). His sense of fun and talent for mimicry, which came to the fore in amateur theatricals, also inspired some of the characters and their use of language in Dickens' novels. It was in this period that Cattermole began to produce the illustrations for his brother Richard's two-volume history, *The Great Civil War of Charles I and Parliament* (1841 and 1855).

Having preferred the company of Royal Academicians to that of his fellow Painters in Water Colours, Cattermole showed increasingly less interest in the society, exhibiting only small drawings through the late 1840s, and then nothing at all in 1851. However, by the end of that year, he had also become confined to his bed with a serious illness.

Following his recovery, Cattermole resigned from the society, and decided to turn towards oils. Yet, he did not enjoy the practice and, as the results of his efforts were not well received, he returned to watercolour. The works that he then produced were bought directly by collectors from the artist rather than through exhibition.

Those exhibitions that did include his work tended to be prestigious and retrospective. So the Paris Exposition Universelle of 1855 included eleven of his works, which were so enthusiastically received that he was awarded a shared *grande médaille d'honneur* with Edwin Landseer. Two years later, the 'Exhibition of Art Treasures of the United Kingdom', held in Manchester, contained thirty-one of his works while, in 1862, the International Exhibition in London contained thirteen works. The breadth of his reputation was also confirmed by his election as a member of both the Academie voor Beelende Kunsten, Amsterdam (1855) and the Belgian Society of Watercolour Painters (1856).

In the summer of 1856, Cattermole took his family on a rare trip abroad, to a villa in Boulogne. When Dickens arrived in the town to work on *Little Dorrit*, he found that the landlord complained 'that the artist always promised but never paid his bills' (Cohen 1980, p 134). This occasion seems to have marked a downturn in his fortunes, as he became anxious over health and money, and thus increasingly retiring.

Soon after the family moved to 4 Cedars Road, Clapham, in the early 1860s, two of Cattermole's children died, due to poverty, so sending him deeper into depression. He died at home on 24 July 1868, leaving his widow, three sons and four daughters.

An auction of Cattermole's paintings, drawings, and books was held at Christie's on 9 March 1869.

One of his sons, Leonardo Cattermole (active 1869-1886), became a painter of Civil War subjects. Richard's son, Charles Cattermole (1832-1900), emulated his uncle's style.

His work is represented in numerous public collections, including the Tate and the V&A; and Manchester Art Gallery and Wiltshire Heritage Museum (Devizes).

Further reading:

Randall Davies, 'George Cattermole (1800-1868)', *Old Water-Colour Society's Club*, 1931-32, vol 9, pp 25-37
Della Clason Sperling, 'Cattermole, George (1800–1868)', H C G Matthew and Brian Harrison (eds), *Oxford Dictionary of National Biography*, Oxford University Press, 2004, vol 10, pp 562-565
Scott Wilcox, 'Cattermole, George (*b* Dickleburgh, Norfolk, 10 Aug 1800; *d* London, 24 July 1868)', Jane Turner (ed), *The Dictionary of Art*, London: Macmillan, 1996, vol 6, pp 90-91

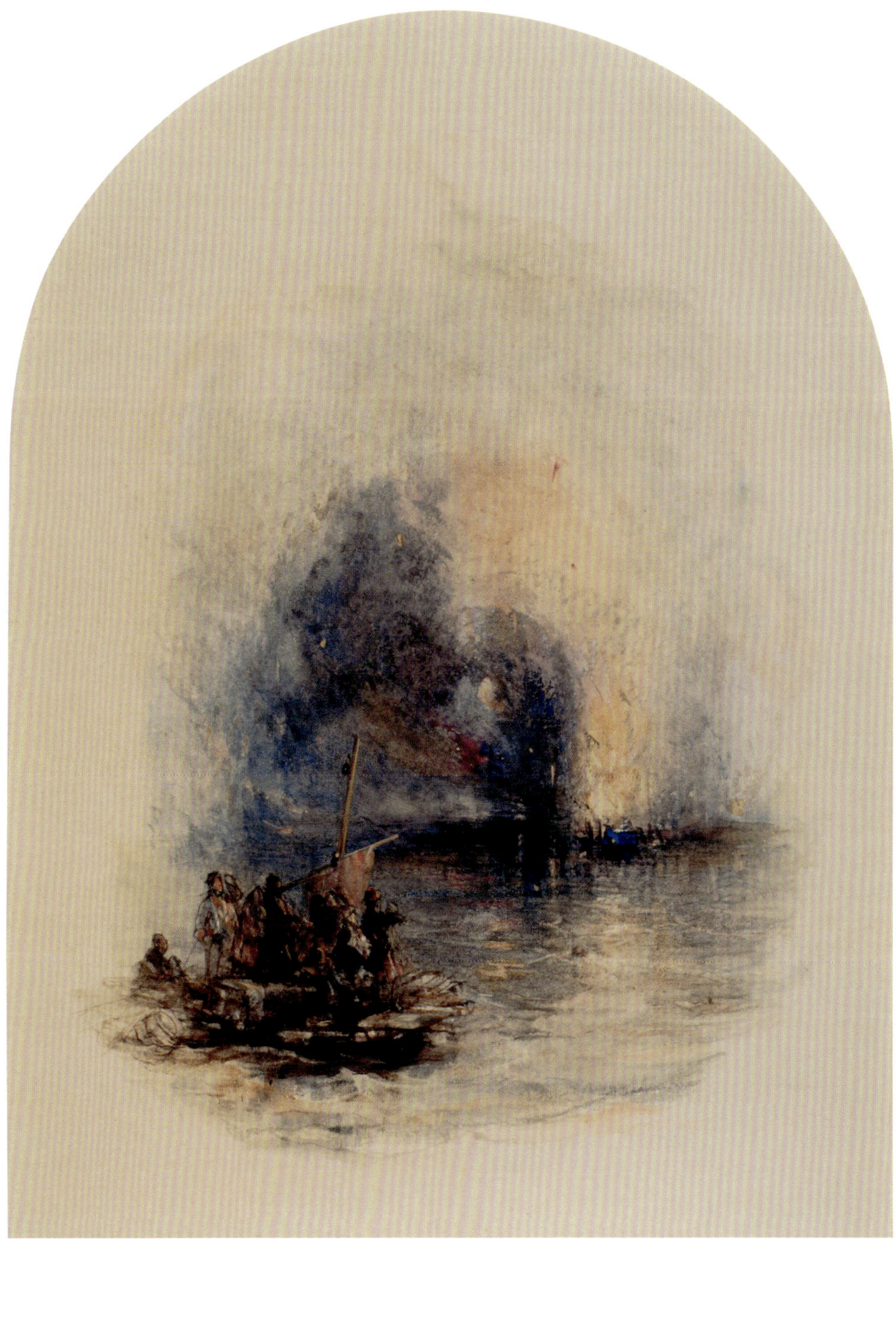

264 SHIPWRECK
watercolour with bodycolour
12 ½ x 9 inches (including arched top)

FREDERICK TAYLER
John Frederick Tayler, PRWS RCAMA (1806-1889)

The painter, printmaker and illustrator, Frederick Tayler gained a high reputation for his genre watercolours, executed with a confident freshness reminiscent of that of his friend Richard Parkes Bonington. These can be divided into three types of scene: sporting, pastoral and historical. The landscape and literature of Scotland, notably the novels of Sir Walter Scott, provided regular inspiration.

One of seventeen children, Frederick Tayler was born in Borehamwood, Hertfordshire on 30 April 1806 (according to Simon Fenwick, in Matthew and Harrison 2004, v 53, p 852, though some sources give 1802). His father had been a country landowner who, ruined by his agent, was forced to go into the army, and died while Tayler was still a child.

Intended for the church, Tayler received a classical education at both Eton College and Harrow School, a circumstance that Martin Hardie has considered 'surely unique' among watercolourists of the time (Hardie 1967, vol 3, p 91).

Determined to become an artist, Tayler studied in London, at Henry Sass's School for Drawing and Painting and at the Royal Academy Schools, and then in Paris under Horace Vernet. He also visited Rome. While in Paris, he lodged with Richard Parkes Bonington, whom he had met in Calais, where Bonington was sketching with LOUIS FRANCIA. It is Bonington who is likely to have encouraged his preference for watercolour. However, he later took lessons in oil painting from William Powell Frith, his junior by some years.

Tayler lived in London for most of his life, and became a member of both the Garrick and Athenaeum clubs. He exhibited at the Royal Academy of Arts (from 1830 to 1865), the British Institution and especially the Society of Painters in Water Colours (known familiarly as an Old Water-Colour Society from 1832, to distinguish it from the New Society). Becoming an associate of the last in 1831, and a full member three years later, he showed five hundred works at its exhibitions, including twelve in collaboration with the landscape painter, George Barret.

Tayler soon developed a distinguished following, headed by Queen Victoria, who purchased work for Windsor Castle, and John Ruskin, who praised him in the first volume of *Modern Painters* (1843), though he later expressed some reservations about his evolving style. He accumulated a number of aristocratic pupils, and became a frequent guest at house parties, particularly in Scotland.

Tayler also became known through his illustrations and prints. As a member of the Etching Club, he issued prints throughout his career, beginning with a series of lithotints collected as *Frederick Tayler's Portfolio* (1844-45). (For a preliminary list of his contributions as an illustrator, please see opposite.)

On the death of COPLEY FIELDING in 1855, Tayler became acting President of the Old Water-Colour Society for a period of eight months. In that capacity, he was called on to help select the British paintings, engravings and lithographs for the Exposition Universelle in Paris, and awarded a Légion d'honneur for his pains. And pains he had indeed, as he had entered into a dispute about the hanging of the drawings, particularly those by John Frederick Lewis, which left him seriously ill from stress.

Lewis then replaced Tayler as President of the Old Water-Colour Society but, when he decided to resign in February 1858, Tayler was unanimously elected to replace him. He remained in office until 1870 but was considered an ineffectual administrator.

Though Tayler exhibited little at this stage in his career, a loan show of his work was held at J & W Vokins of Great Portland Street in 1880. He also published the volume, *Studies in Animal Painting* (1884).

By this time, Tayler had an international reputation. He was an elected member of the Société des Aquarellistes of Belgium and the Pennsylvanian Academy, as well as the Royal Cambrian Academy, and the recipient of awards from Belgium, Bavaria (1859) and Austria (1872).

Late in life, Tayler made heavy losses as a result of unfortunate investments. He died at his home, 63 Gascony Avenue, West Hampstead, London, on 20 June 1889. His remaining works were sold by Christie's on 27 January and 17 February 1890.

Having married in 1837, Tayler had five children, two of whom became artists: Kate Tayler who exhibited at the Society of Women Artists and the Dudley Gallery, and Norman E Tayler, who was elected an associate of the Old Water-Colour Society in 1878.

His work is represented in numerous public collections, including the British Museum and the V&A.

Further reading:

Simon Fenwick, 'Tayler, (John) Frederick (1806–1889)', H C G Matthew and Brian Harrison (eds), *Oxford Dictionary of National Biography*, Oxford University Press, 2004, vol 53, p 852

Martin Postle, 'Tayler, (John) Frederick (*b* Borehamwood, Herts, 30 April 1802; *d* London, 20 June 1889)', Jane Turner (ed), *The Dictionary of Art*, London: Macmillan, 1996, vol 30, p 384

There are few drawings of the present day that involve greater sensations of power than those of Frederick Tayler. Every dash tells and the quantity of effect obtained is enormous in proportion to the apparent means.

John Ruskin, *Modern Painters*, 1843

A Preliminary List of Books Illustrated by Frederick Tayler

1841
Oliver Goldsmith, *The Deserted Village*, London: Etching Club (in collaboration with other members, including John Bell, Charles West Cope, John Callcott Horsley, Richard Redgrave, Charles Stonehouse, Henry James Townsend, Thomas Webster)

1842
James Thomson, *The Seasons*, London: Longman, Brown, Green and Longmans (in collaboration with John Bell, Charles West Cope, Thomas Creswick, John Callcott Horsley, John Prescott Knight, Richard Redgrave, Frank Stone, Charles Stonhouse, Henry James Townsend and Thomas Webster)

1844
The Ancient and Modern Ballads of Chevy Chase (Felix Summerley's Home Treasury), London: Joseph Cundall
[Charles A Cole]; *Puck's Report to Oberon* (Felix Summerley's Home Treasury), London: Joseph Cundall

1846
[Richard Hengist Horne], *The Good-Natured Bear*, London: Joseph Cundall
Oliver Goldsmith, *The Poetical Works*, London: Longman, Brown, Green and Longmans (in collaboration with Charles West Cope, Thomas Creswick, John Callcott Horsley and Samuel Redgrave)

1849
Robert Bloomfield, *Poems*, London: J Van Hoorst (in collaboration with Thomas Sidney Cooper, John Callcott Horsley and Thomas Webster)

1850
Sir Roger de Coverley. By the Spectator, London: Longmans, Brown, Green and Longmans (in collaboration with W Henry Wills)

1851
Oliver Goldsmith, *The Traveller*, London: Art-Union

1864
Anon, *Old English Ballads*, London: Ward & Lock (in collaboration with Myles Birket Foster and Joseph Nash)

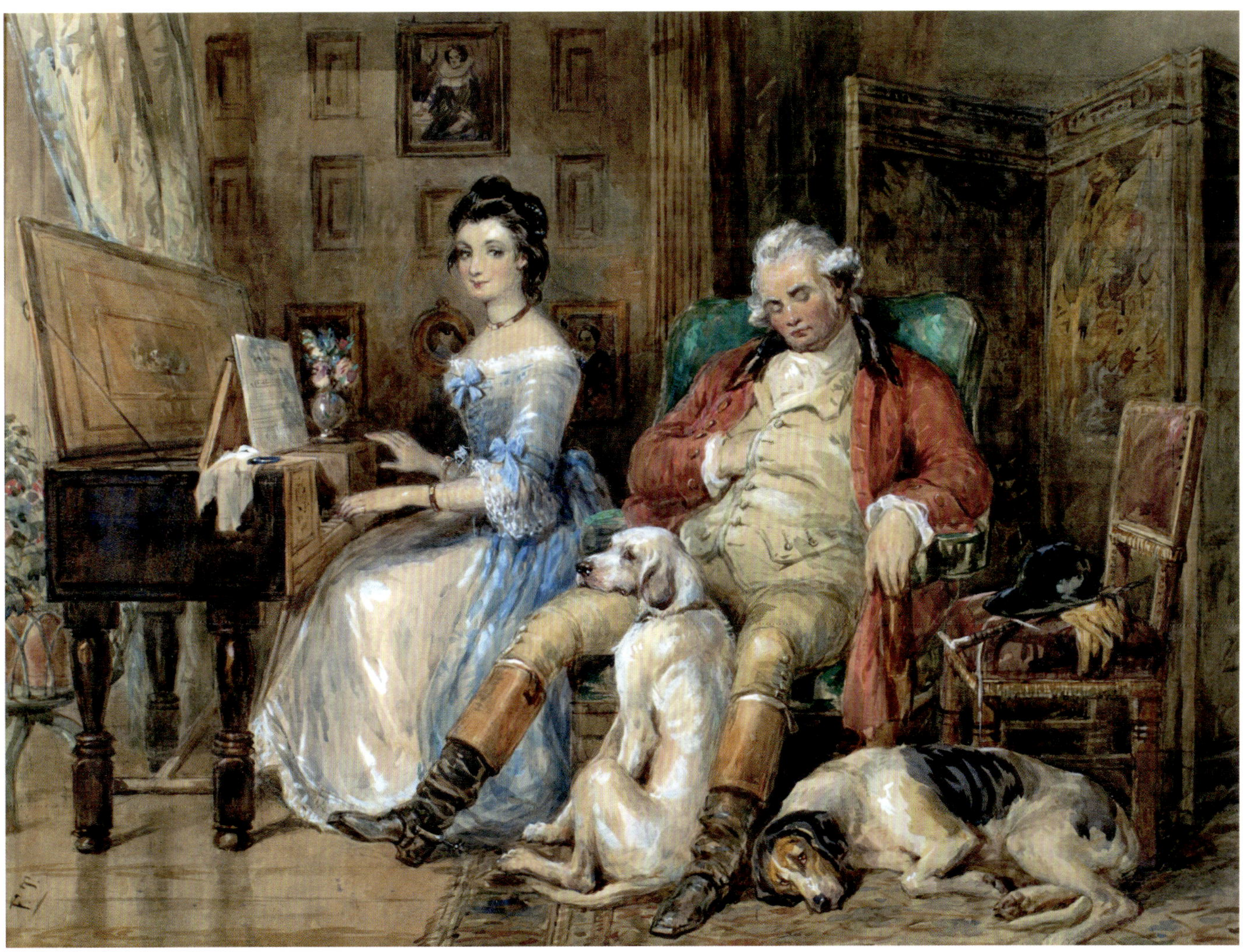

265 SOPHIA AND SQUIRE WESTERN
signed with initials
watercolour
14 ¾ x 19 ¾ inches

THOMAS SHOTTER BOYS

Thomas Shotter Boys, NWS (1803-1874)

The closest follower of Richard Parkes Bonington, Thomas Shotter Boys worked with equal success as a watercolourist and printmaker. His chromolithographs of European cities proved especially innovative and popular.

Thomas Shotter Boys was born in Pentonville, London on 2 January 1803, the son of a salesman. He was apprenticed to the engraver, George Cooke, between 1817 and 1823, and his training in printmaking had an influence on the development of his lucid style of watercolour. Though exhibiting at the Society of British Artists from 1824 (until 1858), he moved to Paris, where he met Richard Parkes Bonington, as well as the Fielding brothers and WILLIAM CALLOW.

As Bonington's friend and protégé, Boys entered an influential artistic circle that included the painter, Eugène Delacroix, and the young writer, Prosper Merimée. While Bonington encouraged Boys to concentrate on watercolours, so he, in turn, may have given lessons in etching to Bonington and the landscape painter, Paul Huet. He exhibited four designs, as engraved by Cooke, at the Paris Salon of 1827-28.

When revolution broke out in Paris in 1830, Boys retreated to London, but returned to the French capital a year later. He soon showed himself – on both sides of the English Channel – to be Bonington's closest follower. He exhibited at the Salon again from 1833, and at the New Society of Painters in Water Colours from 1832 (becoming an associate in 1840, and full member in 1841). He also passed on aspects of the Bonington style directly to his pupils, notably Callow, with whom he shared his studio at 19 rue du Bouloy.

Boys was in Paris at a time when British printmakers were in demand. In addition to his abilities as an etcher, he took lessons in lithography, either at Godefroy Engelmann's Imprimerie Lithographique, or from one of the English artists working for the publisher, J F d'Ostervald. Ever aware of the potential relationship between painting and printmaking, he considered lithography, in particular, as 'painting on stone'. He put his newly learned skills to good use, from 1833, in his contributions to the *Picardie* and *Langeudoc* volumes of Baron Isidore Taylor's *Voyages pittoresques et romantiques dans l'ancienne France.*

Returning to London in 1837 with a large number of watercolours, Boys set about making chromolithographs of them, which Charles Hullmandel published together, two years later, as *Picturesque Architecture in Paris, Ghent, Antwerp, Rouen, etc.* A technically innovative achievement, the project brought him a degree of international fame. *Original Views of London as It Is* (1842) proved equally popular.

However, by 1850, Boys was past his peak. He attempted to revive his work as a painter by taking sketching tours, but had to find work as a drawing master and printmaker. One significant late patron was John Ruskin, for whom Boys prepared the etching plates for *Modern Painters* and the lithographs for *The Stones of Venice.*

Affected by illness and poverty, Boys died at his home – 30 Acacia Road, St John's Wood – on 10 October 1874, leaving a widow.

His work is represented in numerous public collections, including the British Museum and the V&A; and the Yale Center For British Art (New Haven).

Further reading:

Patrick Noon, 'Boys, Thomas Shotter (1803-1874)', H C G Matthew and Brian Harrison (eds), *Oxford Dictionary of National Biography*, Oxford University Press, 2004, vol 7, pp 125-126

Marcia Pointon, 'Boys, Thomas Shotter (*b* Pentonville, London, 2 Jan 1803; *d* London, 2 Oct 1874)', Jane Turner (ed), *The Dictionary of Art*, London: Macmillan, 1996, vol 4, pp 614-615

J Roundell, *Thomas Shotter Boys, 1803-1874*, London: Octopus Books, 1974

A Smart (intro), *Thomas Shotter Boys (1803-1874): Centenary Exhibition*, Nottingham University/London: Thomas Agnew & Sons, 1974

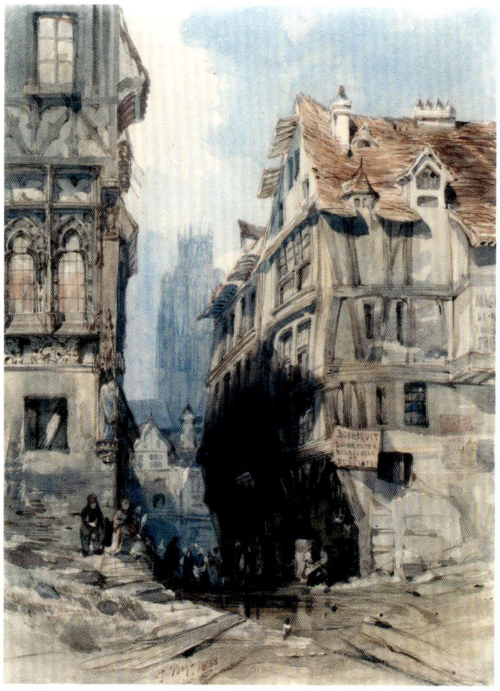

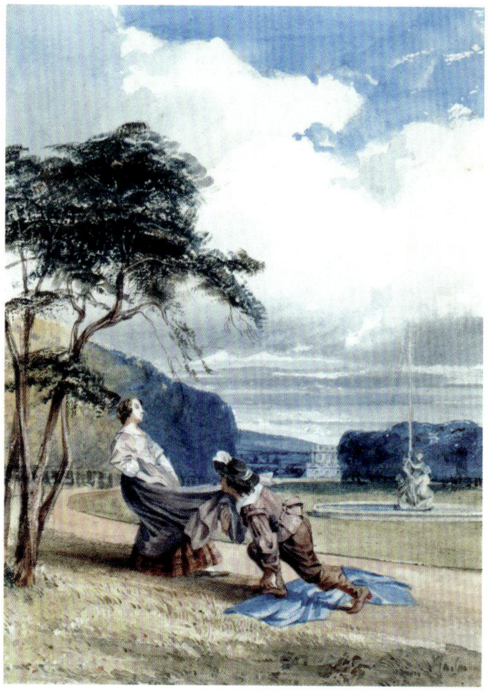

266 RUE MARITAINE, ROUEN
signed and dated 1838
watercolour
12 ¾ x 9 ¼ inches
Literature: James Roundell, *Thomas Shotter Boys*, 1803-1874, London: Octopus Books, 1974, plate 39 (as a soft ground etching)

267 ELEGANT FIGURES IN THE GROUNDS OF A STATELY HOME
watercolour
13 ½ x 9 ½ inches

CHARLES BENTLEY
Charles Bentley, OWS (1805/06-1854)

In engraving works by Richard Parkes Bonington, Charles Bentley learned much about the art of watercolour. The resulting coastal scenes and seascapes – fresh with the salt breeze – have been ranked with those of Copley Fielding and his friend, William Callow.

Charles Bentley was born in Tottenham Court Road, London, the son of a carpenter, and is possibly the child baptised at St James's, Paddington, on 24 August 1806.

In about 1819, Bentley was apprenticed as an engraver to Theodore Fielding, and went on to work in Paris with his brother, NEWTON FIELDING, with whom he engraved a number of watercolours by Richard Parkes Bonington. This experience had a profound influence on his own development as a watercolourist, as did the work of WILLIAM CALLOW, who was also apprenticed to the Fielding brothers, and became a close friend.

In 1827, Bentley set up as an engraver, and worked as an illustrator, though with little financial success. Concentrating instead on watercolour, he was elected an associate of the Society of Painters in Water Colours in 1834, and a full member nine years later. Over thirty years, he exhibited 209 works with the society, also showing work at the Society of British Artists and the New Society of Painters in Water Colours.

Many of these exhibits were the fruits of extensive travels that Bentley made around the coasts of the British Isles, and to the Channel Islands and Normandy – the last in the company of Callow in 1836, 1840 and 1841. Between 1843 and 1846, he shared Callow's home and studio at 20 Charlotte Street (now Hallam Street), before returning to his own address, 11 Mornington Place, Hampstead Road.

A poor businessman, ever in financial difficulties, Bentley left his wife and mother in near poverty when he died at home, of cholera, on 4 September 1854.

His studio sale was held at Christie's on 16 April 1855.

His work is represented in numerous public collections, including the British Museum and the V&A; and The Whitworth Art Gallery (Manchester).

Further reading:

David Cordingly, 'Bentley, Charles (*b* London, 1805-6; *d* London, 4 Sept 1854)', Jane Turner (ed), *The Dictionary of Art*, London: Macmillan, 1996, vol 3, p 745

Jan Reynolds, 'Bentley, Charles (1805/6-1854)', H C G Matthew and Brian Harrison (eds), *Oxford Dictionary of National Biography*, Oxford University Press, 2004, vol 5, pp 276-277

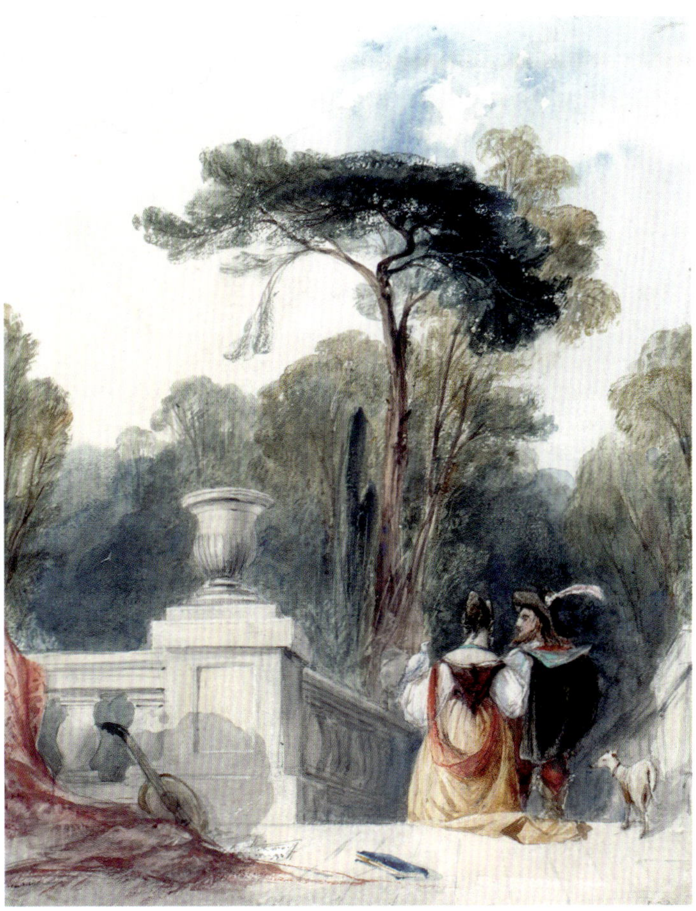

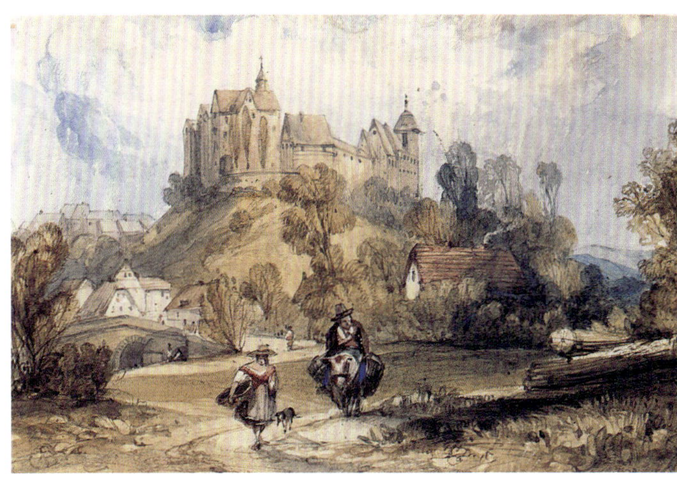

269 TRAVELLERS NEAR A TOWN IN NORTHERN FRANCE
signed with initials
watercolour
4 x 6 inches

268 A COUPLE IN COURTLY DRESS
signed with initials
watercolour
11 ¾ x 8 ½ inches

WILLIAM WYLD
William Wyld, RI (1806-1889)

A diplomat and then a wine merchant, William Wyld was inspired by the example of Richard Parkes Bonington to become a watercolourist. His strongly coloured, virtuoso townscapes and landscapes proved highly influential in the development of watercolour in France.

The son of a businessman, William Wyld was born in London. He entered the diplomatic service, acting as Secretary to the British Consul in Calais, a position previously held by LOUIS FRANCIA who, still living in Calais, gave him lessons in painting. Through Francia and John Lewis Brown, Bordeaux wine merchant and art collector, he was introduced to the work of Richard Parkes Bonington. Absorbing Bonington's influence, he would, in turn, affect the development of watercolour in France.

In 1827, Wyld took charge of a wine business in Epernay, and there began to find patrons for his watercolours. Exhibiting at the Paris Salon in 1831, he settled in the French capital two years later, and became a good friend of the artists, Camille Roqueplan and Horace Vernet. Almost immediately, he and Vernet travelled to North Africa, a journey that resulted in *Voyage pittoresque sans la régence d'Alger pendant l'année 1833*, a collaboration with the lithographer, Emile Lessore. Six years later, he also published twenty lithographs of Paris.

While living in France, Wyld retained his British nationality, and exhibited in London from 1849, becoming an associate of the New Society of Painters in Water Colours in that year, and a full member three decades later. (The NWS became the Royal Institute of Painters in Watercolours in 1881.) He also showed work at the Royal Academy of Arts and the British Institution. Patronised by Queen Victoria, he was invited to Balmoral in 1852, and produced a series of watercolours of the area.

However, Wyld had a more central role in the Parisian art scene, being awarded two medals at the Salon, and given the Légion d'Honneur in 1855. He died in Paris on 25 December 1889

His work is represented in the Royal Collection, and numerous public collections, including the British Museum and the V&A; and Manchester Art Gallery.

Further reading:
Marcia Pointon, *Bonington, Francia and Wyld*, London: Batsford/Victoria & Albert Museum, 1985
Marcia Pointon, 'Wyld, William (*b* London, 1806; *d* Paris, 25 Dec 1889)', Jane Turner (ed), *The Dictionary of Art*, London: Macmillan, 1996, vol 33, pp 451-452

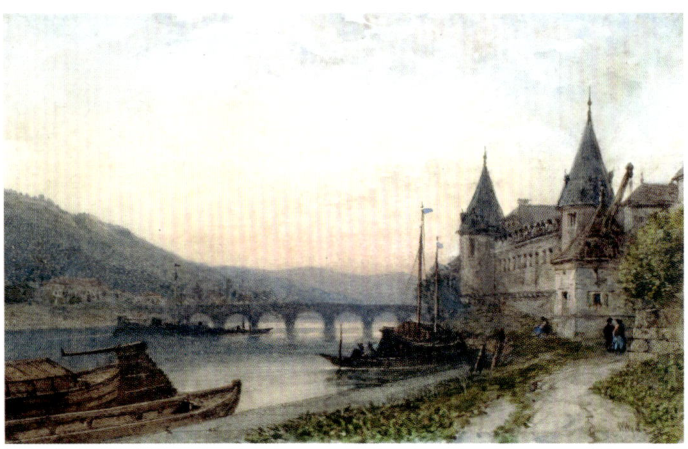

270 A CHATEAU BY THE RIVER
signed
watercolour with bodycolour
6 ½ x 10 ⅜ inches

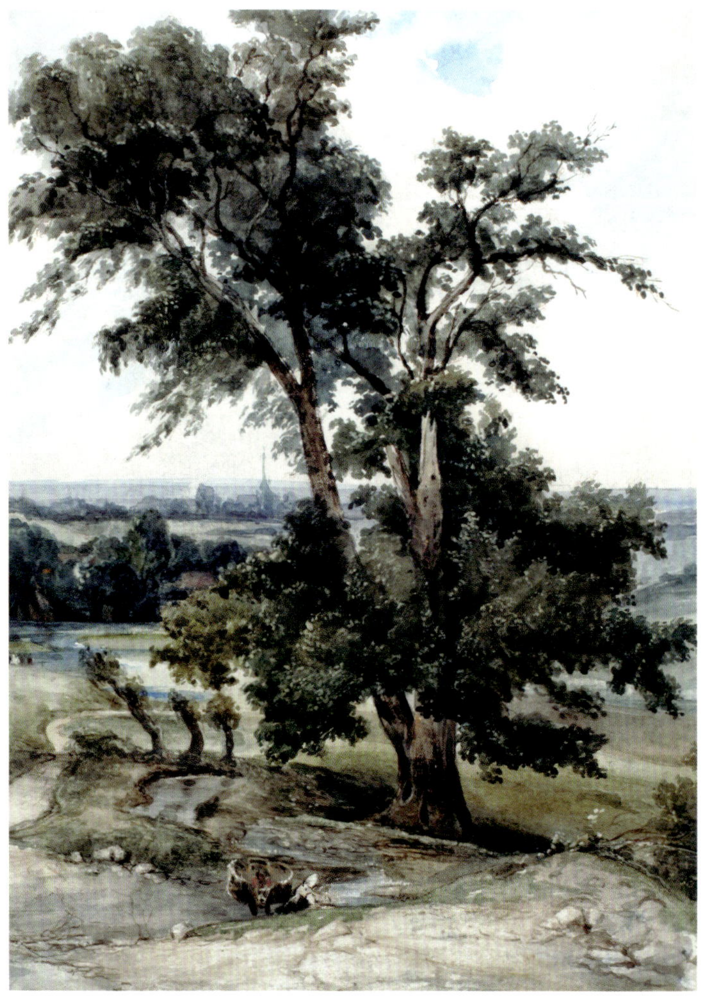

271 LANDSCAPE IN NORTHERN FRANCE
watercolour
14 ¾ x 10 ½ inches

WILLIAM CALLOW
William Callow, RWS FRGS (1812-1908)

Through his watercolours, William Callow reinterpreted the approach of Richard Parkes Bonington to highly popular ends, and ensured that the Bonington tradition thrived until late into the nineteenth century.

William Callow was born in Greenwich, Kent, on 28 July 1812, the elder son of a builder and carpenter who encouraged his artistic talents early on. His younger brother, John, would become a marine watercolourist and drawing master. The Callow brothers grew up the family home in Tottenham Place, off Tottenham Court Road, London.

In 1823, at the age of eleven, Callow began to work under the engraver Theodore Fielding, thus entering a period in which he was strongly influenced and aided by the Fielding brothers. Two years later, he was formally articled to Theodore for instruction in watercolour drawing and aquatint engraving; while in that position he was given his first painting lessons by fellow apprentice CHARLES BENTLEY, and was further encouraged by COPLEY FIELDING. Then, in 1829, he broke with his apprenticeship by taking up the invitation of Thales Fielding to go to Paris to work for the publisher J F d'Ostervald. While there, he began to produce contributions to Charles Heath's *Picturesque Annual: Versailles* (published a decade later in 1839). He lived and worked in Paris with NEWTON FIELDING until 1830, when the outbreak of revolution forced them to return to England.

By February 1831, Callow had returned to Paris and was associating with THOMAS SHOTTER BOYS. He worked in his studio, in rue du Bouloy, and accompanied him on sketching trips. Through him, he found inspiration in the watercolours of Richard Parkes Bonington, who had died in 1828. His early work reinterpreted the approach of Bonington to extremely popular ends. Taking over the studio of Boys, in 1834, he developed a highly profitable practice as a drawing master to members of the French nobility. As a result of exhibiting at the Salon of that year, he was even noticed by King Louis-Philippe who employed him to teach his children, the Duc de Nemours and the Princesse Clémentine.

During the mid 1830s, Callow began a series of long walking and sketching tours, which took him across the Continent and increasingly back to England. In London, in 1838, he was encouraged by John Frederick Lewis to join the Society of Painters in Water Colours and, on submitting some drawings, was promptly elected an associate. (He was elected a full member a decade later, and would act for periods as Secretary and Trustee.)

In 1841, Callow left Paris and set up in London, at 20 Charlotte Street (later Hallam Street). As a drawing master, he again developed a large clientele, which included Lady Beaujolais Berry, Lady Stratford de Redcliffe, Lord Dufferin – and Harriet Anne Smart, whom he married in 1846. At the end of the decade, he began to work in oil as well as watercolour, ambitiously increasing the scale of his works.

In 1854, the Callows moved to Great Missenden, Buckinghamshire, and built a large house, named The Firs, while keeping on their London home. At The Firs, Callow continued to work, both as a drawing master and exhibiting artist, almost until his death. He also continued to make Continental tours, his final visit to Italy taking place in 1892.

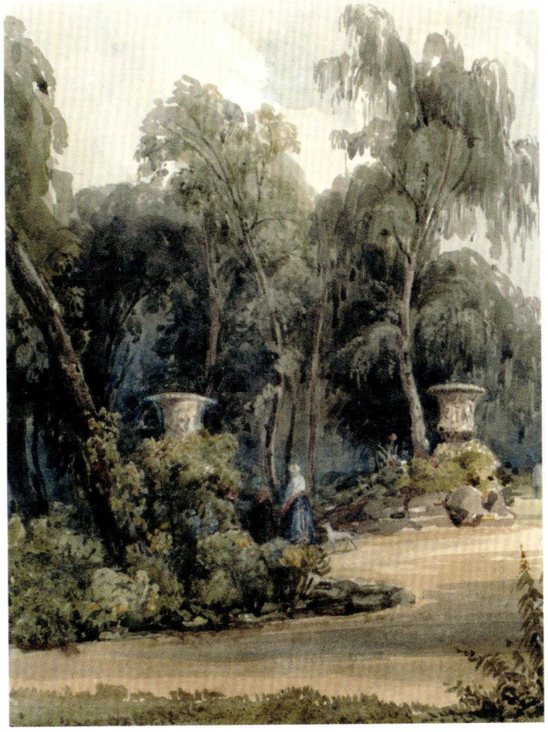

277 IN THE PARK AT ROYAUMONT, NEAR PARIS
inscribed 'Royaumont' on reverse
watercolour, 8 ¼ x 6 inches
Provenance: Albany Gallery, London

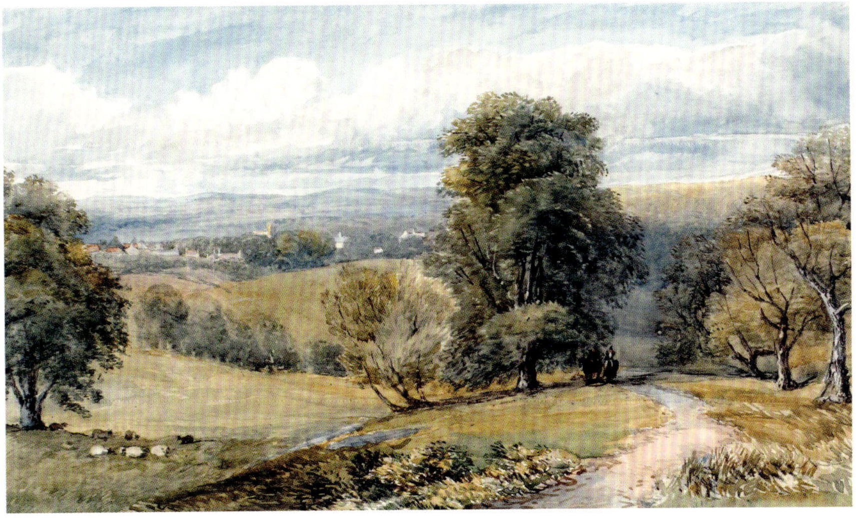

272 A RIDE IN THE COUNTRY
watercolour
10 x 16 ¾ inches

In the Park at Royaumont, near Paris
William Callow stayed at Royaumont with the Vandermere family in August 1833, probably in the company of the painter, Baron Louis-Auguste Schwiter (well known from the large full-length portrait by Eugène Delacroix, now held in the National Gallery). He produced a number of works during his stay, including a number of pencil sketches in the V&A.

Following the death of Harriet in 1883, Callow married Mary Louisa Jefferay, a much younger woman who outlived him.

He died in Great Missenden on 20 February 1908, and his autobiography, edited by H M Cundall appeared in the same year. In the year before, his early work had been exhibited at the Leicester Galleries with such success that it encouraged a reassessment of his career.

His studio sale was held at Christie's on 21 March 1910.

His work is represented in the collections of Eton College, and numerous public collections, including the British Museum, The Courtauld Gallery, Tate and the V&A; Birmingham Museum & Art Gallery, The Fitzwilliam Museum (Cambridge), Manchester Art Gallery and Southampton Art Gallery; and Harvard University Art Museums (Cambridge MA).

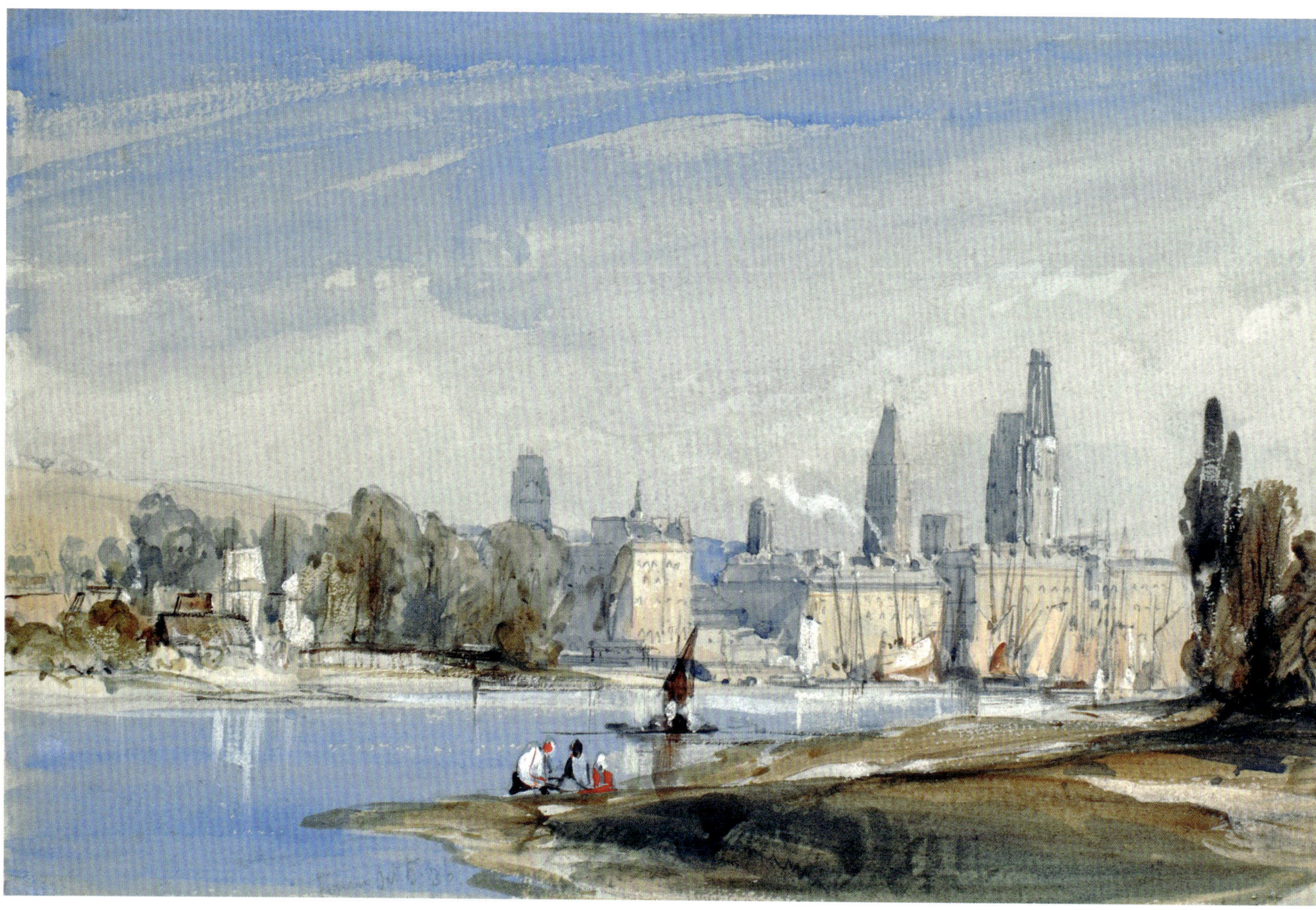

273 ROUEN
inscribed with title and dated 'Oct 5 36'
watercolour with bodycolour
7 x 10 ¼ inches

Rouen

In October 1836, William Callow and Charles Bentley made a sketching tour of Normandy, taking in Rouen and Le Havre. On the same day that he dated this watercolour, Wednesday 5 October, he made two pencil sketches of a fishing boat that are now in the V&A. Another watercolour, with a similar composition, is now in The Fitzwilliam Museum (Cambridge). Callow and Bentley would return to Normandy in 1840 and 1841.

Further reading:
Marcia Pointon, 'Callow, William (b Greenwich, nr London, 28 July 1812; d Great Missenden, Bucks, 20 Feb 1908)', Jane Turner (ed), *The Dictionary of Art*, London: Macmillan, 1996, vol 5, p 439
Jan Reynolds, 'Callow, William (1812-1908)', H C G Matthew and Brian Harrison (eds), *Oxford Dictionary of National Biography*, Oxford University Press, 2004, vol 9, pp 555-557
Jan Reynolds, *William Callow RWS*, London: B T Batsford, 1980

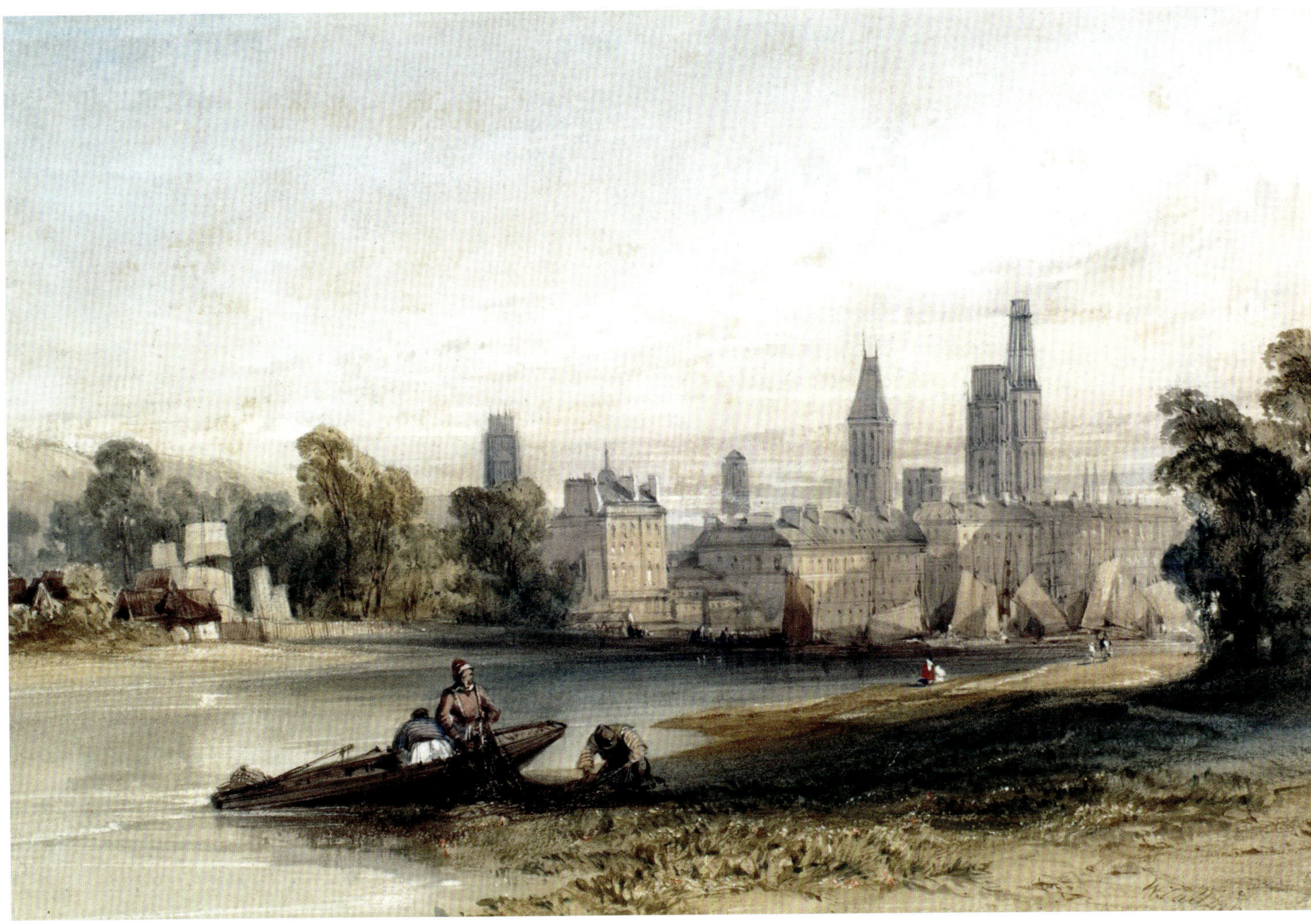

274 CLEANING THE NETS, ROUEN
signed
watercolour
8 ½ x 12 ¼ inches

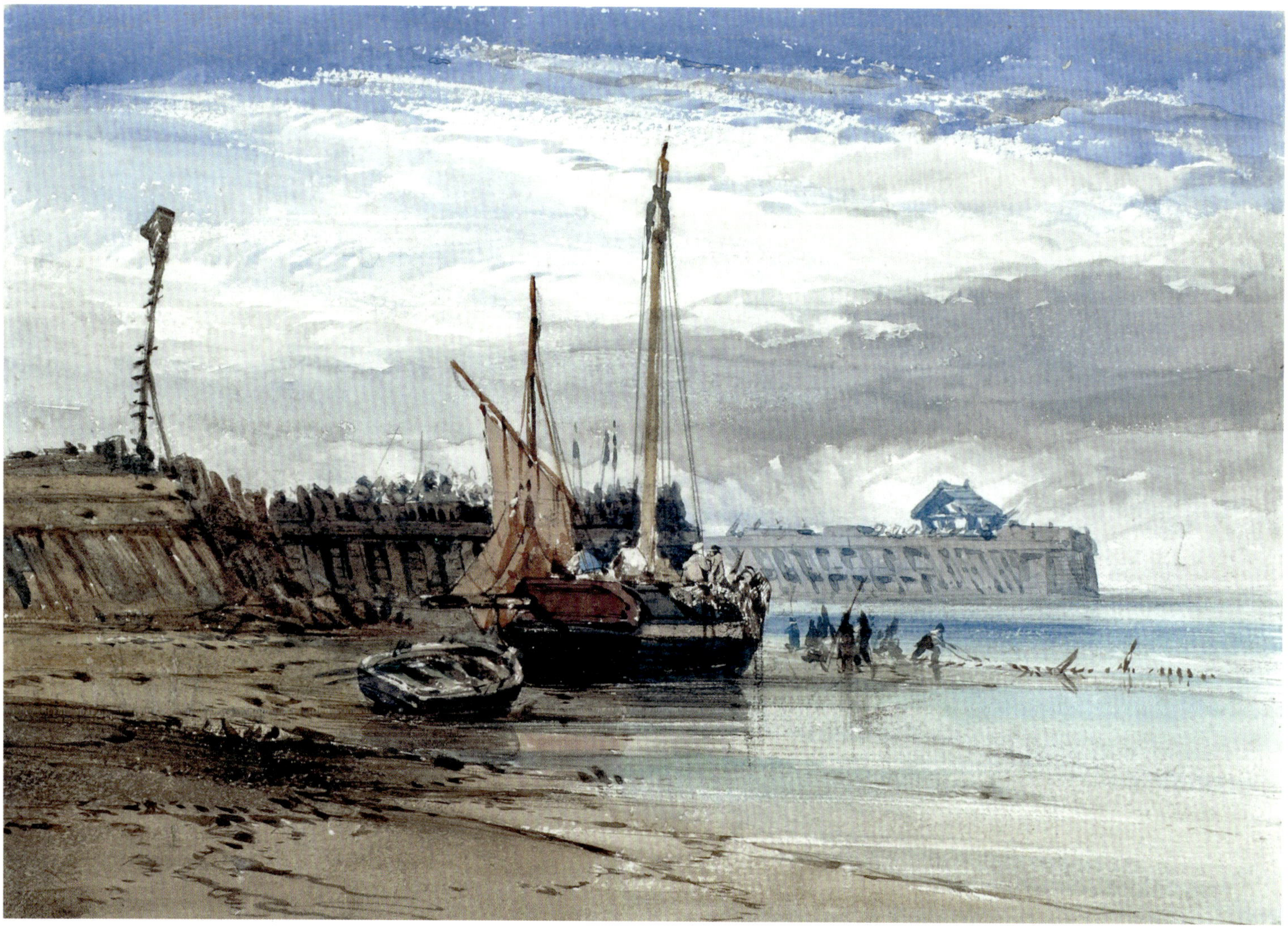

275 BOULOGNE
inscribed with title on reverse
watercolour
6 ¼ x 8 ¾ inches

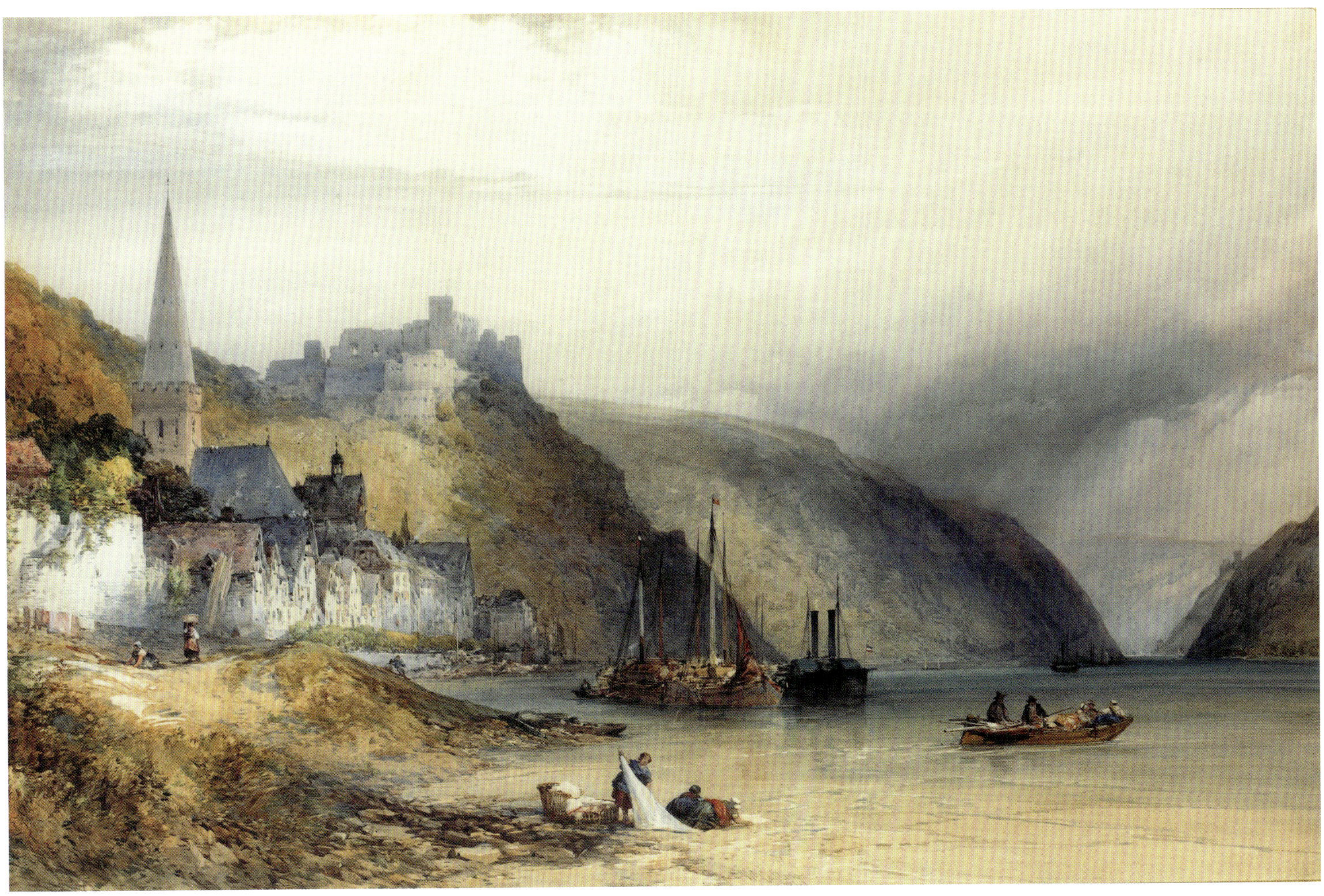

276 RHEINFELS AND VILLAGE OF ST GOAR
signed and dated 1862
inscribed with title and the artist's address on original back label
watercolour with bodycolour
26 ½ x 40 inches
Exhibited: Society of Painters in Water Colours, 1862
The British Institution, 1862, no 371
(also illustrated front endpaper, detail)

Rheinfels and the Village of St Goar
William Callow first visited St Goar on the River Rhine during a walking tour of 1838. The area inspired a number of compositions throughout his career.

SELECT GENERAL BIBLIOGRAPHY

CONTEMPORARY SOURCES

Dayes 1805
Edward Dayes, *The Works of the Late Edward Dayes*, London: Mrs Dayes, 1805

Farington 1978
Kenneth Garlick and Angus Macintyre (eds), *The Diary of Joseph Farington*, New Haven: Yale University Press, 1978-1998 (17 vols)

Gilpin 1768
William Gilpin, *An Essay upon Prints*, London: J Robson, 1768

Sandby 1862
William Sandby, *The History of the Royal Academy of Arts from its Foundation in 1768 to the Present Time, with biographical notices of all the members*, London: Longman, Green, Longman, Roberts & Green, 1862 (2 vols)

Vertue 1934
George Vertue, 'Note Books', vols 3-4, *Walpole Society*, vol 22, 1933-1934

SECONDARY SOURCES

Binyon 1931
Laurence Binyon, *Landscape in English Art and Poetry*, London: Cobden-Sanderson, 1931

Binyon 1933
Laurence Binyon, *English Watercolours*, London: A & C Black, 1933

Broughton 2005
Michael Broughton et al, *The Spooner Collection of British Watercolours*, London: The Courtauld Institute of Art/San Marino: The Huntington Library, Art Collections and Botanical Gardens/ Grasmere: The Wordsworth Trust, 2005

Bryant and Heneage 1994
Mark Bryant and Simon Heneage (compilers), *Dictionary of British Cartoonists and Caricaturists 1730-1980*, Aldershot: Scolar Press, 1994

Cohen 1980
Jane R Cohen, *Charles Dickens and his Original Illustrators*, Columbus: Ohio State University Press, 1980

Everitt 1893
Graham Everitt, *English Caricaturists and Graphic Humorists of the Nineteenth Century*, London: Sonnenschein & Co, 1893 (2nd edition)

Hardie 1967
Martin Hardie, *Water-colour Painting in Britain*, London: B T Batsford, 1967 (2nd edition) (3 vols)

Hawes 1982
Louis Hawes, *Presences of Nature. British Landscape 1780-1930*, New Haven: Yale Center for British Art, 1982

Houfe 1981
Simon Houfe, *The Dictionary of British Book Illustrators and Caricaturists 1800-1914*, Woodbridge: Antique Collectors' Club, 1981 (revised)

Lambourne and Hamilton 1980
Lionel Lambourne and Jean Hamilton, *British Watercolours in the Victoria and Albert Museum*, London: Sotheby Parke Bernet/Victoria and Albert Museum, 1980

Mallalieu 1986
H L Mallalieu, *The Dictionary of British Watercolour Artists up to 1920*, Woodbridge: Antique Collectors' Club, 1986 (2nd edition), vol 1

Matthew and Harrison 2004
H C G Matthew and Brian Harrison, *Oxford Dictionary of National Biography*, Oxford University Press, 2004 (61 vols)

Munro 1994
Jane Munro, *British Landscape Watercolours 1750-1850*, London: The Herbert Press/Cambridge: The Fitzwilliam Museum, 1994

Myrone 2008
Martin Myrone, *Gothic Nightmares. Fuseli, Blake and the Romantic Imagination*, London: Tate Publishing, 2008

Noakes 1954
Aubrey Noakes, *Sportsmen in a Landscape*, London: Bodley Head, 1954

Rosenfeld 1981
Sybil Rosenfeld, *Georgian Scene Painters and Scene Painting*, Cambridge United Press, 1981

Roget 1891
John Lewis Roget, A History of the 'Old Water-Colour' Society, London: Longmans, Green, and Co, 1891 (2 vols)

Sloan 2000
Kim Sloan, *'A Noble Art'. Amateur Artists and Drawing Masters. c1600-1800*, London: British Museum Press, 2000

Stainton 1985
Lindsay Stainton, *British Landscape Watercolours 1600-1860*, London: British Museum Publications, 1985

Turner 1996
Jane Turner (ed), *The Dictionary of Art*, London: Macmillan, 1996 (34 vols)

Wilton 1977
Andrew Wilton, *British Watercolours 1750 to 1850*, Oxford: Phaidon, 1977

Wilton and Lyles 1993
Andrew Wilton and Anne Lyles, *The Great Age of British Watercolours 1750-1880*, London: Royal Academy of Arts/Munich: Prestel, 1993

Wilcox 2005a
Tim Wilcox, *Francis Towne and his Friends*, London: John Spink, 2005

Wilcox 2005b
Tim Wilcox, *The Triumph of Watercolour. The early years of the Royal Watercolour Society 1805-55*, London: Philip Wilson Publishers, 2005

Wood 1978
Christopher Wood, *The Dictionary of Victorian Painters*, Woodbridge: Antique Collectors' Club, 1978 (2nd edition)

INDEX page numbers in **bold** refer to Biographies

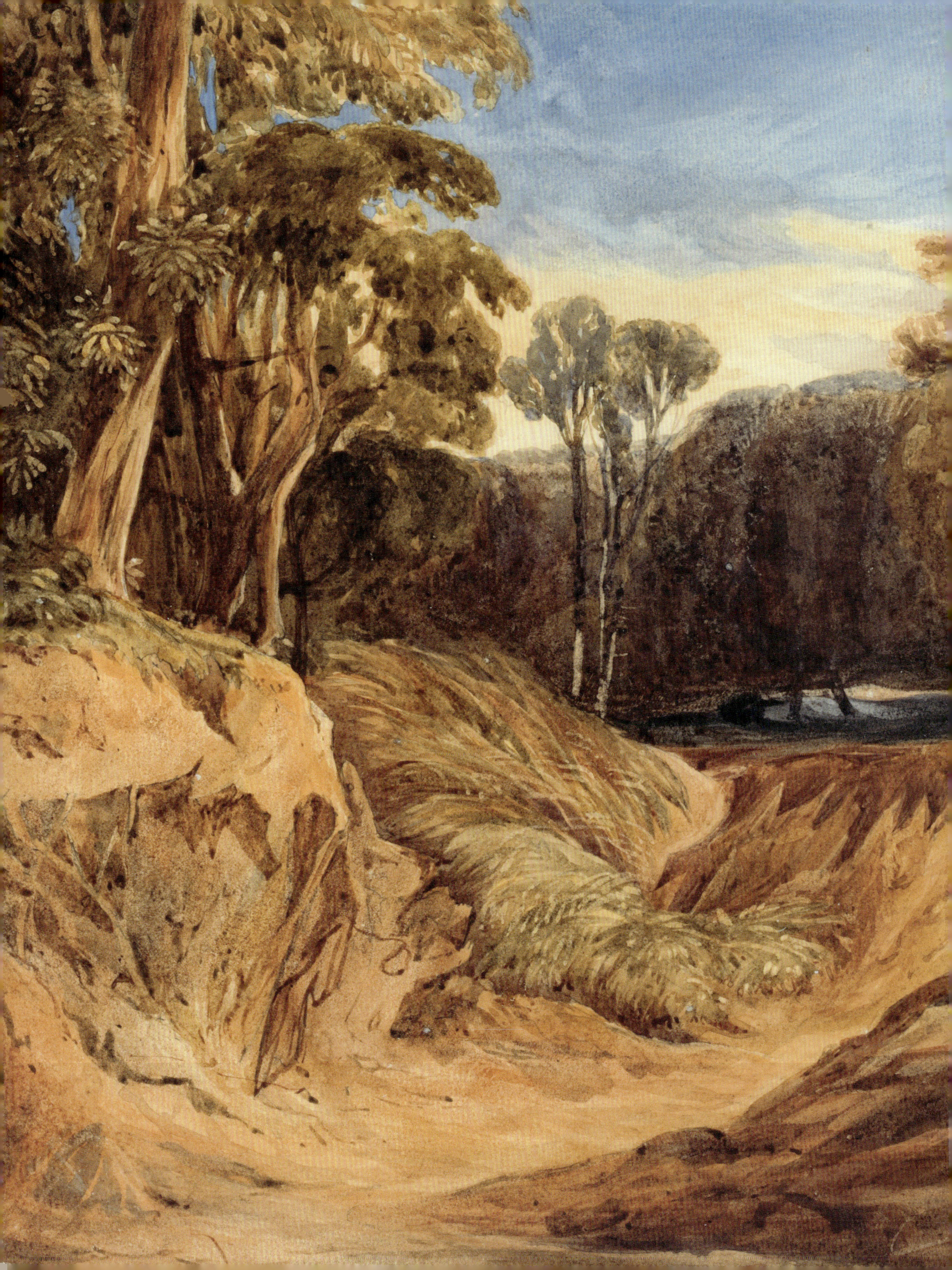